MANAGEMENT

Leading People and Organizations in the 21st Century

CANADIAN EDITION

MANAGEMENT

Leading People and Organizations in the 21st Century

CANADIAN EDITION

Gary Dessler
Florida International University

Frederick A. Starke
University of Manitoba

Dianne J. Cyr
Technical University of British Columbia

Prentice Hall

Toronto

Canadian Cataloguing in Publication Data

Dessler, Gary, 1942–

Management: leading people and organizations in the 21st century

Canadian ed.
Includes index.
ISBN 0-13-016348-1

1. Management I. Starke, Frederick A., 1942–   . II. Cyr, Dianne J. (Dianne Jane), 1952–   . III. Title.

HD31.D4225   2001   658.4   C00-931298-6

ISBN 0-13-016348-1

Vice President, Editorial Director: Michael Young
Executive Acquisitions Editor: Mike Ryan
Marketing Manager: James Buchanan
Developmental Editor: Suzanne Schaan
Production Editor: Marisa D'Andrea
Copy Editor: Susan Broadhurst
Production Coordinator: Janette Lush
Page Layout: Gail Ferreira Ng-A-Kien
Photo Research: Alene McNeill
Art Director: Mary Opper
Interior Design: Alex Li
Cover Design: Alex Li
Cover Image: Hiroshi Yagi/Photonica

1 2 3 4 5   05 04 03 02 01

Printed and bound in U.S.A.

Toronto

Brief Contents

Contents

Chapter 9   Staffing and Human Resource Management   258

Chapter 11 Influencing Individual Behaviour and Motivation   339

Preface

Michael Dell had a vision of a company that would sell high-quality personal computers directly to customers via catalogues and the telephone. Just a few years after starting up operations, Dell Computer had become a billion-dollar corporation. By the mid-1990s, Dell was not only selling computers in almost every country of the world, but a new channel—the Internet—was arising as a potential way to reach its customers directly. Within a year of organizing Dell's new Internet initiative, the company was selling millions of dollars' worth of computers and accessories over the Internet every day. Dell's customers could not only order their equipment directly via the Internet but also track the progress of their orders as they made their way through production and finally to their front doors.

Dell Computer's transformation is just one example of the massive changes that are taking place in the management of organizations today. Globalization, deregulation, and technological advances mean that today's organizations not only have to be more competitive than they've ever been before, but also must be ready to respond quickly to change if they are to thrive in this new, intensely competitive environment. To achieve this responsiveness and competitiveness, new management methods and philosophies have emerged, such as boundaryless organizations, team-based structures, Internet-based managing, scenario planning, and commitment building to supplement traditional control techniques. Leading people and managing organizations in the 21st century will depend on maintaining open, communicative, and responsive organizations; this can only be achieved by sound management practices that recognize the critical importance of the firm's human capital.

Understanding how to manage organizations and people in an environment of rapid change is the focus of this book. We provide students with a practical and concrete explanation of the management concepts and techniques they will need to manage today's new organizations. The book is intended for use in undergraduate courses in management, or in courses that combine management and organizational behaviour. Adopters will find that the book's outline follows the familiar "planning, organizing, leading, controlling" framework, and that its contents and continuing themes stress the leading-edge management concepts and techniques that students will need to manage today's and tomorrow's organizations.

THEMES OF THE TEXT

Within the planning, organizing, leading, and controlling framework, we focus on the following seven themes, which are woven into each chapter:

1. **People are part of managing.** With today's emphasis on competitiveness, on team-based organizations, and on being responsive, managers cannot separate their "people management" responsibilities from their strictly "managerial" ones. Thus, while planning requires the setting of goals, it also requires getting employees to accept those goals. This requires significant leadership and motivational skills on the part of managers. Because of the importance of people in organizations, each chapter contains a boxed insert entitled "The People Side of Managing" that explains why it is so important for managers to deal effectively with people.

2. **Managing today is technology-based and Internet-based.** Everywhere you look today, companies and their managers are relying on the Internet to manage their businesses more efficiently and responsively. Dell Computer, for example, lets

its customers track their own products via the Internet. This does more than simply make things more convenient for Dell's customers; it also eliminates the need to add hundreds of customer relations representatives to handle phone calls as well as the need to house all of those people and provide them with telephone support. Many other companies are using technology to improve their performance. That's why this book contains numerous examples describing how managers are using the Internet or some other technology to improve the performance of their organizations. For example, Chapter 13, Leading Groups and Teams, shows how companies are using the Internet and special groupware software packages to enable geographically dispersed team members to interact in real time, as if they were in the same room. Similarly, each chapter contains several examples of how companies are using the Internet to better manage their business.

3. **Managing change is crucial.** Understanding how to manage under conditions of rapid change is critical for successful management. Managing change is, therefore, a central theme of each chapter in the text. Chapter 14, Leading Organizational Change, is completely devoted to the issue of change management, and numerous examples of managing change are presented in each chapter. Each chapter also contains a boxed insert focusing on "The Challenge of Change."

4. **Entrepreneurship is driving today's economies.** Many college and university graduates will work for smaller firms. Managing a small business is therefore the fourth theme of the text. Examples of effective management in small businesses are found throughout the text, and each chapter contains a boxed insert entitled "The Entrepreneurial Edge" that describes some aspect of entrepreneurial behaviour. These boxes illustrate how entrepreneurs apply the management concepts and techniques that are discussed in that particular chapter.

5. **Diversity must be managed.** As the workforce becomes increasingly diverse, it is important for managers to recognize that diversity is a positive force rather than a negative one. Therefore, a portion of Chapter 3 is devoted to this topic. As well, each chapter contains examples that illustrate the need for techniques to effectively manage diversity.

6. **Teamwork is essential.** Work in organizations is increasingly organized not around traditional organization charts but around teams. A recent survey by the consulting firm Watson Wyatt concluded that the majority of companies depend to some extent on teams to get their work done. Given the importance of teamwork today, we emphasize the importance of teamwork as well as team building skills. Chapter 13 is devoted to managing teams, and additional material on how to organize around teams is found in Chapter 8, Designing Organizations to Manage Change. Each chapter contains examples of how teams can be used to improve decision making, communication, and the formulation of strategies.

7. **Managers manage globally.** Few changes in the past 10 years have had more impact on managers than globalization, and this trend will no doubt continue as the 21st century unfolds. Students are given an early introduction to the concept of globalization and to issues arising from it in Chapter 2. Because today's managers need to view all aspects of business and management from a global perspective, we also provide numerous examples of globalization in every chapter. Here are just a few of the many examples of globalization material contained in the text:

   • Chapter 1, Managing in the 21st Century, discusses the impact on management of changing political systems around the world, including the explosive opening of new markets with hundreds of millions of potential customers.

   • Chapter 2, The Environment of Management: Canadian and Global, is entirely devoted to the impact of globalization on management. It covers the reasons why companies expand operations abroad and their strategies for doing so.

- Chapter 6, Strategic Management, discusses how companies achieve above-average growth rates by aggressively expanding into new geographic markets, both domestically and abroad.

- Chapter 12, Influencing Interpersonal and Organizational Communication, emphasizes that cross-cultural communication is a fact of business life and illustrates how to communicate in different cultures.

- Chapter 15, Controlling and Building Commitment, points out that managing a globally dispersed workforce requires a particularly effective control system and a greater reliance on commitment-building efforts in order to avoid the problems that can arise when employees are far away from the company's central managers.

PEDAGOGICAL FEATURES

The pedagogical features of this text have been carefully designed to reinforce the major themes described above, and to make it easy for students to actively learn and retain what they read. Each chapter contains the following features:

Opening Case.
Each chapter begins with an interesting description of a situation that faced a real organization. The information in the opening case relates to the material in the chapter. For example, the opening case in Chapter 8, Designing Organizations to Manage Change, describes the changes that Canadian Pacific Ltd. made in its corporate structure so that it could more effectively respond to changes in the competitive environment that it is facing. The opening cases convey to students the dynamic environment in which managers work.

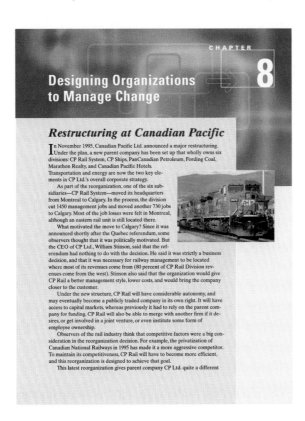

Learning Objectives.

A list of learning objectives is found at the beginning of each chapter. This focuses students' attention on the key items in the chapter.

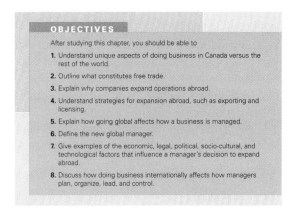

Real-World Management Boxes.

Each chapter contains three boxed inserts describing how ideas discussed in the text are applied in real organizations in Canada and throughout the world. These boxes are organized into three series that run throughout the text. Each chapter contains one box for each of the following series:

- The People Side of Managing (descriptions of current management practices that demonstrate the critical importance of people in the success of organizations)
- The Challenge of Change (examples showing how important it is for managers to anticipate and effectively manage the massive changes that are confronting organizations worldwide)
- The Entrepreneurial Edge (shows how entrepreneurial behaviour is important in the practice of management)

Key Terms.

In each chapter, the key terms that students should know are highlighted and defined in the text and repeated in the margin. Key terms appear in the Glossary and are also listed in bold in the Subject Index at the end of the book.

Weblinks

Web addresses given in the margin direct students to sites where they can learn more about the companies discussed in the text or gather further information about key topics.

Examples.

Each chapter contains numerous examples of current management practices in Canadian and international companies. This feature helps students to understand how management ideas are put into practice. Because globalization has become such an overwhelming feature of organizations in the 21st century, we have included examples from Canadian, U.S., European, and Asian companies. Since the U.S. is such an important trading partner for Canada, we have included continuing examples from well-known U.S. firms such as General Electric, Federal Express, IBM, and Levi Strauss.

Summary of Learning Objectives.

The material in each chapter is concisely summarized to help students understand the main points of the chapter. The summary is organized around the learning objectives listed at the beginning of the chapter.

SUMMARY OF LEARNING OBJECTIVES

1. **Understand unique aspects of doing business in Canada versus the rest of the world.** Several factors must be considered when doing business in Canada, including geographic uniqueness, significant government involvement, a resource-based economy, proximity to the U.S., concerns about foreign ownership, Canada's level of productivity, and the degree of unionization.

2. **Outline what constitutes free trade.** Free trade means that most if not all barriers to trade are removed among countries participating in a mutual agreement. The potential benefit to free trade is that nations have the opportunity for greater economic integration and exchange, as occurs in NAFTA, the trade agreement between Canada, the U.S., and Mexico.

3. **Explain why companies expand operations abroad.** An international business is any firm that engages in international trade or investment. Firms are globalizing for many reasons, including sales expansion, to acquire resources, and to diversify sources of sales and supplies. Other reasons for pursuing international business include reducing costs or improving quality by seeking products and services produced in foreign countries.

4. **Understand strategies for expansion abroad, such as exporting and licensing.** Companies can pursue several strategies for extending operations to foreign markets. Exporting is the route often chosen by manufacturers, but licensing and franchising are two popular alternatives. Licensing occurs when a firm grants another company the right to use its intellectual property or processes for a fee. Franchising is granting the right to start a business based on an original concept or model, as McDonald's does. At some point, a firm may decide to invest its own funds in another country. Joint ventures and wholly owned subsidiaries are two examples of foreign direct investments.

5. **Explain how going global affects how a business is managed.** Globalizing production means dispersing parts of a firm's production process to various locations around the globe. Marketing is likewise more culturally dispersed and sensitive to cultural differences. The aim of globalizing is to take advantage of national differences in the cost and quality of production, and then integrate these operations in a unified system of manufacturing facilities around the world. Companies also are tapping into a new supply of skilled labour in various countries. The globalization of markets, production, and labour coincides with the rise of a new type of global manager, who can function effectively anywhere in the world.

6. **Define the new global manager.** Managers in the global economy are more cosmopolitan, with international exposure. These managers are flexible and

Tying It All Together.

This feature, which goes beyond a simple summary of what was covered in the chapter, emphasizes how the chapter's material relates to the material in the previous and following chapters. It also gives students a continuing reference point so they always know where they stand and how that chapter's material fits in with the material presented in the rest of the book.

Critical Thinking Exercises.

Scenario-based questions at the end of each chapter encourage students to think more deeply about that chapter's concepts and the implications of the ideas that have been presented.

Experiential Exercises.

End-of-chapter exercises promote active learning on either an individual or a team basis.

Internet Exercises.

Each chapter contains an exercise that allows students to use the Internet to investigate some interesting aspect of management. For example, the Internet Exercise in Chapter 2 asks students to go to a Web site that gives information about how different cultures view various types of body gestures. This issue can be very important for managers who must interact with individuals from different cultures.

Case Studies.

Two end-of-chapter case studies give students the opportunity to analyze an actual management situation using the material presented in the chapter to guide their thinking. At the end of each case, several questions are presented to focus student attention in certain areas of analysis.

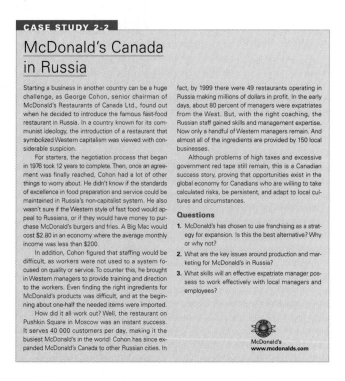

You Be the Consultant.

At the end of each chapter, a continuing case study is presented that focuses on a company called KnitMedia, a music and entertainment company based in New York. This feature asks students to put themselves in the place of KnitMedia's managers and make decisions regarding the future direction of the company. Because these cases are based on information provided by the officers at KnitMedia, they are meaty and realistic.

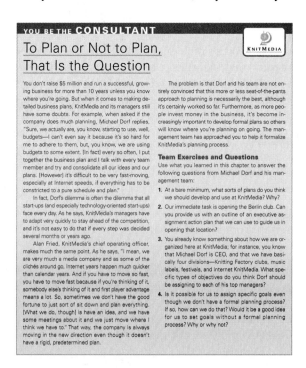

Video Cases.

At the end of each of the five major sections of the text, three video cases are presented. The first two are CBC video cases that describe a Canadian company or management issue. The videos help students understand the dynamic nature of management in the 21st century. Questions that are relevant to one or more of the chapters in the section are found at the end of each case. The third case, entitled "On Location at KnitMedia," is an integrative video case that focuses on KnitMedia. The cases correspond to video clips that were filmed at KnitMedia's offices and edited specifically for use with this text. Most of the CBC segments and the KnitMedia clips are also available on the Companion Website.

SUPPORT MATERIALS

Instructor's Manual.

The Instructor's Manual is designed to guide the educator through the text. Each chapter in the Instructor's Manual includes a topic introduction, an annotated outline that includes space for the instructor's notes, and answers to all critical thinking exercises and cases, including You Be the Consultant. A video guide section provides suggested answers to the case questions for the accompanying CBC video clips and the KnitMedia videos.

Test Item File.

The Test Item File contains about 150 questions per chapter, including multiple-choice, true/false, and essay questions. Every question is page-referenced to the text and is classified as easy, moderate, or difficult to satisfy all classroom needs.

Pearson Education Canada Test Manager.

The Test Manager contains all of the questions in the printed Test Item File. Test Manager is a comprehensive suite of tools for testing and assessment. It allows educators to easily create and distribute tests for their courses, either by printing and distributing through traditional methods or by online delivery via a Local Area Network (LAN) server.

PowerPoint Electronic Transparencies with Teaching Notes.

PowerPoint disks allow access to over 200 figures, exhibits, and text materials.

Colour Transparencies.

Full-colour acetates based on key concepts from the text add a visual element to lectures.

CBC Video Library.

The CBC Video Library for *Management* includes 10 segments from CBC's program *Venture*, which accompany the CBC Video Cases found at the end of each part in the text. These cases focus on Canadian companies and discuss management issues from a Canadian point of view.

On Location at KnitMedia Video.

This customized video, filmed and edited specifically for this text, focuses on a music and entertainment company called KnitMedia. The five video segments correspond to five integrative end-of-part video cases in the text, with an additional video segment that introduces students to KnitMedia.

Companion Website.

The Companion Website for *Management* can be found at www.pearsoned.ca/dessler. This online study guide includes quizzes, Internet exercises, and Weblinks. The CBC videos can also be found on the site, and a special KnitMedia section includes the videos as well as links to the KnitMedia site and other related sites.

ACKNOWLEDGMENTS

The authors and publishers would like to thank the following people who reviewed material for this Canadian edition:

> Kirk L. Bailey, Ryerson Polytechnic University
> Vic de Witt, Red River College/University of Manitoba
> Denny Dombrower, Centennial College
> Geoff Green, Red Deer College
> Kristi Harrison, Centennial College
> Suzanne Kavanagh, George Brown College
> Murray F. Kernaghan, Assiniboine College
> Beverly Linnell, Southern Alberta Institute of Technology
> Kathleen Muller, Humber College
> Eileen B. Stewart, British Columbia Institute of Technology
> Joe Turbic, Ryerson Polytechnic University
> John K. Wilkins, University of Manitoba
> Jeffrey D. Young, Mount Saint Vincent University

Thanks to the American reviewers whose feedback helped shape the original edition on which this text is based, and to Dr. George Puia at Indiana State University for developing some of the end-of-chapter cases. Our thanks are also due to the Prentice Hall staff in the United States who provided files and manuscript for the Canadian authors, especially Jeannine Ciliotta, the U.S. developmental editor, whose good humour, attention to detail, and efficiency in expediting the process were much appreciated.

We are grateful to Michael Dorf, CEO of KnitMedia, and to Alan Fried and the rest of the KnitMedia staff for giving us access to a fascinating business enterprise so that we could create the videos, video cases, and You Be the Consultant features for this text.

The Canadian authors would like to acknowledge the continued support from their editorial team, including Mike Ryan, Lesley Mann, Suzanne Schaan, and Marisa D'Andrea.

At Florida International University Gary Dessler appreciates the moral support he received from all of his colleagues, including Ronnie Silverblatt, Jan Luytjes, Enzo Valenzi, and, of course, Earnest Friday and Richard Hodgetts.

Closer to home, Gary Dessler wants to acknowledge the support of his wife, Claudia, and her willingness to tolerate his disappearance for more evenings and weekends than he should have been gone while he worked on this book. However, when all of the acknowledgments are said and done, if there can be a single inspiration for a book entitled *Management: Leading People and Organizations in the 21st Century*, it is his son Derek, for whom he wrote this book in as practical and useful a way as possible, and whose unswerving support was the only motivation needed.

Gary Dessler (Ph.D. business administration, Bernard M. Baruch School of Business) is Professor of Business at Florida International University. In addition to *Management: Leading People and Organizations in the 21st Century*, he is the author of a number of other books, including, most recently, *Human Resource Management*, 8th edition (Prentice Hall), *Essentials of Human Resource Management* (Prentice Hall), and *Winning Commitment: How to Build and Keep a Competitive Workforce*. His books have been translated into Chinese, Russian, Indonesian, Spanish, and Portuguese, and are being used by students and managers all over the world. He has written numerous articles on employee commitment, organizational behaviour, leadership, and quality improvement, and for 10 years wrote the syndicated "Job Talk" column for the *Miami Herald*.

Fred Starke is an Associate Dean in the Faculty of Management at the University of Manitoba. He earned his B.A. and M.B.A. from Southern Illinois University and his Ph.D. from Ohio State University. He has been actively involved in teaching, research, and administration at the University of Manitoba. His teaching interests focus on organizational behaviour, organization theory, and decision making. He has published research articles in scholarly journals such as *Administrative Science Quarterly*, the *Journal of Applied Psychology*, and the *Academy of Management Journal*. He also writes articles for professional journals such as the *Journal of Systems Management*, *Information Executive*, and the *Canadian Journal of Nursing Administration*. Dr. Starke also devotes time to writing textbooks for university and community college students. His three other texts, *Contemporary Management in Canada, Business Essentials*, and *Business*, are used in universities and community colleges across Canada. Dr. Starke regularly presents seminars on the topics of decision making and goal setting to practising managers in both the public and private sectors.

Dr. Dianne Cyr is an Associate Professor at the Technical University of British Columbia. Her research focuses on joint ventures in North America, as well as on the transition economies of Central and Eastern Europe. Her most recent research has centred on issues of bargaining power in strategic alliances in the high-technology sector and on cultural implications of e-commerce. Dr. Cyr is also the President of Global Alliance Management, a consulting company dedicated to the design structure and implementation of successful strategic alliances. She graduated from the University of British Columbia with a Ph.D. in international alliances. Dr. Cyr is the author of *The Human Resource Challenge of International Joint Ventures* and *Scaling the Ivory Tower: Stories from Women in Business School Faculties*, as well as numerous journal articles. She would like to dedicate this book to Jim, Andrea, Robert and Ryan.

A Note to the Student on KnitMedia

You are not going to learn how to be a manager by reading this book. You can't learn how to do anything—play golf, do calculus problems, or make fine furniture—just by reading about it. Instead, you have to actually *apply* what you read; you have to *practise*. By the time you've completed this book, we'd like you to have had an opportunity to step into a manager's shoes, and to practise what it's like to plan, organize, lead, and control (in other words, to manage) an organization. To help you do this we've created a number of features that focus on a company called KnitMedia.

We find the nature of KnitMedia's business interesting, and we hope that you will, too. KnitMedia is an alternative music and entertainment company whose businesses include an independent record label, and the Knitting Factory—a live music club in New York City that specializes in alternative jazz. As you move through the book you'll see that KnitMedia is involved in other businesses, too, including radio, TV, and Internet and video-conference interactive performances.

Understanding and explaining how to manage a huge enterprise like Inco or Air Canada requires quite a stretch of the imagination for most of us. Most of us can relate more easily to and "get our hands around" the sort of small business that Michael Dorf, the founder and president, is building in KnitMedia. Here are some of the features you'll find in this book that focus on KnitMedia.

You Be the Consultant (found at the end of each chapter) is a continuing case study that focuses on different aspects of KnitMedia from chapter to chapter. As a result, you're going to become very familiar with just about everything about KnitMedia, its competitors, its strengths and weaknesses, its financial situation, and its managers' hopes and dreams. That way, you'll be able to make your decisions not in a vacuum but within the context of what you know about the company. For instance, you'll be able to propose a technique to help the president of the company control his increasingly far-flung enterprise, in the context of what you know about his motives and how he likes to manage.

Integrative Video Cases (found at the end of each major part of the book) let you apply your knowledge of what you've learned from the preceding chapters. The cases are designed to help you think about management in the way that managers actually have to, in a more integrated, "it's all related" fashion.

KnitMedia Videos correspond to the end-of-part integrative cases, and will let you see and hear how KnitMedia's managers and employees are actually managing their company on a day-to-day basis. Your instructor may show the videos in class, or you may view them on the *Management* Website.

The multimedia nature of this KnitMedia component will provide you with a more realistic and concrete way to learn about making management decisions and managing companies. You'll be able to use the text and videos to read about KnitMedia, to actually see the participants at work, and to research your answers to the exercises.

We believe that this integrated package will provide you with an opportunity to apply in practice what you've learned, and thus to actually see what it's like to be a manager. After all, how do you become a manager? Practise, practise, practise.

Your Internet companion to the most exciting, state-of-the-art educational tools on the Web!

The Pearson Education Canada Companion Website is easy to navigate and is organized to correspond to the chapters in this textbook. The Companion Website contains three distinct sections:

1) Student Resources

2) Instructor Resources

3) General Resources

Explore the various modules of this Companion Website. Students and distance learners will discover resources for indepth study, research, and communication, empowering them in their quest for greater knowledge and maximizing their potential for success in the course.

A NEW WAY TO DELIVER EDUCATIONAL CONTENT

Our Companion Website provides students and instructors with a range of options to access, view, and exchange content.

The material is specifically tied to the text, allowing students to review each chapter and test their knowledge. At the same time, it offers opportunities to branch out from the site to explore other Websites for additional and more indepth information.

The site is user-friendly, with **Help** and **Feedback** features that allow users to maximize their experience.

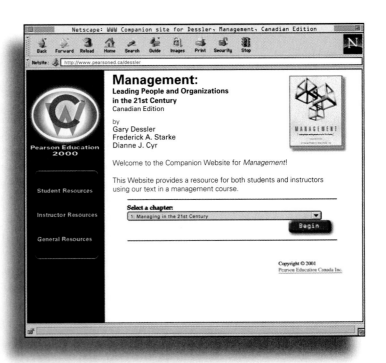

www.pearsoned.ca/dessler

1) Student Resources

The Website acts as an online Study Guide, offering review material, online quizzes, Weblinks, and video cases.

- The review modules cover **Objectives** and **Key Concepts** (including definitions).

- The online quizzes include **True/False**, **Multiple Choice**, and **Essay Questions** for each chapter. These modules provide students with the ability to send answers to a built-in grader and receive instant feedback. In addition, **Internet Exercises** lead students to other Websites where they can apply the ideas learned in the chapter and also discover how real companies deal with these issues.

- The **Web Destinations** module provides further Weblinks related to management issues and specific companies and organizations. **NetSearch** simplifies key term searches using Internet search engines.

- Most of the **CBC Videos** related to the cases in the text plus all of the **KnitMedia Videos** are available for viewing online.

2) Instructor Resources

Syllabus Manager provides instructors with the option to create online classes and construct on online syllabus linked to specific modules in the Companion Website.

3) General Resources

Communications tools can be used in distance learning environments as well as to enhance feedback for on-campus students.

- **Message Board** acts as a national newsgroup allowing students to post and reply to relevant course topics.

- **Live Chat** enables instructor-led group activities in real time. Instructors can display Website content while students participate in the discussion.

The Companion Website can be found at:

www.pearsoned.ca/dessler

PEARSON EDUCATION CANADA
26 Prince Andrew Place
Don Mills, Ontario M3C 2T8

To order:
Call: 1-800-567-3800
Fax: 1-800-263-7733

For samples:
Call: 1-800-850-5813
Fax: (416) 447-2819
E-mail: phcinfo.pubcanada@pearsoned.com

PART 1

Introduction to Managing

Part 1: Introduction to Managing provides an introduction to, and an overview of, the field of management. Managers are critical to the effective functioning of modern society, but they do not receive nearly as much publicity as movie stars, politicians, or sports figures. As a result, many people ask questions like "What do managers do?" and "Why is management important?" In this section, we explain the role of managers and the fundamental importance of management. Since managers are influenced by the environment in which they work, we also examine the important environmental factors—globalization, business ethics, diversity, culture, and social responsibility—that influence them.

We begin in Chapter 1, **Managing in the 21st Century**, by explaining exactly what managers do, and why the study of management is so important. We describe the basic functions that all managers must perform and the different types of managers that are found in organizations. Management is an exciting career, since managers work in a rapidly changing environment that requires them to adapt to continual changes in technology, globalization, and deregulation.

The Appendix to Chapter 1 presents a brief history of the development of modern management thought. Several distinct approaches to management are described, including classical management, behavioural management, the quantitative school, systems theory, and situational management.

In Chapter 2, **The Environment of Management: Canadian and Global**, we look first at the environment of management within Canada, including the key structural features of the Canadian economy that affect managers. We then move on to the international scene and examine issues like why business firms want to sell abroad, the strategies they use to do so, the impact of global strategies on company personnel and structure, and the impact on managers, including those in an international environment. We conclude by discussing the important factors that determine the success of individuals who manage internationally.

Finally, in Chapter 3, **Managing Ethics, Diversity, Culture, and Social Responsibility**, we look at several important but complex areas that are increasingly coming under scrutiny from employees, stockholders, government, and the general public. The focus here is on the human side of management, and on what managers should know about ethics, diversity, culture, and social responsibility in order to effectively carry out their managerial responsibilities.

Managing in the 21st Century

Chapters Turns Over a New Leaf

Toronto-based Chapters Inc. is rapidly accelerating its pace on the Internet, going from a leisurely stroll around cyberspace to a furious run. Strategic activities have included the launch of a new site on the World Wide Web, plans

for an initial public offering to raise capital, and book-selling agreements with two high-profile Web sites—Canoe and Bid.Com—on which it will also advertise. People reading about the Toronto Maple Leafs' drive to the Stanley Cup in Canoe's sports section could see links to Chapters.ca, where they can easily buy books about the team. Chapters.ca is now Canada's largest online book site with over 2 million books, as well as videos, DVDs, music CDs, and software. Bid.Com is an online auction house where Chapters can auction limited-edition and rare books. Chapters' original online venture, launched in November 1998 jointly with the *Globe and Mail,* was ChaptersGlobe.com, which features literary material such as reviews and interviews from the *Globe and Mail*'s book section and also offers access to Chapters e-commerce.

Such partnerships are necessary in a world in which the Internet is quickly becoming the queen of the retail industry. And Chapters deserves applause for its aggressive approach—a rarity among Canadian companies, which tend to creep cautiously forward in the Web domain. Of all the e-commerce ventures, selling books has been one of the most widely accepted. The phenomenal growth of Seattle-based Amazon.com Inc.'s sales and stock has certainly validated the business and its appeal to investors. Canada is in the race to win with companies like Chapters, which demonstrates a new way of doing business in the 21st century.

Chapters
www.chapters.ca

OBJECTIVES

After studying this chapter, you should be able to

1. Explain the management process, including what managers do.

2. Describe the changing role for managers.

3. Describe why the "people side" of management is important.

4. Outline current forces creating turbulence and change for organizations and managers.

5. Discuss the main trends in how modern organizations are changing and managed.

What Managers Do

Business in the 21st century will face a tidal wave of change. As we have seen with Chapters, this process has already begun. New forms of business such as e-commerce are changing the way organizations operate. Globalization continues to increase the pace and complexity of how companies are managed. A shift towards technological advances, increased speed of communications, and changing consumer demands means that whole markets can either appear or disappear almost overnight.

A random crawl through a week's worth of marketing press reveals that a brewer is planning a chain of pubs themed on computer games, TV companies are buying football clubs, and an Internet book shop will start selling toys. Each of these events represents a fundamental shift in how business and industry operates and competes. Yet, without exception, all of them would have been inconceivable to all but the most visionary among us even 18 months ago.[1]

Employees operating in a knowledge-based economy have different expectations and demands than workers of a few years previously. Information technology is changing the way we do work, and the very structure of organizations as a result. Managers face new and complex challenges as they struggle to remain current despite the shifting landscape of how work is done. To help keep pace with the phenomenal changes around you, this book focuses on contemporary management, and how managers will lead people and organizations most effectively in the decade to come.

A **manager** is someone who plans, organizes, leads, and controls the people and the work of an organization with the aim of ensuring that the organization achieves its goals. **Management** refers to two things: (1) collectively, to the managers of an organization; and (2) to the study of what managers do. Managers can have the most remarkable impact on organizations. Consider Dofasco Inc., which along with three other Canadian firms— Enbridge Inc., Suncor Energy Inc., and TransAlta—has emerged as an international leader on the new Dow Jones Sustainability Group Index.[2] Dofasco tops the steel category of the Index, which tracks the performance of the 200 leading sustainability-driven companies in 68 industry groups in 22 countries using innovative technology, corporate governance, shareholder relations, industrial leadership, and social well-being among its criteria for success. Under the leadership of Dofasco's president and CEO, John Mayberry, and others on the management team, the company has steered towards new technologies and excellence in the integration of economic, environmental, and social growth opportunities in Dofasco's business strategies.

manager
Someone who plans, organizes, leads, and controls the people and the work of an organization with the aim of ensuring that the organization achieves its goals.

management
The process of planning, organizing, leading, and controlling a business's financial, physical, human, and information resources in order to achieve designated goals.

Dofasco
www.dofasco.ca

Operators at Dofasco monitor the production of steel products with the latest in high-technology monitoring devices.

International examples of the impact of managers are plentiful. IBM floundered through much of the 1980s and early 1990s, losing market share, seeing costs rise, and watching its stock price dwindle from almost $180 to barely $50 per share. Within three years, new chairman Louis Gerstner revamped the company's product line, dramatically lowered costs, changed the company's culture, and oversaw a quadrupling of IBM's stock price.[3] Dell Computer chairman Michael Dell created a $12 billion company in just 13 years by instituting one of the world's most sophisticated direct-sales operations, eliminating resellers' markups and the need for large inventories, and keeping a vise-like grip on costs while dozens of his competitors were going down the drain.[4] Eleven years after being pushed out of Apple Computer, Steve Jobs returned and totally revitalized the company in barely a year.

Manager effects like these don't happen only at giant corporations. In fact, management occurs in different ways in various types of organizations. Just as it is in for-profit companies, management efficiency is also central in not-for-profit organizations such as government, colleges, or charitable groups. But not all companies are built of bricks and mortar. Today management frequently occurs in **virtual organizations** where employees communicate electronically with the office, lab, or factory by means of their PCs at home. At the Canadian Institute of Chartered Accountants (CICA), information technology is playing a significant role in public accounting.[5] In fact, the Technology Advisory Committee for the CICA recently identified key issues affecting the accounting profession and its practitioners, including electronic commerce, information security, and electronic money. This affects business strategy directly, as well as how work is managed. For example, chartered accountants require the ability to assess complex computer systems for security, as well as the use of technology that safeguards privacy of information for clients.

At this moment, managers at thousands of small businesses such as Internet start-ups, dry cleaners, or restaurants are running their businesses well with courteous, prompt, and first-class service. However, what would happen if you removed the competent managers from those businesses and replaced them with managers without training or skills? You know the answer, because you've probably experienced the effects yourself—businesses with untrained or unprepared staff, orders not prepared on time, or lost reservations. About 90 percent of the new businesses started this year will fail within five years, and business credit analyst Dun & Bradstreet says the reason is generally "poor management."

The effect of good management is really nothing short of amazing. Take an underperforming, even chaotic, organization like the failed Eaton's department stores, install skilled senior managers, and the enterprise could be revitalized. Take a successful enterprise that has been managed well for years by its proprietor—say, a neighbourhood stationery store—and watch as a new, less-competent manager takes over. Shelves are suddenly in disarray, products are out of stock, and bills go unpaid.

Enterprises from Bata Shoes and Air Canada to a restaurant, an Internet business, or the local dry cleaner are all organizations. An **organization** consists of people with formally assigned roles who must work together to achieve stated goals. Organizations, by their nature, cannot simply run themselves. They require managers who are adept at determining goals for an organization, ensuring that those goals are achieved, and envisioning future goals—all the while keeping in mind the fact that people are central to the operation.

The Management Process

Management writers traditionally refer to the manager's four basic functions of planning, organizing, leading, and controlling as the **management process**. The rest of this book will cover each of these topics in detail.

Planning. Planning is setting goals and deciding on courses of action, developing rules and procedures, developing plans (both for the organization and for those who work in it), and forecasting (predicting or projecting what the future holds for the organization).

Organizing. Organizing is identifying jobs to be done, hiring people to do them, establishing departments, delegating or pushing authority to subordinates, establishing a chain

virtual organization
An organization where employees communicate electronically with the office, lab, or factory by means of their PCs at home.

Canadian Institute of Chartered Accountants (CICA)
www.cica.ca

Bata Shoes
www.bata.com

Air Canada
www.aircanada.ca

organization
People with formally assigned roles who must work together to achieve stated goals.

management process
The manager's four basic functions of planning, organizing, leading, and controlling.

of command (in other words, channels of authority and communication), and coordinating the work of subordinates.

Leading. Leading means influencing other people to get the job done, maintaining morale, molding company culture, and managing conflicts and communication.

Controlling. Controlling is setting standards (such as sales quotas or quality standards), comparing actual performance with those standards, and then taking corrective action as required.

You Too Are a Manager

Just as organizations are not necessarily business firms, managers are not always business people. In fact, it is likely that you have already been (or may soon be) in the position of managing others. Let's suppose that you and some friends have decided to spend next summer abroad in France. None of you know very much about France or how to get there, so you have been elected "summer tour master" and asked to manage the trip. Where would you start? (Resist the temptation to call a travel agent and delegate the whole job to him or her, please.)

You might start by thinking through what you have to do in terms of planning, organizing, leading, and controlling. What sorts of plans will you need? Among other things, you will need to plan the dates your group is leaving and returning, the cities and towns in France you will visit, the airline you will use, how you will get around while in France, and where you will stay.

Developing all of those plans will be quite a job, so you will probably want to get some help. In other words, you will need to divide up the work, and to create an organization. For example, you might delegate to Rosa the task of checking airline schedules and prices, put Ned in charge of finding hotels, and make Ruth responsible for determining the sights to see in various cities. However, the job won't get done if everyone works alone. Each individual will require guidance and information from you. For example, Rosa cannot make decisions on airline schedules unless she knows in which city you will be starting the trip. So, you'll have to either schedule weekly "managers meetings" or coordinate all of the work yourself.

In addition, leadership could be a challenge. You will need to make sure your friends get along, work efficiently together, and stay motivated. You will also have to ensure the whole project stays "in control." If something can go wrong, it often will, and that's certainly the case when a group of people is travelling together. At a minimum, all those airline tickets, hotel reservations, and itineraries will have to be checked and checked again to make sure there are no mistakes. From this example you can see that "managing" is something we all do almost every day—often without knowing it.

Types of Managers

Most organizations include several types of managers. In your college or university, for instance, there are presidents, vice-presidents, deans, associate deans, and department chairs, as well as various administrators like human resource managers. At your place of work (if you work) you might find supervisors, financial controllers, sales managers, plant managers, and a president and vice-presidents. These people are managers because they all plan, organize, lead, and control the workers and the work of an organization in such a way that the organization achieves its goals.

There are many ways to classify managers. For example, we can distinguish managers based on their *organizational level, position*, and *functional title* (see Table 1.1).

The managers at the top of the firm are usually referred to as **executives**. Functional titles include President, Chief Executive Officer, Vice-President, and Chief Financial Officer. And new forms of these titles are emerging. Noranda Inc. has a Vice-President of Performance; Ernst & Young has a Chief Knowledge Officer.

Beneath this management level (and reporting to it) may be one or more levels of **middle managers**, positions that typically have the term "manager" or "director" in their titles.

Noranda
www.noranda.ca

Ernst & Young
www.ey.com

executive
A manager at the top of a firm.

middle manager
A manager who usually reports to an executive.

TABLE 1.1 *Types of Managers*

ORGANIZATIONAL LEVEL	POSITION	FUNCTIONAL TITLE
Top Managers (Have managers as subordinates)	Executives	President Vice President, Production Vice President, Sales Vice President, HR Chief Financial Officer
Middle Managers (Have managers as subordinates)	Managers or Directors	Production Manager Sales Manager HR Manager Finance Manager
First-line Managers (Have non-managers as subordinates)	Supervisors	Production Supervisor Regional Sales Manager Assistant HR Manager Chief Bookkeeper

In larger companies like IBM, managers report to directors, who in turn report to top managers like vice-presidents. Examples of some functional titles include Production Manager, Sales Manager, HR Manager, and Finance Manager. The city of Mississauga has a Director of Organizational Effectiveness.

first-line manager
A manager lower on the management ladder; often called a supervisor.

First-line managers are lower on the management ladder. These managers are often called supervisors, and might include Production Supervisors who supervise the assembly-line employees at companies such as Bombardier or Canada Packers.

Regardless of their level and title, managers have a lot in common. They all spend an enormous part of their day with people—talking, listening, influencing, motivating, and attending one-on-one conferences or committee meetings.[6] In fact, even chief executives (whom you might expect to be somewhat insulated from other people, up there in their executive suites) reportedly spend about three-quarters of their time dealing directly with other people.[7]

Managers at different levels use their time differently, however. Top managers tend to spend more time planning and setting goals. Middle managers then take those goals (such as "double the sales in the next two years") and translate them into specific projects (such as "hire two new salespeople and introduce three new products") for their staff to execute. First-line supervisors then concentrate on directing and controlling the employees who work on those projects.

The Manager's Changing Role

The role of the "traditional" manager is obsolete in the 21st century. Old-style managers—middle-aged men who worked in one location with very basic technology, giving orders and expecting obedience—are relics of the past. For one thing, senior and mid-level managers are increasingly apt to be women. And now managers are no longer expected to know all the answers; instead they rely on employees to keep up with the flood of information reaching them each day. Very often, the contemporary manager is not a "command and control" person but a team leader and facilitator, dealing with such complex issues as a culturally diverse workforce, more demanding ethical considerations, and technology as a source of innovation.

Increasingly, CEOs with the "right stuff" are seen as having general management and leadership ability, not specialized knowledge of the industry. They might best be called "portable CEOs." This form of senior manager is hired not because he or she knows the business but because they have leadership skills. They are not afraid to shake things up, and they often move on after they have accomplished what they think is necessary.[8]

The e-CEO

E.piphany
www.epiphany.com

What is it like being an e-CEO, the chief executive of one of the hot new e-commerce companies? To hear the executives tell it, "speed" is the word that sums up their experience best. For example, Roger Siboni is the CEO of E.piphany, a company that creates software to help e-corporations get the most from their customer data. He says, "You're driving too fast—you feel the exhilaration—you must turn left and right at death-defying speed without blinking—never blink—if you go up and down with the news, you'll never make it."[9] E-CEOs also must be "...brutally, brutally honest with yourself and others, because if you let a problem fester a day or two, you'll see someone in your rearview mirror coming after you."

With their markets changing so fast, e-CEOs also must constantly focus their companies' and their employees' attention. These companies are constantly deluged with competitive information and new ideas, so it's relatively easy for the employees to become distracted. It's the e-CEO's job to keep employees focused.

Table 1.2 summarizes why e-CEOs are, in fact, a new breed. For example, they're not just younger and richer than traditional CEOs, but they're also more comfortable with ambiguity and speed. And they're extremely concerned about monitoring market trends and competitors' moves, to ensure their companies aren't blindsided by unanticipated events.

TABLE 1.2 *E-CEOs Are a Brand New Breed*

Operating at breakneck speed in a world with little or no margin for error, e-CEOs need a new set of qualities to thrive.

TRADITIONAL CEO	E-CEO
encouraging	evangelizing
alert	paranoid
cordial	brutally frank
infotech semi-literate (at best)	infotech literate (at least)
clearly focused	intensely focused
fast moving	faster moving
hates ambiguity	likes ambiguity
suffers from technology-confrontation anxiety	suffers from bandwidth-separation anxiety
a paragon of good judgment	a paragon of good judgment
average age: 57	average age: 38
rich	really rich

The People Side of Management

Managing has always been a decidedly behavioural or people-oriented occupation, since managers do their work by interacting with others. In many ways managers have been the brokers of the organization, ensuring that employees are supported, assessed, and recognized for work well done. In today's high-tech and rapidly changing environment, the people side of management is perhaps even more important.

Several years ago the accounting and consulting firm PricewaterhouseCoopers interviewed 400 CEOs whose companies were in the top 2000 in global size.[10] The results are

FIGURE 1.1
What Has the CEO's
Attention?

ACTION	ALL CEOs	U.S. and CANADA	EUROPE and ASIA
Setting vision and strategy	66%	67%	65%
Exploring M&As	51%	51%	51%
Reshaping corporate culture and employee behaviour	47%	48%	45%
Monitoring corporate financial information	45%	47%	43%

summarized in Figure 1.1. As you might expect, a majority of these CEOs devoted a lot of personal time to things like setting corporate strategy, exploring mergers and acquisitions, and monitoring corporate financial results. The surprising thing was that about half actually spent as much or more time trying to shape and influence the people or behavioural side of their businesses as they did monitoring financial results.

More recently, in a 1999 *Globe and Mail* study that surveyed Canadian executives from coast to coast, the key issue that kept senior managers awake at night was related to people.[11] Topping the list were concerns about staffing, recruitment, retraining, and how

THE PEOPLE SIDE OF MANAGING

Dot-coms Turn Up the Heat on Compensation

Dot-com companies and the fast-paced technology sector are putting pressure on employers to reconsider their pay schemes, according to executive compensation consultants at William M. Mercer Ltd.

Many companies face demands for better compensation packages as well as for more frequent payments under annual incentive programs. For instance, some employers are measuring performance for bonuses more often than the usual once-per-year, or offering hiring bonuses. Stock options are a requirement these days in the high-technology world, and employees want earlier vesting and higher payouts of options.

This pressure comes when technology is rapidly advancing, markets are expanding globally, and the economy is shifting from an industrial base towards an information one. These are not new issues, but the emergence of dot-com players has certainly stepped up the pace. Robert Turner, a consultant in the compensation area says, "What we have seen from the dot-coms is the turning up of the switch. These guys move, as they say, at the speed of light."

Dot-coms are scouring established companies for executives and are willing to pay for the talent. They offer potential employees a chance to work in an exciting sector as well as the possibility of massive payoffs from stock options if the company hits it big on the stock market.

The growing competition in compensation "underlies this increased importance of long-term incentives as companies focus on retaining and motivating their employee," says Dawna Townsend, another Mercer consultant.[12]

to create and sustain employee morale. One executive noted, "People are the key to my success and the most talented ones are increasingly hard to find." This is especially true in some industries such as high technology, where the "brain drain" to the United States and other locations provides strategic challenges to companies seeking the best talent in the field.

Why is the people side of management so important today? Perhaps the best way to answer that question is with a real-life example. Our first "The People Side of Managing" feature shows what is happening at some of Canada's dot-com companies in the compensation area as one way to motivate employees.

What Else Do Managers Do?

There are many facets to the manager's role. Over 20 years ago Henry Mintzberg, now a McGill University professor and one of the world's leading management specialists, conducted a study of what managers actually do.[13] He found that as managers went from one task to another they had many duties, including:

The Figurehead Role: Every manager spends part of the time performing ceremonial duties. For example, the prime minister of Canada might greet international delegations, a supervisor might attend the wedding of an administrative assistant, or the sales manager might take an important client to lunch.

The Leader Role: Every manager must also function as a leader, motivating and encouraging employees.

The Liaison Role: Managers also spend a lot of time in contact with people outside their own departments, essentially acting as the liaison between their departments and people within and outside the organization. The assembly-line supervisor might field a question from the sales manager about how a new order is coming along, or the vice-president of sales might meet with the vice-president of finance to make sure a new customer has the credit required to place an order.

The Spokesperson Role: The manager is often the spokesperson for his or her organization. The supervisor may have to keep the plant manager informed about the flow of work through the shop, or the president may make a speech to lobby the local county commissioners for permission to build a new plant on some unused land.

The Negotiator Role: Managers also spend a lot of time negotiating. The head of an airline negotiates a new contract with the pilots' union, or the first-line supervisor negotiates a settlement to a grievance with the union's representative.

More recently, two management experts, Christopher Bartlett and Sumantra Ghoshal, emphasized the importance of managers in creating a responsive and change-oriented company.[14] Successful managers today, say Bartlett and Ghoshal, can't afford to focus just on the mechanical aspects of managing, such as designing organization charts or drawing up plans. Instead, successful managers cultivate three processes aimed at getting employees to focus their attention on creating change: the *entrepreneurial process*, the *competence-building process*, and the *renewal process*.

The Entrepreneurial Process. Entrepreneurship, say Bartlett and Ghoshal, refers to "the externally-oriented, opportunity-seeking attitudes that motivate employees to run their operations as if they own them."[15] In their study of 20 companies in Japan, the United States, and Europe, they found that successful managers focused much of their time and energy on getting employees to think of themselves as entrepreneurs. To do this, managers emphasized giving employees the authority, support, and rewards that self-disciplined and self-directed people need to run their operations as their own.

The Competence-Building Process. Bartlett and Ghoshal also found that "in a world of converging technologies, large companies have to do more than match their smaller competitors' flexibility and responsiveness. They must also exploit their big-company advantages, which lie not only in scale economies but also in the depth and breadth of employees' talents and knowledge."[16]

Successful managers therefore also devote much effort to creating an environment that lets employees really take charge: encouraging them to take on more responsibility, providing the education and training they need to build self-confidence, and allowing them to make mistakes without fear of punishment while coaching them to learn from their mistakes. Part of this competence-building process is aimed at "shaping an environment for collaborative behaviour."[17]

The Renewal Process. Successful managers also concentrate on fostering what Bartlett and Ghoshal call a renewal process—one "designed to challenge a company's strategies and the assumptions behind them."[18] In other words, managers have to make sure that they and all of their employees guard against complacency. Employees should develop the habit of questioning why things are done as they are and whether it might not be better to do things differently.

Despite the importance of managing the renewal process, many Canadian executives are falling behind. A study carried out by Andersen Consulting in June 1999 found that "70 percent of the executives surveyed don't see e-commerce or the Internet as something worthy of a strategic initiative. And yet, 84 percent of them say that within five years the economy will be heavily dependent on the Web."[19] It appears that many Canadian organizations need to revisit their business plans.

Do You Want to Be a Manager?

If you are thinking of being a manager, there is a wealth of research to help you decide whether it would be the right occupation for you.

Personality and Interests. Career counselling expert John Holland says that personality (including values, motives, and needs) is an important determinant of career choice. Specifically, he says that six basic "personal orientations" determine the sorts of careers to which people are drawn.[20] Research with his Vocational Preference Test (VPT) suggests that almost all successful managers fit at least one of the two following personality types or orientations from that group.

The Most Annoying Company in Canada

Sometimes it pays to be obnoxious. Just look at Infolink Technologies Ltd. (formerly Infolink Communications). George Theodore and computer whiz Cesar Correia started the Toronto-based Infolink in 1994. Since then the company has grown into a bustling business by sending out thousands of unsolicited advertisements by fax. In the process, it has managed to tick off almost anyone who owns a fax machine.[21]

Beginning with a couple of rented computers and holed up in a closet-sized office in a warehouse in Toronto, the duo began sending so-called "junk faxes" through their 25 phone lines. Their aim was to serve small businesses that were fed up with the low response rates to newspaper ads. In its first year, Infolink cleared $700 000. Now boasting 800 phone lines and state-of-the-art fax technology designed by Correia, Infolink can transmit up to 40 000 pages of advertisements, press releases, and corporate-disclosure documents to targeted audiences in an hour (about 500 000 pages of information a day) from its spacious downtown office. Such high volume has attracted a client list that includes the Government of Ontario, CIBC Wood Gundy Securities Inc., and Fidelity Investments Canada Ltd.

Whatever one thinks of their "fax blast" methods, Theodore and Correia have certainly been successful. Over the past three years, Infolink has grown 300 percent, and is expecting to generate more than $5 million in revenue. Infolink's quest for a bigger slice of the pie means going head-to-head with broadcasting giants. And Theodore and Correia think they can do just that. As Theodore says, "What we're telling them is that we're faster and we're cheaper."

Social orientation. Social people are attracted to careers that involve working with others in a helpful or facilitative way. Generally speaking, socially oriented people find it easy to talk with all kinds of people, are good at helping people who are upset or troubled, are skilled at explaining things to others, and enjoy doing social things like helping others with their personal problems, teaching, and meeting new people.

Enterprising orientation. Enterprising people tend to like working with people in a supervisory or persuasive way, in order to achieve some goal. They especially enjoy verbal activities aimed at influencing others. Enterprising people often characterize themselves as good public speakers, having reputations for being able to deal with difficult people, successfully organizing the work of others, and being ambitious and assertive. They enjoy influencing others, selling things, serving as an officer of a group, and supervising the work of others.

Competencies. Your competencies will also help determine how successful you might be at managing others. Professor Edgar Schein says that career planning is a continuing process of discovery. Schein also says that as you learn more about yourself, it becomes

career anchor
A concern or value that a worker will not give up if a choice has to be made.

managerial competence
The ability to operate effectively across multiple managerial functions.

apparent that you have a dominant **career anchor**, a concern or value that you will not give up if a choice has to be made. [22]

Based on his study of MIT graduates, Schein concluded that managers had a strong **managerial competence** career anchor. A management position of high responsibility is their ultimate goal. When pressed to explain why they believed they had the skills required to gain such positions, many graduates said they saw themselves as competent in three areas: (1) analytical competence (ability to identify, analyze, and solve problems under conditions of incomplete information and uncertainty); (2) interpersonal competence (ability to influence, supervise, lead, manipulate, and control people at all levels); and (3) emotional competence (the capacity to be stimulated by emotional and interpersonal crises rather than exhausted or debilitated by them, and the capacity to bear high levels of responsibility without becoming paralyzed).

Achievements. Research also suggests that you might gain some insight into your prospects by looking closely at your achievements to date. Industrial/organizational psychologists at AT&T conducted two long-term studies of managers to determine how their pre-management achievements were related to their success on the job. [23]

Employees who had gone to college or university showed much greater potential when first hired for middle and upper management positions than did those who had not. Eight years later the differences between these two groups were even more pronounced. Specifically, those who went to college rose (on average) much faster and higher in management than did those in the non-college sample. Grades were important, too. People with higher college or university grades showed greater potential for promotion early in their careers and, in fact, rose higher in management than did those with lower grades.

Students' college majors was another factor that influenced their later success as managers. Those who had majored in humanities and social sciences initially scored higher as potential managers and eventually moved faster and further up the corporate ladder. [24] Business administration majors ranked second, and math, science, and engineering majors ranked third. More specifically, the skills that seemed important for managerial success included decision making, intellectual ability, written communication skills, creativity in solving business problems, and motivation for advancement. Both the humanities and social science majors and the business administration majors ranked higher than graduates from other fields in leadership ability, oral communication skills, interpersonal skills, and flexibility.

These findings suggest that whatever your major might be, it is important to work on improving decision-making abilities, oral and written communication skills, and other interpersonal skills.

Managing in an Era of Competition and Change

Managers agree that industry is changing at an escalating pace. This is especially true for Canadian banks. A.L. Flood, former chairman and CEO of CIBC, declared:

> This is a time of momentous change in financial services. Our industry is going through massive structural adjustments that amount to a virtual revolution in the way we do business. Incredible advances in information technology are transforming the way we deliver products and services—and require capital investments. Powerful new competitors are entering our markets. Many are financial service giants whose size and resources dwarf those of Canadian banks. [25]

To remain competitive, the banking industry is already realizing the once-futuristic prediction that "virtual banks" would operate solely over telephone lines and in cyberspace, instead of being housed in bricks or mortar. For example, the CIBC has plans to put the infrastructure of a virtual bank in place. Although CIBC does not intend to abandon branch offices, the number will be greatly reduced, in keeping with the forecast by management consultants Deloitte & Touche that half of all bank branches in Canada will close during the next 7 to 10 years.[26] In addition, transactions at branch offices have changed radically: Bank machines are the norm, and the role of traditional bank tellers has changed as a result. Currently, CIBC delivers products and services through 1350 banking centres, a national network of 3800 ATMs, telephone banking, debit and credit cards, PC banking, and the Internet.

CIBC
www.cibc.com

In the wake of rapid change, not all managers are able to move quickly enough. In the past few years hundreds of banks, airlines, computer firms, and other businesses have failed or been gobbled up by stronger competitors. Even some of the strongest brands in the world have not been immune. After spending almost $1 billion in an unsuccessful attempt to make their company more efficient and more responsive, management found that sales at Levi Strauss were heading down instead of up. Faced with smart and fast-moving global competitors like The Gap and Calvin Klein, Levi's sales "fell apart" as its share of the U.S. jeans market dropped from 48 percent in 1990 to 25 percent in 1998. As a result, the plans, organization, leadership, and controls of Levi's top managers were increasingly under critical scrutiny.[27]

The Gap
www.gap.com

What forces are causing such changes and challenges for companies and managers around the world today? We'll look briefly at some important factors: technological innovation, globalization, deregulation, changing political systems, category killers, the new global workforce, cross-cultural management issues, and human capital.

Technological Innovation

Technological innovations are changing the way companies compete. For example, Inter-Design sells plastic clocks, refrigerator magnets, soap dishes, and similar products. Its president explains the impact of *information technology*, which merges communications systems with computers, this way: "In the seventies we went to the post office to pick up our orders. In the early 80s, we put in an 800 number. In the late 80s, we got a fax machine. In 1991, pressured by Target [a customer], we added electronic data interchange." Now, more than half of Inter-Design's orders arrive via modem, straight into company computers. Errors in order entry and shipping have all but disappeared, and both Target and Inter-Design have been able to slash finished goods inventories and, therefore, costs.[28]

technological innovation
Product and service innovation resulting from the use of technology.

Information technology like this has been a boon to many companies but a near-disaster for others. Wal-Mart became the industry leader in the 1990s in part because its managers used information technology to link stores with suppliers to ensure that diminishing stocks could be filled at once. Other companies, such as Canada Safeway or Toronto-based publisher Maclean Hunter (publisher of *Chatelaine* and *Flare* magazines, among others), use technology as a competitive advantage to ensure that supply meets customer demand. As we saw with Chapters, the Internet is revolutionizing how business is done. Software programs, newspapers, and music CDs no longer need to be packaged and delivered to stores, but instead are delivered electronically over the Internet. Airline ticket sales and securities transactions over the Internet already occur in large numbers.

Target
www.target.com

Wal-Mart
www.walmart.com

Without physical stores and staffs, many Internet sellers can offer much lower prices than local bricks-and-mortar stores. And the availability of easily accessible price information means that retailers of thousands of products from clothing to boats must now drive down their costs in order to match Internet sellers' prices, and even develop e-commerce resources of their own. For example, Canadian bookstores have developed Web sites such as Indigo.ca and Chapters.ca to compete with the American online giant Amazon.com. The result is continuing pressure to drive down costs and to manage firms in the most efficient and flexible manner possible.

Globalization

Globalization is important in the context of modern business, and in large part is responsible for enhanced international competition. Throughout the world, firms that once

globalization
The integration of markets globally.

competed only with local firms—from airlines to car makers to banks—have discovered that they must now face an onslaught of new and efficient foreign competitors.

One large Canadian enterprise involved in global export is Abitibi-Consolidated, which sells newsprint and other forest products around the world. Or take, for example, Bombardier of Montreal. This Canadian multinational operates in four areas: transportation equipment, aerospace and defence, motorized consumer products, and financial and real estate services. A diversified company, Bombardier has production facilities in Canada, the United States, Mexico, China, Austria, Belgium, Germany, Switzerland, Finland, France, the Czech Republic, and the United Kingdom. With the help of about 55 000 employees the company markets products on 5 continents, with more than 92 percent of sales coming from markets outside Canada.[29] Bombardier, Abitibi, and other companies in the global arena can no longer focus on single markets, products, or technologies.

The impact of globalization is not limited to large corporations. Many small Canadian companies are also involved in international trade. For example, Seagull Pewter & Silversmiths Ltd. of Pugwash, Nova Scotia, sells pewter giftware in the United States and Europe, while I.P. Constructors Ltd. of Calgary designs and manufactures a complete range of oil and gas processing equipment that is exported.

Deregulation

Recently government involvement in business has decreased through deregulation. **Deregulation** refers to a reduction in the number of laws affecting business activity and in the powers of government enforcement agencies. In Canada, as in other countries, deregulation has occurred in many industries, including airlines, banking, trucking, and communications.

In the communications business, the historic decision by the Canadian Radio-television and Telecommunications Commission (CRTC) to allow competition among long-distance telephone companies has made long-distance calling much cheaper (though this advantage may be offset by the persistent phone calls we receive from various carriers competing fiercely with one another to steal customers). Deregulation in the Canadian airline industry has meant that the government no longer dictates how many airlines there will be and where they will fly. Despite the freedom from regulation, if organizations are not well managed, industry inefficiencies will result. This was clearly illustrated by the dance between Air Canada and Canadian Airlines as they both struggled to survive.

Changing Political Systems

As nations such as the Philippines, Argentina, Russia, and Chile join the ranks of democracy, central planning and communism are being replaced by capitalism. Such political

In the years leading up to the opening of the first McDonald's outlet in Moscow in 1990, McDonald's of Canada had to negotiate in a political environment that was not overly friendly to capitalistic ideology.

changes have in turn triggered the opening of new markets with hundreds of millions of potential customers. For business firms, the opportunities are enormous. But the burgeoning demand for goods and services also brings increased global competition.

One of the first Canadian enterprises to operate in the former Soviet Union was McDonald's of Canada, which opened Moscow's first McDonald's outlet in 1990. Operating in an environment filled with communist ideology proved to be a huge challenge. The negotiations alone took 12 years to complete. And pricing was an issue. At the time the restaurant opened, the price of a Big Mac was $2.80 in an economy where the average monthly income was less than $200.[30] In another example, Volkswagen of Germany formed a joint venture with Skoda in the Czech Republic. The result was the building of a state-of-the-art plant in an area where labour rates remain inexpensive. One of the main challenges was training and motivating a workforce that had operated under a different management system for so many years. [31]

Category Killers: Where Does a 2000-Pound Gorilla Sit?

A 2000-pound gorilla sits wherever it wants to, just like **category killers** such as Office Depot, Burnaby, BC–based Future Shop, Wal-Mart, and Chapters. These mammoth stores rely on economies of scale and wide selections to drive down costs and prices and to attract huge numbers of buyers. Most small competitors—neighbourhood hardware stores, computer stores, and bookstores, for instance—find they can't get their costs or prices low enough to compete, and are without the product range to do so anyway. Most are squeezed out of business by the relentless competition. In Vancouver, this was the case with Duthie's Books. Founded as a family business, the bookstore chain thrived until the giant Chapters stores came to town. Within about one year, the smaller business was forced to close the doors to all but one of its locations.

When Wal-Mart entered Canada many retailers began to worry. In fact, the entry of the superstore caused other Canadian businesses to be more competitive, or to go under. Wal-Mart's presence partly contributed to the demise of Eaton's, which was not able to keep up with the fierce price and volume competition from the megastores. Wal-Mart gives consumers what they want: low prices, good selection, convenience, and fast entry and exit time. Warehouse clubs and other category killers like Home Depot are also challenging traditional distribution and manufacturing practices.

category killers
Retailers who carry large selections with competitive prices in order to attract buyers.

The New Global Workforce

More firms are transferring their operations abroad, not only to seek cheaper labour but also to tap into what *Fortune* magazine calls "a vast new supply of skilled labour around the world."[32] Even today, most multinational firms set up manufacturing plants abroad, partly to establish beachheads in promising markets and partly to use other countries' professionals and engineers. For example, ASEA Brown Boveri (ABB), a $30-billion-a-year Swiss builder of transportation and electric generation systems, has 25 000 new employees in former communist countries and has shifted many jobs from Western to Eastern Europe. Brampton, Ontario–based Nortel Networks has expanded all over the world. Today, Nortel has 16 000 employees in manufacturing, research and development, and sales facilities in 30 countries throughout Europe, the Middle East, and Africa.[33] Bombardier, based in Montreal, has 2000 employees in Mexico alone.[34]

Tapping into overseas labour markets is a two-edged sword for managers and for employers. Employers gain thousands of potential new highly skilled employees, but also must compete for and manage a geographically dispersed workforce. For employees—especially those in Canada—it means competing for jobs with a worldwide labour force.

Nortel
www.nortelnetworks. com

Cross-Cultural Management Issues

It is important to note that the management roles and functions outlined in this chapter vary when applied across different cultures. Management researchers have found culturally based differences in people's values, attitudes, and behaviours. For example, at the Skoda plant mentioned earlier, managers have distinct ways of viewing the world depending on whether they are of Czech or German origin.

The Czechs had lived in a planned economy for about 40 years, and most were unfamiliar with quality control. In fact, efficiency in plant production was sometimes discouraged. The Czechs were hesitant to take on responsibility, but they are proud and wanted to learn to work differently under the new system. The German managers from a free-market economy focused on time and efficiency, and were sometimes impatient with workers who didn't understand the meaning of work in the same way as they did. Figuring out ways to "change the minds" of the workers to a new philosophy of work was key, and depended on cultural understanding. Over time—and with huge amounts of training for the Czechs, improved communication between the Czechs and the Germans, and revised reward systems—the plant and its operations were radically transformed.[35] In an increasingly complex and globally focused business environment, it is imperative that savvy managers understand how to operate within diverse cultural contexts.

Human Capital: A Shift to Service and Knowledge Work

Another trend today is the growing emphasis on **human capital**[36]—the knowledge, training, skills, and expertise of a firm's workers. The emphasis on education and human capital reflects several trends in the business environment. One is the growing importance of service work, where employees provide a service rather than a product. Industries in which service work prevails include retailing, consulting, teaching, and law. Over two-thirds of the Canadian workforce is now involved in producing services, rather than things. Service jobs put a bigger premium on worker education and knowledge than do traditional jobs, and thus they add more to a company's "human capital." As James Brian Quinn, an expert in this area, puts it, "Intellect is the core resource in producing and delivering services."[37]

Human capital is also important in the manufacturing realm, and is transforming traditional jobs in the auto and textile industries. As Bill Gates of Microsoft puts it:

> In the new organization the worker is no longer a cog in a machine but is an intelligent part of the overall process. Welders at some steel jobs now have to know algebra and geometry to figure weld angles from computer-generated designs...new digital photocopiers require the service personnel to have an understanding of computers and the Internet, not just skills with a screwdriver.[38]

Innovation, driven by competition, demands more highly skilled employees. In companies like 3M it is not unusual for more than one-quarter of sales to come from products that are less than five years old. As a result, "innovating—creating new products, new services, new ways of turning out goods more cheaply—has become the most urgent concern of corporations everywhere."[39] In this new era of work, intelligent and creative employees are demanding broader jobs with less structure. In turn, managers are required to manage differently from the "command and control" models of the past.

The Future Is Now

The Modern Organization

Things are moving amazingly fast in the world of business today. In fact, they're moving "at the speed of business," to quote a recent UPS ad. Technology, globalization, deregulation, changing political systems, the new workforce, and a shift to service and knowledge work are putting companies of all types under tremendous pressure to respond faster, and to be ever more cost-effective and competitive. Some of the key changes facing managers are illustrated in Figure 1.2. What does this mean for how companies are actually managed? Perhaps the best way to answer that question is to look at how cutting-edge businesses are being managed today.

Smaller Organizational Units. More people will set up businesses for themselves, and many firms like GM and IBM will continue to downsize. Even within big firms, the operating units will divide into small, self-contained mini-units.

Cypress
Semiconductor
www.cypress.com

Cypress Semiconductor is one example of a firm seeking to be more entrepreneurial. Tom Rogers, president of this California firm, believes that large organizations stifle innovation. So when a new product must be developed, he doesn't do it within the existing corporation. Instead, he creates a separate start-up company under the Cypress umbrella. "I would rather see our billion-dollar company of the 1990s be 10 $100 million companies, all strong, growing, healthy and aggressive as hell," Rogers says. "The alternative is an aging billion-dollar company that spends more time defending its turf than

Explosion of Technological Innovation
- Vast numbers of new patents
- Three new Web sites "born" each minute
- New computers outdated in six months
- New high-tech factories

Globalization of Markets and Competition
- Staggering number of new competitors
- New pressures for quality and productivity
- New opportunities

Deregulation
- Banking
- Telecoms
- Airlines

Changing Demographics
- More diversity
- Two-wage-earner families
- Increasing global workforce

New Political Systems
- Former Soviet Union moves to capitalism
- Rise of European Union, NAFTA, Asia

Leads to

Uncertainty, Turbulence, Rapid Change
- More consumer choices
- Mergers and divestitures
- Joint ventures
- More complexity
- Short product life cycles
- Market fragmentation
- More uncertainty for managers
- Record number of business failures
- From tasks to processes

So Companies Must Be

Fast, Responsive, Adaptive
- Flat organizations
- Downsized
- Quality-conscious
- Empowered
- Smaller units
- Decentralized
- Human-capital oriented
- Boundaryless
- Values- and vision-oriented
- Team-based

FIGURE 1.2
Fundamental Changes Facing Managers
A series of forces—globalized competition, technology revolution, new competitors, and changing tastes—are creating outcomes that include more uncertainty, more choices, and more complexity. The result is that the organizational winners of today and tomorrow will have to be responsive, smaller, flatter, and oriented towards adding value through people.

growing." True to his words, Rogers already has four successful start-ups under development.[40]

Another company that moved to smaller organizational units is Swiss electrical equipment maker ABB, which "dis-organized itself" into mini-units to be more responsive to customer needs. Within two years of taking over this $30-billion firm, former chairman Percy Barnevik "dis-organized" its 215 000 employees into 5000 mini-companies, each averaging only about 50 workers.[41] For instance, the ABB hydropower unit in Finland is a mini-company that serves only its own Finnish customers. Each of ABB's mini-companies is run by a manager and three or four lieutenants. Efficiency and responsiveness are the net results.

New Forms of Control. Sit with Larry Carter, chief financial officer (CFO) of Cisco Systems, and you can see the whole company laid out before you.[42] This is because software manufacturer Cisco Systems is in the vanguard of firms using sophisticated "real-time" computerized financial systems to give their top executives access to data almost instantaneously. As a relatively young company (founded in 1984), Cisco "...doesn't have a bunch of incompatible, old record-keeping systems gumming things up." It therefore started with a clean slate and computerized the entire financial control system.

Canada Post also wants to transform itself to keep pace with the electronic age. Its e-Parcel service automatically calculates the weight of a package and the distance it must travel, and allows users to keep track of deliveries. Canada Post hopes to compete with delivery giant UPS by using the e-postal system to attract direct-mail clients.[43] Vancouver-based Sierra Systems Consultants Inc. is in the business of improving clients' productivity and heightening their competitive position through information technology–based business solutions. This includes better management and control of systems in the areas of human resources, customer information, finances, and health.[44]

Modified Organizational Structures. Instead of the traditional pyramid-shaped organization with its seven or more layers of management, flat organizations with just three or four levels are increasingly likely to prevail. Consider Swiss electrical equipment maker ABB once again. As part of the transformation of that 215 000-employee organization, management levels were shrunk to just three. A 13-member top-management executive committee is based in Zurich. Below this is a 250-member executive level that includes country managers and executives in charge of groups of businesses. Below that is a level consisting of 5000 mini-company managers and their management teams.[45] By slicing out layers of management, ABB is able to be more responsive to customer needs and competitors' moves. Also important is the fact that employees will have more autonomy to do the work for which they are responsible.

Traditional organizational structures, in which managers regularly spend time with employees, have also changed as a result of the growth of virtual organizations in which employees telecommute. Instead of going to work every day, people do some or all or their work away from the office using fax, phone, and computer. **Telecommuting** reduces or eliminates travel time for workers, and enables them to stay "connected" to the workplace while working with less supervision than in traditional organizations.

More and more Canadian companies are taking advantage of telecommuting. B.C. Tel and Bentall Development Inc. jointly developed a satellite telecommuting office in Langley, B.C.[46]

At Nortel, about 5500 of its 75 000 staff participate in a teleworking programme, called HomeBase. According to Mike Taylor, director of HomeBase, a recent survey by the company found that job satisfaction is 30 percent higher among staff taking part in the teleworking scheme. In addition, teleworking frees up expensive office space, and even allows companies to axe some of their offices altogether. Nortel was able to close an entire office in Dallas as demand for its teleworking program took off. Taylor believes that it costs Nortel about $5000 to set up a new teleworker in the U.S. or Canada—which it easily recoups within the first year, largely due to savings in office rent.[47]

telecommuting
A type of work in which people do some or all or their work away from the office using fax, phone, and computer.

team-based organization
A company in which work is organized around teams.

Team-Based Organizations. At GM's subsidiary Saturn Corporation, teams prevail as an important organizational feature. For example, virtually all shop floor work is organized around work teams of 10 to 12 employees. Each team is responsible for a complete task, such as installing door units, checking electrical systems, or maintaining automated machines.

The work teams don't have traditional supervisors. Instead, highly trained workers do their own hiring, control their own budgets, monitor the quality of their own work, and generally manage themselves. Are too many of the door parts not fitting right? Then the team must find the problem and get the parts supplier to solve it. Is a co-worker always late? Then the team must discipline him or her in order to manage its (and its team members') own time.

Teamwork has been enhanced by the growth of virtual organizations, which were discussed earlier. Some teams operate virtually, transcending distance, time zones, and organizational boundaries. Virtual teams evolved as a way to make working across continents and countries an easy and practical way to achieve superior results. In some companies like Nortel, a project can be started in Toronto, then passed to counterparts in different time zones so that work on it can continue around the clock.

Managers As Change Agents. Today's managers need to be facilitators of change. As GE's CEO, Jack Welch, puts it, "You've got to be on the cutting edge of change. You can't simply maintain the status quo, because somebody's always coming from another country with another product, or consumers' tastes change, or the cost structure does, or there's a technology breakthrough. If you are not fast and adaptable, you are vulnerable."[48]

To be effective in the change process, new bases of power are required. According to management theorist Rosabeth Moss Kanter, leaders can no longer rely on their formal positions or authority to get their jobs done.[49] Instead, "success depends increasingly on tapping into sources of good ideas, on figuring out whose collaboration is needed to act on those ideas, and on working with both to produce results. In short, the new managerial work implies very different ways of obtaining and using power."[50] Peter Drucker, often described as "the father of modern management," puts it this way: "You have to learn to manage in situations where you don't have command authority, where you are neither controlled nor controlling."[51] In the new millennium, managers will have to win the respect and commitment of their highly trained and empowered employees.

Emphasis on Vision and Values. Formulating a clear vision and values to which employees can commit will be more important than ever. Managers will need to communicate clearly what is important and unimportant, and what employees should and should not do. As GE's CEO, Jack Welch, noted:

> Every organization needs values, but a lean organization needs them even more. When you strip away the support system of staffs and layers, people need to re-learn their habits and expectations or else the stress will just overwhelm them…values [are] what enable people to guide themselves through that kind of change.[52]

Other experts agree. Peter Drucker says that today's organizations—staffed as they are by professionals and other employees who largely control their own behaviour—require "clear, simple, common objectives that translate into particular actions." In other words, they need a clear vision of where the firm is heading.[53] Even without a lot of supervisors to guide them, employees can then be steered by the company's vision and values.

Knowledge-Based Organizations. Increasingly, organizations rely on teams of highly trained and educated professionals who apply their knowledge to clients' problems, in a setting in which they direct and discipline their own activities. Take for example South River, Newfoundland–based IES Health Technologies Inc. Founders Kim Crosbie and Stephen Mercer grew up in small towns in Newfoundland, and created a computer game that helps children with asthma to manage their condition. Their partner is John Hopkins University in Baltimore. Using skilled teams, they created unique knowledge-based solutions for which distance is irrelevant.[54] Managers in knowledge-based organizations must help their employees get their jobs done by training and coaching them, removing

knowledge-based organizations
Organizations that create and sustain competitive advantage through the application of specialized knowledge.

roadblocks, and getting them the resources they need. You can not simply "boss" teams of professionals.

The change to knowledge-based organizations highlights one major difference between the old and the new manager. Yesterday's manager thinks of himself or herself as a "manager" or "boss." The new manager thinks of himself or herself as a "coach," "team leader," or "internal consultant." The old-style manager makes most decisions alone; the new one invites others to join in the decision making. The old-style manager hoards information to build his or her personal power. The new manager shares information to help subordinates get their jobs done.[55]

Employee Decision Making. Work requires constant learning, "higher-order" thinking, and much more worker commitment. The result is employee empowerment and less of a 9-to-5 mentality.

Experts like Karl Albrecht argue in favour of turning the typical organization upside down.[56] They say that today's organization should put the customer on top and emphasize that every move the company makes must be geared towards satisfying customer needs. To do so, management must empower its front-line employees—the front desk clerks at the hotel, the cabin attendants on the Air Canada plane, and the attendants at Petro-Canada—with the authority to respond quickly to these needs. The main purpose of managers in this "upside-down" organization is to serve the front-line employees, to ensure that they have what they need to do their jobs—and thus to serve the customers.

Let's return to the example of Swiss electrical equipment maker ABB. To speed decision making the 5000 mini-companies were made autonomous and their employees were empowered to make most of their own business decisions. If a customer has a complaint about a $50 000 machine, a mini-company employee can approve a replacement on the spot, rather than having to wait for his or her recommendation for replacement to be reviewed by several levels of management. This not only provides employees with greater responsibility, but also provides better service to the customer.[57]

SUMMARY OF LEARNING OBJECTIVES

1. **Explain the management process, including what managers do.** Managers play a key role in motivating and channelling employees so that they can achieve the goals of the organization. Managers get their work done through people, by planning, organizing, leading, and controlling. Top managers spend more time planning and setting goals, while lower-level managers concentrate more on implementing those goals and directing and controlling employees to achieve them. Managers can be classified according to organizational level (top, middle, or first-line), position (executives, managers or directors, or supervisors), and functional title (vice-president of production, sales manager, or chief bookkeeper).

2. **Describe the changing role for managers.** Increased competition is forcing managers into new and different roles. Rather than being dictators, modern managers are coaches and facilitators. In an increasingly complex world, managers need to rely on workers for assistance and advice, and cannot expect to have all the answers.

3. **Describe why the "people side" of management is important.** The real strength of organizations is people, and for managers to be successful, they must be able to manage people well. More and more, part of the management equation means involving employees in decision-making processes in the organization. As companies move towards new forms of business (i.e., virtual teams, or e-commerce), it will be even more important to create management systems that make people feel part of the organization.

4. **Outline current forces creating turbulence and change for organizations and managers.** Today's managers face numerous challenges, including technological innovation and trying to keep up with the flood of information available, globalization and how to position or reposition a company to take advantage of international opportunities, deregulation, category killers who by virtue of their size have price and volume advantages, a dispersed global workforce, a need to understand cross-cultural management issues, and shifting boundaries to new forms of work, with an emphasis on service and knowledge work.

5. **Discuss the main trends in how modern organizations are changing and managed.** Organizations themselves look and feel different. The main trends in how organizations are changing include smaller organizational units, new forms of control, fewer hierarchical structures, and greater emphasis on teams. In a rapidly transforming environment, managers operate as facilitators of change. There is an emphasis on vision and values, knowledge-based work, and greater decision-making power for employees.

TYING IT ALL TOGETHER

As we have seen in this chapter, managers play a central role in whether organizations are successful. However, in the rapidly changing new world order of business, managers must be flexible, open to new ideas, and willing to embrace novel technologies. Organizations look different than they did in the past, tend to be more decentralized, move faster, and may be staffed by workers who work from home rather than in the office. These changes provide new opportunities for organizations—but only if they are managed well.

This chapter explains what managers do, and describes the trends that are forcing companies and other types of organizations to become more competitive. The fact that companies must be more competitive means that managers must organize and manage their companies to be faster and more efficient. In Chapter 2, The Environment of Management: Canadian and Global, we'll look more closely at globalization and its effects on how managers manage.

CRITICAL THINKING EXERCISE

1. In the 1999 book entitled *The New Thing: A Silicon Valley Story,* Mike Lewis outlines key issues likely to frame the next century. The story itself is about sailing into the future, and focuses on how two different and powerful firms are approaching their journey. Lewis argues that Jim Clark, founder of Netscape, is the model for the future. Clark is seen as a genius "on an endless search for some unattainable solution." Clark is described as having a talent for anarchy that serves him well at this juncture in history. In contrast, Microsoft's Bill Gates is characterized as a passive self-promoter who wants the future "to look exactly like the present." Using Chapter 1 as a guide, speculate on the management models you think will evolve and why? Will the future be the world of Jim Clark or the world of Bill Gates? Predict what a manager might be like by the year 2050.

EXPERIENTIAL EXERCISE

1. In December 1999 Air Canada won government and regulatory approval to acquire its long-time but ailing rival Canadian Airlines after a long battle for su-

premacy of Canada's skies. Canadian Transport Minister David Collenette said that the federal government would allow the $62 million acquisition of Canadian Airlines to proceed, but only with the introduction of legislation to guard against competition in the nation's air industry. The acquisition vaults Air Canada from twentieth to tenth spot among the world's major airlines. Critics of the deal are concerned about a monopoly in the industry and price gouging. But according to Collenette, "The government will not tolerate price gouging. Clearly the best guarantee for reasonable airfares is viable competition. However, the government also believes that measures for dealing with pricing and predatory behaviour can be effectively enshrined in the legislation that will be introduced in February [2000]." What do you think? Will the takeover help Air Canada to compete in the international airline industry? Can legislation be effective in controlling the prices offered to customers? What do you think the future of the airline industry will be?

INTERNET EXERCISE

To learn more about the process of management and issues important to managers in a high-technology company, visit the Web site for the Bulldog Group at www.bulldog.com. Review the home page, as well as the press releases.

1. What are the key and evolving issues for the company?

2. What role do partnerships play for the Bulldog Group?

3. As a technology leader in its category, what does the company do to stay ahead of the competition?

CASE STUDY 1-1

Going E-Postal

Canada's mail service, Canada Post Corp., wants to become a leader in the electronic age. New services are popping up, including e-Parcel, which automatically calculates package weights and the distance they must travel. Customers are also given a wider choice of postal services, itemizing the exact cost and date of arrival. At the end of 1999, an array of online options included electronic money orders, secure couriers, and even an Electronic Post Office that delivers financial statements, direct mail, and bills—with electronic payment options included. The "ugly duckling" of the communications industry, which can trace its often-troubled ancestry back to the creation of the first post office in Halifax in 1755, is struggling to transform itself into the swan of the electronic age.

Sales agents have been zealous in courting direct-mail clients, emphasizing Canada Post's ability to target deliveries. As a result, direct-marketing revenues are predicted to rise from $687 million in 1998–1999 to more than $1.1 billion in 2003–2004. Meanwhile, Canada Post is planning to transform its postal outlets from stamp counters into one-stop operations that will offer everything from Internet access to the Electronic Post Office to basic financial services such as the establishment of registered retirement saving plans with participating banks. "Canada Post has to become much quicker on its feet," says Daniel Sawaya, Canada Post's vice-president of marketing and product development. "This is not a difficult time: it is the biggest single opportunity Canada Post has ever had."

This "opportunity" began with a wake-up call in the mid-1990s, when electronic communications and courier services began to carve chunks out of the postal business. Over the past five years, Canada Post's total annual volume, which includes everything from direct-mail flyers to packages, dropped to 9.6 billion pieces from 11.6 billion. Personal letters are declining at the rate of about 1 percent a year as plugged-in customers

→

switch to the convenience of e-mail. The writing was on the wall. Canada Post had to either transform or perish.

But joining the electronic frenzy has not been easy or simple—if only because Canada Post has had to fight its own lingering reputation as a strike-prone, inefficient relic of another era. In 1981, Ottawa transformed the former government department into a Crown corporation—largely because it was exasperated with the frequent labour disruptions, poor service, and hefty annual deficits. The new corporation's mandate included Ottawa's instructions to deliver the mail on time, improve labour relations—and make money.

The results have been mixed, and it's still unclear how Canada Post's latest transformation will fare. However, the good news is that last year Canada Post made a profit of $50 million, its fourth consecutive year in the black. On the other hand, the postal corporation was still without a president and CEO more than a year after Georges Clermont resigned in December 1998. Former Liberal Cabinet minister André Ouellet has served as interim president and CEO, but his term is due to end soon. The big question now is who will take charge, and lead Canada Post into the electronic age.

Questions

1. What forces and trends are responsible for the changes that Canada Post has made to the way it does business?

2. What are the opportunities and threats for managers facing wide-scale changes in the organization?

3. What issues are involved in leading organizational transformation at Canada Post in the absence of a president and CEO?

Canada Post
www.canadapost.ca

A Canadian Category Killer: Future Shop

Future Shop, based in Burnaby, B.C., is one of North America's largest computer and electronics retailers—and has become a category killer in its own right. Established in 1982, the company has exploded to over 83 stores with approximately 6000 employees in Canada. Its operating strategy is simple: "[T]o provide exceptional value to both the retail and corporate customer by offering a unique combination of guaranteed low pricing, brand name selection and unsurpassed customer service, before, during and after the sale."

In the rapidly changing world of retailing, and now e-commerce, even category killer stores like Future Shop are challenged to change. According to Danny Kucharsky, Future Shop "has figured out how to avoid having its online presence cannibalize sales" in its retail outlets. The family-owned company's strategy of complete integration of its Web site and its stores aims to ensure that in-store sales that are lost to the Web are offset by in-store sales that are won due to information provided on the Web site.

The group manager of Internet marketing at Future Shop, Vida Morkunas, says there are several ways to achieve their competitive goal. This includes a Web site that contains more content about products than is offered in the store, including a "compare tool" that allows browsers to compare features of similar products and weigh the pros and cons of each. An e-zine feature contains independent product reviews and online experts are available to answer questions.

The strategy seems to be working. The Web site has had more than 9 million hits in a single month. And visitors are enticed to continue shopping through invitations to "friends-and-family nights" in Future Shop stores in major cities. By next year, it will be possible to order and pay online and then pick up purchases in the stores. Customers will even be able to return Web-purchased products to stores, or take them to stores for repairs. Web kiosks are also planned within stores, so that sales associates and customers can search the company's Web site for product information. "The face

→

of Future Shop retail will change," Morkunas says. "Compensation will change, incentives to the salespeople and the sales managers of the stores will change. Everything is currently being redesigned."

Questions

1. What are the risks for businesses that are forced to compete with category killers like Future Shop?

2. How do you think management is changing to accommodate the wider use of e-commerce in business?

3. Although not given much attention to date, how do you think Web sites can be developed to take into account the cultural differences of customers?

Future Shop
www.futureshop.ca

YOU BE THE CONSULTANT

KnitMedia Is Up and Running

When it comes to managing a business, there's nothing quite like managing a small, fast-growing enterprise like Michael Dorf's alternative music and entertainment company, KnitMedia. Managing a giant like IBM or GE requires decisions about how to organize, hire, motivate, and keep track of the activities of tens of thousands (and often hundreds of thousands) of employees and of billions of dollars. Managing a small firm like KnitMedia presents a somewhat different set of challenges: only very simple or no support systems (accountants, budget systems, control systems) in place, and only a few or no managers to call on to help get a job done. And in the highly competitive music business environment, you have all of those giants, like AOL/Time Warner and Sony, waiting for you to make a mistake.

At the end of every chapter in this book, you will have an opportunity to meet Michael Dorf and apply that chapter's materials to the challenges faced by his company, KnitMedia, LLC. Its businesses include several independent record labels, a festival division, a NewMedia/Internet division, and a growing chain of Knitting Factory music clubs, including ones in Manhattan and Hollywood and one soon to open in Berlin. You will find a good deal of information about KnitMedia and its businesses in each of the end-of-chapter cases, and more information on KnitMedia's Web site at www.knitmedia.com.

KnitMedia began, to some extent, as a result of

economic necessity. In 1985, while still a college student in Madison, Wisconsin, Dorf began managing the band Swamp Thing. He and the band started Flaming Pie Records to record and distribute their songs. After struggling for two years to get Swamp Thing some exposure, Dorf and his partner, Louis Spitzer, found themselves in New York's downtown SoHo district. They rented a dilapidated office on Houston Street between the Bowery and Broadway, and the Knitting Factory was born. The initial idea (as Dorf describes it in his book *Knitting Music*) was to have an art gallery/performance space that sold coffee, tea, and a small assortment of foods. As he and Spitzer said in their first press release:

> The Knitting Factory is primarily a showcase. Our aim is to weave strands of art mediums into a congruent whole, from the Wednesday night poetry series to the works on the walls. The Knitting Factory is also a café. It serves interesting forms of food like a fondue with fresh fruit. The Knitting Factory considers many things art and is open to suggestions. Hope to see you soon.[58]

Dorf's real motivation at the time was "...To earn enough money to live and to cover the rent for Flaming Pie Records." There wasn't much managing to do, since KnitMedia had few employees. Now, however, it's a different story: After nine profitable years of growth, Dorf and his company recently received an infusion of about $5 million to expand the business. And today KnitMedia, LLC, includes not only several separate businesses, but an executive management team. That team, as of 2000, is made up of Michael Dorf, president and chief executive officer; Allan Fried, chief operating officer; Glen Max, KnitMedia properties programming director; Ed Greer, senior vice-president; Stephanie Oxley, vice-president, KnitMedia labels; Mark Harabedian, vice-president for finance; Victoria DeRose, vice-president for marketing and business development; Chris Shields, director festival division; David Brenner, vice-president of NewMedia; and Mitch Goldman, chief content officer.

These managers know they are in a competitive business, one that is changing very quickly. They also know that as a young company they still have a way to go as far as setting up management systems is concerned. In one recent interview, for instance, Mark Harabedian, the new vice-president for finance, said: "My great challenge, my first great challenge when I got here" was to revamp the whole finance system, so Michael and the other managers could maintain better control over the firm's quickly expanding operations.

Understanding that they face these challenges, the KnitMedia managers have asked you and your team to sign on as consultants. Many of the KnitMedia team have backgrounds in the arts and music, rather than in business, so they're looking forward to drawing on your expanding knowledge of how to plan, organize, lead, and control an organization. Since they're now in the process of planning how KnitMedia will expand in the next few years, their first questions concern the competitive challenges they can expect to face, and the broad management questions that may arise.

Team Exercises and Questions

Use what you learned in this chapter to answer the following questions from Michael Dorf and his management team:

1. Few industries are undergoing as much rapid change as music, entertainment, and Internet/new media— the three industries in which KnitMedia is involved. What are the trends (such as consolidation) taking place today for which we'll have to plan?

2. Who are the key competitors in New York City for the Knitting Factory Club? (*Hint*: Use the Internet to compile a list.)

3. What are the basic management tasks each of our executives can expect to address as part of their day-to-day duties? (*Hint*: What is the management process?)

Appendix

Foundations of Modern Management

The roots of management can be traced back to antiquity. Hunters banded into tribes for protection, the Egyptians used organizations to build pyramids and control the rise and fall of the Nile, and the Romans relied on organizing to build their armies and control their empire. Management is thus a very old idea (as Figure A1.1 illustrates).

2052 B.C. to 1786 B.C. In the Middle Kingdom of Egypt, leaders introduce the subdivision of labour into factories (if papyrus records are to be believed).	Around 59 B.C. Julius Caesar keeps people up-to-date with handwritten sheets and posters around Rome. Ever since, the greatness of leaders has been measured partly by their ability to communicate.	1906 Sears Roebuck opens its Chicago mail-order plant. The Sears catalogue makes goods available to an entirely new audience.	1908 William Hoover sees that automobiles would kill his business, which makes leather accessories for horse-drawn carriages. So he starts the Electric Suction Sweeper Co., creating the mass-market vacuum cleaner.	1955 Ray Kroc likes Mac and Dick McDonald's food stand in San Bernardino, California, so much that he opens his own franchised restaurant and forms McDonald's Corp.	1984 In his dorm room at the University of Texas at Austin, Michael Dell starts selling PCs direct and building them to order.

FIGURE A1.1
The History of Management

Some recurring themes become apparent when we view management over the ages. First, many of the concepts we take for granted today, such as dividing employees into departments, can be traced to the earliest human organizations, including those of the Egyptians and the ancient Greeks. The close supervision and reliance on coercion and rules that management expert Peter Drucker has called "command and control" is also a product of earlier times, in particular of the militaristic organizations of Egypt and ancient Rome.

Second, we will see that the forms that organizations take and the ways that managers manage have always been a product of the time. As futurist Alvin Toeffler has said (in describing 19th-century management):

> Each age produces a form of organization appropriate to its own tempo. During the long epic of agricultural civilization, societies were marked by low transience. Delays in communication and transportation slowed the rate at which information moved. The pace of individual life was comparatively slow. And organizations were seldom called upon to make what we would regard as high-speed decisions.[1]

So management is also an evolutionary process. Let us now look back to the beginning of modern management theory.

SCIENTIFIC MANAGEMENT

Management theory as we know it today is an outgrowth of the first attempts to view the management process with new and almost scientific rigour.

The Industrial Revolution

By 1750, with the advent of the Industrial Revolution, what Toeffler referred to as "the long epic of agricultural civilization" was about to end. The Industrial Revolution was a period of several decades during which machine power was increasingly substituted for human or animal labour. During these years several major trends converged. Scientific and technological discoveries, including the invention of the steam engine and the use of electricity, contributed to enormous increases in productivity and output. England, generally recognized as the epicentre of the Industrial Revolution, had a stable, constitutional government, a sensitivity to laissez-faire (hands-off) economics, and a strong spirit of self-reliance. In his book *The Wealth of Nations*, Adam Smith described the division and specialization of work as a pillar of the burgeoning competitive market system.[2]

The Industrial Environment

For firms in the 1800s, industrialization meant emphasizing resource accumulation and company growth. Division of work and specialization required the high volume and stability that only growth could bring. Growth led to higher profits; as sales, volume, and stability increased, unit costs decreased.

But enlarged operations created new problems for entrepreneurs. They needed management techniques to run their new, large-scale enterprises. These industrialists therefore quickly adopted the structures and principles followed by managers of an earlier day, such as centralized decision making, a rigid chain of command, specialized division of work, and autocratic leadership. All of these had been born in military and religious organizations and subsequently were nurtured for thousands of years.

Frederick W. Taylor and Scientific Management

The race to grow and accumulate resources was particularly pronounced in the United States. The War of 1812 severed the United States from England economically and spurred the growth of domestic manufacturing operations. Technological advances included the steamboat, the cotton gin, the iron plough, the telegraph, the electric motor, and the expansion of a railroad and canal network that opened up new markets for producers. In turn, these new markets provided the volume that was a basic requirement for effective division of work.

Historian Alfred Chandler has pointed out that by the late 1800s many new industries were completing the resource-accumulation stage of their existence and beginning to move into what he calls a rationalization stage.[3] The management focus shifted from growth to efficiency. As organizations became large and unwieldy, and as competition became more intense, managers needed better ways to use the resources they had accumulated. They sought new concepts and techniques to cut costs and boost efficiency. It was out of this environment that the *classical school of management* emerged.

Frederick W. Taylor was among the first of what historians today call the "classical management writers"; he developed a set of principles that became known as *scientific management*. Taylor's basic thesis was that managers should study work scientifically to identify the "one best way" to get the job done. His framework for scientific management was based on four principles:

1. The "one best way." Management, through observation and "the deliberate gathering...of all the great mass of traditional knowledge, which in the past has been in the heads of the workmen...," finds the "one best way" for performing each job.

2. Scientific selection of personnel. This principle requires "the scientific selection and then the progressive development of the workmen." Management must uncover each worker's limitation, find his or her "possibility for development," and give each worker the required training.

3. Financial incentives. Taylor knew that putting the right worker on the right job would not ensure high productivity by itself. Some plan for motivating workers to do their best and to comply with their supervisors' instructions was also required. Taylor proposed a system of financial incentives, in which each worker

was paid in direct proportion to how much he or she produced, instead of according to a basic hourly wage.

4. **Functional foremanship.** Taylor called for a division of work between manager and worker such that managers did all planning, preparing, and inspecting while the workers did the actual work. Specialized experts, or functional foremen, would be responsible for specific aspects of a task, such as choosing the best machine speed, determining job priorities, and inspecting the work. The worker was to take orders from each of these foremen, depending on what part of the task was concerned.[4]

Frank and Lillian Gilbreth and Motion Study

The work of the husband-and-wife team Frank and Lillian Gilbreth also exemplifies the techniques and points of view of the scientific management approach. Born in 1868, Frank Gilbreth passed up an opportunity to attend MIT, deciding instead to enter the contracting business. He began as an apprentice bricklayer and became intrigued by the idea of improving efficiency. By carefully studying workers' motions he developed innovations—for example, in the way bricks were stacked, in the way they were laid, and in the number of motions used—that nearly tripled the average bricklayer's efficiency.[5]

In 1904 Frank married Lillian Moller, who had a background in psychology, and together they began to develop principles and practices to analyze tasks more scientifically. In addition to using stopwatches, they developed various tools, including *motion-study principles*, to assist them in their quest for efficiency. They concluded, for example, that:

1. The two hands should begin and complete their motions at the same time.

2. The two hands should not be idle at the same time, except during rest periods.

3. Motions of the arms should be made at opposite and symmetrical directions and should be made simultaneously.[6]

Therbligs, another tool used by the Gilbreths, were elemental motions like searching, grabbing, holding, and transporting. (The Gilbreths created the term *therblig* by spelling their last name backwards and transposing the *th*.) *Micromotion study* was the process of taking motion pictures of a worker doing his or her job and then running the film forwards and backwards at different speeds so that details of the job could be examined. Used in conjunction with timing devices, micromotion study made it possible to determine precisely how long it took to complete each component activity of a task. Performance could then be improved by modifying or eliminating one or more of these component activities.

Henri Fayol and the Principles of Management

The work of Henri Fayol also illustrates the classical approach to management and work behaviour. Fayol had been a manager with a French iron and steel firm for 30 years before writing his book *General and Industrial Management*. In it, Fayol said that managers performed five basic functions: planning, organizing, commanding, coordinating, and controlling.

He also listed a number of management principles he had found useful during his years as a manager. Fayol's 14 principles are summarized below and include his famous principle of *unity of command:* "For any action whatsoever, an employee should receive orders from one superior only."[7]

1. **Division of work.** The worker, always on the same part, and the manager, concerned always with the same matters, acquired ability, sureness, and accuracy, which increased their output.

2. **Authority and responsibility.** Authority is the right to give orders and the power to exact obedience. Distinction must be made between official authority, deriving from office, and personal authority, compounded of intelligence, experience, moral worth, and ability to lead.

3. **Discipline.** The best means of establishing and maintaining [discipline] are: good superiors at all levels; agreements as clear and fair as possible; sanctions [penalties] judiciously applied.

4. Unity of command. For any action whatsoever, an employee should receive orders from one superior only....

5. Unity of direction. There should be one head and one plan for a group of activities serving the same objective.

6. Subordination of individual interests. In a business, the interests of one employee or group of employees should not prevail over those of the concern.... Means of effecting it are: firmness and good example on the part of superiors; agreements as far as is possible.

7. Remuneration of personnel. Remuneration should be fair and as far as possible afford satisfaction to both personnel and firm.

8. Centralization. The question of centralization or decentralization is a simple question of proportion; it is a matter of finding the optimum degree for the particular concern. What appropriate share of initiative may be left to intermediaries depends on the personal character of the manager, on his moral worth, on the reliability of his subordinates, and also on the conditions of the business.

9. Scalar chain. The scalar chain is the chain of superiors ranging from the ultimate authority to the lowest ranks....It is an error to depart needlessly from the line of authority, but it is an even greater one to keep to it when detriment to the business ensues.

10. Order. For social order to prevail in a concern, there must be an appointed place for every employee and every employee must be in his appointed place.

11. Equity. For the personnel to be encouraged to carry out its duties with all the devotion and loyalty of which it is capable, it must be treated with kindliness, and equity results from the combination of kindness and justice. Equity excludes neither forcefulness nor sternness....

12. Stability of tenure of personnel. Time is required for an employee to get used to new work and succeed in doing it well, always assuming that he possesses the requisite abilities. If, when he has gotten used to it, or before then, he is removed, he will not have had time to render worthwhile service.

13. Initiative. Thinking out a plan and ensuring its success is one of the keenest satisfactions for an intelligent man to experience....This power of thinking out and executing is what is called initiative....It...represents a great source of strength for business.

14. Esprit de corps. "Union is strength." Harmony, union among the personnel of a concern, is a great strength in that concern. Effort, then, should be made to establish it.

Max Weber and Bureaucratic Organization Theory

Max Weber was a contemporary of Taylor, Fayol, and the Gilbreths. His work, first published in Germany in 1921, provides further insight into the ideals of the classical management writers. But unlike most of these writers, Weber was not a practising manager but an intellectual. He was born in 1864 to a well-to-do family and studied law, history, economics, and philosophy at Heidelberg University.

During the 1920s, Weber correctly predicted that the growth of the large-scale organization would require a more formal set of procedures to administer it. At the time, managers had few principles they could apply in managing organizations. Weber therefore created the idea of an ideal or "pure form" of organization, which he called *bureaucracy*. This term did not refer to red tape and inefficiency; instead, *bureaucracy*, for Weber, was the most efficient form of organization. Weber described bureaucracy as having certain characteristics:

1. A well-defined hierarchy of authority.

2. A clear division of work.

3. A system of rules covering the rights and duties of position incumbents.

4. A system of procedures for dealing with the work situation.

5. Impersonality of interpersonal relationships.

6. Selection for employment, and promotion based on technical competence.[8]

Summary: The Classical Approach to Management

The classical approach to management generally focused on boosting efficiency. To Taylor, Fayol, Weber, and the Gilbreths, an efficiently designed job and organization were of prime importance. These writers therefore concentrated on developing analytical tools, techniques, and principles that would enable managers to create efficient organizations. Work behaviour was not unimportant to the classical writers; they simply assumed its complexities away by arguing that financial incentives would ensure motivation. As a result, intentionally or not, the classicists left the impression that workers could be treated as givens in the system, as little more than appendages to their machines. "Design the most highly specialized and efficient job you can," assumed the classicist, and "plug in the worker who will then do your bidding if the pay is right."

THE BEHAVIOURAL SCHOOL OF MANAGEMENT

In the 1920s and 1930s, many changes swept the United States, and indeed the world. Increasing numbers of people moved from farms to cities and thus became more dependent on each other for goods and services. Factories became more mechanized and jobs became more specialized and interdependent.[9] Government became more deeply involved in economic matters, and a number of lawsuits were filed to break up industrial monopolies. Social movements aimed at giving women the right to vote, electing senators by direct popular vote, establishing a minimum wage, and encouraging trade unions. Even the literature of the period became more anti-individualistic, as people questioned whether a philosophy based on hard work, individualism, and maximizing profits—the building blocks of the classical management era—might actually have some drawbacks.

The Hawthorne Studies

In 1927, the *Hawthorne Studies* began at the Chicago Hawthorne Plant of the Western Electric Company. They eventually added an entirely new perspective to the management of people at work. Three main sets of studies took place, one of which became known as the "relay assembly test studies." A group of workers was isolated and studied as a series of changes was made, such as modifying the length of the workday and altering the morning and afternoon rest breaks. Researchers noted with some surprise that these changes did not affect performance greatly, underscoring their growing belief that performance depended on factors other than physical conditions or rate of pay.

The relay assembly test studies led the researchers to conclude that the *social* situations of the workers, not just the *working* conditions, influenced behaviour and performance at work. The researchers discovered, for instance, that in countless ways, their observations had inadvertently made the workers feel that they were "special." The observer had changed the workers' situation by "his personal interest in the girls and their problems. He had always been sympathetically aware of their hopes and fears. He had granted them more and more privileges."[10]

The Hawthorne Effect.
These results have been codified as the Hawthorne effect. This is what happens when the scientist, in the course of an investigation, inadvertently influences the subjects so that it is not the scientist's intended changes that affect the subject's behaviour but rather the way the scientist acts. In the relay assembly test, for instance, the researchers wanted to schedule rest periods when they would be most advantageous. They therefore called a meeting during which they showed the workers their output curves and pointed out the low and high points of the day. "When asked at what times they would like to have their rest, they unanimously voted in favour of ten o'clock in the morning and two o'clock in the afternoon." Accordingly, the investigators agreed to schedule the rests at these times. In ret-

rospect, however, the researchers concluded that the subsequent rise in employee morale and performance was due to more than just the rest breaks; it was also due to the fact that the researchers had involved the workers in the decision.

Hawthorne's Consequences.
The Hawthorne studies were a turning point in the study of management. As the research became more widely known, managers and management experts began to recognize that human behaviour in the workplace is a complex and powerful force. The *human relations movement*, inspired by this realization, emphasized that workers were not just givens in the system but instead had needs and desires that the organization and task had to accommodate.

Environment, Increased Diversity, and Change
Historian Alfred Chandler has suggested that after accumulating and then rationalizing resources, managers traditionally moved to a third stage in which they attempted to better use their organizational resources by developing new products and new markets—by diversifying. In the United States, movement into this third stage was hampered in the 1930s by the Depression. However, excess production capacity did ultimately stimulate research and development. Coupled with the technological and managerial advancements that emerged in the years surrounding the Second World War, this excess capacity finally shifted most U.S. industries into Chandler's *diversification* stage.[11]

To understand evolving management theory, it is important to recognize that this period was characterized by differentiated, complex, and rapidly changing environments. Even before the Second World War, many firms had embarked on extensive research and development to develop new products. For example, at General Electric and Westinghouse, research and development activities resulted in the manufacture of plastics as well as a variety of other products based on electronics. The automobile companies had begun to produce airplane engines, electrical equipment, and household appliances. After the war, companies in the rubber industry—such as United States Rubber and BFGoodrich, which had concentrated on tire manufacturing—entered into systematic research and development and began to market such items as latex, plastics, and flooring.

These changes in the business environment contributed to the development of management theory in several ways. First, the increased rate of change and novelty triggered by diversification meant that managers and management theorists could no longer view organizations as closed systems operating within predictable and unchanging environments.[12] Second, efficiency was no longer a manager's main concern. It was eclipsed by the drives to diversify and then to monitor the activities of previously unrelated companies. Third, the shift towards making organizations more responsive to their environments was characterized by a trend towards *decentralization*, which in essence meant letting lower-level employees make more of their own decisions. Decentralization required a new managerial philosophy: Allowing subordinates to do more problem solving and decision making meant that managers had to rely on their employees' self-control. This change (coming as it did just after Hawthorne's results were popularized) led to a new emphasis on participative, people-oriented leadership and a more behavioural approach to management.

Douglas McGregor: Theory X, Theory Y
The work of Douglas McGregor is a good example of this new approach. According to McGregor, the classical organization (with its highly specialized jobs, centralized decision making, and top-down communications) was not just a product of the need for more efficiency. Instead, it was a reflection of certain basic assumptions about human nature.[13] These assumptions, which McGregor somewhat arbitrarily classified as *Theory X*, held that most people dislike work and responsibility and prefer to be directed; that they are motivated not by the desire to do a good job but simply by financial incentives; and that, therefore, most people must be closely supervised, controlled, and coerced into achieving organizational objectives.

McGregor questioned the truth of this view and asked whether standard management practices were appropriate for the tasks faced by more modern organizations. He felt that management needed new organizations and practices to deal with diversification, decentralization, and participative decision making. These new practices had to be based on a revised set of assumptions about the nature of human beings, which McGregor called *Theory Y*. Theory Y held that people could enjoy work and that an individual would exercise substantial self-control over performance if the conditions were favourable. Implicit in Theory Y is the belief that people are motivated by the desire to do a good job and by the opportunity to affiliate with their peers, rather than just by financial rewards.

Rensis Likert and the Employee-Centred Organization

Researcher Rensis Likert's work is another example of trends in management theory during the post-war years. Likert concluded that effective organizations differ from ineffective ones in several ways. Less effective *job-centred companies* focus on specialized jobs, efficiency, and close supervision of workers. More effective organizations, on the other hand, "focus their primary attention on endeavouring to build effective work groups with high performance goals."[14] As Likert noted, in these *employee-centred companies:*

> The leadership and other processes of the organizations must be such as to insure a maximum probability that in all interactions and all relationships with the organization, each member will, in the light of his background, values and expectations, view the experience as supportive and one which builds and maintains his sense of personal worth and importance.[15]

Chris Argyris and the Mature Individual

Chris Argyris reached similar conclusions, but approached the problem from a different perspective.[16] Argyris argued that healthy people go through a maturation process. As they approach adulthood, they move into a state of increased activity, greater independence, and stronger interests, and they pass from the subordinate position of a child to an equal or superordinate position as an adult. Gaining employees' compliance by assigning them to highly specialized jobs with no decision-making power and then closely supervising them inhibits normal maturation by encouraging workers to be dependent, passive, and subordinate. It would be better to give workers more responsibility and broader jobs.

The Behaviouralist Prescriptions

Behavioural scientists like Argyris, McGregor, and Likert soon translated their ideas into practical methodologies that became the heart of the emerging field of organizational behaviour. Likert emphasized leadership style and group processes. "The low-producing managers, in keeping with the traditional practice, feel that the way to motivate and direct behaviour is to exercise control through authority."[17] In contrast, "the highest-producing managers feel, generally, that this manner of functioning does not produce the best results, that the resentment created by direct exercise of authority tends to limit its effectiveness."[18] Therefore, said Likert, "widespread use of participation is one of the more important approaches employed by the high-producing managers."[19] He found that the value of participation applied to all aspects of the job and of work, "as, for example, in setting work goals and budgets, controlling costs, organizing the work, etc."[20]

McGregor had his own prescriptions. He said that decentralization and pushing decision making down the company hierarchy should be the norm in order to free people from the "too-close control of conventional organization." Management should encourage job enlargement (in which the variety of tasks that an employee performs increases), so that workers' jobs become more challenging and more interesting. Participative management (which McGregor said would give employees some voice in decisions that affect them) would similarly enhance self-control. Finally, McGregor urged using management by objectives (MBO). In MBO, subordinates set goals with their supervisors and are measured on their accomplishment of these goals, thus avoiding the need for close day-to-day supervision.

Bridging the Eras: Chester Barnard and Herbert Simon

The work of Chester Barnard and Herbert Simon does not fit neatly into any one school of management theory. Their research actually spanned several schools and contributed to the development of an integrated theory of management.

The Zone of Indifference.

Chester Barnard used his experience as an executive to develop an important new management theory. He was the president of New Jersey Bell Telephone Company and, at various times, president of the United States Organization (the USO of the Second World War), president of the Rockefeller Foundation, and chairman of the National Science Foundation.

Barnard was the first major theorist after the Hawthorne studies to emphasize the importance and variability of the individual in the workplace. He said, for example, that "an essential element of organizations is the willingness of persons to contribute their individual efforts to the cooperative system." And he added that "the individual is always the basic strategic factor in organization. Regardless of his history or obligations, he must be induced to cooperate, or there can be no cooperation."

Barnard set about developing a theory of how to get workers to cooperate. How do you get individuals to surrender their personal preferences and go along with the authority exercised by supervisors?[21] Barnard believed the answer could be found in what he called the person's *zone of indifference*, a range within each individual in which he or she would willingly accept orders without consciously questioning their legitimacy.[22] Barnard saw willingness to cooperate as an expression of the net satisfactions or dissatisfactions experienced or anticipated by each person. In other words, organizations had to provide sufficient inducements to broaden each employee's zone of indifference and thus increase the likelihood that orders would be obeyed.

But Barnard, in a clear break with the classicists, said that material incentives by themselves were not enough: "The unaided power of material incentives, when the minimum necessities are satisfied, in my opinion, is exceedingly limited as to most men."[23] Several other classes of incentives, including "the opportunities for distinction, prestige, [and] personal power," are also required.

Gaining Compliance.
Whereas Barnard wrote from the vantage point of an executive, Herbert Simon is a scholar who had mastered organization theory, economics, natural science, and political science, and who went on to win the Nobel Prize in economics in 1978. Like Barnard, Simon viewed getting employees to do what the organization needed them to do as a major issue facing managers. He proposed two basic ways to gain such compliance, which can be paraphrased as follows:

> Decisions reached in the highest ranks of the organization hierarchy will have no effect upon the activities of operative employees unless they are communicated downward. Consideration of the process requires an examination of the ways in which the behaviour of the operative employee can be influenced. These influences fall roughly into two categories:

> First, the manager can establish in the employee him- or herself the attitudes, habits and state of mind that lead him or her to reach the decision that is advantageous to the organization. In other words, the manager somehow gets the worker to want to do the job. Or, second, the manager can impose upon the employee decisions reached elsewhere in the organization, for instance by closely supervising everything the person does.[24]

According to Simon, managers can ensure that employees carry out tasks in one of two ways. They can *impose control* by closely monitoring subordinates and insisting that they do their jobs as they have been ordered to do (using the classicists' command and control approach). Or managers can foster employee *self-control* by providing better training, encouraging participative leadership, and developing commitment and loyalty. As rapid change forced employers to depend more and more on employee initiative, fostering such self-control became a major theme in management writings.

THE QUANTITATIVE SCHOOL

After the Second World War, management theorists began to apply quantitative techniques to a wide range of problems. This movement is usually referred to as *operations research* or *management science* and has been described as "the application of scientific methods, techniques, and tools to problems involving the operations of systems so as to provide those in control of the system with optimum solutions to the problems."[25]

The Management Science Approach

Management science has three distinguishing characteristics. First, management scientists generally deal with well-defined problems that have clear and undisputable standards of effectiveness. They want to know, for instance, whether inventory costs have been too high and should be reduced by 20 percent, or whether a specific number of items should be produced at each of a company's plants to minimize transportation costs to customers.

Second, management scientists generally deal with problems that have well-defined alternative courses of action. A company might have four different plants from which to ship products, or various levels of product A and product B that can be produced to maximize sales revenues. The management scientist's task is to recommend a solution. Finally, management scientists must develop a theory or model describing how the relevant factors are related. Like any scientist, management scientists must understand the problem and relationships clearly enough to formulate a mathematical model.

Historian Daniel Wren points out that operations research/management science has "direct lineal roots in scientific management."[26] Like Taylor and the Gilbreths, today's management scientists try to find optimal solutions to problems. Just as Taylor and his people used scientific methods to find the one best way to do a job, management scientists used the scientific method to find the best solution to industrial problems. The difference in the two approaches is twofold. First, modern-day management scientists have much more sophisticated mathematical tools and computers at their disposal. Second, management science's goal is not to try to find a science of management as much as it is to use scientific analysis and tools to solve management problems.

The Systems Approach

The management science approach is closely associated with what is called the systems approach to management. A *system* is an entity—for example, a hospital, a city, a company, or a person—that has interdependent parts and a purpose. *Systems approach* advocates argue that viewing an organization as a system helps managers to remember that a firm's different parts, departments, or subsystems are interrelated and that all must contribute to the organization's purpose.

According to systems advocates like C. West Churchman, all systems have four basic characteristics.[27] First, they operate within an environment, which is defined as those things outside and important to the organization but largely beyond its control. For a company these include clients, competitors, unions, and governments.

Second, all systems are composed of building blocks called elements, components, or subsystems. In an organization, these basic building blocks might be departments, like those for production, finance, and sales. The subsystems may also cut across traditional departmental lines. For example, the marketing subsystem might include sales, advertising, and transportation, because each of these elements has an impact on the task of getting the product to the customer.

Third, all systems have a central purpose against which the organization's efforts and subsystems can be evaluated. For example, the optimal inventory level for a firm that serves top-of-the-line customers would probably be higher than for a firm whose customers want the best buy in town and are willing to wait for shelves to be restocked.

Fourth, focusing on the interrelatedness of the subsystems (and between the subsystems and the firm's environment) is an essential aspect of systems thinking. Interrelatedness emphasizes that a manager can't change one subsystem without affecting the rest—hiring a new production manager might have repercussions in the sales and accounting departments, for instance. Similarly, managers and management theorists need to be sensitive to the way that changes taking place in industrial environments affect the organization and management of the firm.

TOWARDS A SITUATIONAL MANAGEMENT THEORY

In the early 1960s, at about the same time that the systems approach was popular, organizational research studies in England and the United States began to underscore the need for a situational or contingency view of management, one in which the appropriateness of the organization and its management principles were contingent on the rate of change in an organization's environment and technology. In one such study, Tom Burns and G.M. Stalker analyzed a number of industrial firms in England. They concluded that whether what they called a "mechanistic" or an "organic" management system was appropriate depended on the nature of the organization's environment.

Burns and Stalker argued that a *mechanistic management system* was appropriate if the company's tasks were routine and unchanging. Thus, in a textile mill they studied, it was important to have long, stable production runs that kept surprises to a minimum and thereby prevented the necessity of shutting down huge machines. In such unchanging conditions, Burns and Stalker found that a mechanistic (or classical) management approach—characterized by an emphasis on efficiency, specialized jobs, elaborate procedures for keeping behaviour in line, and an insistence that everyone play by the rules—was appropriate.

On the other hand, Burns and Stalker found that the more behavioural *organic management system* was appropriate if innovative, entrepreneurial activities were important. In high-tech electronic firms, for instance, companies and their employees are constantly under pressure to come up with new devices. Burns and Stalker found that management often ran such firms with an approach that emphasized creativity rather than efficiency. These firms placed less emphasis on specialized jobs and issued fewer rules and procedures. Instead, they delegated decisions to employees who then exercised self-control in getting their jobs done.

Also in England, Joan Woodward and researchers from the Tavistock Institute analyzed a group of firms to discover the relationship between an organization and its production technology. The organic, flexible system described by Burns and Stalker again appeared to be more appropriate where dealing with unexpected and unpredictable occurrences was of paramount concern. Thus it was used in small, custom-made job shops, and in large factories that were built to run continuously and in which unexpected breakdowns were a main concern. Woodward and her team found that the mechanistic, classical approach was appropriate where predictability and efficiency were paramount, such as where mass production technologies and assembly lines were used.[28] These findings and others like them culminated in what came to be called a situational, or contingency, approach to management theory, the main findings of which we address in Chapter 8.

The Environment of Management: Canadian and Global

Bombardier Is Buzzing

Bombardier, a diversified Canadian company specializing in transportation, recreational products, aerospace, and financial and real estate services, has an international presence all over the world. The company was founded in 1942 to manufacture tracked vehicles for transportation across snow-covered terrain. Over the years the product line has grown, and in 1991 the company added the world-famous Learjet business aircraft to its portfolio. Now decidedly international in focus, in March 1998 Bombardier International was created to pursue growth—particularly in Asia, Latin America, Eastern and Central Europe, and Russia.

While Bombardier's headquarters are in Montreal, Bombardier employees operate globally. In 1999, 22 000 employees worked in Canada, and there were another 9000 in the United States, 2000 in Mexico, 18 000 in Europe, and 2000 in the Middle East. More than 92 percent of revenues come from markets outside of Canada. As of January 31, 1999, total company assets were $14.2 billion.

Bombardier is on a mission of expansion to accelerate growth in foreign markets. Bombardier International's mandate is to:

- Search for and identify new business opportunities in countries other than North America and Europe;
- Act as an intermediary with government authorities and business communities in foreign locations; and
- Explore opportunities for acquisitions and strategic alliances.

Although Bombardier has done well in international markets, the competition is fierce in the aerospace industry. In the mid-1990s Bombardier held two-thirds of the market for regional jets. But that was before Brazilian rival Embraer captured 45 percent of that market. Embraer was also more successful at landing new clients than was Bombardier. And Bombardier has complained to the World Trade Organization that the Brazilian government is unfairly subsidizing Embraer with $2.5 billion for the manufacture of its jet. To

Bombardier
www.bombardier.com

make matters worse, other competitors are also expected to loom in the market over the next few years. The future is sure to hold a few erratic jet streams for Bombardier.

Globalization is challenging managers and entrepreneurs to examine business in multiple and diverse contexts. As we saw with Bombardier, there are great opportunities in international markets such as Asia, Latin America, and Russia. Among other things, being successful requires vision, creativity to deal with market challenges (such as government subsidies to competitors), and the ability to connect and manage a global workforce.

In the age of e-commerce and technology, "going global" also requires a superior understanding of how to market to a diverse audience, and how to link various international operations using the latest technology. On the west coast of Newfoundland, Innova Multimedia Inc. develops educational software that it sells in China, Chile, and Jordan. Annual revenues are $500 000. Joe Wiseman, Innova's president, makes the pitch and negotiates the details via the Internet as well as by travelling to meet potential clients. "When you're dealing with international markets, location is not an issue. It's not significant to the rest of the world if you're from rural Newfoundland or a city in Ontario," he says. "We can produce software here and ship it to anywhere in the world as easily as if we were in Toronto."[1]

As companies and the managers in them operate internationally, an understanding of different legal systems, different cultures, and different options on how to enter a new market is crucial. Managers must consider different values and motivational systems, and how they vary from one country to the next. To be effective, managers must understand the local culture and how to adapt training programs to suit unique cultural requirements. Simple techniques for planning, organizing, leading, and controlling will not apply in increasingly complex settings.

As companies such as Bombardier enter into countries such as Russia, the success of their operations will depend on planning that includes cross-cultural negotiations. This involves the Western negotiators knowing what is significant to their Russian counterparts, who have lived in a communist system for most of their lives. Priorities and laws are different. Leading in an organization is also different, and Western managers require a good understanding of the local culture. At McDonald's in Russia, training programs that eventually enabled the locals to manage proved very important. The training focused not just on how to make a burger, but also on changing the managers' mindset from a communist framework to one that is market-focused.

In this chapter you will learn more about the international business context and how to manage internationally. You will also learn about strategies for international expansion, and the factors that influence a manager's decision to go global. But first, to provide some context, special issues are presented for managing at home in Canada. How business is done in Canada may also influence our international competitiveness.

Management in the Canadian Context

Business in Canada operates in a unique setting, and the practice of management in Canada is not exactly like that in any other country. Some of the factors that affect management in Canada are geographical uniqueness, significant government involvement, Canada's resource-based economy, proximity to the United States, foreign ownership, productivity, and unionization.

Geographical Uniqueness

Canada is the world's second largest country in terms of area. The majority of the population resides in a narrow east-west band near the U.S. border. As a result, it is difficult to serve a national market effectively. Transportation costs can be a major consideration in management decisions. And the size of the country makes business travel time-consuming.

Significant Government Involvement

The Canadian government has played a large role in industries such as transportation, petrochemicals, fishing, steel making, textiles, and building materials. The biggest Crown corporations have revenues as large as those of Canada's major business firms. Government controls business and also competes with it.

Many managerial jobs are found in government. Critics argue that with no profit motive to guide them, public-sector managers may fail to stress performance, excellence, and output. Government regulations also influence the decision-making processes of private-sector managers.

Canada's Resource-Based Economy

Canada's economy has traditionally been resource-based, although that is gradually changing. This has meant that our main exports have been commodities such as forest products, minerals, or grains. Managing resource-based industries presents a special challenge for planning, because commodity prices are determined by the world market. Consider oil, for example. If the price of oil falls, managers at oil companies cannot do anything about it. Alternately, the service industry is rapidly growing in many sectors of the Canadian business economy. According to Statistics Canada, in 1998 services represented 64 percent of the Canadian economy while resources accounted for only 6 percent. In the service sector, rapidly growing areas include computer and related services and advertising.

Statistics Canada
www.statcan.ca

Proximity to the United States

The United States, with a population 10 times that of Canada's, presents both problems and opportunities. On the positive side, the U.S. offers a very large potential customer base, and is also our biggest trading partner. However, many of the largest U.S. firms operating in

Canada, such as Coca-Cola and IBM, are foreign-owned. In foreign-controlled corporations, Canadian managers must serve two masters—one in Canada and one in the foreign country in which the company is based. Conflicts may arise between how foreign managers and local managers think things should be done.

Foreign Ownership

The control of Canadian corporations by foreigners has always been of concern. In fact, in the early 1970s the Trudeau government passed the Foreign Investment Review Agency to counteract excessive foreign control, which at that time stood at 37.6 percent. The level of foreign control has dropped gradually since then, although it has been on the rise again since the Canada–U.S. Free Trade Agreement was enacted in 1989. While the level of acceptable foreign ownership has been hotly debated in the past, more recently Canadians have been willing to accept globalization and free trade as economic facts.[2]

Canada's Productivity

On the 1999 World Competitiveness Survey, published by the Institute for Management Development, Canada ranked tenth. This is an improvement from 1994 when we stood in twentieth position. The top-ranked countries, in order, are the U.S., Singapore, and Finland, and Russia is in last place. The report indicated that if Canadians want to further improve productivity performance, we will have to do several things, including cutting taxes, reducing government spending, working longer hours, and losing less time to industrial strikes.[3]

Unionization

About 30 percent of Canadian workers belong to unions, which influence the actions of both managers and employees. In a traditional union environment management techniques such as quality circles or employee empowerment have been met with skepticism by the union and its workers. Although in the past relations between union and management have often been adversarial, times are changing and these two groups are attempting to work together to achieve greater competitiveness. For example, to compete in the Japanese market, Mayo Forest Products, a small lumber operation, implemented a performance management system. A union member was part of Mayo's management implementation team.[4]

Understanding International Business

In this section we will examine different forms of international companies; economic integration, with a focus on free trade agreements; and why companies choose to enter into international business.

Forms of International Companies

The multinational corporation is one type of international business enterprise. A **multinational corporation (MNC)** may be defined as an internationally integrated business controlled by a parent corporation, and owned and managed by the nationals of its home country. A MNC operates manufacturing and marketing facilities in two or more countries, but these operations are coordinated by a parent firm, whose owners are primarily based in the firm's home country. Companies like Nortel Networks, General Motors, and Bombardier have long been MNCs. However, thousands of small firms like KnitMedia are now international businesses, too. The Entrepreneurial Edge box provides another example.

multinational corporation (MNC)
An internationally integrated business controlled by a parent corporation, and owned and managed by the nationals of its home country.

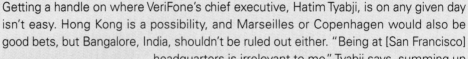
VeriFone, Inc.

Hatim Tyabji, CEO of VeriFone, Inc., regularly travels around the world without losing touch with his 1500 employees. Computers play a major role in his employee communications.

VeriFone
www.verifone.com

Getting a handle on where VeriFone's chief executive, Hatim Tyabji, is on any given day isn't easy. Hong Kong is a possibility, and Marseilles or Copenhagen would also be good bets, but Bangalore, India, shouldn't be ruled out either. "Being at [San Francisco] headquarters is irrelevant to me," Tyabji says, summing up the philosophy of the global manager.

VeriFone manufactures the terminals used for credit-card transactions, and Tyabji takes literally the notion that he and his 2500 employees must stay close to their customers. That's why each new employee is issued a laptop computer. "There is my office," Tyabji says, indicating his own laptop. And even though it sounds like hyperbole, employees learn to "modem in regularly," as one manager put it. Managers average 60 VAX-mail and Internet messages a day, and receiving 200 isn't uncommon.

Requiring employees to hopscotch around the globe might be a disaster for some firms, but not for VeriFone. Despite formidable competitors such as IBM and GTE, the company has a 60 percent market share for card authorization services in the United States. It has also outdistanced rivals in Europe, Asia, and South America, the source of 22 percent of company revenues.

VeriFone employees even use global time differences to their advantage. When VeriFone was competing to design a payment authorization system for German banks, employees around the globe joined in a cooperative effort. The team concluding its workday would forward the project in the direction of the rising sun, and another VeriFone team would then pick up where the first team left off. The effort continued around the clock until the project was completed, at which time the pleasantly surprised bankers awarded the company 80 percent of their business.[5]

global corporation
A corporation that operates as if the entire world (or major regions of it) were a single entity.

Some experts contend that the MNC is slowly being displaced by a special type of multinational enterprise called the global or transnational corporation. The **global corporation** operates as if the entire world (or major regions of it) were a single entity. In fact, about 60 000 transnational businesses with more than half a million overseas affiliates are driving globalization, accounting for an estimated 25 percent of the world's total output. In terms of foreign assets, General Electric is the world's largest global corporation, followed by Ford and Dutch Shell Group. Only three Canadian companies are featured in the world's top 100 transnational companies: Seagram, a beverage company (23rd); BCE Inc., a telecommunications company (49th); and Thomson Corporation, a printing and publishing company (52nd).[6]

Global corporations sell essentially the same things in the same way everywhere. Thus a global corporation such as Sony sells a standardized Walkman around the world, with components made or designed in different countries.[7] Ikea's furniture is much the same the world over. Purdy's chocolate tastes the same everywhere, and Chanel and Lanvin sell the same products around the globe.

However, all global corporations do not look or act the same, even if they do have the same (or similar) global reach and ambitions. In a recent book entitled *The Myth of the Global Corporation*, four experts argue that, while global in reach, such businesses tend to reflect their national roots.[8] For example, when the German investment banking firm Deutsche Bank took over a British investment bank, the traditionally high incentive pay

Deutsche Bank
**http://public.
deutsche-bank.de**

of the British managers created considerable tension among their new lower-paid German bosses. Sensitivity to managing cultural and other differences is therefore one of the great challenges of managing globally.

Economic Integration and Free Trade

The concept of free trade helps explain why business today is increasingly international. **Free trade** means that trade barriers among participating countries are removed.[9] It occurs when two or more countries sign an agreement to allow the free flow of goods and services, unimpeded by trade barriers such as tariffs (special governmental taxes on imports).

The classic explanation for free trade's advantages was presented by political economist and philosopher Adam Smith in his famous book, *The Wealth of Nations*. Writing in 1776, Smith argued that each country, if unhindered by subsidies and tariffs, would specialize in the goods and services it could produce best. Ireland might produce fine glass, Switzerland might manufacture watches, and Japan might specialize in electronics. Such specialization would lead to higher productivity and efficiency, which would lead to higher income, which in turn could be used to purchase imports from abroad. **Economic integration** occurs when two or more nations obtain the advantages of free trade by minimizing trade restrictions between them.

Economic integration occurs on several levels. In a **free trade area**, barriers to trade among member countries are removed, so that goods and services are traded more freely among the member countries. A **customs union** is the next higher level of economic integration, in which members dismantle trade barriers among themselves and establish a common trade policy with respect to non-members. In a **common market**, no trade barriers exist among members, and a common external trade policy is in force. In addition, factors of production, such as labour, capital, and technology, move freely between member countries. These three levels of economic integration are illustrated in Figure 2.1.

- **Europe.** In 1957, the European Economic Community (now called the European Union, or EU) was established by founding members France, West Germany, Italy, Belgium, the Netherlands, and Luxembourg (see Figure 2.2). Their agreement, called the Treaty of Rome, established the formation of a free trade area, the gradual elimination of tariffs and other barriers to trade, and the formation of a customs union and (eventually) a common market. By 1987, the renamed European Community had added six other countries (Great Britain, Ireland, Denmark, Greece, Spain, and Portugal) and signed the Single Europe Act. This act "envisages a true common market where goods, people, and money move among the twelve EC countries with the same ease that they move between Wisconsin and Illinois."[10] Austria, Finland, and Sweden joined in 1995.

  In a 1991 meeting in Maastricht, Netherlands, the countries agreed to submit to their respective legislatures plans for cementing even closer economic ties between them. This included plans for a single European currency, called the Euro (introduced for bookkeeping transactions but not yet in daily use), and free movement of labour across country borders.

  The Soviet Union's breakup around 1989 fragmented that political and trade area. Both Soviet Republic members, such as Russia, Georgia, and the Ukraine, and Eastern European countries that were under the Soviet Union's influence, such as Poland, Hungary, East Germany, Bulgaria, Romania, and today's Czech Republic and Slovakia, have generally pursued their own economic interests. East and West Germany have merged, of course, and several Eastern European countries await admission to the European Union.

- **Asia.** In Asia, the Association of Southeast Asian Nations (ASEAN) was organized in 1967 (see Figure 2.3). It includes Brunei, Indonesia, Malaysia, the Philippines, Singapore, Thailand, and Vietnam. These countries are cooperating to reduce tariffs and liberalize trade, although the results at this point have been limited.[11] Asia also has the Asia Pacific Economic Cooperation (APEC) forum, a loose association of 18 Pacific Rim states that aims to facilitate freer trade in

free trade
Occurs when two or more countries sign an agreement to allow the free flow of goods and services, unimpeded by trade barriers such as tariffs.

economic integration
Occurs when two or more nations obtain the advantages of free trade by minimizing trade restrictions between them.

free trade area
A level of economic integration in which barriers to trade among member countries are removed, so that goods and services are traded more freely.

customs union
A level of economic integration in which members dismantle trade barriers among themselves and establish a common trade policy with respect to non-members.

common market
A level of economic integration in which no trade barriers exist among members, and a common external trade policy is in force.

European Union
www.europa.eu.int

Free trade area

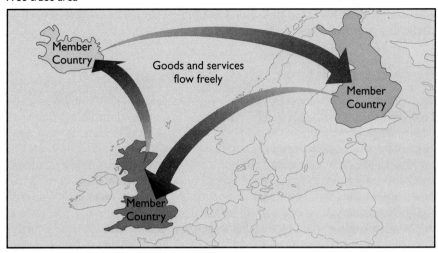

Customs union

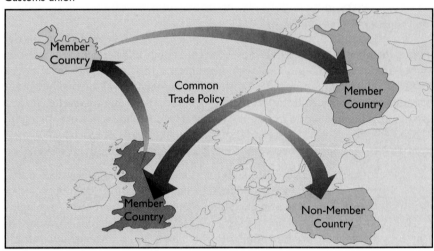

Common market

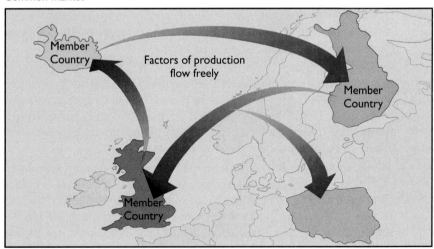

FIGURE 2.1
Levels of Economic Integration

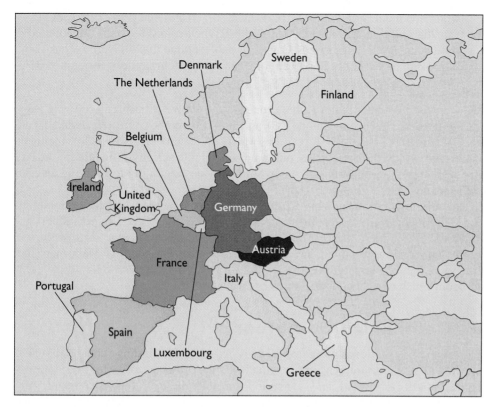

FIGURE 2.2
EU Member Countries

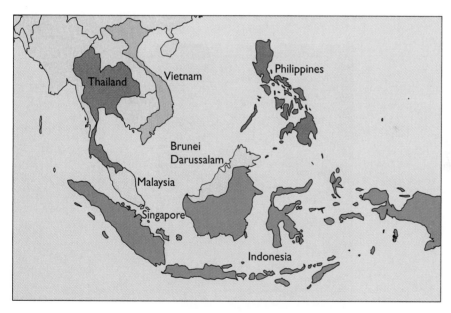

FIGURE 2.3
ASEAN Member Countries

its region. Members include Australia, Canada, Chile, China, Japan, Malaysia, Mexico, Singapore, and the U.S.[12]

■ **North America.** Canada, the United States, and Mexico have established a North American Free Trade Agreement (NAFTA). NAFTA creates the world's largest free market, with a total output of about $6 trillion. What has actually happened since NAFTA took effect? Well, Canadian industry has become more competitive in world markets, and is gradually shedding its image as "hewers of

NAFTA Secretariat
**www.nafta-sec-alena.
org**

wood and haulers of water." Exports have surged and make up 41 percent of Canada's GDP, up from 25 percent in 1991. One job in three is now devoted to producing goods and services. Canadian public opinion about NAFTA has also improved. In 1993 only 37 percent of Canadians favoured the agreement, compared to 67 percent more recently.[13]

Some experts predict that a global economy will evolve with three economic hubs: North America, the European Union (EU), and East and Southeast Asia (including Japan, India, and China).[14] In the mid-1990s, it was widely predicted that Asia would experience the fastest growth of the three areas, but that area ran into serious difficulties in the late 1990s. Although the economies of Asian countries are beginning to rebound, overall growth remains slow.

Economic integration has a big effect on company managers. It can, for example, enhance the rate of growth of a country and its markets. But there are also potential negative effects. For instance, some fear that the EU's existence will lead to a "fortress Europe to which non-EU firms will find it increasingly difficult to export goods."[15] Many managers are therefore entering into joint ventures with European partners to establish local beachheads from which to sell goods and services throughout the EU.

Why Companies Go Abroad

Firms expand internationally for several reasons. Although finding "cheap labour" is often cited as an important goal, this is actually *not* the primary motive for most internationalization efforts. Instead, *sales expansion* is usually the main reason companies decide to enter international markets.[16] For example, firms like Nortel Networks are moving resources to South America because of the relatively fast growth rate of those economies. And stable beer sales in Canada encouraged Canadian breweries such as Labatt to enter foreign markets. About 24 percent of Labatt's beer sales are outside of Canada, mainly in the United States, and Labatt is continuing to expand into other international markets.[17]

Labatt
www.labatt.com

Stable beer sales in Canada mean that Canadian breweries such as Labatt must look for markets outside the country.

Of course, expanding abroad to increase sales can be risky business. In the early 1990s, for instance, several car manufacturers, including Peugeot, Volkswagen, and General Motors, spent billions of dollars building new manufacturing plants in developing countries such as China. Today, demand for all those new Jettas and Buicks is surprisingly weak, and many of these firms are reconsidering their original decisions. Some—like Peugeot—are already trying to bail out.[18] And in 1997–98 scores of global investors, including banks like Citicorp and Deutsche Bank, lost hundreds of millions of dollars when Russia failed to pay its bills.

Firms also go international to seek foreign products and services that help reduce their costs. Toronto-based Bata Shoes, the world's largest manufacturer and retailer of footwear, has manufacturing units in over 65 countries. Many of these operations are in countries where labour and other costs are low. Sometimes high quality drives firms overseas. U.S.-based Apple Computer enlisted Sony's aid in producing parts for its new notebook computer. Companies can also smooth out sales and profit swings by going abroad. A manufacturer of snow blowers might choose to sell its products in Chile, knowing that as demand for its products drops off in the spring in Canada, it rises in Chile, where the seasons are reversed.

Peugeot
www.peugeot.com

Volkswagen
www.vw.com

Types of International Strategies

There are several strategies a company can use to expand internationally. Let's look at the main alternatives: exporting, licensing, franchising, foreign direct investment and multinational enterprises, joint ventures and strategic alliances, and wholly owned subsidiaries.

Exporting

Exporting is often the first choice when manufacturers decide to expand abroad. Exporting means selling abroad, either directly to target customers or indirectly by retaining foreign sales agents and distributors.[19] Exporting increases sales volume and generates funds that can lead to profits. Exporting also reduces the unit cost of production due to increased volume, allows for greater use of plant capacity, lessens dependence on a single market, and provides an opportunity to gain valuable experience in a foreign market.

Abitibi-Consolidated sells newsprint and other forest products around the world, and McCain sells frozen foods. Eicon Technology of Montreal, which designs and manufactures software and hardware for corporate information systems, has won a Canada Export Award several times. Some Canadian firms export more than 80 percent of their products to other countries. By the late 1990s, almost 40 percent of all goods and services produced in Canada were exported. Canada currently ranks first among G7 countries in the proportion of its production that is exported.[20]

But there are also disadvantages to exporting, such as the expense required to develop export markets, modifications to products needed to meet government regulations, the need for further financing, and the need to learn about foreign customs, cultures, and standards. More than half of all world trade is handled by agents and distributors familiar with the local market's customs and customers. However, poorly selected intermediaries can be more trouble than they are worth if, through inexperience, they alienate potential customers. Carefully selecting intermediaries, checking business reputations via local agencies, and then carefully drafting agency and distribution agreements are essential if a company chooses to take this route.[21]

To sum up, whether selling direct or through agents, exporting has advantages and disadvantages. It is a relatively quick and inexpensive way of going international, since it avoids the need to build factories in the host country.[22] It is also a good way to test the waters in the host country and to learn more about its customers' needs. On the other hand,

exporting
Selling abroad, either directly to target customers or indirectly by retaining foreign sales agents and distributors.

Eicon Technology
www.eicon.com

transportation, tariff, and manufacturing costs can put the exporter at a disadvantage, as can poorly selected intermediaries.

Licensing

Licensing is another way to start international operations. International **licensing** is an arrangement whereby a company (the licensor) grants a foreign firm the right to use intangible ("intellectual") property such as patents, copyrights, manufacturing processes, or trade names for a specified period of time, usually for a fee or for a percentage of the earnings, called royalties.[23] Licensing agreements are used when a company does not want to establish a plant or a marketing network in another country. For example, Can-Eng Manufacturing, Canada's largest supplier of industrial furnaces, exports its furnaces under licensing agreements with Japan, Brazil, Germany, Korea, Taiwan, and Mexico.[24]

Licensing arrangements have their pros and cons. For instance, consider a small, underfunded Canadian inventor of a new material for reducing pollution. A licensing agreement with a well-established European environmental products company could allow the Canadian firm to enter the expanding Eastern European market without any significant investment. On the downside, the Canadian firm might not be able to control the design, manufacture, or sales of its products as well as it could if it set up its own facilities in Europe. It is also possible that by licensing its knowledge to a foreign firm, the Canadian firm could eventually lose control over its patented property. This is exactly what happened to Creo Products, a Vancouver-based developer and supplier of high-tech equipment for the printing industry. Creo is suing its Japanese partner, Dainippon Screen, which allegedly used its inside knowledge of Creo to develop and launch competing products.[25]

Franchising

Franchising is another way to start operations overseas, as anyone who has eaten at McDonald's in Moscow or on the Champs Elysées in Paris knows. **Franchising** is the granting of a right by a parent company to another firm to do business in a prescribed manner.[26]

Franchising is similar to licensing, but it usually involves a greater commitment by both parties in terms of time and money. Franchising usually requires the franchisee to follow much stricter guidelines in running the business. In addition, licensing tends to be limited to manufacturers, while franchising is more popular with service firms such as restaurants, hotels, and rental services.

The advantages of franchising are generally the same as those for licensing. Franchising is a quick and relatively low-cost way for a firm to expand into other countries. The one significant disadvantage is maintaining quality control. For example, one early McDonald's franchisee in France was forced to close down its Paris restaurants for failing to maintain McDonald's well-known quality standards.

Foreign Direct Investment and the Multinational Enterprise

Exporting, licensing, and franchising can get most firms only so far. At some point they find that to take full advantage of foreign opportunities they must make a substantial, direct investment. **Foreign direct investment** refers to operations in one country that are controlled by entities in a foreign country. A foreign firm might build new facilities in another country, as Toyota did when it built its manufacturing plant in Cambridge, Ontario. Or a firm might acquire property or operations in a foreign country, as when Wal-Mart bought control of the Wertkauf stores in Germany.

Strictly speaking, a foreign direct investment means acquiring control by owning more than 50 percent of the operation. But, in practice, it is possible for any firm to gain effective control by owning less than 50 percent. In Canada, Americans account for more than half of all foreign ownership.[27] Several industries are more than 50 percent controlled by foreign companies, including the chemical products, automobile, and electronics industries. In any event, a foreign direct investment turns the firm into a multinational enterprise. Joint ventures and wholly owned subsidiaries are two examples of foreign direct investment.

Joint Ventures and Strategic Alliances

The terms *joint venture* and *strategic alliance* are often used interchangeably, although strictly speaking they are not the same thing. **Strategic alliances** are based on reciprocal arrangements in which partners pool, exchange, or integrate specified business resources for mutual gain.[28] Reasons for entering into a strategic alliance include gaining access to new markets or customers, acquiring advanced or new technology, sharing costs and risks of new ventures, obtaining capital, and sharing production facilities. Used in the broadest sense, even licensing or franchising agreements may come under the umbrella of strategic alliances.

Nortel has strategic alliances with several firms, including Daewoo of Korea, Tong Guang of China, and Ascom Hasler of Switzerland. In the airline industry, Star Alliance involves nine partners, including Air Canada, Lufthansa, and United. Working together, the partners are able to share data banks and coordinate bookings. In addition, each individual airline is given security by the strength of the whole.[29]

strategic alliance
A reciprocal arrangement in which partners pool, exchange, or integrate specified business resources for mutual gain.

Star Alliance
www.staralliance.com

THE **CHALLENGE** OF **CHANGE**

Creating Canada's Competitive Advantage Through Technology Alliances

An explosion of alliance activity is occurring in Canada's high-technology sector. Companies must partner to share risks, and to take advantage of synergies in technology, management, or resources. Based on a recent study of alliances in British Columbia's high-technology sector,[30] but with application to other regions, the largest number of alliances are in computer software and biotechnology. Because the high-tech sector is young and quick moving, a full 27 percent of alliances are less than one year old. Most companies are involved in multiple alliances, often with much larger partners. This provides the added benefit of credibility and resources, but often means that the smaller Canadian company has to position itself carefully to retain its bargaining power. Dr. Julia Levy, president and CEO of QLT Phototherapeutics, a biotechnical company specializing in the development and commercialization of proprietary pharmaceutical products for use in photodynamic therapy, says,

> When there's just one alliance and technology is licensed to one company this puts you at risk. A big company has its own agenda. If you rely on one partner and they decide to cut the external budget, they may cut the alliance and you could be finished. If there are too many [alliances] it becomes too much work, as the alliances must be managed carefully.

According to the study, the keys to survival for the smaller partner are (1) retaining unique core capabilities and protection of intellectual property, (2) diversifying to broaden what it can provide to the partner, and (3) building and maintaining multiple alliances. The road may not be easy, but if managed well, the benefits of alliances can be great.

Ballard Power Systems partners with strong, world-leading companies to develop top-of-the-line products.

In contrast, a **joint venture** is a type of strategic alliance in which there is an equity contribution by the partners.[31] A joint venture is "the participation of two or more companies jointly in an enterprise in which each party contributes assets, owns the entity to some degree, and shares risk."[32] In British Columbia, Ballard Power Systems, the world leader in the development and commercialization of fuel cell power systems,[33] has teamed with Daimler-Benz and Ford.

The joint venture of General Motors and Toyota, called New United Motor Manufacturing, Inc. (NUMMI), is another example. Toyota needed to sharpen its U.S. marketing skills and learn about U.S. customers. General Motors, faced with anemic productivity and morale when compared to Japanese car manufacturers, needed to learn more about Japanese manufacturing systems and technology. NUMMI took over a chronically troubled GM plant in Freemont, California, and within two years made it GM's most productive plant.

Joint ventures have advantages. One consultant points out that "in a complex, uncertain world filled with dangerous opponents, it is best not to go it alone."[34] A joint venture arrangement lets a firm like Toyota gain useful experience in a foreign country while using the expertise and resources of a locally knowledgeable company. Joint ventures also help both companies share what could be the substantial costs of starting a new operation.

But, as with licensing, joint venture partners also risk giving away proprietary secrets. And joint ventures almost always mean sharing control. Each partner thus runs the risk that the joint venture may not be managed in the way each would have chosen. Consider the joint venture between Volkswagen and Skoda in the Czech Republic mentioned in Chapter 1 (see page 15). The German partners had specific concerns about quality, time, and efficiency. Czech managers were concerned about maintaining a voice in how things operated in the plant and receiving fair compensation and social benefits for work performed.[35]

Sometimes a joint venture is a necessity. In China, for example, foreign companies that want to do business in highly regulated industries like telecommunications have little choice but to enter into joint ventures with well-connected Chinese partners. The partnership of Britain's Alcatel and Shanghai Bell to make telephone-switching equipment is an example.[36]

Wholly Owned Subsidiaries

As the name implies, a **wholly owned subsidiary** is 100 percent owned by a foreign firm. General Motors of Canada, Ford Motors of Canada, IBM Canada, and Canada Safeway Ltd. are wholly owned subsidiaries of U.S. firms. Canadian business magnate Gerry Schwartz bought Celestica, Inc., an electronics parts manufacturer, and transformed it from a drowsy IBM subsidiary to a global money machine. The Toronto-based company now has branches in Brazil, Malaysia, and the Czech Republic.[37]

Wholly owned subsidiaries have advantages and disadvantages. They provide for tight controls by the foreign firm. Therefore, there is less fear of losing proprietary rights and knowledge. However, subsidiaries are a relatively expensive way to expand into foreign markets, since the company must make the entire investment itself, rather than share with a partner.

wholly owned subsidiary
A company that is 100 percent owned by a foreign firm.

Celestica
www.celestica.com

The Business Team in a Global Economy

Expanding abroad requires a coordinated effort by the company's business team, including the marketing, manufacturing, and human resource managers. Each must analyze how best to manage their functions abroad, while working together to ensure that they achieve the company's overall goals.

Global Marketing

For most companies, marketing abroad is a necessity today. As one expert says, "Even the biggest companies in the biggest countries cannot survive on their domestic markets if they are in global industries. They have to be in all major markets."[38] For NTS Computer Systems, rapid growth depends on developing markets outside of Canada, according to vice-president of finance Pete Donaldson. He outlines, "A lot of our momentum has been the result of keeping our eye on the international markets." Today, NTS manufactures low-cost laptop computers in Ireland and sells them to schools in North America, the UK, Europe, and Puerto Rico.[39]

Successful marketers like Coca-Cola tailor their communications and advertising when they sell their products abroad.

At the same time, mass media, telecommunications, and air travel are conveniently blurring the distinctions that once separated one country's market from another. So for many products "the tastes and preferences of consumers in different nations are beginning to converge on some global norm. Thus, in many industries it is no longer meaningful to talk about the 'German market,' the 'American market,' or the 'Japanese market.' There is only the 'global market.'"[40]

But managers must avoid making the mistake of marketing their products in the same way in all countries. Marketing is culture specific, as Vancouver-based Purdy's Chocolates discovered. Already a well-known brand name in western Canada, a few years ago Purdy's decided to venture into new markets in Taiwan. Problems arose around getting the chocolate onto store shelves without it melting in the tropical climate and the different product preferences and tastes of Taiwanese customers. In addition, the rectangular package that is so common for chocolate in Canada was not well received in Taipei.[41]

Globalization of Production

globalization of production
Dispersing parts of a firm's production process to various locations around the globe.

Canon
www.canon.com

Minolta
www.minolta.com

Ricoh
www.ricoh.com

Globalization of production means dispersing parts of a firm's production process to various locations around the globe. One aim is to provide manufacturing and supply support for marketing efforts abroad. Another is to take advantage of national differences in the cost and quality of production.

Companies today integrate their global operations into a unified and efficient system of manufacturing facilities around the world.[42] Xerox Corporation's worldwide manufacturing system is an example of this. In the early 1980s, each Xerox company in each country had its own suppliers, assembly plants, and distribution channels. Each country's plant managers gave little thought to how their plans fit into Xerox's global needs. This approach became unworkable as international competition in the copier market grew more intense and Canon, Minolta, and Ricoh penetrated Xerox's U.S., Canadian, and European markets with low-cost copiers.

This competitive threat prompted Xerox's senior managers to coordinate their global production processes. They created a central purchasing group to consolidate raw material purchases and thereby cut worldwide manufacturing costs. They instituted a "leadership through quality" program to improve product quality, streamlined and standardized manufacturing processes, and cut costs. Xerox's managers also eliminated over $1 billion of inventory costs by installing a system that linked customer orders from one region more closely with production capabilities in other regions.

McCain Foods Limited is also facing the need to integrate globally. The company that began in Florenceville, New Brunswick, in 1957 with 30 employees now has 16 000 full-time employees worldwide. With a manufacturing capacity of about 1 million pounds of potato product *per hour,* facilities operate in 11 countries on 4 continents.[43]

Responding to the need to integrate on an international basis, McCain has opened facilities all across the globe.

Today, smart managers do not just use their foreign manufacturing facilities as sources of low-cost products. Consider the story of the Hewlett-Packard factory in Singapore. When originally built, its purpose was to produce simple labour-intensive components at low cost. Within several years it was upgraded to produce a complete, low-cost, simple calculator. As the Singapore plant managers became more experienced at manufacturing complete products, they improved their ability to redesign products as well. By redesigning one calculator—the HP 41C—they cut production costs by 50 percent. And by building on their new design capabilities, plant managers and engineers were gradually entrusted with more and more sophisticated assignments by Hewlett-Packard's U.S. headquarters. Today, Singapore is Hewlett-Packard's global centre for the design, development, and manufacture of portable printers for markets worldwide.[44]

Global Staffing

Companies around the world are tapping into wherever in the world the best supply of labour might be located.[45] Thus, Nortel Networks makes telephone equipment in Mexico, 3M makes tapes in Bangalore, India, and Hewlett-Packard assembles computers and de-

THE PEOPLE SIDE OF MANAGING

Managing in Mexico

Managers must carefully weigh behavioural, or "people," factors when staffing far-flung production facilities.[46] Consider some of the following factors involved in setting up a factory in Mexico.

Workplace harmony. The Mexican workplace has a low tolerance for adversarial relations. While "getting along with others" is important in U.S. or Canadian factories, Mexican employers place much more emphasis on hiring employees who have a record of working cooperatively with authority. According to one expert, Mexican employers "...tend to seek workers who are agreeable, respectful, and obedient rather than innovative and independent."[47] This can lead to counterproductive behaviour, even on the part of supervisors. For example, in attempting to preserve the appearance of harmony, supervisors may hide defective work rather than confront the problem or report it to a manager.

Role and status. Mexican employees often put a relatively heavy emphasis on social order and respecting one's status. In a factory in Chihuahua, Mexico, for instance, one manager wore jeans and insisted that everyone call him Jim. He assumed that those around him would prefer that he reduce the visible status gap between himself and the workers, and was therefore amazed to learn that the local employees considered him "uncultured and boorish."[48]

Exercising authority. Mexican employees tend to have a more rigid view of authority than do their Canadian counterparts. Therefore, attempts by Canadian managers to encourage input and feedback from employees may cause confusion. As an expert puts it:

> [Mexican] supervisors seek their role as strictly following orders to the best of their ability, never questioning nor taking matters into their own hands, and this is exactly how they view the proper role of their subordinates. The Mexican supervisor's style is to supervise closely, and look for willing obedience. Opinions expressed by employees are often regarded as "back talk."[49]

signs memory boards in Guadalajara, Mexico. Firms like these aren't just chasing after cheap labour. They are moving plants and jobs overseas to tap into the growing pool of highly skilled employees in Latin America and Asia.

Any decision to do business abroad usually triggers global staffing questions. Setting up factories abroad requires first analyzing employment laws in the host country and establishing a recruiting office. Even a modest expansion abroad requires a global staffing outlook. For example, sending the company's sales manager abroad for several months to close a deal means deciding how to compensate her for expenses abroad, what to do with her house here, and how to make sure she is trained to handle the cultural demands of the foreign assignment.

The Global Manager

Globalization of markets, production, and labour is coinciding with the rise of the global manager. A global manager is one who views markets and production globally and who seeks higher profits for his or her firm on a global basis.[50]

Cosmopolitan Managers

Global managers must be comfortable anywhere in the world; they must be cosmopolitan.[51] *Webster's Dictionary* defines cosmopolitan as "belonging to the world; not limited to just one part of the political, social, commercial or intellectual spheres; free from local, provincial, or national ideas, prejudices or attachments." A cosmopolitan manager's schedule likely involves extensive travel to various parts of the world to negotiate new joint ventures, assessing the firm's foreign manufacturing facilities, opening new plants, hiring new top managers, and meeting with political leaders of the foreign country in which the firm is doing business.

A company's philosophy about international business reflects how cosmopolitan its managers are, and will influence its managers' willingness to take that company global. An ethnocentric management philosophy may manifest itself in an **ethnocentric**, or home-market-oriented, firm. A **polycentric** philosophy may translate into a company that is limited to several individual foreign markets. A **regiocentric (or geocentric)** philosophy may lead a manager to create a more integrated worldwide production and marketing presence.

Do You Have a Global Brain?

To compete successfully around the world today, companies cannot insist that their home-grown ways of doing business are necessarily best. For example, when Volkswagen formed a joint venture with Czech car maker Skoda, it concentrated on training Skoda's managers in Western management techniques, but followed Skoda's suggestions about how business was conducted in the Czech Republic.[52]

A willingness to understand that "going global" means picking and choosing the best solutions from different systems and then applying them to the problems at hand is what management writers mean when they refer to a manager having a global brain. As one expert put it, "A company's goal shouldn't be to operate like a French company in France and a Brazilian company in Brazil. Instead, a company—whether it is a multinational or local—should bring a multinational approach to each business issue."[53] Ernst & Young, a consulting firm, takes exactly that approach. It is developing a global database of "best practices" that can be accessed by its consultants. As one of its officers put it, "a solution that works in India may have a component that works in the UK...sharing best practices helps each office respond more rapidly."[54]

How do managers with global brains behave? For one thing, "global thinkers have a real interest in other cultures...."[55] They also tend to be more sensitive to the possibility of important contributions from other societies, and therefore give ideas from other nations as much credence as those from their own or other Western nations.[56] A manager need not have lived abroad or travelled extensively or be multilingual to have a global brain, al-

ethnocentric
A type of management philosophy that results in a home-market-oriented firm.

polycentric
A type of management philosophy that limits a company to several individual foreign markets.

regiocentric (or geocentric)
A type of management philosopy that may lead a manager to create a more integrated worldwide production and marketing presence.

though such experiences certainly can help. The important thing is that a manager be deeply interested in the larger world, make efforts to learn about other people's perspectives, and take those perspectives into consideration when making decisions.[57] The result might be, for example, "...applying a successful Brazilian marketing solution to a similar situation in Malaysia, or honouring the local communications hierarchy while keeping the appropriate people in your company in the loop."[58]

Would Your Company Pick You to Be an International Executive?

Of course, there's more involved in being picked to be a global manager than simply having the capacity to travel the world or even having a global brain. What do companies look for when trying to identify international executives?

A recent study by behavioural scientists at the University of Southern California provides some answers. The researchers studied 838 lower-, middle-, and senior-level managers from 6 international firms in 21 countries, focusing particularly on personal characteristics. Specifically, the researchers studied the extent to which personal characteristics such as "sensitivity to cultural differences" could be used to distinguish managers who had high potential as international executives.

The results showed that 14 personal characteristics successfully distinguished those identified by their companies as having high potential in 72 percent of the cases. To get a tentative impression of how you would rate, the 14 characteristics (along with sample items) are listed in Figure 2.4. For each sample item, indicate on a scale of 1 to 7 whether you strongly agree (7), strongly disagree (1), or fall somewhere in between.

SCALE	SAMPLE ITEM
Sensitive to Cultural Differences	When working with people from other cultures, works hard to understand their perspectives.
Business Knowledge	Has a solid understanding of our products and services.
Courage to Take a Stand	Is willing to take a stand on issues.
Brings Out the Best in People	Has a special talent for dealing with people.
Acts with Integrity	Can be depended on to tell the truth regardless of circumstances.
Is Insightful	Is good at identifying the most important part of a complex problem or issue.
Is Committed to Success	Clearly demonstrates commitment to seeing the organization succeed.
Takes Risks	Takes personal as well as business risks.
Uses Feedback	Has changed as a result of feedback.
Is Culturally Adventurous	Enjoys the challenge of working in countries other than his/her own.
Seeks Opportunities to Learn	Takes advantage of opportunities to do new things.
Is Open to Criticism	Appears brittle—as if criticism might cause him/her to break.*
Seeks Feedback	Pursues feedback even when others are reluctant to give it.
Is Flexible	Doesn't get so invested in things that he/she cannot change when something doesn't work.

*Reverse scored.

FIGURE 2.4
Do You Have Potential As an International Executive?

Generally speaking, the higher you score on each of these 14 characteristics, the more likely it is that you might have been identified as having high potential to be an international executive in this study.[59]

The Manager in an International Environment

Going international or, certainly, going global presents the manager with new and often perplexing problems. He or she must be adept at assessing a wide array of economic, legal, political, socio-cultural, and technological factors.

The Economic Environment

Managers doing business abroad need to be familiar with the economic systems of the countries in question, the level of each country's economic development, and exchange rates.

The Economic System. In general terms, economic systems are either centrally planned by governments or based on free enterprise and market supply and demand. In some cases, a mixed model may exist. Hong Kong is an example of a market economy. In a pure **market economy**, the quantities and nature of the goods and services produced are not planned by anyone. Instead, the interaction of supply and demand in the market for goods and services determines what is produced, in what quantities, and at what prices.

At the other extreme, the People's Republic of China (PRC) until very recently has been a planned economy. In a **planned economy**, *central planning agencies* such as the government try to determine how much is produced and for whom, by which sectors of the economy, and by which plants. Specific production goals and prices are established for each sector of the economy (for each product or group of products) and for each manufacturing location.

In a **mixed economy**, some sectors of the economy are left to private ownership and free market mechanisms, while others are largely owned by and managed by the government.[60] "Mixed" is, of course, a matter of degree. For example, France is basically a capitalist country, but is mixed to the extent the government still owns shares of industries like telecommunications (France Telecom) and air travel (Air France).

Shifting economic systems can lead to instability, as in Russia. To flourish, free market economies require commercial laws, banking regulations, an independent judiciary, and law enforcement, without which business transactions become difficult. In the former Soviet Union, the first years of transition to a market economy were especially turbulent for business managers. They had to cope not only with competitors, but with criminals, lax law enforcement, and the control of several industries by friends of powerful politicians. Some experts warn of the possibility of similar turbulence in other developing economies in Asia such as South Korea, Malaysia, and Vietnam.[61]

Economic Development. Countries also differ dramatically in levels and rates of economic development. For example, some countries—Canada, Japan, Germany, France, Italy, and the United States, for instance—are large, mature, well-established economies with extensive industrial infrastructures (industry, telecommunications, transportation, and regulatory and judicial systems, for instance). The gross domestic product (the market value of all goods and services that have been bought for final use during a period of time, and therefore the basic measure of a nation's economic activity) for Canada is about $700 billion, for France is $1 trillion, for Germany is $1.5 trillion, for Japan is almost $3 trillion, and for the United States is $7.5 trillion.[62]

However, some countries are growing much faster than others. For example, the

market economy
An economic system in which the quantities and nature of the goods and services produced are not planned by anyone.

planned economy
An economic system in which central planning agencies such as the government try to determine how much is produced and for whom, by which sectors of the economy, and by which plants.

mixed economy
An economic system in which some sectors of the economy are left to private ownership and free market mechanisms, while others are largely owned by and managed by the government.

growth rate of mature economies like those listed above generally averages around 4 percent per year. On the other hand, China, India, and Taiwan are generally growing at just over 7.5 percent, 5.0 percent, and 5.2 percent, respectively. Many multinationals are therefore boosting their investments in these high-growth (and thus high-potential) countries.[63]

Exchange Rates. Managers engaged in international business must also juggle exchange rates. The **exchange rate** for one country's currency is the rate at which it can be exchanged for another country's currency. During the last 20 years, the value of the Canadian dollar has fluctuated a great deal in relation to the currencies of other countries, including the U.S. dollar. In the mid-1970s, the Canadian dollar was worth slightly more than the U.S. dollar, but by the late 1970s it had started on a steady downward path. By 1997 the Canadian dollar was worth only U.S.$0.64. More recently it has risen again to about U.S.$0.67. A drop in the value of the Canadian dollar relative to a foreign currency (say, the British pound) could have a devastating effect on a small Canadian company that suddenly found that it needed 30 percent more dollars to build a factory in Scotland.

exchange rate
The rate at which one country's currency can be exchanged for another country's currency.

The Political and Legal Environment

International managers also must consider the legal and political environments of the countries in which they do business.

Trade Barriers. Trade barriers can dramatically distort the prices companies must charge for their products. **Trade barriers** are governmental influences usually aimed at reducing the competitiveness of imported products or services. **Tariffs**, the most common trade barrier, are governmental taxes levied on goods shipped internationally.[64] The exporting country collects export tariffs, the importing country collects import tariffs, and the country through which the goods are passed collects transit tariffs.

A multitude of non-tariff trade barriers also exists. For example, in addition to the fact that Japan sets high automobile import tariffs, cars not made in Japan must meet a complex set of regulations and equipment modifications. Side mirrors must snap off easily if they come into contact with a pedestrian, for example. And any manufacturer selling 1000 or fewer cars of a particular model annually must test each car individually for gas mileage and emission standards.

Some countries make direct payments to domestic producers. These are called **subsidies**, and they can make an otherwise inefficient producer more cost competitive. Other countries impose **quotas**—legal restrictions on the import of particular goods—as further barriers to trade.[65]

trade barriers
Governmental influences usually aimed at reducing the competitiveness of imported products or services.

tariffs
Governmental taxes levied on goods shipped internationally; the most common trade barrier.

subsidy
A direct payment made by a country to domestic producers in an effort to make them more cost competitive.

quota
A legal restriction on the import of particular goods.

Political Risks. The international manager must be concerned not just with governmental influences on trade, but with political risks as well. For example, companies doing business in Peru must be ever vigilant against terrorist attacks. In 1999 ethnic violence in the former Yugoslavia brought economic activities to a standstill for many companies exporting to that area.[66] Similarly, racial strife in South Africa, civil unrest in Ireland, and religious attacks in Egypt and Israel make doing business in these areas more difficult than it would otherwise be.

Legal Systems. There are important differences in legal systems. Many countries adhere to a system known as common law, which is based on tradition and depends more on precedent and custom than on written statutes. England and Canada (with the exception of Quebec) are examples of countries that use common law.

International law is different, as it is not so much an enforceable body of law as it is agreements embodied in treaties and other types of documents. For example, international law governs intellectual property rights, such as whether music can be reproduced in Japan without permission. Further, legal issues will influence the strategy a manager uses to expand abroad.[67] In some countries where foreign ownership is limited, a Canadian firm can enter the market only through a joint venture.

The Socio-Cultural Environment

People who travel to other countries quickly learn that they must adapt to cultural differences. In Latin America, for instance, *machismo* ("maleness") is defined by virility, zest for action, daring, competitiveness, and the will to conquer. This is translated into business life by demonstrating forcefulness, self-confidence, courage, and leadership.[68] In Japan, saving face and achieving harmony are very important. Indirect and vague communication is therefore preferred, and sentences are frequently left unfinished so the other person may draw his or her own conclusions. In the Middle East, Arabians love the spoken word and tend not to get to the point quickly. This can frustrate Canadian managers, who must be careful not to show impatience or annoyance. And in France, a firm and pumping handshake may be considered uncultured. Instead, a quick handshake with some pressure to the grip is more appropriate. Different cultural orientations influence a wide range of management activities, including planning, organizing, communicating, and training—to name a few.

Cross-Cultural Challenges: An Example. Cultural differences can have very practical consequences. Consider the challenge of negotiating with people abroad. A researcher at Georgetown University assumed, based on previous studies, that there were three basic ways for people to resolve disagreements. The first approach required resolving disputes based on who is more powerful. Alternately, when using the "applying regulations" approach, the parties resolve their differences based on pre-established rules and standardized procedures. A third approach to resolving disagreements focused on taking each party's best interests into consideration, and asking questions to discover the reason for each party's position.[69]

Based on this study, the researcher concluded that Japanese, German, and American managers tend to use very different approaches when resolving workplace conflict. Japanese prefer the power approach, tending to defer to the party with most power. Germans tend to emphasize a more legalistic, "sticking to the rules" approach. Americans tend to try to take all parties' interests into account and to work out a solution that maximizes benefits for everyone.

Needless to say, "these cross cultural differences may complicate life for expatriate managers who find themselves trying to manage conflict in a foreign cultural system."[70] American managers may be shocked to learn that those from other countries are not as interested in finding a solution that benefits everyone. And they may become frustrated while discussing bureaucratic regulations and practices (which Germans did significantly more than Americans). It certainly helps for managers to have global brains when negotiating overseas!

Values. Research by Geert Hofstede[71] shows that a society's values are among the most influential of cultural differences. *Values* are basic beliefs that we hold about what is good or bad, important or unimportant. Values are important because they shape the way we behave. Hofstede says that different societies reflect four basic values, as follows:

power distance
The extent to which the less powerful members of institutions accept and expect that power will be distributed unequally.

individualism vs. collectivism
The degree to which ties between individuals are normally loose or close.

masculinity vs. femininity
The degree to which assertiveness ("masculinity") or quality-of-life issues ("femininity") are valued.

- **Power distance. Power distance** is the extent to which the less powerful members of institutions accept and expect that power will be distributed unequally.[72] Hofstede concluded that the institutionalization of such inequality is higher in some countries (such as Mexico) than it is in others (such as Sweden).

- **Individualism vs. collectivism.** The degree to which ties between individuals are normally loose or close is measured as **individualism vs. collectivism**. In more individualistic countries, "all members are expected to look after themselves and their immediate families."[73] Individualistic countries include Australia and Canada. In collectivist countries such as Indonesia and Pakistan people are expected to care more for the family as well as the larger society.

- **Masculinity vs. femininity.** According to Hofstede, societies differ related to how much assertiveness (which he called "masculinity") or quality-of-life issues ("femininity") are valued. Japan and Austria ranked high in masculinity, while Denmark, Costa Rica, and Chile ranked lower.

- **Uncertainty avoidance. Uncertainty avoidance** refers to whether people in a society are uncomfortable with unstructured situations in which unknown, surprising, novel incidents occur. People in countries such as Sweden, Israel, and Great Britain are relatively comfortable dealing with uncertainty and surprises. People living in other countries (including Greece and Portugal) tend to avoid uncertainty.[74]

uncertainty avoidance
The extent to which people in a society are uncomfortable with unstructured situations in which unknown, surprising, novel incidents occur.

Language and Customs. The international manager must also deal with differences in language. For example, one airline's "Fly in Leather" slogan proved embarrassing when translated as "Fly Naked" for the company's Latin American campaign.[75] A country's traditional manners and customs can also be important. For instance, Campbell's learned that Japanese drink soup mainly for breakfast. A country's predominant religions, cultural orientations (such as styles of music and art), and educational processes can all influence the manner in which business should be conducted in the country. In America or Japan, inviting a business person out for an alcoholic drink is sometimes done, where as in Saudi Arabia such invitations could be shocking.

The Technological Environment

A country's technological environment—and, in particular, the relative ease or difficulty with which technology can be transferred from one country to another—can determine a product's success abroad. **Technology transfer** is the "transfer of systematic knowledge for the manufacture of a product, for the application of a process, or for the rendering of a service, and does not extend to the mere sale or lease of goods."[76]

technology transfer
The transfer of systematic knowledge for the manufacture of a product, for the application of a process, or for the rendering of a service; does not extend to the mere sale or lease of goods.

Successful technology transfer depends on several things. First, there must be a *suitable technology* to be transferred (for instance, filtration devices). Second, *social and economic conditions* must favour the transfer. Pollution-reducing technology that is effective in Canada might be useless in a country where pollution reduction is not a priority. Finally, successful technology transfer depends on the *willingness and ability* of the receiving party to use and adapt the technology.[77] If successfully using pollution-control techniques required chemical engineers who had no access to the receiving country, the technology transfer would fail.

The Process of International Management

Today, almost every manager is an "international manager" because almost every business is involved in some way in international trade (and if that trade spans the globe, then "global manager" would be the better term).

International management means carrying out the management functions of planning, organizing, leading, and controlling on an international scale. Doing business internationally obviously affects the way that each of these functions is carried out. We will present several examples here, and then continue our discussion of international management in subsequent chapters.

international management
Carrying out the management functions of planning, organizing, leading, and controlling on an international scale.

Multinational Planning Issues

Planning means setting goals and identifying the courses of action for achieving those goals. It therefore always requires identifying opportunities and threats, and balancing these with the strengths and weaknesses of the enterprise. Planning in an international arena uses the same basic approach. However, global planning also means dealing with several unique issues.

For one thing, as we have seen, international planners must consider special political, legal, and technological issues. In Germany, for instance, Wal-Mart discovered it was illegal to advertise that it would refund the difference in price to customers if they found the same item elsewhere for less.

There is also the possibility of political instability, since many countries have frequent changes of government.[78] Similarly, currency instability, competition from state-owned enterprises, and pressures from national governments (including changing tariff barriers) can disrupt even the best-laid plans.

Instabilities like these are not just a characteristic of developing countries. Between 1993 and 1995, Italy embarked on a sweeping privatization of its nationalized businesses. During that time, Italy sold banks and companies worth about $60 billion, including some of the country's largest telecommunications, oil and gas, and insurance companies.[79] At the same time, sweeping criminal investigations created havoc among the country's political and managerial elite. The resulting upheaval created enormous opportunities for foreign firms doing business in Italy. But it also increased the risks by boosting both the competitiveness of the newly privatized Italian firms, and the uncertainties of dealing with the country's political institutions.

Other complications arise in international planning.[80] A domestic planner faces a relatively homogeneous home market, while an international planner faces a relatively fragmented and diverse set of foreign customers and needs. For Canadian planners, data are usually available and are relatively accurate and easy to collect. Internationally, collecting information—about demographics, production levels, and so on—can be a formidable task, and the actual data are often of questionable accuracy.

Organizing Issues

How does a manager organize an international business? Figure 2.5 illustrates typical organizational alternatives. These include domestic, export-oriented, international, and multinational organizational forms. Now, with the reality of e-commerce and e-business, the distinctions between these forms of organizations are becoming increasingly blurred. Even a relatively small Canadian company with a Web site is essentially opening its doors to international export.

However, traditionally these various organizational alternatives differ in the way in which authority is maintained over the foreign operations. In the *domestic organization*, each division handles its own foreign sales, which may come largely from unsolicited overseas orders. In response to increasing orders from abroad, the firm may move to an *export-oriented* structure. Here, one department (often called an import-export department) coordinates all international activities such as licensing, contracting, and managing foreign sales. In an *international organization*, the company is divided into separate domestic and international divisions. The international division focuses on production and sales overseas, while the domestic division focuses on domestic markets. This describes the organization of Westcoast Energy International, which has a group focused on Canada and a separate international group emphasizing business in Latin America. Finally, a firm may move to a *multinational* form, in which a subsidiary exists in each country where the firm does business. The oil firm Royal Dutch Shell is organized in this way, with separate subsidiaries for Switzerland and Canada (as well as for many other countries).[81]

Globalization also complicates a firm's human resource management practices. Decisions must be made about who is best suited for a foreign position, and whether this should be a local or foreign manager. Training is complicated by different cultural preferences. And compensation must take into account different taxation issues, depending on where the employee will be located. As we saw Chapter 1, if international teams are operating virtually, then special attention is required to maintain the culture and cohesion of the widely dispersed group.

International executives' relocations can often fail, resulting in a premature return home. Such failures most often occur because the expatriate cannot fathom the customs of a new country, or because his or her family cannot cope with the emotional stress that a relocation entails.[82] Global companies must therefore provide training

Westcoast Energy International
www.westcoastenergy.com/index.html

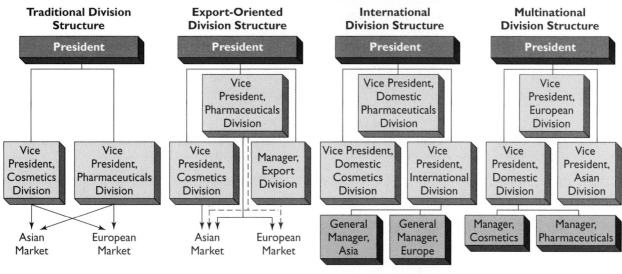

Traditional Division Structure

Here each division handles the minimal existing sales to each market itself.

Export-Oriented Division Structure

Here the export division or department helps to coordinate foreign sales, for instance by assisting with freight forwarding arrangements.

International Division Structure

Here each domestic division produces and sells for the local market. The international division may handle production and sales for foreign markets, or possibly just market abroad products produced in domestic factories.

Multinational Division Structure

Here each country of geographic region is the responsibility of its own officer and division, which handles sales and production within its own geographic boundaries. Increasingly, as we'll see, companies are consolidating production facilities, so that, for instance, more efficient plants in, say, Asia, might supply products worldwide.

FIGURE 2.5
International Organizations
As firms evolve from domestic to multinational enterprises, their increasing international operations necessitate a more globally oriented organization.

that focuses on the impact of cultural differences and on other matters like building language and adaptation skills. In addition, special preparation for the entire family is recommended.

Addressing intercountry differences in labour laws, such as differences in what may be considered sexual harassment, is also important.[83] Yet few firms actually provide such training to their employees.[84]

Leading the International Enterprise

Globalization also influences how to lead people. In Latin America, for instance, bosses are expected to be more autocratic, so participative management (in which employees are encouraged to make work-related decisions) can backfire. At the other extreme, Japanese managers value consensus, and rarely welcome the kind of take-charge leader who wants to personally make all the decisions.

The blending of diverse cultures often results in ambiguity and tension. In a joint venture between Mitsubishi of Japan and Chrysler to build automobiles, one American supervisor summarized the situation this way:

> Probably the biggest thing in terms of joint ventures, or I should say working with the Japanese, or with any other culture, is the fear—the uncertainty of the other culture....There's more emotion involved in coming to work here everyday in a joint venture environment between foreign companies, and working for a foreign company in your own country....It's been difficult. I think it's harder if you're a person that likes direction and continuity...it's always changing here.[85]

Controlling Issues

Maintaining control means monitoring actual performance to ensure consistency with expected standards. This is not an easy task, especially when the people or systems for which you are responsible are 8000 kilometres and an ocean away. In June 1999, for instance, Coca-Cola was hit by a rude surprise, as country after country in Europe required Coke to take its beverages off store shelves. While Coke has some of the industry's highest standards for product quality and integrity, keeping an eye on events at every plant can be a challenge, even for a firm its size. It turned out that chemicals had seeped into the beverages at one of Coke's European plants, and many consumers had apparently become sick as a result.

SUMMARY OF LEARNING OBJECTIVES

1. **Understand unique aspects of doing business in Canada versus the rest of the world.** Several factors must be considered when doing business in Canada, including geographic uniqueness, significant government involvement, a resource-based economy, proximity to the U.S., concerns about foreign ownership, Canada's level of productivity, and the degree of unionization.

2. **Outline what constitutes free trade.** Free trade means that most if not all barriers to trade are removed among countries participating in a mutual agreement. The potential benefit to free trade is that nations have the opportunity for greater economic integration and exchange, as occurs in NAFTA, the trade agreement between Canada, the U.S., and Mexico.

3. **Explain why companies expand operations abroad.** An international business is any firm that engages in international trade or investment. Firms are globalizing for many reasons, including sales expansion, to acquire resources, and to diversify sources of sales and supplies. Other reasons for pursuing international business include reducing costs or improving quality by seeking products and services produced in foreign countries.

4. **Understand strategies for expansion abroad, such as exporting and licensing.** Companies can pursue several strategies for extending operations to foreign markets. Exporting is the route often chosen by manufacturers, but licensing and franchising are two popular alternatives. Licensing occurs when a firm grants another company the right to use its intellectual property or processes for a fee. Franchising is granting the right to start a business based on an original concept or model, as McDonald's does. At some point, a firm may decide to invest its own funds in another country. Joint ventures and wholly owned subsidiaries are two examples of foreign direct investments.

5. **Explain how going global affects how a business is managed.** Globalizing production means dispersing parts of a firm's production process to various locations around the globe. Marketing is likewise more culturally dispersed and sensitive to cultural differences. The aim of globalizing is to take advantage of national differences in the cost and quality of production, and then integrate these operations in a unified system of manufacturing facilities around the world. Companies also are tapping into a new supply of skilled labour in various countries. The globalization of markets, production, and labour coincides with the rise of a new type of global manager, who can function effectively anywhere in the world.

6. **Define the new global manager.** Managers in the global economy are more cosmopolitan, with international exposure. These managers are flexible and

open to new ways of thinking, and are able to operate effectively in different cultural settings.

7. **Give examples of the economic, legal, political, socio-cultural, and technological factors that influence a manager's decision to expand abroad.** International managers must be adept at assessing a wide array of environmental factors. For example, managers must be familiar with the economic systems, exchange rates, and level of economic development of the countries in which they do business. They also must be aware of import restrictions, political risks, and legal differences and restraints. Important cultural differences will also affect the way in which people in various countries act and expect to be treated. Values, languages, and customs are all examples of elements that distinguish people of one culture from those of another. Finally, the relative ease with which technology can be transferred from one country to another is an important consideration in conducting international business.

8. **Discuss how doing business internationally affects how managers plan, organize, lead, and control.** Although the same activities are required of international managers, these activities become more complex as a company goes global. In the area of planning, there are special political, legal, and technological issues. Organizing includes the choice and use of various organizational forms, from domestic to multinational. Leading involves knowledge of multiple cultures, and controlling requires the ability to exert control in a context complicated by time and distance factors.

TYING IT ALL TOGETHER

In this chapter we have seen how the world of business is shrinking—and at the same time becoming more complex—in the context of globalization and new technologies. Canada has some unique characteristics for doing business that affect management both at home and internationally. Contemporary managers need a good understanding of international business, including various options for expansion. Of particular importance to managers is understanding how going global affects how people are managed. Cultural differences must be respected and understood, and economic, political, or legal issues must be considered.

Globalization confronts the manager with new international management issues and challenges. The effectiveness with which he or she deals with these issues—whether they involve planning, organizing, leading, managing human resources, controlling, or managing the behavioural side of a firm—will determine whether the decision to internationalize turns out to be a good one.

Chapter 1 explained how trends like globalization were boosting the level of competition that companies face, and therefore the challenges that managers face in managing their companies successfully. In Chapter 2 we turned the spotlight on managing in a global environment—what globalizing means and, specifically, how "going global" affects what managers do and the skills they need.

One of the main things we learned is that managers must take a society's values and culture into account when dealing with its people. However, cross-cultural issues do not necessarily just involve dealing with people abroad. In today's diverse workforce, differences in values and cultures may be as pronounced in one's own office as they are when dealing with people overseas. That is one reason why, in Chapter 3, we will look more closely at issues related to values and ethics, and how they influence what people do.

1. As we look around the globe, there seems to be war or conflict on most continents. Africa continues to have tribal warfare, poverty is rampant, technology is somewhat rare, and disease is everywhere. In the former USSR, Russia continues to fight with its former satellite countries, while the country itself seems to be falling apart. There is a weakening military, an inadequate food supply for regular citizens, a growing black market, and dissatisfaction among the many unemployed Russians. The European Union (EU) seems to working on the surface, but not without conflict. The United Kingdom and France are boycotting each other's meat and other products. And not all nations have decided to join the EU. For example, Sweden has yet to join. The conflict in Bosnia involved the U.S. and other European nations. In Asia, Pakistan and India have been fighting on a regular basis. Indonesia has been at odds with itself and the people of East Timor. Taiwan and China have different views of the future. And Canada is not without its own problems, ranging from homelessness to child poverty to crime. In terms of business in Canada, you read in this chapter that we are improving our competitive edge, rising to tenth on the World Competitiveness Survey in 1999 from twentieth just five years before. But if we look at the bigger picture, how does the world situation outlined above affect future investment and business opportunities? How would you describe the current global economy? What might the global economy look like in 10 years?

1. You have just accepted an assignment in Russia as a marketing representative. Your company is involved in the development of biotech farming techniques and is located in Ottawa's high-tech community—where progressive agricultural techniques and a sense of social responsibility are industry trademarks. You have a week to prepare to go to St. Petersburg and then on to Moscow. Where would you begin? Would you look at the political turmoil in Russia and its relationships with the former members of the USSR? Would you study the social customs? Would you try to take a crash course in the language? How would you prepare yourself to enter the new world of Russia? Would you interview recent immigrants from Russia? What might reading about Russia's history tell you about how to conduct business meetings there?

2. It is projected that by the middle of the next century, if not before, India will surpass China in population. What do you know about either of these countries? Collectively, they are home to approximately two-fifths of the world's population, and some of the richest and poorest people live in these two nations. Wealth there is not distributed as it is in Canada. China is still a communist country but is developing an entrepreneurial and capitalistic economy. India is a democratic country ruled by religion and other ancient values. How does religion (mainly Confucianism in China and Hinduism in India) affect managerial thinking? How do you think ancient history and religion influence China's and India's respective approaches to business and the global marketplace? What types of governmental structures do these countries have, and how might business be affected as a result? What are the political issues in these regions that would make them potential risks for Canadian investment? In a team of four or five students, research each country's history and current situation. Consider political, social, ethical and moral, economic, technological, and environmental issues. Then, based on your discussion, provide a written recommendation to companies that might wish to invest in either country.

To be successful in international business, managers need to pay attention to differences in national culture. To gain some perspective on various cultural dimensions visit Web of Culture at www.webofculture.com.

Read about different body gestures around the world, and how gestures have different meanings depending on the country in which they are expressed (www.webofculture.com/refs/gestures.html).

1. What do you find most interesting or surprising?

2. How would an understanding of gestures, and more generally of culture, contribute to effective management practice?

CASE STUDY 2-1

Innovation and Internationalization at Nortel Networks

Nortel Networks is an Internet leader that is creating a high-performance Internet that is more reliable and faster than ever before. Through acquisitions, alliances, and research and development the company is successfully executing a four-pronged strategy—Optical Internet, Internet Telephony, Wireless Internet, and Intranet Services—to build a better Internet. It is redefining the economics and quality of networking and the Internet through Unified Networks that promise a new era of collaboration, communications, and commerce. Nortel operates in 150 countries, has 70 000 employees worldwide, and had revenues of U.S.$17.6 billion in 1998. Its sales are growing at about 30 percent per year—faster than rival Lucent Technologies Inc. and close to Cisco Systems, who had expected growth of 36 percent in 1999. In fact, according to the *National Post*, in July 1999 Nortel Networks was ranked the number one Canadian company for creating the most value for its shareholders for a second year in a row.

Part of the growth and internationalization at Nortel Networks is due to CEO John Roth. The soft-spoken 56-year-old engineer has a vision: Virtually all telecommunications will take place on the Internet within 10 years. Since taking over as chief executive of Canada's biggest high-tech company in October 1997, the native of Lethbridge, Alberta, has initiated a radical overhaul of the lumbering maker of phone equipment and transformed it into a fast-growing seller of Internet gear.

To symbolize the transformation of the company, its name was changed from Northern Telecom to Nortel Networks. That was the easy part. The bigger challenge for Roth was attempting to change Nortel's culture. He wants to prove to Nortel's customers, staff, and shareholders that a 104-year-old company headquartered in suburban Toronto can compete and win against the hotshot engineers and hard-driving upstarts of California's Silicon Valley. And one way to build a new culture is to buy into it. That is just what Roth did when he purchased Bay Networks in the U.S.

Manufacturing at Nortel is a global affair. The company operates world-class manufacturing plants in Canada, the U.S., France, Mexico, Brazil, Turkey, and Ireland. Engineering and other product development is conducted at many of these facilities worldwide. As part of an international presence, Nortel Networks has research capabilities around the world, including a network of research and development facilities, joint ventures, and other collaborations that foster innovative product development and advanced design research in 17 countries. The research is paying off for Nortel. In April 1999 it was listed as the most innovative company for the second year running in *Canada's Most Respected*

Companies. It was also named one of the top 10 companies in the country, and one of the five most respected.

Innovation at Nortel Networks is not just confined to technology. As a result there is commitment to a set of principles for how the company operates that includes values-based business practices. Nortel aims to act with integrity by abiding by a code of business conduct. It has made a pledge to environmental sustainability, and has a comprehensive environmental policy that serves as a guide for action. Nortel strives to reduce its impact on the natural world and has won many awards for its efforts in this area.

Nortel also is committed to workforce diversity. The following statement can be found on its Web site: "Our commitment to workforce diversity isn't a cost or an obligation. It's how we work together. We see it as a competitive advantage. Our diverse team of networked employees from widely differing cultures and backgrounds gives us a unique perspective on the world in which we work, do business, and live." The raging success of Nortel Networks is testament to the expansion of a Canadian company with a conscience, commitment to values, and a goal of revolutionizing technology.

Questions

1. Discuss the advantages and disadvantages of global research and development and global manufacturing.

2. What has been CEO John Roth's role in transforming the company? Could the same changes have occurred without a change in leadership? Explain.

3. Discuss how the various strategies relating to social, cultural, or environmental issues can affect overall company success.

Nortel Networks
www.nortelnetworks.com

McDonald's Canada in Russia

Starting a business in another country can be a huge challenge, as George Cohon, senior chairman of McDonald's Restaurants of Canada Ltd., found out when he decided to introduce the famous fast-food restaurant in Russia. In a country known for its communist ideology, the introduction of a restaurant that symbolized Western capitalism was viewed with considerable suspicion.

For starters, the negotiation process that began in 1976 took 12 years to complete. Then, once an agreement was finally reached, Cohon had a lot of other things to worry about. He didn't know if the standards of excellence in food preparation and service could be maintained in Russia's non-capitalist system. He also wasn't sure if the Western style of fast food would appeal to Russians, or if they would have money to purchase McDonald's burgers and fries. A Big Mac would cost $2.80 in an economy where the average monthly income was less than $200.

In addition, Cohon figured that staffing would be difficult, as workers were not used to a system focused on quality or service. To counter this, he brought in Western managers to provide training and direction to the workers. Even finding the right ingredients for McDonald's products was difficult, and at the beginning about one-half the needed items were imported.

How did it all work out? Well, the restaurant on Pushkin Square in Moscow was an instant success. It serves 40 000 customers per day, making it the busiest McDonald's in the world! Cohon has since expanded McDonald's Canada to other Russian cities. In fact, by 1999 there were 49 restaurants operating in Russia making millions of dollars in profit. In the early days, about 80 percent of managers were expatriates from the West. But, with the right coaching, the Russian staff gained skills and management expertise. Now only a handful of Western managers remain. And almost all of the ingredients are provided by 150 local businesses.

Although problems of high taxes and excessive government red tape still remain, this is a Canadian success story, proving that opportunities exist in the global economy for Canadians who are willing to take calculated risks, be persistent, and adapt to local cultures and circumstances.

Questions

1. McDonald's has chosen to use franchising as a strategy for expansion. Is this the best alternative? Why or why not?

2. What are the key issues around production and marketing for McDonald's in Russia?

3. What skills will an effective expatriate manager possess to work effectively with local managers and employees?

McDonald's
www.mcdonalds.com

KnitMedia Goes Global

When it comes to the music industry, "abroad" is one place that a music company has to be. About one-third of the U.S.$50 billion or so in global recorded music sales comes from outside the United States, and all of the major music firms, including Sony, Warner/EMI, and Universal, are expanding into foreign markets. They are setting up joint ventures and company-owned offices, not just to sell music by American performers like Madonna overseas, but also to identify and develop local talent, since it's local talent that music lovers abroad often want to hear. That helps to explain, for example, why Eiffel 65's "Blue "—the number one hit in Italy and across Europe in 1999—was quickly signed by Universal. It hit the U.S. charts at number 6 in January 2000. In Europe, as in the United States, recording companies are continually searching for new talent. You'll find their representatives sifting through the CDs at a music store in London's Camden Town, for example, trying to find the next new break-out band from a small independent label.

"The Knitting Factory is at the center of the international music movement," the *Wall Street Journal* recently noted, and increasingly that's the case. Almost from the beginning, KnitMedia has had international aspirations, but today "going global" is a major part of the company's plans.

In some respects, going global is easier for companies like KnitMedia, but in other respects it's getting a lot more difficult. Technologies like the Internet and videoconferencing make it easier to track what's happening abroad and to communicate across borders and oceans quickly and easily. On the other hand, the industry is also consolidating, making it much more difficult for independents like KnitMedia to break in. Currently the major music companies have consolidated from six to three: Warner Music and EMI (which merged in 2000), Universal and BMG (which merged in 1999), and Sony. Independent record labels ("indies") have about 22 percent of the market, Universal 32 percent, Warner 27 percent, and Sony 17 percent. Independents are increasingly doing battle with companies that have enormous marketing clout.

Michael Dorf and KnitMedia have been doing business overseas since 1990. Going overseas began with a 24-city European tour with bands like Sonny Sharrock, the Jazz Passengers, and Miracle Room. It was a good start, but not everything went smoothly. For one thing,

a first-time agent booked the tour into a venue in Helsingbourd, Sweden, that held only 30 people—barely enough room for Knit's three bands, let alone customers. A performance in East Berlin just before the Berlin Wall fell lost money when German Chancellor Helmut Kohl decided to start the reunification. He offered three East German marks for one Deutsche mark, instead of the six or seven East German mark exchange rate that existed at that time. However, the tour was successful in introducing Europeans to KnitMedia's name and artists, and the company's next tours were much more profitable.

KnitMedia has long had an office in Holland to coordinate its European tours and other operations, and currently plans to move that office to Berlin. The company also devoted considerable time and resources to developing a strategic alliance with the South Bank Centre in London, with the aim of opening Knitting Factory clubs along the Thames in 1997. However, a variety of factors caused KnitMedia to change its plans, and now it will open its first club abroad in Berlin. As more clubs are added, they will be linked to a digital KnitMedia community to provide a global outlet for the company's artists and products.

KnitMedia is also involved in other international operations. "Like other independents," says Dorf, "we're trying to sell American acts abroad and find acts abroad to bring to America. We're working with Tower Records in the United States on a possible strategic alliance that would have Tower opening special KnitMedia kiosks in the jazz sections of more than 100 Tower stores, an idea that can possibly be exported to Europe. And that's not all. Other European tours and festivals are planned, and we're working with telecommunications and Internet firms to develop global Internet music broadcasting." Alliances with companies like Sony Music should help KnitMedia expand to South America, Asia, Africa, and the South Pacific. Given all these possibilities, the KnitMedia executive team would like some advice on how to further its aspirations to expand abroad.

Team Exercises and Questions

Use what you learned in this chapter to answer the following questions from Michael Dorf and his management team:

1. What international strategies have we used thus far to go global? What specific strategies would you suggest KnitMedia use for the next few years, and why?

2. How have the economic, socio-cultural, and technological components of the international environment affected KnitMedia until now? Based on what you know about the international environment in Europe today (or based on what you can find out), what do you think are the main economic, socio-cultural, and technological challenges KnitMedia will face over the next few years?

3. What "international management" challenges do we at KnitMedia seem to have faced to date in planning, organizing, leading, and controlling the company's expansion abroad, and what challenges do you anticipate as we open the new Knitting Factory in Berlin? What specific steps would you suggest we take to meet those challenges?

4. What competition do you see us facing in Europe as KnitMedia expands abroad? How do you suggest we address that competition?

Managing Ethics, Diversity, Culture, and Social Responsibility

Business Ethics in the Canadian Context

Canadian corporations see high technology as the major source of potential ethical misconduct in their organizations, according to a recent KPMG Business Ethics Survey. James Hunter, a partner at KPMG who is charge of the firm's ethics and integrity practice, says that KPMG was "a little bit surprised" by the focus on technology. "People were very concerned about the risks there are in IT [information technology]." On the other hand, he says, such concerns are justified. "Management really has to be concerned about the integrity of books and records. If they allow systems whereby people can play around with the records...it's going to come back to haunt them."

The survey, which was sent to the CEOs of 1000 Canadian companies in the private and public sectors, found that misuse of proprietary knowledge and security of internal communications were cited as the two top risk areas, while failure to report fraud or misconduct was also a major problem area. Despite these problems, only 36 percent of respondents said that their companies had a formal system to allow employees to report misconduct without fear of retribution; 22 percent said they had no system at all in place. "It's a true ethical dilemma," notes Hunter.

Megan Barry, director of business ethics for Nortel Networks, acknowledges that a company with a base of ethical employees is "way ahead of the game." She also believes that the complexity of ethical issues increases with the complexity of technology. For example, she says, Nortel, which recently redrafted its code of conduct written three years ago, is struggling with guidelines for the 40 percent of the company's employees who have Internet access. Nortel even has a toll-free number so that employees can report suspected ethics abuses or seek advice on ethics issues.

KPMG
www.kpmg.com

In Chapter 2 the challenges of managing globally were explained, and problems that can arise from cross-cultural differences in values and points of view were emphasized. In this chapter we will focus more specifically on the subjects of corporate culture, values, and ethics—and why they are important.

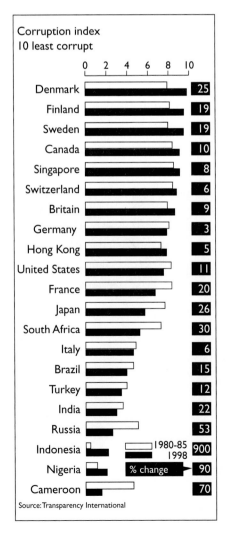

FIGURE 3.1
Bottom Is Worst
As seen in this chart, bribes and unethical behaviour are commonplace in many countries around the world.

Indeed, some managers quickly learn that globalization and ethics are inseparable. For example, consider the international corruption index shown in Figure 3.1. This figure highlights a truism that many managers must deal with every day: Bribes and unethical behaviour are the price of doing business in many countries around the world. For example, it's been estimated that businesses in Albania pay out bribes equal to about 8 percent of their sales (about one-third of their potential profits) as a cost of doing business.[1] Similarly, it's been estimated that in one recent year American businesses lost $15 billion in orders abroad to firms from countries that allow bribes (which are prohibited by the U.S. Foreign Corrupt Practices Act). Business people hope that a number of steps, including an "anti-bribery" treaty recently signed by 34 trading nations, including those responsible for most world trade, will reduce the incidence of corruption.

As we noted in the opening vignette, the advent of technology is creating new and emerging issues around ethics and values that in turn influence the corporate culture of an organization. For instance, what is the current state of Web ethics? How will companies deal with e-mail ethics and other security issues involving the Web? What are the ethical issues around Internet pornography? What role should organizations take to monitor what is condoned as acceptable content on the Web? What is the ethical responsibility of employees to use the Internet appropriately while at work? At this point, we really do not have definite answers to these questions. However, these concerns, as well as broader issues of ethics, corporate culture (which we will refer to simply as culture), and corporate responsibility will be explored as the main topics of this chapter.

What Determines Ethical Behaviour at Work?

We all face ethical choices every day. Consider this dilemma: Your best friend sits next to you in a large college class and cannot afford to miss any more sessions since attendance counts in the final grade. She has just called to ask that you sign the class roll for her tomorrow, and you know that she does in fact have a serious family matter to which she must attend. There are 190 students in the hall, so your chances of getting caught are virtually zero. Should you help your best friend out? Or would it be unethical to do so?

It may not be illegal, but is it unethical for stores to monitor their customers for reasons other than security?

How can you decide? What factors will influence whether you say "yes" or "no"? These are some of the questions we will address in this chapter. Let us look first at the meaning of ethics.

The Nature of Ethics

Ethics refers to "the principles of conduct governing an individual or a group,"[2] and specifically to the standards used to decide conduct. Ethical decisions always involve normative judgments.[3] A **normative judgment** implies "that something is good or bad, right or wrong, better or worse."[4] "You are wearing a skirt and blouse" is a non-normative statement; "That's a great outfit!" is a normative one.

Ethical decisions also always involve **morality**; in other words, society's accepted ways of behaviour. Moral standards differ from other types of standards in five main ways.[5] First, matters of serious consequence to society's well-being are addressed, such as murder, lying, and slander. Second, moral decisions cannot be established or changed by decisions of authoritative bodies like legislatures.[6] Third, self-interest should not be condoned. Fourth, moral judgments are never situational. Something that is morally right (or wrong) in one situation is right (or wrong) in another. Finally, moral judgments tend to trigger strong emotions. Violating moral standards may make you feel ashamed or remorseful. If you see someone else acting immorally, you may feel indignant or resentful.[7]

Ethics and the Law

So there you are, trying to decide whether to sign your friend's name on the class roll. What will you do? Several factors influence whether specific people in specific situations make ethical or unethical decisions. The law is one factor.

Is there a "law" against signing your friend's name? Well, perhaps there is only a college rule, so chances are that other factors will influence your decision. Let us look at them.

Something may be legal but still not right. You can make a decision that involves ethics (such as firing an employee) based on what is legal. However, that does not mean the decision will be ethical, since a legal decision can be unethical (and an ethical one can be illegal). Firing a 38-year-old employee just before she has earned the right to her pension may be unethical, but generally it is legal. Charging a naive customer an exorbitant price may also be legal, but unethical. Alternately, not promoting a pregnant woman to an area of a company where she could be exposed to toxic materials is ethical, but not legal.

Some retailers survey their customers' buying habits through a variety of electronic and infrared surveillance equipment.[8] Videocart, Inc. of Chicago uses infrared sensors in store ceilings to track shopping carts. Other firms compile information from credit card purchases. In other cases, casual conversations between you and a co-worker might be recorded, e-mails might be tracked on your company computer, or casual interactions might be watched in the staff lounge. These activities are not illegal at the present time, but many believe that such encroachment into a person's privacy is unethical.

Individual Standards

People bring to their jobs their own ideas of what is morally right and wrong, so the individual must shoulder most of the credit (or blame) for the ethical decisions he or she makes. Every decision we make and every action we take will reflect, for better or worse, the application of our moral standards to the question at hand.

Remember what happened at Livent, the company that produces shows and owns theatres in Toronto, Vancouver, New York, and Chicago? When Hollywood agent Michael Ovitz expressed an interest in buying Livent, Garth Drabinsky allegedly "cooked the books" to make the company look profitable. The new owners of Livent Inc. sued the company's founders and claimed that Drabinsky had manipulated ticket sales figures to impress stock analysts. This series of less than ethical decisions has resulted in huge losses for the owners, and idle theatres that await grand reopenings.[9]

ethics
The principles of conduct governing an individual or a group and, specifically, the standards used to decide conduct.

normative judgment
A judgment that implies that something is good or bad, right or wrong, better or worse.

morality
Society's accepted ways of behaviour.

A national survey of CEOs of manufacturing firms was conducted to explain the CEOs' intentions to engage (or to not engage) in two questionable business practices: soliciting a competitor's technological secrets and making payments to foreign government officials to secure business. The researchers concluded that the CEOs' ethical intentions were more strongly affected by their personal predispositions than by environmental pressures or organizational characteristics.[10]

It is hard to generalize about the characteristics of ethical or unethical people. However, older people—perhaps because they are more experienced—do tend to make more ethical decisions. In one study, 421 employees were surveyed to measure the degree to which age, gender, marital status, education, dependent children, region of the country, and years in business influenced responses to ethical decisions. (Situations included "doing personal business on company time," "not reporting others' violations of company rules and policies," and "calling in sick to take a day off for personal use.") With the exception of age, none of the variables were good predictors of whether a person would make the "right" decision. Older workers in general had stricter interpretations of ethical standards and made more ethical decisions than younger employees.

This "generation gap" in business ethics has also been found by other researchers.[11] One Baylor University study surveyed 2156 individuals who were grouped by age; those aged 21 to 40 represented the younger group and those aged 51 to 70 represented the older group. As in the previous study, respondents were asked to rate the acceptability of a number of ethics-related vignettes.[12] The following are 5 of the 16 vignettes used in the study.

1. A company president found that a competitor had made an important scientific discovery that would sharply reduce the profits of his own company. He then hired a key employee of the competitor in an attempt to learn the details of the discovery.

2. In order to increase profits, a general manager used a production process that exceeded legal limits for environmental pollution.

3. Because of pressure from his brokerage firm, a stockbroker recommended a type of bond that he did not consider to be a good investment.

4. A small business received one-quarter of its gross revenue in the form of cash. The owner reported only one-half of these cash receipts for income-tax purposes.

5. A company paid a $350 000 "consulting" fee to an official of a foreign country. In return, the official promised assistance in obtaining a contract that should produce a $10 million profit for the contracting company.

In virtually every case, the older group viewed the ethically questionable decision as more unacceptable than did the younger group. Of course, such findings do not suggest that all older employees are ethical, or that all younger ones are unethical. But they do raise the question of whether the younger employees' relative lack of experience leaves them more open to making "wrong" decisions. One danger is that most people view themselves as being more ethical than others. In other words, people tend to have a distorted view of just how ethical they really are.[13]

CMA Canada
www.cma-canada.org

As a counterpoint, CMA Canada surveyed accounting students and asked them to judge the acceptability of 14 business ethics scenarios. Students were asked if things like charging higher prices in poorer areas, using cheap foreign labour, and selling unsafe products overseas were acceptable practices. Only 5 of the 14 scenarios were considered to be acceptable. Female students typically viewed the scenarios as less acceptable than did male students. Older students were less tolerant of questionable behaviour than were younger students.

Students for
Responsible Business
www.SRBnet.org

To examine the complexity in differentiating between ethical and unethical behaviour, you may want to check out a Web site called "Students for Responsible Business." Originally called "Students for Responsible Business," the site was formed by a network of MBA students committed to using the power of business to create a better world.

The Organization Shapes Ethical Practices

Although ethical crises are sometimes caused by unscrupulous employees, most often that is not the case. It is rarely just one employee's character flaws that cause corporate misconduct. More typically, says one ethics expert:

> Unethical business practice involves the tacit, if not explicit, co-operation of others and reflects the values, attitudes, beliefs, language, and behavioural patterns that define an organization's operating culture. Ethics, then, is as much an organizational as a personal issue.[14]

Sears, Roebuck and Company
www.sears.com

Sears, Roebuck and Company provides a good example.[15] In 1992, consumers and attorneys general in more than 40 states accused Sears of misleading customers. The specific complaint was that Sears service writers had sold customers unnecessary parts and services, from brake jobs to front-end alignments. Could so many Sears mechanics and service writers have had ethical lapses?

Research by Sears management and by outside experts suggests that a number of organizational factors contributed to the problem. Faced with declining revenues, Sears management tried to boost the financial results of its auto centres by introducing new quotas and incentives for centre employees. Advisers later reported that those failing to meet quotas would not only lose commissions, but might be transferred to other jobs or have their work hours reduced.

While building pressure for sales, Sears management apparently did not do enough to establish a company culture that would encourage ethical decisions. As Sears' then-CEO Edward Brennan acknowledged, management was responsible for a compensation and goal-setting system that "created an environment in which mistakes did occur."[16] Indeed, the program was probably an honest attempt to boost sales. This is perhaps the scariest lesson of all—that honest people with good intentions can create conditions in which unethical decisions can flourish.

Once the allegations became public, Sears' top management took steps to prevent further occurrences. Unfortunately for Sears and its stockholders, the total cost of set-

THE CHALLENGE OF CHANGE ⇒ ⇒ ⇒

Firms Go on the Offensive in HR War

As the pitch and fervour to obtain highly qualified job applicants escalates, the line between corporate recruiting and headhunting is becoming increasingly blurred for human resource professionals. Technical recruiters are stepping up the methods that they use to attract candidates, especially in industries where competition is most fierce. Hosting a well-publicized open house or advertising on eye-catching billboards were once considered aggressive recruitment methods. But now, according to Personnel Systems, an Ottawa-based human resources management consultancy, "practices are becoming more cut-throat."[17]

Traditionally, headhunters have worked to entice employees away from one company and to sign them up with a competitor. Methods used include soliciting recruits near an employer's property, cold-calling prospects at work, asking new hires for phone lists, and cajoling receptionists. Now some human resources personnel are resorting to the same tactics—even if they are in the vast minority. And while some argue that these activities are in poor form, the counter-argument is that increased competition compels employers to change the standard of HR practices in high demand, high-tech industries.

tling the various lawsuits and providing customer refunds was an estimated $60 million.[18]

In another example, at Cendant Corp. two middle-level managers were asked to "cook the books" by two top managers in their division. When the fraud went public, Cendant's stock dropped nearly 50 percent in one day.[19] And ethical problems do not just occur in for-profit organizations. Take what happened at the Olympics. In December 1998 allegations surfaced that members of the International Olympic Committee had received over $1 million in improper gifts in return for awarding the 2002 Winter Games to Salt Lake City, Utah. A report written by Richard Pound of Montreal said that at least 16 members of the IOC had taken money illegally.[20] And finally, in 1999 Canada's Defence Department admitted that medical files of some Canadian soldiers who had served as peacekeepers in Bosnia had been tampered with, when a letter warning of potential exposure to toxic waste was removed from their files.[21]

Does paying a hefty fine and having the stock price plummet make companies act more ethically the next time around? Apparently not. Sears had to pay out $60 million for its wrongdoing in 1992, but in 1999 the firm was accused of much the same behaviour. Even stockholders do not seem to care. One study focused on what happened after a giant retail food chain had to pay millions of dollars in back wages and civil fines after being accused of child labour violations. The researchers found that the managers "…may dismiss fines and slight declines in stock price as inconsequential…" and that "investors may also be insufficiently grasping the implications of a conviction."[22] Something more than the threat of getting caught and paying a fine is obviously required to ensure ethical behaviour.

The Influence of Top Management

The behaviour of superiors is an important factor influencing ethical decisions.[23] In fact, many managers seem to feel that unethical actions are acceptable if their superior knows about them and says nothing. One writer gives these examples of how supervisors knowingly (or unknowingly) lead subordinates astray on ethical matters.

- Tell staffers to "do whatever is necessary" to achieve results.
- Overload top performers to ensure that work gets done.
- Look the other way when wrongdoing occurs.
- Take credit for others' work or shift blame.
- Play favourites.[24]

Department of National Defence
www.dnd.ca

Canadian athletes, like Mark Tewkesbury, protest against members of the International Olympic Committee after allegations surfaced that members of the IOC had received large amounts of money and gifts to influence them to pick Salt Lake City, Utah as the site of the 2002 Winter Games.

Ethics, Policies, and Codes

The leader's actions may be "the single most important factor in fostering corporate behaviour of a high ethical standard," but surveys rank an ethics policy as very important, too.[25] A policy signals that top management is concerned about ethics and wants to foster a culture that takes ethics seriously.

A survey by KPMG found that two-thirds of Canada's largest corporations have codes of ethics (90 percent of large U.S. firms do). The Canada Deposit Insurance Corp., for example, requires that all deposit-taking institutions have a code of conduct that is periodically reviewed and ratified by the board of directors. The Canadian Competition Bureau, the Canadian Institute of Chartered Accountants, and the Ontario Human Rights Commission all are pushing for the adoption of codes of ethics by corporations.[26]

Canada Deposit
Insurance Corp.
www.cdic.ca

Another study surveyed corporate accountants. The researchers found that 56 percent of the respondents' firms (but only about one-quarter of small firms) had corporate codes of conduct. Some other conclusions from this survey follow.[27]

> *Top Manager's Role.* Top management must make it clear that it is serious about code enforcement.[28] Top management also must ensure that customers, suppliers, and employees are all aware of the firm's stress on ethics.
>
> *Approval of Code.* The researchers concluded that "it is important for the code to be endorsed by executives at or near the top of the organization chart and by employees throughout the organization."[29] In 95 percent of the firms with codes, the code had been approved by the CEO, the board of directors, or both.
>
> *Communication of Code.* To influence employee behaviour, the ethics code must be communicated. The researchers found that the first step was generally to have top management assign responsibility for implementation of the code to a high-ranking manager. He or she in turn communicates the ethics code to employees. Although this is an important step, only about 57 percent of the firms actually sent a copy of their conduct codes to all employees.

Increased workforce diversity may make ethics codes even more important in the future. One expert contends that, with the flow of immigrants across national borders, it may become harder to rely on a shared organizational culture to control ethical behaviour. In other words, to the extent that it is more difficult to infuse common values and beliefs in a diverse workforce, it may become more necessary to emphasize explicit rules, expectations, and ethics codes.[30]

Ethics in Practice

The recurring problems at Sears, as well as those associated with new technologies, show that heading off ethical problems is easier said than done. A recent study found that 56 percent of all workers feel some pressure to act unethically or illegally, and that the problem seems to be getting worse. For example, 60 percent of the workers surveyed said they feel more pressure to act unethically than they did five years before, and 40 percent feel greater pressure than they did just a year before the study was conducted.[31]

How are well-known companies tackling this problem? We can gain a better perspective on how to encourage ethical behaviour by looking at actual corporate ethics programs.

Nortel Networks hired a consultant who spent three years interviewing employees about what they wanted as part of a new company framework. The result was a code of ethics, introduced in 1996, that emphasizes ethical decision making, integrity, respect, and fairness. In fact, employees can be dismissed for ethical infractions. For example, Nortel employees must not accept gifts or other favours from suppliers or potential suppliers, except for promotional items (such as inexpensive pens, mugs, or calendars that bear the company's name). The same standards apply to Nortel's dealings with their customers or potential customers.[32]

Ethical decision making at Johnson & Johnson has long been symbolized by what

Our Credo

We believe our first responsibility is to the doctors, nurses and patients,
to mothers and fathers and all others who use our products and services.
In meeting their needs everything we do must be of high quality.
We must constantly strive to reduce our costs
in order to maintain reasonable prices.
Customers' orders must be serviced promptly and accurately.
Our suppliers and distributors must have an opportunity
to make a fair profit.

We are responsible to our employees,
the men and women who work with us throughout the world.
Everyone must be considered as an individual.
We must respect their dignity and recognize their merit.
They must have a sense of security in their jobs.
Compensation must be fair and adequate,
and working conditions clean, orderly and safe.
We must be mindful of ways to help our employees fulfill
their family responsibilities.
Employees must feel free to make suggestions and complaints.
There must be equal opportunity for employment, development
and advancement for those qualified.
We must provide competent management,
and their actions must be just and ethical.

We are responsible to the communities in which we live and work
and to the world community as well.
We must be good citizens — support good works and charities
and bear our fair share of taxes.
We must encourage civic improvements and better health and education.
We must maintain in good order
the property we are privileged to use,
protecting the environment and natural resources.

Our final responsibility is to our stockholders.
Business must make a sound profit.
We must experiment with new ideas.
Research must be carried on, innovative programs developed
and mistakes paid for.
New equipment must be purchased, new facilities provided
and new products launched.
Reserves must be created to provide for adverse times.
When we operate according to these principles,
the stockholders should realize a fair return.

Johnson & Johnson

FIGURE 3.2
Johnson & Johnson's
Corporate Credo

the company calls "our credo." The credo, presented in Figure 3.2, provides the ethical pillars on which the firm is built and on which it continues to produce its pharmaceutical and health products. It begins with the statement that "we believe our first responsibility is to the doctors, nurses and patients, to mothers and all others who use our products and services."[33] Other elements include "in meeting their needs, everything we do must be of high quality," and "our suppliers and distributors must have an opportunity to make a fair profit."

Stories abound about how the credo provides the moral standards that guide the firm. One story describes how Johnson & Johnson reacted when a few poisoned Tylenol capsules were discovered some years ago. Because "our first responsibility is to the doctors, nurses and patients...," Johnson & Johnson decided to recall all outstanding capsules. The decision cost the firm hundreds of millions of dollars in lost sales. But in five months, the firm had produced a new tamper-resistant Tylenol product and regained 70 percent of its market share. Within several years, its market share was fully restored.

How to Foster Ethics at Work

KPMG's business ethics Web site aims to provide a place to which business people can turn for guidance on ethical issues and problems that threaten progress, as well as the prosperity of organizations. A sample of topics on the Web site includes managing religious diversity, how to guide the business ethics process, whether business ethics can be measured, as well as resources on business ethics. Visitors to the Web site can also access an "Ethics Risk Assessment," as well as information about ethics training and awareness programs.

The University of British Columbia has also developed a comprehensive set of online resources through the Centre for Applied Ethics. Business people can find information on codes of ethics, association codes of ethics, ethics institutions and organizations, publications on ethics, courses, and public-sector ethics.[34]

Centre for Applied
Ethics
www.ethics.ubc.ca/
resources/business

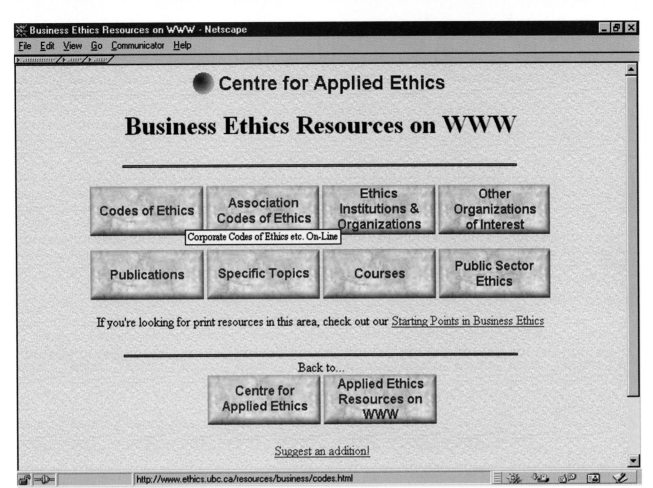

The Web site for the Centre for Applied Ethics at the University of British Columbia offers multiple sources of information pertaining to ethics.

After reviewing the ethics programs at 11 major firms, one study concluded that fostering ethics at work involved five main steps.

1. *Emphasize top management's commitment.* "To achieve results, the chief executive officer and those around the CEO need to be openly and strongly committed to ethical conduct, and give constant leadership in tending and renewing the values of the organization."[35]

2. *Publish a "code."* Firms with effective ethics programs set forth principles of conduct for the whole organization in the form of written documents.[36]

3. *Establish compliance mechanisms.* For example, pay attention to values and ethics in recruiting and hiring, emphasize corporate ethics in training, institute communications programs to inform and motivate employees, and audit to ensure compliance.[37]

4. *Involve personnel at all levels.* For example, use round-table discussions among small groups of employees regarding corporate ethics and surveys of employee attitudes regarding the state of ethics in the firm.[38]

5. *Measure results.* All 11 firms used surveys or audits to monitor compliance with ethical standards.[39] The results of the audit should then be discussed among board members and employees.[40]

Emerging Issues in Ethics

With the introduction of new technologies, new issues are arising in the realm of ethics. Technology is enabling employers to monitor employee behaviour using the Web. According to one study, more than one-third of all major U.S. corporations are monitoring workers' phone lines, reading e-mail, or monitoring through video cameras—and most of this is done without the knowledge of employees. That being said, severe sanctions are imposed for Internet abusers. Lexis-Nexus fired two employees and alerted police after discovering that workers used company computers to traffic in child pornography. Xerox Corp. recently revealed that it has fired more than 40 employees over the last year for inappropriate use of the Web. "We are trying be anything but Big Brother," says Warner Watkins, a security specialist at Coca-Cola. "But we have to set standards."[41]

How does Web monitoring affect companies? According to an article in *Computing Canada*, "the lack of trust demonstrated through monitoring colours the entire corporate culture of an organization. It may create a defensive culture, which has broad and deleterious effects. If employees feel powerless, they will engage in defensive and possibly destructive behaviour. The company then responds with more restrictive rules, and a downward spiral ensues."[42]

Internet security is another issue, and hackers do not respect ethical and appropriate Web behaviour. Consider the recent incident when Microsoft's e-mail system was put on worldwide display. Hackers found a way to open the accounts of 40 million people, including 2.5 million Canadians, who use Microsoft's free Hotmail service. How big was the breach? Well, among the samples posted on a Web site was e-mail from Microsoft president Steve Ballmer. Microsoft was forced to shut down Hotmail for several hours to fix the bug. The giant software maker says that no customers complained about the e-mail tampering, but experts say it is only a matter of time before small operations are compromised in a similar manner.[43]

Hotmail
www.hotmail.com

Creating the Right Culture

You know from your own experience that it is not just what you say that is important, but also what you do. A father can talk about being ethical until he is "blue in the face," but if his children see him cutting ethical corners—bringing home "free" office supplies from work or bragging about buying stocks based on "inside" information, for instance—the lesson his children may learn is that being unethical is acceptable. The same is true in organizations. Whether in regard to ethics or some other matter, the manager—and especially the top manager—creates a culture through what he or she says and does, and the employees then take their signals from that behaviour and culture.

What Is Organizational Culture?

organizational culture
The characteristics, traditions, and values that employees share.

Organizational culture can be defined as the characteristics, traditions, and values that employees share. Values (such as "Be honest," "Be thrifty," and "Don't be bureaucratic") are basic beliefs about what you should or should not do, and what is or is not important. Values guide and channel behaviour. Leading and influencing people and molding their ethical behaviour therefore depends, in part, on influencing the values they use as behavioural guides.

Let us take a closer look at what organizational culture means. To do that, think for a moment about what comes to mind when you hear the word "culture" applied to a country. In France, or China, or Canada, you would probably think of at least three things. Culture means, first, the *physical aspects* of the society, such as art, music, and theatre. Culture also means the *values* a country's citizens share—for instance, the emphasis on equality and fraternity in France, or on democracy and hard work in Canada. By "culture" you would also probably mean the characteristic way the people of a country *behave*—the patience of the people in England, or the emphasis on fine food and art among the people of France.

cultural artifacts
The obvious signs and symbols of corporate culture, such as written rules, office layouts, organizational structure, and dress codes.

We can apply this sort of analogy to get a better feel for the components of organizational culture. **Cultural artifacts** are the obvious signs and symbols of corporate culture, such as written rules, office layouts, organizational structure, and dress codes.[44]

Culture also includes **patterns of behaviour**. These include ceremonial events, written and spoken comments, and the actual behaviours in which the firm's managers and other employees engage (hiding information, politicking, or expressing honest concern when a colleague needs assistance). In turn, these corporate culture signs and behaviours are a product of **values and beliefs**, such as "The customer is always right" or "Don't be bureaucratic." These guiding standards lay out "what ought to be, as distinct from what is."[45] If management's *stated* values and beliefs align with what the managers actually value and believe, this will be demonstrated in their behaviour. For example, Bata Shoes stresses that it will not be satisfied with Canada's high prices to consumers, and advertises that its prices are as low as or lower than those in the U.S. The corporate culture enacts these values by providing competitive prices, as well as providing shoes to customers very quickly.[46] Organizational culture is important to ethics because a firm's culture reflects its shared values, and values help guide and channel people's behaviour. At Sears, for instance, the service advisers and mechanics apparently had little to go by when making decisions other than the "boost sales" incentive plan and quotas that top management had put in place. There wasn't a strong set of shared values throughout the company that signalled, for instance, "Potentially unethical sales practices will not be tolerated," and "The most important thing is to provide our customers with top-quality services that they really need."

The Managers' Influence

Managers play a major role in creating and sustaining a firm's culture, through the actions they take and the comments they make. In some firms, the culture results from the vision of one person. Thomas Watson (IBM), Frank Stronach (Magna International), Larry Clark (Spar Aerospace), Bill Gates (Microsoft), and Jean de Grandpre (BCE) are just a few examples of leaders who have had a strong influence on the culture of their respective organizations.

The following are some specific ways in which managers can shape their organization's culture.

Clarify Expectations. First, managers should make clear their expectations with respect to the values employees must follow. At Hewlett-Packard Canada Ltd., the corporate culture stresses equality, open communication, togetherness, high performance, and profit sharing. The president, Malcolm Gissing, wears a name tag like everyone else. The practice of using first names is part of the "H-P way." The H-P way also assumes that people want to do a good job and be creative, and that they will perform well if given the proper environment in which to work.[47]

Hewlett-Packard
Canada Ltd.
www.hp.com

A firm's values should then guide its behaviour. You may recall that Johnson & Johnson faced a crisis several years ago when someone tampered with its Tylenol capsules. From their credo, it was clear what management had to do: put their responsibility to "patients, to mothers..." first; emphasize high quality; and "be good citizens."[48]

Use Signs and Symbols. **Signs and symbols** are used throughout strong-culture firms to create and sustain the company's culture. Many believe that symbols—what the manager says and does and the signals he or she sends—ultimately do the most to create and sustain a company's culture. "Walking the talk" and doing what is promised is critical. Magna International, a large Canadian producer of auto parts, has a strong culture. The founder, Frank Stronach, is well known for his views about working conditions, day care centres, unions, and profit distribution. Concerning profit sharing, 20 percent goes to shareholders, 2 percent to charities, 7 percent to R&D, 10 percent to employees, and 2 percent to Stronach. The remaining 59 percent is reinvested in the company.[49]

Magna International
www.magnaint.com

At Saturn Corporation—known for its culture of quality, teamwork, and respect for the individual—one of the firm's top managers said this about company culture:

> Creating a value system that encourages the kind of behaviour you want is not enough. The challenge is then to engage in those practices that symbolize those values [and] tell people what is acceptable to do and what not [to do]. Actions, in other words, speak much more loudly than words.[50]

Frank Stronach, the founder of Magna International, is one of Canada's best-known CEOs. His views on profit sharing, working conditions, unions, and day care centres have created a distinctive corporate culture at Magna.

Concrete signs of a company's culture are easily evidenced. Take, for example, any number of high-tech companies where caps, shirts, jackets, or other items prominently display the company logo. At the Molson Centre, championship banners are proudly displayed, and reinforce the message that the Montreal Canadiens are winners.

stories
Company tales that reinforce the company's history and values.

Use Stories. **Stories** illustrating important company values are also widely used to reinforce the firm's culture. Although Walt Disney has been dead for many years, his spirit lives on in stories about how the company was built. Quotations from Disney are affixed to portraits of him placed throughout the company's studios. IBM has its own set of stories, such as how IBM salespeople took dramatic steps, such as driving all night through storms, to get parts to customers.

rites and ceremonies
Company activities such as conferences or annual parties that reinforce the corporate culture.

Use Rites and Ceremonies. **Rites and ceremonies** can also symbolize the firm's values and help convert employees to them. At JCPenney, where loyalty and tradition are values, new management employees are inducted into the "Penney Partnership" at ritualistic conferences, where they commit to the firm's ideology as embodied in its statement of core values. Each inductee solemnly swears allegiance to these values and then receives his or her H.C.S.C. lapel pin. These letters symbolize Penney's core values of honour, confidence, service, and cooperation.

The People Side of Managing box provides an example of culture in action, and how culture can be created by a company's founders and managers.

JC Penney
www.jcpenney.com

Social Responsibility

social responsibility
The extent to which companies should and do channel resources towards improving one or more segments of society other than the firm's own stockholders.

Corporate **social responsibility** refers to the extent to which companies should and do channel resources towards improving one or more segments of society other than the firm's own stockholders. Socially responsible behaviour might include creating jobs for minorities, controlling pollution, or supporting educational facilities or cultural events. A Decima Research survey found that 80 percent of Canadians think a business should give some of its profits to social causes. Corporations in Canada actually account for 10 percent of all money donated to charity. This means that the typical corporation gives less than one-half of 1 percent of its pre-tax profits to charity.[51] Social responsibility is largely an ethi-

Corporate Culture at Procter & Gamble

Procter & Gamble's culture reflects what one management theorist has called the firm's legendary emphasis on "thoroughness, market-testing, and ethical behaviour," values that are transmitted to new employees through selection, socialization, and training processes.[52]

The basic elements of Procter & Gamble's strong corporate culture go back to the company's founders, William Procter and James Gamble. They started P&G in Cincinnati in 1837 to produce relatively inexpensive household products that were technically superior to the competition, quickly consumed, and an integral part of their customer's lifestyle.[53] The intention was to "foster growth in an orderly manner, to reflect the standards set by the founders, and to plan and prepare for the future."[54]

This philosophy was translated into several core P&G values. The emphasis on orderly growth manifests itself in "tremendous conformity."[55] A new recruit soon learns to say "we" instead of "I."[56] This conformity bolsters thoroughness and a methodical approach. Its result, according to one past chairperson, is a "consistency of principles and policy that gives us direction, thoroughness, and self-discipline."[57]

Procter & Gamble's culture manifests itself in and is sustained by various management practices. College graduates are recruited and placed in highly competitive situations. Those who cannot learn the system are quickly weeded out; the remaining employees enjoy the benefits of promotion from within. As a result, no one reaches middle management without 5 to 10 years of close scrutiny and training. This in turn creates what one researcher called "a homogeneous leadership group with an enormous amount of common experience and strong set of shared assumptions."[58]

New recruits may assume major responsibility for projects almost immediately, but the authority for most big decisions is made far up the chain of command, usually by committees of managers. Nearly everything must be approved through a written memo process. Stories abound that reinforce this process; one describes the decision about the colour of the Folger's coffee lid, supposedly made by the CEO after four years of extensive market testing.[59]

Internal competition is fostered by the brand management system: Brands compete for internal resources, have their own advertising and marketing budgets, and act as independent cost centres. The extensive use of memos, the continual rechecking of each other's work, and the rigid timeline for promotions also contribute to (and reflect) P&G's strong culture and emphasis on thoroughness.

cal issue, since it involves questions of what is morally right or wrong with regard to the firm's responsibilities. As you will see, though, there is less unanimity regarding what is right or wrong in this area than there is with respect to traditional ethical issues such as bribery, stealing, and corporate dishonesty. Many perfectly ethical people strongly believe that a company's only social responsibility is to its shareholders.

Social Responsibility Today

Hidden on a small street in Hong Kong's Kowloon area is the tiny headquarters of the Asia Monitor Resource Centre, whose job is to monitor working conditions in mainland China. Its reports often shock huge American firms like Disney, and help to illustrate what socially responsible behaviour means today. Its aim is to uncover and publicized unacceptable working conditions in plants producing products for well-known global firms, and thereby improve working conditions for manufacturing workers in mainland China.

What sorts of unethical practices does the centre report? Its Disney report alleges that some mainland Chinese employed by Disney contractors must work up to 16 hours a day, 7 days a week, and are paid little or no overtime. Another report on China's toy industry describes what some have called "sweatshop Barbie" assembly lines, because of abuses including long hours for workers.

Companies with brands especially vulnerable to such criticism have been among the first to react in a socially responsible way. In fact, the plants of contractors for firms like Disney and Mattel are now reportedly among some the most progressive in mainland China.[60] Both Disney and Mattel have codes of conduct, and Disney has carried out tens of thousands of inspections of its contractors' plants to make sure they comply. Disney even cut off one of its non-complying factories, and Mattel emphasizes that it has received the certificate of workplace standards called for by the Asia Monitor Resource Centre.

Mattel
www.mattel.com

To Whom Should the Corporation Be Responsible?

Mattel's run-in with the Asia Monitor Resource Centre helps to crystallize the dilemma that lies at the heart of social responsibility: To whom should a company be socially responsible? Improving workers' living standards in China is certainly a laudable and socially responsible goal. But would it not be more socially responsible, others ask, for the company to concentrate on boosting its profits, so that its stockholder-owners and their families would gain?

Managerial Capitalism. The classic view of social responsibility is that a corporation's primary purpose is to maximize profits for its stockholders. Today, this view is most often associated with economist and Nobel laureate Milton Friedman, who has said:

> The view has been gaining widespread acceptance that corporate officials and labour leaders have a "social responsibility" that goes beyond the interest of their stockholders or their members. This view shows a fundamental misconception of the character and nature of the free economy. In such an economy, there is one and only one social responsibility of business—to use its resources and engage in activities designed to increase its profits so long as it stays within the rules of the game, which is to say, engages in open and free competition, without deception and fraud. Few trends could so thoroughly undermine the very foundation of our free society as the acceptance by corporate officials of a social responsibility other than to make as much money for their stockholders as possible.[61]

Friedman's position is built on two main arguments.[62] First, stockholders are owners of the corporation and so the corporate profits belong to them and to them alone. Second, stockholders deserve their profits because these profits derive from a voluntary contract among the various corporate stakeholders—the community receives tax money, suppliers are paid, employees earn wages, and so on. Everyone gets his or her due and additional social responsibility is not necessary.

corporate stakeholder
Any group vital to the survival and success of the corporation.

Stakeholder Theory. An opposite view is that business has a social responsibility to serve all the corporate stakeholders affected by its business decisions. A **corporate stakeholder** is "any group which is vital to the survival and success of the corporation."[63] As shown in Figure 3.3, six stakeholder groups are traditionally identified: stockholders (owners), employees, customers, suppliers, managers, and the local community (although conceivably others could be identified).[64]

Whereas Friedman's corporation focuses on maximizing profits, stakeholder theory holds that[65]

The V-Chip and TV Violence

The viewer chip, more commonly known as the v-chip, is a device that allows parents to block the reception of violent television programming that offends their ethical standards. Inventor of the v-chip and entrepreneur Tim Collings, a professor at the Technical University of British Columbia near Vancouver, says, "I think it's very important that we take a look at forces in society and we stand up for what we believe." The v-chip has implications for social responsibility as well, and how we choose to screen out the detrimental effects of children's exposure to violent programs.

A hockey fan who has spent his royalties from the v-chip to buy and refurbish a 1906 Hindman grand piano, Professor Collings invented the v-chip in the aftermath of the 1989 massacre at Montreal's École Polytechnique during which 14 female engineering students were shot. Subsequent research established a link between TV violence and subsequent violent behaviour.

To find a solution to help curb television violence, Collings spent six years developing the v-chip. Aided by a $300,000 research grant from Shaw Cable and the donated use of BCTV facilities, he eventually created, tested, and patented what essentially is a computer program with the ability to block or filter programs based on encoded ratings data. The next step was getting the product to market.

Professor Collings and Simon Fraser University established a spin-off company called Canadian V-Chip Design Inc. that licensed its v-chip technology to Toronto-based Tri-Vision International Ltd. Tri-Vision then signed an agreement with Nichimen Corp. of Japan to promote adoption of the new invention among television manufacturers.

In terms of v-chip adoption, Canada seems to be lagging behind the United States. The good news for Collings and his company is that, under a recent U.S. Congress order, all new television sets sold in the U.S. as of January 1, 2000, (an estimated 25 million to 30 million per year) must be equipped with the v-chip. And the bulk of the U.S. broadcast industry has agreed to implement a voluntary content-based TV ratings system, according to Tri-Vision Vice-President of Marketing Todd Grunberg.

However, Canadian broadcasters do not encode their signals with ratings data and there are no regulatory requirements that televisions be equipped with v-chips, Grunberg explains. As well, he adds, market surveys indicate Canadians "are less concerned about what their children are watching on TV and were less prone and less willing to use electronic devices to block that. They're far more comfortable with their own supervision of their children."

This may change. Professor Collings predicts there will be an increased use of the v-chip within Canada with the introduction of digital television and the future 500-channel universe. That being the case, the dream of one entrepreneur to increase the level of social responsibility in Canada when it comes to television viewing may fast become a reality.[66]

FIGURE 3.3
A Corporation's Major Stakeholders
One view of social responsibility is that a firm must consider and serve all the stakeholders that may be affected by its business decisions.

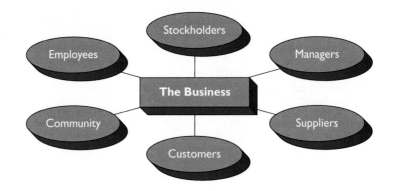

the corporation should be managed for the benefit of [all] its stakeholders: its customers, suppliers, owners, employees, and local communities. The rights of these groups must be ensured, and, further, the groups must participate, in some sense, in decisions that substantially affect their welfare.[67]

The Moral Minimum. Between the extremes of Friedman's capitalism and stakeholder theory is an intermediate position known as the **moral minimum**. Advocates agree that the purpose of the corporation is to maximize profits, but subject to the requirement that it must do so in conformity with the moral minimum,[68] meaning that the firm should be free to strive for profits so long as it commits no harm. By this view, a business would certainly have a social responsibility not to produce exploding cigarette lighters or operate chemical plants that poison the environment. However, it is unlikely that the social responsibilities of the business would extend to donating profits to charity or educating the poor, for instance.

moral minimum
The idea that a firm is free to strive for profits as long as no harm is committed.

How to Improve Social Responsiveness

The question of how to improve a company's social responsibility is not easy to answer because, as we have seen, there is no agreement on what being socially responsible means. Some companies take a proactive approach: "Being socially responsible" is the core of almost all their decisions. Some companies seem to pay as little attention to being socially responsible as they can. Others (such as Disney and Mattel) fall somewhere in the middle: They pursue socially responsible aims after being gently reminded to do so by organizations like the Asia Monitor Resource Centre.

At Bombardier, corporate social commitment is an integral part of its mission. The company fulfils its social and humanitarian responsibilities primarily through the J. Armand Bombardier Foundation, a not-for-profit organization that receives funding equivalent to 3 percent of the corporation's income before taxes. Created in 1965 by the Bombardier family to honour the founder's wishes, a tradition of supporting charitable causes begun by Bombardier's founder is continued. Each year, in addition to funding education in the form of student bursaries and donations to colleges and universities, the foundation supports several charity and relief organizations as well as missionary works.[69]

Corporate Social Monitoring: The Social Audit. Given a commitment to being socially responsible, how can firms ensure that they are in fact responsive? Some firms monitor how well they measure up to their aims using a rating system called a **corporate social audit**.[70]

corporate social audit
An accounting by companies that they uphold acceptable social practices.

The Sullivan Principles for Corporate Labour and Community Relations in South Africa[71] was one of the first such rating systems. The Reverend Leon Sullivan was an African-American minister and a member of General Motors' board of directors. For several years during the 1970s he tried to pressure GM to withdraw from South Africa, whose multiracial population was divided by the government-sanctioned racist policies known as apartheid.

As part of that effort, Sullivan formulated the code that came to be named for him, the purpose of which was "to guide U.S. business in its social and moral agenda in South Africa."[72] The code provided for measurable standards by which companies operating in South Africa could be audited, including non-segregation of the races in all eating, comfort, and work facilities and "equal pay for all employees doing equal or comparable work for the same period of time."[73] In the 1990s he proposed a new code for companies returning to South Africa after apartheid, stressing the protection of equal rights and the promotion of education and job training.

Whistle-Blowing. Many firms have a reputation for actively discouraging **whistle-blowing**, the activities of employees who try to report organizational wrongdoing. Yet many arguments can be made for *encouraging* whistle-blowers. In a firm that adheres to the "moral minimum" view, for instance, whistle-blowers can help the company avoid doing harm. As one writer has put it, whistle-blowers "represent one of the least expensive and most efficient sources of feedback about mistakes the firm may be making."[74] Other firms find that the "benefit of muffling whistle-blowers is illusory."[75] Once the damage has been done—whether it is asbestos hurting workers or a chemical plant making hundreds of people ill—the cost of making the damage right can be enormous.[76]

James Hunter, a partner at KPMG, says that creating a system for employees to report on misconduct is an ethical problem: "Do you speak up and tell your boss what you see, or do you betray a coworker whom you may have known for years? Unless the employer has a system in place to protect [employees], very often they're discriminated against [for speaking out], they can lose promotions or even get fired. It's not a happy ending."[77] Dr. Jeffrey Wigand, the subject of the recent feature film *The Insider*, was fired when he challenged his employer, a U.S. tobacco company, about the fact that they were using additives to increase addiction to cigarettes. He is now going after Imperial Tobacco in Canada for the same reason.[78]

whistle-blowing
The activities of employees who try to report organizational wrongdoing.

Managing Diversity

The workforces of the world are becoming increasingly diverse. In Canada, the various ethnic groups that make up the population include British Isles origin (40 percent), French origin (27 percent), other European (20 percent), Amerindian (1.5 percent), and other, mostly Asian (11.5 percent).[79] This diversity is reflected in the workforce. In the U.S., almost half of the net additions to the workforce in the 1990s were non-white, and almost two-thirds were female.[80] Similarly, it is estimated that minorities comprise 8 to 10 percent of the workforce population in France, 5 percent in the Netherlands, and a growing proportion in Italy, Germany, and much of Europe.[81] Even Japan, historically a homogeneous society averse to immigration, will have to find ways to accommodate many more women in its workforce.[82]

Such diversity will confront managers with challenges—ethical and otherwise—of epic proportions. For one thing, people from different cultures often have values, traditions, and ways of looking at things that are unique to their culture. That is why it is important for managers to have "global brains" (see Chapter 2).

Such diversity is both a blessing and a curse. Bringing together people with different values and views can, for instance, ensure that problems are attacked in a richer, more multi-faceted way. On the negative side, the research findings show that diversity makes it harder to put together a smoothly functioning team. Further, "These findings are consistent with the idea that the more similar people are in background variables such as socio-economic status or attitudes, the more attractive they are likely to be to each other, at least initially."[83] Creating a close-knit and efficient multicultural team can therefore be quite a challenge.

But along with the challenges, diversity creates enormous opportunities. There is, for instance, the opportunity to attract and retain the best possible human talent, and to boost creativity and innovation by bringing different points of view to bear on problems. **Managing diversity** means "planning and implementing organizational systems and

managing diversity
Planning and implementing organizational systems and practices to manage people so that the potential advantages of diversity are maximized while its potential disadvantages are minimized.

practices to manage people so that the potential advantages of diversity are maximized while its potential disadvantages are minimized."[84]

Bases for Diversity

A workforce is **diverse** when it is composed of two or more groups, each of whose members are identifiable and distinguishable based on demographic or other characteristics. The bases upon which groups can be distinguished are numerous. However, when managers talk of "diversity," they usually mean at least the following groups.[85]

- *Racial and ethnic groups.* Asians, aboriginals, and other ethnic groups now comprise a significant minority of the Canadian population. Some ethnic groups are concentrated in certain cities. Asians, for example, constitute a large minority of the ethnic population in cities like Toronto, Winnipeg, and Vancouver.

- *Women* will represent about 48 percent of the Canadian workforce by 2005.

- *Older workers.* In 1996, the median age of the Canadian population was 35 years. This is expected to rise to 50 by 2036, and reflects the rapid aging of the Canadian workforce.

- *People with disabilities.* The Employment Equity Act of 1986 makes it illegal to discriminate against people with disabilities who are otherwise able to do the job. This act has thrown a spotlight on the large number of people with disabilities in the workforce. At Rogers Cablevision, a large workplace area was completely redesigned to accommodate workers who were either visually disabled or in wheelchairs.[86]

- *Sexual orientation.* It has been estimated that about 10 percent of the population is homosexual, which may make homosexuals a larger percentage of the workforce than some racial and ethnic minorities.[87]

Advances in technology have permitted many disabled people to work productively. Nancy Thibeault, telephone operator and receptionist at PAC Corporation, uses specially designed equipment on the job.

Barriers in Dealing with Diversity

Any attempt to manage diversity has to begin with an understanding of the barriers that may prevent a company from taking full advantage of the potential in its diverse workforce. These barriers include the following.

Stereotyping and Prejudice. Stereotyping and prejudice are two sides of the same coin. **Stereotyping** is a process in which specific behavioural traits are ascribed to individuals on the basis of their apparent membership in a group.[88] **Prejudice** is a bias that results from prejudging someone on the basis of some trait.

Most people form stereotyped lists of behavioural traits that they identify with certain groups. Unfortunately, many of these stereotypes (in addition to being inaccurate) carry negative connotations. For example, stereotypical "male" traits might include strong, cruel, aggressive, and loud. Stereotypical "female" traits might include weak, soft-hearted, meek, and gentle.[89] When someone allows stereotypical traits like these to bias them for or against someone, then we say the person is prejudiced.

Ethnocentrism. **Ethnocentrism** is prejudice on a grand scale. It can be defined as a tendency "for viewing members of one's own group as the centre of the universe and for viewing other social groups (out-groups) less favourably than one's own." Ethnocentrism can be a very significant barrier to managing diversity. For example, Caucasian managers have been found to attribute the performance of minority groups less to their ability and effort and more to help they received from others. Conversely, white managers attributed the performance of whites to their own abilities and efforts.[90]

Discrimination. Whereas prejudice means a bias towards prejudging someone based on stereotypical traits, **discrimination** refers to taking specific actions towards or against a person based on the person's group.[91] Of course, in several countries, including Canada, many forms of discrimination are against the law. In Canada it is illegal to discriminate against someone solely based on that person's age, race, gender, disability, or country of national origin.

Discrimination continues to be a barrier to diversity management. For example, many argue that there is an invisible "glass ceiling," enforced by an "old boys' network" and friendships built in places like men-only clubs, that effectively prevents women from breaking into the top ranks of management.

Tokenism. **Tokenism** occurs when a company appoints a small group of women or minority-group members to high-profile positions, rather than more aggressively seeking full workgroup representation for that group. Tokenism is a diversity barrier when it slows the process of hiring or promoting more members of the minority group in question.

"Token" employees often fare poorly. Research suggests, for instance, that token employees face obstacles to full participation, success, and acceptance in the company. There is also a tendency for their performance, good or bad, to be magnified because of the extra attention their distinctiveness creates.[92]

Gender-Role Stereotypes. In addition to problems like glass ceilings, working women confront **gender-role stereotypes**—the tendency to associate women with certain (frequently non-managerial) jobs. In one study, attractiveness was advantageous for female interviewees only when the job was non-managerial. When the position was managerial, a woman's attractiveness tended to reduce her chances of being hired and getting a good starting salary.[93]

Gender stereotypes apply to women choosing technology careers, and to some degree are hampering women's participation in technology sectors. At a Vancouver conference, Cathy Munn, co-founder and director of business development at The Electric Mail Company, pointed out that participation of women in high technology (including biotechnology and other sciences) ranged from 11 percent in Quebec to 27 percent in some provinces. B.C.'s numbers are lower than the national average, as women comprise only 14 percent of the high-tech sector, and only 10 percent of management posi-

stereotyping
A process in which specific behavioural traits are ascribed to individuals on the basis of their apparent membership in a group.

prejudice
A bias that results from prejudging someone on the basis of some trait.

ethnocentrism
A tendency to view members of one's own group as the centre of the universe and to view other social groups less favourably than one's own.

discrimination
Taking specific actions towards or against a person based on the person's group.

tokenism
Occurs when a company appoints a small group of women or minority-group members to high-profile positions, rather than more aggressively seeking full workgroup representation for those groups.

gender-role stereotype
The tendency to associate women with certain (frequently non-managerial) jobs.

tions within this sector. From 1991 to 1996, high technology experienced a 30 percent growth; however, during this same period there was a 2 percent decrease in women's participation.[94] To some degree, this slide can be countered by proactively convincing girls and young women of the opportunities available in high technology. Providing guidance early in the education process and breaking stereotypes that girls "don't do science" are part of the challenge.

Boosting Performance by Managing Diversity

Managing diversity means maximizing the potential advantages of diversity, while minimizing its potential barriers. In practice, doing so includes both compulsory and voluntary management actions.

First, there are many legally mandated actions employers must take to minimize discrimination at work. For example, employers should avoid discriminatory employment advertising (such as "young man wanted for sales position") and prohibit sexual harassment. But, while actions like these can reduce more blatant barriers, blending a diverse workforce into a close-knit community also requires other steps, as illustrated in Figure 3.4. Based on his research, one diversity expert concludes that five sets of activities are at the heart of a managing diversity program.

Provide Strong Leadership. Companies with exemplary reputations are typically led by chief executives who champion diversity. Leadership in this case requires taking a strong personal stand on the need for change, becoming a role model for the behaviours required for the change, and providing the mental energy and financial and other support needed to implement the changes (for instance, in hiring practices). It can also mean writing a statement that defines diversity and explains how diversity is linked to the business.[95]

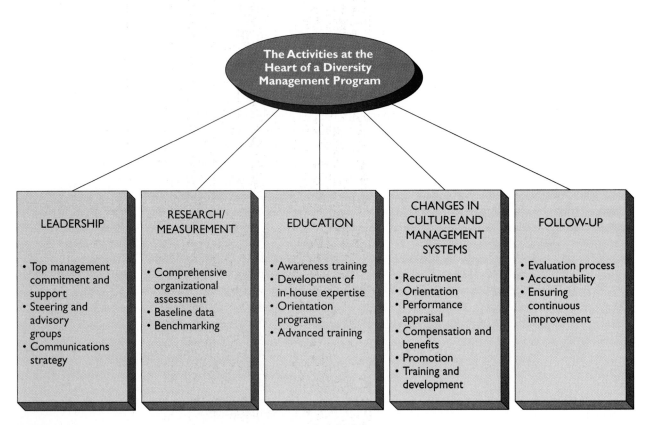

FIGURE 3.4
Activities Required to Better Manage Diversity

Research: Assess the Situation. The company must assess its current situation with respect to diversity management. This might include using surveys to measure current employee attitudes and perceptions about different cultural groups in the company, and about relationships between the groups.

Provide Diversity Training and Education. One expert says, "the most commonly utilized starting point for...managing diversity is some type of employee education program."[96] Employers typically use several types of programs, most often a one- to three-day workshop aimed at increasing awareness and sensitivity to diversity issues.

What might such a seminar cover? Suggestions include involving a diverse group of employees in the process, and asking them the following questions: What does diversity mean to you? Why do you have those perceptions of diversity? What does it mean to our organization? How can we develop an inclusive and positive definition of diversity that will be understood and accepted by everyone?[97] Since disagreements may arise, it is usually best that meetings like this be managed by professional facilitators.

Change Culture and Management Systems. Education programs should be combined with other steps aimed at changing the organization's culture and management systems. For example, the performance appraisal procedure might be changed so supervisors are appraised based partly on their success in minimizing intergroup conflicts. Many companies also institute mentoring programs. **Mentoring** is defined as "...a relationship between a younger adult and an older, more experienced adult in which the mentor provides support, guidance, and counselling to enhance the protégé's success at work and in other arenas of life."[98]

As a specific initiative to enable diversity in Canada, in 1994 the Treasury Board of Canada, in conjunction with the Public Service Commission, implemented the Special Measures Initiatives Programme.[99] Operational delivery of the program was through the Diversity Management Directorate. The program complemented the federal government's larger Employment Equity Program established in 1983, and focused on the development, advancement, and retention, as well as recruitment, of a diverse workforce. It also considered ways to change the corporate culture of organizations in order to support diversity. To date, several key achievements have resulted from the program, including:[100]

1. Partnership building—166 initiatives were co-funded with federal departments;

2. Internet technology—Piloted Web-site initiatives in the Public Service Commission. Operation site hits worldwide now range from 9000 to 11 300 per month, representing about 5 percent of the total traffic on the Public Service Commission's site.

3. Accessibility—Pioneered the development of the Accessibility Self-Evaluation Test, and provided information on employment-equity and diversity-management documents, tools, and software.

4. Career consultation—Conducted 3880 career consultations with group-designated members.

This all goes to prove that diversity initiatives can work if they are managed and implemented effectively.

Evaluate the Diversity Program. This stage is aimed at measuring the diversity management program's results. For example, do surveys now indicate an improvement in employee attitudes towards diversity? How many employees have entered into mentoring relationships, and do these relationships appear to be successful?

What effects do programs like these have on employee attitudes and points of view? Do they actually boost mutual understanding? In the case of the federal government's diversity program outlined above, an evaluation was conducted in 1997 and the conclusion was that cultural awareness had increased.

mentoring
A relationship between a younger adult and an older, more experienced adult in which the mentor provides support, guidance, and counselling to enhance the protégé's success at work and in other arenas of life.

Treasury Board of Canada
www.tbs-sct.gc.ca

Public Service Commission
www.psc-cfp.gc.ca

1. **Explain the nature of ethical decisions, including what makes a decision a moral one.** Managers face ethical choices every day. Ethics refers to the principles of conduct governing an individual or a group. Ethical decisions always include both normative and moral judgments. Being legal and being ethical are not necessarily the same thing. A decision can be legal but still be unethical, or be ethical but still be illegal.

2. **Discuss the factors that influence whether specific people in specific organizations make ethical or unethical decisions.** The individual making the decision must ultimately shoulder most of the credit (or blame) for any ethical decision he or she makes. However, the organization itself—including its leadership, culture, and incentive/compensation plan—will also shape an individual employee's behaviour.

   Ethics policies and codes are important. They send a strong signal that top management is serious about ethics, and are a sign that the company wants to foster a culture that takes ethics seriously. There are several steps that managers take to foster ethics at work, including emphasizing top management's commitment to ethics, publishing a code of ethics, establishing compliance mechanisms, involving personnel at all levels, and measuring the results of ethics initiatives.

3. **Explain how to create a company's culture.** Organizational culture may be defined as the characteristic traditions, norms, and values that employees share. Values are basic beliefs about what you should and should not do, and what is and is not important. Several things contribute to creating and sustaining the corporate culture. One is a formal core values statement such as Johnson & Johnson's credo. Leaders also play a role in creating and sustaining culture, a process that often goes back to the firm's founders, who established the firm's cultural beginnings. One of a leader's most important functions is to influence the culture and shared values of his or her organization. Managers use signs, symbols, stories, rites, and ceremonies to create and sustain their companies' cultures.

4. **Explain the main approaches to corporate social responsibility.** Social responsibility is largely an ethical issue, since it involves questions of what is morally right or wrong with regard to the firm's responsibilities. People differ in answering the question, "To whom should the corporation be responsible?" Some say a company should be responsible solely to stockholders, some say to all stakeholders, and some take an intermediate position. This last group agrees that the purpose of the corporation is to maximize profits, but that it must do so in conformity with the moral minimum.

5. **Discuss techniques that managers can use to manage workforce diversity.** As the workforce becomes more diverse, it becomes more important to manage diversity so that its benefits outweigh any potential drawbacks. Potential barriers to managing diversity include stereotyping, prejudice, and tokenism. Managing diversity involves taking steps such as providing strong leadership, assessing the situation, providing training and education, changing the culture and systems, and evaluating the program.

TYING IT ALL TOGETHER

In this chapter we have considered the importance of ethics from both a personal and an organizational perspective. To a large degree the organization, and the senior management in those organizations, have a key role in ensuring employee compliance with ethical standards and behaviours. With the advent of technology, some of the ethical boundaries are shifting, and it is more difficult to both monitor and determine what is ethical. Codes of ethics are one way to standardize ethical and acceptable behaviour in organizations. In addition, many Canadian companies are concerned about providing information about ethics to employees through training and other programs. We have also seen how the corporate culture of a company sets the values and behaviours of acceptable behaviour, including norms for decision making around ethics. The extent to which companies value "giving back to society" is an indication of corporate social responsibility—and is increasingly on the minds of Canadian managers.

Organizations and their employees get things done within an environment that is continually shifting. Outside forces such as globalization, deregulation, and technological change all contribute to the creation of a competitive environment. In this chapter we have focused in particular on values, ethics, social responsibility, and corporate culture. Collectively, Chapters 1 to 3 examine the "outside" and "inside" environments of a firm, and how they affect what managers and employees do.

In the chapters ahead, we will turn our attention to a detailed examination of what managers do and how they do it—in others words, to the management topics of planning, organizing, leading, and controlling. Since making good decisions underlies just about everything else managers do, we turn first to Making Decisions.

CRITICAL THINKING EXERCISE

1. You work in the marketing department of a medical genetics research firm. You love your job: The location is great, the hours are good, and the work is challenging and flexible. In addition, you receive a much higher salary than you ever had anticipated. One day, you hear via the rumour mill that the company's elite medical team is working on how to clone humans. You are not sure you are in favour of cloning. You joined the firm because of its moral and ethical reputation. The image presented to you was one of research and development of life-saving drugs and innovative medical procedures. The thought of cloning was never on your mind until now. What are the ethical and cultural issues involved? What will you do? Do you think that managers in Japan, Sweden, Chile, or France would manage the issue of cloning in the same way? Why? Do you think cloning will become an even more controversial ethical and moral issue in the future?

EXPERIENTIAL EXERCISE

1. In teams of four or five, research and then write a report on the ethical philosophies and attitudes towards business of the following nations: Russia, India, Egypt, Israel, the Congo, Norway, Saudi Arabia, and Australia. Compare these countries' respective approaches to ethics and corporate social responsibility and explain why there are differences.

INTERNET EXERCISE

Ethics and social responsibility are important parts of doing business. In this chapter we have also considered how technology has added a new dimension to workplace ethics. To learn more about this topic, go to the Centre for Applied Ethics at the University of British Columbia at www.ethics.ubc.ca/resources/business.

Once there, go to the "Codes of Ethics," where you will find a list of companies and their corporate codes of ethics. Focus on Nortel, Johnson & Johnson, and Texas Instruments.

1. What are the key features of a company's code of ethics?

2. How do the codes of ethics differ between Nortel, Johnson & Johnson, and Texas Instruments?

3. How do the ethics codes affect employees and how they work?

Going to the Wall with China

The Three Gorges Dam, a mammoth $45 billion undertaking in the heart of China, has been described by one Chinese official as "Canada's project." The reason for this peculiar distinction? The Canadian government provided crucial financial and technical support for the project, and Canadian engineers were the first foreigners to work on it. The Canadian participants included Agra International, a division of the Calgary-based engineering giant Agra Inc., General Electric Canada of Toronto, and Teshmont Consultants Inc. of Winnipeg. Canadian involvement has a lot to do with prestige—the dam is, after all, one of the largest engineering feats in history. In China, it is the most ambitious project since the construction of the Great Wall.

There is an additional twist to Canada's involvement: A Toronto-based environmental and human rights group, Probe International, is one of the world's most vocal critics of the dam. Building the dam has meant diverting the mighty Yangtze River, and consequently the eventual resettlement of more than 1 million Chinese citizens to make way for a massive reservoir that will stretch 100 kilometres longer than Lake Superior and submerge entire cities. Families will be forced to abandon their land with little compensation. The reservoir will submerge 13 cities, 140 towns, 320 villages, 650 factories, and 28 000 square kilometres of farmland. The dam also may have an impact on rare fish and wildlife in the area. And most ominously, given China's spotty track record in construction quality, fears abound that the dam may collapse, unleashing a torrent that will kill tens of millions of people who live downstream.

The Three Gorges project could enrich foreign participants, but also damage their reputations at home and abroad. Agra's involvement has endeared the company to Chinese officials who hold the purse strings for future contracts. At the same time, however, Agra risks being targeted by environmental groups and becoming a corporate scapegoat. The threat of such a backlash is real, even though Agra sees its role in the Three Gorges Dam as humanitarian.

In Canada, various foreign aid and credit agencies—including the Canadian International Development Agency (CIDA) and Canada's Export Development Corp. (EDC)—have pledged money and support to the Three Gorges project. In contrast, the U.S. equivalent of EDC, the Export-Import Bank of the United States, voted against lending funds to the Three Gorges project in 1996. This occurred after American environmentalists claimed that participation would violate the U.S. Endangered Species Act and threatened to sue. As a result, no large U.S. firms are directly involved in the project, although General Electric found a way in through its Canadian subsidiary. "When the Americans pulled back, Canada very smartly stepped in," says Agra Vice-President Peter Mayers. "There's no question the benefit to Canada has been enormous."

Questions

1. What responsibility do companies have to adhere to standards of social and environmental responsibility?

2. Should the same standards of ethics and social responsibility apply in Canada and in China, even if the rules in China for human rights and preservation of the environment differ?

3. As existing partners in this project, what do you think Agra and others should do now?

Agra International
www.agra.ca

General Electric Canada
www.ge.com

Teshmont Consultants Inc.
www.teshmont.ca

Export Development Corp.
www.edc.ca

Building an Employee-centric Culture

Common business logic dictates that the customer always comes first. However, in an industry burdened with a serious skills shortage, Canada's high-tech firms need to rethink this philosophy and, instead, build a corporate culture that puts workers first. The old adage, "You're only as strong as your weakest link and as good as your best people," provides support for this reasoning. If the right people with the right training are in place, high levels of customer service and profitability will follow.

As straightforward as this may seem, employing a "people first" strategy is a huge departure for many information technology (IT) companies. An employee-centric approach means more than aggressive recruiting strategies and competitive salaries. It also means infusing the approach into all aspects of a business. If a company has an attractive corporate culture, then recruiting and retaining talented IT workers becomes a self-fulfilling prophecy.

In 1999 two separate surveys found that Canada's personal income tax rates may not be a significant factor affecting the staff shortages in Canadian IT firms. Instead, computer science and engineering graduates say they would rather have interesting jobs at a company that provides a "cool" place to work—even if it means they will earn less.

Paul Maasland, a principal of Toronto-based Daedalian Systems Group Inc., says that a "cool place to work can be defined by several factors: the opportunity to do interesting and challenging work; a company that commits to technical and professional development; and a progressive compensation package." At Daedalian Systems Group Inc. the human resources department is responsible not only for recruiting new job candidates, but for nurturing existing employees. Employee interests and strengths are identified to match the qualities required in project work.

On the topic of money, compensation must be competitive. And these days, especially in the high-tech sectors, stock options, performance bonuses, and profit sharing are often included. All of this costs money, but Daedalian Systems believes it is worth it. According to Maasland, "Investing in a rich environment with limitless resources is a considerable cost to incur. When we make an investment of this nature, every employee becomes a highly valuable resource."

Questions

1. How will the various activities and offerings at Daedalian help to create a corporate culture that supports and retains employees?

2. What is the role of the leader in creating a company's culture?

3. In what ways is creating and sustaining a culture in a high-tech company unique?

Daedalian Systems Group Inc.
www.daedalian.com

Ethics and Con Edison

One of the many differences between managing a small business like KnitMedia and a giant like GE is this: Your local electric utility rarely comes in and shuts off the power when you are the president of GE.

The Knitting Factory faced a dilemma as Con Edison, New York City's electric utility, came close to putting the club out of business, at least for one weekend. With bills of about $2000 a month, the Knitting Factory was occasionally late with its payments. Con Edison reacted by demanding an $800 deposit, and even Michael Dorf's letters, formal complaint, and visit to the local Con Ed office weren't enough to get Con Ed to change its mind. Now it is 5:45 on Friday afternoon, the start of the Knitting Factory's heavy weekend schedule. Four refrigerators are filled with chilled products. A Con Edison employee has just come into the bar, saying he is there to read the meter. He proceeds to turn off the Knitting Factory's electric service.

Michael Dorf has an ethical and managerial dilemma. On the one hand, it's too late to pay Con Ed, but a company of KnitMedia's size simply cannot afford to walk away from a full weekend of performances. There is one choice: There is a living area above the club, and the electricity is still turned on in that space. Dorf and his managers could quickly rig up extension cords running from the apartment and keep the Knitting Factory open all weekend. Doing so would raise some questions, however. For instance, is that the ethical thing to do? And what would be the ethical and moral implications if the electric lines overheated and something went wrong? Michael Dorf asks you what to do.

Team Exercises and Questions

Use what you learned in this chapter to answer the following questions from Michael Dorf and his management team:

1. Assume that the Knitting Factory will incur a substantial loss without electric power for the weekend, and that Con Ed was aware of that. Do you believe that Con Ed's decision to cut off the power was an ethical one? Regardless of the decision to cut off the power, do you think the *manner* in which Con Ed cut off the power was ethical?

2. Given the fact that Con Ed cannot be contacted until the following Monday, should KnitMedia go ahead and run the extension lines down from the apartment to keep the club open? Why or why not? What are the ethical and moral pros and cons of this solution?

CBC VIDEO CASE 1-1

E-Commerce: Retail's Risky Venture?

The world of business is rapidly changing—and e-commerce is leading the way. One estimate projects that the global e-commerce market will reach $1.2 trillion by 2001. In the first quarter of 1999, e-commerce sales increased a whopping 127 percent to reach $37.5 billion. The U.S. is leading in Internet buying, but Canada is catching up quickly.

Businesses of all types are going online in order to compete. Future Shop, which sells electronic equipment and accessories, went online in November 1998, and business has ballooned since. With 104 000 products available online, there is a lot of choice. Web shopping allows consumers to fully research products and prices, and people can shop at leisure, compare prices, and make informed buying decisions.

Despite the apparent advantages to consumers, it is not clear to retailers exactly how much money they can make—especially given the high start-up costs of e-commerce. As David Pecault of Boston Consulting Group says, "There is enormous range as for what it costs to go online. You'll see small retailers, some of them start to put up Web sites for under $100 000 and begin to sell products online, shipping one and two at a time via United Parcel Service or something like that. But for the bigger retailers it can be very expensive."

Consider Chapters, the national book chain. CEO Larry Stevenson has spent $22 million to date on the Internet division, which is rapidly under expansion. "It's really an amazing misconception, I think by most people who are not in e-commerce, that it's two guys in a garage," says Stevenson. "I think that what we are trying to do is to make sure that we are the Canadian leader in e-tailing. And the way to do that is to spend enough to be there."

→

To succeed in e-commerce the prevailing strategy is to get in the game early, and to go big. There are significant expenses, including implementing new technology, hiring or retraining staff, marketing and advertising, and maintaining distribution and warehousing. Building a highly automated warehouse cost Chapters $10 million. Then there are the concerns about security and credit card transactions. David Pecault, who advises companies in Europe, the U.S., and Canada on how to do e-commerce, cautions, "Companies had better have deep pockets with their investors or venture capitalists to be able to stay the course."

And if the costs don't kill retailers, then dealing with tough and impatient online shoppers might. In the past shoppers have tended to be relatively passive, but now the Internet is changing all that. Psychologists and marketing experts are finding that while online shoppers are some of the same people who buy from bricks and mortar stores, their behaviour online is different. Now tougher and impatient,

they whiz through online shopping sites and indicate their displeasure with the click of a mouse. And they talk back. "I can have a Web site that says, 'Company X Stinks' and there's not much anyone can do about it," says Donna L. Hoffman, co-director of the Electronic Commerce Research Center at Vanderbilt University. "That's profound. In fact, that's revolutionary."

Questions

1. You have read about issues facing managers, such as technological innovation, information overload, globalization, and category killers. How do these issues apply to e-commerce?

2. In what ways do you think managers must consider the socio-cultural aspects of e-commerce?

3. As noted in the text, there are ethical implications for e-commerce. Discuss what you think they are.

Video Resource: "E-Commerce: Retail's Risky Venture?" *Venture* #723 (October 5, 1999).

Fear and Loathing on Bay Street

The issue of ethics in business is a pervasive topic, one that some business people would rather sweep under the carpet. But they might want to consider whether businesses have a duty to be truthful, forthright, and act in ways that are corporately responsible to employees, customers, shareholders, or others.

One example of a business deal gone awry occurred with Alberta-based Bre-X Minerals Ltd. The company, which once claimed to have found the world's largest gold deposit, was exposed as a fraud in 1997 after no gold was found at its Busang deposit in Indonesia. The market value of Bre-X, once estimated at $6.1 billion, fell to nothing—investors were burned. After a two-year investigation of the scandal, the RCMP said that no charges would be laid. "There is no doubt

a fraud took place, but we have no evidence," said RCMP spokesman Peter Macaulay. "A lot of the witnesses lived outside Canada. There are no laws to make them speak or come here."

Another example of questionable ethics, and perhaps even outright fraud, occurred with Livent Inc., an entertainment company. At the centre of the controversy is Garth Drabinsky. Livent filed for bankruptcy protection in Canada and the United States in November 1998 after the company's new managers filed a $225 million civil suit against Livent co-founders Drabinsky and Gottlieb. This suit alleges a $100 million fraud and $7.5 million in kickbacks. As a result of this turmoil, Livent's investors lost a lot of money.

Livent's accounting staff, as well as Drabinsky,

faced a number of civil and criminal charges linked to alleged "accounting irregularities." Said one of Livent's officers, "Drabinsky, in particular, was well known amongst the accounting team as the directing mind of Livent, who micro-managed all aspects of the business, including Livent's accounting, budgeting and financial reporting." Drabinsky and Gottlieb denied the charges. However, despite their denials, they were indicted in the U.S. on 16 counts of fraud and conspiracy relating to what the U.S. federal authorities described as a "massive" and "brazen" scheme to manipulate Livent's books.

Difficulties also extended to how employees were treated under the guise of running a legitimate business. Five former Livent employees claimed that they were "coerced and intimidated" into the fraud by senior management. This raises questions about the corporate culture at Livent, and the core values that existed within the company.

Apart from shareholders, investors, and employees, other people are hurt by less-than-ethical business practices. Former financial analyst Alex Winch decided to leave his job, and the financial industry altogether, after a run-in with Livent. In a letter sent to *Forbes* magazine, Winch said that Livent was stretching the rules of accounting. Livent sued Winch for $10 million. After fighting the libel suit for about a year, Winch decided to give up. However, he had to agree to not talk publicly about Livent for three years and to publish an apology. Winch had little power to wield against a company with much deeper pockets than his.

Questions

1. What are key ethical issues in the examples of Bre-X and Livent?

2. What steps should companies take to ensure that ethical standards are met, and to reduce the occurrence of outright fraud?

3. Can investors, employees, or other stakeholders protect themselves against ethical irregularities? If so, how?

Video Resource: "Fear and Loathing on Bay Street," *Venture* #725 (October 19, 1999).

Managing in a Global Environment

The Knitting Factory, an alternative downtown jazz club in New York City, is also the heart of what *Inc.* magazine calls "a wildly growing business" under the leadership of its co-founder and CEO, Michael Dorf. KnitMedia, the holding company, includes a Web site, a Webcast operation, a recording studio, four record labels, touring and festival promotion operations, videoconferenced educational programs for high schools and colleges, and new Knitting Factory clubs in Los Angeles and abroad. Plans for the future include additional European clubs, a not-for-profit foundation to provide (among other things) health insurance to Knitting Factory performers, retail KnitMedia merchandise, and a stronger Internet presence via jazzE.com and a broadband media project that will provide both audio and video. Dorf envisions the Knitting Factory as the pre-eminent jazz "brand"—a name that jazz lovers everywhere will associate with a downtown culture that he calls "more than a zip code—it's a philosophy."

KnitMedia took its first steps into the international marketplace with an office in Amsterdam, opened several years ago to develop relationships with local

European musicians, agents, promoters, and retailers. Plans for opening the first Knitting Factory club in London recently fell through due to difficulties with the site that was chosen, but Dorf's business plan has not changed at all, he says. A new club is set to open in Berlin, and to streamline the European operation the Amsterdam office will soon be moved to Berlin. London is still a likely home for a future club, and Paris may be as well, although Dorf is aware of French concerns over U.S. "cultural imperialism," the tendency for U.S. cultural values and icons to swamp respected national traditions when they are exported abroad.

Like the Knitting Factory club in Los Angeles, each European club will have its own local general manager, and its own contacts with local musicians and the music and retail communities. Each will report to the central New York operation.

One of the consequences of KnitMedia's rapid growth over the last several years is the increased complexity of the management tasks and issues at every level of the business. The organization has changed, by necessity, from a loose and informal structure with Dorf at its centre to a layered, hierarchical structure with Dorf at the top. Its members now do many of the tasks that Dorf once did himself, as he finds it increasingly necessary to delegate. The number of employees has nearly doubled, and the size of the management staff has tripled. Communication has become more formal, with increasing use of the written word, particularly in the form of e-mail. Budgets are constructed and plans are made. Formal goals are set, and an employee evaluation system is under way.

All of these internal changes are taking place at a time when close links between the Internet and the music industry are offering KnitMedia ever more ways to reach a worldwide audience. As excited as the organization's managers are about using technology, however, they agree that nothing can substitute for the thrill of a live performance. Knitting Factory clubs will continue to be at the forefront of KnitMedia's international expansion efforts.

Listen as Dorf describes the difficulties of operating abroad now that KnitMedia's success has put it "in the spotlight." You will also hear from Mary Noelle Dana, festival programming director, Jazzchool coordinator, and a native of France, as she contrasts the United States and France in terms of their cultural differences and approaches to financial support for the arts. Consider how some of these factors will affect KnitMedia's global expansion and prospects for success in Europe. Other managers address the organization's internal culture and the dedication to music that draws people to work there, sometimes via unlikely paths. Think about how expansion abroad will affect, and be affected by, KnitMedia's changing culture.

Questions

Based on this case, the video, the text chapters you've read so far, and your knowledge from other sources, answer the following.

1. What issues do KnitMedia managers face in deciding to open a club in Europe?

2. How would you describe the culture at KnitMedia?

PART

2 Planning

Part 2: Planning provides an overview of the planning function. It includes a description of the planning process, an analysis of strategic planning, and an in-depth look at the essence of management—decision making. In the opening cases of Chapters 4, 5, and 6, you will read about Urs Zimmerman, Ray Loewen, and Edgar Bronfman, Jr., and how the decisions they made have affected other people.

We begin in Chapter 4, **Making Decisions**, by describing the different types of decisions that managers are called upon to make, the rational decision-making process, and several decision-making techniques that are available to managers. We also make suggestions as to how managers can make better decisions and how they can use groups in decision making. The Appendix to Chapter 4 explains several popular quantitative techniques that are used by managers to improve their decision making.

Next, in Chapter 5, **Planning and Setting Objectives**, we describe the planning process and the central role that managers play in it, the importance of goal setting in management, the various types of plans that managers create, and the management by objectives approach.

Finally, in Chapter 6, **Strategic Management**, the process of making strategic management decisions is described, and the various strategic options that are available to managers are explained.

Making Decisions

Decision Making in a Crisis

On the night of September 2, 1998, Swissair flight 111 took off from New York bound for Geneva, Switzerland. At 10:11 p.m. the pilot and co-pilot smelled smoke in the cockpit. Urs Zimmerman, a veteran Swissair pilot, immediately instituted a lengthy by-the-book decision-making procedure that

included working through a checklist and other time-consuming procedures, such as flying out over the ocean to dump fuel. The co-pilot, Stefan Lowe, wanted to scrap the rules, head for Halifax (which was only 110 kilometres away), and land as quickly as possible. He thought they should descend rapidly and dump fuel quickly so the jet wouldn't be too heavy to land.

Zimmerman decided to follow the checklist. As the crisis worsened, both the pilot and co-pilot donned oxygen masks. Although air traffic controllers cleared the plane to descend to 10 000 feet, Zimmerman told Lowe not to descend too quickly. That the men were under a great deal of stress was revealed by their respiration rate, which was measured by their oxygen masks. Zimmerman's respiration rate had increased to 25 breaths per minute; Lowe's was a more moderate 11 breaths per minute. At 10:22 p.m., a crucial decision needed to be made: Should the plane make a steep descent into the Halifax airport and land immediately, or should it circle over the ocean and dump fuel before landing? The former choice would mean that the plane would be on the ground within five minutes. The latter choice would mean extending the flight time by 20 minutes or more. The decision was made to head out over the ocean and dump fuel. At 10:30 p.m., the plane crashed, killing all 229 passengers aboard.

OBJECTIVES

After studying this chapter, you should be able to

1. Understand the importance of decision making in the manager's job.

2. Differentiate between programmed and non-programmed decisions.

3. Describe the rational decision-making process.

4. Compare rational decision making and decision making in practice.

5. Identify the barriers to effective decision making.

6. Explain five guidelines for making better decisions.

7. Understand how to use groups more effectively in the decision-making process.

Understanding Decision Making

The decision facing the pilots of Swissair flight 111 was a dramatic one. But we all face the need to choose—the route to school, the job to accept, the computer to buy, for instance. A **decision** is a choice from among the available alternatives. **Decision making** is the process of developing and analyzing alternatives and making a choice.

Most decisions are prompted by problems. A *problem* is a discrepancy between a desirable situation and an actual situation. For example, if you need $50 for a show and you only have $10, you have a problem. A decision doesn't necessarily involve a problem, although this is often the case. On the other hand, problem solving always involves making decisions, so we'll use the terms "decision making" and "problem solving" interchangeably in this book. *Judgment* refers to the cognitive or "thinking" aspects of the decision-making process.[1] We'll see in this chapter that the decision-making process is often subject to distortions and biases, precisely because it is usually a judgmental, not a purely mechanical, process.

As noted at the end of Chapter 3, we've focused to this point on the things that surround and influence what managers do: specifically, on outside and inside forces such as globalization, deregulation, and values, culture, and ethics. Now, in Chapter 4, we begin a more detailed discussion of what managers actually do. Since making good decisions underlies just about everything we do, we've turned first to making decisions.

decision
A choice from among the available alternatives.

decision making
The process of developing and analyzing alternatives and making a choice.

Decisions and the Management Process

Decision making is at the heart of what managers do. Planning, organizing, leading, and controlling are the basic management functions. However, as illustrated in Table 4.1, each of these calls for decisions to be made—which plan to implement, what goals to choose, and which people to hire, for instance.

Every manager on the company's business team makes decisions. This is illustrated in Table 4.2. The accounting manager decides what outside auditing firm to use, and how many days a customer can be allowed to wait before it pays its bills. The sales manager decides which sales representatives to use in each region, and which advertising agency to hire.

TABLE 4.1 *Decisions in the Management Functions*

MANAGEMENT FUNCTION	TYPICAL DECISIONS MANAGERS FACE
Planning	What are the organization's long-term objectives? What strategies will best achieve these objectives? What should the organization's short-term objectives be? How difficult should individual goals be?
Organizing	How many subordinates should I have report directly to me? How much centralization should there be in the organization? How should jobs be designed? When should the organization implement a different structure?
Leading	How do I handle employees who appear to be low in motivation? What is the most effective leadership style in a given situation? How will a specific change affect worker productivity? When is the right time to stimulate conflict?
Controlling	What activities in the organization need to be controlled? How should these activities be controlled? When is a performance deviation significant? What type of management information system should the organization have?

TABLE 4.2 *Some Decisions Business-Team Managers Make*

MANAGER	EXAMPLES OF DECISIONS THESE MANAGERS FACE
Accounting Manager	What accounting firm should we use? Who should process our payroll? Should we give that customer credit?
Finance Manager	What bank should we use? Should we sell bonds or stocks? Should we buy back some of our company's stock?
Human Resource Manager	Where should we recruit for employees? Should we set up a testing problem? Should I advise settling the equal employment complaint?
Production Manager	Which supplier should we use? Should we build the new plant? Should we buy the new machine?
Sales Manager	Which sales rep should we use in this district? Should we start this advertising campaign? Should we lower prices in response to our competitor's doing so?

The production manager chooses between alternative suppliers and decides whether to recommend building a new plant. Nearly everything a manager does brings him or her to a decision that must be made.

Programmed and Non-Programmed Decisions

Any decision a manager makes can be classified as either a *programmed decision* or a *non-programmed decision.* The two differ in the extent to which the decision must be handled as a completely new situation.[2]

Programmed Decisions. Luckily for managers, not every decision must be handled as a brand new situation. Instead, many decisions can be classified as programmed decisions. **Programmed decisions** are repetitive and routine and can be solved through mechanical procedures such as by applying rules. For example, to expedite the refund process, a department store may use this rule: "If the customer returns a jacket, you may give that person a refund if the tag is not removed, if the jacket is not damaged, and if the purchase was made within the past two weeks." Other examples include the personnel at the University of Calgary deciding how to register students each fall, Canada Customs and Revenue determining an appropriate auditing procedure for income tax returns, and Kasba Lake Lodge in the Northwest Territories deciding how to schedule float plane flights to bring tourists to the lodge each Saturday.

Up to 90 percent of management decisions are programmed.[3] In many universities, for example, the question of which students to admit is made by mathematically weighting each candidate's test scores and grades. In most companies, the calculation of overtime pay and weekly payroll benefits is made by computer software. In fact, the advent of computers has dramatically boosted the number of decisions that can now be "programmed." For example, when your credit card is "swiped" at a point of purchase, the decision to accept it is generally computerized. The decision is referred to a credit manager only if your credit limit has been reached. It makes sense for managers to try to determine whether particular decisions can be programmed, and if so, the decisions can be left to subordinates.

Non-Programmed Decisions. In contrast, **non-programmed decisions** are unique and novel. The Toronto Stock Exchange made a non-programmed decision when it decided to install state-of-the-art equipment for tracking stock transactions, as did IBM when it de-

programmed decision
A decision that is repetitive and routine and that can be solved through mechanical procedures such as by applying rules.

Toronto Stock
Exchange
www.tse.com

non-programmed decision
A unique and novel decision that relies on judgment.

The decision to install state-of-the-art computer equipment at the Toronto Stock Exchange is an example of a non-programmed decision.

cided to enter the home computer market. Algonquin College made a non-programmed decision when it decided to introduce a new program of studies for students, and the province of Manitoba did the same when it imposed border duties on liquor purchased in the U.S.

Non-programmed decisions are generally "...the kinds of [major] decisions which managers are paid to address..."[4] They rely on judgment and focus on the firm's long-term strategic development and survival. With the big and unexpected changes of the past few years—deregulation, global competition, and downsizings, for instance—such decisions are increasingly common. Table 4.3 compares programmed and non-programmed decision making.

Top-level managers tend to face more non-programmed decisions, while lower-level

Algonquin College
www.algonquinc.on.ca

TABLE 4.3 *Comparing Programmed and Non-Programmed Decisions*

	PROGRAMMED	NON-PROGRAMMED
Type of Decision	Programmable; routine; generic; computational	Non-programmable; unique; innovative
Nature of the Decision	Procedural; predictable; well-defined information and decision criteria	Novel; unstructured; incomplete channels information; unknown criteria
Strategy	Reliance on rules and computation	Reliance on principles; judgment; general problem solving
Decision-Making Techniques Emphasized	Management science; capital budgeting; computerized solutions; rules	Judgment; intuition; creativity

THE CHALLENGE OF CHANGE

Advanced RISC Machines: A Non-Programmed Decision to Stay Flexible

Advanced RISC Machines www.arm.com

You are faced with the following problem: How does your firm navigate a path through the unpredictable peaks and valleys of semiconductor chip demand and avoid getting stuck with millions of surplus microchips? The decision for one firm in this fast-changing industry was to let other firms make the chips it designed.

Advanced RISC Machines (ARM) of Cambridge, England, is one such chip-making company. ARM decided to create a company based on what it perceived to be the changes occurring in the semiconductor marketplace. A private company of 140 employees with $16 million in annual revenues, ARM focuses on supplying chips for products with "embedded intelligence"—cyberspeak for things like smart telephones, Internet TVs, pocket computers, and "intelligent" kitchen devices. Because such devices need to be light and portable, their microprocessors must be tiny and energy efficient, running for hours on a few volts of battery power.

Chips built by larger semiconductor companies (such as Motorola and IBM) tend to be more powerful, but also bigger and more expensive—and thus impractical for carry-anywhere devices like the Apple Newton. ARM chips don't work quite so fast but are much cheaper. ARM's simplest chip is two to three times cheaper than competing products and one-tenth the price of Intel's Pentium chip.

The company currently has this niche almost to itself, and the future looks rosy. However, the product life of most of the devices that use ARM's chips is quite short. The company's managers must therefore continually apply good judgment lest ARM itself get stuck with excess chips.[5] ARM's non-programmed decision to subcontract production has helped it land big-name customers, including Texas Instruments and Samsung, while allowing it a profit almost from its first day in business.

managers face more programmed ones, as illustrated in Figure 4.1. Lower-level managers tend to spend more time addressing programmed decisions, such as "How many employees should I put on the assembly line today?" Top managers face more decisions like "How should we respond to our competitor's moves?"

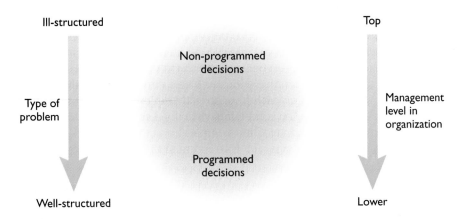

FIGURE 4.1
Top managers tend to confront more ill-structured, ambiguous situations and so make more non-programmed decisions; lower-level managers tend to confront more structured decisions and make more programmed decisions.

The "Rational" Decision-Making Process

Suppose you are the owner of a big retail store and must decide which of several delivery vehicles to buy. What process would you use to select among the many alternatives? The answer depends on how rational you believe you are. The idea that managers are entirely rational has a long and honourable tradition in economic and management theory. Early economists needed a simplified way to explain economic phenomena, like how supply and demand were related. Their solution was to accept a number of simplifying assumptions about how managers made decisions. Specifically, they assumed that the rational manager:

1. Had complete or "perfect" information about the situation, including the full range of goods and services available on the market and the exact price of each good or service;

2. Could perfectly define the problem and not be confused by symptoms or other obstacles;

3. Could identify all criteria and accurately weight all of the criteria according to the manager's preferences;

4. Knew all possible alternatives and could accurately assess each against each criterion; and

5. Could accurately calculate and choose the alternative with the highest perceived value.[6]

The "rational" manager's approach to making a decision includes the following steps:

1. Define the problem.[7] Managerial decision making is usually sparked by the

identification of a problem. Perhaps you need to expand your retail chain, or you are faced with increased advertising by competitors. Identifying the problem is not always easy, however. Common mistakes here include emphasizing the obvious, or being misled by symptoms.[8]

Here is a classic example that illustrates these decision-making mistakes. Office workers in a large downtown building were upset because they had to wait so long for elevators. A consulting team was called in to solve the problem. The owners of the building told the consultants that the problem was that "the elevators were running too slowly," but the consultants wisely decided to define the problem as "workers are upset because they have to wait for elevators." The consultants decided on a relatively inexpensive solution: install full-length mirrors next to the elevators on each floor so that employees could look at themselves while they waited. The complaints virtually disappeared, even though waiting times were just as long. This example shows that managers must be careful when they define problems. The Entrepreneurial Edge box provides another example.

2. **Identify the criteria.** In most decisions you'll want to achieve several objectives or satisfy several criteria (see Figure 4.2). In buying a computer, for instance, you may want to maximize reliability, minimize cost, obtain adequate support, and so on.

3. **Weight the criteria.** Some criteria may be more important to you than others. For example, minimizing cost may be more important than having continuing service support. Rational decision-makers will weight each of the decision criteria, as shown in Figure 4.2.

4. **Develop alternatives.** Whether you are choosing between alternative plans, job candidates, cars, or computers, the existence of some choice is a prerequisite to

THE ENTREPRENEURIAL EDGE

Rewriting the Software Code

Some software entrepreneurs, seeing the success of superstores for products like building supplies and office equipment, might ask themselves, "How big a retail store can we build to sell software, and thereby knock off our smaller competitors?" But that's not how David Prais and Tim Burton saw the problem. As they saw it, "the software-retail system breeds big inefficiencies," and "no one is looking five years out." They therefore created chumbo.com, which became the first company to sell Windows 98 and Microsoft Office 2000 over the Web, and the first to let customers pre-order software.

This Web site was soon offering about 15 000 titles from almost 500 publishers, and its sales were approaching $20 million per year. The strategy Prais and Burton chose for their company was guided in large part by the needs of the hardware (not software) manufacturers themselves. When a company like IBM sells an Aptiva computer, for instance, many of its customers go to IBM's Web site to find out about buying new software. Prais and Burton decided to build their new Web site in part around servicing those hardware companies' Web sites. So now when you click on Aptiva's site, you're first guided to IBM's online easychoice.com, which then has chumbo.com supply the software. This proved to be a good decision for two entrepreneurs who decided not to define their problem as "How to sell software through bigger stores."[9]

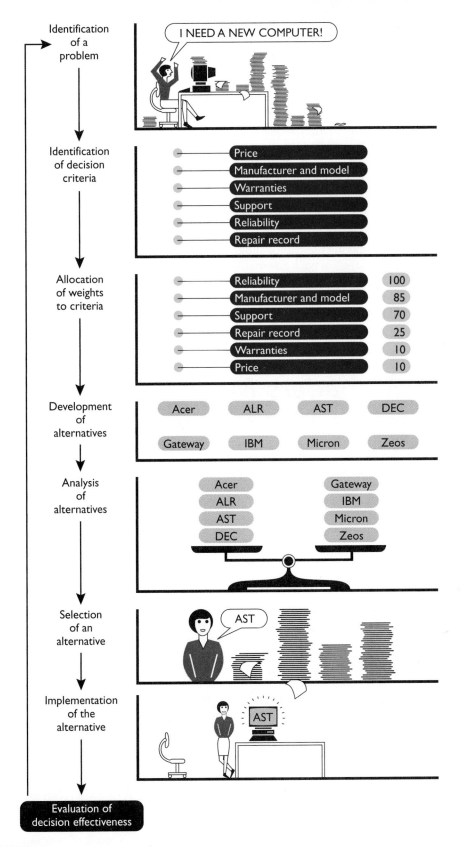

Identification of a problem

I NEED A NEW COMPUTER!

Identification of decision criteria

- Price
- Manufacturer and model
- Warranties
- Support
- Reliability
- Repair record

Allocation of weights to criteria

Reliability	100
Manufacturer and model	85
Support	70
Repair record	25
Warranties	10
Price	10

Development of alternatives

Acer   ALR   AST   DEC

Gateway   IBM   Micron   Zeos

Analysis of alternatives

Acer
ALR
AST
DEC

Gateway
IBM
Micron
Zeos

Selection of an alternative

AST

Implementation of the alternative

AST

Evaluation of decision effectiveness

FIGURE 4.2
The Rational Decision-Making Process

effective decision making. In fact, when a manager has no choice, there really isn't any decision to make—except perhaps to "take it or leave it." Developing good alternatives is no easy matter; it takes a great deal of creativity and judgment, as we'll see later in this chapter.

5. **Analyze the alternatives.** The next step is to analyze the alternatives. Should you buy the IBM or the ACER? Should the factory buy machine A or machine B? How does each alternative stack up, given the criteria on which the decision is to be based? One expert says, "This is often the most difficult part of the decision-making process, because this is the stage that typically requires forecasting future events."[10] Under the most perfectly rational conditions, a decision-maker would be able to carefully assess the potential consequences of choosing each alternative. However, such perfect conditions rarely exist.

6. **Make a choice, and then implement and evaluate the decision.** Under perfect conditions, making the choice should be a straightforward matter of computing the pros and cons of each alternative and choosing the one that maximizes your benefits. However, in practice, as you know, making a decision—even on a relatively clear-cut matter like the choice of a computer—usually cannot be done so accurately or rationally. To see why, let's look at decision making in practice.

How Managers Make Decisions: The Limits to Rationality

Many factors limit just how rational a decision-maker can be. That does not mean that the rational model is useless; most managers probably do try to make rational analyses. But in practice we know there are many barriers to rationality, including:

- individual differences
- decision-making shortcuts
- how the problem is framed
- anchoring
- psychological set
- organizational barriers
- escalation of commitment

Individual Differences

The ability to absorb, analyze, and generally "process" information varies from person to person, and is also quite limited. In one series of laboratory studies, subjects were required to make decisions based on the amount of information transmitted on a screen.[11] Most people quickly reached a point at which "information overload" occurred, and they then began adjusting in several ways. Some people omitted or ignored some of the information transmitted on the screen; others began making errors by incorrectly identifying some of the information; others gave only approximate responses (such as "about 25" instead of "24.6").

Perception. The way someone perceives a situation is a good example of how individual differences influence the way decisions are made. **Perception** is the selection and interpretation of information we receive through our senses and the meaning we give to the information. Many things, including our individual needs, influence how we perceive a stimulus. A thirsty person in the desert may perceive faraway heat waves as a mirage, whereas his healthy rescuer sees nothing but sand. In organizations, a person's prior ex-

perception
The selection and interpretation of information we receive through our senses and the meaning we give to the information.

periences and position in the company can have a big effect on how the person perceives a problem and reacts to it.

In a classic study of this phenomenon, 23 executives, all employed by a large manufacturing firm, were asked to read a business case.[12] The researchers found that a manager's position influenced how he or she defined the "most important problem" facing the company. For example, of six sales executives, five thought the most important problem was a sales problem. "Organization problems" were mentioned by four out of five production executives, but by only one sales executive and no accounting executives.

Findings like these illustrate the importance of the people side of management. In this study a person's experiences and functional role molded and influenced how he or she "saw" the problem. The managers looked at the same data but interpreted or saw it differently, and each would probably have taken action based on his or her own view of the problem. You know from your experience that things like this happen every day: You might be a lot less happy with a B in a course after finding out that your friend got an A with more or less the same test grades.[13]

Systematic vs. Intuitive Decision Styles. Individuals also differ in how they approach decision making. **Systematic decision-makers** tend to take a more logical, structured, step-by-step approach to solving a problem.[14] At the other extreme, **intuitive decision-makers** use a more trial-and-error approach. They disregard much of the information available and rapidly bounce from one alternative to another to get a feel for which seems to work best.

One study compared systematics (those who took a systematic approach to searching for information, and to slowly and thoroughly evaluating all alternatives) with intuitives (those who sought information non-systematically or selectively, and quickly reviewed the data on just a few alternatives). The study clearly showed that, for most situations, the intuitive approach was definitely best.[15] The lesson seems to be that plodding through all of the options may be fine if time permits, but in the real world there's a lot to be said for not letting yourself get overly involved in the process.

systematic decision-makers
Those who tend to take a more logical, structured, step-by-step approach to solving a problem.

intuitive decision-makers
Those who use a more trial-and-error approach.

Decision-Making Shortcuts

Decision-making shortcuts also distort how decisions are made. People take shortcuts when solving problems by applying simplifying rules or **heuristics**. For example, a banker might follow the heuristic, "People should not spend more than 30 percent of their disposable income on mortgage and interest expenses."[16] Applying this heuristic may expedite decision making, but it may also mean that an otherwise qualified applicant is rejected.

The use of heuristics may lead to errors in decision making. For example, a manager might predict someone's performance based on that person's similarity to other individuals with the same ethnic background that the manager has known in the past.

heuristics
Shortcuts, or rules of thumb, used when solving problems.

How the Problem Is Framed

Misdefining the problem may be the biggest barrier to making good decisions. Remember how much money the building owners would have wasted if their elevator consultants had accepted at face value the owners' claim that the problem was "slow-moving elevators!" Here's how three decision-making experts put it:

> The greatest danger in formulating a decision problem is laziness. It's easy to state the problem in the most obvious way, or in the way that first pops into your mind, or in the way it's always been stated in the past. But the easy way isn't necessarily the best way.[17]

In other words, managers need to work hard to understand what the "problem" really is.

Care to test your framing skills? Since you should be an expert at solving "mirror" problems by now, here's another one for you. You just bought a new but small apartment, and you'd like to make it look roomier. On your right as you enter is a three-metre-wide closet with a set of two bifold doors. Mirrors make a room look bigger, so your significant other has suggested you have mirrors mounted on the door panels. Unfortunately, the estimates you've gotten so far are much too high. So, you are about to give up. But first you ask, "Did I frame the problem correctly?"

Well, probably not. What did you do wrong? For one thing, you've defined the problem as "How do we mount mirrors on the door panels?" Even if we assume that mirroring the closet is the best way to make your apartment look roomier, why limit yourself to accomplishing that by *mounting* mirrors on the closet doors? You don't really care if you *mount* mirrors there, do you? The problem really is this: "What's the best way to put mirrors where we now have closet doors?" A quick trip to your local building supply store uncovers a set of inexpensive sliding-door mirror panels that will replace your bulky doors, and that slide back and forth on a track you install yourself. Total cost: one-half the previous estimates.

Anchoring

Errors in framing are sometimes caused by **anchoring**, which means unconsciously giving disproportionate weight to the first information you hear.

Anchors pop up in the most unexpected ways. Let's say you're selling your car, which you know is worth about $10 000. Joe has responded to your classified ad; when he arrives he offhandedly remarks that the car is only worth about $5000. What would you do? On the one hand, you know that Joe is probably just positioning himself to get a better deal, and you know that $5000 is absolutely ridiculous. On the other hand, Joe is the only game in town at the moment (one other person called but never showed up) and you don't really feel like spending any more weekends placing ads and waiting around for buyers who don't show up. So, you start bargaining with Joe: He says $5000, you say $10 000, and before you know it you've arrived at a price of $8000, which Joe graciously points out is "better than splitting the difference" from your point of view.

What happened here? Without realizing it, you gave disproportionate weight to Joe's "offhand" comment, and your decision making (and bargaining) from that point on revolved around his price, not yours. (What should you have done? One response might have been "$5000? Are you *kidding*? That's not even in the *ballpark*!" It might not have worked, but at least you'd have loosened that subliminal anchor, so the bargaining could have been on your terms, not his.)

Psychological Set

The tendency to focus on a rigid strategy or point of view is called *psychological set*.[18] This mental trait can severely limit a manager's ability to think of alternative solutions. A classic example is presented in Figure 4.3. Your assignment is to connect all nine dots with no more than four straight lines running through them, and to do so without lifting your pen from the paper. Hint: Don't fall into the trap of taking a rigid point of view. The answer is provided in Figure 4.4 on page 112.

FIGURE 4.3
Looking at the Problem in Just One Way

Organizational Barriers

All too often it's the company itself—how it's organized, or its policies and procedures, for instance—that undermine employees' ability to make good decisions. You've probably experienced that yourself. For example, you ask a salesperson at a department store to make a simple change and you're told, "You'll have to get that approved first by customer service." Microsoft went through a major reorganization in 1999, in part to ensure that lower-level managers could make more decisions themselves, without having to refer to Bill Gates.

In a recent study, nearly two-thirds (62 percent) of 773 hourly workers surveyed said their organizations were operating with half or less than half the employee brain power available to them. This observation was shared by 63 percent of the 641 managers who responded to the survey. About 40 percent of all employees listed "organizational politics" as one of the three big barriers to effective thinking in their firms. Time pressure and a lack of involvement in decision making were the other two big barriers. Less important barriers included lack of rewards, lack of skills, procedures/work rules/systems, lack of training, and unclear job expectations. Obviously managers can undermine decision making in many ways if they aren't careful.

Escalation of Commitment

Escalation of commitment refers to the situation in which a manager becomes increasingly committed to a previously chosen course of action even though it has been shown to be ineffective. A good example of this is Expo '86, the world's fair that was held in British Columbia. When the project was first conceived, the deficit was projected at about $56 million. Over the next few years, the projected deficit kept rising, until it was over $300 million. In spite of this, the project went forward.

escalation of commitment
The situation in which a manager becomes increasingly committed to a previously chosen course of action even though it has been shown to be ineffective.

There are various reasons why supposedly rational managers get into difficulties like these: because they are success-oriented, they are motivated to defend their initial decision; they are reluctant to admit they made a mistake; they fear that their career will be harmed if their project fails; or they believe that they simply haven't worked hard enough to ensure the success of the project.

Managers can avoid overcommitment by setting specific goals ahead of time that deal with how much time and money they are willing to expend on the project. The existence of specific time and money goals makes it harder for the manager to interpret unfavourable news in a positive light.

Expo '86 is an example of escalation of commitment. In spite of information showing that the fair would incur a large deficit, the decision was made to go forward.

Decision Making: How It Should Be Versus How It Actually Is

The existence of these decision-making barriers means that the ideal "rational" model of what management decision making *should be* must be modified to take into consideration how managers *actually* make decisions. Herbert Simon and his associates say that, in practice, "bounded rationality" more accurately represents how managers actually make decisions. **Bounded rationality** means that a manager's decision making is only as rational as his or her unique values, capabilities, and limited capacity for processing information permit him or her to be—rationality is bounded or limited, in other words.

Satisficing is another important idea. To **satisfice** means that managers in practice tend to be concerned with discovering and selecting *satisfactory* alternatives, and only in exceptional cases with finding *optimal* alternatives.[19] This is not to say that managers don't try to be rational; it simply recognizes the fact that, in practice, their attempts to be rational will be limited or "bounded" by the sorts of decision-making barriers discussed above. Luckily, several decision-making tools are available to help minimize the adverse effects of these barriers and thus improve a manager's decisions.

bounded rationality
A manager's decision making is only as rational as his or her unique values, capabilities, and limited capacity for processing information permit him or her to be.

satisfice
Discovering and selecting satisfactory alternatives, rather than finding optimal alternatives.

How to Make Better Decisions

Some people assume that good judgment is like great singing—either you can do it or you can't. But overcoming the decision-making barriers we've identified can lead to better decisions being made by almost anyone. Techniques like the ones we discuss next can help you avoid problems at every step of the decision-making process.

Be Creative

creativity
The process of developing original, novel responses to a problem.

Creativity—the process of developing original, novel responses to a problem—plays a big role in making good decisions. It is essential for decision-making activities like framing the problem and developing new alternatives. Remember the consultant's creative redefinition of the "slow-moving elevators" problem. Creativity *can* be cultivated, as shown in The People Side of Managing box. Here are some additional suggestions.

Check Your Assumptions. Decision-making barriers like anchoring and psychological set can be avoided in part by forcing yourself to check your assumptions. Let's look again at the problem of the nine dots in Figure 4.3 on page 110. Psychological set, the tendency to take a rigid view of a problem, may be the decision-making barrier at work here. Most people tend to view the nine dots as a square, but this of course limits the solutions. In fact, there is no way to connect all of the dots with just four lines as long as you make this assumption.

Figure 4.4 shows one creative solution. The key to this solution is breaking through

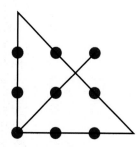

FIGURE 4.4
The Advantage of Not Just Looking at the Problem in One Way

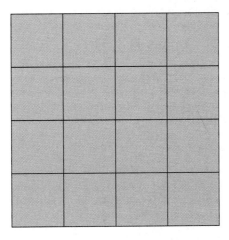

FIGURE 4.5
Using Creativity to Find a Solution
How many squares are in the box? Now, count again. Only 16? Take away your preconception of how many squares there are. Now, how many do you find? You should find 30!

Nurturing Creativity at Hallmark Cards Inc.

Hallmark Cards Inc.
www.hallmark.com

When you're in the business of developing greeting cards, you simply must encourage employee creativity. That's exactly what Hallmark Cards Inc., the world's largest greeting card company, does. Consider the experience of Robert Hurlburt, a 17-year employee. He was given a three-month sabbatical to do whatever he wanted to develop his creative spark. He chose to learn pottery. Although his pottery will probably never be sold commercially, Hallmark hopes that when he returns to his regular duties, the company will see a return in terms of increased creativity. Hallmark's biggest competitor, American Greetings Inc., has similar programs for its employees.

The sabbatical program is available to many writers and artists at Hallmark. And it is not the only program available. Other creativity-enhancing ideas include having workers get together away from the workplace to exchange ideas, giving workers free movie passes, sending workers overseas to absorb new cultures, and having retreats far away from the head office where employees do fun activities like building bird houses. The wackiest extreme is found in the Shoebox Cards division, where teams of writers and editors start their day by watching videotapes of popular TV shows like David Letterman. They also look at magazines and have exercise sessions during the day.

But there are serious business goals behind all these creativity-enhancing activities. The Shoebox group, for example, is expected to develop 70 new greeting cards each week. To achieve that goal, they usually have to develop at least 150 ideas. At the end of each day, new greeting-card ideas are screened at a meeting led by the senior editor. He or she reads each card aloud and then, based on the reaction of the group, either accepts or rejects it.

The success of each card that actually makes it to the market is assessed through surveys and information gathered from store cash registers. Therefore, each employee knows how well his or her card ideas are selling.

your assumptions about how the problem needs to be solved. In fact, one managerial decision-making expert refers to creativity as, in essence, "...an assumption-breaking process."[20] Now try to solve the problem in Figure 4.5. Remember: Always check your assumptions.

Think Through the Process. Forcing yourself to think through the decision and each of its consequences, as if you were actually there experiencing them, can also help you be more creative. Consider this problem: An extraordinarily frugal person named Joe can make one whole cigar from every five cigar butts he finds. How many cigars can he make if he finds 25 cigar butts? Before you answer "five," think through Joe's cigar-making process, step by step. There he sits on his park bench, making (and smoking) each of his five cigars. As he smokes each cigar, he ends up with one new cigar butt. Thus, in smoking his five handmade cigars, Joe ends up with five new butts, which of course he combines into his sixth, and in this case final, whole new cigar.[21]

This problem illustrates how "process analysis" can boost creativity and insight. Process analysis means solving a problem by thinking through the process involved from beginning to end, imagining what actually would happen at each step.[22] In this case, process analysis meant envisioning Joe sitting on his park bench, and thinking through each of the steps he would take as if we were there. By using process analysis to look over his shoulder in this way, we boosted our creativity and discovered that he made a sixth cigar.

Increase Your Knowledge

"Knowledge is power," someone once said, and that's particularly true when it comes to making decisions. Even the simplest decisions—mapping your route to work in the morning or deciding which cereal to buy, for instance—become problems if you lack basic information, such as the distances involved or the costs of each of the various products. And making major, more complex life decisions of course depends even more on what you know about the situation. For example, Ed was a medical doctor who practised for many years in one location. He then accepted a job with a group of young doctors in another province, only to find that what he was expected to do and the hours he had to work were not at all what he had anticipated. After less than a year of being run ragged he had to leave, albeit as a wiser man. Knowledge is power, and the more you know about the elements of the decision before you make that decision, the better the decision will be. Increasing your knowledge will increase your ability to carry out the steps in the rational decision-making process (for example, by being aware of more alternatives).

That's easy to say, of course, but how do you go about getting the knowledge you require? There are several things you can do. First, ask, ask, ask. In formulating your questions, always keep the six main "question" words in mind: Who, What, Where, When, Why, and How. Then, even for a smaller decision like buying a used car, make sure to do your research. Who is selling the car, and who has owned it? What do similar cars sell for? What, if anything, is wrong with this car? Where has it been serviced? Why does the owner want to sell it? How well has the car been maintained? And how much does the owner want to sell it for? Think of how much trouble Dr. Ed could have saved himself if he had asked his prospective partners a few incisive questions about the job!

Second, get experience. For many endeavours, there's simply no substitute for getting some experience. That's certainly true on a personal level: Many students find that interning in a job similar to the occupation they plan to pursue can help enormously in clarifying whether that's the right occupation for them. And it's certainly true when it comes to managing organizations. In Chapter 2 we saw that some companies expand abroad by opening their own facilities, while others enter into joint ventures. What do you think determines which route a company's managers choose? It turns out that experience has a lot to do with it. Multinational corporations that already have a great deal of experience in doing business in a particular country generally opt for full ownership of foreign affiliates. Less experienced companies tend to establish joint ventures in foreign markets, in part so they can get the necessary expertise.[23]

Third, do your research. Whether the decision involves a new job, a new car, expanding abroad, or the sorts of issues now facing Chapters (such as whether to expand its Web site and, if so, how), there is a wealth of information out there that managers can tap into. Pierre Lessard, the CEO of Metro-Richelieu, knows the value of research and the information that it yields. He meticulously analyzes statistics before making important decisions for his company. Good information increases the chance that a decision will be a good one.[24]

On a more personal level, you might be thinking of moving from Vancouver to Moncton. How do salaries in Moncton compare with those in Vancouver? That question is easily answered on an Internet Web site such as Human Resources Development Canada's Labour Market Information site (http://lmi-imt.hrdc-drhc.gc.ca). Want to know what your used car is worth? Then tap into Kelley Blue Book's Web site (www.kbb.com).

Fourth, use consultants. In fact, that's basically what business consultants are for. The consultants' experience in some areas (such as personnel testing or strategic planning) can be used to supplement the managers lack of experience in those areas. And the "consultants" needn't be management consultants, of course. If Dr. Ed had had the foresight to meet with an employment lawyer to draw up an employment contract before taking his new job, the lawyer probably would have asked a lot of the questions Ed had neglected to ask. Sometimes just talking the problem over with other people can also help, particularly if they've had experience solving similar problems.

Use Your Intuition

Overemphasizing rationality and logic can actually backfire by blocking you from using your intuition. **Intuition** can be defined as a cognitive process whereby a person unconsciously make a decision based on accumulated knowledge and experience. Here is what the psychiatrist Sigmund Freud had to say about making important decisions:

> When making a decision of minor importance I have always found it advantageous to consider all the pros and cons. In vital matters, however, such as the choice of a mate or a profession, the decision should come from the unconscious, from somewhere within ourselves. In the important decisions of our personal life, we should be governed, I think, by the deep inner needs of our nature.[25]

Another expert says you can usually tell when a decision fits with your inner nature, for it brings an enormous sense of relief. Good decisions, he says, are the best tranquilizers ever invented; bad ones often increase your anxiety. So always consult your inner feelings: Never disregard your intuition.[26]

Intuitiveness can be measured. The short test in Figure 4.6 provides an approximate reading on whether you are more rational or intuitive in your decision making.[27]

Don't Overstress the Finality of Your Decision[28]

Very few decisions are forever; there is more "give" in most decisions than we realize. While many major strategic decisions are certainly hard to reverse, most poor decisions won't lead to the end of the world, so don't become frozen in the finality of your decision.

In fact, it's the manager's job to see that a decision needs changing, and to drive through the change. For example, Jean Monty, CEO of Bell Canada Enterprises (BCE), wants to ensure that his company will be competitive in the high-tech communications field. He says that the Internet is going to be pervasive in everything that BCE does. And it's not just talk. BCE sold off Nortel Networks and has made deals with Yahoo! and Lycos to reinforce its position on the Internet. BCE will now focus on providing communication services.[29]

Knowing when to quit is sometimes the smartest thing a manager can do. London, England's, city government recently lost millions as its efforts to automate the London Stock Exchange collapsed due to technical difficulties. Experts studying the problem sub-

intuition
A cognitive process whereby a person unconsciously makes a decision based on accumulated knowledge and experience.

Yahoo!
www.yahoo.com

Lycos
www.lycos.com

London Stock Exchange
www.londonstockexchange.com

What Is My Orientation?

You can get a rough idea of your relative preferences for the rational and intuitive ways of dealing with situations by rating yourself on four items. For each statement, rank yourself on a six-point scale from 1 (never), 2 (once in a while), 3 (sometimes), 4 (quite often), 5 (frequently but not always), to 6 (always) and place your response in the box to the right of the item:

1. When I have a special job to do, I like to organize it carefully from the start. ☐
2. I feel that a prescribed, step-by-step method is best for solving problems. ☐
3. I prefer people who are imaginative to those who are not. ☐
4. I look at a problem as a whole, approaching it from all sides. ☐

Now add the values for the first two items for one total and for the last two items for another total. Subtract the second total from the first. If your total has a positive value, your preference is Rational by that amount, and if your total has a negative value, your preference is Intuitive by that amount. Ten represents the maximum possible rational or intuitive score from the equally preferred midpoint (0). Mark your position on the range of possible scores:

Intuitive ←——————— | ———————→ Rational

−10 −9 −8 −7 −6 −5 −4 −3 −2 −1 0 1 2 3 4 5 6 7 8 9 10

These items are taken from a 30-item Personal Style Inventory (PSI) assessment of preferences for Rational and Intuitive behaviour created by professor William Taggert.

FIGURE 4.6
Are You More Rational or More Intuitive?

sequently said that the venture might have been a victim of escalation of commitment.[30] So don't let fears that the decision is "forever" scare you into not making a decision. And once the decision is made, stick with it if you believe you're on the right track, but "know when to fold" if the decision turns out to be a poor one.

Make Sure the Timing Is Right

You've probably noticed that, as with most people, your decisions are affected by your mood. For example, when deliberately cut off by another driver while speeding down the highway, even a usually conservative driver might unwisely decide to engage in some retaliation. At work, a small business owner, who we'll call Tom, is famous (or maybe infamous) among his workers for his mood swings. After a bad night on the home front or after losing a big sale, the mercurial Tom is usually ready to lash out at anyone and anything around him, so his managers learned long ago to steer clear of asking him for a decision when he's in one of his dark moods. Researchers know that when people feel "down" their actions tend to be aggressive and destructive. When they feel good, their behaviour swings towards balance and tolerance. Similarly, people tend to be lenient when they're in good spirits, and tough when they are grouchy. How would you like to have your class presentation evaluated by a professor who is in a particularly bad mood?

Decision-makers in general (and managers in particular) can derive a lesson from this: It's important to take your emotions into account when making important decisions. Whether it's appraising an employee, hiring a supervisor, or buying a new machine, do a quick reality check to make sure you're not in the midst of an unwelcome mood swing. Good managers usually have stable, mature personalities. And the successful ones know enough to take their moods into consideration before making a decision.

Using Groups to Make Better Decisions

In organizations, decisions can be made by one person or by a group of people working together. Laurent Beaudoin, CEO of Bombardier, is an autocrat who does not share power, so there is little group decision making at that firm.[31] At CP Rail, by contrast, an executive committee makes major decisions affecting the firm.[32]

Groups at Work

Whether they are called work groups, teams, or committees, groups accomplish much of the work in organizations. Since we've focused on individual decision making up to now, it's important that we turn our attention to using the power of groups to make better decisions.

Although we'll discuss groups in more detail in Chapter 13, some working definitions are in order now. A **group** is two or more persons who interact together for some purpose and in such a manner that each person influences and is influenced by each other person. Thus the board of directors of Inco is a group, as is the work team that installs the dashboards in Daimler-Chrysler's vans at its Windsor, Ontario, plant.

Groups are important at work in part because of the effect they have on their members. For example, pressure by other group members can cause a member to raise or lower his or her output. In turn, the extent to which a group can influence its members depends on several things, including the **cohesiveness** of the group—the attraction of the group for its members—and on the group's **norms**—the informal rules that groups adopt to regulate and regularize members' behaviour.[33]

group
Two or more persons who interact together for some purpose and in such a manner that each person influences and is influenced by each other person.

cohesiveness
The attraction of the group for its members.

norms
The informal rules that groups adopt to regulate and regularize members' behaviour.

Pros and Cons of Group Decision Making

You probably have found from your own experience that groups to which you belong can and do influence how you behave and the decisions you make. It is therefore not surprising that having groups make decisions has its pros and cons. These pros and cons are summarized in Figure 4.7.

Advantages of Using Groups to Make Decisions. The old saying that "two heads are better than one" can be true when you bring several people together to make a decision. Pooling the experiences and points of view of several people can lead to more points of view regarding how to define the problem, more possible solutions, and more creative decisions in general. Groups that analyze a problem and come up with their own decisions also tend to "buy into" those decisions; this acceptance boosts the chance that the group will work harder to implement the decision once it's put into effect.[34] Overall, groups can better cope with the problems of anchoring, psychological set, and perceptions because of the various perspectives that individuals in groups bring to the decision-making process.

PROS	CONS
• "Two heads are better than one"	• Pressure for consensus
• More points of view	• Dominance by one individual
• Fosters acceptance	• Escalation of commitment: pressure to "win your point"
• Group may work harder to implement decisions	• More time consuming
	• Groupthink

FIGURE 4.7
Summary of Pros and Cons of Using Groups to Make Decisions

Better decisions sometimes result from consultation with others, particularly if they are more knowledgeable or more experienced in dealing with similar problems.

Disadvantages of Using Groups to Make Decisions. Although group-decision-making advocates say that "two heads are better than one," detractors reply that "a camel is a horse put together by a committee." This is a reference to the fact that using a group can sometimes actually short-circuit or distort the decision-making process.

Several things can go wrong when groups make decisions. The desire to be accepted tends to silence disagreement and to favour consensus, a fact that can actually reduce creative decisions instead of enhancing them.[35] In many groups, a dominant individual emerges who effectively cuts off debate and channels the rest of the group to his or her point of view. Escalation of commitment can be a problem, too. When groups are confronted by a problem, there is often a tendency for individual members to become committed to their own solutions; the goal then becomes winning the argument rather than solving the problem. Groups also take longer to make decisions. The process can therefore be inherently more expensive than having an individual make the decision.

One of the hazards of a cohesive work group is the phenomenon known as "groupthink."[36] **Groupthink** occurs when members of a group voluntarily suspend their critical-thinking abilities and repress any conflict and disagreement that could challenge group solidarity. Groupthink is a problem because it suppresses minority opinions and unpopular views, both of which can help the group to critically examine its decision-making processes.

Eight symptoms of groupthink have been identified (see Table 4.4). When these symptoms are evident in the group, the likely outcome is poor development and analysis of alternatives, a poor choice of decision, a failure to consider the difficulties in implementing the decision, and a failure to re-examine the assumptions that were used to make the decision.

Groupthink can occur in any highly cohesive group. It has been observed in business firms that made poor competitive decisions, and in not-for-profit organizations that adopted inappropriate strategies. Groupthink is probably best known for some spectacular examples of poor decision making. In the case of the space shuttle *Challenger*, for example, engineers warned that the air temperature on the morning of the rocket launch was low enough to cause hardening of "O-rings," which could cause hot gases to escape from the fuel tank and cause an explosion. But these warnings were ignored by NASA management, who felt pressure to stay on schedule for the launch, and the engineers did not pursue the issue. So, the shuttle was launched and seven astronauts died when the O-rings failed.

groupthink
Occurs when members of a group voluntarily suspend their critical-thinking abilities and repress any conflict and disagreement that could challenge group solidarity.

The likelihood that groupthink will develop can be reduced if certain strategies are adopted (see Table 4.5). These strategies require that group members accept the view that conflict and disagreement—while time-consuming and perhaps uncomfortable—

TABLE 4.4 *Symptoms of Groupthink*

SYMPTOMS	EXPLANATION
1. Illusion of invulnerability	Group members believe that they are invulnerable to any actions that opponents or competitors might take.
2. Rationalization	Group members develop rationalizations to reassure themselves that the decision they made was the right one.
3. Moralization	Group members believe that their chosen course of action is "right" and is therefore justified.
4. Stereotyping	Group members view the enemy or competition as evil, incompetent, weak, or ineffective.
5. Pressure	Group members apply pressure to anyone in the group who expresses doubts about the group's illusions.
6. Self-censorship	Group members say nothing about their misgivings and minimize the importance of their own decisions.
7. Illusion of unanimity	Group members have the feeling that they alone have doubts about the wisdom of the decision, and that everyone else in the group is in favour of it.
8. Mindguards	Some group members take it upon themselves to protect other group members from negative information that might jolt the group out of its complacency.

TABLE 4.5 *Remedies for Groupthink*

REMEDIES	EXPLANATION
1. Legitimize dissent	The group leader should assign the role of critical evaluator to every member of the group.
2. Stress impartiality	The leader should adopt an impartial stance on major issues instead of stating preferences at the outset.
3. Divide group into subgroups	The group should be divided into subgroups that meet separately and then come together to work out their differences.
4. Consult constituents	Each member should be required to discuss the group's tentative consensus with members of the unit he or she represents.
5. Consult outside experts	Outside experts should be invited to meetings to give their views and to challenge the views of group members.
6. Assign devil's advocate role	The devil's advocate role should be assigned on a rotating basis to group members.
7. Assess warning signals	One or more sessions should be devoted to assessing the warning signals from enemies or competitors.
8. Give "last chance" opportunity	After a tentative consensus has been reached a "last chance" meeting should be held to allow group members to express any doubts they may have.

must be encouraged if bad decisions are to be avoided. Legitimizing dissent is the underlying theme of the strategies listed in Table 4.5.

Tools for Improving Group Decision Making

The manager's job is to use groups in such a way that the advantages of group decision making outweigh the disadvantages. For this there are several group decision-making tools in the manager's tool box.[37]

Brainstorming. **Brainstorming** is one way to amplify the creative energies of a group. It has been defined as a group problem-solving technique whereby group members introduce all possible solutions before evaluating any of them.[38] The technique is aimed at encouraging everyone to introduce solutions without fear of criticism; it uses four rules: (1) avoid criticizing others' ideas; (2) share even wild suggestions; (3) offer as many suggestions and supportive comments as possible; and (4) build on others' suggestions to create your own.[39] Interestingly, brainstorming can produce more creative solutions even if group members feel too inhibited to make wild suggestions.[40]

Brainstorming is not without shortcomings. In fact, studies during the 1960s and 1970s consistently showed that brainstorming actually produced fewer and lower-quality ideas than did individuals working alone. But a new, high-tech variation of brainstorming—

electronic brainstorming—overcomes these problems by having group members type ideas into a computer. These ideas then show up simultaneously on the computer screens of other group members. Studies of electronic brainstorming show that performance increases as group size increases. As well, the problems of production blocking (not everyone in the group can talk at once, and people forget ideas because they can't immediately express them) and evaluation apprehension (fear of having your idea ridiculed) are almost completely eliminated in electronic brainstorming.

Executives from Metropolitan Life who gathered at Queen's University spent their time seated side-by-side in front of microcomputers. They typed in ideas for how their firm could improve operations. The company's vice-president estimated that the managers accomplished in one day what would normally have taken five days using traditional methods. Many other Canadian firms are also using electronic brainstorming. In fact, IBM Canada, Royal Trust, and Sears Canada have set up their own electronic meeting rooms.[41]

Devil's-Advocate Approach. One way to guard against the tendency for one group member's efforts to stifle debate is to formalize the process of criticism. The devil's-advocate approach is one approach. An advocate defends the proposed solution while a "devil's" advocate is appointed to prepare a detailed counter-argument listing what is wrong with the solution and why it should not be adopted.

The Delphi Technique. The Delphi technique maximizes the advantages of group decision making while minimizing its disadvantages. Basically, the opinions of experts who work independently are obtained, with the expert's written opinions from one stage providing the basis for the experts' analyses of each succeeding stage. In a typical Delphi analysis, the steps are as follows: (1) a problem is identified; (2) experts' opinions are solicited anonymously and individually through questionnaires (for example, on a problem such as "What do you think are the five biggest breakthrough products our computer company will have to confront in the next five years?"); (3) the experts' opinions are then analyzed, distilled, and resubmitted to other experts for a second round of opinions; (4) this process is continued for several more rounds until a consensus is reached.

This can obviously be a time-consuming process; on the other hand (as in electronic brainstorming), problems like groupthink can be reduced by eliminating face-to-face meetings.

The Nominal Group Technique. The nominal group technique is a group decision-making process in which participants do not attempt to agree as a group on any solution, but rather meet and secretly vote on all the solutions proposed after privately ranking the proposals in order of preference.[42] It is called the "nominal" group technique because the "group" is a group in name only: Members vote on solutions not as a group but individually. The process is this: (1) each group member writes down his or her ideas for solving the problem at hand; (2) each member then presents his or her ideas orally and the ideas are written on a board for the other participants to see; (3) after all ideas have been presented, the entire group discusses all ideas simultaneously; (4) group members individually and secretly vote on each proposed solution; and (5) the solution with the most individual votes wins.

The Stepladder Technique. The stepladder technique also aims to reduce the potentially inhibiting effects of face-to-face meetings. Group members are added one by one at each stage of the process so that their input is untainted by the previous participants' points of view. The process involves these steps: (1) individuals A and B are given a problem to solve and each produces an independent solution; (2) A and B meet and develop a joint decision, then meet with C, who had independently analyzed the problem and arrived at a decision; (3) A, B, and C jointly discuss the problem and arrive at a consensus decision, then are joined by D, who has individually analyzed the problem and arrived at his or her own decision; (4) A, B, C, and D arrive at a final group decision.[43]

How to Lead a Group Decision-Making Discussion

The person leading the group discussion can have a big effect on whether the group's decision is useful. If a committee chairperson monopolizes the meeting and continually shoots down others' ideas while pushing his or her own, it's likely that other members' points of view will go unexpressed. An effective discussion leader has a responsibility to do the following:

1. Ensure that all group members participate. As a discussion leader, it is your responsibility to ensure that all group members actively participate in the discussion by having an opportunity to express their opinions. Doing so can help ensure that different points of view emerge and that everyone "takes ownership" of the final decision.

2. Distinguish between idea generation and idea evaluation. Studies conclude that evaluating and criticizing proposed solutions and ideas actually inhibits the process of generating new ideas. Yet in most group discussions, there's a tendency for one person to present an alternative and for others to begin immediately discussing its pros and cons. As a result, group members quickly become apprehensive about suggesting new ideas. Instituting brainstorming rules—in particular, forbidding criticism of an idea until all ideas have been presented—can be useful here.

3. Do not respond to each participant or dominate the discussion. Remember that the discussion leader's main responsibility is to elicit ideas from the group, not to supply them. As a discussion leader, you should therefore work hard to facilitate a free expression of ideas and to consciously avoid dominating the discussion.

4. See that the effort is directed towards overcoming surmountable obstacles. In other words, focus on solving the problem rather than on discussing historical events that cannot be changed. For example, some discussion groups make the mistake of becoming embroiled in discussions concerning who is to blame for the problem or what should have been done to avoid the problem. Such discussions can't lead to solutions, because the past can't be changed. Instead, as a discussion leader, your job is to ensure that the group focuses on obstacles that can be overcome and on solutions that can be implemented.[44]

1. **Understand the importance of decision making in the manager's job.** Decision making is at the heart of what all managers do. To properly carry out the four basic functions of management—planning, organizing, leading, and controlling—good decisions must be made.

2. **Differentiate between programmed and non-programmed decisions.** Programmed decisions are recurring decisions about relatively routine matters, and are made using established procedures that the manager is familiar with. Non-programmed decisions are one-time decisions for which no routine or standard procedure exists.

3. **Describe the rational decision-making process.** The rational decision-making process includes the following steps: (1) define the problem, (2) identify the criteria to be used in making the decision, (3) weight the criteria, (4) develop alternatives, (5) analyze the alternatives, and (6) make a choice and implement the chosen alternative.

4. **Compare rational decision making and decision making in practice.** Rational decision making assumes ideal conditions such as accurate definition of the problem and complete knowledge of all relevant alternatives and their values. In contrast, decision making in reality is limited by several barriers (see point 5 below). Bounded rationality describes decision making in reality and often implies satisficing, or accepting satisfactory, as opposed to optimal, alternatives.

5. **Identify the barriers to effective decision making.** Barriers to effective decision making include (1) *individual differences* (people's ability to absorb information is limited), (2) *decision-making shortcuts* (using heuristics, which lead to faster, but possibly poorer, decisions), (3) *framing* (misdefining the problem), (4) *anchoring* (giving undue weight to certain sources of information), (5) *psychological set* (using a rigid strategy to try to solve a problem), (6) *organizational barriers* (inflexible company policies and procedures), and (7) *escalation of commitment* (becoming overcommitted to a course of action even when there is evidence that it is not working).

6. **Explain five guidelines for making better decisions.** Guidelines for making better decisions include: (1) *be creative* (be willing to make novel responses to problems), (2) *increase your knowledge* (make sure you have all relevant information before making a decision), (3) *use your intuition* (consult your inner feelings, especially when making important decisions), (4) *don't overstress the finality of your decision* (be willing to change your mind if it becomes necessary), and (5) *ensure the timing is right* (take your mood into account when making decisions).

7. **Understand how to use groups more effectively in the decision-making process.** A group consists of two or more persons who interact for some purpose and who influence each other in the process. Group decision making can result in the pooling of resources and strengthened commitment to the decision. Tools for better group decisions include brainstorming, the devil's advocate approach, the Delphi technique, the nominal group technique, and the stepladder technique.

In this chapter we moved from the environment of the manager's job to a more detailed discussion of what managers actually do. Since all of the management functions (planning, organizing, leading, and controlling) require making decisions, we began this part of the book with Making Decisions—the process, the barriers, and the techniques you can use to make better decisions.

Decisions underlie everything managers do. Everything revolves around decisions. It's not coincidental that we placed the decision-making chapter at the start of Part 2, which focuses on planning. After all, the decisions we make when planning are among the biggest decisions we will ever make, whether the plans concern a choice of career or which new products to introduce.

CRITICAL THINKING EXERCISES

1. To paraphrase philosopher Bertrand Russell, there are two kinds of workers: those that roll the rock up the hill and those that tell them to do so. Since you are probably in college or university as you read this textbook, let's assume that you wish to be the one giving the directions (the brain work) rather than rolling the rock (the brawn work). The brain-based economy reinforces the necessity of education if you wish neither to roll the rock up the hill nor have it roll down on you. Times are continuously changing. As a result, there are many things you need to know as a manager to make good decisions. How do you think managerial decision making is different in a brain-based economy than in an industrial or brawn-based one? What are the most important factors or variables that go into making managerial decisions in the 21st century? What do you think decision making will be like in the year 2100? Will the rational model prevail or will some form of creativity and innovation displace the time-honoured tradition of Western thought and Descartes' dictum: "I think, therefore I am"? Be prepared to discuss these questions in class.

2. In his provocative book, *Managing as a Performing Art*, Peter Vaill argues that there are seven myths in managing organizations. Three of these are as follows.

   The myth of a single person called "the manager" or "the leader." Vaill contends that all kinds of people without the title or power have opportunities for management and leadership in modern organizations.

   The myth that what the leader leads and the manager manages is a single, free-standing organization. Vaill states that thinking of organizations as singular things allows us to ignore the fact that they are a part of their environment and therefore must be aware of their impact on that environment.

   The myth of rational analysis as the primary means of understanding and directing organizations. Intuition is important; change is so constant and discontinuous that we must be creative constantly, and there is much mystery in our decisions today.

   Analyze and discuss the points made by Vaill in light of what you now know about decision making and organizations.

EXPERIENTIAL EXERCISES

1. The world is becoming more competitive every day. Management expert Rosabeth Moss Kanter uses an analogy of "Alice in Wonderland" in *When Giants Learn to Dance* to explain her perspective on the "game of change" that managers find themselves playing.

To some companies, the contest in which they are now entered seems increasingly less like baseball or other traditional games and more like the croquet game in *Alice in Wonderland*—a game that compels the player to deal with constant change. In that fictional game, nothing remains stable for very long, because everything is alive and changing around the player—an all-too-real condition for many managers. The mallet Alice uses is a flamingo, which tends to lift its head and face in another direction just as Alice tries to hit the ball. The ball, in turn, is a hedgehog, another creature with a mind of its own. Instead of lying there waiting for Alice to hit it, the hedgehog unrolls, gets up, moves to another part of the court, and sits down again. The wickets are card soldiers, ordered around by the Queen of Hearts, who changes the structure of the game seemingly at whim by barking out an order to the wickets to reposition themselves around the court.

Substitute technology for the mallet, employees and customers for the hedgehog, and everyone else from government regulators to corporate raiders for the Queen of Hearts, and the analogy fits the experience of a growing number of companies.

Divide the class into teams of five to seven. Assign one of the following companies to each group: Microsoft, Nortel, GM Canada, Levi Strauss, Home Depot, Johnson & Johnson, Cott Cola, McDonald's, Canadian National Railways, Corel Corp., Air Canada, Four Seasons Hotels, Maclean-Hunter, and Hudson's Bay Company. Each group should research its company, applying the *Alice in Wonderland* analogy, and generate a two- to three-page analysis to be presented in class describing examples of how the analogy applies and how it affects organizational decision making.

2. As a team, analyze the following story by Taoist thinker Chuang-tse:

While sitting on the banks of the P'u River, Chuang-tse was approached by two representatives of the Prince of Ch'u, who offered him a position at court. Chuang-tse watched the water flowing by as if he had not heard. Finally, he remarked, "I am told that the Prince has a sacred tortoise, over two thousand years old, which is kept in a box, wrapped in silk and brocade." "That is true," the officials replied. "If the tortoise had been given a choice," Chuang-tse continued, "which do you think he would have liked better—to have been alive in the mud, or dead within the palace?" "To have been alive in the mud, of course," the men answered. "I too prefer the mud," said Chuang-tse. "Good-bye."

In our rapidly changing world, we must all make a number of decisions as to how we wish to live our lives. As a class project, research decision making as it relates to career choices and life choices.

INTERNET EXERCISE

Every company makes key decisions on the path to success, failure, or mediocrity. Intel is a success story, based on a series of interesting decisions. To find out more about Intel and the history of the microprocessor go to www.intel.com/intel/museum/25anniv/index.htm.

Once there, go to the "Interact with History" link. Use the HMTL version, as that will take you to an interactive walk through the history of Intel and the company decisions that were made.

1. To what extent would you have made the same decisions or taken the same actions?

2. Is decision making at Intel planned and rational, or based to some degree on intuition? Why?

Voisey's Bay: Field of Dreams or Nightmare?

In 1993, two diamond prospectors under contract to Diamond Field Resources (DFR) stumbled on one of the world's richest nickel finds in the rolling hills of northeast Labrador. After word of the discovery got out, the price of DFR's stock rose from $4 to $41 per share.

In 1996, Inco decided to buy controlling interest in DFR for $4.3 billion in order to maintain Inco's dominant position in the world nickel mining industry. Unfortunately, once Inco gained control of the nickel deposit, things began to go wrong. In 1997, Inco's stock price dropped 50 percent because of declining world nickel prices, and because Inco had issued additional shares to pay for the purchase of Voisey's Bay. Also in 1997, Inco announced that it would have to delay development of the project because of a time-consuming and expensive environmental review process. The government of Newfoundland had also gotten into the act, demanding that Inco build a smelter in the province to smelt the ore it mined. The Innu Nation then demanded a 3 percent smelter royalty and a guarantee that the mine would be in operation for 25 years.

At Inco's annual meeting in 1998, chairman Michael Sopko had to cope with hostile questions from union and aboriginal leaders, shareholders, environmentalists, and political leaders. Rumours began circulating that Inco would have to take a massive writedown on the project.

By 1999 things were again looking up. Nickel prices (and Inco's stock price) had risen dramatically since 1997, and Inco had returned to the bargaining table with provincial politicians to try to work out an agreement. Because of its improved financial condition, Inco was apparently willing to talk about building the smelter in Newfoundland after all. As of late 1999, it looked like Inco was finally going to be able to begin production at Voisey's Bay sometime in the year 2000.

However, in February 2000 Inco announced it was closing its Newfoundland office because it had been unable to reach an agreement with Newfoundland Premier Brian Tobin about the conditions under which Inco would be allowed to mine the nickel at Voisey's Bay. Inco also said that it was shifting more than $1 billion to its nickel operations in the South Pacific.

Questions

1. What criteria did Inco likely use when they originally decided to spend $4.3 billion to gain control of the Voisey's Bay nickel deposit?

2. Did Inco make a rational decision when they first bought Voisey's Bay? Explain.

3. In 1996, did it look like Inco had made a good decision? How did this decision look in 1998? In 2000? Explain.

Should BP Shareholders Approve This Proposal?

Shareholders of British Petroleum (BP) were faced with a major decision. BP's CEO, Sir John Browne, had recommended that the venerable British company purchase its long-time American competitor Amoco for $57 billion. Browne had led BP in the purchase of Atlantic Richfield for $27 billion just six months earlier. If the shareholders approved the deal, BP-Amoco would become the second largest oil producer in the world. Not bad for a company that had been in serious financial trouble just seven years previously.

In a presentation to press and industry analysts, Browne stated that the merger would make BP a "super-major" oil company, holding the third-largest volume of oil and gas reserves. Browne portrayed the new company as having distinctive assets, global reach, and strongly competitive returns. The company would be restructured somewhat as part of the deal. The resulting synergies gained by the new firm would result in $2 billion in pre-tax savings. The merger would also geographically diversify BP, improving the balance in its revenues between the U.S., Europe, and the rest of the world. BP's profits in 1997 were $4.6 billion and Amoco's totalled $2.7 billion. Combined revenues of the two giants would total $108 billion. The current combined market capitalization (the total value of its shares) of some $110 billion would create Britain's largest company.

Critics of the proposal suggested it wasn't such a good idea. Among other issues, Browne needed to develop a strategy for BP's natural gas assets. The merger was scheduled to make BP the world's third largest producer of natural gas (smaller only than the Russian giant Gazprom and the U.S.'s Exxon). Analysts had predicted that demand for natural gas would grow twice as fast as that for oil, yet there were questions about BP's knowledge and skills in this area. Former Amoco executives said the company did not understand the global nature of the gas business.

There was also concern that Browne might not be able to grow the new business. He had shown great skill in cutting costs and gaining efficiencies, but analysts were concerned because different sets of skills are required to cut costs and to grow a company. For all of his success, Browne had not clearly demonstrated to everyone's satisfaction that he could move a company to sustained growth.

Still, the numbers were impressive. Browne was careful to document the sources of the estimated $2 billion in cost savings, providing assurances that these moves were well planned. Further, the management team suggested that its numbers were conservative, as they did not reflect any synergies that might occur in revenue generation, but only those that came from cost cutting. As a result, the projected $2 billion improvement in profit might be conservative. Further, the management team at BP had linked their own management compensation to meeting their strategic cost targets.

In describing the merger to BP shareholders, Browne described the BP-Amoco link as "a superb alliance of equals with complementary strategic and geographical strengths which effectively creates a new super-major that can better serve our millions of customers world-wide."

There was a great deal of information to consider, and there were strong opinions both for and against the acquisition. What should the shareholders decide?

Questions

1. What criteria did BP use in making its decision? Would you consider their decision to be rational?

2. What criteria might you use as an investor that would be different than BP's?

3. What decision do you think the shareholders should make?

British Petroleum
www.bp.com

YOU BE THE CONSULTANT

Where to Open Next?

Some of the biggest decisions Michael Dorf and his executive team have to make concern the locations of their new Knitting Factory music clubs. Indeed, much of the millions of dollars they recently raised from private investors is earmarked to go towards building new clubs, so the decisions that KnitMedia makes regarding these clubs will have a big effect on the company's success.

When one talks to Dorf, it's apparent how complicated making a decision about one of these club locations can be. For example, for many years KnitMedia worked on opening its first club abroad in London, but it never happened. Why? According to Dorf, "The real estate deal fell through. It was a joint venture with the South Bank, which is a publicly supported arts institution that gets its funding from the British Arts Council, which receives its funding from the lottery, and due to all kinds of political reasons beyond our control, the lottery did not grant to the Arts Council, which in turn didn't grant to the South Bank, the funding for them to do their whole complex and renovation of which we were to be part."

It therefore looks like KnitMedia's first club abroad will open in Berlin, Germany. But as Dorf explains it, opening a club anywhere—and particularly abroad—is "not as easy as building a Web site. You know, there are local laws and local politics and numerous elements that go into a large facility like a Knitting Factory." Just building the balcony for the new club in Hollywood involved over 200 tonnes of steel, for instance, plus dealing with building codes, union regulations, and inspections. And construction problems are just part of the overall decision-making process when it comes to deciding where to open a new club.

Dorf is a very, very smart person whose business has thrived so far in large part because of his decision-making ability. However, he wants to make sure that he's using all the decision-making tools he can when it comes to deciding where to open his next club abroad. He wants your advice.

Team Exercises and Questions

Use what you learned in this chapter to answer the following questions from Michael Dorf and his management team:

1. We want to make sure we don't make any unnecessary errors. What are the main stumbling blocks to good decision making that we ought to be on the lookout for?

2. In our opinion, the problem we want to address here is: "Where should we open our next Knitting Factory abroad?" Do you agree that we've defined the problem accurately? If not, what do you think the problem statement should be?

3. You've told us that information is very important in making decisions. What specific kinds of information do you think we need to make a decision about the location of our new club abroad? Where specifically do you think we ought to get that information?

4. We obviously ran into unanticipated consequences in opening the London Knitting Factory (or in *not* opening the London Knitting Factory, as it turned out). What do you think we did wrong in London? Did we choose the wrong location? Did we not manage the process properly? How can we avoid making the same mistakes again?

Appendix

CHAPTER

4

Quantitative Decision-Making Aids

Many decisions (particularly programmed ones) lend themselves to solution through quantitative analysis. Here are several of the more popular quantitative decision-making techniques.

BREAK-EVEN ANALYSIS

In financial analysis, the break-even point is that volume of sales at which revenues equal expenses and there is neither a profit nor a loss. **Break-even analysis** is a decision-making aid that enables a manager to determine whether a particular volume of sales will result in losses or profits.[1]

break-even analysis
A decision-making aid that enables a manager to determine whether a particular volume of sales will result in losses or profits.

Break-Even Charts

Break-even analysis makes use of four basic concepts: fixed costs, variable costs, revenues, and profits. Fixed costs (such as for plant and machinery) are costs that basically do not change with changes in volume. In other words, you might use the same machine to produce 10 units, 50 units, or 200 units of a product. Variable costs (such as for raw material) do rise in proportion to volume. Revenue is the total income received from sales of the product. For example, if you sell 50 dolls at $8 each, then your revenue is $8 × 50 or $400. Profit is the money you have left after subtracting fixed and variable costs from revenues.

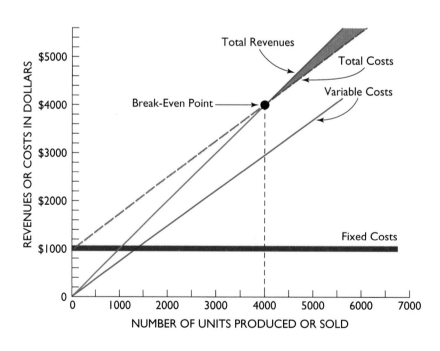

FIGURE A4.1
A Break-Even Chart
The break-even point is that number of units sold at which total revenues equal total costs.

A **break-even chart** is a graph that shows whether a particular volume of sales will result in profits or losses (see Figure A4.1). The fixed-costs line is horizontal, since fixed costs remain the same regardless of level of output. Variable costs, however, increase in proportion to output and are shown as an upward-sloping line. The total-costs line is equal to variable costs plus fixed costs at each level of output.

The **break-even point** is the point at which the total-revenues line crosses the total-costs line. Beyond this point (note the shaded area in Figure A4.1), total revenues exceed total costs. In this example, an output of about 4000 units is the break-even point. Above this, the company can expect to earn a profit. But if sales are fewer than 4000 units, the company can expect a loss.

break-even chart
A graph that shows whether a particular volume of sales will result in profits or losses.

break-even point
The point at which the total-revenues line crosses the total-costs line.

Break-Even Formula

The break-even chart provides a picture of the relationship between sales volume and profits. However, a chart is not required for determining break-even points. Instead, you can use a formula:

$$P(X) = F + V(X)$$

where

F = fixed costs

V = variable costs per unit

X = volume of output (in units)

P = price per unit

Rearranging this formula, the break-even point is $X = F/(P - V)$. In other words, the break-even point is the volume of sales where total costs equal total revenues. If, for example, you have a product in which:

F = fixed costs = $1000

V = variable costs per unit = $0.75

P = price per unit = $1 per unit

then the break-even point is $1000/$1 - $0.75 = 4000 units.

LINEAR PROGRAMMING

Break-even analysis is only one of many decision techniques. Decision-science techniques are a second category of programmed decision-making aids, all of which are distinguished by their reliance on mathematics. For example, **linear programming** is a mathematical method used to solve resource allocation problems. These arise "whenever there are a number of activities to be performed, but limitations on either the amount of resources or the way they can be spent."[2] For example, linear programming can be used to determine the best way to:

linear programming
A mathematical method used to solve resource allocation problems.

- distribute merchandise from a number of warehouses to a number of customers;
- assign personnel to various jobs;
- design shipping schedules;
- select the product mix in a factory to make the best use of machine and labour hours available while maximizing the firm's profit;
- route production to optimize the use of machinery.

In order for managers to apply linear programming successfully, the problem must meet certain basic requirements: There must be a stated, quantifiable goal, such as "minimize total shipping costs"; the resources to be used must be known (a firm could produce 200 of one item and 300 of another, for instance, or 400 of one and 100 of another); all the necessary relationships must be expressed in the form of mathematical equations or inequalities; and all these relationships must be linear in nature. An example can help illustrate this technique:

Shader Electronics has 5 manufacturing plants and 12 warehouses scattered across Canada. Each plant is manufacturing the same product and operating at full capacity. Since plant capacity and location do not permit the closest plant to fully support each warehouse, Shader would like to identify the factory that should supply each warehouse in order to minimize total shipping costs. Applying linear programming techniques to this problem will provide an optimum shipping schedule.

WAITING-LINE/QUEUING TECHNIQUES

Waiting-line/queuing techniques are mathematical decision-making techniques for solving waiting-line problems. For example, bank managers need to know how many tellers they should have. If they have too many, they are wasting money on salaries; if they have too few, they may end up with unhappy customers. Similar problems arise when selecting the optimal number of airline reservation clerks, warehouse loading docks, highway toll booths, supermarket checkout counters, and so forth.

STATISTICAL DECISION THEORY TECHNIQUES

Statistical decision theory techniques are used to solve problems for which information is incomplete or uncertain. Suppose a shopkeeper can stock either brand A or brand B, but not both. She knows how much it will cost to stock her shelves with each brand, and she also knows how much money she will earn (or lose) if each brand turns out to be a success (or failure) with her customers. However, she can only estimate how much of each brand she might sell, so her information is incomplete. Using statistical decision theory, the shopkeeper would assign probabilities (estimates of the likelihood that the brand will sell or not) to each alternative. Then she could determine which alternative—stocking brand A or brand B—would most likely result in the greatest profits.

Three Degrees of Uncertainty

Statistical decision theory is based on the idea that a manager may face three degrees of uncertainty in making a decision. Some decisions are made under conditions of **certainty**. Here, the manager knows in advance the outcome of the decision. From a practical point of view, for example, you know that if you buy a $50 Canada Savings Bond, the interest you will earn to maturity on the bond is, say, 6 percent. However, managers rarely make decisions under conditions of certainty.

At the opposite extreme, some decisions are made under conditions of **uncertainty.** Here, the manager cannot even assign probabilities to the likelihood of the various outcomes. For example, a shopkeeper may have several new products that could be stocked, but no idea of the likelihood that one brand will be successful or that another will fail. Conditions of complete uncertainty are also relatively infrequent.

Most management decisions are made under conditions of **risk**. In these situations, the manager can at least assign probabilities to each outcome. In other words, the manager knows (either from past experience or by making an educated guess) the chance that each possible outcome (such as product A being successful or product B being unsuccessful) will occur.

Decision Tree

A **decision tree** is one technique for making a decision under conditions of risk. With a decision tree like the one shown in Figure A4.2, an expected value can be calculated for each alternative. **Expected value** equals the probability of the outcome multiplied by the benefit or cost of that outcome.

For example, in Figure A4.2 it pays for our shopkeeper to stock brand B rather than brand A. Stocking brand A provides a 70 percent chance of making an $800 profit, so the shopkeeper has to balance this $560 profit she could make against the possibility of a $90 loss (30 percent × possible loss of $300). The expected value of stocking brand A is thus $470. However, the expected value of stocking brand B is a relatively higher $588.

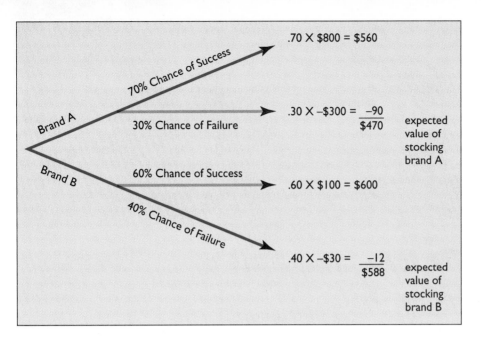

.70 × $800 = $560

.30 × –$300 = −90 / $470

expected value of stocking brand A

60% Chance of Success

.60 × $100 = $600

.40 × –$30 = −12 / $588

expected value of stocking brand B

FIGURE A4.2
Example of a Decision Tree
The expected value of each alternative is equal to the chance of success or failure multiplied by the expected profit or loss.

Planning and Setting Objectives

The Rise and Fall of Loewen Group Inc.

Ray Loewen started with one funeral home in Manitoba, and then acquired hundreds more in the U.S. and Canada during the 1980s and 1990s. Eventually, Loewen Group Inc. became the second largest funeral home chain in North America, with more than 750 funeral homes and 8000 employees. Loewen's expansion strategy served him well for quite a few years, but the company ran into trouble after it got involved in a seemingly minor legal wrangle with a funeral home owner in the state of Mississippi. The legal fight—which Loewen lost in 1996—eventually ended up costing the company $175 million. Loewen claimed that the settlement wouldn't have a negative impact on the company, but analysts were skeptical. By the middle of 1998, the company's stock had dropped sharply.

Confidence in the company continued to erode, and Loewen began hinting that the company might be for sale. This was a major change from his claim a year earlier that he would never sell the company. SCI, the largest funeral home in the U.S., which had unsuccessfully tried to buy Loewen in 1997 at $45 per share, indicated that it might still be interested, but at a much lower price. In October 1998 Ray Loewen was removed as president of Loewen Group Inc. The company's stock price by that time had dropped to $13 per share.

What happened to Ray Loewen? Why didn't his expansion strategy work? Apparently, he was the classic entrepreneur who was unable to delegate authority to his subordinates. His tight control of everything in the company prevented subordinate managers from properly running the business. He also tried to grow too fast, spending over $500 million per year on acquisitions during the peak of his expansion. Even after Loewen's resignation, the company continued to experience financial difficulties.

SCI
www.sci-corp.com

Loewen Group
www.loewengroup.com

OBJECTIVES

After studying this chapter, you should be able to

1. Define planning and describe the different types of plans companies use.

2. Explain the five steps in the planning process.

3. Recognize effective goals.

4. Explain three techniques for developing the premises upon which plans are built.

Planning, the subject of this chapter, is often called the "first among equals" of the four management functions (planning, organizing, leading, and controlling), since it establishes the goals that are the bases of all these functions. The people you hire, the incentives you use, and the controls you institute all relate to what you want to achieve and to the plans and goals you set. In this chapter we'll focus on planning, and on the techniques for how to set goals and objectives. Then, in the following chapter, we'll turn to the crucial subject of strategic planning; in other words, how to set long-term, company-wide plans for an enterprise.

The Nature and Purpose of Planning

Why Plan?

Plans are methods formulated beforehand for achieving a desired result. All plans specify goals (such as "boost sales by 10 percent") and courses of action (such as "hire a new salesperson and boost advertising expenditures by 20 percent"). Plans should specify (at a minimum) what you will do, how you will do it, and by when you'll get it done.[1] **Planning,** therefore, is "the process of establishing objectives and courses of action, prior to taking action."[2] **Goals,** or **objectives,** are specific results you want to achieve. Wal-Mart's data warehouse helps its managers forecast what its customers will buy, and therefore helps them to achieve its plan to have that merchandise in their stores when it is needed. In this section we'll look at the nature of planning, and then turn to the methods managers use to forecast the future.

Planning and decision making (the subject of Chapter 4) are closely intertwined. Planning means choosing your objectives and the courses of action that will get you there. In other words, when you make a plan, what you're really doing is deciding ahead of time what you (or your company) are going to do in the future. A plan is thus a group of premade decisions that will allow you to achieve a future goal. So, if you're planning a trip to Paris, your plan might include the following decisions: the date you leave, how to get to the airport, your airline and flight, the airport of arrival, how to get into Paris, your hotel, and a fairly detailed itinerary (or plan) for each day you're in Paris.

You could just "wing it," and some people do. Don't decide ahead of time how you'll get to or from the airport, or what you'll be doing on each of your days in Paris. What will happen? Perhaps nothing. More likely, though, you'll find yourself having to make a lot of last-minute decisions under stressful conditions. Instead of arranging ahead of time to have a friend take you to the airport, you may be scrambling at the last minute to find a cab. Instead of researching and pricing your options ahead of time, you may find yourself at Orly Airport, tired and faced with a bewildering variety of buses and cabs—including some high-priced uncertified "gypsy" cabs. And instead of deciding ahead of time in the comfort of your home what you'll do each day, you may kill two hours or more on each day of your trip deciding what to do and finding out what is open.

The point, again, is this: Planning gives you the luxury of deciding ahead of time what you're going to do. You don't have to plan; but if you don't, you're going to find yourself scrambling, probably under less-than-hospitable conditions, to make those decisions on the run. And that can lead to lots of errors.

Here's another example. You're probably reading this book as part of a management course. And why are you taking this course? Chances are that the course is part of your program of studies. This program is *planned.* It identifies your goal (say, getting a diploma or degree in business in two years), and it identifies how you will get that degree by specifying the courses you'll need to graduate.

You may also have a broader goal, a vision of where you're headed in life. If you do,

plan
A method formulated beforehand for achieving a desired result.

planning
The process of establishing objectives and courses of action, prior to taking action.

goal (objective)
A specific result you want to achieve.

then your degree may just be one step in a longer-term plan. For example, suppose you dream of running your own management consulting firm by the time you are 35. Ask yourself, "What do I have to do to achieve this goal?" The answer may be to work for a nationally known consulting firm, thus building up your experience and your reputation in the field. So here is your plan: Take this course to get the degree, get the degree to get the consulting job, and then work hard as a consultant to achieve your dream.

What Planning Accomplishes

In discussing the trip to Paris, we mentioned one big benefit of planning: You *get to make your decisions ahead of time*, in the comfort of your home or office, and with the luxury of having the time to do research and weight your options. Here are a few other benefits of planning:

Planning Provides Direction and a Sense of Purpose. "If you don't know where you're going, any path will get you there," Alice is told as she stumbles into Wonderland. The same is true for all your endeavours. In the career example above, knowing ahead of time that your goal is to have your own consulting firm provides a sense of direction and purpose for all the career decisions you have to make, such as what to major in and what experience you'll need along the way. This helps you avoid piecemeal decision making. It's a lot easier to decide what to major in and what courses to take when you've got a clear career objective.

The same is true in management. A plan provides a unifying framework against which decisions can be measured. For example, in the 1990s Canada's major banks began to increase their emphasis on electronic banking. They knew that this would likely mean fewer branches over time, but electronic banking would also make them more efficient and able to compete in global financial markets.

Planning Reduces Piecemeal Decision Making. A plan also provides a unifying framework against which decisions can be assessed. The result, as one expert put it, is that "planning channels effort toward desired results, and by providing a sequence of efforts, [it] minimizes unproductive behavior."[3]

Electronic banking has become a familiar sight in Canada. The change to electronic banking will mean fewer traditional bank branches, but it will make Canadian banks more efficient and better able to compete in global financial markets.

Planning Reveals Future Opportunities and Threats. Management theorist Peter Drucker says that planning can help identify potential opportunities and threats and at least reduce long-term risks.[4]

Planning Facilitates Control. Control means ensuring that activities conform to plans; it is a three-step process in which standards are set, performance is measured against these standards, and deviations are identified and corrected.

Planning is the first step in this cycle—specifying what is to be achieved. For example, a company's five-year plan may specify that its profits will double within five years. This goal can then be a standard against which to measure and control the president's performance.

Types of Plans

While all plans specify goals and the courses of action chosen for reaching them, the plans themselves come in all shapes and sizes. They differ in format, in their time horizon, and in their frequency of use.

Different Formats. Plans differ in format, or the way they are expressed. Perhaps the most familiar plans are **descriptive plans**; like the career plan above, they state in words what is to be achieved and how. Plans stated in financial terms are called **budgets**. **Graphic plans** show in charts what is to be achieved and how.

Different Time Horizons. Plans also differ in the spans of time they cover. Top management usually engages in long-term (five- to ten-year) strategic planning. For example, the planning process for Bombardier's Global Express executive jet started in 1991, when the company first saw an opportunity in the ultra long-range executive jet market.[5] Before Bombardier committed to building the new jet, it assessed the views of potential buyers like large international companies, heads of state, and extremely wealthy individuals. The Global Express was finally ready for sale to customers in 1996.

A **strategic plan** specifies the business or businesses the firm will be in, and the major steps it must take to get there. Middle managers typically focus on developing shorter-term tactical plans (of up to five years' duration). **Tactical plans** (sometimes called **functional plans**) show how top management's plans are to be carried out at the departmental level; for instance, by the managers responsible for sales, finance, and manufacturing. First-line managers then focus on shorter-term **operational**, or detailed day-to-day, **planning**. These plans might show, for instance, exactly which workers are to be assigned to which machines or exactly how many units will be produced on a given day.

Different Frequency. Some plans must be developed specially for one-of-a-kind situations, while other plans can be used over and over again. **Single-use plans** are developed for a specific, one-time purpose and will not be used again. The plan developed by the Canadian Forces to deal with the Mohawk blockade at Oka, Quebec, in 1990 was a single-use plan. So was the United Nations' plan to enter Kosovo and keep the peace in 1999.

Standing plans are intended for repeated usage. Policies, procedures, and rules are examples of standing plans. A **policy** is a guide to action; it suggests in general terms what managers should do in various situations. For example, a company might have a policy that "purchasing agents will not accept gifts from suppliers that are sufficient to cause undue influence on the decisions of the purchasing agent." This policy does not tell the purchasing agent how large a gift he or she can accept from a supplier, but it does convey the principle that accepting gifts can lead to problems. **Procedures**, as the name implies, specify how to proceed if some specific situation arises. For example, "Before refunding the customer's purchase price, the salesperson must carefully inspect the garment and then obtain approval from the floor manager for the refund." Finally, a **rule** is a highly specific guide to action. For example, "Under no condition will the purchase price be refunded after 30 days."

descriptive plan
A plan that states in words what is to be achieved and how.

budget
A plan stated in financial terms.

graphic plan
A plan that shows in charts what is to be achieved and how.

strategic plan
A plan that specifies the business or businesses a firm will be in, and the major steps it must take to get there.

tactical (functional) plan
A plan that shows how top management's plans are to be carried out at the departmental level.

operational planning
Shorter-term planning by first-line managers regarding staffing and production levels, for example.

single-use plan
A plan developed for a specific, one-time purpose that will not be used again.

standing plan
A plan, such as a policy, procedure, or rule, intended for repeated usage.

policy
A guide to action.

procedure
Specifies how to proceed if some specific situation arises.

rule
A highly specific guide to action.

The Management Planning Process

Steps in Planning

As shown in Figure 5.1, the planning process consists of a logical sequence of five steps.

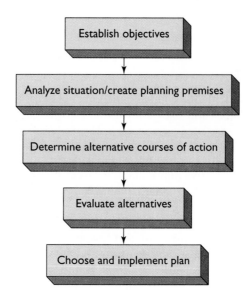

FIGURE 5.1
The Planning Process

Step 1: Set Organizational Objectives. Plans are methods formulated beforehand for achieving a desired result. In a business, the first step in planning is therefore to establish objectives for the entire enterprise and then, through the process of planning, to establish goals in turn for subordinate units, each of which will develop its own plans.

Objectives focus employee attention on tasks that are consistent with the organization's mission. The goal at Royal Airlines is to fill every seat on every flight.[6] Shell Canada Ltd. set the objective of changing its fossil fuel companies to energy companies that will put as much effort into solar and wind power as they will into oil and gas exploration.[7] The managers at Imperial Oil's Dartmouth, Nova Scotia, plant were given one year to improve their refinery's status from one of the worst to one of the best. The workers got "real clarity" that day about what goals would have to be achieved to keep the plant open. Nine months later, management and workers at the refinery had achieved their goal.[8]

Step 2: Identify the Gap Between Desired and Actual Positions. Managers need to determine how well organizational objectives are being achieved. The focus may be on the entire company, a department within the company, or an individual within a department. For example, a year-end financial analysis will determine whether the company reached its profitability objectives. At the end of a recruiting period, a department can assess whether it reached its hiring objectives of four new people. An annual performance appraisal of an individual will tell the boss and subordinate whether the subordinate reached his or her goals for the year. Once the magnitude of the gap is determined, the manager must then decide how the gap will be closed. This involves developing various types of plans.

Step 3: Develop Plans to Achieve Objectives. As we saw at the beginning of the chapter, plans are methods formulated beforehand for achieving a desired result. While objectives indicate *what* results are desired, plans indicate *how* these objectives are to be achieved. Plans also indicate the activities that are required, the individual or group that will carry them out, and the deadline for their completion.

Royal Airlines
www.royalairlines.com

Step 4: Choose and Implement Plans. The steps that we have discussed so far all require managers to think about what is to be accomplished. At some point, however, this thinking must be converted into action. This is the point at which many managers encounter problems, because implementing plans almost always involves introducing change, and this is likely to meet with resistance. We discuss this important issue in Chapter 15.

Step 5: Evaluate Planning Effectiveness. The final step in the planning process is assessing the effectiveness of the plans the organization has developed. This requires comparing actual results with planned performance. Without such an assessment, little will be learned about how the plans helped or hindered the organization. Stated most generally, a plan is effective if it helps the organization reach its objectives.

The Planning Hierarchy

Step 4 in Figure 5.1 (implement the plan) means that top management's goals become the targets for which subsidiary units must formulate derivative plans. One result of the planning process is, therefore, a **hierarchy of plans**. The hierarchy includes (1) the enterprise-wide plan and objectives, and (2) subsidiary units' derivative plans and objectives, each of which contributes to achieving the enterprise-wide plan and objectives. In practice, a hi-

hierarchy of plans
Broad and specific plans that work together to achieve overall organizational goals.

THE PEOPLE SIDE OF MANAGING

The Need for Teamwork in Planning

Because each manager's plans should complement those of his or her colleagues and also contribute to making the company's overall goals a reality, effective planning is enhanced by teamwork.

DaimlerChrysler's recent success in introducing new models while boosting profitability provides an example.[9] Many credit DaimlerChrysler's recent strong performance (including increased market share and a dramatic rise in profit per vehicle) to the close-knit camaraderie of DaimlerChrysler's top management team. In the car business, where huge investments are required, product planning requires especially close teamwork.

At DaimlerChrysler, product planning starts with market research information from sales head James Holden. That information helped design head Thomas Gale and his group to create the successful "cab-forward" design, which in turn was implemented by engineering head François Castaing and his department. They then worked closely with parts supply chief Thomas Stallkamp and manufacturing head Dennis Pawley to develop a comprehensive product design/engineering/production/sales plan.

The first stage in the cab-forward design of DaimlerChrysler's 1998 Concorde. Cross-functional planning teams are responsible for implementing new designs like this one.

Daimler-Chrysler
www.daimler chrysler.com

Anything less than close cooperation—disruptive interdepartmental rivalries, for instance, or political manoeuvring by any of the department heads—could have slowed development and led to a less successful product launch. At DaimlerChrysler, as at other enterprises, successful plans are usually the result of close cooperation among members of a cross-functional planning team.

erarchy of plans literally evolves. Several years ago the Sunbeam Corporation (which makes kitchen appliances) decided to drive down costs by at least 20 percent by dramatically reducing the size of the firm ("downsizing," in other words). What evolved was a top-management plan to reduce the number of employees by half, roll out 30 new products per year, and shrink the number of factories and warehouses from over 40 to just 13.

With that framework as a guide, lower-level plans then had to be crafted. For the coming year, for instance, managers for each product group had to formulate and have approved plans regarding the new products they would add, and the ones they'd drop. The production head had to craft plans showing which plants would close.

Once these second-level plans were in place, third-level operational plans were needed. Once she knew which plants would be closed, for instance, the HR manager would need to formulate specific plans for handling the dismissals. And each plant manager would need specific monthly production plans, once he or she knew the targets that top management had set for the facility. In this way, a hierarchy of plans of increasing specificity

TABLE 5.1   *Executive Assignment Action Plan for Achieving Long-Term Objective*

Long-Term Objective: Have a minimum of 55 percent of sales revenue from customized products by 2003.

EXECUTIVE ASSIGNMENTS/ DERIVATIVE OBJECTIVES	ACCOUNTABILITY		SCHEDULE		RESOURCES REQUIRED			FEEDBACK MECHANISMS
	Primary	Supporting	Start	Complete	Capital	Operating	Human	
1. Complete market study on sales potential for customized products	VP Marketing	VP Sales	Yr 1	**Year 1**		$10 000	500 hrs	Written progress reports
2. Revise sales forecasts for Years 1, 2, and 3 to reflect changes	VP Sales	VP Marketing		**Year 1**			50 hrs	Revised forecasts
3. Convert Building C to customized manufacturing operation	VP Mfg	VP Engineering VP Admin	Yr 1	**Year 2**	$500 000	$80 000	1100 hrs	Written progress reports
4. Change compensation structure to incentivize customized sales	VP HR	VP Sales	Yr 1	**Year 1**		$50 000	100 hrs	Revised structure report
5. Train sales staff in new technology	Director of Training	VP Sales	Yr 2	**Year 2**		$50 000	1000 hrs	Training plan reports
6. Expand production of customized products —to 25 percent —to 30 percent —to 40 percent —to 50 to 55 percent	VP Mfg	VP Engineering	Yr 1	**Year 2** **Year 2** **Year 3** **Year 3**		Budgeted	Budgeted	Production reports
7. Increase sales of customized products —to 25 percent —to 30 percent —to 40 percent —to 55 percent	VP Sales	VP Marketing	Yr 1	**Year 2** **Year 2** **Year 3** **Year 3**				Sales reports
8. Revise sales forecasts	VP Sales	VP Marketing		**Year 3**				Revised forecasts

Note: This executive assignment action plan shows the specific executive assignments required to achieve top management's long-term objective: "Have a minimum of 55 percent of sales revenue from customized products by 2003."

(and increasingly short-term) would evolve from the top of the firm to the bottom.

Table 5.1 shows an executive assignment action plan for linking management's goals at one level to the derivative plans at the next level down.[10] In this case, one of top management's long-term objectives is to "have a minimum of 55 percent of sales revenue from customized products by 2003." The action plan in Table 5.1 summarizes the derivative targets to be achieved by each department if that long-term objective is to be met. Thus, the vice-president of marketing is to "complete market study on sales potential for customized products" within one year. The VP for manufacturing is to "convert building C to customized manufacturing operation" within one year.

Each vice-president's assigned goals then become the target for which they must develop their own plans. This is illustrated in Table 5.2. Here the manufacturing vice-president's goal of converting building C to a customized manufacturing operation by 2003 is the target for which derivative plans must be formulated. For instance, converting building C will entail completing a feasibility study, purchasing and installing new equipment, and training a production staff.

The Hierarchy of Goals. As you can see, the planning process produces a hierarchy, or chain, of goals from the top to the lowest-level managers.[11] This is illustrated in

TABLE 5.2 *Action Plan for Specific Executive Assignment*

Executive Assignment: Convert Building C to customized manufacturing operation by 2003.

ASSIGNMENTS/ DERIVATIVE OBJECTIVES	ACCOUNTABILITY		SCHEDULE		RESOURCES REQUIRED			FEEDBACK MECHANISMS
	Primary	Supporting	Start	Complete	Capital	Operating	Human	
1. Complete feasibility study on conversion requirements	Director Engineering	VP Engineering	Yr 1	**Year 1**		$10 000	100 hrs	Written progress reports
2. Complete converted production line design and equipment specifications	Director Engineering	VP Engineering		**Year 1**		$50 000	500 hrs	Design review meetings
3. Purchase and install new equipment	Purchasing	VP Mfg	Yr 1	**Year 1**	$400 000		100 hrs	Written progress reports
4. Modify existing equipment	VP Mfg	VP Engineering	Yr 1	**Year 1**	$100 000	$10 000	100 hrs	Written progress reports
5. Train production staff	Director of Training	VP Mfg	Yr 1	**Year 1**		$10 000	300 hrs	Training plan reports
6. Initiate customized production line	VP Mfg	VP Engineering				Budgeted	Budgeted	Production reports
7. Increase production of customized products —to 25 percent —to 30 percent —to 40 percent —to 50 to 55 percent	VP Mfg	VP Engineering	Yr 1	**Year 2** **Year 2** **Year 3** **Year 3**		Budgeted	Budgeted	Production reports
8. Reassess future production capacity	VP Mfg	VP Engineering		**Year 3**				Production forecast

Note: This action plan shows the subsidiary assignments required to achieve the specific executive assignment: "Convert Building C to customized manufacturing operations by 2003."

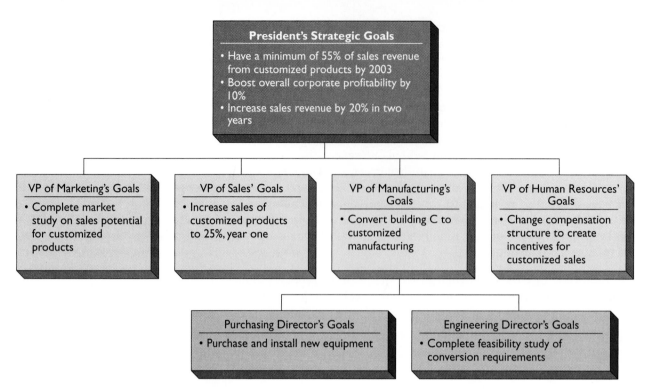

President's Strategic Goals

• Have a minimum of 55% of sales revenue from customized products by 2003
• Boost overall corporate profitability by 10%
• Increase sales revenue by 20% in two years

VP of Marketing's Goals

• Complete market study on sales potential for customized products

VP of Sales' Goals

• Increase sales of customized products to 25%, year one

VP of Manufacturing's Goals

• Convert building C to customized manufacturing

VP of Human Resources' Goals

• Change compensation structure to create incentives for customized sales

Purchasing Director's Goals

• Purchase and install new equipment

Engineering Director's Goals

• Complete feasibility study of conversion requirements

Note: A hierarchy of goals like this is one important by-product of the planning process. This figure shows some (not all) of the supporting goals that need to be formulated to help achieve the company's overall goal of having a minimum of 55 percent of its sales revenue from customized products by 2003.

FIGURE 5.2
Hierachy of Goals

Figure 5.2. At the top, the president and his or her staff set strategic goals (such as to have a minimum of 55 percent of sales revenue from customized products by 2003), to which each vice-president's goal (such as convert Building C to customized manufacturing operation) is then tied. Similarly, a hierarchy of supporting departmental goals down to tactical/functional goals and finally short-term operational goals is then formulated.

Contingency Planning

contingency planning
Identifying possible future outcomes and then developing a plan for coping with them.

Managers have no guarantee that future outcomes will be favourable, but they can at least develop plans for what to do if they are unfavourable. **Contingency planning** involves identifying possible future outcomes and then developing a plan for coping with them. Marlin Fast Freight might have a contingency plan to rent a delivery truck if one of its own trucks breaks down unexpectedly. Imperial Tobacco might have a much more elaborate contingency plan for dealing with possible government legislation that is detrimental to cigarette sales. Air Canada has an elaborate contingency plan. Its Systems Operations Control (SOC) continuously tracks all of the company's aircraft; if a snowstorm develops, the SOC goes into action to ensure that Air Canada's planes do not get stranded at snowed-in airports.[12] Manitoba Telephone System developed a contingency plan that involved getting customers to sign long-term leasing agreements so that MTS wouldn't be negatively affected when it lost its monopoly because of deregulation in the telephone industry.[13]

How to Set Objectives

Why Set Objectives?

If there is one thing on which every manager can expect to be appraised, it is the extent to which he or she achieves his or her unit's goals or objectives. Whether it's a work team or a giant enterprise, the manager in charge is expected to move his or her unit ahead, and this means visualizing where the unit must go—and helping it get there. Organizations exist to achieve some purpose, and if they fail to move forward and achieve their aims, to that extent they have failed. As Peter Drucker puts it, "There has to be something to point to and say, we have not worked in vain."[14]

Effectively setting goals is important for other reasons. Objectives are the targets towards which plans are aimed, and the anchor-points around which the hierarchy of objectives is constructed. Objectives can also aid motivation. Employees—individually and in teams—focus their efforts on achieving concrete goals with which they agree, and usually perform better with goals at which to aim. In fact, when performance is inadequate, it is often not because the person or team is loafing, but because the individual or team doesn't know what the job's goals are. Therefore, all managers today require a good working knowledge of how to set objectives.

Types of Objectives

The range of activities for which objectives may be set is virtually limitless. Peter Drucker argues that organizations should set objectives in eight key result areas (see Table 5.3).[15]

One thing apparent in Table 5.3 is that "profit maximization" is not by itself a good enough guide to management action. It is true that in economic theory, and in practice, managers aim to maximize profits (although other goals, including social responsibility, are crucial too). However, managers also require specific objectives in areas like market penetration and customer service if they are to have any hope of boosting profits.

How to Set Motivational Goals

Goals are useful only to the extent that employees are motivated to achieve them. Managers can do several things to ensure that the goals they set do motivate employees. Studies conducted by psychologists Edwin Locke and Gary Latham and their associates provide a vivid picture of how managers should set goals. We can summarize the implications of these studies as follows.

Assign Specific Goals. Employees who are given specific goals usually perform better than those who are not. One study that illustrates this was conducted in a logging operation.[16] The subjects were truck drivers who had to load logs and drive them to the mill. An analysis of the truckers' performance showed that they often did not fill their

TABLE 5.3 *Objectives for Key Result Areas*

KEY RESULT AREA	EXPLANATION
1. Market share	The proportion of the total market for a product or service that the company controls.
2. Innovation	The development of new products or services.
3. Productivity	Maximizing the amount of goods or services produced while minimizing the resources necessary to produce them.
4. Physical resources	Physical facilities and their most effective use.
5. Financial resources	Sources of funds and how these funds will be used.
6. Profitability	Monetary gain resulting from organizational activity.
7. Human resource development	Attract and develop high-quality managers and employees.
8. Social responsibility	Concern for issues like ethical behaviour and good corporate citizenship.

trucks to the maximum legal net weight. The researchers believed this happened largely because the workers were urged just to "do their best" when it came to loading the truck. Therefore, the researchers arranged for a specific goal ("94 percent of a truck's net weight") to be communicated to each driver. The drivers were told that this was an experimental program, that they would not be required to make more truck runs, and that there would be no retaliation if performance suddenly increased and then decreased. No monetary rewards or benefits, other than verbal praise, were given for improving performance. The drivers and their supervisors got no special training of any kind.

The results of the study were impressive. Performance (in terms of the weight loaded on each truck) jumped markedly as soon as the truckers were assigned specific high goals, and it generally remained at this much higher level. This and other evidence shows that setting specific goals with subordinates, rather than setting no goals or telling them to "do their best," can substantially improve performance in a wide range of settings.[17]

Assign Measurable Goals.[18] Wherever possible, goals should be stated in quantitative terms and include target dates or deadlines for accomplishment. In that regard, goals set in absolute terms (such as "an average daily output of 300 units") are less confusing than goals set in relative terms (such as "improve production by 20 percent"). If measurable results will not be available, then "satisfactory completion"—such as "satisfactorily attended workshop" or "satisfactorily completed his or her degree"—is the next best thing. In any case, target dates or deadlines for accomplishment should always be set.

Assign Challenging but Doable Goals. Researcher Gary Yukl says that goals should be challenging but not so difficult that they appear impossible or unrealistic.[19] Particularly in areas such as sales management, where immediate and concrete performance is both obvious and highly valued, goals consistent with past sales levels—realistic yet high enough to be challenging—are widely espoused.[20]

When is a goal too difficult? Yukl recommends considering prior performance by the same person, performance by people in comparable positions, available resources, likely conditions that will affect performance, and the amount of time until the deadline. As he suggests:

> A goal is probably too easy if it calls for little or no improvement in performance when conditions are becoming more favorable, or if the targeted level of performance is well below that of most other employees in comparable positions. A goal is probably too difficult if it calls for a large improvement in performance when conditions are worsening, or if the targeted level of performance is well above that of people in comparable positions.[21]

Encourage Participation Where Possible. Should managers assign their subordinates' goals, or should they permit their subordinates to participate in developing their own goals? Research evidence on this point has been mixed, but we can reach five conclusions concerning the relative superiority of goals set through participation versus assigned goals.

First, employees who participate in setting goals do, in fact, tend to perceive themselves as having had more impact on the setting of those goals than do employees who are simply assigned goals.[22] Second, goals set through participation tend to be higher than the goals a supervisor would normally have assigned.[23] Third, even when goals set through participation are more difficult than the assigned ones, they are not perceived as such by the subordinates.[24] Fourth, goals set through participation do not consistently result in higher performance than assigned goals nor do assigned goals consistently result in higher performance than ones set through participation. However, when the goals set through participation are higher and more difficult than the assigned goals, as is usually the case, then they usually lead to higher performance. (The fact that the goal is more difficult seems to account for the higher performance, not the fact that it was set through participation.[25]) Finally, goals unilaterally assigned by managers can trigger employee resistance, regardless of the goal's reasonableness. Insofar as participation creates a sense of ownership of the goals, it can reduce resistance.[26]

How to Express the Goal

Knowing how to express the goal is important. As illustrated in Table 5.4, it is important to distinguish between an *area to be measured* (such as sales), a *yardstick* (such as sales revenue), and a *goal* (such as $85 000 per month). There are usually several possible yardsticks for any measurable area. The area of "sales" could be measured in terms of sales revenue or market share. Remember to state any goal in measurable terms.

Planning expert George Morrisey presents a four-point model for use in formulating objectives. It is presented in Table 5.5, along with several examples. A well-crafted goal should contain four types of information.

TABLE 5.4 *Example of Yardsticks and Goals*

AREA	YARDSTICK	STANDARD/GOAL
Sales	Sales revenue	$85 000 per month
Production	Productivity	Produce at least 5 units per labour hour
Customer reactions	Satisfaction	Zero complaints
Quality	Number of rejects	No more than 3 rejects per 100 items produced
Employee behaviour	Absenteeism Accidents Turnover	No more than 3% absences/week No serious accidents 10% turnover maximum
Finances	Profitability Turnover	20% profit margins Sales – inventory = 8%
Expenses	Phone bill Raw materials Supplies	$300 per month maximum 20% of sales 5% of sales

TABLE 5.5 *Model and Examples of Well-Stated Objectives*

MORRISEY'S FOUR-POINT MODEL

To (1) (*action verb*)	(2) (single measurable *result*)
by (3) (*target* date/time span)	at (4) (*cost* in time and/or money)

EXAMPLES OR OBJECTIVES THAT FOLLOW THE MODEL

- To (1, 2) complete the Acme project by (3) December 31 at a (4) cost not to exceed $50 000 and 500 work hours.

- To (1) decrease the (2) average cost of sales by a minimum of 5 percent, effective (3) June 1, at an (4) implementation cost not to exceed 40 work hours.

- To (1, 2) release product A to manufacturing by (3) September 30 at a (4) cost not to exceed $50 000 and 5000 engineering hours.

- To (1) reduce (2) average turnaround time on service requests from 8 to 6 hours by (3) July 31 at an (4) implementation cost of 40 work hours.

Management by Objectives

Management by objectives (MBO) is a technique used by many firms to assist in the process of setting organization-wide objectives and goals for subsidiary units and their employees. Supervisors and subordinates jointly set goals for the latter and periodically assess progress towards those goals. A manager may engage in a modest MBO program by setting goals with his or her subordinates and periodically providing feedback. However, the term MBO almost always refers to a comprehensive organization-wide program for setting goals, one usually reserved for managerial and professional employees.

Investors Group Financial Services uses MBO to motivate its sales force in selling financial services. The MBO process begins when the vice-president of sales develops general goals for the entire sales force. This sets the stage for Planning Week, which is held annually at regional centres across Canada. During Planning Week, sales representatives review their past accomplishments and set financial goals for the coming year.[27]

In most companies, the MBO process consists of five steps:

1. *Set organization's goals.* Top management sets strategic goals for the company.

2. *Set departments' goals.* Department heads and their superiors jointly set supporting goals for their departments.

3. *Discuss departments' goals.* Department heads present departments' goals and ask all subordinates to develop their own individual goals.

4. *Set individual goals.* Goals are set for each subordinate, and a timetable is assigned for accomplishing those goals.

5. *Give feedback.* The supervisor and subordinate meet periodically to review the subordinate's performance and to monitor and analyze progress towards his or her goals.[28]

Managers can do several things to make an MBO program more successful. They can state the goals in measurable terms, be specific, and make sure each person's goals are challenging but attainable. Most experts also agree that goals should be reviewed and updated periodically, and that the goals should be flexible enough to be changed if conditions warrant.[29]

Again, however, an effective MBO program requires more than just setting goals. The main purpose is to integrate the goals of the individual, of the unit in which the individual works, and of the company as a whole. In fact, to Peter Drucker, the creator of MBO, the method was always more a philosophy then a rigid sequence of steps. As he said, "The goals of each manager's job must be defined by the contribution he or she has to make to the success of the larger unit of which they are part." His MBO technique therefore basically gives managers a road map for how to link the goals at each level and across the firm's departments, and thereby to create the company's hierarchy of goals.

Developing Planning Premises

Good plans—whether for a career, a trip to Europe, or an expansion by Wal-Mart into Europe—are built on **premises**, assumptions we make about the future. Managers use several techniques to produce the premises on which they build their plans. These include forecasting, marketing research, and competitive intelligence.

Sales Forecasting Techniques

IBM's strategy in the new century reflects the assumptions it made regarding what the demand for mainframe computers would be. **Forecasting** means to estimate or calculate in advance or to predict.[30] In business, forecasting often starts with predicting the direction and magnitude of the company's sales.

Errors in forecasting can cause major problems. In 1989 the Ontario Workers Compensation Board forecast that its unfunded liability (the difference between its assets and the future costs of worker compensation claims already on the books) would be reduced to zero by the year 2007. In 1993 the Board made a new prediction: The unfunded liability would be $50 billion by the year 2014! Ontario Hydro has also made some wildly inaccurate forecasts. In the 1960s it predicted that it would need 80 000 megawatts of capacity by 2000; the actual number was closer to 30 000 megawatts.[31]

There are two broad classes of sales forecasting methods: quantitative and qualitative. **Quantitative forecasting** methods use statistical methods to examine data and find underlying patterns and relationships. **Qualitative forecasting** methods emphasize human judgment.

Quantitative Forecasting Methods.
Quantitative methods like time-series methods and causal models forecast by assuming that past relationships will continue into the future. A **time series** is a set of observations taken at specific times, usually at equal intervals. Examples of time series are the yearly or monthly gross domestic product (GDP) of Canada over several years, a department store's total monthly sales receipts, and the daily closing prices of a share of stock.[32]

If you plot time-series data on a graph for several periods, you may note various patterns. For example, if you were to plot monthly sales of air conditioning units, you would find seasonal increases in late spring and summer and reduced sales in the winter months. For some types of time series, there may also be an irregular pattern, such as a sudden "blip" in the graph that reflects unexplained variations in the data. The basic purpose of all time-series forecasting methods is to remove irregular and seasonal patterns so that management can identify fundamental trends.

Managers often need to understand the causal relationship between two variables, such as their company's sales and an indicator of economic activity, such as disposable income. **Causal methods** develop a projection based on the mathematical relationship between a company factor and those variables that management believes influence or explain the company factor.[33] The basic premise of causal methods is that a particular factor—such as company sales of television sets—is directly influenced by some other, more predictable, factor or factors—such as the number of people unemployed in a province, or the level of disposable income in Canada.[34] **Causal forecasting** thus estimates the company factor (such as sales) based on other factors (such as advertising expenditures, or level of unemployment). Statistical techniques such as correlation analysis (which shows how closely the variables are related) are generally used to develop the necessary relationships.

Simulation involves developing a model of an actual situation and working through the simulation to see what kind of outcome results. The model may be a computer model, an algebraic formula, or a miniature physical model. A computer simulation is used by the Canadian Forces to train fighter pilots at Cold Lake, Alberta. The system simulates high-speed chases, gunfire, tracer shells, and changes in gravity as the pilot's "airplane" manoeuvres. The pilots must shoot down an aggressor aircraft before it fires on them.[35]

Companies like Wal-Mart use sophisticated technology to forecast sales; Wal-Mart's data warehouse is a good example of how Wal-Mart does this. The data warehouse collects information on point-of-sale, inventory, products in transit, and product returns from Wal-Mart's 3000 stores. These data are then analyzed to help Wal-Mart's managers analyze trends, understand customers, and more effectively manage inventory.

How is this information used? As one example, Wal-Mart is implementing a new demand-forecasting system. Its data warehousing tracks the sale of 100 000 Wal-Mart

---

forecasting
To estimate or calculate in advance or to predict.

quantitative forecasting
Using statistical methods to examine data and find underlying patterns and relationships.

qualitative forecasting
Forecasting methods that emphasize human judgment.

time series
A set of observations taken at specific times, usually at equal intervals.

causal method
Develops a projection based on the mathematical relationship between a company factor and those variables that management believes influence or explain the company factor.

causal forecasting
Estimates the company factor (such as sales) based on other factors (such as advertising expenditures, or level of unemployment).

simulation
Developing a model of an actual situation and working through the simulation to see what kind of outcome results.

products by store. This powerful system lets Wal-Mart managers examine the sales of individual items in individual stores, and also creates seasonal profiles for each item. Armed with this information, managers can more accurately plan what items will be needed for each store, and when.

Wal-Mart is also teaming with vendors like Warner-Lambert to create an Internet-based collaborative forecasting and replenishment (CFAR) system. Wal-Mart extracts data (on things like sales by product and by store, and seasonal trends) for its sales of Warner-Lambert products. Managers at Wal-Mart and Warner-Lambert then collaborate to develop forecasts of sales by store for Warner-Lambert products such as Listerine. Once Warner-Lambert and Wal-Mart planners decide on mutually acceptable figures, a purchase plan is finalized and sent to Warner-Lambert's manufacturing planning system. So far, CFAR has helped cut the supply cycle time for Listerine from 12 weeks to 6, and that means less inventory, lower costs, and better buys for Wal-Mart customers.[36]

Qualitative Forecasting Methods. Time series and causal forecasting have three big limitations. First, they are virtually useless when data are scarce, such as for a new product with no sales history. Second, they assume that historical trends will continue into the future.[37] Third, they tend to disregard unforeseeable, unexpected occurrences. Yet it is exactly these unexpected occurrences that often have the most profound effects on companies.

Qualitative forecasting techniques emphasize human judgment. They gather, in as logical, unbiased, and systematic a way as possible, all the information and human judgment that can be brought to bear on the factors being forecast.[38] (See Table 5.6 for some expert forecasts that didn't quite work out.)

The **jury of executive opinion** technique is one such qualitative technique. It involves asking a "jury" of key executives to forecast sales for, say, the next year. Generally, each executive is given data on forecasted economic levels and anticipated changes. Each jury member then makes an independent forecast. Differences are reconciled by the president or during a meeting of the executives. In an enhancement of this approach, experts from various departments gather to make the forecast.

The **sales force estimation** method is similar to the jury of executive opinion, but it gathers the opinions of the sales force regarding what they think sales will be in the forthcoming period. Each salesperson estimates his or her next year's sales, usually by product and customer. Sales managers then review each estimate, compare it to the previous year's data, and discuss changes with each salesperson. The separate estimates are then combined into a single sales forecast for the firm.

Warner-Lambert
**www.warner-lambert.
com**

jury of executive opinion
A qualitative forecasting technique that involves asking a "jury" of key executives to forecast sales for, say, the next year.

sales force estimation
A qualitative forecasting technique that gathers the opinions of the sales force regarding what they think sales will be in the forthcoming period.

TABLE 5.6 *Expert Predictions That Went Amiss*

1. "There is no reason for any individual to have a computer in their home." (Ken Olson, 1977, president of Digital Equipment Corporation, speaking at the convention of the World Future Society)

2. "Man will never reach the moon, regardless of all future advances." (Dr. Lee DeForest, inventor of the auditron tube, quoted in the *New York Times*, February 25, 1957; early in his career, DeForest had been told that the auditron tube was a scientific impossibility)

3. "The radio craze will die out in time." (Thomas Edison, 1922)

4. "I cannot imagine any condition which would cause a ship to founder. Modern ship-building has gone beyond that." (Captain Edward J. Smith, 1906, future commander of the *Titanic*)

5. "Man will not fly for 50 years." (Wilbur Wright, to his brother Orville, in 1901)

6. "The horseless carriage is at present a luxury for the wealthy, and although its price will probably fall in the future, it will never, of course, come into as common use as the bicycle." (*Literary Digest*, October 14, 1899)

7. "Well-informed people know it is impossible to transmit the voice over wires and that were it possible to do so, the thing would be of no practical value." (Editorial in the *Boston Globe*, 1865, commenting on the arrest of Joshua Coopersmith for fraud as he attempted to raise funds for work on a telephone)

Marketing Research

Tools like causal models and scenario planning can help managers explore the future to develop more accurate planning premises. However, there are times when, to formulate plans, managers want to know not just what may happen in the future, but what their customers are thinking right now. **Marketing research** refers to the procedures used to develop and analyze new customer-related information that helps managers make decisions.[39]

Harlequin Enterprises Ltd., which started in Winnipeg in 1949, is now the leading company in the romance novels industry. When deciding whether to enter a foreign country, Harlequin does market research to determine whether a distribution system is in place, whether there is access to TV and print media (so that demand can be stimulated through advertising), and whether the company will be able to convert local currency into Canadian dollars.[40]

Marketing researchers depend on two main types of information, as summarized in Figure 5.4 on page 148. One source is **secondary data**, information that has been collected

marketing research
The procedures used to develop and analyze new customer-related information that helps managers make decisions.

Harlequin Enterprises
www.eharlequin.com

secondary data
Information that has been collected or published already.

Scenario Planning

Some companies, such as Shell Oil, must make major investments, although the firm's future may be very unpredictable. One way to manage change under such conditions is to make projections based on scenario planning. Scenarios have been defined as

> hypothetical sequences of events constructed for the purpose of focusing attention on causal processes and decision points. They answer two kinds of questions: (1) precisely how might some hypothetical situation come about, step by step, and (2) what alternatives exist, for each situation at each step, for preventing, diverting, or facilitating the process?[41]

Shell Oil Company is one firm that uses scenario planning. As one of its officers has said, "the Shell approach to strategic planning is, instead of forecasting, to use scenarios, which are 'stories' about alternative possible futures. These stories promote a discussion of possibilities other than the 'most likely' one, and encourage the consideration of 'what-if' questions."[42]

In developing its current scenarios, Shell looked at "the world...in terms of geopolitical change, international economics, and the environment." It saw such things as international economic tensions (as symbolized by some increase in trade tariffs) and increasing pollution concerns. Out of its analysis came two scenarios: "global mercantilism" and "sustainable world."

global mercantilism
A scenario in which regional conflicts and frustration with international failures lead to more government intervention in managing international trade.

sustainable world
A scenario in which international economic frictions are resolved and economic trade flows freely.

These two scenarios are summarized in Figure 5.3. In **global mercantilism**, the new post–cold war "international order proves to be too weak to withstand serious political and economic shocks and setbacks." As a result, regional conflicts and frustration with similar international failures lead to more government intervention in managing international trade. For a company like Shell (whose crude oil is a key traded commodity), this managed system could lead to "intermittent overcapacity and undercapacity and a price 'roller coaster.'" In the **sustainable world** scenario, international economic frictions are resolved and economic trade flows freely. But here, concern about environmental problems leads to tightened emissions regulation and higher quality standards for energy products. In either case, scenario planning provides Shell managers with a better basis for managing change, by letting them view various futures and the consequences these futures might have for the firm and its products.

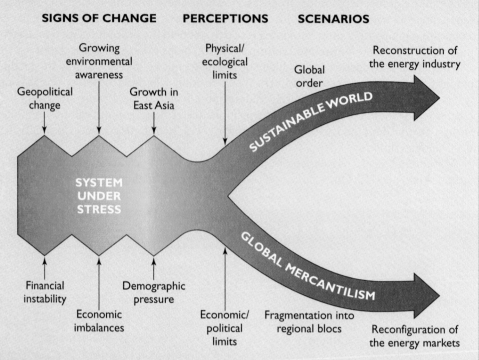

FIGURE 5.3
Scenarios Used by Royal Dutch Shell
Scenario planning involves looking at the events of the world and creating likely scenarios (such as "sustainable world" and "global mercantilism") along with the implications each of these scenarios would have for the company.

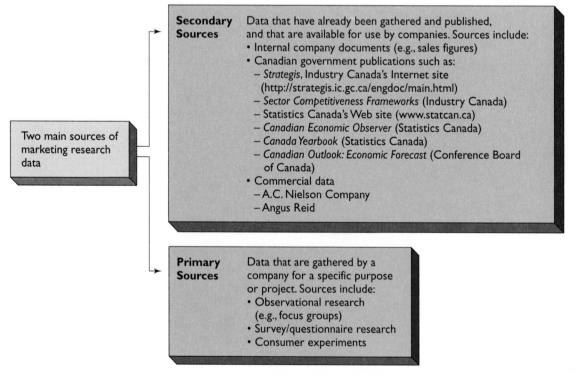

FIGURE 5.4
Sources of Secondary and Primary Data

or published already. Good sources of secondary data include libraries, trade associations, and company files and sales reports. **Primary data** refer to information specifically collected to solve a current problem. Primary data sources include mail and personal surveys, in-depth and focus-group interviews, and personal observations (like watching the reactions of customers who walk into a store).[43]

primary data
Information specifically collected to solve a current problem.

Competitive Intelligence

Developing useful plans requires knowing as much as possible about what competitors are doing or are planning to do. **Competitive intelligence** is a systematic way to obtain and analyze public information about competitors. Although "competitive intelligence" sounds (and is) a lot like legalized spying, it's become much more popular over the past few years. According to one report, the number of large companies with competitive intelligence groups has tripled since 1988 to about 10 percent.[44]

competitive intelligence
A systematic way to obtain and analyze public information about competitors.

Competitive intelligence (CI) practitioners use a variety of techniques to find out what their clients' competitors are doing. These include keeping track of existing and new competitors by having specialists visit their facilities, hiring their workers, and questioning their suppliers and customers. CI firms also do sophisticated Internet searches to dig up all available Internet-based information about competitors, as well as more mundane searches like reading stock analysts' reports on the competitors' prospects.

As illustrated in Table 5.7, CI consultants provide a range of information. For example, this particular firm can help client companies learn more about competitors' strengths and vulnerabilities, product strategies, investment strategies, financial capabilities, and current or prior behaviour. Other CI services include evaluating the capabilities, weaknesses, and reputation of potential or existing joint venture partners; identifying the major players in a new market or industry that the firm is thinking of entering; and helping planners boost sales opportunities, for instance by identifying the decision-makers who actually do the purchasing and the critical factors they look for in vendors.

Managers using competitive intelligence must beware of slipping into activities that are ethically, morally, or legally wrong. Reading brokers' analytical reports on a com-

Focus groups, in which a moderator leads a group of typical customers in a discussion or trial of the firm's products, are a good source of primary marketing research information. Sometimes, as here, special rooms equipped with one-way observation windows allow executives to monitor the process.

TABLE 5.7 *Competitive Intelligence: Kroll's Business Intelligence and Analysis Services and Capabilities*

CI CAN ADDRESS FOUR CRITICAL MANAGEMENT CONCERNS	BY PROVIDING INTELLIGENCE LIKE THIS ON COMPANIES, INDUSTRIES, AND COUNTRIES
Competition: Learning enough about competitors to devise proactive and reactive strategies, including competitors' strengths and vulnerabilities, product strategies, investment strategies, financial capabilities, operational issues, and anti-competitive behaviour.	**Operations:** Nature of business, sales, locations, head count. **Financial:** Ownership, assets, financing, profitability.
Business Relationships and Transactions: Evaluating the capabilities, weaknesses, and reputation of potential or existing joint venture partners, strategic alliances, acquisitions, distributors, licensees/licensors, critical suppliers/vendors, and project finance participants.	**Management:** Organizational structure, decision-makers, integrity/reputation, management style, history as partner, political connections. **Marketing/Customers:** Market position, major accounts, pricing, distribution, sales force, advertising.
Entry into New Markets: Developing entry strategies into new geographic and/or product markets, including identifying players in an industry, analyzing industry structure and trends, assessing local business practices, ascertaining entry barriers, government regulations, and political risk.	**Manufacturing:** Plant and equipment, capacity, use, sourcing materials/components, shifts, labour costs, unions. **Technology:** New products and processes, R&D practices, technological assessment.
Sales Opportunities: Maximizing opportunities to win contracts, develop major new customers, or maintain existing ones, including identifying purchasing decision-makers and critical factors, determining current suppliers, understanding the competition, and assessing the status of bids.	**Strategic Directions:** Line of business priorities, diversification, geographic strategy, horizontal/vertical integration, strategic relationships. **Legal:** Lawsuits, judgments, potential liabilities, environmental exposure.

petitor or finding information about it on the Internet would probably be viewed as legitimate by almost everyone. However, when CI practitioners dig through the target's trash on public property to search for planning memos, or hire former employees to pick their brains, ethical alarms start ringing.

Planners in Action

So far in this chapter we've explained the planning process, and some techniques for setting goals and for predicting the future. In this final section we turn to a discussion of how planners actually plan; in other words, to illustrations of planners and planning departments in action.

Who Does the Planning?

The answer to this question depends a lot on the size of the firm. The basic process—set goals, develop background information such as forecasts, develop and evaluate alternatives, and finalize the plan—is pretty standard. However, in a small business the entrepreneur will likely do most of the planning him- or herself, perhaps informally bouncing around ideas with a few employees (see The Entrepreneurial Edge box). In larger firms, there's usually a central corporate planning group (some call it corporate central) whose role is to work with top management and each division to continually challenge and refine the company's plans.

Over the past few years, most large companies have made dramatic changes in the way they do their planning. For example, most large companies have moved from centralized

Planning Under the Gun

When Gary Steele joined Internet start-up Netiva, the company looked like a sure bet. It had big-name venture-capital backers, and a product, the Netiva Internet application system, that let larger companies build databases in Java programming language.

Steele soon discovered, though, that most of the company's plans were based on erroneous assumptions. Its software was designed for the customer to run and maintain, but that meant that Netiva's technical people had to get deeply involved up front in selling the software, and the deals were taking too long to complete. The original business plan also assumed that customers would develop multiple applications based on Netiva's software (and thereby have to pay multiple licence fees); that wasn't happening, so Netiva was doing a lot of work for a one-time licence fee of $25 000.

Steele quickly concluded that the company was doomed unless drastic measures were taken. He laid off 40 percent of the employees the next week. Then, working mostly on his own, Steele produced an eight-point plan of action, laying out what the company had to do in the following six weeks. Several weeks later he and four members of his executive team held 75 fact-finding meetings with executives at medium- and large-sized firms to get the information they required about what customers wanted, and thus what Netiva's plans should be. ServicePort was one new product to come out of these meetings. It is basically a Web portal for consulting firms to enable their employees (who are often out of town) to conveniently plug into their company's databases and share things like client reports.

Portera
www.portera.com

Now called Portera, the company is back up to 70 employees, and Steele has raised another chunk of cash, thanks in large part to his ability to pretty much single-handedly develop his company's new plan.[45]

to decentralized planning.[46] The people doing the actual planning are generally not specialists housed in large, centralized planning departments at headquarters. Instead, the actual planning is carried out by product and divisional managers, often aided by small advisory groups at headquarters. Pushing planning down from centralized planning departments to product managers reflects the fact that the latter are usually in the best position to sense changes in customer, competitive, and technological trends and react to them.

What Planners Do

Most large companies still have small central planning departments, and these planners still play a crucial role in those organizations. For example, the corporate-central planning departments of multinational firms like GE engage in several basic planning activities.[47]

- *Act as "information central."* They compile and monitor all planning-related data such as on divisions' progress towards meeting planned financial targets, and competitor intelligence.
- *Conduct competitor and market research.* They help the divisions analyze global competition; for instance, by identifying major global competitors.
- *Develop forecasts.* They develop forecasts that are applicable company-wide.
- *Provide consulting services.* They help divisions conduct industry analyses and provide divisional planners with training in the techniques they could or should be using.

- *Create a common language.* They devise corporate-wide planning reports and forms, so that the divisions' plans are comparable in terms of the information they provide.
- *Communicate company-wide objectives.* They communicate company-wide objectives to divisional managers. The latter then formulate plans for achieving their assigned objectives.

Planning in Action

The idea that planning is done by lower-level managers rather than a planning department is in fact somewhat misleading, since the actual process in larger firms involves much give and take. Based on input from product and divisional managers and other sources, top management sets an overall strategic direction for the firm. The resulting objectives then become the targets for which the product and divisional managers formulate specific tactical and operational plans. Strategic planning and direction setting are still mostly done by top managers, usually with the planning unit's assistance. However, more of the premising, alternatives-generating, and product-planning input goes up the hierarchy than in previous years.

General Electric's recent planning activities provide a "big company" example. In 1998–99, three themes guided organization-wide planning at GE: globalization, product-services, and "six-sigma quality" (what GE calls its quality improvement–cost minimization process.)

These basic themes or "growth initiatives" provided the guidelines for the top managers of GE's various divisions (such as Aerospace, GE Capital, and NBC). For example, with Asia in economic crisis in 1998, several of GE's divisions moved quickly to take advantage of extraordinary global opportunities in Japan. GE's Edison Life quickly became a force in the Japanese insurance industry, acquiring over $6 billion of Japanese insurance assets. Company-wide, GE also wants to move to providing more high-value, information technology–based productivity services. Several GE divisions have therefore invested hundreds of millions of dollars to allow them to provide services to upgrade the competitiveness and profitability of customers as wide-ranging as utilities, hospitals, railroads, and airlines. Finally, the first of GE's six-sigma-guided products are now coming to market from various GE divisions. One, the LightSpeed scanner, dramatically reduces (from 3 minutes to 17 seconds) the time a trauma patient must spend being scanned to diagnose an illness such as a pulmonary embolism.[48]

Planning in action, in other words, is really an interplay between headquarters and divisions, particularly in large, multi-business firms. In a typical company, top management and the board might formulate a few guiding themes at the start of the year. The divisions might then complete reviews of their businesses in April, and forward these to corporate planning. In June the board adopts a set of planning assumptions and guidelines prepared by the corporate planning department. At the same time, central planning might be preparing various financial forecasts, again based in part on projections from the divisions.

In July, the board reviews and sets the firm's financial objectives, and in early August these goals are sent to each business unit. The units then use these financial targets (as well as other guidelines, like GE's three growth initiatives) to prepare their own plans. These are submitted for approval in January. Once adopted, the plans are monitored by central planning, perhaps via quarterly reports from the operating units. Once their broad divisional plans are approved, the divisions and their departments develop shorter-term tactical plans.

There's No "One Best Way"

Planning can sometimes be more trouble than it's worth. Even with something as simple as a trip to Paris, for instance, blind devotion to a plan could cause you to miss a great opportunity that pops up at the last minute. In a company, such inflexibility can be even more dangerous: For example, department stores like The Bay would be foolish to ig-

The Bay
www.hbc.com

nore the possibility of Internet catalogue sales just because the word "Internet" didn't appear in their long-term plans two or three years ago.

A recent *Harvard Business Review* article explains some other ways that misguided planning can destroy a company's value. An extensive and time-consuming planning process can be a waste of time and money unless top management and its planning group can coax divisional managers to do things differently than they would have done on their own. Yet, "...at many companies, business unit plans get through the process largely unscathed." The result is that a lot of time and money has been spent, for very little gain. The opposite is also true: If they're not careful, top managers and central planning may insist on counterproductive changes in the division managers' plans. Top managers, after all, can spend only a fraction of their time understanding the details of each of the many separate businesses of the company, so "the potential for misguided advice is high, especially in diversified companies."[49]

Problems like these don't have to happen. One way to avoid them, says one expert, is to remember that a planning process that works for one company won't necessarily work for another. A good planning process, he contends, "...is not a generic process but one in which both analytic techniques and organizational processes are carefully tailored to the needs of the businesses as well as to skills, insight, and experiences of senior corporate managers. A mature electrical-products business, for example, has different planning needs than a fast growing entertainment business or a highly cyclical chemicals business."[50]

What this means is that a company must develop a planning process that's right for it. Most important is to think through what it wants its planning process to achieve. The planning process at Granada, a British conglomerate that has businesses in television programming and broadcasting, hotels, catering, and appliances, emphasizes *not* relying on comparing or "benchmarking" its financial results to the industry. When you do that, "you lock yourself into low ambitions" the CEO says.[51] Granada's planning process is therefore built around challenging business managers to find ways to achieve huge leaps in their divisions' sales and profitability. "Planning is about raising ambitions and helping businesses get more creative in their search for ways to increase profits."[52]

On the other hand, Dow Chemical Corporation's planning process is aimed at finding small, incremental improvements in processing costs—such as a 2 percent saving in maintenance costs—because in the slow-growing chemicals industry costs are what is important. The whole planning process at Dow is therefore much more formal, analytical, comparative, and numbers-oriented. The point, says one planning expert, is that managers must define what they want to achieve from their planning before establishing a planning process.

Granada Group
www.granada.co.uk

Dow Chemical
www.dow.com

If a planning team is separated by distance, videoconferencing can offer an effective way to communicate and thereby build cohesiveness.

1. **Define planning and describe the different types of plans companies use**. Plans are methods formulated beforehand for achieving desired results. Planning is the process of establishing objectives and courses of action prior to taking action. Plans differ in terms of their format, time horizon, and frequency of use.

2. **Explain the five steps in the planning process.** The five steps are (1) set organizational objectives, (2) identify the gap between desired and actual positions, (3) develop plans to achieve the objectives, (4) implement the plans, and (5) evaluate the effectiveness of planning.

3. **Recognize effective goals.** To be effective, goals must be specific, measurable, time-framed, and challenging. Whenever possible, managers should allow employees to participate in setting the goals that affect them.

4. **Explain three techniques for developing the premises upon which plans are built.** The three techniques are forecasting, marketing research, and competitive intelligence. Within *forecasting*, there are quantitative forecasting methods—which use statistical methods to examine data and find underlying patterns and relationships—and qualitative forecasting methods—which emphasize human judgment. *Marketing research* refers to the procedures used to develop and analyze customer-related information that helps managers make decisions. *Competitive intelligence* is a systematic way to obtain and analyze public information about competitors.

TYING IT ALL TOGETHER

We saw in this chapter that planning and decision making are closely intertwined. Planning means choosing your objectives and the courses of action that will get you there, and doing this ahead of time. So a plan is actually a set of prior decisions.

This chapter focused on the overall planning process and goals, and on the hierarchical nature of corporate planning. We saw that all companies' plans tend to revolve around and service top management's longer-term strategic plan. Setting strategy—deciding what businesses the company will be in and how it will compete—is a primary management function, one that we discuss in more detail in the next chapter.

CRITICAL THINKING EXERCISES

1. Consider an ancient country with a long tradition of religious philosophy, an ethic of hard work, and strong warrior instincts. Imagine this country, one with over 1.2 billion consumers, emerging into the world marketplace almost overnight. Many of its citizens have a per capita income of only $500, but economists estimate that as many as 200 million middle-class consumers have disposable income to spend on a variety of products. There are believed to be at least 1 million millionaires in this socialistic-capitalistic country. Many people are concerned with the civil and intellectual rights of the people of this country, which has imposed government sanctions on demonstrators and has a history of human-rights violations.

   The country, of course, is the world's largest: China. There is great potential and opportunity for business here, but there are also threats. Using the concepts presented in the chapter, explain how you would go about developing a plan for doing business in China for the next five years. (Assume that you are a manager in a consumer products company, and that your firm sells low-priced goods such as candy.)

2. The Internet is increasingly a part of our lives. We can bank with it; shop for groceries, cars, and homes; go to college or university; be our own travel agents; research topics; talk with others in chat rooms; etc. The long-term implications of the Internet are amazing, as it can provide a much more flexible and convenient lifestyle for many people. But there are potential downsides, too. What happens to all of the jobs that are displaced by technology? For example, many of us have not been inside a bank for years because we use ATMs. And now we can bank over the Internet from home. We can pay our bills, and can shop and have goods delivered. Critical questions arise for companies, individuals, and society in terms of planning and setting objectives. What will happen to displaced workers? Describe how the Internet will affect the planning process of business firms.

EXPERIENTIAL EXERCISES

1. One chronic complaint of employers about prospective employees, especially those just out of college or university with limited work experience, is that they don't have well-honed presentation skills. A recent issue of *Fast Company* outlines an eight-point program for presentations guaranteed to keep listeners on the edge of their seats:[53]

   - Incite, don't inform. Effective presentations don't end with nodding heads and polite applause. They end with *action*.
   - Don't talk to strangers. Know your audience by doing research prior to the presentation.
   - First (and last) impressions are everything. The two most important parts of your presentation are the first 30 seconds and the last 15 seconds.
   - Simpler is better. Make your presentations shorter and more candid.
   - Perform, don't present. The impact of a typical presentation is 55 percent visual (how you look), 38 percent vocal (how you talk), and only 7 percent verbal (what you say). In other words, you don't deliver presentations, you *perform* them.
   - The show must go on. Concentrate on the performance factor.
   - There's one in every crowd—that is, a hostile member you must handle. The first rule is to disagree without being disagreeable, and don't pick a fight.
   - Practice, practice, practice.

   Select a topic from this chapter and prepare a five-minute presentation following the rules outlined here. Be ready to give your presentation to your class.[54]

2. As noted in the chapter, we plan all day long without really knowing we are doing it. So, for the next three days, keep track of your planning. On the first day, write down what, how, when, and where you accomplished the goals you had informally set out for the day. That night write out what goals you wish to accomplish the next day. At the end of the second day, write down what happened. Now write out what goals you wish to accomplish and a specific, hour-by-hour plan to accomplish those goals. At the end of the day, see how you have done on each of the three days and what you have learned about how you do or do not plan, and how planning can help you manage your time better. If you already plan your time, try not planning so carefully and see what happens. What new things did you learn about yourself?

INTERNET EXERCISE

To find out more about planning and organization in a large company, visit the world and Canadian sites for Kodak at www.kodak.com and www.kodak.ca, respectively.

1. What is the CEO's role in the corporate structure as described in the Web site?

2. What are some of the company's major goals as communicated in Web site press releases and other information? Which goals are long term? Which are short term?

3. Based on your explorations of the Web sites, what value does the company place on research and development? Explain.

Cin-Made, Inc.

The main thing Bob Frey learned during his career at a big consumer-products company was that he hated bureaucracy. So when he bought Cin-Made, a paper and cardboard package manufacturing company, he decided that he would shun formal training and keep track of everything in his head.

That turned out to be a mistake. For the next three years Cin-Made careened through the market from product to product while profit margins shrank. It finally dawned on Frey that he needed a business plan.

He began by analyzing the packaging market and where his company might fit into it. In doing so, he discovered that Cin-Made was one of many firms making a standard commodity that was subject to cutthroat pricing from the lowest-cost producers. He also discovered a big change in one of his prime packaging markets that made him think he could set his company apart.

Specifically, when motor oil cans went from paper to plastic containers, Frey decided to make the investment required to convert to manufacturing plastic chemical canisters. Since customers for such canisters wanted custom features, they usually didn't quibble about price as long as Frey could deliver the goods. He decided to refocus his company's mission on providing specialty packaging needs that his non-custom competitors couldn't provide. With the growing success of his new strategy, it became easier for Frey to make the decisions that had to be made. For instance, he eventually decided to permit bales of standard packages to diminish so he could concentrate on custom products and use his new custom-built machinery.

Other decisions followed from Frey's new focus on custom packaging. For example, "To properly exploit our premium niche strategy, we have to plow more into R&D," Frey says. "That yields products with higher price tags to reflect our larger investment in custom-built machines."

Not surprisingly, Cin-Made's operations are now directed by very specific business-planning summaries that Frey creates. These one-page synopses circulate from the shop floor to the boardroom. While each plan covers targets up to five years out, the plans are updated at least monthly, and sometimes more often.

Frey's plans reflect the sort of step-by-step approach that's usually required to achieve objectives over time. For example, Cin-Made is committed to premium pricing, in keeping with its emphasis on custom products, so it won't be drawn into a pricing war for its high-end products. Because the firm spent a lot of money on non-custom packaging equipment before Frey adopted his custom-niche strategy, Frey still has a plan to compete for high-volume, traditional packaging business. His aim is to recoup his investment until Cin-Made's newer custom products carve out enough of a market to carry the firm.

Cin-Made's new strategy and planning have paid off. Pre-tax profit margins have increased fivefold. Even better, new products may double the company's revenues. And today Frey seems to enjoy the new discipline that comes with being a planner instead of a manager who tries to keep all of his ideas in his head.

Questions

1. In what ways does Bob Frey's planning approach differ from the more formal five-step process outlined in this chapter?

2. Based on what you know about Cin-Made, create several objectives using the Morrisey model discussed in this chapter (see page 143).

3. Overall, what do you think of Frey's planning method? Do you think it could be improved using any of the methods discussed in this chapter? How?

High Spirits

Karl Kaiser is the co-owner and wine maker at Inniskillin Wines Inc. at Niagara-on-the-Lake. As he looks out over the vineyards, he notes that last summer was not a good one, with unseasonably cool weather, too much rain, and two hailstorms that devastated about 60 percent of the grapes. Kaiser says it's difficult to watch one hailstorm wipe out all your hard work. But he notes that the year before, the weather was great, and the company had its best harvest ever.

The weather is difficult to control, but there are other things the company can do something about. Donald Ziraldo, the firm's president, recently announced a merger with Cartier Wines & Beverages, Canada's second largest wine producer. The merger will give Inniskillin access to Cartier's network of 47 retail stores. And Karl Kaiser has just purchased two additional grape presses and three fermenters in Europe to increase production of the firm's well-known ice wine. It was an ice wine from Inniskillin that won one of the 19 Grands Prix d'Honneur at the 1989 VinExpo in Bordeaux, France, and put Canadian ice wine on the map. Inniskillin's president said it was like winning an Academy Award.

Positive news like this is something of a surprise. Just a few years ago, there was much doom and gloom in the industry because of the Canada–U.S. Free Trade Agreement. When the FTA first took effect in 1989, the price differentials between Canadian and foreign wines were eliminated. It was thought that this might destroy the Canadian industry. Indeed, the market share of Canadian firms did decline, vineyard hectarage was reduced, and some vintners closed their doors. But the increased competition forced the remaining firms to increase product quality and, in so doing, find new markets for Canadian wine.

The quality improvement has occurred because *vitis labrusca*, the native North American grapevine, has been banned from table wines. It has been replaced with *vitis vinifera*, a higher-quality and more delicate stock. While Canadian wineries can get up to $1200 per tonne for *vinifera*, and only $200 per tonne for *labrusca*, replanting all the vineyards is an expensive and time-consuming process. It takes five years to get a new *vinifera* crop into production, and five to seven more years to recover initial investment costs. Bad weather along the way can extend the time even further.

Other uncertainties continue to create problems for the Canadian wine industry. For one thing, the 42 percent market share within Canada now held by Canadian companies is a far cry from the 75 percent share they held in their heyday in the 1960s. For another, the quota program in B.C. that ensures that wineries will purchase the entire grape crop from provincial growers was phased out in 1995. Buyers are now able to purchase wine juice from foreign producers if they wish. And consumers are still not convinced that Canadian wine has the quality that French or California wines do.

Questions

1. How is the planning process in the wine industry similar to that in an industrial firm?

2. What kinds of contingency plans are necessary in the wine business?

3. In what areas of the wine business should plans be made, and over what time frames should the plans extend?

Inniskillin Wines Inc.
**www.inniskillin.com/
default.html**

To Plan or Not to Plan, That Is the Question

You don't raise $5 million and run a successful, growing business for more than 10 years unless you know where you're going. But when it comes to making detailed business plans, KnitMedia and its managers still have some doubts. For example, when asked if the company does much planning, Michael Dorf replies, "Sure, we actually are, you know, starting to use, well, budgets—I can't even say it because it's so hard for me to adhere to them, but, you know, we are using budgets to some extent. [In fact] every so often, I put together the business plan and I talk with every team member and try and consolidate all our ideas and our plans. [However] it's difficult to be very fast-moving, especially at Internet speeds, if everything has to be constricted to a pure schedule and plan."

In fact, Dorf's dilemma is often the dilemma that all start-ups (and especially technology-oriented start-ups) face every day. As he says, KnitMedia's managers have to adapt very quickly to stay ahead of the competition, and it's not easy to do that if every step was decided several months or years ago.

Alan Fried, KnitMedia's chief operating officer, makes much the same point. As he says, "I mean, we are very much a media company and as some of the clichés around go, Internet years happen much quicker than calendar years. And if you have to move so fast, you have to move fast because if you're thinking of it, somebody else's thinking of it and first player advantage means a lot. So, sometimes we don't have the good fortune to just sort of sit down and plan everything. [What we do, though] is have an idea, and we have some meetings about it and we just move where I think we have to." That way, the company is always moving in the new direction even though it doesn't have a rigid, predetermined plan.

The problem is that Dorf and his team are not entirely convinced that this more or less seat-of-the-pants approach to planning is necessarily the best, although it's certainly worked so far. Furthermore, as more people invest money in the business, it's become increasingly important to develop formal plans so others will know where you're planning on going. The management team has approached you to help it formalize KnitMedia's planning process.

Team Exercises and Questions

Use what you learned in this chapter to answer the following questions from Michael Dorf and his management team:

1. At a bare minimum, what sorts of plans do you think we should develop and use at KnitMedia? Why?

2. Our immediate task is opening the Berlin club. Can you provide us with an outline of an executive assignment action plan that we can use to guide us in opening that location?

3. You already know something about how we are organized here at KnitMedia; for instance, you know that Michael Dorf is CEO, and that we have basically four divisions—Knitting Factory clubs, music labels, festivals, and Internet KnitMedia. What specific types of objectives do you think Dorf should be assigning to each of his top managers?

4. Is it possible for us to assign specific goals even though we don't have a formal planning process? If so, how can we do that? Would it be a good idea for us to set goals without a formal planning process? Why or why not?

Strategic Management

Planning and Strategy at Seagram

On June 20, 2000 the French conglomerate Vivendi SA purchased Montreal-based Seagram Co. for approximately $33 billion in stock. Seagram had been one of Canada's largest companies, with over 30 000 employees and annual sales of over $12 billion. The company was started in the 1920s by Sam Bronfman, who sold liquor by mail order. His son, Edgar Bronfman, Sr., became CEO in 1957. Until the early 1990s, the company's activities were focused largely on the production of wine, distilled spirits, and orange juice. But in the mid-1990s, the company, now led by Edgar Bronfman, Jr., began making some dramatic strategic moves. These moves turned the company away from its traditional products and moved it towards the high-risk entertainment business.

The move into entertainment occurred partly because Edgar Bronfman has both an artistic and a business temperament. He is friends with some well-known show-business types, including Michael Douglas, and he has long had a fascination with Hollywood. Bronfman is well aware that more than a few third-generation heirs have dissipated family fortunes, and he was determined that he would not make those mistakes. But he has also refused to simply make cautious investments; rather, he embarked on a strategy to make Seagram a stronger company.

Some of his decisions startled company observers. For example, he paid more than $2 billion for 15 percent of Time Warner in 1993, leading some to think that he might try a hostile takeover of that company. But he then unexpectedly sold those shares a short time later. He also sold a large block of DuPont shares that Seagram had held for many years. In 1995, he bought MCA Inc. (now Universal) for $5.7 billion.

In 1997, Seagram decided to embark on an ambitious plan to process orange juice in China through its Tropicana Beverages Group. The plan was to form a joint venture with a Chinese organization to finance and build an orange juice processing plant. Seagram was also to build a technology centre and seedling nursery, and was to provide technical assistance to farmers who wanted to raise orange trees. But in 1998, Seagram indicated that it might sell shares in Tropicana as an initial public offering (IPO) that would help raise funds to pay for its Polygram acquisition. Market analysts thought that the IPO

Seagram
www.seagram.com

Polygram
www.umusic.com

would raise between $3.5 and $4 billion. Seagram announced a few months later that it was simply selling Tropicana to PepsiCo Inc. for $3.3 billion in cash. The deal allowed PepsiCo to compete head-on with Coca-Cola (which owns the Minute Maid orange juice brand).

In 1998, Bronfman took a giant step into the world of entertainment with the $10.6 billion acquisition of Polygram NV, a company whose artists are as diverse as the Three Tenors, Elton John, and U2. With the acquisition of Polygram, Seagram instantly became the world's largest music company. The company thought that Polygram's international music operations would fit perfectly with Universal's music business, which is strongest in North America. Seagram continued to focus on the entertainment industry, with the development of theme parks in the U.S., Japan, Spain, and China.

But were all these strategic changes a good idea? Industry observes note, for example, that the DuPont stock that Bronfman sold for $8.8 billion in 1995 would have been worth $20 billion in 1998 if the dividends had been reinvested. And critics of the Tropicana decision say that Seagram waved goodbye to a steady source of income and traded it for the uncertain revenue of the music business. In 1999, Bronfman countered the criticisms by noting that Seagram's stock was at its highest level in a year, and that an investment in Seagram made at the same time he sold off his DuPont stock was worth more than an investment made in DuPont.

The sale of the company to Vivendi is financial vindication for Edgar Jr. Vivendi handed over stock worth about $75 a Seagram share, which was well above the high $40s that Seagram stock was trading for just prior to the sale. But one of Canada's largest and most famous companies has suddenly disappeared.

OBJECTIVES

After studying this chapter, you should be able to

1. Describe the five steps in the strategic management process.

2. Describe the three steps needed to create strategic plans.

3. Identify four strategic planning tools.

4. Explain the three main types of strategies.

5. Understand the important factors in strategy implementation.

Planning, as we saw in Chapter 5, means setting objectives and deciding on the courses of action for achieving them. We saw that plans are usually hierarchical; the firm's long-term strategic plan provides the framework within which its other plans must fit. So, if you define your occupational strategy as "management consultant," you will make short-term plans (for example, about which school to attend and which courses to take) that are vastly different than they would be if your strategy is to become a dentist. In business management, too, says management guru Peter Drucker, top management's primary task is

> thinking through the mission of the business, that is, of asking the question "What is our business and what should it be?" This leads to the setting of objectives, the development of strategies and plans, and the making of today's decisions for tomorrow's results.[1]

In this chapter, we therefore turn to strategic planning. Planning and strategic planning have much in common. Both involve assessing the situation today and predicting the future. Both involve setting objectives. And both involve crafting courses of action to get you from where you are today to where you want to be tomorrow. But we'll see in this chapter that strategic planning is also in a class of its own because a successful strategy is rarely ever created simply because an organization carried out a sound planning process.

Why? Because, unlike shorter-term plans (such as choosing your next term's courses), strategic planning (such as deciding what occupation is best for you after you graduate) requires looking far ahead and using insight and creativity to make sense of a great many imponderables. For your personal strategic plan, these might include answering the questions "Will I be a good consultant?" "Will I enjoy that career?" and "Will there be enough jobs to make being a consultant worth my while?" As two experts put it, "Planning processes are not designed to accommodate the messy process of generating insights and modeling them into a winning strategy."[2] So, do not be misled into believing that strategic planning is simply a mechanical process. Insight and creativity always play a very big role.

The Strategic Management Process

How do firms know what strategy they should pursue to stay competitive?

Strategic management is the process of identifying and pursuing the organization's mission by aligning the organization's internal capabilities with the external demands of its environment.[3] As shown in Figure 6.1, the strategic management process consists of five tasks: defining the business and developing a vision and mission; translating the mission into specific goals; crafting a strategy to achieve the goals; implementing and executing the strategy; and evaluating performance, reviewing the situation, and making adjustments.

We'll look at each step in turn.

strategic management
The process of identifying and pursuing the organization's mission by aligning the organization's internal capabilities with the external demands of its environment.

THE FIVE STRATEGIC MANAGEMENT STEPS

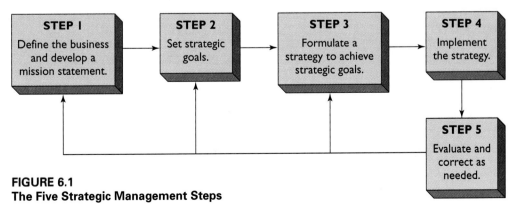

FIGURE 6.1
The Five Strategic Management Steps

Step 1: Define the Business and Develop a Mission Statement[4]

Two companies can be in the same industry but still answer the question "What is our business?" in different ways. For example, Ferrari and Toyota both make cars, but there the similarity ends. Ferrari specializes in high-performance cars, and its competitive advantage is built on handmade craftsmanship and high-speed performance. Toyota produces a wide range of automobiles, as well as many of its own supplies and parts; its competitive advantage is built on cost-efficient production and a strong worldwide dealer network.

The first step in strategic management is to define the business. It is not enough to say, "We make cars." Toyota and Ferrari both make cars, but their missions are quite different.

vision
A general statement of an organization's intended direction that evokes emotional feelings in organization members.

Similarly, Timex and Rolex both produce watches, but they do so in very different ways. Timex sells low-cost reliable watches in department stores, discount stores, and drugstores, while Rolex sells high-quality, high-priced fashion watches only in selected jewellery stores.

Answering the question, "What business should we be in?" requires both a vision statement and a mission statement (although the two are often similar). The organization's **vision** is a "general statement of its intended direction that evokes emotional feelings in organization members."[5] As Warren Bennis and Bert Manus say:

> To choose a direction, a leader must first have developed a mental image of a possible and desirable future state for the organization. This image, which we call a vision, may be as vague as a dream or as precise as a goal or mission statement. The critical point is that a vision articulates a view of a realistic, credible, attractive future for the organization, a condition that is better in some important ways than what now exists.[6]

Carrier Canada is a leading supplier of residential and commercial heating and cooling equipment. The company is committed to the vision of being "the biggest and the best." This vision is realized by constantly reminding all stakeholders, especially employees, of Carrier's objectives and the need to perform better. Dr. Edwin Land, who invented the Polaroid camera, had a vision of a company built on providing instant photographs in self-contained cameras. Rupert Murdoch has a vision of an integrated global news-gathering, entertainment, and multimedia firm. Bill Gates had a vision of a software company serving the needs of the then-fledgling microcomputer industry.

The firm's **mission statement** operationalizes the top manager's vision. A mission statement "broadly outlines the organization's future course and serves to communicate 'who we are, what we do, and where we're headed.'"[7] Examples of mission statements are presented in Table 6.1.

mission statement
Broadly outlines an organization's future course and serves to communicate who the organization is, what it does, and where it's headed.

TABLE 6.1 *Examples of Mission Statements*

Bell Canada's mission is to be a world leader in helping communicate and manage information.

Transit Windsor is a company that provides public transportation for the City of Windsor and adjacent areas. Our mission is to continually improve public transportation services for the people of Windsor at a reasonable cost to both the customer and the taxpayer.

The business mission of **Atco Ltd.** is to achieve an international reputation for excellence by providing products and services to the energy and resource industries and to invest principally in energy-related assets in North America.

Noverco is a Quebec public company with a North American vocation. It was formed with the purpose of acquiring, financing, and managing large-scale companies, which will afford its shareholders solid guarantees for the future and excellent rates-of-return, in various activities principally related to the energy field.

The business mission of **Investors Group** is to satisfy clients in need of general and comprehensive financial planning. Through product development and a well-trained sales distribution organization, investors will assist in implementing financial plans and providing effective ongoing service.

Step 2: Set Strategic Goals

The next strategic management task is to translate top management's vision and mission into strategic goals. Strategic goals for a typical business firm usually include elements like growth in earnings per share, commitment to customers, achieving superior rates of return, having a strong balance sheet, and balancing the business by customer, product, and geography.

When new CEOs take over, they often state very explicit strategic goals. For example, when Anthony Comper became CEO of the Bank of Montreal in 1999, he indicated that he wanted the bank to achieve a return on equity (ROE) of 18 to 20 percent over the next four years. (The bank had only been achieving an ROE of about 15 percent.) To achieve this goal, he decided that the Bank of Montreal should focus its capital on lines of business that had a high profit margin, such as residential mortgages and small business loans, and get out of lines of business that made only a marginal return, like corporate lending.[8] When Wallace McCain took control of Maple Leaf Foods Inc., he set three strategic goals: to make Maple Leaf a bigger company through acquisitions, to build larger animal processing plants, and to cut labour costs.[9]

Step 3: Formulate a Strategy to Achieve the Strategic Goals

A **strategy** is a course of action that explains how the enterprise will move from the business it is in now to the business it wants to be in (as stated in its mission), given its op-

strategy
A course of action that explains how the enterprise will move from the business it is in now to the business it wants to be in (as stated in its mission), given its opportunities and threats and its internal strengths and weaknesses.

John Hunkin was chosen as the CEO of CIBC because he could effectively implement a strategy to improve the company's operations. The strategy places less emphasis on wholesale banking, and more on retail banking.

portunities and threats and its internal strengths and weaknesses. For example, Wal-Mart decided to pursue the strategic goal of moving *from* being a relatively small southern U.S.–based chain of retail discount stores *to* becoming the national leader in Canada and the U.S. in low cost and price. One of Wal-Mart's strategies was to reduce distribution costs and minimize inventory and delivery times through a satellite-based distribution system.

Step 4: Implement the Strategy

Strategy implementation means translating the strategy into actions and results. Doing so requires drawing on all of the functions in the management process, namely, planning, organizing, leading, and controlling. For instance, employees will have to be hired and motivated and budgets formulated so that progress towards strategic goals can be measured.

When CIBC needed a top executive who could effectively execute a strategy to improve its operations, it chose John Hunkin.[10] He was seen by some as a risk taker, but he is not reckless. Rather, he takes calculated risks. He decided to focus the activity of CIBC on wealth management and e-commerce. The overall strategy will be to have less emphasis on the wholesale side of banking (for example, brokerages) and more emphasis on the retail side (for example, branch banking).[11]

Step 5: Evaluate Performance and Correct as Needed

CIBC
www.cibc.com

strategic control
Assessing progress towards strategic goals and taking corrective action as needed.

Finally, **strategic control**—assessing progress towards strategic goals and taking corrective action as needed—keeps the company's strategy up-to-date. Strategic control should also ensure that all parts and members of the company are contributing in a useful way towards the strategy's implementation.

Managing strategy is thus an ongoing process. Competitors introduce new products, technological innovations make production processes obsolete, and societal trends reduce demands for some products or services while boosting demand for others. Managers must therefore be alert to opportunities and threats that might require modifying or totally redoing their strategies.

strategic planning
The process of identifying the business of the firm today and the business it wants for the future, and then identifying the course of action it will pursue, given its opportunities, threats, strengths, and weaknesses.

Strategic Planning

Strategic planning is part of the overall strategic management process that was described at the beginning of this chapter. It consists of the first three strategic management tasks illustrated in Figure 6.1: defining the business and developing a mission, translating the mission into strategic goals, and crafting a strategy or course of action to move the organization from where it is today to where it wants to be. **Strategic planning** is, therefore, the process of identifying the business of the firm today and the business it wants for the future, and then identifying the course of action it will pursue, given its opportunities, threats, strengths, and weaknesses.

Creating Strategic Plans

The Three-Stage Strategic Planning Process

Like any planning, strategic planning involves making decisions today about where you want to be tomorrow. Defining the problem correctly is therefore crucial. You need to ask: "What are the main issues our plan must address?" You would not, for instance, want to aim your new strategy at selling more supplies through office supply stores when the real problem is, "How can we sell more supplies on the Internet?"

Strategic planning therefore usually starts with *identifying the driving forces in a firm's environment*. As we'll see in a moment, these driving forces include the economic, demographic, technological, and competitive forces that shape a company's strategy. We'll review the tools you can use to identify and assess these forces, but it's important to avoid being too mechanical in your approach. You don't want to miss potentially important forces. Encouraging insight and creativity is therefore important.

Brainstorming (discussed in Chapter 4) can be a useful tool at this stage. One strategy expert suggests having the top management team spend several hours brainstorming all of the possible forces that might influence the firm, being sure to avoid criticizing or disposing of any until their potential usefulness and impact have been thoroughly considered.[12]

In the next stage (stage two) the *strategy itself is generally formulated*. Here again brainstorming is a useful tool for generating strategic options. It's hard to overestimate the importance of the strategy formulation stage. A recent *Fortune* magazine article emphasizes that the 17 companies that topped the Fortune 1000 in shareholder return did so in large part based on brilliant strategies. For example, "While many of its competitors in the biotech industry let the disease lead them to the science, Amgen stays ahead by taking the opposite approach. It develops its drugs by identifying areas of promising research that may lead to breakthrough products."[13] Similarly, "Worldcom saw there was more than one way to be a telephone company. By offering customers not only long distance but also local and Internet services, it broke out of the pack and became a powerhouse in the U.S. telecommunications industry."[14] Here's another example: "Seeing opportunity and a market made up of mom-and-pop hardware stores, Home Depot launched a national chain of mega stores. Economies of scale let the giant retailer offer better prices, selection, and service to the home-improvement crowd."[15] For a view of the Internet's effect on strategy, see The Challenge of Change box.

In the final stage, stage three, strategic planning cycles back to the overall planning process: You turn to *creating plans for actually implementing the strategy*. This brings the strategic planner back to the hierarchical planning process discussed in Chapter 5. Specific strategy-related goals are formulated and assigned to the company's managers, who in turn are responsible for crafting plans to ensure those goals are achieved.

Strategy and Uncertainty

Strategic planning always involves predicting the future, but some futures are more predictable than others. For example, the president of Air Canada needs a strategy for dealing with low-cost airlines such as WestJet entering the market. While such planning involves some uncertainty, this situation and the range of Air Canada's strategic options are fairly clear-cut. But Air Canada would face a far more uncertain range of options if, for instance, it was considering entering emerging markets such as Russia. The number of im-

How the Internet Drives Change

Strategies can't be crafted today without considering how information technology (IT) and the Internet could and should affect the company's strategy.

This is nothing new: Wal-Mart has grown so quickly thanks to its satellite-based warehouse and distribution system. UPS, the world's largest air and ground package distribution company, has maintained its competitive edge largely due to the almost $2 billion it invested between 1992 and 1996 in information technology. UPS drivers use hand-held computers to capture customers' signatures, along with pickup, delivery, and time card information, and automatically transmit this information to headquarters via a cellular telephone network. For companies like these and thousands more, IT lies at the heart of their strategies.

But it's likely that the Internet's effect on companies' strategies will be even more profound in the future. Online companies like Amazon.com are perhaps the most obvious examples here. Consider how the strategies of traditional booksellers like Chapters and countless smaller ones have had to change in reaction to Amazon.com. Chapters has had to create its own online bookstore, and many smaller booksellers have had to reconsider whether they can or even want to remain in business given the new competitive landscape.

Take another example: Two experts writing in the *Harvard Business Review* recently pointed out that "newspaper companies exist as intermediaries between the journalist and the reader because there are enormous economies of scale in printing and distribution. But when high resolution electronic tablets advance to the point where readers consider them a viable alternative to newsprint, those traditional economies of scale will become irrelevant. Editors—even journalists—will be able to e-mail content directly to the reader."[16] Written in 1997, this projection is already "old news." Numerous papers (including the *New York Times* and *Wall Street Journal*) already sell their "papers" online.

And it's not just "information businesses" that must adapt to the Internet. Two experts argue that even businesses not widely considered to be information businesses are (or will be) highly dependent on the Internet. For example, General Electric's divisions used to purchase their supplies from suppliers with which they had long and established relationships. Today, GE has created special online purchasing Web sites, and any supplier may bid on GE's orders. Doing this drives down GE's purchasing costs and gives it a new competitive advantage; meanwhile, its former suppliers must adapt their strategies to make themselves a lot more Web-friendly.[17]

ponderables would be enormous, from potential political instability to criminal activities to economic collapse.

Sometimes, the future is "clear enough." For example, if you were the president of Air Canada and wanted to develop a strategy to deal with the possible entrance of a low-cost no-frills airline into one of your major markets, what strategies might you pursue as a response? Possibilities include introducing a low-cost service of your own, surrendering the low-cost niche to the new entrant, or competing more aggressively on price and service in an attempt to drive the entrant out of the market.[18]

What kind of information will you need to make your decision? Generally, the sort of information provided by traditional planning tools. For example, you'll need market research on the size of the different customer segments and on the likely response of customers in each segment to different combinations of pricing and service, and information about the new entrant's competitive objective. Strategic planning tools you might use would include SWOT analysis, the environmental scan, benchmarking, and portfolio analysis.

SWOT Analysis. **SWOT analysis** is used to list and consolidate information regarding the firm's external opportunities and threats and its internal strengths and weaknesses. As illustrated in Figure 6.2, potential strengths might include adequate financial resources, economies of scale, and proprietary technology. Potential internal weaknesses include lack of strategic direction, obsolete facilities, and lack of managerial depth and talent.

Formulating a strategic plan is largely a process of identifying strategies or strategic actions that will balance these strengths and weaknesses with the company's external opportunities and threats. Opportunities might include the possibility of serving additional customers (market penetration), the chance to enter new markets or segments (market development), or falling trade barriers in attractive foreign markets. Threats might include the likely entry of new lower-cost foreign competitors, rising sales of substitute products, and slowing market growth. The manager considers all of these facts, summarizes them on the four quarters of a SWOT chart, and uses this information to help develop a corporate strategy.

SWOT analysis
A strategic planning tool used to list and consolidate information regarding a firm's external opportunities and threats and internal strengths and weaknesses.

POTENTIAL STRENGTHS
- Market leadership
- Strong research and development
- High-quality products
- Cost advantages
- Patents

POTENTIAL WEAKNESSES
- Large inventories
- Excess capacity for market
- Management turnover
- Weak market image
- Lack of management depth

POTENTIAL OPPORTUNITIES
- New overseas markets
- Falling trade barriers
- Competitors failing
- Diversification
- Economy rebounding

POTENTIAL THREATS
- Market saturation
- Threat of takeover
- Low-cost foreign competition
- Slower market growth
- Growing government regulation

FIGURE 6.2
Example of a Company's Strengths, Weaknesses, Opportunities, and Threats

The Environmental Scan. The **external environment** of an organization is the set of forces with which that organization interacts.[19] These external forces include those things—like economic trends, regulatory policies and laws, and competitors' actions—that may influence a company by providing an opportunity for it to expand or a threat to which it must plan to react. Environmental scanning means obtaining and compiling information about those environmental forces that might be relevant to the company's strategic planners.

In general, six key areas of the company's environment are "scanned" to identify the forces or factors that may be opportunities or threats (see Figure 6.3).

external environment
The set of forces with which that organization interacts.

1. *Economic trends:* These are factors related to the level of economic activity and to the flow of money, goods and services, information, and energy. For example, recently there has been a trend for people living in Asia to hoard more of their money in gold and gold items. What opportunities and threats would such a trend imply, for instance, for bankers or for companies in the business of selling gold items?

2. *Competitive trends:* Included here are all those factors that involve actions taken or possibly taken by current and potential competitors, as well as related questions regarding, for instance, market share. For example, the trend towards increased consolidation in the airline industry is driving more and more airlines to consider partnerships or mergers.

Economic Trends
(such as: recession; inflation; employment; monetary policies)

_____
_____
_____
_____
_____

Competitive Trends
(such as: competitors' strategic changes; market/customer trends; entry/exit of competitors; new products from competitors)

_____
_____
_____
_____

Political Trends
(such as: national/local election results; special interest groups; legislation; and regulation/deregulation)

_____
_____
_____
_____

Technological Trends
(such as: introduction of new production/distribution technologies; rate of product obsolescence; trends in availability of supplies and raw materials)

_____
_____
_____
_____

Social Trends
(such as: demographic trends; mobility; education; evolving values)

_____
_____
_____
_____

Geographic Trends
(such as: opening/closing of new markets; factors affecting current plant/office facilities; location decisions)

_____
_____
_____
_____

FIGURE 6.3
Worksheet for Environmental Scanning

3. *Political trends:* These are factors related to the use or allocation of political power among people, including dealings with local, national, and foreign governments. For example, major cigarette manufacturers like Imperial Tobacco must closely monitor trends in the regulation of cigarette smoking around the globe.

4. *Technological trends:* This category includes all those factors related to the development of new or existing technology, including electronics, machines, tools, processes, and know-how in general. Several years ago, Microsoft's Bill Gates noticed that the Internet's explosive growth provided both opportunities and threats to his company. The threat lay in the possibility that computer users might increasingly rely on the Internet itself for computer processing and thus

Social trends such as the values people hold and how they live are important environmental forces that must be taken into account when organizations are developing their overall strategy.

need less-sophisticated personal computers and Microsoft programs. The opportunity lay in the possibility of linking more and more Microsoft programs directly to the Internet, thus making Microsoft, instead of competitors like Netscape, the gateway to the Internet.

5. *Social trends:* These are factors that affect and reflect the way people live, including what they value. In Canada, for example, the proportion of people who are Asian or aboriginal is rising. What impact might such trends have on major advertising companies and on makers of consumer products?

6. *Geographic trends:* This includes factors related to topography, climate, natural resources, and so forth. The possibility of global warming, for example, may mean a northward expansion of agriculture on Canada's prairies. Conversely, a cooling trend in Florida would mean a reduced possibility of continuing to grow oranges there.

Such scanning can be done in several ways. Employees can be assigned to track particular subsectors, perhaps by monitoring publications like *The Globe and Mail* or *Canadian Business*, as well as the Internet, consultants' reports, information services, and industry newsletters. Increasingly, outside experts called environmental scanners (individuals who read and abstract a wide variety of publications) are retained to search for environmen-

The Globe and Mail
www.theglobeandmail.com

Canadian Business
www.canbus.com/index.shtml

tal changes that could affect the firm. Internet news services can be used to continuously and automatically screen thousands of news stories and provide precisely the types of stories in which scanners are interested.

Managers in practice use several techniques to gather this sort of information—to "scan" their environments, in other words. Premise-building techniques like forecasting, marketing research, and competitive intelligence (discussed in Chapter 5) are certainly useful. Benchmarking and portfolio analysis, to which we now turn, can also provide useful input here.

benchmarking
A process in which a company learns how to become the best in one or more areas by carefully analyzing the practices of other companies who excel in that area.

Benchmarking. Sometimes it is important to build plans and strategies based on a knowledge of the very best that your competitors and others have to offer. **Benchmarking** is a process in which a company learns how to become the best in one or more areas by carefully analyzing the practices of other companies who excel in that area (called best-practice companies). For example, Toronto Hospital gathered performance data on 26 indicators from various Canadian hospitals so that it could determine how well it was performing compared to other organizations in the health care industry.[20] Executives from Ford, Chrysler, and General Motors frequently tour Toyota manufacturing facilities as they try to figure out how Toyota makes cars so efficiently.

The basic benchmarking process typically follows several guidelines:[21]

1. Focus on a specific problem and define it carefully. For example, a specific problem might be, "What order-fulfilment technology do best-practices companies use in the mail-order business?" (Best-practice companies are those that are widely agreed to excel in a particular process or practice. For instance, L.L. Bean is viewed as a best-practice company for the way it expeditiously and courteously answers prospective customers' questions and fulfils their orders.)

2. Use the employees who will actually implement those changes in your company to identify the best-practices companies and to conduct the on-site studies of their best practices. For example, companies interested in benchmarking the best order-fulfilment technology might plan visits to L.L. Bean and Dell Computers. Having employees who will actually implement the best practices do the study helps ensure commitment to needed changes.

3. Studying best practices is a two-way street, so be willing to share information with others.

4. Avoid sensitive issues such as pricing, and don't look for new product information.

5. Keep information you receive confidential.

Portfolio Analysis. How does a company decide which businesses to keep? Several portfolio analysis aids are used to help managers decide, including the BCG Matrix and the GE Business Screen.

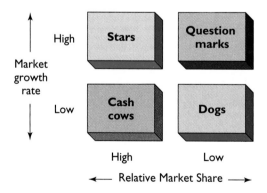

FIGURE 6.4
BCG Matrix
Once the position of each of the company's businesses is plotted, a decision can be made regarding which businesses will be cash sources and which will be cash users.

The BCG Matrix, developed by the Boston Consulting Group (BCG), helps to identify the relative attractiveness of each of a firm's businesses. As shown in Figure 6.4, it compares business growth rate and relative competitive position (market share) for each of the company's businesses. Each business is usually placed in a quadrant and represented by a circle proportional to the size of the business.

Once all of the businesses have been plotted on the matrix, a decision can be made as to whether each is a "star," "question mark," "cash cow," or "dog," to use the technique's terminology. **Stars** are businesses in high-growth industries in which the company has a high relative market share. For example, Intel's microprocessor business (microprocessors are the heart of computers such as IBM's pentium-driven PCs) has a high growth rate, and Intel has a relatively high market share. Star businesses usually require large infusions of cash to sustain growth. However, they generally have such a strong market position that much of the needed cash can be generated from sales and profits.

Question marks are businesses in high-growth industries, but with low market share. These business units (such as the computer business started by Exxon Oil several years ago) face a dilemma: They are in attractive high-growth industries, but they have such low market shares that they lack the clout to fend off larger competitors. The company must either divert cash from its other businesses to boost the question mark's market share or get out of the business.

Cash cows are businesses in low-growth industries that enjoy a high relative market share. Their being in a low-growth, unattractive industry argues against making large cash infusions into these businesses. However, their high market share generally allows them to generate high sales and profits for years, even without much new investment. Cash cows can thus be good cash generators for the company's question mark businesses.

Finally, **dogs** are low-market-share businesses in low-growth, unattractive industries. Having a low market share puts the business in jeopardy relative to its larger competitors. As a result, dogs can quickly become "cash traps," absorbing cash to support a hopeless and unattractive situation. They are usually sold to raise cash for stars and question marks.

The GE Business Screen, shown in Figure 6.5, is another strategic portfolio analysis aid. This is a nine-cell matrix originally used by GE to analyze its own business portfolio. Each company is plotted into the appropriate cell according to its (1) industry attractiveness and (2) business unit position. Industry attractiveness (as illustrated) reflects criteria such as industry size, market growth, and industry profitability. Business unit position reflects criteria such as relative size, market share, and profitability.

Like the BCG matrix, the GE Business Screen focuses on whether the company will boost or reduce its investment in each business. For this reason, it is also called the GE Stop Light Strategy. As in the upper left of Figure 6.5, businesses in attractive industries that are

star
A business in a high-growth industry in which the company has a high relative market share.

question mark
A business in a high-growth industry, but with low market share.

cash cow
A business in a low-growth industry that enjoys a high relative market share.

dog
A low-market-share business in a low-growth, unattractive industry.

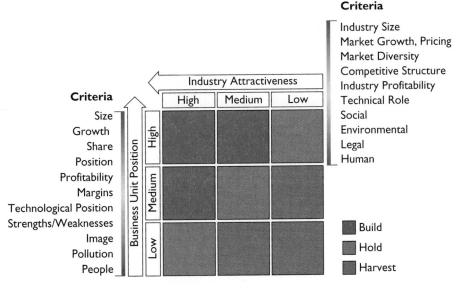

FIGURE 6.5
Company Position/Industry Attractiveness (GE) Screen

relatively strong competitors justify further investment and a growth strategy like market development. Businesses in the cells in the lower right of the matrix no longer deserve investment: They either become cash cows or are divested. Those falling in the three diagonal cells need to be monitored for any changes in industry attractiveness or business strengths. Such changes might signal the need for increased or decreased investment.

Types of Strategies

Dylex Ltd.
www.dylex.com

corporate-level strategy
Identifies the group of businesses that will comprise the corporation, and the ways in which these businesses will relate to each other.

competitive strategy
Identifies how to build and strengthen the business' long-term competitive position in the marketplace.

functional strategy
Identifies the basic courses of action that each functional department will pursue to contribute to attaining the business' competitive goals.

There are three types of strategies, as summarized in Figure 6.6. Many companies consist of several businesses; for example, Dylex Ltd. includes Harry Rosen, Fairweather, Bi-Way, and Thrifty's. A **corporate-level strategy** identifies the group of businesses that will comprise the Dylex corporation, and the ways in which these five businesses will relate to each other.

Each of these businesses (such as Harry Rosen) then has its own business-level competitive strategy. A **competitive strategy** identifies how to build and strengthen the business' long-term competitive position in the marketplace. It identifies, for instance, how Tip Top Tailors will compete with Moore's, or how Microsoft will compete with Netscape.

Each business is in turn composed of departments, such as manufacturing, marketing, and human resources. **Functional strategies** identify the basic courses of action that each functional department will pursue to contribute to attaining the business' competitive goals. We'll look at each type of strategy in turn.

Corporate-Level Strategies

Every company must choose the number of businesses in which it will compete and the relationships that will exist among those businesses. These decisions are driven by the firm's corporate-level strategy, which identifies the portfolio of businesses that will comprise the company. Companies can pursue one or more of the following corporate strategies when deciding what businesses to be in and how these businesses should relate to each other.

Concentration. A concentration strategy means the company focuses on one product or one product line. Organizations that have successfully pursued a concentration strategy include McDonald's and Kentucky Fried Chicken. Recently, Canadian National Railways

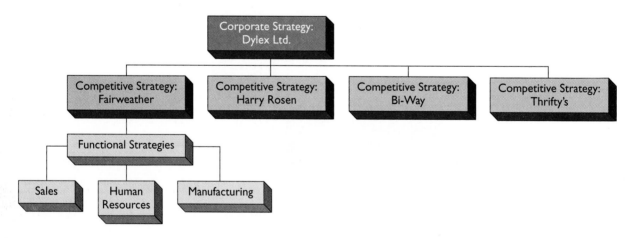

FIGURE 6.6
Relationships among Strategies in Multiple-Business Firms
Companies typically formulate three types of strategies. Corporate strategies identify the mix of business in which the firm will engage. The business level/competitive strategies identify how each of the firm's businesses will compete; and each business then has several functional strategies identifying how the unit's manufacturing, sales, and other functions will contribute to the business' strategy.

(CN) has vigorously pursued a concentration strategy by moving to acquire two large U.S. railroads—the Illinois Central and the Burlington Northern Santa Fe. CN is now a railroad giant in North America, with more than 80 000 kilometres of track and over $18.5 billion in annual revenue.[22]

The main advantage of a concentration strategy is that the company can focus its strengths on the one business it knows well, allowing it to do that one thing better than its competitors. Gerber's baby food, for example, stresses that "baby foods are our only business." The main disadvantage is the risk inherent in putting all of one's eggs into one basket. Concentrators must always be on the lookout for signs of decline. After years of concentrating in the hamburger franchise business, McDonald's Corporation tried (unsuccessfully) to diversify into franchising children's play areas in covered shopping malls.

Concentrating in a single line of business need not mean that the firm won't try to grow. Indeed, some traditional concentrators like the Coca-Cola Company have achieved very high growth rates through concentration.

Four strategies can contribute to growth.[23] Single business companies can grow through **market penetration**. This means taking steps to boost sales of present products by more aggressively selling and marketing into the firm's current markets. **Geographic expansion** is another alternative. Many U.S.-based companies like McDonald's, Wal-Mart, and Midas Muffler have grown by expanding their operations into Canada and other countries. Growth can also be achieved through **product development**, which means developing improved products for current markets. **Horizontal integration**, acquiring ownership or control of competitors in the same or similar markets with the same or similar products, is another option. For example, Hudson's Bay Company purchased Kmart's 112 stores in 1998 (it had previously purchased Zellers' 298 stores as well).

Vertical Integration. Instead of staying in one business, a firm can expand into other businesses through a vertical integration strategy. **Vertical integration** means owning or controlling the inputs to the firm's processes and/or the channels through which the products or services are distributed. (The former is backwards integration, while the latter is forward integration.) Thus, major oil companies like Shell not only drill and produce their own oil but also sell it through company-controlled outlets across Canada.

Diversification. **Diversification** means expanding into related or unrelated products or market segments.[24] Diversifying helps to move the organization into other businesses or industries or perhaps just into new product lines. In any case, it helps the firm avoid the problem of having all of its eggs in one basket by spreading risk among several products or markets. However, diversification adds a new risk of its own: It forces the company and its managers to split their attentions and resources among several products or markets instead of one. To that extent, diversification may undermine the firm's ability to compete successfully in its chosen markets.

Several forms of diversification are widely used. **Related diversification** (also called concentric diversification) means adding new, but related, products or services to an existing business. For example, CN diversified into trucking, an activity that is clearly related to railway operations. Campbell's Soup purchased Pepperidge Farm Cookies because it felt that Pepperidge's customer base and channels of distribution were a good fit with its existing customers. And Maple Leaf Gardens Ltd., which already owned a professional hockey team (the Toronto Maple Leafs), acquired a professional basketball team (the Toronto Raptors).

Conglomerate diversification, in contrast, means diversifying into products or markets that are *not* related to the firm's present businesses or to one another. For example, Bell Canada decided to diversify by forming BCE Inc., which then acquired interests in such unrelated businesses as trust companies, pipelines, and real estate. The opening case of this chapter describes the many different businesses that Seagram Company has been involved in during its history.

Conglomerate diversification is not as popular as it was 20 years ago. Businesses are now focusing their attention on a few core activities. For example, TransCanada Pipelines Ltd. got rid of its chemical division, and Alcan divested itself of its non-core businesses so it could focus on aluminum production.[25]

market penetration
Taking steps to boost sales of present products by more aggressively selling and marketing into the firm's current markets.

geographic expansion
Expanding a company into new geographic areas or foreign countries.

product development
Developing improved products for current markets.

horizontal integration
Acquiring ownership or control of competitors in the same or similar markets with the same or similar products.

vertical integration
Owning or controlling the inputs to the firm's processes and/or the channels through which the products or services are distributed.

diversification
Expanding into related or unrelated products or market segments.

related diversification
Adding new, but related, products or services to an existing business.

conglomerate diversification
Diversifying into products or markets that are *not* related to the firm's present businesses or to one another.

Status Quo Strategies. Unlike other growth-oriented strategies, a stability or status quo strategy indicates that the organization is satisfied with its rate of growth and product scope. Operationally, this means that it plans to retain its present strategy and, at the corporate level, to continue focusing on its present products and markets, at least for now.

Investment Reduction Strategies. Whether caused by overexpansion, ill-conceived diversification, or some other financial emergency, investment reduction and defensive strategies are corrective actions. They are taken to reduce the company's investments in one or more of its lines of business. For example, in the 1980s Federal Industries was a conglomerate with interests in trucking, railways, metals, and other product lines, but it has now retrenched and focused on a much more limited set of products and customers.

There are several ways to reduce investment. **Retrenchment** means the reduction of activity or operations. IBM engaged in a massive retrenchment effort, dramatically reducing (downsizing) the number of its employees and closing many facilities. **Divestment** means selling or liquidating individual businesses. (Divestment usually denotes the sale of a viable business, while liquidation denotes the sale or abandonment of a non-viable one.)

Strategic Alliances and Joint Ventures. Sometimes benefits can be obtained by forming a partnership with another company, rather than by growing internally. In such cases, strategic alliances and joint ventures are corporate strategic options. As we noted in Chapter 2, either term generally refers to a formal agreement between two or more separate companies that enables the organizations to benefit from complementary strengths.

The Virtual Corporation. For many firms encountering rapid change, the ultimate strategic alliance is the **virtual corporation**, "a temporary network of independent companies—suppliers, customers, even erstwhile rivals—linked by information technology to share skills, costs, and access to one another's markets."[26] Virtual corporations don't have headquarters staffs or organization charts or the organizational trappings that we associate with traditional corporations. In fact, virtual corporations are not "corporations" at all, in the traditional sense of common ownership or a chain of command. Instead, they are networks of companies, each of which lends the virtual corporation/network its special expertise. Information technology (computer information systems, fax machines, electronic mail, and so on) then helps the virtual corporations' often far-flung company constituents to stay in touch and quickly carry out their contributions.[27]

When managed correctly, the individual contributors aren't merely impersonal suppliers or marketers. Instead, successful virtual corporation relationships are built on trust and on a sense of "co-destiny." This means that the fate of each partner and of the virtual corporation's whole enterprise is dependent on each partner doing its share.[28]

Virtual corporations abound today. AT&T called on Japan's Marubeni Trading Company to help it link up with Matsushita Electronic Industrial Company when it wanted to speed production of its Safari notebook computer (itself designed by Henry Dreyfuss Associates).[29] Unable to produce its entire line of PowerBook notebooks, Apple turned to Sony Corporation to manufacture one version, thus merging Sony's miniaturization manufacturing skills (its core competencies) with Apple's easy-to-use software.[30]

When start-up company TelePad came up with an idea for a hand-held, pen-based computer, a virtual corporation was its answer for breathing life into the idea. An industrial design firm designed the product; Intel brought in engineers to help with some engineering details; several firms helped develop software for the product; and a battery maker collaborated with TelePad to produce the power supply.[31]

But there are dangers in becoming a virtual organization. The biggest one is that the independent contractors may start competing with the organization that contracted with them. Also, companies that contract out a lot of work may find that they lose control of the technology of the product. The classic example of the advantages and disadvantages of the virtual organization is IBM's development of the personal computer.

IBM developed the PC in 1981 by contracting out most of the work on the major components. The microprocessor was bought from Intel and the operating system from Microsoft (which was at that time a small company). The PC's architecture was "open," which meant that the components used in the product were widely available. This open architecture was originally a big selling point for the PC.

By contracting out, IBM got their new PC to market in only 15 months. The PC was sold not only in IBM Product Centres, but also through retailers like Computerland and Sears. The PC was initially a big hit. By 1984, IBM had one-quarter of the PC market, and by 1985, over 40 percent.

However, over the next few years, "IBM-compatibles" like Compaq, Dell, and AST started coming to the market. These competitors purchased the same components from Intel and Microsoft that IBM did, and began selling their products through the same retail outlets as IBM. And they competed vigorously on price. Over the next 10 years, IBM's advantage slipped away. By 1995, IBM had less than 10 percent of the PC market.

Competitive Strategies

Whether a company decides to concentrate on a single business or to diversify into several different ones, it should develop competitive strategies for each of its businesses. Strategic planning expert Michael Porter defines competitive strategy as a plan to establish a profitable and sustainable competitive position against the forces that determine industry competition.[32] The competitive strategy specifies how the company will compete; for instance, based on low cost or high quality. Porter says three basic or generic competitive strategic options are possible: cost leadership, differentiation, and focus.

Cost Leader. Just about every company tries to hold down costs. In this way, a company can price its products and services competitively. **Cost leadership** as a competitive strategy goes beyond this. A business that pursues this strategy is aiming to become *the* low-cost leader in an industry. Its unique characteristic is emphasis on obtaining absolute cost advantages from any and all possible sources. Wal-Mart is a typical industry cost leader. Its distribution costs are minimized through a satellite-based warehousing system, store location costs are minimized by placing most stores on relatively low-cost land outside small- to medium-sized towns, and the stores themselves are very plain.

Pursuing a cost leadership strategy requires a tricky balance between pursuing lower costs and maintaining acceptable quality. Southwest Airlines, for instance, keeps its cost per

cost leadership
A competitive strategy in which a company aims to become *the* low-cost leader in an industry.

Cost leadership is Wal-Mart's competitive strategy.

passenger mile below those of most other major airlines while still providing service as good as or better than those of its competitors.

Differentiator. In a **differentiation strategy**, a firm seeks to be unique in its industry along some dimensions that are valued by buyers.[33] In other words, it picks one or more attributes of the product or service that its buyers perceive as being important, and then positions itself to meet those needs. In practice, the dimensions along which a firm can differentiate itself range from the "product image" offered by some cosmetics firms to concrete differences, such as the product durability emphasized by Caterpillar Tractor. Volvo stresses safety, Apple Computer stresses usability, and Mercedes-Benz emphasizes quality. Firms can usually charge a premium price if they successfully stake out their claim to being different in some way.

Focuser. Differentiators like Volvo and low-cost leaders like Wal-Mart generally aim their business at all or most potential buyers. A business pursuing a **focus strategy** selects a market segment and builds its competitive strategy on serving the customers in its market niche better or more cheaply than its competitors. The basic question in choosing whether to pursue a focus competitive strategy is this: By focusing on a narrow market, can we provide our target customers with a product or service better or more cheaply than can our generalist competitors?

Examples of focusers abound. Pea in the Pod, a chain of maternity stores, focuses on selling stylish clothes to pregnant working women. By specializing in "working woman maternity clothes," the company is able to provide a much wider range of such clothes to its target customers than those customers would find in generalist competitors such as The Bay or Zellers. Other focusers are E.B. Eddy Forest Products Ltd. and Fraser Inc., both of which focus on producing the high-quality, durable, lightweight paper that is used in bibles.[34]

The Five Forces Model. To formulate a competitive strategy, the manager must understand the competitive forces that together determine how intense the industry's rivalries are and how best to compete. Based on that analysis, the company must find a sustainable **competitive advantage**; that is, a basis on which to identify a relative superiority over competitors. Strategy expert Michael Porter argues that how a company competes—its competitive strategy—depends on the nature and intensity of the competition in its industry. When competition was not as keen in the auto industry years ago, GM was not as concerned with competing on cost and quality.

Competitive intensity, says Porter, reflects five competitive forces, shown in Figure 6.7. The task is to analyze them so that management can decide how best to compete in that industry.[35] We'll look at each of the five forces.

1. Threat of Entry.
Intensity of industry competition depends first on the threat of new entrants to the industry. In general, the more easily new competitors can enter the business, the more intense the competition. However, several things can make it harder for new competitors to enter an industry. For example, it's not easy to enter the auto industry, because of the high investment needed in plant and equipment. Making it more expensive for customers to switch to a competitor is another entry barrier. For instance, once a travel agent signs up for one of the major airlines' computerized reservation systems, it's expensive for that agent to switch to another system.

2. Intensity of Rivalry Among Existing Competitors.
Rivalry among existing competitors manifests itself in tactics like price competition, advertising battles, and increased customer service.[36] The rivalry in some industries is more intense and warlike than in others.

3. Pressure from Substitute Products.
Intensity of competition also depends on substitute products. For example, frozen yoghurt is a substitute for ice cream, and rayon is a substitute for cotton. Substitute products perform the same or similar functions. The more substitute products there are, then, in effect, the more competitive the industry is. To the extent that few substitutes are available

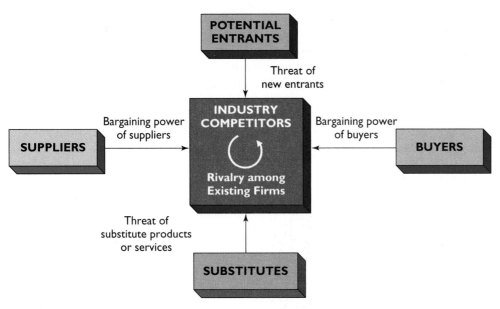

FIGURE 6.7
Forces Driving Industry Competition

(as would be the case with certain patented drugs), rivalry is reduced and the industry is more attractive and less cutthroat.

4. Bargaining Power of Buyers.
The buyers' power is another factor. For example, a buyer group is powerful if it purchases large volumes relative to the seller's sales: Toyota has a lot of clout with its suppliers, for instance. Similarly, when the products purchased are standard or undifferentiated (such as apparel elastic), and when buyers face few switching costs or earn low profits, then buyers' bargaining power (over suppliers) tends to be enhanced.

5. Bargaining Power of Suppliers.
Suppliers can also influence an industry's competitive intensity and attractiveness, for instance by threatening to raise prices or reduce quality. Suppliers tend to have greater bargaining power when they are dominated by a few firms and are more concentrated. When few substitute products are available, when the buying industry is not an important customer of the supplier group, and when the supplier's product is an important input to the buyer's business, then the supplier's power rises.

Applying the Model.
Analyzing an industry using the five forces model helps a company choose competitive strategy options. For example, where rivalry among existing competitors is very intense or there is a real threat of new entrants, a competitive strategy of boosting product differentiation is a sensible option. That's why image-oriented advertising is important to cosmetics firms. Boosting switching costs (as American Airlines did when it convinced thousands of travel agents to use its SABER computerized reservation system) can also reduce rivals' (or new entrants') ability to compete, even when the product or service itself is fairly undifferentiated.

Functional Strategies

At some point, each business' choice of competitive strategy (low-cost leader, differentiator, or focuser) is translated into supporting functional strategies for each of its departments to pursue. (Note that in some very large firms similar businesses are first grouped into strategic business units [SBUs] for control purposes. A **strategic business unit** is an organizational entity that contains several related businesses. For instance, the forest products SBU at a firm might include separate fine papers, newsprint, and pulp businesses. As another example, chemical companies such as CIL Inc. produce several chemical prod-

strategic business unit (SBU)
An organizational entity that contains several related businesses.

ucts. One division produces fertilizer, and within this division the producers of bagged lawn fertilizer would be an SBU.)

A functional strategy is the basic course or courses of action that each department is to follow in enabling the business to accomplish its strategic goals. Wal-Mart has chosen to compete as the industry's low-cost leader. To implement this competitive strategy, it had to formulate departmental functional strategies that made sense in terms of moving Wal-Mart towards its desired position. Thus, the distribution department pursued a strategy (satellite-based warehousing) that ultimately drove distribution costs down to a minimum; the company's land development department found locations that fit the firm's customer profile and kept construction costs to a minimum; and the merchandise buyers found sources capable of providing good quality merchandise at the lowest possible prices. Notice that functional strategies cannot be formulated intelligently unless the business has a clear direction in terms of the competitive strategy it wants to pursue. Then those functional strategies must "fit" the competitive strategy.

Implementing the Strategy

Creating a strategic plan is just the first part of the strategy management process. Whether at the corporate or competitive level, the strategy must then be implemented. Implementation requires several things, including (1) achieving a strategic "fit" between the strategy and the company's functional activities, (2) leveraging the firm's core competencies, and (3) providing the top management leadership required to implement the plan.

Achieving "Strategic Fit"

Strategic planning expert Michael Porter says managers can't just formulate a competitive strategy and expect it to be implemented. Instead, all of the firm's activities must be tailored to or "fit" that strategy, because this is how firms create competitive advantage. As he says, "All differences between companies in cost or price derive from the hundreds of activities required to create, produce, sell, and deliver their products or services, such as calling on customers, assembling final products, and training employees. Cost is generated by performing activities, and cost advantage arises from performing particular activities more efficiently than competitors."[37]

Let's look at two examples—Interprovincial Pipelines of Edmonton and WestJet of Calgary. Interprovincial Pipelines operates the largest petroleum pipeline system in Canada and the U.S. The company wanted to expand its business beyond simply transporting liquid hydrocarbons; it also wanted to be the industry leader by being proactive in safety and environmental protection. To achieve these long-term goals, Interprovincial implemented several strategies:

- identifying and developing key growth areas
- increasing efficiency and effectiveness through continuous improvement programs
- improving relations with shippers
- working with regulators to create a more positive regulatory climate
- ensuring that the company's human resources were appropriately trained to achieve the company's objectives.

All of these strategies work together to facilitate the goal of being the industry leader. The company also recognizes that its continued success depends on recognition of the company's people and equipment as key assets.[38]

WestJet is modelled after U.S.–based Southwest Airlines, which pioneered cheap air travel. WestJet's strategy is to appeal to price-sensitive travellers who make up the so-called "VFR" market (visiting friends and relatives). By setting prices very low (as low as one-sixth of what Air Canada charges), WestJet believed it could entice many more people to fly a commercial airline. In fact, the travel market in western Canada has doubled on the routes that WestJet flies.

WestJet's low-price, no-frills style fits well with its strategy of occupying a specific niche in the Canadian air travel market. The company has been successful almost from the day it started. Although it is tiny compared to industry giant Air Canada, it is a fearsome competitor because it has a very low cost structure that allows it to make a profit even though it offers ultra-cheap fares.[39]

Ideally, the relationship between competitive strategy and the firm's activities is reciprocal. In formulating the strategy, the manager considers the company's unique "core competencies" or strengths and weaknesses, such as a highly trained workforce. In the other direction, implementing the strategy requires managing every activity so it contributes to achieving the competitive strategy.[40]

Achieving strategic fit is important at the corporate level, too. Consider McDonald's competitive strategy of expanding overseas. Employees with knowledge and skills in the new markets had to be recruited and trained, and new reward systems were needed to inspire and motivate employees (for instance, to move overseas). For finance and accounting, it meant that control systems had to be modified to include what were now far-flung facilities around the globe. Entrepreneurs must also implement strategies, and The Entrepreneurial Edge box explains how successful women entrepreneurs do so.

THE ENTREPRENEURIAL EDGE

Women Entrepreneurs Focus on Business Growth

Women entrepreneurs are focused on profitability and building strong and growing businesses, according to a study released by IBM Canada Ltd. and the Women Business Owners of Canada. The study focuses on key business issues facing Canadian women entrepreneurs, including technology, recruitment, and international trade.

Based on the results, the top five strategic business issues and concerns for Canadian women entrepreneurs are maintaining business profitability (97 percent), managing cash flow (89 percent), the state of the economy (70 percent), gaining access to technology (65 percent), and finding and keeping quality employees (62 percent).

According to Margret Kennedy, market relationship manager of the small business division of IBM Canada, "this study shows the integral value that technology plays in building and growing a small business. Nearly 95 percent of the respondents use computers, and the majority are using the Internet, either for research or business transactions, and have Web sites."

And women entrepreneurs are not confining their activities to the local scene. Women business owners are looking towards international trade as an important strategy for growth and future opportunities. In fact, almost one-third are currently involved in international activities. This is especially so in larger firms (those with more than 10 employees and/or with annual sales of more than $500 000), where an average of 42 percent are going international. Along these lines, Deborah Schmidt, president of the Women Business Owners of Canada, says, "Women business owners understand the potential of global markets to remain competitive and to help grow the business."

Madeleine Paquin, president and CEO of Montreal-based Logistec Corp., was named Canada's top woman entrepreneur by Canadian Business.

Strategy as Stretch and Leverage

Strategy experts Gary Hamel and C.K. Prahalad caution that in planning and implementing strategy, firms should not be preoccupied with strategic fit.[41] They agree that every company "must ultimately effect a fit between its resources and the opportunities it pursues."[42] However, they argue that a preoccupation with fit can unnecessarily limit growth. The concept of "stretch" should supplement that of fit. Hamel and Prahalad argue that leveraging resources—supplementing what you have, and doing all that's possible, or more, with what you have—can be more important than just fitting the strategic plan to current resources.

As Hamel and Prahalad observe, if limited resources were really a deterrent to competitiveness, large companies like GM, Phillips, and IBM would not have found themselves on the defensive against Honda, Sony, and Compaq. Similarly, Kmart would not have found itself overtaken by Wal-Mart. Companies, they say, can **leverage** their resources by concentrating them more effectively on key strategic goals. Wal-Mart focused its relatively limited resources on building a satellite-based distribution system and gained a competitive advantage that helped it overtake Kmart.

Hamel and Prahalad believe that a company's core competencies should be leveraged. They define **core competencies** as "the collective learning in the organization, especially [knowing] how to coordinate diverse production skills and integrate multiple streams of technologies."[43]

Canon Corporation provides one example. Over the years it has developed three core competencies: precision mechanics, fine optics, and microelectronics. These reflect collective learning and skills that cut across traditional departmental lines, and result from hiring and training in such a way as to create accumulated knowledge and experience in these three core areas.

Canon draws on its core competencies to produce core component products such as miniature electronic controls and fine lenses. Its businesses—cameras, computers, and faxes—are then built around these core products. The businesses use the core products to create end products such as electronic cameras, video still cameras, laser printers, and the laser fax.

"Growing" its businesses out of a handful of core competencies this way makes it

leverage
Concentrating limited organizational resources on a few key strategic goals.

core competencies
The collective learning in the organization, especially knowing how to coordinate diverse production skills and integrate multiple streams of technologies.

Leadership and Strategic Change

The quality of the company's leadership will ultimately determine whether a new strategy succeeds or fails. Using core competencies and achieving fit are certainly important. Ultimately, however, each employee must be motivated to focus on and contribute to accomplishing the company's strategies, and for this effective leadership is required. **Leadership** may be defined as one person influencing another to work towards some predetermined objective.

leadership
One person influencing another to work towards some predetermined objective.

Although leadership is explored more fully in Chapter 10, several aspects of leadership particularly apply to implementing strategic change such as we have discussed in this chapter. These include the following.

Provide a Vision. Leaders should provide a vision or dream of what the company can and will be, one that each employee can understand and link to his or her activities. We'll see later that vision-setting is essential to what behavioural scientists today call transformational leadership. **Transformational leadership**, as discussed in Chapter 10, is the process of influencing major changes in the attitudes and assumptions of organization members and building commitment for the organization's mission, objectives, and strategies.[46]

transformational leadership
The process of influencing major changes in the attitudes and assumptions of organization members and building commitment for the organization's mission, objectives, and strategies.

Set and Communicate Limits.[47] Michael Porter points out that "deciding which target group of customers and needs the company should serve is fundamental to developing a strategy. But so is deciding *not* to serve other customers or needs and not to offer certain features or services." The leader therefore must set limits in order to channel his or her managers' decisions. Doing so involves (1) clarifying the company's business and mission, (2) teaching managers when to say "no" when something doesn't fit with that mission, and (3) providing the policies to ensure that managers have guidelines to follow (such as "15-minute gate turnarounds" at Southwest Airlines).

Communicate the Strategy. The leader also communicates the strategy. As Porter puts it, "one of the most important functions of an explicit communicated strategy is to guide employees in making choices..."[48]

Overcome Resistance to Change. A number of years ago social psychologist Kurt Lewin formulated a model of organizational change that emphasized what he called the need for "unfreezing" the organization. By unfreezing, he meant reducing the forces that maintain the status quo. Overcoming resistance to change is an important part of leading strategic change. Such resistance may stem from many sources, including a preference for a habitual way of doing things or a feeling that one's personal power or security is at stake. In any case, leaders can and should influence employees so that resistance is eliminated or at least reduced. In Chapter 14, Leading Organizational Change, we'll explain some techniques used to overcome resistance to change.

Develop Political Support. A new strategy can threaten the balance of power in an organization, thus resulting in political conflicts and struggles.[49] For example, Louis Gerstner's strategy of downsizing IBM meant dismissing tens of thousands of long-term IBM employees. As chairman, Gerstner certainly was in a powerful position. However, as a shrewd leader, he also understood the wisdom of building political support for the downsizing strategy—among his top managers and other IBM board members, for instance.

Motivate Employees. The most brilliant strategy is worthless unless the company's managers and employees are motivated to implement it. In Chapter 11, we'll see that leaders use many techniques to motivate employees. One simple but powerful technique, say two change experts, is for the leader to convey "credible positive expecta-

→

tions" for the change, in terms of specific behavioural outcomes that the manager expects from his or her employees. Another is to express his or her confidence that the employees can achieve those outcomes.[50]

easier for Canon's managers to quickly change its product mix. Regardless of how demand for products shifts—for instance, from one type of fax machine to another—Canon's "eggs" are in its core competencies. Canon can thus quickly sense changes in customer demand and reach across departmental lines to marshal its core competencies. Suppose Canon's managers sense the need for a tiny new consumer electronic product like a compact "fashion" camera. Its managers can reach across departmental lines and "harmonize know-how in miniaturization, microprocessor design, material science, and ultra thin precision casting—the same skills it applies in its miniature card calculators, pocket TVs, and digital watches—to design and produce the new camera."[44]

Companies can get into trouble if they try to go beyond their core competencies. Arrow Manufacturing Inc. of Montreal had a core competency in making men's belts, but when it tried to enter the luggage business, it ran into problems. Arrow discovered that although both products were made of leather the similarity ended there. To sell luggage required large amounts of space for inventory, as well as a new sales force. After losing money in the luggage business, Arrow returned to its core competency of making belts.[45]

The Importance of Top Management Leadership

While strategic techniques like core competencies analysis are important in strategy implementation, the people side of managing is important too, as a survey of 9144 employees illustrates. The results showed that the vast majority of surveyed employees understood their employers' goals (83 percent) and their own job responsibilities (87 percent), both of which are potentially important factors in getting employees to cooperate in implementing a firm's strategies. Unfortunately, most employers were probably failing to take full advantage of this knowledge. Less than half of the employees (43 percent) said they were given the skills and information required to achieve their goals. The problem, of course, is that having a strategy that's widely known and understood is of little value if the employees don't have the wherewithal to implement it.

Findings like these illustrate two main points. First, people are central to implementing the company's strategy, and it looks like not enough employers are taking the time or effort to make sure their employees can do their job if they want to. Second, implementing strategy depends on more than just good planning: the other management functions—organizing, leading, and controlling—are the vehicles through which the company breathes life into its strategy.

SUMMARY OF LEARNING OBJECTIVES

1. **Describe the five steps in the strategic management process.** The five steps are: define the business and develop a mission statement; translate the mission into strategic goals; formulate a strategy to achieve the strategic goals; implement the strategy; and evaluate performance.

2. **Describe the three steps needed to create strategic plans.** The three steps are identify the driving forces in a firm's environment, formulate a strategy, and create plans for actually implementing the strategy.

→

3. **Identify four strategic planning tools.** The four strategic planning tools are SWOT analysis (used to list and consolidate information regarding the firm's external opportunities and threats, and internal strengths and weaknesses); environmental scanning (obtaining and compiling information about environmental forces that might be relevant to the company's strategic planners); benchmarking (the process by which a company learns how to become the best in one or more areas by carefully analyzing the practices of other companies who excel in that practice); and portfolio analysis (used to decide which businesses a company should keep and which ones it should get out of).

4. **Explain the three main types of strategies.** *Corporate-level strategies* identify the portfolio of businesses that in total will comprise the corporation and the ways in which these businesses will relate to each other. Generic corporate strategies include concentration, market penetration, geographic expansion, product development, horizontal integration, vertical integration, and diversification, as well as status quo and retrenchment strategies. *Competitive strategies* identify how to build and strengthen the business' long-term competitive position in the marketplace. Generic competitive strategies include being a low-cost leader, differentiator, or focuser. The five forces model helps managers understand the five main forces of competitive pressure in an industry. *Functional strategies* identify the basic courses of action that each of the business' functional departments will pursue to contribute to the attainment of the business' goals.

5. **Understand the important factors in strategy implementation.** Implementing the organization's strategy involves several activities, among them achieving strategic fit, leveraging the company's core competencies, and effectively leading the change process.

TYING IT ALL TOGETHER

Creating the strategic plan is just the first step in the process; like any plan, it must then be implemented. This requires achieving strategic fit; that is, crafting functional plans so that all of the firm's activities—from maintenance to sales to finance—contribute in an orderly and coordinated way to what the company wants to achieve.

But achieving strategic fit is itself, of course, just one element in implementing the plan. Work assignments have to be made; authority must be delegated to carry them out; employees must be hired, trained, and motivated; and the final results must be compared to the plan and adjusted if required (in other words, *controlled*). *Implementing the company's plans ultimately depends on how good a job the manager does with the management functions of organizing, leading, and controlling.* In the following chapters we'll consider the fundamentals of organizing.

CRITICAL THINKING EXERCISES

1. You are a strategic management planner for General Motors. In the late 1990s you noted the merger of DaimlerChrysler. By the fall of 1999 the Germans had taken greater control of the company and removed some Chrysler people from the board of directors. The Chrysler CEO also departed. Rumour has it that the viewpoints of the two companies did not completely "merge" as had been projected earlier. Now there is a rumour that Ford and Toyota are thinking of merging. What would you recommend that GM do? Using the concepts presented in the chapter, analyze the situation and make recommendations to the GM board of directors.

2. Imagine an organization in which everyone is involved in strategic planning. Seasoned managers are on committees with new employees so that the experience of the past can be blended with fresh impressions and new ideas. On other committees, retirees, customers, stockholders, and managers from all parts of the company participate. How might this approach challenge the traditional approaches to strategic planning? How might it create management problems as well as strengths?

EXPERIENTIAL EXERCISES

1. With three to four other students in the class, form a strategic management group for your college or university. In a two-hour time period, identify what "business" your college or university is in, where it is in terms of implementing a strategy, and where it needs to be headed strategically. Prior to meeting to develop your plan, look at what your college or university has developed in the way of a strategic plan by interviewing some administrators, faculty, and students about their knowledge of the strategic plan. From the information gathered, prepare a database for the other students to use to assess the strategy in a class "brainstorming" session.

2. You are the newest member of the design team for a major toy manufacturer. You just saw a piece on the television news that identified the most popular toys of the 20th century. The top five, in ascending order, were Playdo, Lionel Trains, Barbie, the Crayon, and the Yo-Yo. Your job is to design a new toy that could be the top toy of the 21st century. In a team of four to five students, formulate a strategy for developing, designing, advertising, marketing, and evaluating such a toy.

INTERNET EXERCISE

To remain competitive, companies must be both strategic and innovative. London Drugs takes pride in its ability to change and adapt over time. Visit the Web site for London Drugs at www.londondrugs.com. Refer to the corporate information, including the history of the company.

1. In what way has the company innovated and why?

2. Perform a SWOT analysis of the company. In other words, what are London Drug's strengths, weaknesses, opportunities, and threats?

3. To what extent does London Drugs have an online presence? To what degree is this sufficient to compete in the current flood of e-commerce?

Harrison Products and the Question of Alliances

Edward Harrison and his management team had some important strategic decisions to make. While the company had the best products on the market for filtering poisonous gases from special chemical processes, its marketing efforts were limited by its small size and the enormous clout of some of its bigger competitors. While competitors like Dow Chemical might not have superior products, they did have global sales networks, and their salespeople generally overwhelmed the meagre efforts of the independent sales reps who represented Harrison Products.

Over the past two months, however, something interesting had been happening at Harrison. Officers of three separate competitors had met with Edward Harrison and his management team. Each of these officers basically made the same pitch, which was as follows: "We now offer many types of filters but want to fill in the holes in our product line by adding your excellent sophisticated filters. However, if you go into partnership with us it must be on an exclusive basis, so you won't be able to sell through anyone else—we'll do all your marketing for you. A big advantage for you and for us is that we'll become a one-stop shop: unlike your small company, we can provide not just filters but the entire housing and piping that goes into the installation."

Edward and his management team had some decisions to make.

Questions

1. Assuming that these suitors want to create, as they say, "one-stop shops," what sort of corporate strategies are they really recommending for Harrison Products?

2. Use Porter's five forces model to try to develop a competitive strategy that you think would work for Harrison if it decided not to form a partnership with one of the three larger firms.

3. Based on this brief case incident, and on whatever you may know about environmental protection and pollution control trends, complete an environmental scan for Harrison Products. Explain what implications your conclusions might hold for Edward Harrison and his management team.

How Many Brand Names Can a Company Successfully Manage?

The merger of Daimler and Chrysler created a unique auto maker. Daimler, the maker of the Mercedes brand, has long been respected for its quality engineering and high reliability, but it has often been criticized for the rather "boxy" design of its autos. While somewhat successful in the sales of its expensive Mercedes automobiles in North America, Daimler has been losing market share to Lexus and BMW (even agent 007, James Bond, has switched from his British Aston-Martin to a BMW). Daimler has not had a successful strategy for penetrating the lucrative North American auto market.

Chrysler Corporation, the number three domestic auto maker behind Ford and GM, has long been recognized for its innovative design. Chrysler was the first to produce a minivan, and its Jeep brand was the first SUV. While successful in these areas, Chrysler has been less successful in establishing a global presence. While the marriage of Daimler and Chrysler seemed a natural strategic fit, the question remained: Would the new DaimlerChrysler be able to exploit the synergies created by the merger?

The newly merged company was faced with an unusual situation—it had several successful brand names in its camp, including Mercedes, Chrysler, Plymouth, and Jeep. Brand names are powerful assets. A well-known brand, when placed on a new product, signals to the customer that the new product can be trusted. Many consumers develop brand loyalty, and when faced with a new purchase decision they buy the familiar brand they can trust. Brand management is not free, however. To maintain a brand requires constant advertising and promotion.

Consumers have known for some time that Chrysler and Plymouth have many overlapping designs. Yet, there exist Plymouth owners who are loyal to Plymouth. The most recent Plymouth product lineup included Neon, Breeze, Voyager, Grand Voyager, and Prowler. In an attempt to establish a more consistent global image, DaimlerChrysler made the decision to drop the Plymouth brand name. This will allow the company to focus more of its considerable marketing resources on the Chrysler brand. Daimler wants to establish a strong brand image for small and mid-size cars worldwide, and does not feel that it can accomplish that for more than one brand. It has selected Chrysler as its world car for the future. "Our goal is to increase our automotive presence around the world, and to do that, we need to focus our resources and our efforts on our growth opportunities," said company president James P. Holden. "The Chrysler brand has tremendous worldwide growth potential for cars."

Has DaimlerChrysler made the right decision in dropping the Plymouth brand?

Questions

1. Perform a SWOT analysis on DaimlerChrysler. What are the company's greatest strengths? Its greatest weaknesses?

2. In what ways might the decision to drop the Plymouth brand strengthen DaimlerChrysler?

3. What are the risks in dropping the Plymouth brand?

KnitMedia's Strategies for Growth and Expansion

KNITMEDIA

Up to now, you might say that KnitMedia's remarkable growth has been vision-based rather than strategy-based. Looking back, it seems apparent that Michael Dorf had a vision of a vertically integrated music company, one in which a new artist could be discovered, showcased in the Knitting Factory clubs, recorded by KnitMedia's record labels, publicized by KnitMedia's festivals division, and marketed by KnitMedia's marketing arms. Therefore, as chief operating officer Allan Fried puts it, leveraging KnitMedia's name and its artists is at the heart of everything the company does. The Knitting Factory is not just a club: "It's an entertainment destination that was leveraged over the Internet, and that was leveraged in what became the Knitting Factory festivals. So, it's leveraging or expanding the [KnitMedia] brand that we're looking to do." That's why KnitMedia launched the new Web site jazze.com, which started with alternative jazz and now is moving into what Fried calls "more commercial, more smooth jazz."

Basically, therefore, KnitMedia hopes that the synergies created by the integration of the company's various divisions will enable it to compete better in the marketplace and to provide a single source of management, promotion, and distribution for its products and services. In fact, some of KnitMedia's literature presents the company's strategy in terms of a pyramid: In a triangle at the top of the pyramid are the Knitting Factory clubs and the studios whose live recordings and artists, filmmakers, shows, and stories generate the content for everything the company does. Just below this content source are the "brick and mortar" distribution divisions, including record labels and music festivals. These distribute the content generated by the top of the pyramid. At the base are

→

KnitMedia's many online operations, including jazze.com, knittingfactory.com, jazzschool.com, knit-films.com, and knitradio.com. Along with Internet partners like AOL and Bell Atlantic, KnitMedia's managers plan to use these online properties to deliver KnitMedia's content directly to consumers.

As Dorf and his team explain it, the company's basic strategies for growth and expansion include offering a broad, integrated family of products and services; leveraging existing products, artists, and expertise; expanding international businesses; expanding and strengthening merchandising businesses; expanding and strengthening product licensing; and continuing to target consumers, especially those aged 25 to 49.

However, several recent events have been a little unnerving for the KnitMedia management team. For one thing, in 1999 and 2000 most of the large record companies around the world merged, so that today there are basically only three major record companies left: Warner Music/EMI, Universal/BMG, and Sony Music. Independent record labels still account for about one-quarter of all record companies' market share, but competing with the marketing and distribution resources of these giants is becoming increasingly demanding. Perhaps even more disconcerting was the merger, announced in early 2000, of AOL and Time Warner, a merger that gives Time Warner and its library of hits automatic access to AOL's tens of millions of customers.

So, part of the strategic question facing Michael Dorf and his team is whether a company the size of KnitMedia is really up to competing with giants like Universal and Warner, and if so what strategy it should pursue. On the one hand, these giant businesses are, as Dorf has said, relatively slow and ponderous when it comes to finding new talent and making decisions. It's also true that the Internet is certainly making it easier for independent record labels like KnitMedia to distribute content directly to consumers. On the other hand, the giants do have the financial and human resources to buy the top talent and then market and distribute it effectively.

In a nutshell, Dorf and his team want to make sure they don't end up getting steamrollered while KnitMedia is busy spreading itself across so many businesses. They need your strategic advice.

Team Exercises and Questions

Use what you learned in this chapter to answer the following questions from Michael Dorf and his management team:

1. Of the generic corporate strategies that strategic planning experts use, which ones are KnitMedia currently pursuing? Do you think pursuing these strategies is a good idea? Why or why not?

2. Do you think KnitMedia will be able to achieve the sorts of vertical integration synergies it desires (for instance, by having its clubs spotlight talent that can then be put under contract, recorded, and sent on music tours)? Why or why not? What do you see as the pros and cons of KnitMedia pursuing this integration strategy?

3. Based on what you know about the company, about strategic planning, and about the music business and the Internet, what corporate strategy would you recommend that KnitMedia pursue? Why? What competitive strategy do you think KnitMedia should pursue for each of its separate sub-businesses? Why?

Earth Buddy

Thoughts of bankruptcy, scandal, and personal disaster raced through Anton Rabie's mind as he faced the prospect that loomed before him. The buying office of the U.S. retail giant Kmart appeared to be having second thoughts about placing an order with Anton's fledging manufacturing company. The product Anton's company hoped to sell Kmart was a novelty product called Earth Buddy that Anton, together with four of his closest friends, had developed for the retail fad market.

The Earth Buddy was manufactured by stuffing sawdust and grass seed inside a nylon stocking. The stock was then decorated with two eyes, glasses, a nose, and a mouth and placed in a colourful cardboard box. After purchasing an Earth Buddy the customer watered it and then watched as it sprouted its grassy toupee in the ensuing weeks.

To date Anton and his four business cohorts had sold thousands of Earth Buddies to several of the largest retail operations in Canada, including Zellers. Tremendous demand for the product had netted the company nearly $400 000 profit in only four short months of operation.

With this healthy momentum behind them, Anton and company had set their collective sights on even bigger targets south of the border in the huge U.S. market. Combining persistence with panache, he had recently enticed Kmart U.S. to consider placing an order for 500 000 units. This order was several times larger than anything the company had handled to date.

The Kmart order was not without its problems, however. Foremost was Kmart's insistence on the order's timely delivery. This was a problem because of the comparatively small-scale runs the company was used to. Producing half a million buddies was almost inconceivable. Further complicating the demand for timely delivery was Kmart's unwillingness to make a firm written commitment to the order. This resulted in Anton's company having to begin the manufacture of the order on speculation that the written purchase order would be forthcoming.

Faced with these two uncertainties Anton and his friends decided to risk all and began manufacturing hundreds of thousands of Earth Buddies in the hope that the Kmart order would actually materialize. In order to realize their objective of 500 000 units, the company needed to produce about 16 000 units each day.

This production objective required Michelle and Ben, the two manufacturing managers, to hire and train an additional 140 employees.

In the early weeks of manufacturing the order another problem had surfaced: raw material stockouts. Secure, sufficient, and balanced supplies of each of the key raw inputs were not always on hand. At one point, a shortage of sawdust had resulted in most of the company's production employees having to be sent home early and in a shortfall of several thousand finished Earth Buddies.

However, the worst problem associated with the Kmart order was its perpetual uncertainty. While Anton had been assured of a purchase order from the U.S. giant, he still had not received written confirmation of Kmart's commitment to the sawdust-based pals. With the majority of the order now complete, Anton felt both relieved and worried. What if the Kmart order fell through? Fresh out of business school, he had only limited experience in dealing with giant corporations and the giant orders they placed. What, if anything, could he do to secure the Kmart order?

Questions

1. What is a mission statement? How would you articulate the mission employed by the makers of Earth Buddy?

2. What is a contingency plan? How well do the makers of Earth Buddy appear to plan for possible contingencies?

3. List and briefly describe the *corporate-level strategies* that a company might use. What is Earth Buddy's corporate-level strategy?

4. List and briefly describe the *competitive-level strategies* that a company might use. What is Earth Buddy's competitive-level strategy?

5. Mintzberg's research shows that top managers are extremely busy people, that they work at an unrelenting pace, and that their work is often interrupted by crises that arise. How do the managers at Earth Buddy compare with the top managers that Mintzberg studied?

Video Resource: "Earth Buddy," *Venture* #518 (December 11, 1994).

Spinmaster Toys

In 1993, Anton Rabie and a couple of friends from business school began manufacturing the Earth Buddy—a sawdust and grass-seed filled novelty that competed with products like Chia Pet. The firm had some early successes selling Earth Buddies to large Canadian retail operations like Zellers. Then the U.S. retail giant Kmart indicated that they would like to place an order for half a million units. Although Anton did not have a firm purchase order in hand, he decided to take the risk and began manufacturing hundreds of thousands of Earth Buddies in the hope that Kmart would actually send in an order. To achieve the production volume that was required, Anton had to hire an additional 140 people and had to manage a production system that was producing at a far higher level than anything the company had experienced before.

What has happened to Anton's company since 1993? Well, the news is very positive. The company eventually got the Kmart order and made $500 000 profit from it. By the end of 1998, the company—now called Spinmaster Toys—was selling several different lines of toys, and its annual sales had reached the $10 million mark. During December 1998, Spinmaster had another mega Christmas hit toy on its hands, and Anton was scrambling to try to fill orders from retailers across North America who were desperate to stock the product on their shelves. The product was Air Hogs, a toy plane powered by compressed air that is manufactured in China. Spinmaster never planned for a toy that would be so in demand, so the company has had to dramatically increase output at the Chinese factory where it is made.

In February 1999 Spinmaster took part in the Toy Fair in New York City. The idea was to push the toys that Spinmaster was selling, and to look for new toy ideas. The latest product (an obvious extension of Air Hogs) is an air pressure–powered toy car, which Spinmaster demonstrated to retailers at the Toy Fair.

Wal-Mart, Toys 'R' Us, and Price-Costco all expressed a lot of interest in the various air-powered toys that Spinmaster has available.

Yet another twist has developed. Spinmaster is now looking at a water-powered rocket that uses the same basic propulsion idea as the air-powered cars and airplanes. Toys 'R' Us thinks it can sell a couple million units of the water-powered rocket. It wants a partnership with Spinmanster, and will commit to an Air Hogs toy section in its retail outlets. Sales for these products could reach $50 to $60 million. That scale would be far greater than anything Spinmaster has seen so far. Anton's dream is to have an Air Hogs section in every toy store.

In December 1999, Spinmaster produced yet another hit toy. This one was called finger bikes, which are miniature (collectible) models of real bikes. Anton Rabie is always looking for that next hit toy product. So far, he has been very successful.

Questions

1. Is Anton Rabie making programmed or non-programmed decisions? Explain.

2. Describe the three activities that are required in the strategic planning process. What kinds of things would Anton Rabie need to do at Spinmaster Toys to complete these steps?

3. Explain the concept of environmental scanning and the six key factors in the environment of business firms. Which of these factors are likely to be most important for Spinmaster Toys?

4. Six different corporate-level strategies are described in the text. Which of these best describes Spinmaster's approach? Explain.

Video Resource: "High Flyers," *Venture* #739 (February 15, 2000).

Planning and Setting Objectives

Planning—the process of setting goals, developing procedures, and forecasting outcomes—is in a state of evolution at KnitMedia. From its small and loosely structured beginnings, the organization has nearly doubled in size and grown in complexity. Its goals have broadened considerably, to take advantage of a fruitful overseas market for U.S. jazz music and explosive growth in the power of the Internet. Its managers are still finding new ways of planning, organizing, leading, and controlling efficiently in the process of all of this expansion. At the same time that they are creating new positions, shaping an organizational hierarchy, and adding to staff, KnitMedia's managers also face an ever-increasing pace of change. This phenomenon, experienced by every business firm today, is particularly evident at the vibrant crossroads of music and technology that KnitMedia occupies.

All of these factors combine to raise planning at KnitMedia to a new level of importance. Planning for the long term receives perhaps the most attention. Long-term goals include opening Knitting Factory clubs in new markets, as we saw in the video case in Part 1, and leveraging the Knitting Factory brand into new ventures and new media, such as electronic commerce and interactive Webcasts. As Chief Operating Officer Allan Fried points out, KnitMedia's vision changes as the Internet changes and grows, and as its capabilities for reaching and interacting with audiences become clearer. At the same time, it's important for KnitMedia's managers to keep in touch with their market, and with the rate at which the new communication technologies they are exploring are being adopted by consumers.

Some planning still takes place on an ad-hoc basis. Good ideas may just pop up at night or on a weekend, for example. However, most of KnitMedia's managers expect that they will be doing more formal planning in the future, not less. Dave Brenner, vice-president of new media, follows a coherent plan for creating new Web sites with his designers that includes setting goals with them and checking periodically to see whether the work is on schedule and the goals are still realistic. Everyone has noticed that there are more meetings than there were in the past.

Brenner also recognizes that flexibility is a key characteristic of good planning, particularly when looking several years ahead. If audiences don't have the hardware necessary to receive super-fast media streams on the Internet, for instance, Brenner foresees scaling back the technology part of the Webcasting goal and refocusing that plan on the audience as it exists at the time, wherever that audience may be in terms of technological capability. The overall goal, however, is likely to remain the same as in CEO Michael Dorf's original vision—to make the Internet a conduit between the artist and the consumer. As Dorf sees it, only the tools are changing.

The speed of business also dictates flexibility in planning, according to Ed Greer, senior vice-president of club operations. KnitMedia is working hard to create more proactive plans and do less reacting, or catching up, to events and opportunities that arise without warning. While no one can accurately predict every new trend or spot every new talent, the organization still wants to be in a position to develop plans that help it respond in time to rapid changes in its environment. Greer believes that KnitMedia has strengthened its planning function in this respect over the last five years.

More KnitMedia managers are preparing and using budgets, essentially financial plans. Dorf believes that KnitMedia must and will remain "fast and nimble" in order to stay ahead of the curve. He recognizes, however, that tighter planning will only help the process of delegation that the organization's growth has made necessary. Now he regularly prepares and revises his business plan and coordinates the plans of each of his managers. In this way he ensures that the team is achieving the proper balance between formalized planning and "gut" innovation that makes KnitMedia a dynamic and successful operation.

Questions

Based on this case, the video, the text chapters you've read so far, and your knowledge from other sources, answer the following questions:

1. Dave Brenner, VP for New Media, wants a more formal planning process for his department. How can he achieve it?

2. What are some of the goals at KnitMedia?

3. Describe the decision making process at KnitMedia.

3 Organizing

Part 3: Organizing provides an overview of what is involved in the organizing function of management. It includes a look at both "hard" issues like organizational structure, and "soft" issues like the informal organization and the people who work in organizations. In the opening cases of Chapters 7, 8, and 9, you'll learn how the operations of companies like Starbucks, Canadian Pacific, and Cisco Systems are influenced by the management function of organizing.

Beginning in Chapter 7, **Fundamentals of Organizing**, we explain what organizational structure is and how managers carry out the organizing function. We describe various bases for creating departments in organizations, as well as several techniques for ensuring that the diverse work of these departments is coordinated. The nature of authority and how it is delegated in organizations is also explained.

Chapter 8, **Designing Organizations to Manage Change**, describes recent developments in innovative organization types, including team-based organizations, network organizations, boundaryless organizations, and virtual organizations. The impact of the firm's external environment on the structure of the firm is also analyzed.

This section concludes with Chapter 9, **Staffing and Human Resource Management**, which focuses on the process of mobilizing people—the most valuable asset in an organization. We discuss the key elements in human resource management, including planning for human resources, staffing the organization, developing and compensating the workforce, and providing human resource services.

Fundamentals of Organizing

Starbucks on the Move

Starbucks Coffee buys and roasts high-quality coffee beans and sells them at its retail outlets. It also sells freshly brewed coffee, pastries and confections, and coffee-related equipment at company-owned retail outlets. Starbucks is a familiar sight to Canadians who cruise the malls, and to shoppers who browse at Chapters superstores.

The company's objective is to become the most recognized and respected brand in the world. Indeed, it is difficult to escape Starbucks. The company has outlets across Canada and the U.S., and the Starbucks Coffee International division operates stores in Japan, China, Kuwait, Taiwan, New Zealand, Malaysia, Singapore, and the Philippines.

Starbucks began operations in 1971 in Seattle, Washington, in an open-air farmer's market. Growth was slow at first, and in 1987 the company had only 17 stores. But then the expansion began in earnest. By 1995 there were 676 stores, and by 1998 Starbucks operated 1886 stores. The company now operates over 2200 retail stores and plans to continue to rapidly expand its retail operations.

Maintaining the company's innovativeness in the face of this dramatic expansion is no easy task. For example, an effective training department turns college students into café managers. Training seminars are held regularly, and employees learn how to brew the perfect cup of coffee. The company has a lot of rules, and partners have to memorize them. Milk must be steamed to between 150 and 170 degrees Fahrenheit, and every espresso must be pulled within 23 seconds or thrown away. All of these things are stressed in a "Retail Skills" seminar, which is an eight-hour series of lectures, demonstrations, and hands-on practice for trainees.

How to organize this training—as well as the myriad other activities that must be done to make Starbucks successful—is therefore not just an academic issue to Howard Schultz, CEO of Starbucks. He must give serious attention to how his company is organized so that it can achieve the objectives he has set for it.

Schultz has discovered that planning and organizing are inseparable. When

Starbucks
www.starbucks.com

his firm was small, its strategy focused on offering high-quality coffee drinks through small, specialized neighbourhood coffee houses. This strategy in turn suggested the main jobs for which Schultz had to hire his lieutenants—for example, store management, purchasing, finance, and accounting. Departments then grew up around those jobs.

As Schultz's strategy evolved to include geographic expansion, his organization also had to evolve. Regional store management divisions were established to oversee the stores in each region. Today, with Starbucks-brand coffee also sold to airlines, bookstores, and supermarkets, its structure is evolving again, with new departments organized to sell to and service the needs of these new markets. What Schultz is discovering, in other words, is that the organization's structure is determined by the plan: Strategy determines structure.

OBJECTIVES

After studying this chapter, you should be able to

1. Define organizing.

2. Describe the steps in the organizing process.

3. Describe and draw examples of the basic alternatives for creating departments.

4. Explain what coordination is and how managers achieve coordination between departments.

5. Identify the different types of authority in organizations.

6. Explain what is meant by decentralization.

From Planning to Organizing

We All Organize

The planning-organizing link applies, whether the company in question is General Motors, Starbucks, or a small start-up business. Let's go back to the management task we first addressed in Chapter 1—your assignment as "summer tour master." What is your organization's strategic mission? To plan, organize, and execute a successful trip to France. What job assignments will that require? One way to organize (and the one we chose in Chapter 1) is to break the job into the main functions that must be performed, thus putting Rosa in charge of airline scheduling, Ned in charge of hotels, and Ruth in charge of city sightseeing.

How might your organization change if your strategic mission was different? Suppose that next year you are in charge of simultaneously planning several trips—to England, to Sweden, and to the south of France. Your organization's strategic mission therefore has changed, too, as it's now to plan, organize, and execute three successful trips, and to do so more or less simultaneously. How would you organize now? Perhaps you'd put each of last year's trusted lieutenants in charge of a country (say, Rosa in charge of England, Ned in charge of Sweden, and Ruth in charge of the south of France). You'd then have a sort of "regional" organization, and each lieutenant might in turn hire trusted friends to arrange for airline tickets, hotels, and sights to see. Again, the tasks to be done, and thus how you organize, have flowed logically out of your plan.

What Is Organizing?

organization
Exists when two or more people decide to cooperatively work towards achieving some goal.

Think for a moment about the organizations of which you are a member—a college or university, an intramural sports team, a musical group, a volunteer organization, a church, a military unit, or a business firm. An **organization** exists when two or more people decide to cooperatively work towards achieving some goal. The fans attending a Toronto Blue Jays baseball game do not constitute an organization, but the team's players and the managers do. Organizations exist because people can accomplish more working together than they can working alone.

All organizations have a purpose (providing a product or service), a structure (which defines a hierarchy of authority), and a division of labour (the work that is to be done is broken down into specialized jobs that can be performed by individuals with specific training). Every organization also has both formal and informal features. The formal features are defined by the organization chart, rules, objectives, procedures, etc., while the informal aspect is the network of social relationships that spontaneously arises.

organizing
The process of deciding which specific functions must be performed, and how these functions should be coordinated so that organizational goals are achieved.

Organizing is the process of deciding which specific functions must be performed, and how these functions should be coordinated so that organizational goals are achieved. The organizing process has four steps, as shown in Figure 7.1

The usual way of depicting an organization is with an **organization chart**, as shown in Figure 7.2. It shows the structure of the organization, specifically, the title of each manager's position and, by means of connecting lines, who is accountable to whom and who is in charge of what area.

organization chart
Shows the structure of the organization, specifically, the key positions in the organization and interrelationships among them.

The organization chart also shows the **chain of command** (sometimes called the *scalar chain* or the *line of authority*) between the top of the organization and the lowest positions in the chart. The chain of command represents the path a directive should take in travelling from the president to employees at the bottom of the organization chart, or from employees at the bottom to the top of the organization chart.

chain of command
The path a directive should take in travelling from the president to employees at the bottom of the organization chart, or from employees at the bottom to the top of the organization chart.

Organization charts do *not* indicate how much authority each of the positions on the chart possesses, what the organization's objectives are, what the significant factors in the organization's external environment are, what technology is used, what the comparative importance of the jobs in various departments is, or how much horizontal interaction occurs between departments.

informal organization
The informal, habitual contacts, communications, interpersonal relationships, and ways of doing things that employees always develop.

Perhaps most importantly, organization charts do not show the informal organization. The **informal organization** is the informal, habitual contacts, communications, interpersonal relationships, and ways of doing things that employees develop. At the New York Metropolitan Opera, for example, musicians and singers play poker during the intermissions. Hands are played quickly, with most pots in the $30 to $40 range. Luciano Pavarotti, the famed tenor, once played and lost big.[1] In a business firm, a salesperson might develop the habit of calling a plant production supervisor to check on the status of an order. The salesperson might find this quicker than adhering to the chain of command, which would entail having the sales manager check with the plant manager, who in turn would check with the supervisor.

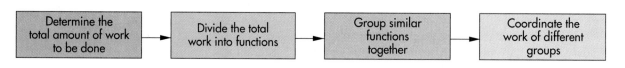

FIGURE 7.1
The Organizing Process

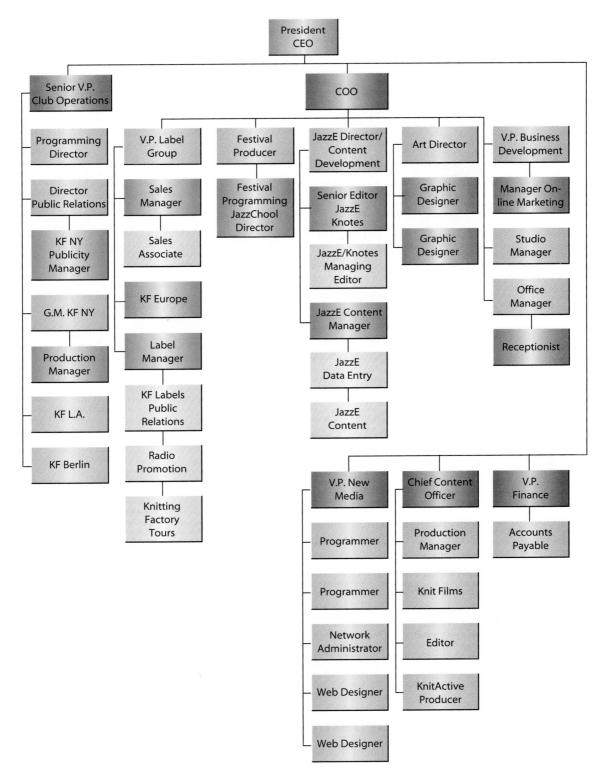

FIGURE 7.2
KnitMedia's Organization Chart
An organization chart like this one shows the title of each manager's position and the departments they manage, as well as who reports to whom.

The informal organization, which does not appear on any organizational charts, consists of the informal contacts among themselves that employees use to get the job done.

Creating Departments

Every enterprise—including your summer tour organization—must carry out various activities to accomplish its goals. In a company, these activities might include manufacturing, selling, and accounting. In a city, they might include the activities of agencies like the fire, police, and health protection departments. In a hospital, they include nursing, medical services, and radiology. **Departmentalization** is the process through which an enterprise's activities are grouped together and assigned to managers; it is the organization-wide division of work. Departments—logical groupings of activities—are often called divisions, units, or sections.

The basic question is this: Around which activities should you organize departments? Should you organize your people around functions such as airline scheduling and hotels, or around places to visit such as England, Sweden, and France? In a manufacturing company, should departments be established for sales and manufacturing? Or should there be separate departments for industrial and retail customers, each of which then has its own sales and manufacturing units? As we'll see next, many options are available.

Creating Departments Around Functions

Functional departmentalization means grouping activities around basic functions like manufacturing, sales, and finance. Figure 7.3 shows the organizational structure for ABC Car Company and for Summer Tour Masters (STM). In the car company, each department is organized around a different business function—sales, finance, and production. The production director reports to the president. He or she manages ABC's production plants and its one foreign-based assembly plant. Other directors carry out the sales and production functions.

Service businesses like STM can be built around business functions, too (see Figure 7.3). In this case, Rosa is in charge of airline scheduling, Ned is in charge of hotel reservations, and Ruth is in charge of sightseeing. These three activities are the basic functions that a company like STM has to do well in order to succeed. In another service firm, for example, a

departmentalization
The process through which an enterprise's activities are grouped together and assigned to managers.

functional departmentalization
Grouping activities around basic functions like manufacturing, sales, and finance.

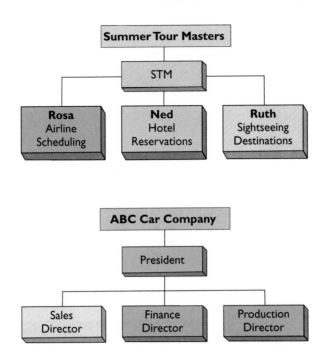

FIGURE 7.3
Functional Departmentalization: ABC Car Company and Summer Tour Masters
These organizational charts show *functional* organizations with departments for basic functions: finance, sales, and production in the manufacturing organization; scheduling, reservations, and destination-planning in the service organization.

bank, the basic business functions include operations, control, and loans. In a university, the basic functions include academic affairs, administration, and student affairs.

There are other types of "functions" as well. For example, building departments around managerial functions means putting supervisors in charge of departments like planning, control, and administration. Departmentalization based on technological functions means grouping activities such as plating, welding, or assembling. The basic idea of any functional departmentalization is to group activities around the elemental functions the enterprise must carry out.

Advantages. Organizing departments around functions has several advantages. It is simple, straightforward, and logical; it makes sense to build departments around the basic functions in which the enterprise must engage. Functional organizations usually have single departments for sales, production, and finance that serve all of the company's products, rather than duplicate facilities for each product. Because the volume in these departments is relatively high, the firm typically gets increased returns to scale—in other words, employees become more proficient (from doing the same job over and over again), and the company can afford larger plants and more efficient equipment. Functional organizations are therefore often associated with greater efficiency.

The managers' duties in each of the functional departments tend to be more specialized (a manager may specialize in finance or production, for instance); the enterprise therefore needs fewer general managers—those with the breadth of experience to administer several functions at once. This can simplify both recruiting and training. Functional department managers also tend to receive information on only part of the big picture of the company, that which concerns their own specialized functions. This can make it easier for top management to exercise tight control over the department managers' activities.

Disadvantages. Functional organizations also have disadvantages. Responsibility for the enterprise's overall performance rests on the shoulders of one person, usually the

Functional areas include but are not limited to (a) sales, (b) finance, (c) human resources, and (d) manufacturing.

president. He or she may be the only one in a position to coordinate the work of the functional departments, each of which is only one element in producing and supplying the company's product or service. This may not be a serious problem when the firm is small or does not work with a lot of products. But as size and diversity of products increase, the job of coordinating, say, production, sales, and finance for many different products may prove too great for one person; the enterprise could lose its responsiveness. Also, the tendency for functional departments to result in specialized managers (finance experts, production experts, and so forth) makes it more difficult to develop managers with the breadth of experience needed for general management jobs like president. These advantages and disadvantages are summarized in Table 7.1.

Creating Departments Around Products

With product departmentalization, departments are organized for each of the company's products or services, or for each product line. For example, Bombardier has three major product lines—mass transit, recreational and utility vehicles, and rail products. Each of these product lines is managed by an executive who has specialized knowledge about the product line.[2] Department heads in this type of organization are responsible for both creating and marketing a product, family of products, or services. Figure 7.4 shows the organization charts for STM and for North Atlantic Inc. As you can see, a president heads North Atlantic Inc. Three product divisions report to this person: one for drugs and pharma-

TABLE 7.1 *Advantages and Disadvantages of Functional Departmentalization*

ADVANTAGES	DISADVANTAGES
1. Managers are functionally specialized and therefore are more efficient	1. Responsibility for overall performance lies with chief executive only
2. Less duplication of effort	2. Can overburden chief executive and lead to slower decision making and less responsiveness
3. Increased returns to scale	3. Reduces the attention paid to specific products, customers, markets, or areas
4. Simplified training	4. Results in functionally specialized managers rather than general managers.
5. Simple and proven over time	
6. Tight control by chief executive	

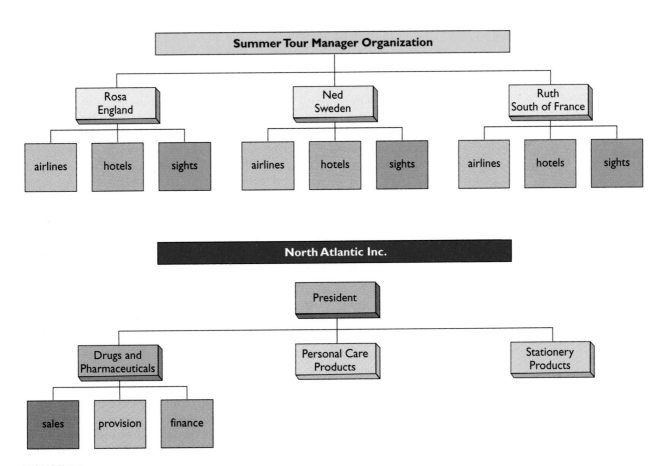

FIGURE 7.4
Product Departmentalization
With product departmentalization, separate departments or divisions are set up for products.

ceuticals, one for personal care products, and one for stationery products. Each of these three product divisions then has its own staff for activities such as production, sales, and finance.

Arranging departments around products in this way is often called **divisionalization**. Divisionalization exists when the firm's major departments are organized so that each can manage all of the activities needed to develop, manufacture, and sell a particular product, product line, or service. The head of such a division usually has functional departments—say, for production, sales, and personnel—reporting to him or her. To the extent that he or she does so, each of these product divisions is self-contained. Each has control of all or most of the resources it needs to create, produce, and supply its product or products.

At Nortel Networks, CEO Jean Monty reorganized the company into four divisions—public carrier networks (the phone companies); broadband networks (cable-TV companies and all of the long-distance companies that have sprung up since deregulation); enterprise networks (internal communication for government agencies and business firms); and wireless networks. Splitting the company into four divisions is one way to ensure that customers are not ignored. It will also help Nortel find out what customers think of the company and the products and services it produces.[3]

Netscape provides a good example of how a company went from a functional to a product organization (see The Entrepreneurial Edge).

Advantages. In product departmentalization, a single manager is charged with overseeing all of the functions required to produce and market each product. Each product division can therefore focus its resources on being more sensitive and responsive to the needs of its particular product or product line. (The manager in charge of North Atlantic's drugs and pharmaceuticals group shown in Figure 7.4, for example, has his or her own sales, production, and finance departments. As a result, the division can usually respond quickly when, for instance, a competitor brings out a new and innovative product.) The manager need not rely on sales, production, or finance managers who are not within his or her own division. Divisionalization is thus appropriate where quick decisions and flexibility (rather than efficiency) are paramount.

Also, performance is more easily judged. If a division is doing well (or not doing well), it is clear who is responsible, because one person is managing the whole division. Related to this, being put in charge of the whole ball game can help motivate the manager to perform better. Self-contained divisions can also be good training grounds for an enterprise's executives because they are exposed to a wider range of problems, from production and sales to personnel and finance. Finally, divisionalization helps shift some of the management burden from top management to division executives. Imagine if the president of a company had to coordinate the tasks of designing, producing, and marketing each of the company's many products. The diversity of problems he or she would face would be enormous. Therefore, virtually all very large companies, as well as many small ones with diverse products and customers, have divisionalized.[4]

Disadvantages. Organizing around divisions can also produce disadvantages. Divisions breed an expensive duplication of effort. The fact that each product-oriented unit is self-contained implies that there are several production plants instead of one, several sales forces instead of one, and so on. Related to this, the company's customers (such as a drugstore) may become annoyed at being visited by many salespeople representing different divisions.

Divisionalization may also diminish top management's control. The division heads often have great autonomy because they are in charge of all phases of producing and marketing their products. Top management, therefore, tends to have less control over day-to-day activities. A division might run up excessive expenses before top management discovers that there is a problem. In fact, striking a balance between providing each division head with enough autonomy to run the division and maintaining top management control is crucial.

Divisionalization also requires more managers with general management abilities. Each product division is, in a sense, a miniature company, with its own production plant,

divisionalization
Exists when the firm's major departments are organized so that each can manage all of the activities needed to develop, manufacture, and sell a particular product, product line, or service.

How Netscape Organized on Internet Time

Between May 5, 1994 (when it started corporate life as Mosaic Communications) and March 1999 (when it was bought by AOL), Netscape went from nothing to a company valued at over $10 billion. How it built its organization in such a short time provides some interesting insights into how start-up companies organize to grow rapidly under conditions of hyper-change.[5]

Like most start-ups, Netscape began with a simple functional organization, with separate departments for activities like marketing, development, legal, and finance. However, even at this early date, one of the company's big challenges was maintaining the intensity of a start-up, so the development group was divided into small teams of around six engineers, with each group enjoying considerable autonomy.

The company even used the Internet to create a virtual development organization. For example, in 1994 Netscape had only 115 employees, and so didn't really have the resources to test and debug its new Netscape browser. It therefore posted a beta version of its browser on the Internet in October 1994, thus allowing users to serve as a sort of virtual quality assurance team. Within a month, over 1.5 million users had given Netscape Navigator a trial run and its design engineers gained invaluable information about what needed to be changed.

As the company grew, its functional organization was replaced by a structure built around product divisions. As one researcher points out, Netscape executives did this in part because "...they believed that combining the functional groups needed to build a product under a single general manager will enable the product groups to be closer to customers, to focus more effectively on specific markets and competitors, and act more autonomously."[6]

As the size of the product divisions increased, Netscape's top managers needed a more formal way to coordinate the activities of its different groups. In early 1998, various organizational changes were made to add more formality. For example, a new position was created for "quality and customer satisfaction," and the company began to emphasize a more systematic, longer-term way of looking at things by building activities around 36-month plans.

sales force, personnel department, and so forth; therefore, divisional managers cannot just be sales, production, or personnel specialists. Companies with divisional structures and strong executive development programs therefore tend to be prime hunting grounds for executive recruiters.

The advantages and disadvantages of product departmentalization (divisionalization) are summarized in Table 7.2.

Creating Departments Around Customers

Customer departmentalization is used when an organization wants to focus on the needs of specific types of customers. By organizing on the basis of those needs, the firm can do a better job of satisfying them. A firm selling electronics equipment might departmentalize on the basis of consumer, government, and industrial buyers (see Figure 7.5). Universities and colleges typically focus on customers (students) by organizing faculties

customer departmentalization
Used when an organization wants to focus on the needs of specific types of customers.

TABLE 7.2 Advantages and Disadvantages of Product Departmentalization

ADVANTAGES	DISADVANTAGES
1. One unit is responsible for giving continuous, undivided attention to the product, so the unit is more sensitive and responsible to the unique needs of the product.	1. Duplication of effort and perhaps reduced efficiency. In some situations, customers may also be bothered by representatives of more than one division.
2. Part of the burden is lifted from the shoulders of the top manager.	2. Finding and training people to head each division is a more difficult job.
3. Performance is more easily identified and judged; this in turn may motivate good performance.	3. Since division heads now do their own coordinating without checking with the top manager, the latter could begin to lose control. He or she no longer coordinates and oversees the day-to-day activities of managers, just the end results—whether the division makes a profit at the end of the year.
4. Provides a good training ground for future top executives.	

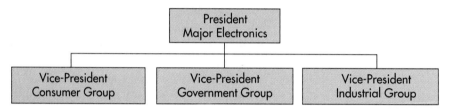

FIGURE 7.5
Departmentalization by Customer

and divisions to offer different majors or patterns of study. A law firm might departmentalize on the basis of commercial, criminal, or corporate law activity.

Advantages and Disadvantages. Organizing around customers has several advantages. As in product departmentalization, a manager is charged with giving his or her continuous, undivided attention to a customer or group of customers. This can result in faster, more satisfactory service to each of the company's customers, particularly when their needs are substantially different. As in product departmentalization, the main disadvantage is duplication of effort. The company may have several production plants instead of one and several sales managers, each serving the needs of his or her own customers, instead of one. This can reduce overall corporate efficiency.

Creating Departments Around Marketing Channels

marketing-channel departmentalization
In which top-level departments are organized around each of the firm's marketing channels.

marketing channel
The conduit through which a manufacturer distributes its products to its ultimate customers.

With **marketing-channel departmentalization**, top-level departments are organized around each of the firm's marketing channels. A **marketing channel** is the conduit (wholesaler, drugstore, grocery, or the like) through which a manufacturer distributes its products to its ultimate customers.

Marketing-channel departmentalization, illustrated in Figure 7.6, is similar to customer departmentalization, but there are several differences. In customer departmentalization, each customer-oriented department is usually responsible for both manufacturing and selling its own product to its own customers. In marketing-channel departmentalization, the same product (such as soap) is typically marketed through two or more channels. Usually one department is chosen to manufacture the product for all of the other marketing-channel departments.

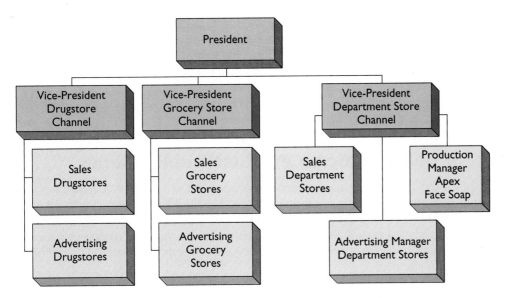

FIGURE 7.6
Marketing-Channel Departmentalization
With marketing channels, the main departments are organized to focus on particular marketing channels, such as drugstores and grocery stores.
Note: Only the department store channel produces the soap, and each channel may sell to the same ultimate consumers.

Organizing around marketing channels assumes that it is the marketing channel's unique needs that must be catered to. For example, Revlon may sell through both department stores and discount drugstores. Yet the demands of these two channels are quite different. The department store may want Revlon to supply specially trained salespeople to run concessions in its stores. The discount druggist may just want quick delivery and minimal inventories. Putting a manager and department in charge of each channel can help ensure that diverse needs are met quickly and satisfactorily. As in product and customer departmentalization, the resulting duplication—in this case, of sales forces—is the main disadvantage.

Revlon
www.revlon.com

General Motors has often been criticized because it takes so long to develop new car models. In 1998, the company reorganized because it needed a simpler organizational structure. GM merged its two big, independent automotive units for North America and the rest of the world into one unit called GM Automotive Operations. The new unit is made up of four regional divisions: Europe, Asia-Pacific, Latin America–Africa–Mideast, and North America.[7]

Creating Departments Around Geographic Areas

With geographic or territorial departmentalization, separate departments are organized for each of the territories in which the enterprise does business. For example, the Personal Services Division of Montreal Trust is organized around four regions—Atlantic, Quebec, Central, and BC/Western regions. Regional vice-presidents in the marketing function at Air Canada are organized into western, central, eastern, Atlantic Canada, U.S., and European regions.

Territorial departments are often examples of divisional departmentalization, with each geographic area tending to be self-contained, perhaps with its own production, sales, and personnel activities. Thus, if STM decided to put Rosa in charge of England, Ned in charge of Sweden, and Ruth in charge of France, the company would be departmentalized on the basis of geographic areas.

Advantages and Disadvantages. The main advantage of territorial departmentalization is that one self-contained department focuses on the needs of its particular buyers—in this case, those in its geographic area. This can led to speedier, more responsive, and better service. A department store chain like The Bay might organize territorially to cater to the tastes and needs of customers in each area. Like product, customer, and marketing-channel departmentalization, territorial departmentalization is advantageous insofar as it ensures quick, responsive reaction to the needs of the company's clients. Also like these forms, however, territorial departmentalization may create duplication of effort. And, again, these types of divisions need to hire and train general managers capable of managing several functions (like production, sales, and personnel).

From Geographic to Product Departments

To some extent, organizing geographically was a product of a time when inadequate communications made it difficult to communicate across borders, and particularly across international borders. Taking the pulse of consumers' needs and monitoring operations in a far-flung global operation is no easy task; many global companies departmentalized so that managers could run their separate regional or country businesses as more or less autonomous companies.

Trends are making that sort of geographic organization less practical today. First, competition on a global basis is becoming much more intense, so it is increasingly important for a company to be able to apply product improvements it obtains in one locale to another. So, if H J Heinz in Japan, for instance, discovers a new way to formulate one of its soups, it will want to make sure that the improvement is also implemented in the company's other markets. A geographic organization—with its relatively compartmentalized country divisions—may hamper such implementation.

Second, information technology is reducing the impediments to cross-border communication. With today's videoconferencing, e-mail, fax, and computerized monitoring of operations, an executive in one region can more easily keep his or her finger on the pulse of operations in countries around the world.

Many companies are therefore switching from a geographic to a product departmentalization. For example, Heinz's new CEO, William Johnson, said that he will end the company's system of managing by country or region.[8] Instead, he will manage the company by products or categories. For instance, tuna managers in Europe will work with tuna managers in Asia and other regions so that the best ideas from one region can be quickly spread to other regions.

Procter & Gamble recently announced that it was taking the same approach. Its new organization eliminates the company's four business units based on regions of the world, and instead puts profit responsibility in the hands of seven executives who will report directly to Durk Jurgen, the new CEO. Each executive will manage global products units such as baby care, beauty, and fabric and health care. The reorganization will speed decision making and get products to market faster.[9]

Companies like Heinz can use the Internet in many ways to improve global communications; videoconferencing is one of them. For the cost of a local telephone call, companies today can have global, face-to-face communications and thereby can help eliminate the barriers that distance formerly placed in the way of such face-to-face talk.[10]

CU-SeeMe is one of the systems that companies use to hold multi-party videoconference meetings over the Internet. This system uses a "reflector" program, which sends simultaneous transmissions to every participant. While this system is used primarily for "talking head" meetings (each participant appears on the screen in a separate box), it provides an inexpensive and effective way to hold long-distance meetings.

The World Bank
www.worldbank.org

The World Bank, which is headquartered in Washington D.C., is one organization that uses this particular system. With offices or partners in 180 countries, the World Bank has an urgent need to communicate quickly and efficiently across borders. It uses the CU-SeeMe technology to conduct small meetings and "virtual seminars." While the images may be small and the video may not always be very smooth, the system's low cost and ease of use makes it easy for the World Bank and other organizations and companies to communicate instantly and face to face around the globe. To that extent, it reduces the need to depend so heavily on global organization structure.

In 1999, CIBC named John Hunkin as CEO, to succeed the retiring Al Flood. Hunkin immediately began to reorganize the bank, cut costs, and flatten the management structure. At CIBC, there have been two distinct parts of the business—the conservative and traditional retail/commercial banking side, and the more volatile investment banking side. Hunkin wanted to break down the walls between these two areas. He did so by drawing on managers from both areas in his new plans. CIBC is now organized around product lines like other Canadian banks.[11]

Creating Matrix Organizations

A **matrix organization** (also known as **matrix management**) is defined as the imposition of one form of departmentalization on top of another.[12] In one familiar example, illustrated in Figure 7.7, product departments are superimposed over a functional departmentalization. This company's automotive products division is functionally organized, with departments for functions like production, engineering, and personnel. But superimposed over this functional departmentalization are three product groups—for the Ford project, the Chrysler project, and the GM project. Each of these product groups has its own project manager (PM). Employees from each functional department (like production and engineering) are temporarily assigned to each project. The PM has some authority over

matrix organization (matrix management)
The imposition of one form of departmentalization on top of another.

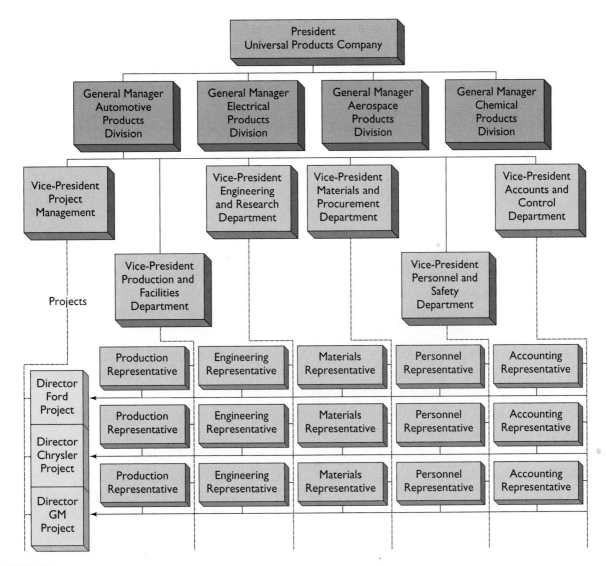

FIGURE 7.7
Matrix Departmentalization
With a matrix organization, a project structure is often superimposed over a functional organization.

the people on the project, but the functional managers also retain some authority over the workers. Since workers have two bosses, the potential for conflict exists between the project manager and the functional line manager.

Genstar Shipyards in Vancouver specializes in the custom building and repair of icebreakers, research vessels, ferries, tugs, and barges. Construction periods for ships vary from four months to two years. Each ship is treated as a project that is overseen by a project manager (PM). The PM is responsible for developing the master schedule for the building of the ship. The workers that actually build the ship report to their own line supervisor. If the supervisor and the PM disagree about something, they can appeal to their common superior (the superintendent). If the disagreement is about how many workers should be assigned to the project, the PM usually prevails, but if the disagreement is about something like trade practices, the supervisor usually prevails.[13]

Combining customer and geographic organizations is another common matrix approach.[14] For example, one bank is organized geographically, with separate officers in charge of the bank's operations in each of several countries. At the same time, the bank has a customer structure superimposed over this geographic organization. Project heads for major bank customers such as IBM lead teams consisting of bank employees from each country who concentrate on the local and worldwide financial interests of IBM. Bank employees in each country may report to both their country managers and their project head managers.

Some matrix organizations are more formal than others. Sometimes temporary project managers are assigned to provide coordination across functional departments for a project or customer. Other firms sometimes add semi-permanent administrative structure (including, for instance, project employee appraisal forms) to help build the project teams' authority.[15]

The project organization is used extensively by Canadian firms, although it is much less common than the functional structure. It is very likely to be used in the construction of hydroelectric generating stations like those developed by Hydro-Québec on the La Grande River and those developed by Manitoba Hydro on the Nelson River. When the generat-

The project organization structure is typically used in construction projects like the Nelson River hydro-electric generating station in northern Manitoba.

ing station is complete, it becomes part of the traditional structure of the provincial hydroelectric utility.

Advantages and Disadvantages. Matrix departmentalization can help give bigger companies some of the advantages of smaller ones. For example, a self-contained project group can devote its undivided attention to the needs of its own project, product, or customer, yet the entire organization need not be permanently organized around what may turn out to be temporary projects. Another advantage is that management avoids having to establish duplicate functional departments for each of the several projects.

However, matrix organizations can also trigger problems that, although avoidable, are potentially serious. These problems can be summarized as follows:

- *Power struggles and conflicts.* Since authority tends to be more ambiguous and up for grabs in matrix organizations, struggles between managers who head the functional and project groups may be more commonplace than in traditional organizations.
- *Lost time.* Matrix organizations tend to result in more intragroup meetings and therefore often seem to be indecisive and time-consuming.
- *Excessive overhead.* Matrix organizations may tend to raise costs because hiring more managers and secretaries raises overhead.

Departmentalization in Practice: A Hybrid

In practice, most organizations use multiple bases of departmentation. No one form of departmentation meets the needs of firms such as Bell Canada, Bristol Aerospace, Canada Customs and Revenue Agency, The Bay, Saskatchewan Telephones, or Montreal Trust. The organization of Montreal Trust illustrates how multiple bases of departmentation can be used within one organization (see Figure 7.8). At the top (divisional) level, departments are organized mainly on the basis of the customers the firm sells to. Within the personal services division, functional departmentation is used, while the branch offices in the personal services division are departmentalized on a territorial basis.

Montreal Trust
www.montrealtrust. com

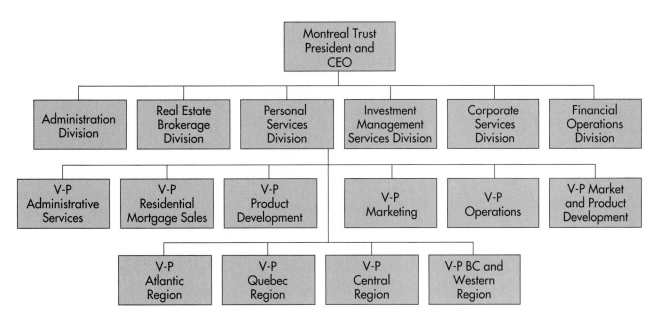

FIGURE 7.8
Combination Departmentalization

Achieving Coordination

Coordination: What It Is and Why It's Important

coordination
The process of achieving unity of action among interdependent activities.

Congratulations: You have split or divided the tour work to be done into several departments. Now—as with your assignments to Rosa, Ned, and Ruth—that work must be coordinated. **Coordination** is the process of achieving unity of action among interdependent activities. Coordination is required whenever two or more interdependent individuals, groups, or departments must work together to achieve a common goal. For example, what good would it do for your trip to France if Rosa got airline tickets that weren't coordinated with Ned's hotel reservations or Ruth's sightseeing plans? The only way your efforts (and the trip) will work is if Rosa's, Ned's, and Ruth's activities are coordinated by you, so that all of the dates in the schedule make sense and your group arrives for its hotel reservations on the days that it's supposed to.

Coordination is important for all kinds of organizations. Wescam Inc. of Ontario makes cameras that are designed to give good-quality pictures even when filming is done from unsteady objects like helicopters, boats, and cars. Wescam cameras were used in the helicopters that filmed the police chasing O.J. Simpson down a Los Angeles freeway. In recent years, the company has grown by acquiring several other firms. For Wescam to be effective, it must coordinate the work of these newly acquired firms so that corporate objectives are achieved.[16] The same is true for Abitibi-Consolidated, which was created by the merger of Abitibi-Price and Stone Consolidated. CEO Ronald Oberlander had to oversee the integration of the two companies into one effective unit.[17]

Departmentalization thus creates the need for coordination, but some types of departmentalization create the need for more coordination than others. Functional departmentalization tends to create departments that are highly interdependent and that rely heavily on someone to make sure the work is coordinated. This is the case with your group's trip to France. You had better coordinate the work of your three lieutenants, or you may well find that your group arrives in Paris on Tuesday but the hotel reservations don't begin until Friday. Similarly, review the Air Canada organizational chart shown in Figure 7.9. Notice that there are separate vice-presidents for finance, operations, and marketing. If Air Canada wants to introduce a new service, each department's activities must be

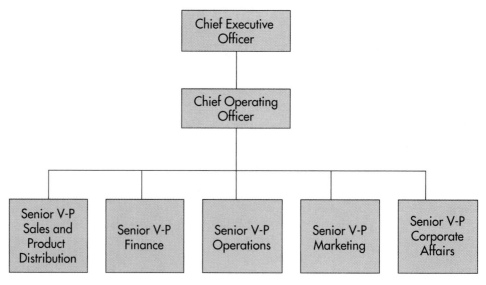

FIGURE 7.9
Departmentalization by Function (Air Canada)

210 PART 3 Organizing

closely coordinated by the chief operating officer. If the marketing vice-president projects revenues of $200 million from the new service next year, then the operations vice-president must take steps to make sure that the new service can actually be provided, and the finance vice-president must be sure that the funds are available to introduce the new service.

Coordination tends to be simpler with divisional types of departments. In the case of your three-country trip, for instance, putting each lieutenant in charge of his or her own country means that, at least within each country, you can be fairly sure that all of the plans will be coordinated without much input from you. Rosa will make sure that all of the airline, hotel, and sightseeing plans within England make sense. As another example, the separate customer divisions established by Major Electronics are pretty much self-contained. Although not shown in Figure 7.10, each division has its own research, production, and sales units. In such a divisionalized organization, each division can be managed more or less as an autonomous business. The job of achieving coordination between the autonomous divisions is relatively simple, because it is not essential for the divisions to work in unison on most day-to-day matters.

Techniques for Achieving Coordination

There are many techniques that managers use to achieve coordination, including mutual adjustment, rules and procedures, direct supervision, divisionalization, staff assistants, liaisons, committees, independent integrators, and standardization.

Mutual Adjustment. **Mutual adjustment** means achieving coordination by relying on face-to-face interpersonal interactions in both simple and complex situations. In a simple situation (such as two people moving a heavy piece of equipment), coordination can be achieved simply by having one person count "1-2-3, lift," at which time both people lift the equipment. Or, for an organization like STM, you could have Rosa, Ned, and Ruth meet before making any final decisions on the trip to France.

Mutual adjustment is also used in more complex situations. A military unit, for example, may follow formal procedures and stick to the chain of command during normal day-to-day activity. But when it hits the beach during an invasion, coordination will most likely take place through an ongoing process of mutual adjustment, with the soldiers continually interacting with and responding to each other as they deal with problems they encounter.

Rules and Procedures. If the work can be planned in advance, you can specify ahead of time what actions your subordinates should take. Rules and procedures are useful for coordinating routine, recurring activities. They specify the course of action each subordinate should take if a particular situation arises. Thus, a restaurant manager could have a rule that tables should be cleared as soon as people are finished eating. This ensures that the table is ready for the next customer.

Direct Supervision. Direct supervision allows one person to coordinate the work of others, issuing instructions and monitoring results.[18] When problems arise that are not

mutual adjustment
Achieving coordination by relying on face-to-face interpersonal interactions in both simple and complex situations.

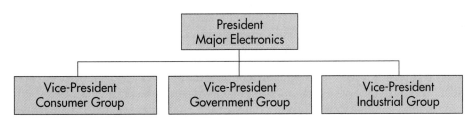

FIGURE 7.10
Departmentalization by Customer

The coordination of effort needed for complex tasks like this barn-raising is the result of a communication process called mutual adjustment.

covered by rules or procedures, subordinates bring the problem to the manager. In addition to using rules and mutual adjustment, all managers use the chain of command to achieve coordination.

Divisionalization. Functional departmentalization creates additional demands for managerial coordination, since the work of the functional departments is both specialized and interdependent. Divisional types of departments tend to reduce such interdependence, and take the burden of coordination off the president. For example, in a divisional organization, the president does not have to work as hard at coordinating the efforts of the product divisions because they are each relatively independent.

Staff Assistants. Some managers hire a staff assistant to make the job of coordinating subordinates easier. When subordinates bring a problem to the manager, the assistant can compile information about the problem, research it, and offer advice on available alternatives. This effectively boosts the manager's ability to handle problems and coordinate the work of his or her subordinates.

Liaisons. When the volume of contacts between two departments grows, some firms use special liaisons to facilitate coordination. For example, the manager of the sales department might appoint a salesperson to be his or her liaison with the production department. This liaison is based in the sales department but travels frequently to the factory to learn as much as possible about the plant's production schedule. When an order comes in to the sales department, the sales manager can then quickly determine what the production schedules are and will know whether a new order can be accepted.

Committees. Many firms achieve coordination by appointing interdepartmental committees, task forces, or teams. These are usually composed of representatives of five or six interdependent departments. They meet periodically to discuss common problems and ensure interdepartmental coordination.

independent integrator
An individual or group that coordinates the activities of several interdependent departments.

Independent Integrators. An **independent integrator** is an individual or group that coordinates the activities of several interdependent departments.[19] Integrators differ from liaison personnel in that integrators are independent of the departments they coordinate. They report to the manager who oversees those departments.

This technique has proved useful in high-tech firms where several interdependent departments must be coordinated under rapidly changing conditions. In the plastics industry, for instance, developing new products requires close coordination between the research, engineering, sales, and production departments in a situation where competitors are always introducing new and innovative products. Some firms have thus established new-product development departments. Their role is to coordinate (or integrate) the research, marketing analysis, sales, and production activities needed for developing and introducing a new product.

Standardized Targets, Skills, or Shared Values. Firms also achieve coordination by standardizing their employees' efforts. First, you can standardize the *goals or targets* the employees are to reach. For example, as long as the sales, finance, and production managers reach the goals for their specific areas, the president can be reasonably sure that their work will be coordinated, because adequate financing and production will be provided to meet the sales target.

Standardizing *skills* also facilitates coordination. That's one reason why firms like Saturn spend millions of dollars training workers. Whether a work team is installing door panels or solving a problem, training ensures that each team member knows how his or her efforts fit with the others and how to proceed. Standardized skills reduce the need for outside coordination.[20]

Creating *shared values* is another approach. For example, every year Unilever brings 300 to 400 of its managers to its executive development centre and also gives 100 to 150 of its most promising overseas managers temporary assignments at corporate headquarters.[21] This gives the visiting managers a strong sense of Unilever's strategic vision and values. Such knowledge helps to ensure that, wherever they are around the world, Unilever managers will contribute in a coordinated way to that vision, while adhering to the values of the firm. As one of Unilever's managers put it, "The experience initiates you into the Unilever club and the clear norms, values, and behaviors that distinguish our people—so much so that we really believe we can spot another Unilever manager anywhere in the world."[22]

Authority in Organizations

Authority is the right to take action, to make decisions, and to direct the work of others. It is an essential part of organizing because managers and employees must be authorized to carry out the jobs assigned to them. What use would it be for you to put Rosa in charge of airline scheduling if you don't also authorize her to check with the airlines and to make reservations?

authority
The right to take action, to make decisions, and to direct the work of others.

Sources of Authority

Authority derives from several sources, one of which is a person's position. For example, the president of Ford Motor of Canada, Bobbie Gaunt, has more authority based on rank than does one of her senior vice-presidents. In a corporation, the shareholders choose a board of directors and authorize them to choose corporate officers. The board then chooses these officers and authorizes them to run the company.

But authority can stem from other sources, too. Some people have authority because of personal traits, such as intelligence or charisma. Others are acknowledged experts in some area or have some knowledge that requires others to depend on them. Thus, even the president of Ford Motor of Canada might have to defer some highly technical matters to the head of R&D.

Some management writers argue that authority must come from the bottom up and be based on the subordinate's acceptance of the supervisor's orders. Theorist Chester Barnard was an early proponent of this view. Barnard argued that for orders to be carried out, they must lie within the subordinate's "zone of acceptance" (in other words, they must be viewed as acceptable). From a practical point of view, there is a great element of truth in this. A president might have considerable authority based on rank but be unable to get anyone to follow orders. Experts such as Rosabeth Moss Kanter and Tom Peters argue that getting employees' acceptance is increasingly important today, given the growing emphasis on empowered workers and team-based organizations.

Line and Staff Authority

line managers
Managers in charge of essential activities and authorized to issue orders to subordinates.

staff managers
Managers who assist and advise line managers.

In organizations, managers distinguish between line and staff authority. **Line managers**, like the president, production manager, and sales manager, are always in charge of essential activities, such as sales. They are always authorized to issue orders to subordinates. **Staff managers**, on the other hand, generally cannot issue orders down the chain of command (except in their own departments); they can only assist and advise line managers. For example, an HR manager—even a senior vice-president—can advise a production supervisor regarding the types of employee selection tests to use. However, it would be unusual for the HR manager to order the supervisor to hire a particular employee. On the other hand, the production supervisor's boss—the production manager—could issue such orders.

functional authority
The ability to issue orders down the chain of command within the very narrow limits of the staff manager's authority.

There is an exception to this rule: A staff manager (such as an HR manager) may have functional authority. **Functional authority** means that the staff manager can issue orders down the chain of command within the very narrow limits of his or her authority. For example, the president might order that no employee screening tests be administered without first getting the HR manager's approval. The HR manager then has functional authority over the use of personnel tests.

Line and Staff Organizations

A line-staff organization is one that has both line managers and staff experts. In Figure 7.11, the line managers are represented by solid lines and the staff managers are represented by dotted lines. In the Canadian Forces, for example, the line officers are the ones who actually engage in battle. The staff officers perform functions like military intelligence that support the activities of the line officers. At Iron Ore of Canada, the line managers oversee the extraction and marketing of iron ore. Staff managers, like safety officers, support the line managers by making sure that the mines are safe so that production operations can be carried out.

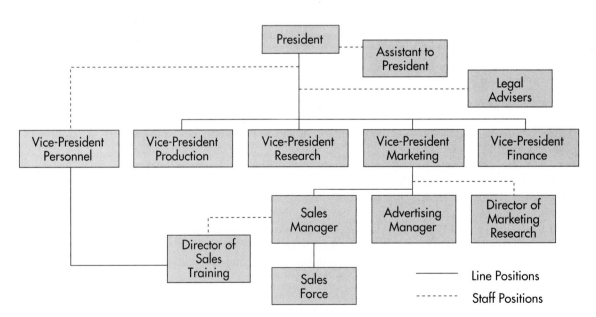

FIGURE 7.11
Typical Line-Staff Structure in a Production-Oriented Organization

We can distinguish between line and staff managers if we keep in mind the goals of the particular organization. At Aluminum Company of Canada, the director of personnel is a staff manager because the personnel department supports the primary functions of producing and marketing aluminum. However, at an employment agency like Office Overload, the director of personnel is a line manager because the primary goal of that firm is to provide personnel to other firms. The legal staff at Canadian National Railways are staff people, but at a law firm like Shewchuk & Associates, they are line people.

Line-staff conflict refers to disagreements between a line manager and the staff manager who is giving advice. For example, a production manager may want to use a particular personnel test but the HR manager insists that the test not be used. Conflict usually results when line managers feel that staff managers are encroaching on their duties and prerogatives. For their part, staff managers may feel that line managers are unnecessarily resisting their good advice. One way to reduce such conflict is to make clear who is responsible for what.

line-staff conflict
Disagreements between a line manager and the staff manager who is giving him or her advice.

The Delegation Process

Organizing departments would be useless without **delegation**, which is the pushing down of authority from supervisor to subordinate. The assignment of responsibility for some department or job traditionally goes hand in hand with the delegation of authority to get the job done. It would be inappropriate, for example, to assign a subordinate the responsibility for designing a new product and then deny him or her the authority to hire designers to create the best design.

delegation
The pushing down of authority from supervisor to subordinate.

But while authority can be delegated, responsibility cannot. A manager can assign responsibility to a subordinate. However, the manager is still ultimately responsible for ensuring that the job gets done properly. Since the supervisor retains the ultimate responsibility, delegation of authority always entails the creation of accountability. Subordinates become accountable—answerable—to the supervisor for the performance of the tasks assigned to them, particularly if things go wrong.

Today, the terms *delegation* and *empowerment* are intertwined; however, empowerment is the broader term. Specifically, **empowerment** means authorizing and enabling workers to do their jobs. Assembly workers at Toyota do not just have the authority to solve problems on the line. They are also given the training, tools, and management support required to enable them to solve problems. In this way, Toyota workers are empowered to continuously improve production quality.

empowerment
Authorizing and enabling workers to do their jobs.

Centralized and Decentralized Organizations

In every organization, management must decide how authority will be distributed throughout the hierarchy. **Centralization** occurs when top management makes all decisions regarding the hiring and firing of personnel, the purchasing of equipment and supplies, and other key decisions. Lower-level managers and workers do what is required to ensure that top-level decisions are followed. For example, Cedric Ritchie, the former CEO of the Bank of Nova Scotia, knew all details of the bank's operations and made many decisions that CEOs of other banks delegate to subordinates.[23] Most Japanese business firms are very centralized, and their overseas managers do not have much discretion.

centralization
Occurs when top management makes all decisions regarding the hiring and firing of personnel, the purchasing of equipment and supplies, and other key decisions.

Decentralization occurs when the right to make decisions is pushed down to the middle and lower levels of the management hierarchy. When Paul Tellier became president and CEO of Canadian National Railways, he introduced many changes in an attempt to return the railroad to profitability. One of these changes involved decentralizing the organization because it was too head-office-oriented. Decentralizing means putting responsibility for running trains at the regional level.[24] At the Bank of Montreal, bank branches have been organized into "communities" of branches in a specific geographic area. Each community is managed by an area manager who actually works close to the branches in that

decentralization
Occurs when the right to make decisions is pushed down to the middle and lower levels of the management hierarchy.

General Electric
www.ge.com

community. This allows the Bank of Montreal to respond quickly and intelligently to the needs of local customers.[25]

At General Electric's Bromont, Quebec, plant every effort has been made to get employees involved in a wide range of decision making.[26] Traditional jobs like supervisor and foreman don't exist at the plant, and all hiring is done by committees made up of workers. Some workers spend only 65 percent of their time on production work; the other 35 percent is spent on training, on planning, and in meetings. At Hymac Ltée., a Laval, Quebec, producer of pulp-processing machinery, managers encourage employees to meet with customers to determine how Hymac can more effectively serve them.[27] U.S. jeans maker Levi Strauss has aggressively competed internationally by delegating to foreign managers the authority they need to compete in their respective markets.[28] Even Japanese business firms are starting to move towards decentralization. Managers at Honda's U.S. subsidiary, for example, are allowed considerable discretion when making marketing and production decisions.[29]

Decentralization has advantages and disadvantages. Centralization generally fosters consistent employee behaviour, reduces the risk of costly mistakes, and allows for tight control of the organization's operations. Decentralization generally enables faster de-

---

THE **CHALLENGE** OF **CHANGE** →→ →→ →→

Cirque du Soleil Manages Globally

It is a great challenge to manage an organization globally. For example, employment laws that apply in one country may not apply in another. What if your organization operates from Las Vegas to Amsterdam, from Montreal to Asia? One company that does so is Cirque du Soleil, Inc., which produces an internationally celebrated travelling circus of sophisticated and daring performers.

Cirque du Soleil is headquartered in Montreal, with 2100 employees worldwide and offices in Amsterdam and Las Vegas. How do you manage such an enterprise? The answer for this firm is combining decentralization with a small-company atmosphere.

Most of the 2100 employees are attached to local "product division" tours, with two-thirds of the workforce outside of the company's headquarters. Employees represent 40 different countries and speak 25 languages. Decision making for such areas as human resources is decentralized to the tour managers because employment law, for example, can vary drastically from country to country. The company maintains cohesion through its strong culture of shared beliefs. Open jobs are posted on the Internet, employees write the company newspaper, and members of, say, Las Vegas' finance department can videotape themselves on the job and swap tapes with the casting crew in Montreal to keep that community feeling.[30]

Cirque du Soleil
**www.cirquedusoleil.
com**

cision making, decisions that are adapted to local conditions, higher motivation and professionalism on the part of managers, and more time for top management to do strategic planning.

Strategy and Organizational Structure

People who study organizations today generally agree that the way a company is organized depends on that company's strategy.[31] The classic, and still the most influential, study in this area was conducted by economic historian Alfred Chandler; his findings have received widespread empirical support.[32]

Chandler analyzed the histories of about 100 industrial enterprises. Information was obtained from sources such as annual reports, articles, and government publications, as well as interviews with senior executives. Chandler wanted to find out why some companies had adopted decentralized, divisionalized organizational structures, while others had remained functionally departmentalized.

Based on his analysis, Chandler concluded that "structure follows strategy"; in other words, a company's organizational structure had to fit its strategy. He concluded, for instance, that

> The prospect of a new market or the threatened loss of a current one stimulated [strategies of] geographical expansion, vertical integration, and product diversification. [In turn] expansion of volume...growth through geographical dispersion...[and finally] the developing of new lines of products...brought the formation of the divisional structure...[33]

It was the amount of new-product development and technological change with which the company's strategy required its managers to cope that apparently explained the strategy-structure link. In the steel industry, for instance, managers followed a strategy of concentrating on just one product, and the main strategic objective was to boost the company's efficiency. Here the sort of duplication inherent in setting up separate product divisions was unnecessarily inefficient, so these companies generally stayed with functional departmentalization.

At the other extreme, Chandler found that companies in the electronics and chemical industries emphasized research and development, product development, and a strategy of expansion through product diversification. This meant that companies had to market an increasingly diverse range of products to an increasingly diverse range of customers. Having to deal with so many products and customers rendered these firms' original functional structures obsolete. As one early Westinghouse executive pointed out to Chandler, for example:

> All of the activities of the company were [originally] divided into production, engineering, and sales, each of which was the responsibility of a vice president. The domain of each vice president covered the whole diversified and far-flung operations of the corporation. Such an organization of the corporation's management lacks responsiveness. There was too much delay in the recognition of problems and in the solution of problems after they were recognized.[34]

The Span of Control

The **span of control** refers to the number of subordinates that report directly to a manager. Managers who have relatively few subordinates have a narrow span of control, while managers with a large number of subordinates have a wide span of control.

There is a direct relationship between the span of control and the "shape" of an organization. In a *tall structure*, there are many levels of management, but each manager has a narrow span of control. In a *flat structure*, there are fewer levels of management, but each manager has a wider span of control. In Figure 7.12, there are 29 employees in both organizations, yet one organization is tall (seven levels), while the other is flat (only three levels of management). The taller the organization, the more managers are required.

span of control
The number of subordinates that report directly to a manager.

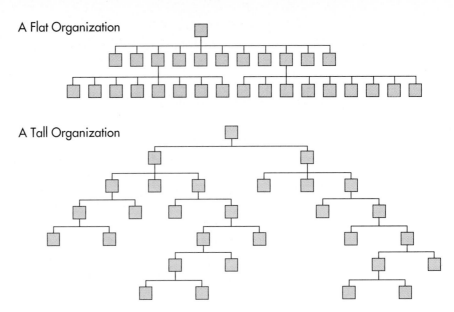

FIGURE 7.12
Flat and Tall Organizational Structures

Narrow spans permit close supervision of employees, but they create vertical communication problems because information must be filtered through many management levels. Wide spans give more discretion to employees, but they also create the possibility for bad decisions on the part of inexperienced people. Overall, wide spans are more *efficient*, but at some point they become less *effective*.

In the downsizing of the 1990s, many jobs held by middle managers disappeared as companies flattened organizational hierarchies in their drive to be more competitive. Downsizing may mean that entire levels of management are eliminated. Toyota Motor Company, for example, removed two complete layers of management from its hierarchy, downsizing to only seven levels in order to speed up decision making and make the company more competitive.[35] In the 1990s, many firms began looking more like pancakes than pyramids.

Downsizing often results in increased spans of control for those managers who remain with the company. At General Electric and Reynolds Aluminum, for example, spans of control are now twice as large as they were 20 years ago.[36] Because spans of control are wider, corporate structures are flatter after downsizing. Michael Cowpland, CEO of Corel Systems Corp., leads a firm with a very flat structure (only three layers of management). Cowpland's office is right in the middle of the action and his door is open to anyone at any time.[37]

Corel Systems Corp.
www.corel.com

Organizing's Impact on Employee Stress

How would you feel if, after you had reported to a vice-president for two years, your company reorganized and you ended up reporting to one of her subordinates? For many people, organizational changes like these can create stress.

Excessive employee stress can be a serious problem at work. Stress—which psychologists define as the psychological state that develops when an individual is confronted with situations that exceed his or her perceived ability to handle—often results in a predictable sequence of reactions.[38] The body exhibits numerous physical changes, including elevated heart rate, blood pressure, and respiration.[39] If the stress is perceived as sufficiently severe and unrelenting it can at worst lead to physical, behavioural, and psychological problems and to decreased performance.[40] Under the worst of conditions the stress may prove so debilitating that the employee actually must escape the workplace, either by physically leaving it or by retreating into a shell and isolating himself or herself from the source of the problem.

Levels of employee stress increased during the 1990s because workers were subjected to stress-inducing factors such as too much work to do in too little time, concerns over how long their jobs would last, and uncertainty about whether their skills would continue to be needed by the company. A study conducted by the Canada Health Monitor found that workers are twice as likely to report work-related stress as they are a physical illness.[41]

We'll see in later chapters that many factors—called *stressors*—can trigger stress and its consequences. Some jobs, such as air traffic controller, are inherently more stressful than are others. The physical work environment (such as extreme heat or cold) can cause stress, too. Excessive corporate politics and a particularly loathsome boss are some other obvious stressors.

The way the company is organized—its structure—is a particularly important potential source of stress, but one that is manageable if the person doing the organizing knows what to look for. Some guidelines for managing organization-based stressors follow.

Reduce Role Conflict. Even "management experts" in antiquity advised against putting anyone in the position of having to "serve two masters." Most people become uncomfortable when they receive incompatible instructions from two or more bosses. **Role conflict** is defined as a situation in which two or more sets of demands are placed on an employee in such a manner that compliance with one demand makes it difficult to comply with the other.[42]

role conflict
A situation in which two or more sets of demands are placed on an employee in such a manner that compliance with one demand makes it difficult to comply with the other.

The way that companies organize can trigger role conflict in several ways, since there are several types of role conflict.[43] There may be conflict between the person and the role, such as when someone's personality or training doesn't fit the job: Introverts tend to make poor salespeople, for instance. Inter-role conflict means that demands are placed on an employee such that complying with one makes it hard to comply with the other: Having your boss tell you to complete a report by tomorrow morning and then having her boss tell you to finish another project instead is an example.

Such role conflicts can't always be eliminated, nor do they necessarily have to be. But, in general, reducing role conflict is advisable. Doing so includes ensuring that employees have clear job assignments, that employees are properly screened and trained for their jobs,

$\rightarrow$

and that employees feel secure enough to express their discomfort if they do receive contradictory orders.

Make Job Assignments Clear. Sometimes the problem is a lack of clarity regarding what the employee is to do or how he or she is to do it; this is called **role ambiguity**. For example, consider how you would feel if you took a college class and weren't told the basis on which you were to be graded, or what you could do to get a better grade: You would probably exhibit some of the stress associated with role ambiguity.

Empower Employees. Stress can also be triggered by the perception that one has little or no control over important aspects of one's job, such as work schedule, work pace, or the decisions one can make. For example, consider the plight of a newly appointed sales manager who has just discovered that she doesn't have the authority to hire or fire salespeople, develop sales plans, or evaluate the sales staff in any way.

This sales manager would probably experience the stress associated with not having enough authority to do her job. Empowerment is one solution. In this case, empowerment might include (1) delegating more authority to the sales manager and allowing her to appraise her salespeople, to hire new ones, and (with her supervisor's approval) to dismiss those who are underperforming; (2) providing her with supervisory training in the areas of employee appraisal and interviewing; and (3) reinforcing with other managers the fact that she is now in charge of appraising, hiring, and dismissing members of her sales force.

role ambiguity
A lack of clarity regarding what the employee is to do or how he or she is to do it.

SUMMARY OF LEARNING OBJECTIVES

1. **Define organizing.** Organizing is the arranging of an enterprise's activities in such a way that they systematically contribute to the enterprise's goals. An organization consists of people whose specialized tasks are coordinated to contribute to the organization's goals.

2. **Describe the steps in the organizing process.** There are four steps: (a) determine the total amount of work to be done, (b) divide the total work into functions, (c) group similar functions together, and (d) coordinate the work of the different groups.

3. **Describe and draw examples of the basic alternatives for creating departments.** Departmentalization is the process through which an enterprise's activities are grouped together and assigned to managers. The basic alternatives for grouping are functions, customer groups, marketing channels, or geographic areas.

4. **Explain what coordination is and how managers achieve coordination between departments.** Coordination is the process of achieving unity of action among interdependent activities. It is required when two or more interdependent entities must work together to achieve a common goal. The techniques for achieving coordination include mutual adjustment, rules or procedures, direct supervision, departmentalization, staff assistants, liaisons, committees, independent integrators, and the standardization of targets, skills, or shared values.

5. **Identify the different types of authority in organizations.** Authority is the right to take action, to make decisions, and to direct the work of others. Managers usually distinguish between line and staff authority. Line authority is held by line managers like presidents, vice-presidents, and production and sales man-

agers. Staff authority is held by staff managers like legal staff, accountants, and human resource managers; it is more restricted, and usually involves staff managers giving advice to line managers.

6. **Explain what is meant by decentralization.** Decentralization occurs when the right to make decisions is pushed down to the middle and lower levels of the management hierarchy. The more decision-making rights that middle and lower level managers have, the more decentralized the organization is.

TYING IT ALL TOGETHER

Planning (Chapters 4 to 6) helps to determine what tasks must be done, and therefore the activities around which you should organize. For example, a plan to expand to Europe may mean organizing new departments for European sales and manufacturing. In this chapter we covered the fundamentals of organizing, in particular setting up departments, providing coordination, and delegating authority down the chain of command. In today's fast-changing world, new ways of organizing are required if a firm is to be able to respond quickly enough to competitive and technological changes. We turn to *organizing to manage change* in the following chapter.

CRITICAL THINKING EXERCISES

1. The book *Creative Organization Theory* offers a series of mind-stretchers. Among them is the following exercise.

   Conventional texts on management often define organizations as groups of people united by a common goal. This kind of definition eliminates almost all the interesting features of organizations in practice. They are rarely so rational and so united as the definition suggests. How would you define an organization?

2. Think about the college or university you are attending. How is it organized? Could it be organized more efficiently using the concepts discussed in this chapter? How would you reorganize the organization to be more effective and efficient for all stakeholders?

EXPERIENTIAL EXERCISES

1. You have been hired to reorganize and redesign ABC Corporation, which has had a single product line, women's dress shoes, for over four decades. It is a traditional tall organization with authority at the top (the CEO is a former designer) and a functional structure of sales, design, marketing, human resources, customer relations, finance and accounting, and production. Lately, sales have been falling off because styles in women's shoes have changed. Using the information provided in the chapter, propose how a new organization might help avoid further dips in sales.

2. How managers structure organizations to accommodate a changing set of circumstances is increasingly important to company survival. New organizational models are required. In less turbulent times, the bureaucracy, with its top-down control and hierarchically arranged roles and authority, was relatively efficient and effective. But with the advent of the global economy, rapidly changing technology, and immense competitive pressures, managers are looking for ways to more effi-

ciently and effectively structure the flow of work in their organizations. One of the most frequently touted means is the use of groups or teams. In a book entitled *Organizing Genius: The Secrets of Creative Collaboration*, Warren Bennis and Patricia Ward Biederman explore the inner workings of famous collaborations from what they call "Troupe Disney" to the Manhattan Project (the building of the atomic bomb). Their thesis is that "None of us is as smart as all of us." They come to a number of interesting conclusions, including the following: Greatness starts with superb people; great groups and great leaders create each other; every great group has a strong leader; leaders of great groups love talent and know where to find it; and great groups see themselves as winning underdogs and always have an enemy. In the new millennium, all of our brainpower and creativity will be needed to survive. Given the structures discussed in the chapter and the information about groups provided in *Organizing Genius*, design a new structure to accommodate the following industries: retail sales, the aerospace industry, hospitals, automobile manufacturing, and construction.

INTERNET EXERCISE

The Body Shop International operates in 47 countries with over 1500 outlets. Visit the international and Canadian Web sites at www.int.the-body-shop.com and www.thebodyshop.ca, respectively.

1. How are products organized? What are the key marketing channels?

2. How do the product sites reflect the corporate values of The Body Shop?

CASE STUDY 7-1

Jersak Holdings Ltd.

Vaclav Jersak was born in Prague, Czechoslovakia, in 1930. His family had long been active in the retail trade in that city. The Jersak family was very close, but the 1930s and 1940s were a time of great turbulence in central Europe. In 1938, Hitler's troops invaded Czechoslovakia and five years of war followed. After the war, Czechoslovakia came under the influence of the Soviet Union, and capitalistic ventures that had been such an integral part of the Jersak family were severely restricted. By the early 1960s, there were some hints of a return to a more capitalistic economy. To Jersak's dismay, these were snuffed out by the Soviet Union's invasion of Czechoslovakia in 1968.

The invasion was the last straw for Jersak, who had felt for some years that the environment for private business activity was very poor. At age 38, he decided to leave Czechoslovakia for a better life in Canada. He arrived in Toronto in December 1968, determined to apply his entrepreneurial talents in a more promising business environment.

Jersak quickly discovered the freedom that entre-

preneurs had in Canada. He started a small gas station, and over the next three years he opened several more. In 1971, he purchased a franchise of a major fast-food outlet, and by 1977 he owned four fast-food restaurants. His entrepreneurial instincts led him into a wide variety of business operations after that. From 1977 to 1991, he expanded his activity into the manufacture of auto parts, microcomputers, textiles, and office furniture. He purchased five franchises of a retail auto parts store, two automobile dealerships, and a carpet business that sells to both residential and commercial users. A mining company, a soft drink bottling plant, and a five-store chain of shoe stores are also part of Jersak Holdings Ltd.

As each new business venture was added, Jersak hired a person to manage the operating company. He also added individuals with expertise in accounting, finance, marketing, and production in his head office. Currently, Jersak Holdings Ltd. contains 17 operating companies, each headed by a manager (see Figure 7.13). Employment ranges from five to ten people in

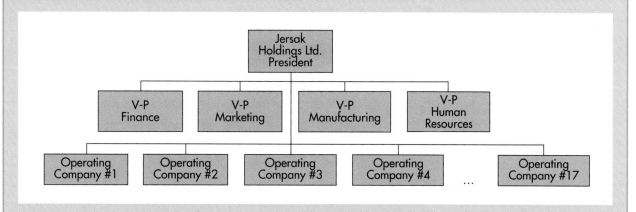

FIGURE 7.13
Organization of Jersak Holdings Ltd.

each company. In 1999, sales totalled $37 million and profits were $4.7 million.

Head office staff make most of the strategic decisions in the firm. Jersak and the other top executives have frequent informal meetings to discuss matters of importance to the firm. Discussions usually continue until a consensus is reached on a course of action. The operating managers are expected to put into practice the strategic plans that are made at head office.

As Vaclav Jersak looks back on the last 30 years, he feels a great sense of satisfaction that he has accomplished so much. He has been thinking of retiring, but he is not sure how well the company will perform once he is gone. He recognizes that the top management group operates smoothly because the people have worked together for many years. But he feels that areas of authority should be more clearly defined so that when changes occur in top management because of retirements, the new people will know exactly what they are responsible for.

Some of Jersak's business acquaintances are of the view that he should delegate considerably more authority to the managers of the operating companies. In effect, they recommend that he turn these operating managers into presidents of their own firms, each of them being responsible for making a profit in their particular enterprise. His acquaintances point out that giving the managers of the operating companies this level of responsibility will motivate them to achieve much more than they are now. Also, it should motivate the employees in these firms because they will have more discretion as well. Jersak sees some real benefits in

this approach, but worries that the current managers of the operating companies haven't had much experience in making important decisions. He also fears that head office will lose control of the operating companies. Jersak feels that it is important for head office staff to know some of the details of each operating company. Without this knowledge, he feels that the head office staff will be unable to make good decisions regarding the operating companies.

Other friends of Jersak argue that the time has come to centralize control at head office because the firm has gotten so large and is so diverse. Only in this way, they argue, will top management be able to effectively control all of the activities of Jersak Holdings Ltd.

Jersak is uncertain about what to do, but he feels he must do something to ensure that his life's work will not disappear when he retires.

Questions

1. Discuss the advantages and disadvantages of centralization and decentralization as they relate to Jersak Holdings Ltd.

2. Which basic approach—centralization or decentralization—should Jersak Holdings Ltd. adopt? Defend your answer.

3. What problems are evident in the current organizational structure of Jersak Holdings Ltd.? Design a new organization chart for the company that will solve these problems.

ABB: Organizing for Business in 100 Countries

How should a company based in Zurich, Switzerland, that employs about 170 000 people in more than 100 countries organize itself to compete globally? That was the problem faced by Asea Brown Boveri (ABB) leaders Percy Barnevik, chairman, and Gorean Lindahl, president and CEO. ABB's complexity goes far beyond its geographic scope. Much of the company's revenue comes from custom projects that may not necessarily generate repeat business. ABB is not a household name in Canada or the U.S., but it should be. Lindahl was recently named *Industry Week*'s CEO of the year, the first non-U.S. CEO to win this honour. Previous recipients of the award include IBM's Lou Gerstner, Dell Computer's Michael Dell, GE's Jack Welch, and Microsoft's Bill Gates. The award is the top honour bestowed by *Industry Week*.

In its report to ABB shareholders, the company describes its approach to business as helping customers to be more successful by providing them with the resources of a fully globalized company. These global resources are then delivered locally by ABB employees who understand the unique needs of the local customer—technically and culturally.

ABB originally had a regional management structure. The task of the regional managers was to establish a market presence and brand reputation for ABB worldwide. Each regional manager had a geographic territory for which he or she was accountable. This system worked so well that ABB decided that it had in fact accomplished its mission—it had become a truly global company.

But as a global company, ABB felt that perhaps it was not sufficiently responsive to customers. The firm wanted to serve its customers better, and to do that it needed to move faster. ABB wanted to organize its resources to exploit its unique combination of speed and flexibility. As a result, ABB decided to eliminate its regional management level. The new structure is shown in Figure 7.14.

ABB prides itself on its decentralized management culture. Managers at the local level are encouraged to make tough and important decisions. Organizational structure was something that ABB decided needed to change from the top.

Questions

1. How would you characterize ABB's current structure?

2. Do you think ABB's decision to remove its regional managers was a prudent one? Defend your answer.

3. What are the strengths and weaknesses of the new structure?

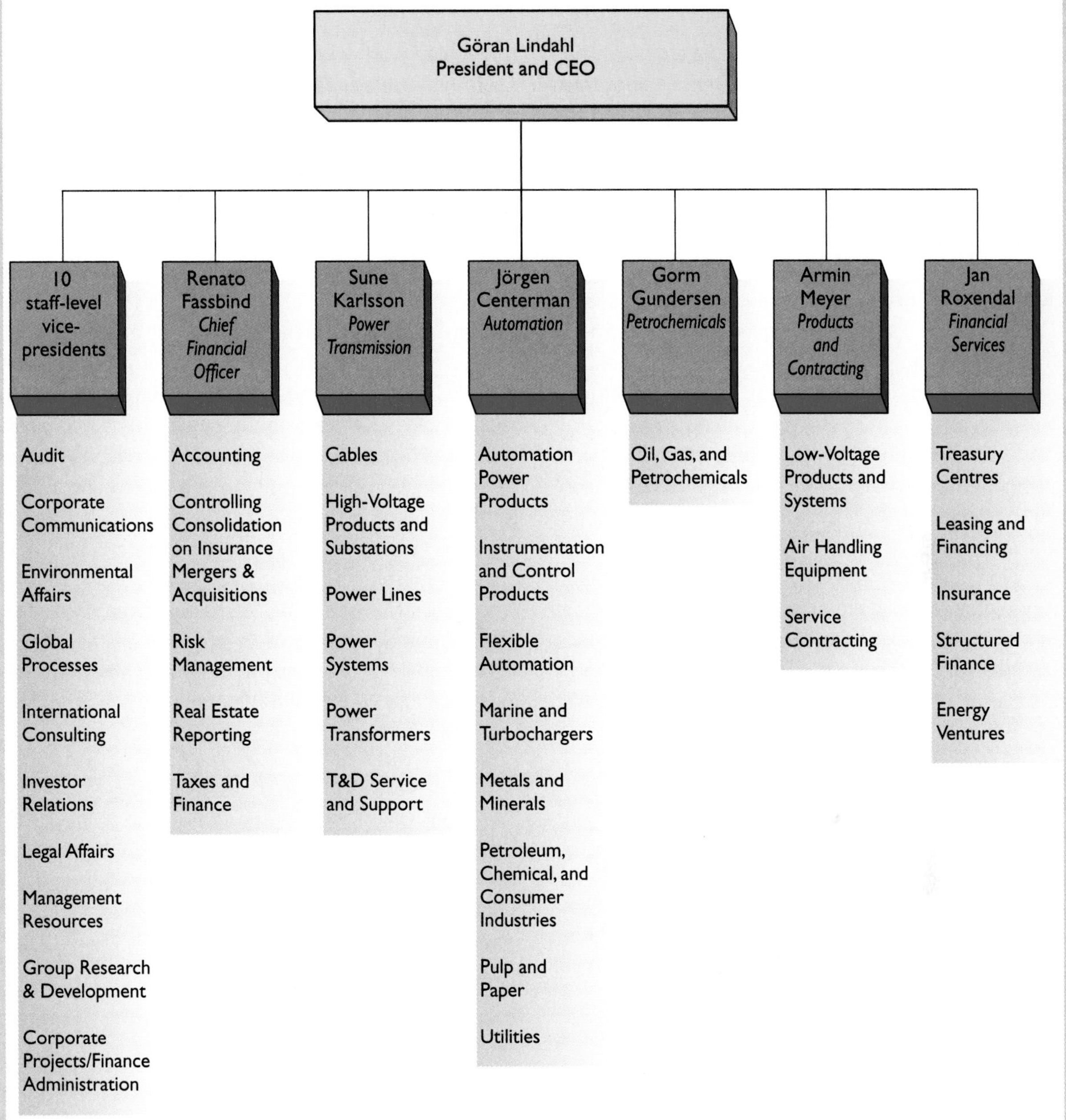

FIGURE 7.14
Organizational Structure at ABB—Key Personnel

KnitMedia Gets Organized

In terms of the numbers, KnitMedia's growth has been phenomenal. For example, revenues shot from $269 000 in 1994 to over $7 million in 1999 and the number of staff members increased from 11 to almost 100. KnitMedia has therefore gone from a traditional "mom and pop" type of organization, in which the owner-founder (in this case, Michael Dorf) could stand in the middle of all the action and make all of the decisions himself, to a larger company with the type of organization chart presented in Figure 7.2 (see page 197). In the organization chart, as you can see, Michael Dorf is president and CEO, and he has reporting to him Ed Greer as senior vice-president of club operations, Allan Fried as chief operating officer, Dave Brenner as vice-president of new media, Mitch Goldman as chief content officer, and Mark Harabedian as vice-president of finance.

While the chart is a fairly accurate representation of how things really are at KnitMedia, two important things must be taken into consideration. First, since a lot of the plans and vision are still in Michael Dorf's head, a company like this has to be careful that not a lot happens that Michael Dorf doesn't know about. Here's how Dorf puts it:

> Having a chief operating officer in place has certainly freed me up to do more, for instance to work in the finance side of the business, and maybe more of what I like to do, which is in strategic deal making, and less on the operational side of managing the club, the record label, even some of the festival day-to-day [activities]. So in some respects, when it comes to these things I feel a little clueless although at the same time, you know, I like to drill down to really look at what is actually happening and selling so we can make an analysis of whether we're doing the job correctly.

In other words, the new organization has freed Michael Dorf to help the company grow, but it also, in some respects, took him away from the day-to-day operations.

The second important thing to remember is that with a company growing this fast, everyone has to pitch in to do things that may not, strictly speaking, be their job on the organizational chart. For example, Ed Greer is senior vice-president of club operations, but he might also work with Mark Harabedian on a financial systems problem. Greer is also responsible for juggling the operations of the lucrative New York Knitting Factory club, as well as those Knitting Factory clubs in Los Angeles, Berlin, and the other sites under development.

To hear Michael Dorf tell it, opening the clubs outside of New York actually helped KnitMedia breathe life into its organization chart. "[Opening the Hollywood/L.A. site has been a great exercise, one] I'd recommend to anybody trying to learn how to manage a company. Leaving for three months [while Dorf was in Hollywood opening the new club] helped us all understand what [our] roles were and forced the proper delegation. When I'm in that office, how easy it was for someone to go around Allan and talk to me. [With me in Hollywood for three months] there wasn't any opportunity for that, so it was a great exercise."

Great exercise or not, Dorf and his team want to make sure that creating the organization chart in Figure 7.2 was the right way to proceed, and also that the new structure won't stifle the company's responsiveness. They'd like your advice.

Team Exercises and Questions

Use what you learned in this chapter to answer the following questions from Michael Dorf and his management team:

1. What are the benefits and potential drawbacks to KnitMedia of having organized in the manner depicted in the organization chart in Figure 7.2?

2. How would you suggest we avoid the potential drawbacks you mentioned in your answer to question 1 above?

3. The Knitting Factories are basically the "cash cows" that produce the revenues we use to build KnitMedia's other operations. Given that fact, and the fact that more of these clubs are going to be opened abroad, should we reorganize KnitMedia in such a way as to include a separate executive who can handle international operations? What would be the pros and cons of doing so?

4. Let's suppose we decide to throw away our organization chart and come up with a new one. What kind of new organization chart would you suggest for KnitMedia?

Designing Organizations to Manage Change

Restructuring at Canadian Pacific

In November 1995, Canadian Pacific Ltd. announced a major restructuring. Under the plan, a new parent company has been set up that wholly owns six divisions: CP Rail System, CP Ships, PanCanadian Petroleum, Fording Coal, Marathon Realty, and Canadian Pacific Hotels. Transportation and energy are now the two key elements in CP Ltd.'s overall corporate strategy.

As part of the reorganization, one of the six subsidiaries—CP Rail System—moved its headquarters from Montreal to Calgary. In the process, the division cut 1450 management jobs and moved another 730 jobs to Calgary. Most of the job losses were felt in Montreal, although an eastern rail unit is still located there.

What motivated the move to Calgary? Since it was announced shortly after the Quebec referendum, some observers thought that it was politically motivated. But the CEO of CP Ltd., William Stinson, said that the referendum had nothing to do with the decision. He said it was strictly a business decision, and that it was necessary for railway management to be located where most of its revenues come from (80 percent of CP Rail Division revenues come from the west). Stinson also said that the organization would give CP Rail a better management style, lower costs, and would bring the company closer to the customer.

Under the new structure, CP Rail will have considerable autonomy, and may eventually become a publicly traded company in its own right. It will have access to capital markets, whereas previously it had to rely on the parent company for funding. CP Rail will also be able to merge with another firm if it desires, or get involved in a joint venture, or even institute some form of employee ownership.

Observers of the rail industry think that competitive factors were a big consideration in the reorganization decision. For example, the privatization of Canadian National Railways in 1995 has made it a more aggressive competitor. To maintain its competitiveness, CP Rail will have to become more efficient, and this reorganization is designed to achieve that goal.

This latest reorganization gives parent company CP Ltd. quite a different

Canadian Pacific
www.cp.ca

look than it had as recently as 10 years ago. Then, it was involved in all sorts of diverse businesses, including mining (Cominco), forest products (Canadian Pacific Forest Products), airlines (Canadian Pacific Airlines), and communications (Unitel). All these business operations have been sold during the last decade.

Also as a result of the reorganizations, the 11 layers of management in the company have been compressed to six. As well, costs will be cut by reducing the scale of activities in various locations around North America, including Toronto, Vancouver, Minneapolis, and Albany, New York. The reorganization will save the firm $100 million each year in administrative costs. Overall, industry analysts think the reorganization will give CP Ltd. a much clearer corporate strategy. It will also give CP Rail a tighter focus and greater earning power.

OBJECTIVES

After studying this chapter, you should be able to

1. Give examples of the initial redesign steps for making organizations more responsive.

2. Explain how to organize and lead team-based organizations.

3. Give examples of network-based and boundaryless organizations.

4. Describe horizontal and federal organizations.

5. List the factors affecting how organizations are designed and structured.

A Wave of Reorganizations

Canadian Pacific is just one of the many companies that have downsized and restructured during the last decade. Downsizing and restructuring are part of a wave of reorganizations—actually disorganizations—that are sweeping businesses as managers grapple with the challenge of managing rapid change. For example, Asea Brown Boveri (ABB), based in Zurich, Switzerland, cut its headquarters staff by 95 percent and "deorganized" 215 000 people into 5000 largely independent profit centres that average only 50 people each. At IBM, CEO Louis Gerstner stripped away the ponderous central staff and bureaucratic procedures that helped to slow IBM's responsiveness, and substituted instead decentralized decision making and smaller organizational units.[1]

Al Flood, former chairman of Canadian Imperial Bank of Commerce, described his job as "managing through change." This meant staying on the leading edge to ensure that the bank was not hurt by new developments in information technology. Marti Smye, president of People Tech Consulting, estimates that 90 percent of Canadian corporations have recently initiated significant change like a merger, acquisition, restructuring, downsizing, or development of a new corporate strategy.[2]

Many companies are creating new means of organizing their operations. They hope this will help them respond better to competitors' innovations, and thus help them manage change. Chapter 7 covered the fundamentals of organizing, such as the basic ways to departmentalize and how to provide coordination and delegate authority. However, those are just the basic building blocks and language of how to organize. Now we turn to *organiz-*

ing to manage change, and to the new ways of organizing that companies are using to help them respond better to competitive, technical, and political change.

Moving Beyond Traditional Organizations

Early, "classical" management theorists were not oblivious to the fact that organizations had to be responsive—at least occasionally. Most of these experts, such as Henri Fayol, Frederick Taylor, and Luther Gulick, were managers or consultants. They were therefore experienced enough to know that there are times when sticking to the chain of command simply results in too ponderous a response. Henri Fayol, for instance, said that orders and inquiries should generally follow the chain of command. However, in very special circumstances a "bridge" communication could take place, say, between a salesperson and a production supervisor, if a decision was required at once.

Prescriptions like these worked fairly well as long as abnormal situations were not the rule. If a company was operating in an environment in which novel, unexpected occurrences were minimal, then giving every employee a specialized job and achieving coordination by making most people stick to the chain of command was an effective way to do things. But as the number of unexpected problems and issues—new competitors, new product or technological innovations, customers suddenly going out of business, and so on—becomes unmanageable, a mechanistic organization becomes overloaded and errors start to mount. Today, says management expert Tom Peters, success in the marketplace "is directly proportional to the knowledge that an organization can bring to bear, how fast it can bring that knowledge to bear, and the rate at which it accumulates knowledge."[3] In other words, companies must be organized to respond to rapid change, and to respond very quickly.

As a result, today you might say that we are moving beyond even organic organizations. Product divisions, flexible lines of authority, less specialized jobs, and decentralized decisions—all features of organic structures—are often not enough today to provide the fast response time that companies need.

Managers—even those whose firms already had organic types of structures—initially reacted to today's more rapid change in several ways. Many downsized. **Downsizing** means dramatically reducing the size of a company's workforce.[4] Often, at the same time, they and others modified the existing structures by (1) reducing the levels of management, thus flattening their companies' structures; (2) reorganizing around small mini-units; (3) reassigning support staff from headquarters to the divisions, thus decentralizing decisions; and (4) further decentralizing by empowering workers. We'll address these initial attempts at boosting responsiveness next, and then move on to the team-based, network-based, and boundaryless structures that define designing organizations for managing change in the following three sections.

downsizing
Dramatically reducing the size of a company's workforce.

Reduce Layers of Management

Reducing layers of management is perhaps the most widespread tactic used to manage change. As we saw in Chapter 7, Toyota Motor Co. and Corel Systems Corp. are just two of the companies that have reduced the number of management layers in order to speed up decision making and improve communication between managers and workers.

Keep in mind that delayering is not always a panacea. For many years organizational experts emphasized the advantages of cutting out layers of "useless" managers whose only function was to check and recheck the decisions of those below them. "Why not cut out those useless barriers and just let empowered lower-level employees make more of their own decisions?" the thinking went. Many, many companies ended up doing just that.

The results have not always been favourable. For example, recall the debacle several years ago when the "rogue trader" Nicholas Leeson brought down Barings Bank by losing over $1.4 billion through a series of fraudulent trades. As one reviewer recently put it, "Numerous organizations have been removing layers of management—layers sometimes depicted as performing no useful function...but as [Leeson's book] *Rogue Trader* underlines, management may also provide experience and judgment, curbing actions on the part of enthusiastic, novice employees that may otherwise have disastrous consequences..."[5]

Establish Mini-Units

Many managers reacted to the need to manage change better by reorganizing their companies into smaller mini-companies. These smaller units tended to be more entrepreneurial: Everyone (including the top executive) knew everyone else, layers of management weren't required for an approval, and interactions and communications were more frequent, given the greater likelihood of employees knowing each other and working in close proximity. At Intuit the new CEO broke the company into eight separate businesses, each with its own general manager and mission.[6]

Reassign Support Staff

Mars, Inc.
www.mars.com

Many firms also move headquarters staff such as industrial engineers out of headquarters and assign them to the divisional officers of their business units. For example, candy maker Mars, Inc., is a $7 billion company with only a 30-person headquarters staff. Mars does have staff employees, but as is true in more and more firms, these staff employees are assigned directly to the individual business units. Here they can help their business units be successful in the marketplace rather than act as gatekeepers who check and recheck divisional managers' plans for the firm's top executives. When Percy Barnevik took over as CEO of Sweden's ASEA, it had a central staff of 2000, which he quickly reduced to 200. When his firm then acquired Finland's Stromberg company, its headquarters staff of 880 was reduced within a few years to 25.[7]

Widen Spans of Control

Squeezing out management layers results in wider spans of control. The typical span of control in North American business firms has been 1 supervisor to 10 workers, but in Japan the ratio is often 1 to 100 and sometimes 1 to 200.[8]

Building Team-Based Structures

team
A group of people who work together and share a common work objective.

Increasingly today, steps such as empowering, widening spans of control, or establishing mini-units are no longer enough. Managers are therefore using teams, networks, and "boundaryless" structures to redesign their organizations so as to manage change better. Many firms boost responsiveness by organizing most of their activities around self-contained and self-managing work teams. A **team** is a group of people who work together and share a common work objective.[9]

For example, when Tim Adlington became the new operations manager at the Black Diamond cheese factory in Ontario, he decided to run every department with employee teams that would be organized to address problems such as waste reduction, productivity, excessive rework, lost time for accidents, and customer returns.[10] Under this system, managers became facilitators rather than order-givers. Managers who used to spend all of their time watching workers to ensure they did what they were supposed to do now spend most of their time facilitating and organizing work, and chairing meetings that are designed to improve operations.

In the traditional management structure, if something went wrong, the proposed so-

lution would have to go up the chain of command for approval by management. But in many firms, teams are empowered to make decisions like recruiting new workers, formulating the team's budget, making capital investment proposals, developing quality and productivity standards, and coordinating their work with other teams.

Under a similar program at Chesebrough-Ponds USA, a functional organization was replaced with multi-skilled, cross-functional, self-directed teams that now run the plant's four production areas. Hourly employees make employee assignments, schedule overtime, establish production times and changeovers, and even handle cost control, requisitions, and work orders. They are also solely responsible for quality control under the plant's Continuous Quality Improvement Challenge, a program in which employees can post suggestions or challenges to improve quality. Employee Sherry Emerson summed up employee sentiments: "The empowerment is exciting. If we see something that will affect the quality to customers, we have the freedom to stop a process. They [management] trust us."

The results have been extraordinary. Quality acceptance is 99.25 percent. Annual manufacturing costs are down $10.6 million, work-in-process inventory has been reduced 86 percent, and total inventory is down 65 percent.[11]

Nature of Team-Based Organizations[12]

As these examples suggest, team-based organizations are different from the traditional departmentalized and hierarchical organizations described in Chapter 7. Companies were traditionally organized with individuals, functions, or departments as their basic work units. This is evident in the typical organization chart, which might, for example, show separate boxes for each functional department, down to separate tasks for individual workers at the bottom of the chart.

In team-based organizations, however, the team is the basic work unit. The employees, working together as a team, will do much of the planning, decision making, and implementing required to get their assigned jobs done, and be responsible for activities like receiving materials, installing parts, and dealing with vendors who ship defective parts.

Teamwork at Eicon

Eicon Technology Inc. has succeeded in building a better mousetrap—a low-cost ISDN modem. The project could not have been completed if the company's purchasing and engineering teams had not been able to work together effectively. The Montreal-based company entered the ISDN market about three years ago when it got feedback from its major telecommunications customers that its products were too expensive, and that the company needed to change. Frederick Gasoi, director of hardware products development at Eicon, said that the goal was to design a less expensive version of a current product, with the same functionality and quality, while still turning a profit.

Effective teamwork was integral to the strategy. In prior projects, engineering would ask purchasing, manufacturing, and other departments for their opinions, but usually near the end of the project. There was not always time for meetings to develop the best sources of parts at the lowest cost.

But in this project, operating as a team from the start was critical. Engineering, purchasing, cost accounting, manufacturing, quality assurance, and project management participated in formal sit-down reviews for the lowest-cost modem. The meetings were seen as pivotal, turning the spotlight on both design and departmental issues that could undermine the project. Another issue was the lack of effective communication between purchasing and engineering.

Along the way the team had multiple challenges, such as realizing that a redesign feature proved too costly. Gasoi said, "It was a frustration to lose a month, but it made sense." The team felt fortunate that key dialogue had taken place early on, so that the necessary changes could be made in time. Even distributors became part of the team, and they agreed to hold inventory at no charge, moving it directly from Eicon's warehouse to subcontractors as needed. Distributors agree that the system works. "From a forecasting point of view, it's been good," said John Walsh, sales representative for Arrow Electronics, Inc. in Montreal. It appears that teamwork contributed not only to lower costs, but to other system efficiencies as well.

Eicon Technology
www.eicon.com

Arrow Electronics
www.arrow.com

Designing Organizations to Support Teams[13]

No manager can create a team-based organization without providing the supporting mechanisms that will allow the teams to flourish. Management has to provide at least five organizational supporting mechanisms to enable work teams to do their jobs and therefore ensure the proper functioning of the team-based organization: organizational philosophy, organizational structure, systems, policies, and skills (see Figure 8.1). In a nutshell, here is what each entails:

- **Organizational philosophy.** Companies in which work teams flourish are characterized by a management philosophy and core values that emphasize high em-

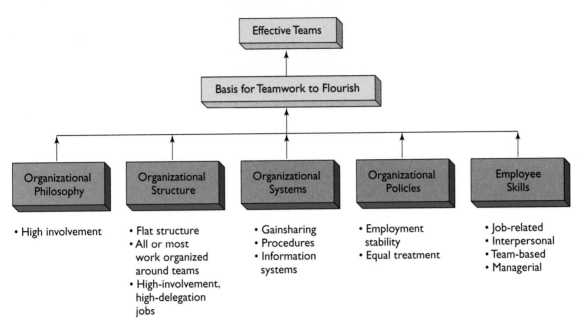

FIGURE 8.1
Designing Organizations to Manage Teams

ployee involvement and trust. For example, many companies like Saturn and Toyota emphasize values such as "People can be trusted to make important decisions about their work activities."

■ **Organizational structure.** Team-based organizational structures are flat, with few supervisors and delegation of much decision-making authority to the work teams themselves. In turn, the work teams in firms like Chesebrough-Ponds carry out tasks ranging from scheduling overtime to actually doing the work. Organizational charts are often nonexistent.

■ **Systems.** The company's systems (and especially its reward systems) should also support the team-based approach. For example, in team-based companies like Toyota, "gainsharing" incentives—which pay employees a portion of the savings incurred by their hard work—are paid to the team as a whole rather than to individual employees. This supports the idea that teamwork is rewarded. Other important, team-oriented systems decisions include internal TV systems to keep employees informed and team-friendly procedures such as "Consult those making a product before making engineering changes to the product."

■ **Policies.** Building close-knit cohesive work teams takes time and therefore requires company policies that support and encourage teamwork. For example, "equal treatment" policies—no reserved parking spaces, minimal status differences in offices and dress, employee evaluations of supervisors and vice versa—help to encourage a sense of community. Most team-based organizations also emphasize policies of employment stability. At a Toyota plant, for example, slack demand might mean that more employees spend time being trained to develop new skills rather than simply be laid off until more work develops.

■ **Skills.** Work teams typically have wide-ranging responsibilities (such as scheduling their own time, hiring their own team members, installing their own units, and so on); therefore, it is important that all team members have a wide range of skills. This includes (1) the job skills to actually do the job (such as welding); (2) the interpersonal skills to work in a healthy manner with and in the team (listening, communicating, and so on); (3) team skills (such as problem solving and running decision-making meetings); and (4) management skills (including planning, leading, and controlling, for instance).

Building Network-Based Organizations

Many firms today superimpose "organizational networks" over their existing structures. In general, an *organizational network* is a system of interconnected or cooperating individuals.[14] In this section we describe three types of networks: formal organizational networks, informal organizational networks, and electronic information networks. The network is, in essence, superimposed over the existing organizational structure, thus enhancing the likelihood that the work of far-flung units can be carried out promptly and in a coordinated way if quick decisions on some matters must be made.

Whether formal or informal, organizational networks share the same basic idea: to link managers from various departments, levels, and geographic areas into a multidisciplinary team whose members communicate across normal organizational boundaries. Let us first compare informal and formal networks.

Formal Networks

formal organizational network
A recognized group of managers assembled by the CEO and the senior executive team and drawn from across the company's functions, business units, and geography, and from different levels of the hierarchy.

A **formal organizational network** has been defined as "a recognized group of managers assembled by the CEO and the senior executive team.... The members are drawn from across the company's functions, business units, and geography, and from different levels of the hierarchy. The number of managers involved almost never exceeds 100 and can be fewer than 25—even in global companies with tens of thousands of employees."[15]

The cross-functional nature of formal networks is illustrated in Figure 8.2. Note the number of organizational levels and departments represented by the blue boxes.

Formal networks differ from teams, cross-functional task forces, or ad hoc groups in three ways.[16] First, unlike most task forces, networks are not temporary. In fact, it is each manager's continuing experience in the network that helps build the shared understanding among members and explains the network's effectiveness.

Second, unlike most teams and task forces, networks take the initiative in finding and solving problems. In other words, they do not just solve the specific problems they are given.

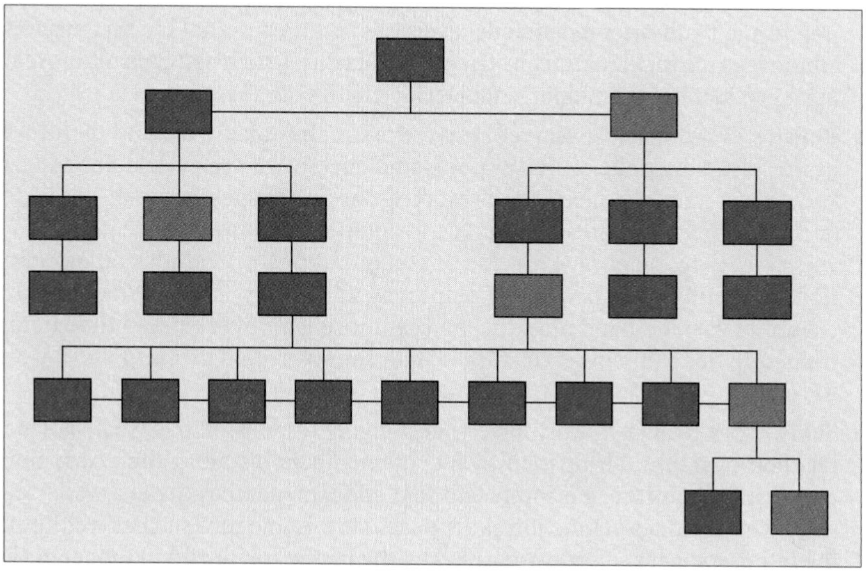

FIGURE 8.2
How Networks Reshape Organizations—For Results
The members of a formal network may be selected from various departments and organizational levels.

Third, the existence of the formal network changes—or should change—the nature of top management's job. With the networks in place, CEOs "no longer define their jobs as making all substantive operating decisions on their own."[17] Instead, although CEOs still make many decisions, the network can handle more of the inter-unit coordinating that the CEO might otherwise have to do, leaving him or her more time for strategic planning.

One such formal network might be set up so that 19 middle managers from various departments and levels constitute the firm's operating committee, which is actually a formal network. The managers influence most of the firm's key operating decisions through this committee. They meet for several hours on Monday mornings. Here they review and decide on tactical issues (delivery schedules and prices, for instance) and work on longer-term issues such as five-year business plans.

The experience of Electrolux illustrates how networks can be used to support a company's strategy. When Leif Johansson took over an Electrolux division that stretched from Norway to Italy, he inherited a daunting task. Electrolux's line included 20 products, numerous acquired companies, and more than 200 plants in many countries. Each presented unique market positions, capabilities, plant capacity, and competitive situations. Johansson recognized that his strategy had to be to create strengths across functional and geographic borders if he was to derive maximum economies of scale from the multi-product, multi-plant, multinational operation.

Local managers convinced him that abandoning local brands would jeopardize existing distribution channels and customer loyalty. But how could he derive the benefits of Electrolux's large multi-country scale while maintaining local brands' autonomy? His solution was to appoint a *formal network* comprising managers from various countries. Johansson's network structure helped to keep operations flexible and responsive. Local managers still had wide authority to design and market local brands. But the formal network helped to provide the overall multinational and multi-product coordination that helped Electrolux obtain economies of scale.[18]

Informal Networks

Networks needn't be formally assigned, and indeed many firms, particularly multinationals, encourage the growth of informal organizational networks. "Here," as one expert puts it, "creating confidence in the work of colleagues around the world and building up personal relationships are the key factors."[19] Unlike formal networks, with their assigned membership and purpose, **informal organizational networks** consist of cooperating individuals who are interconnected only informally. They share information and help solve each other's problems based on their personal knowledge of each other's expertise.

There are several ways to nurture the personal relationships on which informal networks are built. For example, multinationals like Phillips and Shell build personal relationships through international executive development programs, bringing managers from around the world to work together in training centres in New York and London. Other firms, like Olivetti, have international management development centres in their home cities, to which they bring their managers.

Moving managers from facility to facility around the world is another way to build informal networks. Transferring employees enables managers to build lasting relationships around the globe, and some firms, such as Shell, transfer employees around the world in great numbers. In one case, for instance:

> [International mobility] has created what one might call a "nervous system" that facilitates both corporate strategic control and the flow of information throughout the firm. Widespread transfers have created an informal information network, a superior degree of communication and mutual understanding between headquarters and subsidiaries and between subsidiaries themselves, as well as a stronger identification with the corporate culture, without compromising the local subsidiary cultures.[20]

Development programs like these help to build informal networks in several ways. Perhaps most notably, the socializing that takes place builds personal relationships among

informal organizational network
A group of cooperating individuals who are interconnected only informally and who share information and help solve each other's problems based on their personal knowledge of each other's expertise.

managers from the firm's facilities around the world. Such personal relationships then facilitate global networking and communications. So, if a new Shell Latin America sales manager needs to see a new client, she might call a Shell Zurich manager she knows who has a contact at the client firm.

Electronic Networking

The rise of the Internet and of special "collaborative computing" networking software lets companies make better use of existing formal and informal networks and, indeed, encourages all employees throughout the firm to network. The advantages of such computer-based networking aren't limited to businesses, of course. For example,

> science advisors to legislators joined together with technical professional societies, federal labs and public interest research groups to form Legitec Network. ...[Using the network], for example, one [northern U.S.] state posed the question: "What are alternatives to road salt for dealing with icy highways without polluting water supplies?" Another state, having recently dealt with the problem, responded, as did associations and labs that knew of relevant research on the topic. Other frost-belt states joined the topic to get the benefit of inquiry responses that might help their states as well....[21]

Electronic networking is at the heart of many business organizations today. For example, Price Waterhouse's 18 000 accountants stay in touch with each other thanks to electronic bulletin boards on over 1000 different subjects. Thus, a Dublin employee with a question about dairy plant accounting might have her question answered by a networked colleague half a world away.[22] Group decision support systems allow employees—even those in different countries—to brainstorm ideas and work together on projects.[23]

Networking software products do more than simply link employees, customers, suppliers, and partners electronically. They enable companies to create what amount to electronic networked organizations, ones in which communications and relationships ignore traditional departmental boundaries, and in which even the traditional boundaries separating the company from its customers and its suppliers largely cease to exist. Companies today use the Internet, intranets, and similar links between themselves, customers, and suppliers to communicate in what two experts call **hyperarchies.** The effect of such networking is illustrated in Figure 8.3. In a hyperarchy, the network is so complete that basically everyone can communicate with anyone else, and is encouraged to do so. As these experts put it, "Hyperarchy challenges all hierarchies, whether of logic or of power, with the possibility (or the threat) of random access and information symmetry."[24] In other words, everyone from first-line employees on up can communicate digitally with everyone else. The result is an organization in which communication isn't restricted by the organization chart or the chain of command—a sort of digital boundaryless organization.

To Microsoft's Bill Gates, ensuring that employees can communicate is a good example of knowledge management. Here's how he puts it:

> Knowledge management is nothing more than managing information flow, getting the right information to the people who need it so they can act on it quickly....And, knowledge management is a means, not an end. The end is to increase institutional intelligence, or corporate IQ. In today's dynamic markets a company needs a high corporate IQ to succeed. By corporate IQ I don't mean simply having a lot of smart people at your company—although it helps to start with smart people. Corporate IQ is a measure of how easily your company can share information broadly and of how well people within the organization can build on each other's ideas....The workers in a company with a high corporate IQ collaborate effectively so that all of the key people on a project are well-informed and energized.

hyperarchy
A network so complete that everyone can communicate with anyone else, and is encouraged to do so.

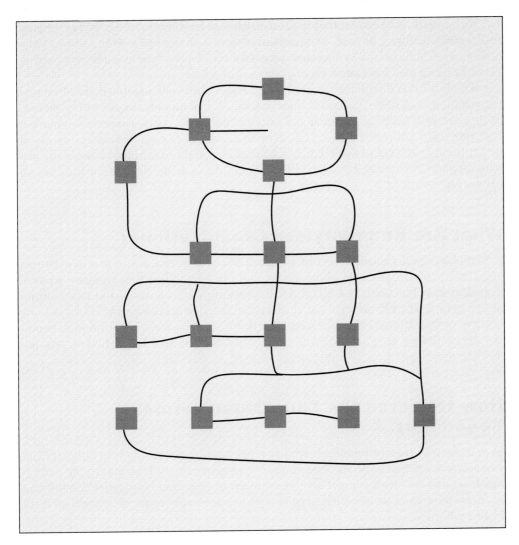

FIGURE 8.3
Hyperarchies

The ultimate goal is to have a team develop the best ideas from throughout an organization and then act with the same unity of purpose and focus that a single, well-motivated person would bring to bear on the situation.[25]

Boundaryless Organizations

"Old-style" organizations have various boundaries. Vertically, the chain of command implies clearly defined authority boundaries: The president gives orders to the vice-president, who gives orders to the managers, and so on down the line. There are also clearly delineated horizontal or departmental boundaries such that most companies are separated into what some call "smokestacks": the production department has its own responsibilities, the sales department has its, and so on. Similarly, if the company happens to be divisionalized, then the work of each division is self-contained and each division often proceeds on the assumption that it can (and should) do its job with little or no interaction with the other product divisions.[26]

We've seen that such boundary-filled organizations once served a useful purpose. Jobs were specialized, lines of communication were well defined, and the slow-arriving problems could be solved in a relatively mechanical, step-by-step manner by an organization in which everyone knew exactly where they stood.

For most firms, things are different today. Rapid change demands a more responsive organization. As a result, yesterday's neat organizational boundaries need to be pierced, as they are with teams and formal and informal networks. As two experts summarized it, "Companies are replacing vertical hierarchies with horizontal networks; linking together traditional functions through interfunctional teams; and forming strategic alliances with suppliers, customers, and even competitors."[27] In so doing, they are creating boundaryless organizations.

What Are Boundaryless Organizations?

boundaryless organization
An organization in which the widespread use of teams, networks, and similar structural mechanisms means that the boundaries that typically separate organizational functions and hierarchical levels are reduced and made more permeable.

A **boundaryless organization** is one in which the widespread use of teams, networks, and similar structural mechanisms means that the boundaries that typically separate organizational functions and hierarchical levels are reduced and made more permeable.[28] In fact, taken to the extreme, the boundaryless company is one in which not only internal organizational boundaries but also those between the company and its suppliers and customers are stripped away. (Recall our discussion of the virtual corporation in Chapter 6.)

How to Pierce the Four Organizational Boundaries

In practice, four specific boundaries must be pierced if the company is to obtain full advantage of teams and networks: the authority boundary, the task boundary, the political boundary, and the identity boundary.[29] A summary of these four boundaries and the managerial tensions and feelings that must be addressed in order to pierce them is shown in Figure 8.4.

Nortel Networks manufacturing plant in Mexico. Note the Canadian, Mexican, and U.S. flags on the back wall of the plant.

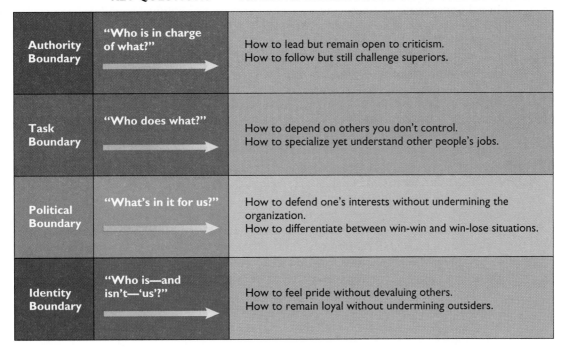

FIGURE 8.4
The Four Organizational Boundaries That Matter
In setting up a boundaryless organization, four boundaries must be overcome, but doing so means dealing with the resulting tensions.

The Authority Boundary. Superiors and subordinates—even those found in self-managing teams or formal networks—always meet at an **authority boundary** in every company.

Therein lies the problem: To achieve the responsiveness required of a team-based or network structure, just issuing and following orders "is no longer good enough."[30] For example, a manager in a formal network who happened to be a vice-president would inhibit the network's effectiveness if she demanded the right to give orders based solely on the fact that she was the highest-ranking person in the network. Doing so would undermine the collaboration and the reliance on experts that are two advantages of teams and networks.

Piercing the authority boundary thus requires three things. Bosses must learn how to lead while remaining open to criticism. They must be willing to accept "orders" from lower-ranking employees who happen to be experts on the problems at hand. And "subordinates" must be trained and encouraged to follow but still challenge superiors if an issue must be raised.

The Task Boundary. Creating a boundaryless organization also requires managing the **task boundary**, which means changing the way that employees feel about who does what when employees from different departments must divide up their work. Specifically, managing the task boundary means training and encouraging employees to rid themselves of the "it's not my job" attitude that typically compartmentalizes one employee's area from another's:

> Indeed, their own performance may depend on what their colleagues do. So, while focusing primarily on their own task, they must also take a lively interest in the challenges and problems facing others who contribute in different ways to the final product or service.[31]

The Political Boundary. Differences in political agendas often separate employees as well. For example, manufacturing typically has a strong interest in smoothing out the demand for its products and in making the firm's products as easy to produce as possible. Sales, on the other hand, has an equally legitimate interest in maximizing sales (even if it means

authority boundary
The boundary at which superiors and subordinates always meet.

task boundary
The boundary defining how employees from different departments feel about "who does what" as the necessary work is divided up.

accepting a lot of custom or rush orders). The result of such opposing agendas in a traditional organization can be a conflict at the departments' **political boundary**.

Members of each special-interest group in a boundaryless firm may still ask, "What's in it for us?" when a decision must be made. But they must be encouraged to take a more collegial, consensus-oriented approach, defending their interests without undermining the best interests of the team, network, or organization.

The Identity Boundary. Everyone identifies with several groups. For example, a GM Canada accountant might identify with her colleagues in the accounting profession, with her co-workers in the GM accounting department, and perhaps with General Motors Corporation itself, to name a few. The **identity boundary** means that we tend to identify with those groups with which we have shared experiences and with which we believe we share fundamental values.

Unfortunately, such identification tends to foster an "us" versus "them" mentality. The problem at the identity boundary arises because people tend to trust those with whom they identify but distrust others. Attitudes like these can undermine the free-flowing cooperation that responsive, networking, or team-based organizations require.

Achieving boundarylessness thus also means piercing the identity boundary, and there are several ways to do this. One is to train and socialize all of the firm's employees so that they come to identify first with the company and its goals and ways of doing things: "The company comes first" becomes their motto. Another is to emphasize that while team spirit may be laudable, employees must avoid "devaluing the potential contribution of other groups."[32]

The Horizontal Corporation

In many firms today, boundarylessness translates into what management experts call a horizontal corporation. As illustrated in Figure 8.5, the **horizontal corporation** is a structure organized around customer-oriented processes such as new-product development, sales and fulfilment, and customer support. Employees work together in multidisciplinary teams; each team performs one or more of the processes. In its purest form, a horizontal corporation structure eliminates functional departments, instead sprinkling functional specialists

political boundary
The boundary defining what different departments want, based on who will benefit from an activity and who will not.

identity boundary
The boundary identifying those who share values and experiences from those who do not.

horizontal corporation
A structure organized around customer-oriented processes such as new-product development, sales and fulfilment, and customer support.

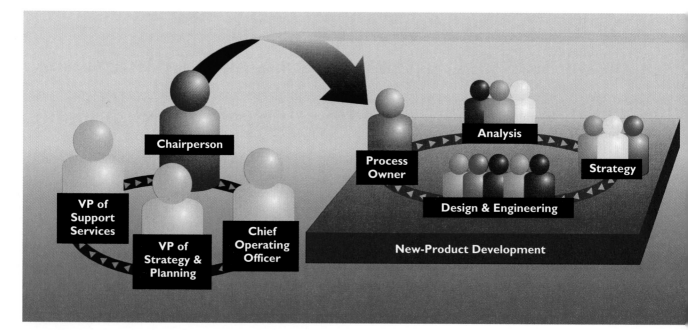

FIGURE 8.5
The Horizontal Corporation
In the horizontal corporation the work is organized around cross-functional processes with multi-function teams carrying out the tasks needed to service the customer.

throughout the key process teams. They then work together on those teams with other functional specialists to accomplish the process-oriented team's mission, be it product development, sales and fulfilment, customer support, or some other goal. The horizontal structure usually has a small team of senior executives to ensure strategic direction and to provide essential staff support functions like human resource management.[33]

Horizontal Corporations in Practice. Companies organize horizontally for several reasons. Many firms found that downsizing did not change the fundamental way that their departments accomplished their work. The work of the organization—from getting the sales order to processing an invoice—was still handed from department to department like a baton in a relay race. At truck rental firm Ryder Systems, for instance, purchasing a vehicle for subsequent leasing required as many as 17 handoffs, as the relevant documents made their way from one department to another. Since such handoffs occurred both horizontally and vertically, the amount of time and energy wasted was enormous until Ryder reduced it by establishing a multi-specialist horizontal "vehicle purchase" group.

Ryder Systems
www.ryder.com

Horizontal structures also help to obliterate the organizational boundaries we mentioned earlier. Even in divisionalized firms, functional areas tend to grow into fiefdoms in which protecting one's turf takes priority over satisfying customer needs. Such territorial thinking is less likely to occur where the "departments" are not departments at all, but essentially multi-functional teams organized to provide basic customer-oriented processes. Thus the horizontal new-product-development process team might replace the new-product-development sequence, in which each department (such as engineering, production, and sales) did its part and then passed the responsibility to the next department.

Several companies are moving towards the horizontal model. For example, General Electric's lighting business is organized around multidisciplinary teams, each carrying out more than 100 processes, from new-product design to improving the efficiency of manufacturing machinery. As shown in Figure 8.6, the essence of creating a horizontal corporation is defining the firm's core processes and then organizing teams around these while linking each process team's performance to specific customer-related objectives. Once the horizontal heart of the organization is in place, the firm eliminates the functions, levels, and staff departments that do not directly contribute to the work of the process-oriented teams.

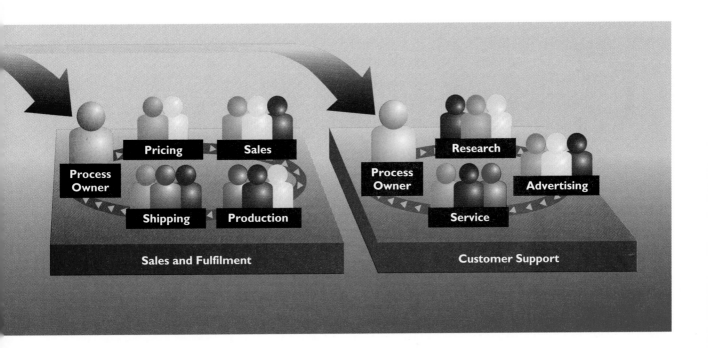

| Identify strategic objectives. | Analyze key competitive advantages to fulfil objectives. | Define **core processes**, focusing on what's essential to accomplish your goals. | **Organize around processes, not functions.** Each process should link related tasks to yield a product or service to a customer. | **Eliminate all activities that fail to add value or contribute to the key objectives.** |

THE PEOPLE SIDE OF MANAGING

Organizing Horizontally

Many companies organize around complete, horizontal processes to speed decision making and get orders out faster to the customers, but doing so requires more than just reorganizing.[34] In successful reorganizations, management fosters what researchers in one study call a "collective sense of responsibility." In other words, the employees took an active interest in their colleagues and in improving the outcome of their mutual efforts. They were willing to offer their colleagues a helping hand and to work hard so the team would not be let down.

How do you cultivate that kind of collective responsibility in a horizontal organization? In four ways, these researchers found:[35]

- *Make responsibilities overlap.* Design individual jobs as broadly as possible and keep the number of job titles to a minimum. That way, responsibility boundaries blur, and employees are more inclined to pitch in and help each other.

- *Base rewards on unit performance.* In this study the most successfully reorganized companies based employees' rewards (salaries, incentives, recognition) on the performance of the units to which they belonged. That helped to emphasize the importance of everyone working together.

- *Change the physical layout.* In other words, don't just reorganize. Change the physical layout so that it promotes collective responsibility, such as by letting people see each other's work.

- *Redesign work procedures.* Work procedures should encourage collective responsibility. Provide computer terminals so that employees can communicate more readily; use the e-mail network to keep employees informed of how they're doing as a team; and make sure managers are available if the team or any member has an issue to discuss.

Two experts say that some managers do underestimate the difficulty of breaking the functional mindset. They spend all of their time fine-tuning new (process-oriented) tasks, instead of concentrating on the people side of the problem:

Such managers overlook the importance of changing their organizations' culture. They fail to see that collective responsibility is an attitude, a value, a concern. It means taking an interest in one's colleagues and in improving the outcome of mutual (as opposed to individual) efforts. People who feel collectively responsible are willing to work especially hard to not let the team down. They will take the initiative in offering a colleague a helping hand with a work problem, even though doing so might make it more difficult for them to meet their own deadlines.[36]

| Cut function and staff departments to a minimum, preserving key expertise. | Appoint a manager or team as the "owner" of each core process. | Create multidisciplinary teams to run each process. | Set specific performance objectives for each process. | Empower employees with authority and information to achieve goals. | Revamp training, appraisal, pay, and budgetary systems to support the new structure and link it to customer satisfaction. |

FIGURE 8.6
How to Create a Horizontal Corporation
Creating a horizontal organization involves several steps, starting with determining the firm's strategic objectives, and including flattening the hierarchy and using teams to accomplish the work.

Can a Job Be Too Interesting?

job enrichment
Building opportunities for achievement into a job by making it more interesting and challenging.

Organizational behaviour experts tend to assume that the interesting and "enriched" jobs that result from change-oriented team-based structures are on the whole a good thing. For example, psychologist Frederick Herzberg recommends **job enrichment**, by which he means building opportunities for achievement into a job by making it more interesting and challenging. This is often accomplished by giving a worker more autonomy and allowing him or her to do more of the planning and inspecting normally done by the supervisor.[37] And, of course, such job enrichment often results when decisions are pushed down to decision-making teams.

Unfortunately, having a more interesting job is not always what it's cut out to be. For one thing, there's considerable evidence that putting too many demands on someone can actually lead to so much stress it can backfire.

A recent study of 418 full-time employees illustrates the problem. The researchers focused on the extent to which the scope of the employees' jobs—for instance, how many skills were needed to perform the jobs and how much autonomy employees had—was related to the amount of job stress the employees reported. The findings suggest that managers should use caution before dumping too much autonomy on employees.

The researchers basically drew three conclusions from their findings:

1. There is a U-shaped relationship between job scope and stress (see Figure 8.7). In other words, when the job is too narrow, too boring, and too routine, job stress is high, but the opposite is also true: If the job is too enriched and the employee has too much responsibility and autonomy, that also triggers job stress. Managers have to design into jobs the right level of autonomy, decision-making authority, and responsibility to keep job stress to a minimum.

2. Particularly when dealing with wide-scope jobs, it's crucial to have a good fit between (1) the demands of the job, and (2) the employee's ability to handle these demands. The more that employees perceived a misfit between the two, the more stress they experienced. Managers must therefore be particularly careful to put people into jobs that they can do and then provide the training to ensure they then can do their jobs well.

3. It's not just the broader jobs and increased autonomy of team-based structures that can lead to job stress; downsizing can cause it, too. The process is as follows: A company

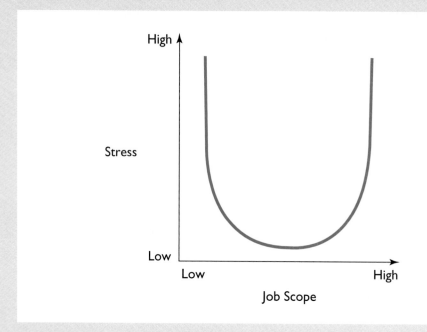

FIGURE 8.7
The Relationship Between Job Scope and Stress

downsizes; several layers of middle managers are squeezed out; the remaining employees each end up doing their previous work plus the work of one or more of their former colleagues; and job stress rises.

Job stress and its accompanying emotional exhaustion are not problems to be taken lightly. Quite aside from the very considerable human cost of exposing employees to job stress, the financial impact in terms of absences, hospitalization, and so on can be enormous.[38]

How can such adverse results be avoided? We'll discuss this further in later chapters, but based on this study the implications for managers are as follows:

1. Don't assume that more autonomy is always a good thing. Giving too much autonomy too fast can trigger job stress.

2. Provide adequate training, raise competence levels, and help ensure that employees have the skills they need to do their jobs.

3. Monitor the enrichment program carefully for signs of stress.

4. Be prepared to provide special support (counselling, for instance) for employees who remain with the firm after it downsizes.[39]

Creating Federal Organizations

For some companies, managing change means moving to what we might call federal organizations. In **federal organizations** (as in federal governments), power is distributed between a central authority and a number of constituent units, but the central unit's authority is intentionally limited.[40] Organizing and disbursing power in this way enables a company to marshal resources and bring them to bear quickly, while giving the remote units the authority and flexibility they need to respond quickly to local challenges.

We've already discussed one example. At ABB, the former CEO broke his company into 5000 profit centres, each containing about 50 employees. Each unit had wide authority to act more or less like a mini-company in its dealings with customers and suppliers. However, the parent firm retained control over matters like company-wide strategy and financing major projects. Let's look at two more recent federal organizations.

federal organization
An organization in which power is distributed between a central authority and a number of constituent units, but the central unit's authority is intentionally limited.

Virtual Organizations

It often happens that a company has to organize considerable resources to accomplish a significant project, but can't afford the time or expense of acquiring and owning those resources itself. The question then becomes, "How can we accomplish that?" For many firms, the answer (as we first saw on page 174) is a virtual corporation, "a temporary network of independent companies—suppliers, customers, perhaps even rivals—linked by information technology to share skills, costs, and access to one another's markets."[41] Virtual corporations usually are not "corporations" at all in the traditional sense, but rather networks of companies, each of which brings to the virtual corporation its special expertise. For example, AT&T worked with Matsushita Electronics Industrial Co. to speed production of its Safari notebook computer, which itself was designed by Henry Dreyfuss Associates.

Organizationally, virtual organizations have two main features. First, "the central feature of virtual organizations is their dependence on a federation of alliances and partnerships with other organizations."[42] "A virtual organization operates as a federated collection of enterprises tied together through contractual and other means, such as partial ownership arrangements. Specific arrangements include joint ventures, strategic alliances, minority investments, consortia, coalitions, outsourcing, and franchises."[43]

The virtual organization's second feature stems from this first characteristic: Corporate self-interest (rather than authority) generally plays a major role in maintaining organizational integrity. In traditional (non-virtual) organizations, authority is dispersed down the chain of command and employees who actually do the work are generally expected to follow legitimate orders. In virtual organizations, on the other hand, it's not a company's employees who are doing the work, but the principals and employees of its virtual partners, so that "giving orders" and relying solely on a chain of command is usually not a constructive way to get things done. Instead, assignments are made, partners are chosen for competence and reliability, and arrangements that provide for equitable incentives are negotiated.[44]

The Cellular Organization

Do you remember your biology lessons from high school? If you do, it will be easier to understand what some experts have called cellular organizations.

In biology, cells are the microscopic structural units of the body, just as bricks are the building blocks of a house. But there the similarity ends. Cells are not just building blocks but also independent functional units, each able to live, grow, repair itself, and often learn and thus adapt on its own. All cells have certain things in common (such as nuclei and cell membranes), yet cells also differ markedly in the jobs they have to do. Complex organisms (like humans) are composed of billions and billions of specialized cells (skin, hair, eyes, and so on), each making its own unique contribution to the organism's functioning.

Cellular organizations are much the same. "Cells"—often small independent companies, but also self-managing teams—are the basic building blocks of cellular organizations. As in biology, each cell in a cellular organization is organized to be self-sufficient, to live and adapt, and to perform a specialized function. And (also as in biology), each individual cell contributes to the overall functioning of the company, while simultaneously deriving needed resources from the parent firm.

While team-based organizations and mini-unit structures (such as the ones at ABB) have cellular features, **cellular organization** usually denotes something more. For example, consider the cellular organization at Technical and Computer Graphics Company (TCG), which develops a wide variety of products such as portable and hand-held data terminals.[45] TCG is organized around 13 individual small firms: "Like a cell in a large organism, each firm has its own purpose and ability to function independently, but shares features and purposes with all of its sister firms."[46]

Figure 8.8 summarizes how TCG's cellular structure works. At TCG, each individual firm continually searches for new product and service opportunities. Then, when a particular venture—say, developing and selling a new product—shows concrete progress, the initiating firm acts as project leader for what the company calls its triangulation process. Triangulation means that the initiating firm creates and leads a three-way partnership consisting of (1) one or more of TCG's firms, (2) an external joint venture partner, and (3) a principal customer for the product or service.[47] Specifically,

> the first step in the triangulation process is to identify and collaborate with a joint-venture partner, a firm with expertise in the proposed technology. TCG receives partial funding for the project from the joint-venture partner, and also gains access to technical ideas and distribution channels. Next, the project leader firm identifies an initial large customer for the new project....according to TCG's governance principles, the project leader is also expected to search among the other TCG companies for additional partners—not only because they are needed for their technical contribution, but also because the collaboration itself is expected to enhance overall organizational knowhow.[48]

cellular organization
A structure in which independent companies or self-managing teams (cells) are self-sufficient and perform specialized functions. Each cell contributes to the overall functioning of the company.

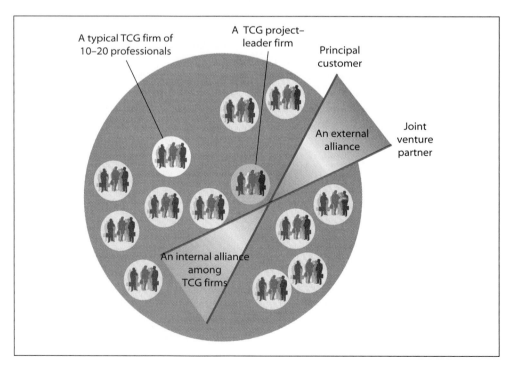

FIGURE 8.8
TCG's Cellular Organization

While TCG is thus essentially composed of its 13 individual, self-contained "cells," the triangulation process and mutual support among the 13 firms help make TCG more than just the sum of its parts. For example, the firms learn from one another, gain access to each other's customers, and help to capitalize and fund each other's projects.

In turn, TCG's cellular approach is based on three underlying principles: (1) Each individual firm must accept its entrepreneurial responsibilities; for instance, with respect to identifying new project opportunities and pursuing customers; (2) Each individual firm is "self-organized"; in other words, it is a self-contained and functioning firm with "both the ability and freedom to reach deeply into its own know-how to create responses to a continuously evolving set of customer and partner needs"; and (3) Each firm has the responsibility to be profitable and the opportunity to invest in (and even own stock in) the other TCG firms.

Fitting the Organization to the Task

The fact that many firms today are becoming "boundaryless," "team-based," or "horizontal" so as to become more highly responsive could give the impression that the "old-style" bureaucratic organization is gone for good. In fact, nothing could be further from the truth. Yes, responsiveness (for instance, Amazon.com being able to respond quickly to Barnes and Noble's Internet innovations) does generally demand the kind of loose, networked relationships that only such modern organizations can provide. However, there are still many situations (in manufacturing, for instance) where efficiency is king, and where you'll still find that the classical approach applies.

Barnes and Noble
www.bn.com

What this means, of course, is that you have to fit the organization to the demands of the task. In other words, you have to take a "contingency approach" to how you organize. It is certainly true that "strategy determines structure," and that the organization structure grows out of the plan (recall your summer tour assignments to Rosa, Ned, and Ruth, for instance). This also means that in practice the company's strategy determines the competitive playing field on which you compete, and some playing fields require a lot quicker responses than do others.[49] Recall from Chapter 7 that Chandler, in his strategy-determines-structure study (see page 217), found that companies with diversification strategies competed on so many fronts that they had to set up decentralized product divisions to deal with them all. Others stayed in one business where efficiency was king, and so stayed with the classical, functional organization.

In addition to Chandler, three other organizational theorists have conducted important studies regarding how to fit the structure to the task, and it's appropriate that we end this chapter by briefly reviewing them.

Organization and Environment: The Burns and Stalker Studies

Researchers Tom Burns and G.M. Stalker studied about 20 industrial firms in the United Kingdom a number of years ago. Their goal was to determine how the nature of a firm's environment affected the way in which the firm was organized and managed. They found that a stable, unchanging environment demanded a different type of organization than did a rapidly changing one.[50] We can illustrate Burns' and Stalker's findings by focusing on two contrasting environments that they studied: the stable environment and the innovative environment.

Organizing in a Stable Environment. A stable environment can be characterized as follows:

1. Demand for the organization's product or service is stable and predictable.

2. There is an unchanging set of competitors.

3. Technological innovation and new-product developments are evolutionary rather than revolutionary; necessary product changes can be predicted well in advance and the required modifications can be made at a leisurely pace.

4. Government policies regarding regulation and taxation of the industry change little over time.

Burns and Stalker found that a rayon manufacturer they studied operated in such a stable environment. To be successful in this industry, the parent firm had to keep costs down and be as efficient as possible. Its existence, therefore, depended on keeping unexpected occurrences to a minimum, so as to maintain steady, high-volume production runs.

Burns and Stalker found that the rayon mill's organizational structure seemed to reflect this stable, unchanging environment and emphasis on efficiency. The organization was a "pyramid of knowledge" in that top management made most decisions and communicated them downward. Decision making in the plant was highly centralized, and the plant was run on the basis of an elaborate network of policies, procedures, rules, and tight production controls. Job descriptions were carefully defined, and everyone from the top of the organization to the bottom had a very specialized job to do.[51] Coordination was accomplished via the chain of command.

Organizing in an Innovative Environment. An innovative environment is characterized by the following factors:

1. Demand for the organization's product or service can change drastically, sometimes overnight, as competitors introduce radically improved products.

2. Sudden, unexpected changes in the nature of the organization's competitors.[52]

3. An extremely rapid rate of technological innovation and new-product development. Organizations in innovative environments usually rely heavily on research and development for their survival.

4. Quickly evolving government policies regarding regulation and taxation that try to keep pace with the stream of new and more technologically advanced products being introduced by firms.

Innovative environments are typical of industries such as Internet software, electronics, and computers; the space industry (satellites, space platforms); the deep-sea industry (new sources of food and minerals); and the gene industry (high-yielding crops, "oil-eating" bacteria).

Burns and Stalker found that several of the electronics firms they studied were competing in an innovative environment. Their existence depended on being able to continually introduce innovative electronic components. They also had to be constantly on the alert for innovations by competitors, so responsiveness and creativity (rather than efficiency) were paramount.

In these firms, the researchers found a "deliberate attempt to avoid specifying individual tasks."[53] Each worker's job, in other words, might change daily, as employees rushed to respond to the "problem of the day." Most important, all employees recognized the need for sharing common beliefs and goals, and these common goals (such as "Let's make sure we only produce first-rate products") helped ensure that all could work together with little or no guidance.

This pervasive self-control helped the firm to adapt quickly and unbureaucratically to its rapidly changing environment. When a problem arose, an employee took the initiative to solve it, or took it to the person he or she felt was in the best position to solve it (just like is done in today's boundaryless organizations). This often meant bypassing the formal chain of command. The head of one such firm attacked the idea of an organization chart as inapplicable to his concern and as a dangerous method of thinking about industrial management. According to him, the first requirement of management was that it make the fullest use of the capacities of its members; an individual's job should be defined as little as possible so that it will "shape itself" to his or her special abilities and initiative.[54]

Mechanistic and Organic Organizations. Their findings led Burns and Stalker to distinguish between two types of organizations, which they called mechanistic and organic. The rayon firm was typical of mechanistic, classic organizations; the electronics firms were typical of the organic organizations. **Mechanistic organizations**, they said, are characterized by:

- Close adherence to the chain of command.
- A functional division of work: The problems and tasks facing the concern as a whole are broken down into specialized activities.
- Highly specialized jobs.
- Use of the formal hierarchy for coordination.
- Detailed job descriptions that provide a precise definition of rights, obligations, and technical methods for performing each job.
- A tendency for interaction between employees to be vertical, "between superior and subordinate."
- A tendency for behaviour to be governed by the instructions and decisions issued by superiors.

Organic organizations are characterized by:

- Little preoccupation with the chain of command.
- A more self-contained, divisionalized structure of work.
- Job responsibility not viewed by employees as a limited field of rights, obligations, and methods. (Employees do not respond to requests by saying, "That's not my job.")
- Jobs that are not clearly defined in advance but instead are continually adjusted and redefined as the situation demands.
- A network or matrix structure of communication.
- Lateral rather than vertical communication and an emphasis on consultation rather than command. Communication generally consists of information and advice rather than instructions and decisions.
- A pervasive commitment to the organization's tasks that motivates employees to maintain self-control (as opposed to having performance controlled through a system of rewards and penalties, as is often the case in mechanistic organizations).[55]

In terms of organizational structure, the Burns and Stalker findings can be summarized as follows:

1. *Lines of authority.* In mechanistic organizations, the lines of authority are clear and everyone closely adheres to the chain of command. In organic organizations, employees' jobs are always changing and the lines of authority are not as clear. There is less emphasis on the chain of command and more emphasis on speaking directly with the person who might have an answer to the problem.

2. *Departmentalization.* In mechanistic organizations (with their emphasis on efficiency), functional departmentalization prevails. In organic organizations (where flexibility is the rule), product/divisional departmentalization prevails.

3. *Degree of specialization of jobs.* In mechanistic organizations, each employee has a highly specialized job at which he or she is expected to become an expert. In organic organizations, "job enlargement" is the rule.

mechanistic organization
An organization that stresses highly structured work, clearly stated authority relations, centralized authority, and vertical communication.

organic organization
An organization that puts little emphasis on hierarchical authority and encourages managers and subordinates to work together as a team to solve problems.

4. *Delegation and decentralization.* In mechanistic organizations, most important decisions are centralized. In organic organizations, more important decisions are made at lower levels; they are more decentralized.

5. *Span of control.* The span of control is narrow in mechanistic organizations, and there is close supervision. Spans of control are wider in organic organizations, and supervision is more general.

Organization and Technology: The Woodward Studies

British researcher Joan Woodward's contribution lies in her discovery that a firm's production technology (the processes it uses to produce its products or services) affects the way in which the firm should be organized.

Almost from the outset Woodward and her associates confronted a dilemma: Organizational structure seemed at first to have no relationship to success for the firms they studied. The research team spent months analyzing data on each company's history and background, size, and policies and procedures. None of these factors seemed to explain why some successful firms had classic, mechanistic structures while others had organic ones. Finally, Woodward's team decided to classify the companies according to their production technologies, as follows:

1. *Unit and small-batch production.* These companies produced one-at-a-time prototypes and specialized custom units to customers' requirements (like fine pianos). They had to be very responsive to customer needs.

2. *Large-batch and mass production.* These companies produced large batches of products on assembly lines (like Ford cars). Here efficiency was emphasized.

3. *Process production.* These companies produced products such as paper and petroleum products through continuously running facilities. Here highly trained technicians had to be ready to respond at a moment's notice to any production emergency.

Once the firms were classified, it became clear that a different type of organizational structure was appropriate for each type of technology. Some of Woodward's findings are summarized in Table 8.1. Note that organic structures were usually found in the unit and process production firms; mass production firms usually had mechanistic structures.

In terms of organizational structure, the Woodward findings can be summarized as follows:

1. *Lines of authority.* The lines of authority and adherence to the chain of com-

TABLE 8.1 *Summary of Woodward's Research Findings*			
	UNIT AND SMALL-BATCH FIRMS (EXAMPLE: CUSTOM-BUILT CARS)	LARGE-BATCH AND MASS PRODUCTION (EXAMPLE: MASS-PRODUCED CARS)	PROCESS PRODUCTION (EXAMPLE: OIL REFINERY)
Chain of Command	Not Clear	Clear	Not Clear
Span of Control	Narrow	Wide	Narrow
Departmentalization	Product	Function	Product
Overall Organization	Organic	Mechanistic	Organic

mand are rigid in mass production firms, but more informal and flexible in unit and process production firms.

2. *Departmentalization.* There is functional departmentalization in mass production firms, and product departmentalization in unit and process production firms.

3. *Degree of specialization of jobs.* Jobs are highly specialized in mass production firms, and less so in unit and process production firms.

4. *Delegation and decentralization.* Organizations tend to be centralized in mass production firms, and decentralized in unit and process production firms.

5. *Span of control.* Unit and process production firms have narrower supervisory-level spans of control than do mass production firms.

In Summary: A Contingency Approach to Organizing

The Burns and Stalker findings, and Woodward's, suggest that different organizational structures are appropriate for, or contingent on, different tasks.[56] At one extreme are organizations dealing with predictable, routine tasks like running a rayon firm.[57] Here, efficiency is emphasized, and successful organizations tend to be mechanistic. They stress adherence to rules and to the chain of command, are highly centralized, and have a more specialized, functional departmentalization.

At the other extreme, some organizations have more unpredictable tasks and are constantly faced with the need to invent new products and respond quickly to emergencies. Here creativity and entrepreneurial activities are emphasized, and to encourage these activities such organizations tend to be organic. Like many of today's boundary-less and team-based organizations, they do not urge employees to "play it by the rules" or stick to the chain of command. Decision making is decentralized and jobs and departments are less specialized.[58] These differences are summarized in Table 8.2.

TABLE 8.2 *Summary of Contingency Approach to Organizing*		
	TYPE OF ORGANIZATION	
CHARACTERISTICS	**Mechanistic**	**Organic**
Type of Environment	Stable	Innovative
Comparable to	Classical Organization	Behavioural Organization Emphasis on Self-Control
Adherence to Chain of Command	Close	Flexible—Chain of Command Often Bypassed
Type of Departmentalization	Functional	Divisional
How Specialized Are Jobs?	Specialized	Unspecialized—Jobs Change Daily with Situation
Degree of Decentralization	Decision Making Centralized	Decision Making Decentralized
Span of Control	Narrow	Wide
Type of Coordination	Hierarchy and Rules	Committees, Liaisons, and Special Integrators

1. **Give examples of the initial redesign steps for making organizations more responsive.** Managers can make a number of basic structural changes to make their organizations operate more responsively. Simplifying or reducing structure by reducing layers of management, creating mini-units, reassigning support staff, and widening spans of control while empowering workers are examples.

2. **Explain how to organize and lead team-based organizations.** Some managers find that to manage change, innovative organizational structures are advisable. Team-based organizations built around self-managing teams are an example. Here the team is the basic work unit, and teams do much of the planning, decision making, and implementing required to get their assigned jobs done. Management has to provide at least five organizational supporting mechanisms to enable teams to do their jobs: organizational philosophy, organizational structure, systems, policies, and skills.

3. **Give examples of network-based and boundaryless organizations.** Many firms superimpose organizational networks over existing structures. A network is a system of interconnected or cooperating individuals. A formal network is made up of a group of managers drawn from across the company's functions, business units, and geography. Informal networks are made up of individuals who are interconnected only informally. They share information and help solve each other's problems based on their personal knowledge of each other's expertise. An electronic network has recently been made possible with the rise of the Internet and collaborative computing software. It allows all employees throughout the firm to network. Taken to its logical conclusion, a networked organization results in a boundaryless organization, which makes widespread use of teams, networks, and similar structural mechanisms such that the boundaries that typically separate organizational functions and hierarchical levels are reduced and made more permeable. In the boundaryless organization, managers have taken the steps required to pierce the organizational boundaries that often inhibit networked communication and decision making: the authority boundary, the task boundary, the identity boundary, and the political boundary.

4. **Describe horizontal and federal organizations.** The horizontal organization is a structure organized around basic processes such as new product development, sales fulfilment, and customer support. Everyone works together in multidisciplinary teams, with each team assigned to perform one or more of the processes. Federal organizations are ones in which power is distributed between a central authority and a number of constituent units, but the central unit's authority is intentionally limited. Virtual organizations and cellular organizations are two examples. A virtual organization is a collection of independent enterprises tied together by contracts and other means, such as partial ownership arrangements (e.g., a joint venture). In a cellular organization, small independent companies are the basic building blocks, and while each is self-sufficient, they all contribute to each other's success and to the parent firm's success.

5. **List the factors affecting how organizations are designed and structured.** Research suggests that different organizational structures are appropriate for, or contingent on, different tasks. Routine, efficiency-oriented tasks seem best matched with mechanistic organizational structures. These are characterized by adherence to rules and to the chain of command, centralization, and more specialized, functional departmentalization. At the other extreme, rapid change and technological innovation seem more suited to organic organizational structures. Here, employees are not urged to "play it by the rules" or to abide closely to the chain of command. Decision making is more decentralized and jobs and departments are less specialized.

Once plans are made, managers have to organize the work that needs to be done. In Chapter 7 we focused on the fundamentals of organizing, including departmentalization (by function or product, for instance), coordination, and delegation. In this chapter we turned to *designing organizations to manage change,* and to structures like boundaryless and cellular organizations.

However, designing the organization and organization chart is only part of the overall job of creating an organization. Having a box on an organization chart that says "Finance Department" doesn't really tell you very much about what the employees in that department actually do on a day-to-day basis. Nor will an organization chart be of much use without employees to fill its positions. In Chapter 9 we therefore turn to *staffing,* and to the methods that managers use to find and select employees to do the organization's jobs.

CRITICAL THINKING EXERCISES

1. This chapter introduced new organizational structures that have been created to deal with accelerated changes in technology and the environment. Here are two examples that illustrate some of those structures.

   • At American Express, a program called "One Enterprise" led to a range of projects where peers from different divisions worked together on cross-marketing, joint purchasing, and cooperative product and market innovation. Employees' rewards were tied to their One Enterprise efforts. Executives set goals and could earn bonuses for their contributions to the results of other divisions.

   • At Alcan, managers and professionals from line divisions formed screening teams to consider new-venture proposals to aid the search for new uses and applications for its core product, aluminum. A venture manager chosen from the screening team took charge of concepts that passed muster, drawing on Alcan's worldwide resources to build a new business. In one case of global synergy, Alcan created a new product for the Japanese market using Swedish and U.S. technology and Canadian manufacturing capacity.[59]

   What types of organizational restructuring are illustrated by the above examples?

2. Max Weber, the German sociologist, is considered by most to be the "Father of the Mechanistic or Bureaucratic Organization." Writing in the late 1800s and the early 1900s, Weber was analyzing the ushering in of what 1990s management expert Charles Handy has called "The Century of Organizations." For Weber it was a time when the new revolution of large-scale organizations would emphasize the importance of authority in the system: "In the past the man has been first, in the future the system must be first." What do you think he meant by that statement? How would he see the new revolution of today's boundaryless organizations? How might today's new structures change the relationship between the system and the human beings?

EXPERIENTIAL EXERCISES

1. In *The Horizontal Organization*, Frank Ostroff argues that the vertical organizational design is outdated and that the horizontal organization is the organization of the future. The vertical organization has inherent shortcomings in our competitive, technological, and workforce environment. Among the shortcomings are (1) its internal focus on functional goals rather than an outward-looking concentra-

tion on delivering value and winning customers; (2) the loss of important information as knowledge travels up and down the multiple levels and across the functional departments; (3) the fragmentation of performance objectives brought about by a multitude of distinct and fragmented functional goals; (4) the added expense involved in coordinating the overly fragmented work and departments; and (5) the stifling of creativity and initiative of the workers at lower levels. Ostroff sees the horizontal corporation as the structure for today and the future. Among the reasons given are that (1) horizontal organizations organize around cross-functional core processes, not tasks or functions; (2) they install process owners or managers who will take responsibility for the core process in its entirety; (3) teams, not individuals, are the cornerstone of the organizational design and performance; and (4) they empower people by giving them the tools, skills, motivation, and authority to make decisions essential to the team's performance. Compare this list with the analysis of horizontal organizations in the chapter. What do you think? Would you rather work in a vertical or horizontal organization? Why? Which structure do you think will survive better in the future? Why?

2. There is a new system of organizing—called "open book management"—that gets every employee thinking like a businessperson; that is, like a competitor.[60] In a nutshell, open-book management is a way of running a company that gets everyone to focus on helping the business make money. There are three essential differences between this approach and conventional approaches to management: (1) every employee sees—and learns to understand—the company's financial records, along with all of the other numbers that are critical to tracking the business' performance; (2) employees learn that, whatever else they do, part of their job is to move those numbers in the right direction; and (3) employees have a direct stake in the company's success: If the company makes a profit, they get a share; if it doesn't, they don't.

   You work for an old-line industrial firm with a mechanistic organizational structure that has been managed by basically the same management team for the last 30 years. The company has developed a paternalistic culture where employees are expected to do their jobs, but not question the whys and wherefores. Financial data, including salaries and compensation packages, are kept secret. In fact, if you share information about your pay with others, you may be fired. Your competitors seem to have a very motivated workforce and aggressive sales and marketing people, as well as technologically sophisticated products. As the newest member of the management team, you are very interested in introducing new ideas (like those discussed in this chapter) about organizational design, including open-book management.

   Your assignment is to write a brief report on how you would introduce these new concepts into this organization. The report should only be two pages and should outline the issues and your recommendations based on concepts from the chapter. You should be ready to present your report either to a group in class or to the whole class.

INTERNET EXERCISE

The look and feel of organizations is rapidly changing. As companies strive to be more responsive and flexible, telecommuting is becoming an important structural option. To learn more about telecommuting and telework visit www.nbs.ntu.ac.uk/staff/lyerj/list/hrtc.htm.

   Once there, go to "Smart Valley Guide to Telecommuting." This site serves as an introduction to telecommuting. Read about what constitutes telecommuting and why workers and employers are doing it.

   Also go to "Telecommuting, Teleworking, and Alternative Officing," an extensive offering of worldwide sources. Read "Do You Want to Telecommute" to gain a flavour of what telecommuting entails. Also read "Do You Manage Telecommuters?" and "Managers and Management FAQ" to find out about some of the issues facing managers who are responsible for employees who telecommute.

1. Would you like to be a telecommuter, or do you prefer a more traditional office arrangement? Why?

2. What are the main issues for managers to consider with regards to telecommuting?

3. How do you think managers can motivate employees despite the decentralized structure of a telecommuting system?

CASE STUDY 8-1

Lions Gate Entertainment Corp.

How can a small Canadian entertainment company compete with U.S. giants like Warner Brothers and Disney? Lions Gate Entertainment Corp. has two organizational strategies for taking its competitors to the mat: Imitate the best of the existing structures and use external networks of resources to make up for your smaller size.

Like its U.S. competitors, Lions Gate Entertainment employs an integrated media model. That is, it has a series of operating divisions that can deliver stand-alone products or provide support services to each of its other divisions. The four main operating groups at Lions Gate are motion pictures, television, animation, and studio facilities.

Recent projects demonstrate how a smaller firm like Lions Gate can use networked resources to strengthen its market position. To produce and distribute class-A feature films (larger budget films with international distribution), Lions Gate developed a joint venture—Mandalay Pictures—with a major U.S. film producer. The venture's first film was *Sleepy Hollow*, which starred Johnny Depp and Christina Ricci and opened as the number two film in the U.S. with a first-weekend take of over $30 million.

In a similar move for the television market, Lions Gate formed a partnership with Paramount International Television and signed a contract with the Fox Family Network before the first episode of its new TV series was filmed. The TV series, *Higher Ground*, began its life with a full-season 22-episode agreement with the Fox Family Channel.

Like most film companies, Lions Gate uses a network of banks and financial institutions to finance its projects. Single banks are often uncomfortable financing projects as risky as major films, but by arranging a consortium of lenders, film companies can receive financing without a single bank having to bear all of the risk associated with a project. The company also uses its network for film distribution. Since Lions Gate has no distribution system of its own, it relies on its network partners for the theatrical release of its films.

Questions

1. In what ways does Lions Gate benefit from having a network structure?

2. What limitations would Lions Gate face without its networking capabilities?

3. Could a small firm like Lions Gate be competitive using just its own resources?

Lions Gate Entertainment
www.lionsgate-ent.com

Mandalay Pictures
www.mandalay.com

The Future Is Now: How to Fine-Tune Your Crystal Ball

Skandia Group is a 140-year-old Swedish financial services giant with $7 billion in revenue in 1996. In 1992, the company appointed Lief Edvinsson the world's first director of intellectual capital. He rapidly set out to revolutionize corporate accounting by establishing a framework for measuring such "intangibles" as customer relations and organizational knowledge. Edvinsson has now moved on to reinventing strategic planning.

He started a new unit, Skandia Futures Centers (SFC), with a hand-picked team of 30 people from around the world. Their mission is to explore five driving forces of the business environment: the European insurance market, demographics, technology, the world economy, and organization and leadership. Their goal is to present a vision of the future to Skandia's corporate council, which consists of 150 of the company's senior managers.

The team represents diverse functional roles, organizational experiences, and cultural backgrounds, and every age from 20 to 60. In Edvinsson's experience, some of the most potent lessons have come from the young and inexperienced—those typically excluded from such ventures. As Edvinsson notes: "We need people who can understand the archeology of the future.... That's why we have these 25-year-olds in our program. They already have that vision—they carry the icons of tomorrow with them."

Questions

1. How might other companies implement Edvinsson's approach and prosper? Why haven't more done so?

2. What resistance might his approach meet in traditional companies?

3. In what ways has Edvinsson redesigned Skandia to analyze strategic alternatives and better manage change?

How Can We Organize without Losing It?

KnitMedia is at the epicentre of several industries that are undergoing very rapid change. Record distribution and music publishing are two related industries that are rapidly consolidating, with giants like Warner, Sony, and Universal now responsible for over three-quarters of total industry revenues. New media, including music Web sites and music cybercasts, are undergoing similar explosive growth. Not only are substantial players like KnitMedia increasingly active in this industry, but so are tiny "one person bands" with their own Web sites and—at the other extreme—the Web sites and networks of giants like Viacom, Sony, and Apple Computer.

KnitMedia therefore finds itself competing in a marketplace dominated by both multinational corporations and tiny independent operations. The large corporations have enormous resources, but their great size may also be a potential weakness. As KnitMedia's management has said: "Due to the multinationals' international structures, they are restricted in their ability to react quickly to market demands. This has historically caused late entry for major record labels in many new markets. Because the size of the large organizations also precludes them from a certain familiarity with a consumer, this has created an inability to see shifts in a marketplace."[61]

On the other hand, particularly with all of those tiny independent bands and labels using the Internet to distribute their music, KnitMedia also has to guard against the same sort of institutional isolation setting in as it grows larger. In other words, it has to make sure that its organization is such that Michael Dorf and his management team don't become isolated from the consumer so that they are no longer able to see shifts in the marketplace and react quickly and appropriately.

Dorf and his management team certainly recognize this potential problem and have tried to make sure that it doesn't occur. For one thing, KnitMedia tries to take a team approach to most of its activities. For example, in describing the job of Ed Greer, chief operating officer, Allan Fried put it this way: "Ed Greer's been around, I think, for about 13 years. So to say, 'Ed, you should just be involved with the clubs and we don't want your opinion on anything else,' would just be wasting his talent, his intelligence, his energy, and because . . . people are passionate about what goes on here, they all have good ideas and we like to think that the best idea wins, not just my idea because it's my idea. I think we're all fighting for a common cause [and I think, overall] that we're very much a team."

Of course the problem is that saying you're operating like a team is one thing, and actually putting it in practice is another, particularly when you start with the fairly conventional KnitMedia organization chart depicted in Figure 7.2 (see page 197). Michael Dorf and his team certainly want to take advantage of the latest thinking when it comes to designing organizations to manage change; the question is how to do that. They've come to you for advice.

Team Exercises and Questions

Use what you learned in this chapter to answer the following questions from Michael Dorf and his management team:

1. Do you think KnitMedia's current organization chart provides our company with the ability to manage rapid change? Why or why not?

2. We want to be more team-oriented in the way that we organize and deal with problems. What, exactly, can we do to inject more of a team orientation in the way we organize?

3. Would it be helpful for us to also apply the latest thinking with regard to network-based organizations, boundaryless organizations, and/or horizontal organizations at KnitMedia? Why or why not? If so, how would you suggest we do it?

Staffing and Human Resource Management

Cisco Systems

When it comes to leading-edge, quickly changing companies, it's hard to think of one more on the edge than Cisco Systems. Cisco is the worldwide leader in Internet networking, and it supplies the network solutions that let people transfer information over the Internet.

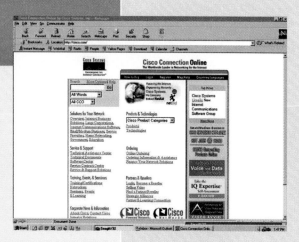

With offices in over 115 countries worldwide and growing at hyper-speed, Cisco has a constant need to hire the best of the best computer specialists. And, as you'd expect from the world's Internet networking leader, much of its recruiting and initial screening takes place via the Internet.

On its Web page, Cisco provides information to prospective employees in its "hot jobs" feature. These are jobs that are critical for Cisco to fill, and include titles like board designer, embedded software development, software development test manager, software engineer, and human resource manager. A human resource manager, for example, would work with senior management in various business units to create the organizational capabilities that are necessary for Cisco to meet the business challenges it faces. An e-mail address is provided, where applicants can send their résumés.

Cisco's Web page also includes information about the company's mission, its commitment to communication through all levels of the organization, its willingness to support flextime and telecommuting, its commitment to diversity, its programs and facilities, its stock option plan, and its medical plans.

Information and places where Cisco will be recruiting in person are also provided to prospective employees. These are typically job fairs, conferences, seminars, trade shows, and career invitation events. For example, Cisco took part in the Ottawa HiTech Career Fair at the Ottawa Congress Centre in January 2000.

Cisco Systems
www.Cisco.com

1. Explain why human resource management (HRM) is now a core function.

2. Understand the legal framework within which HRM must operate.

3. Use five methods to recruit a pool of good candidates.

4. Know how to use testing in selecting new employees.

5. List and briefly discuss the main steps in conducting an employment interview.

6. Describe three other important employee selection techniques.

7. Explain what is involved in employee orientation and training.

8. Explain what is involved in appraising and compensating employees.

Human Resource Management as a Core Function

Human resource management (sometimes called **HRM**, staffing, or personnel management) is the management function devoted to acquiring, training, appraising, and compensating employees. All managers are, in a sense, personnel managers, because they all get involved in activities like recruiting, interviewing, selecting, and training. But most larger firms also have HR departments with their own human resource managers. These HR departments typically are responsible for activities like industrial and labour relations, employee relations, organization development and employee training programs, compensation management, and employee benefits.

As we saw earlier, companies are flattening their pyramids, relying more on self-managing work teams, and getting closer to their customers, in part by empowering employees and giving them more authority to handle customer complaints and requests. Actions like these boost the need for motivated, self-directed, and committed employees. As workers become more fully empowered, the HR function thus grows in importance. We'll see in this chapter that HR plays a central role in molding a company's workforce into a motivated and committed team, one that can help the company and its management to manage change more effectively.

The fact that employees today are central to helping companies achieve competitive advantage and manage change has led to the emergence of strategic human resource management. **Strategic human resource management** has been defined as "the linking of HRM with strategic goals and objectives in order to improve business performance and develop organizational cultures that foster innovation and flexibility. . . ."[1] Strategic HR means accepting the human resource function as a strategic partner in formulating the company's strategies, as well as in executing those strategies through HR activities like recruiting, selecting, training, and rewarding personnel.

human resource management (HRM)
The management function devoted to acquiring, training, appraising, and compensating employees.

strategic human resource management
The linking of HRM with strategic goals and objectives in order to improve business performance and develop organizational cultures that foster innovation and flexibility.

HR's Role in Formulating Strategy

In many companies, HR management already plays a crucial role in formulating strategy. HR management is in a unique position to supply competitive intelligence that may be useful in the strategic planning process. Details regarding advanced incentive plans being used by competitors, opinion surveys from employees that elicit information about customer complaints, and information about pending legislation like labour laws or mandatory health insurance are some examples.

HR also participates in strategy formulation by supplying information regarding the company's internal strengths and weaknesses. For example, IBM's decision to buy Lotus was prompted in part by IBM's conclusion that its own human resources were inadequate to enable the firm to reposition itself as an industry leader in networking systems, or at least to do so quickly enough.

HR's Role in Executing Strategy

Federal Express
www.fedex.com/
ca_english

Human resource management also plays a pivotal role in successfully executing a company's strategic plan. For example, Federal Express's competitive strategy is to differentiate itself from its competitors by offering superior customer service and guaranteed on-time deliveries. Since basically the same technologies are available to UPS, DHL, Purolator, and FedEx's other competitors, it is FedEx's workforce that necessarily gives FedEx a crucial competitive advantage. This means that the firm's HR processes and its ability to create a highly committed, competent, and customer-oriented workforce are crucial to FedEx being able to execute its strategy.

Human resource management supports strategic implementation in numerous other ways. For example, HR today is heavily involved in the execution of most firm's downsizing and restructuring strategies through outplacing employees, instituting pay-for-performance plans, reducing health care costs, and retraining employees. And in an increasingly competitive global marketplace, instituting HR practices that build employee commitment can help improve a firm's responsiveness. In summary, HR today plays a central role as a strategic partner, helping top management formulate and then implement its strategies.[2]

FedEx's human resources—its employees—provide the firm with its competitive advantages of superior customer service and on-time deliveries. For this firm, human resource management is the key to the strategic plan.

Human Resource's Legal Framework

More than any other management function, personnel is subject to numerous constraints in the form of federal and provincial laws. These laws affect recruiting practices, how employees are paid, sexual harassment, employee safety and health, labour-management relations, and employment laws in general. Each of these areas is discussed briefly in the following sections.

Recruiting

When recruiting, firms must be careful not to violate anti-discrimination laws. The key federal anti-discrimination legislation is the **Canadian Human Rights Act** of 1977. The goal of this act is to ensure that any individual who wishes to obtain a job has an equal opportunity to compete for it. The act applies to all federal agencies, federal Crown corporations, any employee of the federal government, and business firms that do business interprovincially. Thus, it applies to such firms as the Bank of Montreal, Air Canada, Telecom Canada, Canadian National Railways, and many other public and private sector organizations that operate across Canada. Even with such wide application, the act affects only about 10 percent of Canadian workers; the rest are covered under provincial human rights acts.

The Canadian Human Rights Act prohibits a wide variety of practices in recruiting, selecting, promoting, and dismissing personnel. The act specifically prohibits discrimination on the basis of age, race and colour, national and ethnic origin, physical handicap, religion, gender, marital status, or prison record (if pardoned). Some exceptions to these blanket prohibitions are permitted. Discrimination cannot be charged if a blind person is refused a position as a train engineer, bus driver, or crane operator. Likewise, a firm cannot be charged with discrimination if it does not hire a deaf person as a telephone operator or as an audio engineer.

These situations are clear-cut, but many others are not. For example, is it discriminatory to refuse women employment in a job that routinely requires carrying objects that weigh more than 50 kilograms? Ambiguities in determining whether discrimination has occurred are sometimes dealt with by using the concept of "**bona fide occupational requirement**." An employer may choose one person over another based on overriding characteristics of the job in question. If a fitness centre wants to hire only women to supervise its women's locker room and sauna, it can do so without being discriminatory because it established a bona fide occupational requirement.

Even after referring to bona fide occupational requirements, other uncertainties remain. Consider three cases: Would an advertising agency be discriminating if it advertised for a male model about 60 years old for an advertisement that is to appeal to older men? Would a business firm be discriminating if it refused to hire someone as a receptionist because the applicant was overweight? Would a bank be discriminating because it refused to hire an applicant whom the human resources manager felt would not fit in because of the person's appearance?

We might speculate that the advertising agency is not discriminating, the business firm might or might not be discriminating, and the bank could probably be accused of discrimination, but we can't be sure. The human rights legislation cannot specify all possible situations; many uncertainties remain over what the law considers discriminatory and what it considers acceptable. Nevertheless, the spirit of the legislation is clear, and managers must try to abide by it.

Enforcement of the federal act is carried out by the Canadian Human Rights Commission. The commission can either respond to complaints from individuals who believe they have been discriminated against, or launch an investigation on its own if it has reason to believe that discrimination has occurred. During an investigation, data are gathered about the alleged discriminatory behaviour and, if the claim of discrimina-

Canadian Human Rights Act
Ensures that any individual who wishes to obtain a job has an equal opportunity to apply for it.

Canadian Human Rights Act
www.chrc-ccdp.ca/ Legis&Poli/chra-lcdp. asp?1=e

bona fide occupational requirement
When an employer may choose one applicant over another based on overriding characteristics of the job.

tion is substantiated, the offending organization or individual may be ordered to compensate the victim.

Each province has also enacted human rights legislation to regulate organizations and businesses operating in that province. These provincial regulations are similar in spirit to the federal legislation, with many minor variations from province to province. All provinces prohibit discrimination on the basis of race, national or ethnic origin, colour, religion, sex, and marital status, but some do not address such issues as physical handicaps, criminal record, or age. Provincial human rights commissions enforce provincial legislation.

The **Employment Equity Act of 1986** addresses the issue of discrimination in employment by designating four groups as employment disadvantaged—women, visible minorities, aboriginal people, and people with disabilities. Companies covered by the act are required to publish statistics on their employment of people in these four groups.

The Bank of Montreal recently became the first company outside the U.S. to win a prestigious award for promoting women's careers. Women represented over half of executive level promotions at the bank in 1993. The Bank of Montreal has introduced initiatives such as flexible working hours, a mentoring program, a national career information network, and a gender awareness workshop series.[3]

Companies are increasingly making provisions for disabled employees. At Rogers Cablevision, a division of Rogers Communications Inc., a large workplace area was completely redesigned to accommodate workers who were either visually disabled or in wheelchairs. Special equipment was also installed—a large print computer for workers with partial sight, and a device that allows blind workers to read printed materials.[4]

Comparable Worth

In spite of recent advances, women, on average, still earn only about three-quarters of what the average man earns; *single* women, however, earn 99 percent of what single men earn. In 1969, women earned only 59 percent of what men earned. The most recent gains by women have occurred because men lost four of every five jobs that disappeared during the early 1990s. But most top jobs in the public and private sector continue to be held by men.[5] As well, women continue to have difficulty moving out of low-paying jobs. A 1998 Statistics Canada report showed that one-third of the men who had low-paying jobs in 1993 had been able to get a better paying job by 1995, but only 17 percent of the women were able to do so. Only 12 percent of *single-parent women* were able to get a better paying job.[6]

Comparable worth is a legal concept that aims at paying equal wages for jobs that are of comparable value to the employer. This might mean comparing dissimilar jobs, such as those of nurses and mechanics or secretaries and electricians. Proponents of comparable worth say that all the jobs in a company must be evaluated and then rated in terms of basic dimensions such as the level of skill they require. All jobs could then be compared based on a common index. People in different jobs that rate the same on this index would be paid the same. Experts hope that this will help to reduce the gap between men's and women's pay.

Critics of comparable worth say that it ignores the supply and demand aspects of labour, and that forcing a company to pay people more than the open market price for their labour (which may happen in jobs where there is a surplus of workers) is not economically sound. A study prepared for the Ontario Ministry of Labour estimates that it will cost approximately $10 billion for the public and private sectors in Ontario to establish equitable payment for jobs of equal value. Yet the cost defence cannot be easily used. In one case, the Quebec Human Rights Commission ruled that 234 female office employees of the Quebec North Shore Paper Company were performing work of equal value to that done by male production workers. The company was required to increase the secretaries' salaries by $701 annually and give them over $1000 each in back pay.[7]

In 1999, the Canadian Human Rights Tribunal ruled that the federal government must pay a total of more than $3 billion to thousands of civil servants because it discriminated against workers in female-dominated job classifications. About 85 percent of these workers were women.

Employment Equity Act of 1986
Federal legislation that designates four groups as employment disadvantaged—women, visible minorities, aboriginal people, and people with disabilities.

Employment Equity Act
canada.justice.gc.ca/ STABLE/EN/Laws/ ChapE/E-5.4.html

comparable worth
A legal idea that aims to pay equal wages for work of equal value.

Ontario Ministry of Labour
www.gov.on.ca/LAB/ main.htm

Canadian Human Rights Tribunal
www.chrt-tcdp.gc.ca

Sexual Harassment

Sexual harassment doesn't simply mean insisting on sexual favours in return for some reward, as many people believe. Instead, it is defined as unwelcome sexual advances, requests for sexual favours, and other verbal or physical conduct of a sexual nature that occurs under conditions including the following: (1) when such conduct is made, either explicitly or implicitly, a term or condition of an individual's employment; (2) when submission to or rejection of such conduct by an individual is used as the basis for employment decisions affecting the individual; or (3) when such conduct has the purpose or effect of unreasonably interfering with an individual's performance or creating an intimidating, hostile, or offensive work environment. In other words, if it makes the other person feel uncomfortable, it may be sexual harassment.

Managers cannot be complacent about the activities of employees towards one another, and they must remember that the Canadian Human Rights Act takes precedence over any policies the company might have developed in this area. If a manager in a company is found guilty of sexual harassment, the company is also liable, even if it didn't condone or know about the behaviour. This is because the manager is an agent of the company. The most reasonable and prudent course of action for a company to take is to establish a clear policy against harassment and then to enforce that policy vigorously.

A company may be liable even if one employee is harassing another. At Levac Supply Ltd. of Kingston, Ontario, one employee harassed another over a period of many years. A board of inquiry ruled that the company was jointly responsible for the harassment with the employee who had done the harassing. The woman who was harassed received a settlement of $448 273.[8]

Dealing with Sexual Harassment at Work. There are a number of steps that employers and individuals can take to avoid or deal with sexual harassment when it occurs. Here are some strategies.

What the employer should do:

1. First, take all complaints about harassment seriously. As one sexual harassment manual for managers and supervisors advises, "When confronted with sexual harassment complaints or when sexual conduct is observed in the workplace, the best reaction is to address the complaint or stop the conduct."[9]

2. Issue a strong policy statement condemning such behaviour.

3. Inform all employees about the policy prohibiting sexual harassment and of their rights under the policy.

4. Establish a complaint procedure so that employees understand the chain of command when it comes to filing and appealing sexual harassment complaints.

5. Establish a management response system that includes an immediate reaction and investigation by senior management when charges of sexual harassment are made.

6. Begin management training sessions with supervisors and increase their own awareness of the issues.

7. Discipline managers and employees involved in sexual harassment.

An employee who believes that he or she has been sexually harassed can also take several steps to eliminate the problem:

1. Make a verbal request to the harasser and the harasser's boss that the unwanted overtures cease because the conduct is unwelcome.

2. Write a letter to the harasser providing a detailed statement of the facts and a statement that the employee wants the harassing activities to end immediately (the letter should be delivered in person and, if necessary, a witness should accompany the employee).

3. Report the unwelcome conduct and unsuccessful efforts to get it to stop to the harasser's manager or to the HR director (or both), verbally and in writing.

4. Finally, consult an attorney about suing the harasser and possibly the employer.

Employee Safety and Health

Employee safety and health programs help to reduce absenteeism and labour turnover, raise productivity, and boost morale by making jobs safer and more healthful.

In Canada, each province has developed its own workplace health and safety regulations. The purpose of these laws is to ensure that employees do not have to work in dangerous conditions. These laws are the direct result of undesirable conditions that existed in many Canadian businesses at the close of the 19th century. While much improvement is evident, Canada still has some problems with workplace health and safety. In one study of six Western industrialized nations, Canada had the worst safety record in mining and construction and the second worst record in manufacturing and railways.

Government regulations about employee safety are getting stricter. Ontario, which loses more than 7 million working days yearly because of on-the-job injuries, has passed amendments to the Ontario Occupational Health and Safety Act. Officers and directors of companies are now held personally responsible for workplace health and safety and are subject to punishment by jail terms and fines for permitting unsafe working conditions.[10]

Some industrial work—logging, construction, and mining—can put workers at risk of injury in obvious ways. But other work, such as typing or lifting, can also cause painful injuries. Repetitive strain injury is becoming much more common. At Cuddy Food Products (the sole supplier of poultry products to McDonald's), as many as 44 workers per month became disabled from repetitive strain injury. The company instituted a plan to redesign how workers performed their jobs and trained people to avoid injuries. During one nine-month period after the training, not a single repetitive strain injury was reported. At CP Rail, injuries were reduced 50 percent when employees did 10 minutes of warm-up exercises before beginning work.[11]

The Ontario Occupational Health and Safety Act illustrates current legislation in Canada. It requires that all employers ensure that equipment and safety devices are used properly. Employers must also show workers the proper way to operate machinery. At the job site, supervisors are charged with the responsibility of seeing that workers use equipment properly. The act also requires workers to behave appropriately on the job. Employers have the right to refuse to work on a job if they believe it is unsafe; a legal procedure exists for resolving any disputes in this area.

In most provinces, the Ministry of Labour appoints inspectors to enforce health and safety regulations. If the inspector finds a sufficient hazard, he or she has the authority to clear the workplace. Inspectors may come to a firm unannounced to conduct an inspection.

Safety in Practice. Companies can take a number of steps to improve the safety and health of their workforces. Important examples include:

- *Reduce unsafe conditions that can lead to accidents.* This is an employer's first line of defence. For example, is material piled in a safe manner? Are there safety feet on straight ladders? Do stairways have guardrails?

- *Hire safety-prone people.* Employee selection and testing can be used to hire people who are less likely to have accidents, particularly on accident-prone jobs like driving heavy equipment. For example, psychological tests—especially tests of emotional stability—have been used to screen out accident-prone taxi drivers.[12] Similarly, tests of muscular coordination are important for jobs such as lumberjack, and tests of visual skills are important for drivers and employees operating machines.

- *Emphasize safety.* Use safety posters and continual reminders from top management that safety is paramount.

- *Use training to improve safety.* Safety training, such as instructing employees in safe practices and procedures and warning them of potential hazards, can help employees act more safely at work. At one Subaru-Isuzu automotive plant, employees engage in a series of stretching exercises before starting work, in part to keep work-related injuries to a minimum.

- *Set specific loss-control goals.* Analyze the number of accidents and safety incidents and then set specific safety goals to be achieved; for instance, a maximum for time lost due to injuries.

- *Formulate and enforce safety rules.* Set specific safety rules, such as "Safety hats must be worn in construction area" and "Oil spills must be wiped up promptly," and actively enforce these rules.

- *Conduct safety and health inspections regularly.* Similarly, investigate all accidents and "near misses" and have a system in place to allow employees to notify management about hazardous conditions.

Labour-Management Relations

Under the laws of Canada and many other countries, workers are permitted to organize into labour unions—groups of individuals working together to achieve job-related goals such as higher pay, shorter working hours, and better working conditions. In Canada, Privy Council Order 1003 recognizes the right of employees to bargain collectively, prohibits unfair labour practices on the part of management, establishes a labour board to certify bargaining authority, and prohibits strikes except in the course of negotiating a collective agreement. Each province also has a labour relations act that regulates labour activity within the province.

Other Employment Law Issues

The Canada Labour Code is a comprehensive piece of legislation that applies to the labour practices of firms operating under the legislative authority of Parliament. The code sets out guidelines in areas such as fair employment practices, vacations and holidays, employee safety, and industrial relations regulations. It also addresses the issue of child labour. In Canada, for example, young people under the age of 17 may work, but only if

According to Canadian Labour Laws, employees under the age of 17 cannot work between the hours of 11 p.m. and 6 a.m.

(a) they are not required to attend school under the laws of their province, and (b) the work is not likely to endanger their health or safety. No one under the age of 17 is permitted to work between 11 p.m. and 6 a.m.

Staffing the Organization

staffing
Filling a firm's open positions.

The term **staffing** is often used to refer to actually filling a firm's open positions, and it includes six steps (as summarized in Figure 9.1): job analysis, personnel planning, recruiting, interviewing, testing and selection, and training and development.

Job Analysis

job analysis
The procedure used to determine the duties of jobs and the kinds of people (in terms of skills and experience) who should be hired for them.

Developing an organization chart (discussed in Chapters 7 and 8) results in creating jobs to be filled. **Job analysis** is the procedure used to determine the duties of jobs and the kinds of people (in terms of skills and experience) who should be hired for them.[13] These data are then used to develop a **job description**, or a list of duties showing what the job entails, and **job specifications**, a list of the skills and aptitudes sought in people hired for the job. A job description like the one in Figure 9.2 identifies the job, provides a brief job summary, and then lists specific responsibilities and duties of the job.

job description
A list of duties showing what the job entails.

job specifications
A list of the skills and aptitudes sought in people hired for the job.

job analysis questionnaire
A questionnaire used by managers and administered to employees to determine the duties and functions of a job.

Job Analysis in Practice. How do managers determine the duties and functions of a job? A **job analysis questionnaire**, such as the one shown in Figure 9.3 (see pages 268–69), is often used. This one requires employees to provide detailed information on what they do, such as briefly stating their main duties in their own words, describing the conditions under which they work, and listing any permits or licences required to perform the duties assigned to their positions.

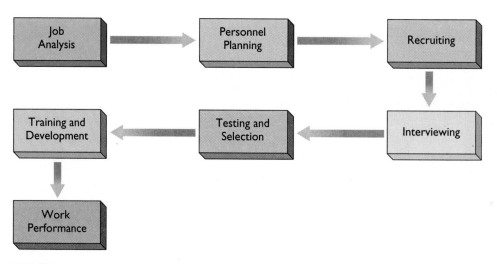

FIGURE 9.1
Steps in the Staffing Process
The term "staffing" is often used to refer to the steps taken to actually fill a position—from job analysis to training and development.

COMPUTER CORPORATION

Supervisor of Data Processing Operations	*Exempt*	*012.168*
Job Title	Status	Job Code

July 3, 1997	*Main Office*
Date	Plant/Division

Arthur Allen	*Information*
Written By	*Data Processing—Systems*
	Department/Section

Juanita Montgomery	*12*	*736*
Approved By	Grade/Level	Points

Manager of Information Systems	*22 000–Mid 24 000–26 000*
Title of Immediate Supervisor	Pay Range

SUMMARY

Directs the operation of all data processing, data control, and data preparation requirements.

JOB DUTIES*

1. Follows broadly based directives.
   (a) Operates independently.
   (b) Informs Manager of Information Systems of activities through weekly, monthly, and/or quarterly schedules.
2. Selects, trains, and develops subordinate personnel.
   (a) Develops spirit of cooperation and understanding among work group members.
   (b) Ensures that work group members receive specialized training as necessary in the proper functioning or execution of machines, equipment, systems, procedures, processes, and/or methods.
   (c) Directs training involving teaching, demonstrating, and/or advising users in productive work methods and effective communications with data processing.
3. Reads and analyzes wide variety of instructional and training information.
   (a) Applies latest concepts and ideas to changing organizational requirements.
   (b) Assists in developing and/or updating manuals, procedures, specifications, etc., relative to organizational requirements and needs.
   (c) Assists in the preparation of specifications and related evaluations of supporting software and hardware.
4. Plans, directs, and controls a wide variety of operational assignments by five to seven subordinates; works closely with other managers, specialists, and technicians within Information Systems as well as with managers in other departments with data needs and with vendors.
   (a) Receives, interprets, develops, and distributes directives ranging from the very simple to the highly complex and technological in nature.
   (b) Establishes and implements annual budget for department.
5. Interacts and communicates with people representing a wide variety of units and organizations.
   (a) Communicates both personally and impersonally, through oral or written directives and memoranda, with all involved parties.
   (b) Attends local meetings of professional organizations in the field of data processing.

*This section should also include description of uncomfortable, dirty, or dangerous assignments.

FIGURE 9.2
Sample Job Description

JOB QUESTIONNAIRE
IMPERIAL MANUFACTURING COMPANY

YOUR NAME _____ PRESENT JOB TITLE _____

DEPARTMENT _____ EMPLOYEE NUMBER _____

SUPERVISOR'S NAME _____ SUPERVISOR'S TITLE _____

I. SUMMARY OF DUTIES: State briefly, in your own words, your main duties.

_____

_____

2. SPECIAL QUALIFICATIONS: List any licences, permits, certifications, etc. required to perform duties assigned to your position.

_____

_____

3. EQUIPMENT: List any equipment, machines, or tools (e.g., computers, motor vehicles, lathes, fork lifts, drill presses, etc.) you normally operate as a part of your position's duties.

MACHINE	AVERAGE NO. HOURS PER WEEK

4. REGULAR DUTIES: In general terms, describe duties you regularly perform. Please list these duties in descending order of importance and give the percentage of time spent on them per month. List as many duties as possible and attach additional sheets, if necessary.

_____

_____

_____

5. CONTACTS: Does your job require any contacts with other department personnel, other departments, outside companies or agencies? If yes, please define the duties requiring contacts and how often.

_____

_____

6. SUPERVISION: Does your position have supervisory responsibilities? ( ) Yes ( ) No. If yes, please fill out a *Supplemental Position Description Questionnaire* for Supervisors and attach it to this form. If you have responsibility for the work of others but do not directly supervise them, please explain.

_____

_____

_____

7. DECISION MAKING: Please explain the decisions you make while performing the regular duties of your job.

_____

_____

_____

(a) What might be a likely result of your making (a) poor judgment(s) or decision(s), or (b) improper actions?

_____

_____

(continued)

FIGURE 9.3
Job Analysis Questionnaire for Developing Job Descriptions
A questionnaire like this one can be used to interview job incumbents or may be filled out by them.

8. REPORTS AND RECORDS: List the reports and files you are required to prepare or maintain. State for whom each report is intended.
   (a)   REPORT   INTENDED FOR
   _____
   _____
   _____

   (b)   FILES MAINTAINED
   _____
   _____
   _____

9. FREQUENCY OF SUPERVISION: How frequently must you confer with your supervisor or other personnel in making decisions or in determining the proper course of action to be taken?
   ( ) Daily   ( ) Weekly   ( ) Monthly   ( ) Never

10. WORKING CONDITIONS: Please describe the conditions under which you work—inside, outside, air-conditioned area, etc. Be sure to list any disagreeable or unusual working conditions.
    _____
    _____

11. JOB REQUIREMENTS: Please indicate the minimum requirements you believe are necessary to perform satisfactorily in your present position.
    (a) Education: (b) Experience:
        Minimum schooling _____   Type _____
        Number of years _____   Number of years _____
        Specialization or major_____
    (c) Special training:
                    TYPE   NUMBER OF YEARS
    _____
    _____

    (d) Special Skills:
        Computer programs: _____
        Other: _____

12. ADDITIONAL INFORMATION: Please provide additional information, not included in any of the previous items, that you feel would be important in a description of your position.
    _____
    _____
    _____
    _____

    EMPLOYEE'S SIGNATURE_____ DATE:_____

FIGURE 9.3 cont'd

Planning for Human Resources

Human resource planning consists of three activities: (1) forecasting personnel requirements (in terms of future open positions); (2) forecasting the supply of outside candidates and internal candidates; and (3) producing plans that describe how candidates will be hired, trained, and prepared for the jobs that will be opening up.

Thanks to computers, human resource planning today is becoming increasingly sophisticated. Many firms maintain computerized data banks that contain information about hundreds of employee traits (like special skills, product knowledge, work experience, training courses, relocation limitations, and career interests).[14] The availability of so much employee data facilitates planning for and filling positions in big companies. It also has intensified the need to protect the privacy of the personal data that are sorted in the firm's data banks.

human resource planning
Forecasting personnel requirements (in terms of future open positions); forecasting the supply of outside candidates and internal candidates; and producing plans that describe how candidates will be hired, trained, and prepared for the jobs that will be opening up.

Will Companies Become "Jobless"?

Many of the trends that we've discussed so far in this book suggest that someday the job as we know it may disappear. Workers won't get jobs with neat listings of duties on job descriptions, say some experts.[15] Instead, they may be assigned to teams on which their duties may shift from day to day, and on which the lines between "my" job and "yours" may blur and disappear.[16]

We've already seen evidence of this shift in previous chapters. Flattening organizations and establishing self-contained mini-units often make employees' responsibilities much broader and less confined. Similarly, re-engineering business processes and organizing the work to be done around teams usually mean that workers' jobs are designed to overlap so that they'll all pull together. Boundaryless organizations similarly foster a willingness on the part of employees to think of their jobs in terms of what the worker must do to get the work done.

Job descriptions will undoubtedly be around for some time. However, increasingly HR managers must help the company to manage change by designing "jobs" that are broad and flexible enough to encourage team-based employees to work together and share each others' load. And HR has to see that the right employees are hired and properly trained for these more demanding jobs.

Employee Recruiting

recruiting
Attracting a pool of viable job applicants.

Recruiting—attracting a pool of viable job applicants—is very important. If you only have two candidates for two openings, you may have little choice but to hire them. But if 20 or 30 applicants appear, you can use techniques like interviews and tests to hire the best one. The main sources of applicants are discussed next.

Internal Sources of Candidates. Although recruiting often brings to mind employment agencies and classified ads, current employees are often the largest source of recruits.

Filling open positions with inside candidates has both benefits and drawbacks. On the plus side, employees see that competence is rewarded and morale and performance may thus be enhanced. Inside candidates are also known quantities in terms of their performance and skills, and they may already be committed to your company and its goals. On the other hand, current employees who apply for jobs and do not get them may become discontented. Furthermore, promotion from within can lead to inbreeding: When an entire management team has been brought up through the ranks, there may be a tendency to maintain the status quo when innovation and a new direction could be needed.

job posting
Publicizing an open job to employees and listing its attributes, such as qualifications, supervisor, working schedule, and pay rate.

To be effective, promotion from within requires job posting.[17] **Job posting** means publicizing an open job to employees (often by literally posting it on bulletin boards) and listing its attributes, such as qualifications, supervisor, working schedule, and pay rate. Some union contracts require job posting to ensure that union members get first chance at new and better positions. Job posting can also be a good practice even in non-union firms if it facilitates the transfer and promotion of qualified inside candidates.[18]

Advertising. As you know from the many help-wanted ads that appear in your local newspaper, advertising is a major source of attracting applicants. The main issue here is selecting the best advertising medium, be it the local paper, *The Globe and Mail*, or a technical journal. The medium chosen depends on the type of job. The local newspaper is usually the best source for blue-collar help, clerical employees, and lower-level administrative employees. For specialized positions, employers can advertise in trade and professional journals like *Sales Manager* and *Chemical Engineering*. Executive jobs are often advertised in *The Globe and Mail*.

Employment Agencies. An employment agency is an intermediary whose business is to match applicants with employers' open positions. Employment agencies charge fees for each applicant they place. These fees are usually posted in the agencies' offices. Whether the employer or the candidate pays the fee is mostly determined by market conditions. However, the trend in the last few years has been towards "fee-paid" jobs in which the employer and not the candidate pays the fees. Such agencies are important sources of clerical, white-collar, and managerial personnel.

Executive Recruiters. **Executive recruiters** (also ominously known as *headhunters*) are agencies retained by employers to seek out top management talent. They fill jobs in the $50 000 and up category.

> **executive recruiter**
> An agency retained by employers to seek out top management talent.

These firms can be very useful. They have many business contacts and are especially adept at contacting qualified candidates who are employed and not actively looking to change jobs. They can also keep a client firm's name confidential until late in the search process. The recruiter saves management time by doing the preliminary work of advertising for the position and screening what could turn out to be hundreds of applicants.

The executive recruiting process typically starts with the executive recruiter meeting with the client's executives to formulate a clear written description of the position to be filled and the sort of person needed to fill it. The recruiter will then use various sources and contacts to identify viable candidates, interview these people, and present a short list of three or four candidates to the client's executives for final screening.

Two trends—technology and specialization—are changing the executive search business. Top firms used to take up to seven months to complete a search, with much of that time spent shuffling between headhunters and researchers who dig up the initial "long list" of candidates.[19] This often takes too long in today's fast-moving environment. Most search firms are therefore establishing Internet-linked computerized databases, the aim of which, according to one senior recruiter, is "to create a long list by pushing a button."[20]

Referrals or Walk-ins. Particularly for hourly workers, walk-ins—people who apply directly at the office—are a major source of applicants. Encouraging walk-in applicants may be as simple as posting a handwritten "Help Wanted" sign in your office or plant window. On the other hand, some organizations encourage walk-in applicants by mounting employee referral campaigns. Here, announcements of openings and requests for referrals are made in the company's newsletter or posted on bulletin boards.

College and University Recruiting. Sending employers' representatives to college and university campuses to pre-screen applicants and create an applicant pool from each school's graduating class is an important source of management trainees, promotable candidates, and professional and technical employees. One recent study of 251 staffing professionals concluded, for instance, that about 38 percent of all externally filled jobs requiring a college degree were filled by new college graduates.[21]

Exactly which traits to look for in candidates will depend on the company's specific needs. Traits to assess include motivation, communication skills, education, appearance, and attitude.[22]

Many college students get their jobs through college *internships,* a recruiting approach that has grown dramatically in recent years. Internships can be win-win situations for both students and employers. For students, it may mean being able to hone business skills, check out potential employers, and learn more about their likes (and dislikes) when it comes to choosing careers. And employers, of course, can use the interns to make useful contributions while they're being evaluated as possible full-time employees.

Duncan Group, Inc.

"One day," as Melba J. Duncan recalls, "I woke up, and I knew: this is a business!"[23] After years as an administrative assistant to CEOs at companies like Wall Street's Lehman Brothers, Duncan decided to strike out on her own. She correctly believed that top-ranked administrative/executive assistants were an overlooked region of the retained-search industry. Today her company successfully places administrative assistants who command salaries ranging from US$55 000 to US$130 000 per year, not counting bonuses and benefits. Clients include IBM, Home Depot, Bankers Trust, and the Boston Consulting Group.

With years as a top assistant herself, Duncan combines a complete understanding of what the job calls for with a comprehensive system for selecting great candidates. For Duncan, it all starts with recruiting: She knows that to send 3 great finalists to a client, she'll need to start with a pool of 100. Her recruiters therefore work the phones "like air-traffic controllers," and review their files and their network of contacts. An initial screening cuts the original candidate pool to about 50; these complete a 15-page questionnaire, after which the pool is further cut to about 15.[24]

The screening doesn't stop there. Those 15 then go through a 4-hour testing and profiling process, which helps to highlight their written and oral communication skills, clerical skills, and management aptitude and personality. A clinical psychologist spends two days a week in Duncan's office, interviewing candidates and compiling profiles. Clients usually get the first three solid prospects within five days of the official opening of the search, along with a complete file on each candidate's background and work history.[25]

Workforce
www.workforce.com

NEC Electronics
www.nec.com

Unisys Corp.
www.unisys.com

The Internet. A large and growing proportion of employers recruit on the Internet. In one survey, 32 percent of the 203 respondents said they were using the Internet as a primary recruitment source.[26]

A multitude of Internet job-placement and recruiting sources are available today. For example, the personnel journal *Workforce* has a Web site (www.workforceonline.com/postajob/) that will take you to various sites, including "best Internet recruiter," general recruitment sites, college recruitment sites, and specific industry recruitment sites, and will also let you place your own help-wanted ad online. Yahoo! (http://employment.yahoo.com/) is just one of the other possible sites on which you can place and access employment classified ads.

Employers are using Internet recruiting in various ways. NEC Electronics, Inc., Unisys Corp., and LSI Logicorp have all posted Internet-based "cyber fairs" to recruit applicants.[27] As noted earlier, Cisco Systems, Inc.'s Web site contains a Cisco Employment Opportunities page, which offers links to hot jobs (job descriptions for hard-to-fill positions), Cisco culture (a look at Cisco work life), Cisco College (information on internships and mentoring programs), and jobs (job listings).[28]

But collecting résumés via the Internet is only part of it. At peoplesoft company, for instance, applications sent via the World Wide Web or fax are automatically deposited in a database (those submitted on paper are first scanned into a computer). When a hiring manager selects an applicant for interview, the system automatically phones that person and asks him or her to select an interview time by punching buttons on a touch-tone phone. After the call, the database system notifies the interviewer of the appointment and sends a reminder on the day of the interview—all without human interaction.

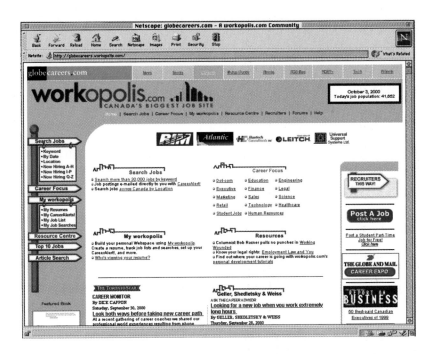

The Globe and Mail's job-search site allows job hunters to efficiently search for jobs that are appropriate for their skill levels and interests.

Recruiting a More Diverse Workforce. Recruiting a diverse workforce is not just socially responsible: It's a necessity, given the rapid growth of minority and female candidates. Smart employers will actively recruit a more diverse workforce. This means taking special steps to recruit older workers, minorities, and women.

There are several reasons why more employers are looking to older workers as a source of recruits. For one thing (because of buyouts and early retirements), many workers have retired early and are ready and willing to re-enter the job market.[29] Furthermore, over the next 10 or 15 years the number of annual retirees will double. As a result, "there will be, I guarantee it, many boomers who will have to work beyond age 65 because they simply haven't saved enough money to retire," says a demographer.[30] Fewer 18- to 25-year-olds are entering the workforce,[31] and this has caused many employers to harness "grey power" by encouraging retirement-age employees not to leave, or by actively recruiting employees who are at or beyond retirement age.[32]

Most companies are also actively recruiting minorities and women. There are many things an employer can do to become more attractive to minorities. Because some minority applicants may not meet the educational or experience standards for a job, many companies offer remedial training in basic arithmetic and writing.[33] Diversity data banks or nonspecialized minority-focused recruiting publications are another option.

Employers are also implementing various "welfare-to-work" programs to attract and assimilate former welfare recipients. The key to a welfare-to-work program's success seems to be the employer's "pre-training" assimilation and socialization program, during which participants receive counselling and basic skills training.[34] Marriott International has hired 600 welfare recipients under its "Pathways to Independence" program. The heart of the program is a six-week pre-employment training program that teaches work and "life" skills designed to rebuild workers' self-esteem and instill positive attitudes about work.[35]

Selection and Placement Techniques

With a pool of applicants, the employer can turn to screening and selecting. These processes use one or more techniques, including application forms, interviews, tests, and reference checks, to assess and investigate an applicant's aptitudes, interests, and background. The company then chooses the best candidate, given the job's requirements.

Employee selection is important for several reasons. For a manager, his or her job performance will always hinge on the subordinate's performance. A poor performer will drag a manager down, and a good one will enhance the manager's performance. Therefore, the time to screen out undesirables is before they have their foot in the door—not after.

Screening applicants is also expensive, so it is best to do it right the first time. Hiring a manager who earns $60 000 a year may cost as much as $40 000 or $50 000 once search fees, interviewing time, and travel and moving expenses are added up. In fact, the cost of hiring even non-executive employees can be $3000 to $5000 each or more.

Application Forms

The selection process usually starts with an application form, although some firms first require a brief screening interview. The **application form** requests information about factors like education, work history, and hobbies.[36] It is a good means of quickly collecting verifiable and therefore fairly accurate historical data from the candidate.

Testing for Employee Selection

A **test** is basically a sample of a person's behaviour, skills, characteristics, capabilities, and aptitudes. It is used in human resource management for predicting a person's success on the job. The use of tests for hiring, promotion, or both has increased in recent years after two decades of decline.[37] It appears that about half of all employers use tests of some sort for employee screening: About two-thirds use skills tests (such as typing tests), while only about 17 percent use so-called personality tests.

Many types of tests are available to be used at work. For example, intelligence (IQ) tests are designed to measure general *intellectual abilities*. Common ones are the Stanford-Binet test or the Wechsler or Wonderlic tests.

For some positions, ability or aptitude tests may be part of the initial screening process. When Toyota hired workers for its Cambridge, Ontario, plant, applicants were put through a series of tests to determine their math, verbal, and communication skills and their ability to work on a team. Even though most of the workers hired had never worked for an automobile firm before, they are now producing the highest-rated car in North America.[38]

For some jobs, managers will also be interested in testing an applicant's other abilities. For example, the Bennett Test of Mechanical Comprehension (illustrated in Figure 9.4) helps to assess an applicant's understanding of basic mechanical principles and might be useful for predicting success on a job such as machinist or engineer. A test like the Stromberg Dexterity Test is used to measure the applicant's speed of finger, hand, and arm movements. This would be useful if the job in question involves manipulating small items (for instance, assembling computer circuit boards).

It is also sometimes useful to measure the applicant's *personality and interests*. For example, you probably would not want to hire someone for an entry-level job as an accounting clerk if he or she had no measurable interest in working with figures.[39] With the burgeoning number of service workers these days, service management expert Karl Albrecht says that jobs with high levels of emotional labour will increase. *Emotional labour* is any work in which the employee's feelings are the tools of his or her trade (for instance, an airline reservation clerk would be expected to deal courteously with each and every caller). Most of us have had some experience dealing with service people who are obviously not well suited psychologically for such jobs. A personality test might have screened them out.

Assessment Centres. A **management assessment centre** is another approach to selection. In such centres, about a dozen management candidates spend two or three days per-

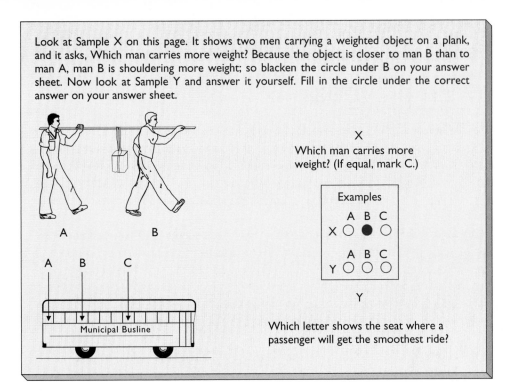

Look at Sample X on this page. It shows two men carrying a weighted object on a plank, and it asks, Which man carries more weight? Because the object is closer to man B than to man A, man B is shouldering more weight; so blacken the circle under B on your answer sheet. Now look at Sample Y and answer it yourself. Fill in the circle under the correct answer on your answer sheet.

X
Which man carries more weight? (If equal, mark C.)

Examples
A B C
X ○ ● ○

A B C
Y ○ ○ ○

Y

Which letter shows the seat where a passenger will get the smoothest ride?

A B

A B C

Municipal Busline

FIGURE 9.4
Bennett Test of Mechanical Comprehension, Example
Human resource managers often use personnel tests, like this one, to measure a candidate's skills and aptitudes.

forming realistic management tasks (like making presentations) under the observation of expert appraisers. Each candidate's potential for management is thereby assessed.[40] The centre's activities might include individual presentations, objective tests, interviews, and participation in management games. Here participants would engage in realistic problem solving, usually as members of two or three simulated companies that are competing in a mock marketplace.

Video Assessment. In this new technique, potential new hires view videos that show a series of realistic work situations portrayed by actors. For example, one scenario shows a department manager's assistant trying to convince the supervisor of the word processing pool to give his job top priority. The supervisor refuses and the assistant goes back to the boss, asking him to intercede. At the end of each situation, the potential hire chooses one of four courses of action to resolve the problem presented in the video. The test administrator then uses the computer to score the candidate's choices, much like a university or college instructor would grade student exams. Video assessment is fast, reliable, and relatively inexpensive. Videos take about an hour to complete and cost between $25 and $100. Canadian firms using video assessment include Weyerhaeuser, Reebok, Nortel Networks, and B.C. Hydro.[41]

Interviews

Both before and after any testing occurs, several interviews will usually be in order. Although the interview is probably the single most widely used selection device, its usefulness is often questioned. One doubt centres on reliability: Will different people interviewing the same candidate come to similar conclusions about the applicant's acceptability for the job? A second question concerns validity: Do the results of the interview accurately predict success on the job?

Hiring Happy Employees

With all the aptitudes, skills, and traits for which managers can test applicants, there is still one thing that's usually not tested for but that perhaps should be—at least if some recent research findings are valid. Particularly in companies being rocked by downsizings and competitive pressures, there's something to be said about hiring people who are inclined to remain happy even in the face of unhappy events. And, a recent line of research suggests that it may be possible to do so.

Basically, this line of research suggests that happiness seems to be largely determined by the person's genetic makeup—that, in other words, some people are simply born to be somewhat happier than others.[42] The theory, in a nutshell, says that people have a sort of "set-point" for happiness, a genetically determined happiness level to which the person quickly gravitates, pretty much no matter what failures or successes the person experiences. So, confront a high-happiness-set-point person with the prospect of a demotion or unattractive lateral transfer and he or she will soon return to being relatively happy once the short blip of disappointment has dissipated. On the other hand, send an inherently low-happiness-set-point person off on a two-week vacation or give him or her a sizable raise or a new computer and chances are he or she will soon be as unhappy as before the reward.

Several lines of research lend support to this set-point theory. For example, a study of lottery winners found that they were on the whole no happier a year after their good fortune than they were before. Several studies show that even people with spinal-cord injuries tend to rebound in spirits.[43] Studies of identical twins led one psychologist to conclude that life circumstances, like salary, education, or marital status, predicted only 2 percent of the happiness variation within each pair of twins, and that much of the rest was simply determined by the person's genes. In fact, the results of several long-term studies that followed people over many years suggest that the people who are happiest today will also be the happiest 10 years from now.

Like testing employees for any traits, coming up with a set of tests or interview questions to identify happier, high-set-point people requires careful consideration and probably the help of a licensed psychologist. However, following are several questions that may help provide some insight into a person's tendency to be relatively happy.

Indicate how strongly (high, medium, low) you agree with the following statements:

- "When good things happen to me, it strongly affects me."
- "I will often do things for no other reason than they might be fun."
- "When I get something I want, I feel excited and energized."
- "When I'm doing well at something, I love to keep at it."

Agreeing with more statements, and agreeing with them more strongly, *may* correlate with a higher happiness set-point.[44]

How to Be a Better Interviewer. A manager can boost the reliability and validity of selection interviews by following sound interviewing procedures.[45] These can be summarized as follows:

Plan the interview.

Begin by reviewing the candidate's application and résumé, and note any areas that are vague or may indicate strengths or weaknesses. Review the job specification and plan to start the interview with a clear picture of the traits of an ideal candidate.

If possible, use a structured form. A structured interview like that shown in Figure 9.5 (pages 278–80) usually results in the best interviews.[46] At a minimum, you should write out your questions prior to the interview.

The interview should take place in a private room where telephone calls are not accepted and interruptions can be minimized.

Also, plan to delay your decision. Interviewers often make snap judgments even before they see the candidate—on the basis of his or her application form, for instance—or during the first few minutes of the interview. Plan on keeping a record of the interview and review this record afterwards. Make your decision then.[47]

Establish rapport.

The main purpose of the interview is to find out about the applicant. To do this, start by putting the person at ease. Greet the candidate and start the interview by asking a non-controversial question—perhaps about the weather or the traffic conditions that day. As a rule, all applicants—even unsolicited drop-ins—should receive friendly, courteous treatment, not only on humanitarian grounds but also because your reputation is on the line.

Be aware of the applicant's status. For example, if you are interviewing someone who is unemployed, he or she may be exceptionally nervous and you may want to take additional steps to relax the person.[48]

Ask questions.

Try to follow your structured interview guide or the questions you wrote out ahead of time. A menu of questions to choose from (such as "What best qualifies you for the available position?") is presented in Figure 9.6, page 281.

Some suggestions for how to ask questions include the following:

Avoid questions that can be answered "yes" or "no."

Don't put words in the applicant's mouth or telegraph the desired answer (for instance, by nodding or smiling when the right answer is given).

Don't interrogate the applicant as if the person were a criminal, and don't be patronizing, sarcastic, or inattentive.

Don't monopolize the interview by rambling, and don't let the applicant dominate the interview so you can't ask all of your questions.

Listen to the candidate and encourage him or her to express thoughts fully.

Draw out the applicant's opinions and feelings by repeating the person's last comment as a question (such as "You didn't like your last job?").

When you ask for general statements of a candidate's accomplishments, also ask for examples.[49] Thus, if the candidate lists specific strengths or weaknesses, follow up with, "What are specific examples that demonstrate each of your strengths?"

Close the interview.

Towards the close of the interview, leave time to answer any questions the candidate may have and, if appropriate, to advocate your firm to the candidate.

Try to end the interview on a positive note. The applicant should be told whether there is an interest in him or her and, if so, what the next step will be. Similarly, rejections should be made diplomatically; for instance, with a statement like "Although your background is impressive, there are other candidates whose experience is closer to our re-

APPLICANT INTERVIEW GUIDE

To the interviewer: This Applicant Interview Guide is intended to assist in employee selection and placement. If it is used for all applicants for a position, it will help you to compare them, and it will provide more objective information than you will obtain from unstructured interviews.

Because this is a general guide, all of the items may not apply in every instance. Skip those that are not applicable and add questions appropriate to the specific position. Space for additional questions will be found at the end of the form.

The Canadian Human Rights Act prohibits discrimination on the basis of age, race and colour, national and ethnic origin, physical handicap, religion, gender, marital status, or prison record (if pardoned). Interviewers should take care to avoid any questions that suggest that an employment decision will be made on the basis of any such factors.

Job Interest

Name _____ Position applied for _____

What do you think the job (position) involves? _____

Why do you want the job (position)? _____

Why are you qualified for it? _____

What would your salary requirements be? _____

What do you know about our company? _____

Why do you want to work for our company? _____

Current Work Status

Are you now employed? ____Yes ____ No. If not, how long have you been unemployed? _____

Why are you unemployed? _____

If you are working, why are you applying for this position? _____

When would you be available to start work with our company? _____

Work Experience

(Start with the applicant's current or last position and work backwards. All periods of time should be accounted for. Go back at least 12 years, depending on the applicant's age.)

Current or last
employer_____ Address _____

Dates of employment: from _____ to _____

Current or last job title _____

What are (were) your duties? _____

Have you held the same job throughout your employment with that company? ____Yes ____No. If not, describe the various jobs you have had with that employer, how long you held each of them, and the main duties of each. _____

_____

What was your starting salary? _____ What is your current salary? _____ Comments _____

_____

Name of your last or current supervisor _____

What did you like most about that job? _____

What did you like least about it? _____

Why are you thinking of leaving? _____

    Why are you leaving right now? _____

    Interviewer's comments and observations _____

_____

What did you do before you took your last job? _____

    Where were you employed? _____

    Location _____ Job title _____

(continued)

FIGURE 9.5
Structured Interview Guide

Duties _____

Did you hold the same job throughout your employment with that company? ____Yes ____No. If not, describe the jobs you held, when you held them and the duties of each. _____

_____

What was your starting salary? _____What was your final salary? _____

Name of your last supervisor _____

May we contact that company? ____Yes ____No

What did you like most about that job? _____

What did you like least about that job? _____

Why did you leave that job? _____

Would you consider working there again? _____

Interviewer: If there is any gap between the various periods of employment, the applicant should be asked about it.

_____

Interviewer's comments and observations _____

_____

What did you do prior to the job with that company? _____

What other jobs or experience have you had? Describe them briefly and explain the general duties of each.

_____

Have you been unemployed at any time in the last six years? ____Yes ____No. What efforts did you make to find work?

_____

What other experience or training do you have that would help qualify you for the job you applied for? Explain how and where you obtained this experience or training. _____

_____

Educational Background

What education or training do you have that would help you in the job you are applying for? _____

_____

Describe any formal education you have had. (If relevant, interviewer may substitute technical training.) _____

_____

Personal

Would you be willing to relocate? ____Yes ____No

Are you willing to travel? ____Yes ____No

What is the maximum amount of time you would consider travelling? _____

_____

Can you work overtime? _____

What about working on weekends? _____

Self-Assessment

What do you feel are your strong points? _____

_____

What do you feel are your weak points? _____

_____

(continued)

FIGURE 9.5 cont'd

Interviewer: Compare the applicant's responses with the information given on the application for employment. Note any discrepancies. _____

Before the applicant leaves, the interviewer should provide basic information about the organization and the job opening. The applicant should be given information on the work location, work hours, the wage or salary, type of remuneration (salary or salary plus bonuses, etc.), and other factors that may affect the applicant's interest in the job.

Interviewer's Impressions

Rate each characteristic from 1 to 4, with 1 being the highest rating and 4 being the lowest.

Personal Characteristics	1	2	3	4	Comments
Poise, manner					
Speech					
Cooperation with interviewer					
Job-related Characteristics					
Experience for this job					
Knowledge of job					
Interpersonal relationships					
Effectiveness					

Overall rating for job

1	2	3	4	5
_____ Superior	_____ Above Average (well qualified)	_____ Average (qualified)	_____ Marginal (minimally qualified)	_____ Unsatisfactory

Comments or remarks _____

_____

Interviewer _____ Date _____

FIGURE 9.5 cont'd

quirements." If the applicant is still being considered but a decision can't be reached at once, say this. If it is your policy to inform candidates of their status in writing, do so within a few days of the interview.

Review the interview.
After the candidate leaves, review your interview notes, fill in the structured interview guide (if this was not done during the interview), and review the interview while it's fresh in your mind.

Remember that snap judgments and negative emphasis are two common interviewing mistakes: Reviewing the interview shortly after the candidate has left can help you minimize these two problems.

Guidelines for Interviewees. Before you get into a position where you have to interview applicants, you will probably have to navigate some interviews yourself. Here are some hints for excelling in your interview.

The first thing to understand is that interviews are used primarily to help employers determine what you are like as a person. In other words, information regarding how you get along with other people and your desire to work is of prime importance in the interview; your skills and technical expertise are usually best assessed through tests and a study of your educational and work history. Interviewers will look first for articulate answers. Specifically, whether you respond concisely, cooperate fully in answering questions, state personal opinions when relevant, and keep to the subject at hand are by far the most important elements influencing the interviewer's decision.

There are seven things to do to get that extra edge in the interview.

1. Did you bring a résumé?
2. What salary do you expect to receive?
3. What was your salary in your last job?
4. Why do you want to change jobs or why did you leave your last job?
5. What do you identify as your most significant accomplishment in your last job?
6. How many hours do you normally work per week?
7. What did you like and dislike about your last job?
8. How did you get along with your superiors and subordinates?
9. Can you be demanding of your subordinates?
10. How would you evaluate the company you were with last?
11. What were its competitive strengths and weaknesses?
12. What best qualifies you for the available position?
13. How long will it take you to start making a significant contribution?
14. How do you feel about our company—its size, industry, and competitive position?
15. What interests you most about the available position?
16. How would you structure this job or organize your department?
17. What control or financial data would you want and why?
18. How would you establish your primary inside and outside lines of communication?
19. What would you like to tell me about yourself?
20. Were you a good student?
21. Have you kept up in your field? How?
22. What do you do in your spare time?
23. What are your career goals for the next five years?
24. What are your greatest strengths and weaknesses?
25. What is your job potential?
26. What steps are you taking to help achieve your goals?
27. Do you want to own your own business?
28. How long will you stay with us?
29. What did your father do? Your mother?
30. What do your brothers and sisters do?
31. Have you ever worked on a group project and, if so, what role did you play?
32. Do you participate in civic affairs?
33. What professional associations do you belong to?
34. What is your credit standing?
35. What are your personal likes and dislikes?
36. How do you spend a typical day?
37. Would you describe your family as a close one?
38. How aggressive are you?
39. What motivates you to work?
40. Is money a strong incentive for you?
41. Do you prefer line or staff work?
42. Would you rather work alone or in a team?
43. What do you look for when hiring people?
44. Have you ever fired anyone?
45. Can you get along with union members and their leaders?
46. What do you think of the current economic and political situation?
47. How will government policy affect our industry or your job?
48. Will you sign a non-compete agreement or employment contract?
49. Why should we hire you?
50. Do you want the job?

FIGURE 9.6
Interview Questions to Expect

Preparation is essential.
Before the interview, learn all you can about the employer, the job, and the people doing the recruiting. At the library or on the Internet, look through business periodicals and Web sites to find out what is happening in the employer's company and industry.

Uncover the interviewer's real needs.
Spend as little time as possible answering your interviewer's first questions and as much time as possible getting him or her to describe his or her needs. Determine what the person is looking to accomplish and the type of person he or she feels is needed. Use open-ended questions such as "Could you tell me more about that?"

Relate yourself to the interviewer's needs.

Once you know the type of person your interviewer is looking for and the sorts of problems he or she wants solved, you are in a good position to describe your own accomplishments *in terms of the interviewer's needs*. Start by saying something like, "One of the problem areas you've said is important to you is similar to a problem I once faced." Then state the problem, describe your solution, and reveal the results.

Think before answering.

Answering a question should be a three-step process: pause, think, speak. *Pause* to make sure you understand what the interviewer is driving at, *think* about how to structure your answer, and then *speak*. In your answer, try to emphasize how hiring you will help the interviewer solve his or her problem.

Remember that appearance and enthusiasm are important.

Appropriate clothing, good grooming, a firm handshake, and the appearance of controlled energy are important.

Make a good first impression.

Studies show that, although they should wait, in most cases interviewers make up their minds about the applicant during the early minutes of the interview. A good first impression may turn to a bad one during the interview, but it is unlikely. Bad first impressions are almost impossible to overcome. Remember: You only have one chance to make a good first impression. One expert suggests paying attention to these key interviewing considerations:

Appropriate clothing

Good grooming

A firm handshake

The appearance of controlled energy

Pertinent humour and a readiness to smile

A genuine interest in the employer's operation and alert attention when the interviewer speaks

Pride in past performance

An understanding of the employer's needs and a desire to serve them

The display of sound ideas

Ability to take control when employers fall down on the interviewing job

Sample questions that you can ask are presented in Figure 9.7. They include "Would you mind describing the job for me?" and "Could you tell me about the people who would be reporting to me?"

Watch your nonverbal behaviour.

Remember that your *nonverbal behaviour* may broadcast more about you than the verbal content of what you say. Maintaining eye contact is very important. Speak with enthusiasm, nod agreement, and remember to take a moment to frame your answer (pause, think, speak) so that you sound articulate and fluent.[50]

Other Selection Techniques

Various other selection techniques are used to screen applicants.

Checking References. Most employers (estimates range up to 93 percent) do at least some reference checking on final candidates. These background checks can take many forms. However, most companies at least try to verify an applicant's current or previous position

1. What is the first problem that needs the attention of the person you hire?
2. What other problems need attention now?
3. What has been done about any of these to date?
4. How has this job been performed in the past?
5. Why is it now vacant?
6. Do you have a written job description for this position?
7. What are its major responsibilities?
8. What authority would I have? How would you define its scope?
9. What are the company's five-year sales and profit projections?
10. What needs to be done to reach these projections?
11. What are the company's major strengths and weaknesses?
12. What are its strengths and weaknesses in production?
13. What are its strengths and weaknesses in its products or its competitive position?
14. Whom do you identify as your major competitors?
15. What are their strengths and weaknesses?
16. How do you view the future for your industry?
17. Do you have any plans for new products or acquisitions?
18. Might this company be sold or acquired?
19. What is the company's current financial strength?
20. What can you tell me about the individual to whom I would report?
21. What can you tell me about other persons in key positions?
22. What can you tell me about the subordinates I would have?
23. How would you define your management philosophy?
24. Are employees afforded an opportunity for continuing education?
25. What are you looking for in the person who will fill this job?

FIGURE 9.7
Interview Questions to Ask

and salary with his or her current employer by telephone. Others call current and previous supervisors to discover more about the person's motivation, technical competence, and ability to work with others. Some employers also get background reports from commercial credit-rating companies; this can provide information about an applicant's credit standing, indebtedness, reputation, character, and lifestyle. The most commonly verified background areas are legal eligibility for employment (in compliance with immigration laws), dates of prior employment, military service (including discharge status), education, and identification (including date of birth and address).[51]

Computer databases have made it easier to check background information of candidates. There was a time when the only source of background information was what a candidate provided on the application form and (in some cases) what the employer could obtain through the use of private investigators. Today so-called pre-employment information services use databases to accumulate mounds of information about matters such as worker's compensation histories, credit histories, and conviction records. Employers are increasingly turning to these information services in order to make the right selection decision.

To many people, the ethics of using such information is debatable. For example, *Theftnet* is a database being tested by several large retailers including Home Depot and JC Penney Company. The database contains the names of workers who have either been prosecuted for theft or who have signed admissions statements with former employers.[52]

On its face, using a database like Theftnet should be straightforward, focusing as it does on convictions and written admissions. Yet in practice using such a database raises several serious issues. For example, one attorney says that supplying information to the database could make an employer liable for defamation and retaliation claims unless it has "clear proof" of an employee's guilt.[53] Similarly, employees who have signed admissions statements may in fact be guilty, but also may have signed for unrelated reasons such as coercion or promises by the employer. Sources like these must therefore be used with considerable caution.

Honesty Testing. With so many employees working in jobs in which honesty is important—such as in banks, retail stores, and restaurants—paper-and-pencil "honesty testing" has become an important mini-industry.[54] Several psychologists have expressed concern about the proliferation and potential misuse of such tests. However, the American Psychological Association recently reported that "the preponderance of the evidence" supports the notion that some of the tests work, meaning that they can predict which prospective employees may prove undependable or dishonest.[55]

These tests ask questions aimed at assessing a person's tendency to be honest. For instance, a test might ask a series of questions such as "Have you ever made a personal phone call on company time?" Sometimes the test assumes that someone who answers all such questions "no" may not be entirely honest, although the person may actually be telling the truth.

Health Exams. A physical examination and drug screening are often two of the final steps in the selection process. A pre-employment medical exam is used to confirm that the applicant qualifies for the physical requirements of the position and to discover any medical limitations that should be taken into account in placing the applicant. By identifying health problems, a physical exam can also reduce absenteeism and accidents and detect communicable diseases that may be unknown to the applicant.

Because drug use can be a serious problem at work, many companies use drug tests, even though they are increasingly coming under fire for doing so. In 1998, for example, the Ontario Divisional Court decided that Imperial Oil's drug policy—which included pre-employment drug testing that made offers of work conditional on a negative result—was unlawful because Imperial failed to prove that a positive drug test would indicate a failure to perform essential duties. Imperial's policy also required random drug and alcohol testing, but that was also judged to be discriminatory because the company could not prove that such testing was necessary to deter alcohol or drug impairment on the job.[56]

Toronto Dominion Bank wanted to give drug tests to all new employees because it felt that drug use was a growing problem in society, and because it wanted to have the public's trust. But a federal court ruled that TD Bank's policy was discriminatory and that it wasn't related closely enough to job performance.[57]

Orientation and Training

Once employees have been recruited, screened, and selected, they must be prepared to do their jobs; this is the purpose of employee orientation and training.

Employee **orientation** means providing new employees with basic information about the employer. In many companies, employees receive an orientation handbook to facilitate this. It contains information like that summarized in Figure 9.8 on pages 286–87. Orientation aims to familiarize the new employee with the company and his or her co-workers; provide information about working conditions (coffee breaks, overtime policy, and so on); explain how to get on the payroll, how to obtain identification cards, and what the working hours are; and generally reduce the sort of first-day jitters that are commonly associated with starting a new job.

This initial orientation is usually followed by a **training program**, one aimed at ensuring that the new employee has the basic knowledge required to perform the job satisfactorily. Some companies find that they must retrain their current employees because of changes in products and markets. When Honeywell Ltd.'s Scarborough, Ontario, plant won a mandate to export to the U.S. and Europe, the plant had to become more competitive. To achieve this goal, the company offered training opportunities to its workers. When it offered 30 spaces in after-work classes in English as a second language, it received 130 applications. Two hundred applications were received for a computer aware-

orientation
Providing new employees with basic information about the employer.

training program
A program aimed at ensuring that the new employee has the basic knowledge required to perform the job satisfactorily.

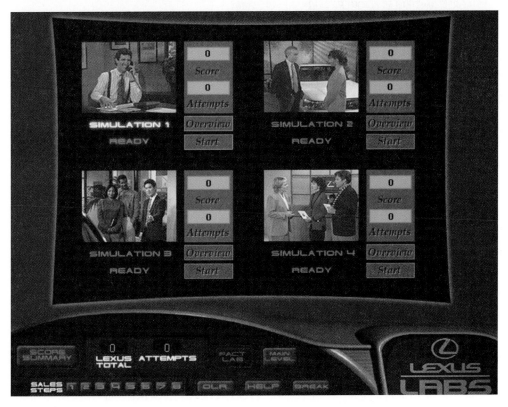

Second Cup Ltd. runs Coffee College where recruits learn about all aspects of the retail coffee business.

Computerized simulation training allows employees to practise job-related skills before they actually have to interact with co-workers or customers. The Lexus computerized simulation training shown here is just one example of this kind of training.

ness course. Sixty people signed up for a course designed to increase the workers' ability to work in teams.[58]

On-the-job training occurs while the employee is actually at work. Ford Motor of Canada trained 140 workers for a year to work in a new aluminum casting plant in Windsor, Ontario. Because workers needed to know many jobs, they needed a lot of training.[59] Much on-the-job training is unplanned and informal, as when one employee shows another how to use the new photocopier.

Off-the-job training, by contrast, is performed at a location away from the work site. For example, refresher courses are offered for managers of McDonald's Canadian restau-

on-the-job training
Training that occurs while the employee is actually at work.

off-the-job training
Training that is performed at a location away from the work site.

Orientation Checklist
(Small western supply company)

HOURLY & SALARIED EMPLOYEE ORIENTATION GUIDE CHECKLIST
NOTE: ALL INFORMATION MUST BE DISCUSSED
WITH EACH NEW EMPLOYEE

SUPERVISOR: This form is to be used as a guide for the orientation of new employees in your department.

In order to avoid duplication of instruction the information indicated below has been given to the employee by the Personnel Department.

PERSONNEL DEPARTMENT

INSURANCE PROGRAM BOOKLET	PAY, SALARY, PROMOTIONS, AND TRANSFERS	
SALARY CONTINUANCE INSURANCE BOOKLET	TRANSPORTATION	
SAFETY BOOKLET	TIME SHEET	
PENSION PLAN BOOKLET	PERSONAL RECORDS	
EMPLOYEE HANDBOOK/LABOUR AGREEMENT/RULES BOOKLET	BULLETIN BOARDS	
MATCHING GIFTS	PERSONAL MAIL, E-MAIL	
EDUCATIONAL ASSISTANCE PROGRAM	PARKING FACILITIES	
PATENT AGREEMENT	ABSENCES, TARDINESS	
I.D. CARD	CHARITABLE CONTRIBUTION	
CREDIT UNION	VACATIONS	
STOCK PURCHASE PLAN	JURY DUTY	
SAVINGS BOND PLAN	SICK BENEFITS — A & S — LIMITATIONS, ETC.	
PROBATIONARY PERIOD	LEAVE OF ABSENCE, MATERNITY, MEDICAL, BEREAVEMENT, ETC.	
SERVICE AWARDS	DIFFICULTIES, COMPLAINTS, DISCRIMINATION & GRIEVANCE PROCEDURES	
VISITORS	MILL TOUR	
HOLIDAYS	TERMINATION NOTICE AND PAY, ESP. VACATION ALLOWANCE (VOLUNTARY RESIGNATION)	
FOOD SERVICES	INTRODUCTION TO GUARDS	

(continued)

FIGURE 9.8
Contents of Orientation Program
In many organizations, new employees receive a package of orientation materials or a handbook, containing information on matters like the ones shown in this checklist.

FIRST AID & REQUIREMENTS OF REPORTING INJURY	(OTHERS)		
SIGNATURE OF EMPLOYEE:	WITNESS:		DATE

SUPERVISOR: The following is a checklist of information necessary to orient the new employee to the job in your department. Please check off each point as you discuss it with the employee and return to the Personnel Department within three days following employee placement on the job:

INTRODUCTION TO FELLOW EMPLOYEES		HOURS OF WORK, OVERTIME, CALL-IN PROCEDURES	
TOUR OF DEPARTMENT		REST, LUNCH PERIODS	
EXPLANATION OF NEW EMPLOYEE'S JOB. RESPONSIBILITIES AND PERFORMANCE EVALUATIONS		SUPPLY PROCEDURES	
LAVATORY		LINE OF AUTHORITY	
PHONE CALLS — PERSONAL/COMPANY			
SIGNATURE OF SUPERVISOR:			DATE

I have received a copy of the appropriate materials listed above and have had explained to me the information outlined. I understand this information concerning my employment with (Company name). Also, in case of voluntary separation (resignation) I understand the Company's policy, that in order to be eligible for any due vacation allowance, I must give my supervisor at least two weeks' notice in writing prior to my last day of work.

SIGNATURE OF EMPLOYEE:	WITNESS:		DATE

FIGURE 9.8 cont'd

rants at the Canadian Institute of Hamburgerology. Second Cup Ltd., Canada's largest retailer of specialty coffee, runs Coffee College, where franchisees and managers learn a lot of details about coffee. They also learn how to hire workers, keep the books, detect employee theft, and boost Christmas sales.[60] At Toronto Plastics Ltd., machine operators must continually assess the performance of their equipment as part of a new emphasis on statistical process control. To help the employees do a better job, the company trained 75 machine operators in statistics and mathematics.[61]

Statistics Canada reports that 16 percent of Canadian adults cannot read the majority of written material they encounter in everyday life, and that 22 percent do not have the reading skills to deal with complex instructions. Companies like Nortel Networks and CCL Custom Manufacturing are finding that they have to train workers because the equipment they must use is increasingly complex.[62] A study by the Conference Board of Canada found that, on a per-employee basis, large Canadian companies spend only half as much on training as U.S. firms do. And U.S. firms, in turn, spend only a fraction of the amount that Japanese firms spend.[63]

Other activities that come under the general heading of training and orientation are *management development programs* (training managers to be more effective in their work), *mentoring* (helping younger managers learn the ropes and benefit from the experiences of older managers), and *networking* (improving informal interactions among managers).

Appraising and Compensating Employees

Employee Appraisal

performance appraisal
Evaluating an employee's current or past performance relative to his or her performance standards.

Once employees have been at work for some time, their performance should be appraised, or evaluated. **Performance appraisal** is defined as evaluating an employee's current or past performance relative to his or her performance standards. You've probably already had experience with performance appraisals. For example, most colleges and universities ask students to rank instructors on scales like the one shown in Figure 9.9. Do you think this is an effective scale? Do you see any way to improve it? These are two of the questions you should be better able to answer by the end of this chapter.

Probably the most familiar approach is to use a performance appraisal form like the one shown in Figure 9.10. This form (traditionally called a "graphic rating scale") lists several job characteristics (like quality of work) and provides a rating scale (from outstanding to unsatisfactory) along with short definitions of each rating. This particular appraisal form is relatively objective, because it calls for specific ratings. However, the form also provides space for more subjective examples of particularly good or particularly bad employee performance.

360-degree feedback
A appraisal technique in which performance information is collected "all around" an employee, from his or her supervisors, subordinates, peers, and internal or external customers.

Companies use other appraisal techniques today. For example, with **360-degree feedback**, performance information is collected "all around" an employee, from his or her supervisors, subordinates, peers, and internal or external customers.[64] The feedback is generally used for training and development, rather than for pay increases.[65] Most 360-

---

Classroom Teaching Appraisal by Students

This questionnaire is designed to improve teaching effectiveness. Please do not sign your name—participants are to remain anonymous.

Rate your instructor on each item. The highest rating (10) reflects exceptional teaching, while the lowest (1) indicates very poor teaching. Use the rating that most clearly expresses your view.

Use the blank lines for any additional qualities you would like to rate.

Instructor _____   Course _____

Semester _____   Academic Year _____

Exceptional				Good				Very Poor		Don't Know
10	9	8	7	6	5	4	3	2	1	X

_____ Do the course objectives reflect the lesson assignments?

_____ Are the instructing methods used by the teacher effective?

_____ Is the instructor competent in the subject matter?

_____ Are the classes organized and well-planned?

_____ Are the classes designed to challenge and stimulate?

_____ Does the instructor welcome differing viewpoints?

_____ Does the instructor show interest in helping you in and out of class?

_____ Rate the fairness and effectiveness of the grading system employed by the instructor.

_____ Does the instructor show genuine interest in the subject matter?

_____ _____

_____ _____

FIGURE 9.9
An Example of a Teaching Appraisal by Students

degree feedback systems contain several common features. Appropriate parties—peers, supervisors, subordinates, and customers, for instance—complete survey questionnaires on an individual. The questionnaires can take many forms but often include supervisory skill items such as "returns phone calls promptly," "listens well," or "my manager keeps me informed."[66] Computerized systems then compile all of this feedback into individualized reports that are presented to the person being rated.[67]

Do Performance Appraisals Work? Managers usually assume that performance appraisals lead to increased worker productivity. But there has always been a nagging concern that performance appraisals may work only for the people who are top performers, and that appraisals simply deflate the sense of self-worth of everyone else. A 1997 survey of 2004 Canadian workers found that:

- 40 percent of employees did not understand the measures that were used to evaluate their performance.
- 43 percent thought that their performance was not rated fairly.
- 53 percent felt that managers did not express goals clearly.
- 58 percent said that appraisals were not timely.
- 61 percent felt that appraisals were not helpful in improving their performance.
- 81 percent did not think there was a clear link between their performance and their pay.[68]

Overall, performance appraisals cause stress for both managers and employees. Employees often see appraisals as a whip in the hands of managers. But there are some strong arguments supporting the idea of performance appraisals:[69]

- Appraisals may be necessary as a foundation for dismissal of problem employees.
- A favourable evaluation serves as a motivator for those who are doing well.
- An unfavourable evaluation identifies problems early so an employee can begin working to correct deficiencies.
- Part of the appraisal involves setting performance goals for the next time period, and this should improve performance.

While performance appraisals should probably not be done away with, certain improvements are necessary. Perhaps the key improvement is more effective communication between managers and their subordinates. Improving communication opens the door for increased understanding between managers and their subordinates, increased goodwill on the part of employees towards the company, and increased commitment and effort on the part of employees.

Basic Forms of Compensation

A major factor in retaining skilled workers is a company's **compensation system**—what it offers employees in return for their labour. Wages and salaries are a key part of any compensation system, but most systems also include features such as incentives and employee benefit programs. We will explore each of these elements in this section. Bear in mind, however, that finding the right combination of elements is complicated by the need to make employees feel valued while simultaneously keeping company costs at a minimum. Thus, compensation systems are highly individualized, depending on the nature of the industry, the company, and the type of workers involved.

compensation system
What a firm offers its employees in return for their labour.

Wages and Salaries. Wages and salaries are the dollar amounts paid to employees for their work. **Wages** are dollars paid for time worked or for number of units produced. Workers who are paid by the hour receive wages. Canadian manufacturing workers are among the highest paid workers of that type in the world. Only German workers receive higher wages.

wages
Dollars paid based on the number of hours worked or the number of units produced.

Performance Appraisal for:

Employee Name _____ Title _____

Department _____ Employee Payroll Number _____

Reason for Review: ☐ Annual ☐ Promotion ☐ Unsatisfactory Performance
                    ☐ Merit   ☐ End Probation Period ☐ Other _____

Date employee began present position _____ / _____ / _____

Date of last appraisal _____ / _____ / _____   Scheduled appraisal date _____ / _____ / _____

Instructions: Carefully evaluate employee's work performance in relation to current job requirements. Check rating box to indicate the employee's performance. Indicate N/A if not applicable. Assign points for each rating within the scale in the corresponding points box. Points will be totalled and averaged for an overall performance score.

RATING IDENTIFICATION

O – Outstanding – Performance is exceptional in all areas and is recognizable as being far superior to others.

V – Very Good – Results clearly exceed most position requirements. Performance is of high quality and is achieved on a consistent basis.

G – Good – Competent and dependable level of performance. Meets performance standards of the job.

I – Improvement Needed – Performance is deficient in certain areas. Improvement is necessary.

U – Unsatisfactory – Results are generally unacceptable and require immediate improvement. No merit increase should be granted to individuals with this rating.

N – Not Rated – Not applicable or too soon to rate.

GENERAL FACTORS	RATING	SCALE	SUPPORTIVE DETAILS OR COMMENTS
1. **Quality** – The accuracy, thoroughness, and acceptability of work performed.	O ☐ V ☐ G ☐ I ☐ U ☐	100–90 90–80 80–70 70–60 below 60	Points
2. **Productivity** – The quantity and efficiency of work produced in a specified period of time.	O ☐ V ☐ G ☐ I ☐ U ☐	100–90 90–80 80–70 70–60 below 60	Points
3. **Job Knowledge** – The practical/technical skills and information used on the job.	O ☐ V ☐ G ☐ I ☐ U ☐	100–90 90–80 80–70 70–60 below 60	Points

(continued)

FIGURE 9.10
Performance Appraisal Chart
This is a page from a typical performance appraisal form. Supervisors use it to rate the employee's performance on factors like quality and productivity.

4. Reliability – The extent to which an employee can be relied upon regarding task completion and follow up.	O ☐ V ☐ G ☐ I ☐ U ☐	100–90 90–80 80–70 70–60 below 60	Points
5 . Availability – The extent to which an employee is punctual, observes prescribed work break/meal periods, and the overall attendance record.	O ☐ V ☐ G ☐ I ☐ U ☐	100–90 90–80 80–70 70–60 below 60	Points
6. Independence – The extent of work performed with little or no supervision.	O ☐ V ☐ G ☐ I ☐ U ☐	100–90 90–80 80–70 70–60 below 60	Points

FIGURE 9.10 cont'd

Salary is the money an employee receives for getting a job done. An executive earning $100 000 per year may work five hours one day and fifteen the next. Such an individual is paid to get a job done rather than for the specific number of hours or days spent working. Salaries are usually expressed as an amount to be paid per year but are often paid each month or every two weeks.

> **salary**
> Dollars paid at regular intervals in return for doing a job, regardless of the amount of time or output involved.

In setting wage and salary levels, a company must consider several factors. First, it must take into account how its competitors compensate their employees. A firm that pays less than its rivals may soon find itself losing valuable personnel.

Within the company, the firm must also decide how wage and salary levels for different jobs will compare. And within wage and salary levels, managers must decide how much to pay individual workers. Two employees may do exactly the same job, but the employee with more experience may earn more, in part to keep that person in the company and in part because the experienced person performs better. Some union contracts specify differential wages based on experience. Note that the basis for differential pay must be job-related, however, not favouritism or discrimination.

The profession of management can be very rewarding from a financial perspective. A survey of executive salaries, for example, showed that the highest paid Canadian executive in 1998 (Peter Munk of Barrick Gold Corp.) earned $38.9 million in total compensation. Other executives in the top 10 earned between $8.4 million and $34.1 million. The twenty-sixth ranked CEO (Israel Asper of Canwest Global Communications Corp.) earned over $2.7 million in 1998. Even the seventy-third ranked executive (David Johnson of Encal Energy) made over $1 million.

Barrick Gold Corp.
www.barrick.com

Canwest Global
www.canwestglobal.com

Canadian CEOs make much less than their U.S. counterparts, but more than the CEOs in some other countries. The typical CEO of a U.S. corporation with sales revenue of $250 to $500 million receives about $1 million per year. A Canadian CEO in a company of the same size receives about $500 000, and a German CEO about $400 000. Canadian CEOs are also in the middle of the range when it comes to their pay as a multiple of the typical manufacturing employee. Brazilian CEOs make 50 times more than a typical manufacturing employee, Canadian CEOs about 15 times, and German CEOs about 10 times.

Is there a relationship between CEO pay and company performance? Sometimes, but it is not hard to find examples where executive pay went up while company profit went down. The average compensation for executives in the top 100 list went up 26 percent from 1997 to 1998, but earnings at Canada's 135 biggest companies declined 18 percent.[70]

incentive program
Any program in which a company offers its workers additional pay over and above the normal wage or salary level in order to motivate them to perform at a higher-than-normal level.

Incentive Programs. The term **incentive programs** refers to special pay programs designed to motivate high performance. The use of incentive programs has increased recently, largely because of concern for productivity.

Sales bonuses are a typical incentive. Under such a program, employees who sell a certain number or dollar amount of goods for the year receive a special payment. Employees who do not reach this goal earn no bonus. Similarly, *merit salary systems* link raises to performance levels in non-sales jobs. For example, many baseball players have clauses in their contracts that pay them bonuses for hitting over .300, making the All-Star team, or being named Most Valuable Player. Executives commonly receive stock options and bonuses as an incentive.

gain-sharing plan
An incentive program in which employees receive a bonus if the firm's costs are reduced because of greater worker efficiency and/or productivity.

Some incentive programs apply to all employees in a firm. **Gain-sharing plans** distribute bonuses to all employees in a company based on reduced costs from working more efficiently. Palliser Furniture Ltd. introduced a gain-sharing plan that rewards employees for increasing production. Any profit resulting from production above a certain level is split 50-50 between the company and the employees.[71]

profit-sharing plan
An incentive program in which employees receive a bonus depending on the firm's profits.

Profit-sharing plans are based on profit levels in the firm. Profits earned above a certain level are distributed to employees. Stock ownership by employees serves as an incentive to lower costs, increase productivity and profits, and thus increase the value of the employee's stock.[72]

Employee Benefits

benefits
What a firm offers its workers other than wages and salaries in return for their labour.

A growing part of nearly every firm's compensation system is **benefits** programs—compensation other than wages and salaries. Benefits now often comprise over half a firm's total compensation budget. Most companies are required by law to provide workers' compensation, holiday pay, and Canada Pension Plan and employment insurance contributions. Most businesses also voluntarily provide extended health, life, and disability insurance. Many also allow employees to buy stock through payroll deductions at a slightly discounted price. Many firms also provide vision care and dental benefits to employees. Some even provide free legal services.

Starbucks is a good example of how managers use benefits to help build a loyal workforce. Howard Schultz, Starbuck's CEO, places great emphasis on a benefits package that features fully company-paid physicals, dental coverage, eye care, and company-paid disability and life insurance. Also included are stock options, training programs, career counselling, and product discounts for all employees, full-time and part-time. Even though the benefits are generous, they make up only a quarter of Starbucks' labour costs and have stabilized there. Schultz sees benefits as the bond that ties workers to the company and inspires loyalty. Perhaps more important, he thinks that employees who are treated right treat customers right. "The future of Starbucks," says Schultz, "lies in increasing shareholder value—and increasing employee value will [do that]."[73]

Benefits are an important part of most compensation programs. Some are provided by the employer, while others are mandated by the government. A new parental leave provision allows either parent to take up to 10 weeks of paid leave after the birth or adoption of a child.

cafeteria benefits
A flexible approach to providing benefits in which employees are allocated a certain sum to cover benefits and can "spend" this allocation on the specific benefits they prefer.

As the range of benefits has grown, so has concern about containing their cost. Businesses are experimenting with a variety of procedures to cut benefit costs, while maintaining the ability to attract, retain, and maintain the morale of employees.[74] One new approach is the use of **cafeteria benefits**. These plans provide a set dollar amount in benefits and allow employees to pick among alternatives. Employees at Toyota's Cambridge, Ontario, plant are given the opportunity once each year to structure their benefits packages. For example, they can give more weight to dental coverage if they have young children, or to life insurance or disability coverage, depending on their circumstances.[75] At companies like Canada Life Assurance and KPMG Canada, employees actually have the option of taking their benefit dollar figure as cash.[76]

More and more firms are using "temporary" workers on a long-term basis. Since they are not covered by most companies' benefits plans, temporary workers allow businesses to keep staff levels high and benefits costs low.

Retirement. Some employees are ready for retirement much earlier than others. But because most retirement plans are based on an employee's age, some workers who should retire earlier stay on the job while others, who are still useful workers, leave before they would like to. This policy is short-sighted. A compromise is to grant year-to-year extensions to productive employees who want to continue working but who have reached retirement age. Recently several workers in different locations across Canada have successfully challenged mandatory retirement rules. Their employers must allow them to work even though they are past the traditional retirement age.

In spite of these individual exceptions, Canadians generally are retiring earlier than they used to. In the period 1976–80, for example, the median retirement age in Canada was 64.9 years, but in the period 1991–95 that figure dropped to 62.3 years.[77] Two other interesting facts: Workers over age 65 are nearly four times as likely to die from work-related causes than younger workers, and older workers have double the health care costs that workers in their forties do.[78]

Miscellaneous Services. Human resources departments also provide many other services, which vary widely among firms. These range from setting policies to deal with allegations of sexual harassment on the job to helping employees arrange car pools.

Promotions, Terminations, and Discipline

Performance appraisal often leads to personnel actions such as promotion, termination, and discipline. A **promotion** generally means rewarding an employee's efforts by moving that person to a job with increased authority and responsibility. Ideally, promotions (like rewards in general) should be awarded based on proven competence.

Unfortunately, that is often not the case today, for two reasons. First, with the downsizings and consolidations of the past few years, there are often not enough middle management (and higher) positions available into which a firm can promote worthy employees. As a result, companies today are relying more on lateral "promotions" to broaden employees' experiences and to help them gain additional skills. Being transferred from a post such as sales manager to one such as personnel manager may not have the same impact as a traditional promotion. However, it can at least reignite the initial interest and excitement that the employee felt in his or her first job, and it gives the person additional skills that may be useful later.

promotion
Rewarding an employee's efforts by moving that person to a job with increased authority and responsibility.

grievance
A complaint that an employee lodges against an employer, usually regarding wages, hours, or some condition of employment like unfair supervisory behaviour.

Discipline and Grievances. A **grievance** is a complaint that an employee lodges against an employer, usually regarding wages, hours, or some condition of employment like unfair supervisory behaviour. Most union contracts contain a grievance procedure that provides an orderly system of steps, whereby employer and union determine whether some clause of the contract has been violated. Steps typically include discussing the problem with one's supervisor, then referring the matter to the department head, the personnel department, and finally to the employer's head of the facility. Thus, a supervisor may fire an employee for excessive absences. The employee might then file a grievance stating that the supervisor had issued no previous warnings or discipline related to excessive absences as was called for in the union agreement and that the firing was thus unwarranted. Many non-unionized companies also offer grievance procedures.

Supervisors sometimes have to discipline subordinates, usually because a rule or procedure was violated. A company should have clear rules (such as "No smoking allowed when dealing with customers") as well as a series of progressive penalties that all employees know will be enforced if the rule is broken.

One way to set up a discipline system is to follow the so-called FRACT model: Get the *facts*, obtain the *reason* for the infraction, *audit* the records, pinpoint the *consequences*, and identify the *type* of infraction before taking remedial steps.

discipline without punishment
A discipline technique that makes the employee aware that a company rule has been broken, but that does not monetarily punish the employee for having broken the rule.

A recent innovation in this area is called **discipline without punishment**. With this disciplinary technique, for example, an employee first gets an oral reminder for breaking the rule and then a written reminder if the rule is broken again. Then a paid one-day "decision-making leave" is mandated if another incident occurs in the next few weeks. If the rule is broken again, then the employee may be dismissed.

dismissal
The involuntary termination of an employee's employment with the firm.

Dismissal—the involuntary termination of an employee's employment with the firm— is the most dramatic disciplinary step an employer can take towards an employee. In general, the dismissal should be *just*, in that sufficient cause should exist for it. Furthermore, the dismissal should occur only after all reasonable steps to rehabilitate or salvage the employee have failed. However, there are undoubtedly times when immediate dismissal is required—such as for gross insubordination.

Companies must be very careful when dismissing employees. A general manager at Jumbo Video Inc., who was fired when he refused to take a large pay cut, was awarded more than $226 000 in damages. The manager had earlier signed a contract containing certain stipulations that the company later tried to void because of financial problems. The judge ruled that the company had reneged on the contract.[79]

Legislation on unjust dismissal in the Canada Labour Code requires the company to prove that it had "just cause" in firing the person. However, some strange rulings have been handed down. One Canadian Imperial Bank of Commerce employee was fired because of the people she associated with while she was not at work. Police burst into her apartment at precisely the same time that five men were dividing the loot from a CIBC robbery. A Labour Canada adjudicator ruled that CIBC did not have "just cause" to fire her because she hadn't actually done anything wrong herself. A supervisor at another bank got her job back even after she admitted that she had planned to steal customers' money.[80]

SUMMARY OF LEARNING OBJECTIVES

1. **Explain why human resource management (HRM) is now a core function.** Human resource management is the management function devoted to acquiring, training, appraising, and compensating employees. As workers become more fully empowered, the HRM function has grown in importance.

2. **Understand the legal framework within which HRM must operate.** In hiring, training, compensating, and/or dismissing workers, managers must obey many laws. Equal employment opportunity and equal pay laws forbid discrimination other than that based on legitimate job requirements. Controversy over what constitutes discrimination in paying men and women who hold different jobs is

a current issue. Managers are also required to provide employees with a safe working environment.

3. **Use five methods to recruit a pool of good candidates.** Staffing—filling a firm's open positions—starts with job analysis and personnel planning. Recruiting—including the use of internal sources, advertising, employment agencies, recruiters, referrals, college and university recruiting, and recruiting a more diverse workforce—is then used to create a pool of applicants.

4. **Know how to use testing in selecting new employees.** With a pool of applicants, the employer can turn to screening and selecting, using one or more techniques—including application forms, interviews, tests, and reference checks—to assess and investigate an applicant's aptitudes, interests, and background.

5. **List and briefly discuss the main steps in conducting an employment interview.** To be effective, an interviewer must do the following: plan the interview (familiarize yourself with the applicant's qualifications), establish rapport (put the applicant at ease), ask questions (follow questions you have prepared ahead of time), close the interview (on a positive note), and review the interview (consult the notes that you took during the interview).

6. **Describe three other important employee selection techniques.** These include checking references, conducting a video assessment, honesty testing, and health exams (possibly including drug tests).

7. **Explain what is involved in employee orientation and training.** Once employees have been recruited, screened, and selected, they must be prepared to do their jobs. This is the role of employee orientation and training. Orientation means providing new employees with basic information about the employer, while training ensures that the new employee has the basic knowledge required to perform the job satisfactorily.

8. **Explain what is involved in appraising and compensating employees.** Once they have been on the job for some time, employees are appraised. Performance appraisal forms and 360-degree feedback are two methods for appraising performance. Performance appraisal can lead to actions such as promotions, termination, or discipline. Employee compensation refers to all work-related pay or rewards that go to employees. It includes direct financial payments in the form of wages, salaries, incentives, commissions, and bonuses, and indirect payments in the form of financial fringe benefits like employer-paid insurance and vacation.

TYING IT ALL TOGETHER

After planning what's to be done, managers must create an organization. We covered Planning in Chapters 4 to 6, and in this part of the book (Chapters 7 to 9) we focused on how to design an organization and an organization chart. Of course, "an organization" is more then just a chart of reporting relationships and positions. It's the people who make the organization, and so in this chapter we focused on the staffing methods that managers use to recruit, select, and train employees to fill the organization's positions. Once the organization is staffed with competent and well-trained individuals, the manager's job is still not complete: Employees must then be inspired, motivated, and led, the topics we turn to in the next part of this book.

1. You are now a citizen of the 21st century. The rules of the job and career game appear to be changing as rapidly as machines such as ATMs replace bank tellers. You can now bank and pay bills with your computer and you can order all sorts of products over the Internet, including groceries. In groups of five students, preferably from different majors, explore how you think your job choice will change in the future. Also discuss what you think the profession you are now preparing for will look like 10 years from now and 30 years from now. Be prepared to compare your discussion with that of other groups.

2. *Fast Company*'s September 1999 issue is all about the future and is entitled "21 Rules for the 21st Century." Among the articles is one called "2004: A Personal Odyssey." The article begins with the following questions: "What are *your* expectations five years from now? As the 21st Century arrives, are you feeling confident about your career and sure of your future? Or does the prospect of ever-more-powerful technology and never-ending change leave you wishing you could return to the simpler days of the Old Economy? The *Fast Company*–Roper Starch worldwide survey found the answers to these questions and more." First, think where you will be in 2004 and where you want to be. Then find *Fast Company* in the library or on the Internet and look at the survey. When you get to the questions, answer them yourself prior to looking at the results the survey found. Then compare your responses with others that took the survey. You may wish to discuss these matters in small groups in class or as a class discussion.

1. Human resource management is an increasingly challenging area. As the following scenario describes, human resources can be pulled into very difficult circumstances.

   > It's midday in Kuwait, but it's unnaturally dark. As far as the eye can see, blazing oil-field fires spew up tornadoes of black smoke. A blanket of sooty, acid clouds seal in the hundreds of miles of desert. On the ground, an army of Bechtel Corporation workers toil amid the heat, providing support activities to the actual fire fighters. They construct roads for the trucks, create pipelines pumping water, build hospitals for the workers, and cook and serve meals to the cadre of smoke-coated personnel.

   > More than 7000 miles away from the flame and wreckage of the Gulf War, in a 14th-floor office in San Francisco's financial district, men and women of Bechtel Corporation sweat over 30 000 employee files and resumes. Culling through 105 000 phone-in inquiries, the HR staff works frantically to supply the necessary manpower to the Middle-East operation. The debris here isn't burned rubber and charred metal: it's fax paper and plastic coffee cups used by the HR staff as it dispatches calls from San Francisco to Bangkok, so that it can hire and assign foreign-contract personnel. Gathering and transferring employee information from headquarters to ground operations in Kuwait, human resources managers mobilize more than 16 000 Americans, Britons, Filipinos, Australians—people from 37 countries in all—to rectify the Kuwait disaster.[81]

   Your task as human resources recruiter for Bechtel is to devise a plan to recruit, select, and deploy your resources and then explain how you would implement it. You may wish to form a team of experts from your class for this exercise.

   You may want to visit the Internet and research this specific case. Go to www.bechtel.com. Then click on Bechtel project experience. Once you are there, click on Search. Type in the word "Kuwait" and read the information presented. Include this information in your analysis.

2. Interview a human resource manager at a local company. Select a position for which the firm is currently recruiting applicants and identify the steps in the selection process. Also obtain a copy of an employment application. Examine it carefully to determine how useful it might be in making a hiring decision.

INTERNET EXERCISE

In many companies the HRM function is now aided by the use of technology. At Dell Computer Corporation, employees are provided with online information about job postings, training, and benefits. To gain a window on what the company offers to employees visit www.us.dell.com/careers/index.asp. Go to "Working at Dell" and view "Benefits."

1. How do fast-moving companies like Dell attract and retain good employees?

2. If you were an employee at Dell, or any other company, which benefits would you find most attractive? Why?

3. Most high-tech companies offer employees profit-sharing and stock option plans. To what extent do you think this would motivate employees to stay with the company? Is there a "downside"?

4. How effective do you think self-paced online courses such as those offered at Dell's corporate virtual university are?

To learn even more about HRM at Dell, refer to the article in *HR Magazine* at www.shrm.org/hrmagazine/articles/0499dell.htm.

CASE STUDY 9-1

Freelancing

When people think about careers, they usually think of going to work full-time for a company and, if they like it, staying at that company for many years. In fact, until recently the notion of "lifetime employment" was touted as the wave of the future. Even if a person didn't stay at one firm, the idea still was that the person would work full-time for a company for at least a few years.

But times are changing. A growing number of workers are becoming freelancers—individuals who contract with a company for a set period of time, usually until a specific project is completed. After the project is completed, the freelancer moves on to another project in the firm, or to another firm. Statistics Canada estimates that 30 percent of working adults are doing non-standard work such as freelancing.

Why is this happening? The main reason is that competitive pressures are forcing firms to reduce their costs and increase their productivity. The current buzz-word is "flexibility" and this can often be achieved by hiring freelancers to solve specific company problems. This allows a firm to maintain a minimum number of full-time workers and then supplement them with freelancers.

Some people freelance because they can't get full-time work with one company, but others freelance by choice. Accomplished freelancers can control their own destiny, make above-average incomes, and have a strong sense of flexibility and freedom. Typically, freelancers don't get paid company benefits like full-time workers do, but pressures are building to change this. In 1994, the province of Saskatchewan became the first in Canada to require companies to pay contract and part-time workers at least some benefits.

Many banks and insurance companies have trouble seeing the needs of contract workers. To them, it may appear that the contract worker is not really employed on a steady basis because they work for so many different companies. Creative Art Management Service is a firm that fills this void. It offers business advice, financial planning, budgeting, and legal services for contract workers. The firm takes the view that freelancing, if properly planned and executed, is the best security in the new economy of the 21st century.

While the work of technical or professional employees is often contracted out to freelancers, the management of various functions may also be contracted out. The Halifax District School Board contracted out the management of custodial services for the district's 42 schools to ServiceMaster Canada Ltd. The school district expects to save more than half a million dollars each year. And Manpower Temporary Services manages a packaging department for a pharmaceutical firm that sometimes numbers up to 130 people, and sometimes as few as 70, depending on demand. A Manpower manager is on site at the pharmaceutical firm; she recruits the temporary workers, does some of the necessary training, conducts performance appraisals of temporary workers, and handles the payroll.

Management experts predict that freelancing will increase in importance. With the massive layoffs that have been evident in recent years, workers are beginning to realize that job security is not provided by large firms. Rather, security comes from having confidence in your own knowledge and skills, and marketing yourself in innovative ways. Freelancing has been facilitated by the recent advances in information technology, since workers do not necessarily have to be at the workplace in order to do their work.

There are both positive and negative aspects to freelancing. From the worker's perspective, those with marketable skills will find that freelancing will result in high pay and satisfying work. For those without marketable skills, freelancing will likely mean part-time work in low-paying service jobs. Those individuals who lack either the ability or interest to capitalize on freelancing will find that there is much uncertainty in their careers.

From the organization's perspective, a conclusion about the value of freelancing means weighing the value of long-term employee loyalty and commitment against the benefits of the increased flexibility that is possible with part-time freelancers.

Questions

1. What kind of people are most likely to want freelance work?

2. What are the pros and cons of freelance work from the individual's perspective? From the organization's perspective?

3. Is it unethical to hire freelancers in order to avoid paying company benefits to them?

Monster.com: Can a Firm Outsource Its Recruiting?

Most Canadians became familiar with Monster.com when the company ran its famous advertisements during the 2000 Super Bowl. The advertisements challenged viewers to take stock of their careers with its "When I Grow Up" spots. The ads featured children musing about what they wanted to be when they grew up. Each child described a particularly distasteful aspect of a job, saying "I want to file all day," or "I want to claw my way up to middle management." The spots have been successful in building a brand identity for Monster.com, the online recruitment leader.

Behind the successful image campaign at Monster.com is a well-organized corporate entity. The company is a subsidiary of TMP Worldwide, the world's largest yellow page advertising agency and a highly respected provider of direct marketing services. The "Monster" subsidiary, a natural extension of their advertising business, is drawing 9.6 million unique visits per month to its job-search Web site. Independent research has estimated that Monster.com's share of the Web job-search market is over 40 percent.

For job seekers, Monster.com can form a career

network, providing instantaneous access to many progressive companies. The firm also offers interactive, personalized tools to facilitate the job search process, including résumé planning and management, a personal job search agent, chats and message boards, privacy options, and expert advice on job seeking. In high turnover industries it is conceivable that an individual could use Monster.com as a lifelong career agent.

One of the most attractive features for employers is the ability to attract high-tech employees. Only candidates with a computer, a browser, and access to the Internet are likely to use the forum. There are other benefits as well. The Internet can provide instantaneous information, allowing firms to post last-minute openings. A firm can also provide links to its own Web site, offering a prospective employee far more information than is available in a print ad. Monster.com can also offer résumé-screening services, routing, and searching. Currently, Monster.com has over 1 million active résumés from job seekers in its database.

The more traditional method of recruiting employees is to place an advertisement in a local or regional paper. National publications like trade magazines often require 30-day lead times for ads. Once the ads have gone out, the company needs to allow time for potential employees to respond. It is not uncommon for an organization to wait 60 days before it begins the interview process. Delays like this could prove costly in highly competitive industries.

It is common for companies to outsource areas that are not part of their core competence or areas in which they have difficulty being competitive. Given that Monster.com already has over 1 million résumés in its database and the ability to instantly post for jobs, will more and more companies outsource their recruiting to Monster.com?

Questions

1. What strengths does Monster.com bring to the recruiting process that a company might not have?

2. Why might a company outsource its recruiting to Monster.com?

3. Why would a company decide to keep its recruiting "in house"; that is, what are the limitations of Monster.com?

Implementing a Staffing/HR Program at KnitMedia

If you review KnitMedia's latest organization chart, you'll probably note one department that is conspicuous by its absence. Like most companies with around 100 or so employees, KnitMedia has no separate HR/personnel department. Historically, companies have about 1 HR person for each 100 employees, but that ratio has been drifting upwards as companies have tried to become more efficient. At KnitMedia, there simply aren't enough employees yet to make having an HR manager economically feasible.

This presents several problems. For one thing, from a practical point of view, keeping track of the personnel needs of about 100 employees isn't easy. Think, for instance, about the challenge of simply keeping track of 100 employees' vacation time, sick leave, pension plans, and salary adjustments. That's a lot of paperwork and record keeping.

More important perhaps is the fact that when a lot of people have to be hired, how can you be sure that you are hiring the best ones to do the job? For example, here's how Chuck Brownley, the general manager of the Knitting Factory club in New York, puts it: "How do we plan for how many staffers we need? It actually starts from the programming when you speak to Glenn, our programming manager....The different artists that we have booked in different programs or events dictates the manpower...if we need extra sound people, or extra technical people or extra door people or extra bar staff to accommodate the overflow." In other words, staffing tends to be an informal process at KnitMedia. That could be a problem if some people who shouldn't be hired are hired.

→

There are also legal factors to consider. For example, with about 100 employees, KnitMedia is certainly covered by the various federal, state, and New York City laws regarding equal employment opportunity. Unless the company carefully adheres to these laws and regulations, it could run into problems in the future.

The company has taken some steps to organize its human resource operations. For example, there is a six-page employee manual that covers KnitMedia's policies regarding matters such as security, the environment, probationary periods, at-will employment, and time off. Allan Fried recently finished developing a performance appraisal form that the company will use to evaluate employees. These steps notwithstanding, though, Michael Dorf and his management team are concerned about whether they're doing enough to formalize their HR process, and they've come to you for advice.

Team Exercises and Questions

Use what you learned in this chapter to answer the following questions from Michael Dorf and his management team:

1. What are the main HR areas we should be addressing at KnitMedia and what, in outline form, do they involve?

2. Do you think we're doing an effective job of selecting employees? If not, how exactly would you suggest we go about selecting employees in the future?

3. How would you propose the HR function should be administered at KnitMedia? Why?

CBC VIDEO CASE 3-1

Downsizing

For the last 15 years or so, companies have pursued a strategy of downsizing in an attempt to cope with increasingly competitive markets. Middle managers are often downsized because they don't get big severance packages when they are let go, and it is often not clear what will be lost when they are gone.

One thing, however, has become clear about downsizing: it seems to cause an increase in employee fraud. Why? When a company lets go a lot of middle managers, there are simply fewer managers left to check the work of other employees. Opportunities for fraud therefore increase. Also, with fewer managers, the remaining managers have more power, and they can more easily engage in fraud.

Because companies lose an important fraud-detecting capability when they lay off middle managers, they often hire private detectives to ferret out fraud. Consider what happened at a company that had two managers handling rent cheques on buildings it owned. After one manager was laid off to save money, it wasn't too long before the remaining manager began cheating the company. Apartments that were shown as vacant on the books actually had tenants, and the rent cheques were directed into the manager's pocket. The company lost more in the fraud than they saved from the salary of the manager who was laid off.

Many companies are surprised when layoffs lead to increased fraud, assuming "it couldn't happen to me." It has reached the point where insurance companies now get worried because policyholders are making big claims. With fewer middle managers on the job, any fraudulent activity is likely to go undetected for longer periods of time, costing the company more money. Increasingly, insurance companies are pressuring their clients to resolve their fraud problems.

Fraud isn't the only difficulty associated with downsizing. Because a level of supervision is often removed in downsizing, employees may not be able to work as effectively afterwards. One Ontario shipbuilding company found that productivity dropped after downsizing because there were no longer enough supervisors to provide proper management for workers.

Employee morale also takes a beating during downsizing. Employees who survive downsizing wonder if they're going to be next, and spend a lot of time and energy worrying about losing their jobs. Downsizing usually means more work for those who remain, but they are reluctant to let go of any work for fear that they will appear dispensable.

Why don't companies avoid all these problems and simply hire back some of the middle managers they laid off? The answer is simple: competition. With the move towards "lean and mean" companies, the pressure is on to operate with as little personnel as possible, even when it is common sense that some unanticipated negative outcomes may result.

Questions

1. What is downsizing? What unanticipated negative consequences can arise because of downsizing?

2. What is the span of control? How might downsizing affect the span of control in a company?

3. What can managers do to reduce the chance that employees who remain after downsizing do not engage in fraudulent behaviour?

4. "A company that is profitable does not need to engage in downsizing." Do you agree or disagree? Explain.

Video Resource: "Revenge of Middle Managers," *Venture* #724 (October 12, 1999).

CBC VIDEO CASE 3-2

Keepers

In Canadian high-tech companies, 60-hour weeks are not uncommon. Couple that with demanding bosses and customers, and families that are unseen for days, and you have a recipe for employee turnover. Anne Graham is vice-president of Human Resources at Kanata-based Dy4 Systems, a company that builds specialized computers for use in deserts, oceans, and battlefields. One of her important goals is to keep employees from leaving Dy4 and moving to the competition. Turnover is high in this industry—25 percent—and rapid growth in many firms is stretching employees to the breaking point.

Dy4 has hired Daniel O'Connor of Keepers Inc., a firm that specializes in helping employees determine what is causing friction and unhappiness in their lives and how to resolve that friction. O'Connor, who has spent more than 12 years looking deeply into workers' lives, strives to practise what he preaches about balance. Currently, he is writing a romantic comedy that is set in a business firm.

O'Connor first meets with employees one-on-one and tries to determine what is bothering them. He has found a common theme: employees have lost their sense of control in the workplace. As a result, they

feel disempowered and subject to the whims of others.

At Dy4, O'Connor meets three typical employees. *Grant* manages one of Dy4's product lines. O'Connor meets with him and listens to his concerns. Grant feels overwhelmed and anxious because he has so many meetings that he must attend. O'Connor asks Grant if perhaps he is allowing this to happen. This week's "assignment" is for Grant to think about that possibility and what he might do about it.

Michelle manages Dy4's Human Resource department. She feels that demands from her bosses have pulled her in too many directions. She also feels frustrated, chasing after people to ensure they do what they are supposed to. For her, cutting back hours has been difficult. She leaves the building at the end of the day feeling she should have done more.

Ernie is a veteran engineer at Dy4. He feels that he doesn't have enough time with his family, and that he needs a better work–family balance. Ernie's "assignment" is to keep track of his time for a week.

After a period of time has passed, O'Connor meets again with the three individuals to check on their progress. After two months, *Grant*'s situation has somewhat improved. The company has allowed him

→

to hire an assistant, and this has made a noticeable difference. But he is still looking for ways to get more control over his schedule, because he continues to spend a great deal of time in meetings. He also notes that he had to work three 12-hour days just to be able to take a week's vacation. O'Connor emphasizes the need for Grant to make change happen.

O'Connor takes the data that *Ernie* provided and converts it into a pie chart so he can clearly see where Ernie is spending his time. Ernie learns that seeing his life mapped out in pie chart form can be very startling (he spent 61 hours at work one week, leaving little time for his family). Ernie sees a new perspective on what over-commitment means and the importance of balancing home and work life.

When *Michelle* meets with O'Connor again, she decides to resolve her dilemma by setting a goal to at least do the tasks that are necessary so that other people who are counting on her are not let down. She will cut back on some other things that do not impact other people.

After two months of O'Connor's coaching, the employees at Dy4 seem to be slowly turning their lives around. They are now focusing on maintaining their

new "life rules" after O'Connor leaves. Dy4 is counting on it to keep their talent under their roof.

Questions

1. Explain how Dy4 could use an assessment centre to resolve some of the difficulties it is having with turnover.

2. What role might orientation and training play in helping employees cope with the rapid pace of change and the heavy workload at Dy4?

3. What actions other than counselling can Dy4 take to reduce turnover?

4. Re-read the "Hiring Happy Employee" insert on p. 276 of the text. Then consider the following statement: "Coaching people about how to better manage their jobs will not have much affect on their life's happiness because a person's genetic makeup largely determines whether or not they are happy." Do you agree or disagree with this statement? Explain.

Video Resource: "Keepers Inc.," *Venture* #742 (March 7, 2000).

KNITMEDIA

Fundamentals of Organizing and Staffing

Although many large business firms have downsized in recent years—thus reducing their staffing needs and flattening their organizational structures—it will be a long time before KnitMedia adopts such a strategy. The company is growing profitably, and its managers are managing its increase in size by developing a structure that is becoming more, not less, hierarchical. As Ed Greer, senior vice-president of club operations, observes, however, KnitMedia can't afford to stand still while it consolidates its new structure. Its business environment is changing too fast for that. So KnitMedia

grows organically, its structure evolving as it goes along.

There are now four major divisions in the organization: new media, festival operations, club operations, and the label group. There are also separate organizational units for the JazzE Web site, art and graphics, marketing, production, and finance. New positions like chief content officer and chief operating officer have been created, and some jobs have grown big enough to be performed by two people instead of one. There is also an official organization chart. We've seen that instead of being at the centre of a loose and rather informal structure, as he was a few years ago, Michael Dorf is now at the top of a more conventional hybrid organization.

This new structure actually allows KnitMedia to grow. One of its chief benefits is that it creates a way for Dorf to delegate authority to others, who can keep the organization's operations running smoothly while Dorf continues to seek new ventures, new business partners, and new ways to bring KnitMedia's products to a growing audience. One of the drawbacks is that the layers of hierarchical structure tend to distance Dorf from others in the company who had become used to having more frequent and more informal contact with him.

An interesting test of the benefits and drawbacks of KnitMedia's increasingly formal structure occurred during Michael's recent three-month trip to Los Angeles. Interviewed for the video on the day of his return to New York, Dorf noted that his absence had been helpful in forcing a certain amount of delegation to take place. It also revealed the difference between those employees who could shoulder their responsibilities and those who couldn't. KnitMedia's organizational culture still provides a great deal of freedom, including the freedom to fail, and it lacks the easy out that a large corporate safety net provides. Thus it is self-motivated individuals who tend to thrive in its still relatively small and constantly evolving environment.

Staffing an organization like KnitMedia presents some interesting challenges. It is an indication of the firm's coming of age as a major force on the Internet that employees are no longer being hired away by record companies; most of those who leave now go to work for Internet start-ups. Turnover can be high in a fast-paced environment where the stakes and the responsibilities are great. Dorf believes that "the cream rises to the top," however, and he is committed to retaining those employees who have proven their worth to the firm.

A deep commitment to "non-commercial music" and the chance to be creative in many different ways are two of the major draws that bring people from a variety of fields to work at KnitMedia. Competitive salaries, improved benefits, and, for the management team, a stock option plan are some of the rewards that keep them there. In the video you'll hear Ed Greer tell of a receptionist's recruitment and promotion to a more responsible position in the JazzE unit. Mary Noelle Dana, festival programming director and Jazzchool coordinator, talks about the process by which she was hired and how, later, her job grew big enough to be split in half. Sometimes, when the need arises, managers like Mitch Goldman, chief content officer, will hire freelancers who cost the organization less than staff employees and perform valuable short-term services. Recent college graduates work as interns, "floating" throughout the New York office and Knitting Factory club, helping where they are needed and picking up valuable skills.

Questions

Based on this case, the video, the text chapters you've read so far, and your knowledge from other sources, answer the following questions:

1. What are some of the advantages and disadvantages of KnitMedia's increasingly hierarchical structure?

2. Do you see any negative aspects to high turnover rates at the Knitting Factory?

3. Do you think authority has been pushed down too far or is it about right?

Part 4: Leading provides an overview of the "people" side of management. It considers what effective leadership involves, how to successfully motivate and communicate with subordinates, how to gain the benefits of teams, and how to lead organizational change.

We begin in Chapter 10, **Being a Leader**, by noting the importance of leadership and explaining how to think like and act like a leader, the importance of understanding the foundations of leadership, and how to provide a vision for subordinates.

Next, in Chapter 11, **Influencing Individual Behaviour and Motivation**, we present several important theories that help leaders understand and motivate employees. We also describe a variety of practical suggestions about how to actually motivate employees in the workplace. The Appendix to Chapter 11 focuses on how individual differences complicate the manager's job, and how factors like personality, perception, attitudes, abilities, and job satisfaction affect employee performance.

In Chapter 12, **Influencing Interpersonal and Organizational Communication**, we explain the basic communication process and what a manager must know about communicating to be an effective leader. We describe the interpersonal and organizational barriers to communication and how to overcome them. The chapter concludes with a discussion of the impact of technology on communication.

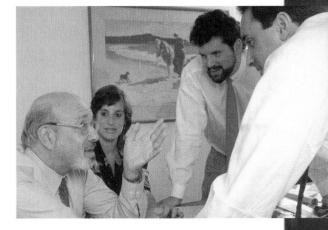

In Chapter 13, **Leading Groups and Teams**, we illustrate the various kinds of teams that are found in organizations and the group dynamics the leader should take into account when building and leading productive teams.

Finally, in Chapter 14, **Leading Organizational Change**, we describe the need for change in organizations, why people resist change, and practical suggestions for helping managers lead change in their organizations. The chapter also examines the topics of conflict and organization development, and how these areas relate to organizational change.

Being a Leader

Breaking the Glass Ceiling

During the 1990s, much was written about the "glass ceiling" that prevents women from achieving top jobs in industry. But as we enter the new millennium, the winds of change are blowing and numerous breakthroughs have

been achieved by women who now occupy top-ranking jobs in major industrial firms. In the Canadian automobile industry, for example, the CEOs of two of the three North American manufacturers are women. Maureen Kempston Darkes, the president of General Motors of Canada, started with GM in 1975 and worked her way up through the legal and government affairs side of the company. Bobbie Gaunt, the CEO of Ford Motor of Canada, is a 25-year veteran of Ford and a world-class marketer.

In 1999, New Brunswick native Cynthia Trudell (pictured) was appointed chair and president of Saturn Corp., a subsidiary of GM. She was the first woman ever to head up a fully integrated subsidiary of a North American auto maker. Also in 1999, Carly Fiorina was named president and CEO of Hewlett-Packard. She was the first woman to become CEO of a company in the Dow Jones Industrial Average. Shortly after her appointment, Fiorina offered the opinion that there really isn't a glass ceiling any more. She also said that her gender was not an issue, and that individuals who believe they are limited by their gender will actually limit themselves.

Fiorina's opinions may not be widely accepted, but the fact is that more and more women are earning high-level leadership positions. The Canadian CEOs of Home Depot, General Foods, EDS, and Kraft are all women. Linda Hasenfratz is president of Linamar Corp. and Nancy Southern is deputy CEO of ATCO Ltd. Other prestige jobs just below the CEO level are also increasingly held by women. Gail McGovern is the head of AT&T's $26 billion consumer business, and Lois Juliber is the head of North American and European operations for Colgate-Palmolive. Both of these women have a chance to become CEOs in a few years.

A survey of 461 female executives found that four strategies were important in breaking through the glass ceiling: consistently exceeding performance expectations, developing a style with which male managers are comfortable, seeking difficult or high-visibility work assignments, and having an influential

General Motors
www.gm.com

Kraft
www.kraft.com

AT&T
www.attcanada. com

Colgate-Palmolive
www.colgate.com

mentor. The same survey found that male CEOs thought that women didn't advance to the very top ranks of management because they lacked general management experience, and because women had not been in the "pipeline" long enough. Women, on the other hand, felt that the key barriers to their success were male stereotyping of women, the exclusion of women from informal networks, and an inhospitable corporate culture.

The Challenge of Leading

Once your organization is staffed with competent employees, those employees must be inspired, motivated, and led. In this part of the book, we'll therefore turn to leadership.

Leadership is an easy concept to define but a difficult one to study and understand. It is easy to define since leadership means influencing others to work willingly towards achieving objectives. What makes leadership a challenging concept to master is the need to understand a variety of leadership theories, and to translate these into leadership skills through application and practice. In outline form, the leadership theories and skills we'll discuss in this chapter are as follows:

leadership
Influencing others to work willingly towards achieving objectives.

1. *How to think like a leader.* How to review a leadership situation in which you find yourself and identify what is happening, account for what is happening, and formulate leader actions.

2. *What are the foundations of leadership?* Two important foundations or prerequisites of leadership are power and the right mix of leadership traits, such as drive and self-confidence.

3. *How leaders provide a vision.* Leaders provide a general statement of their organization's intended direction and, often, a "road map" for how to get there.

4. *How leaders act like leaders.* To influence followers to work towards the vision, leaders engage in a number of characteristic leader behaviours, such as providing *structure* and *consideration*, being *participative* when the situation warrants it, and adapting their leadership style to the situation.

Leaders Fill Many Roles

Being a leader requires more than just knowing about leadership theories like those covered in this chapter. That's why all of Part 4 of this book is called "Leading," even though it also includes chapters on motivating, culture, groups, conflict, and change. These topics are part of leadership because effective leaders must simultaneously perform many duties: motivating and communicating with subordinates, managing groups and their interaction, managing conflicts between individuals and groups, and introducing changes that are needed by the organization.

The leadership knowledge presented in this chapter is only part of what you must know to be an effective leader, but it will give you a good start. To have a reasonably complete understanding of leading you also need to understand the material in the following chapters. Remember that there are a large number of leadership and behavioural science theories, each helping to explain how the effective leader should act. Think of each theory as a tool in your leadership toolbox, each useful in its own way and under the right conditions.

Leaders and Managers

Managers plan, organize, lead, and control, and so "leading" and "managing" are inseparable in management theory. Leading is part of managing: Managing means planning, organizing, leading, and controlling the work of others so the company's aims are achieved. But if you can't influence and inspire people to work towards those aims, then all your planning and organizing will be for naught. "Leading" is thus the distinctly behavioural and "influencing" part of what managers do.

Having leadership skills but no management skills does not work either. Setting a direction and saying, "Here's where we've got to go" is usually not enough. In other words, no matter how inspiring you happen to be, management skills—such as ensuring that salaries, incentives, and other rewards make it worthwhile for employees to try hard, and ensuring that employees have the tools to do their jobs—are crucial, too, if the organization is to accomplish its aims.[1]

There is no generally accepted or proven theory describing how leaders effectively blend such tasks and lead organizations. However, Figure 10.1 provides a model you may

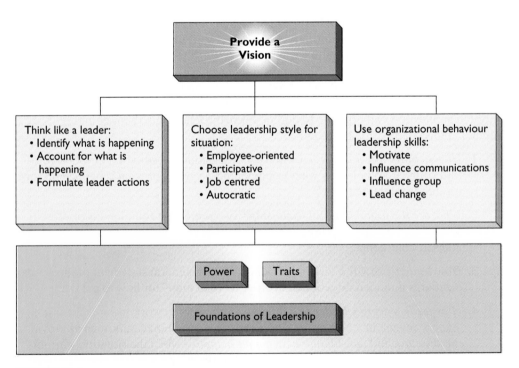

FIGURE 10.1
The Building Blocks of Being a Leader
Note: Leaders with the power and personal traits required to be effective can provide leadership by engaging in four sets of activities: provide a vision, think like a leader, use the right leadership style, and then use the organizational behaviour leadership skills such as motivating and leading change, as explained in the next four chapters.

find useful for organizing your thoughts. Those with the power and personal traits to be effective in a leadership situation can lead by engaging in four sets of activities: provide a vision; think like a leader; use the right leadership style; and then use organizational behaviour skills such as motivating.

How Leaders Provide a Vision

As you can see, showing the way out of the wilderness—providing direction—has always been a crucial leadership task. Each year when he teaches seasoned executives in the Advanced Management Program and the International Senior Management Program at the Harvard Business School, Professor Renato Tagiuri polls them to compile what he calls a list of conditions for effective leadership. "Clarify the mission, purposes, or objectives of your employees' assignments" and "Describe assignments clearly" head the list.[2] We discussed setting objectives in Chapters 5 and 6. We saw that the leader must provide a goal that his or her followers can work towards. Whether that "goal" is a statement of vision, a mission, or objectives depends largely on what the leader wants to achieve and the level at which he or she is acting.

Sometimes what's required is a **vision**, a general statement of the organization's intended direction that evokes positive emotional feelings in organization members. Bill Gates' vision of Microsoft offering Internet-based software helped provide the sense of direction employees, owners, and bankers all required, and around which they could rally. When he became CEO of CN, Paul Tellier conveyed the vision of CN as a highly efficient railroad, able to compete with the best railroads in North America.

Communicating a vision is especially important in today's changing environment, where business conditions are "volatile and carry in them the seeds of rapid and potentially hostile change."[3] Here, "the faster the chief executive officer can conceive a future vision where new products are positioned within emerging product markets the greater is the ability of the firm to control its destiny and affirm a sense of direction."[4] And e-CEOs have to do just that, "at death-defying speed."

We've seen that the firm's **mission statement** defines and operationalizes the top manager's vision. A mission statement "broadly outlines the organization's future course and serves to communicate who we are, what we do, and where we're headed."[5] Mission state-

> **vision**
> A general statement of the organization's intended direction that evokes positive emotional feelings in organization members.

> **mission statement**
> A statement that broadly outlines the organization's future course and serves to communicate "who we are, what we do, and where we're headed."

Paul Tellier, CEO of Canadian National Railways, emphasizes his vision of CN as a well-run railroad that is able to compete with the best in North America.

objectives
Specific results a leader
wants the group to
achieve.

ments like one elevator firm's ("Our mission is to provide any customer a means of moving people and things up, down, and sideward over short distances....") are meant to communicate the purpose of the company. Then too, the leader's task might require that he or she provide **objectives,** which are specific results he or she wants the group to achieve.

At CN, for example, Paul Tellier set an objective of reducing CN's operating ratio (the amount of money it costs to generate $1 of revenue) from 81.5 percent to something much lower so that CN could effectively compete with U.S. Railroads. When Anthony Comper became CEO of the Bank of Montreal, he set an objective to increase the bank's return on equity from 15 percent to nearly 20 percent.

THE CHALLENGE OF CHANGE

Chris Sinton at Cisco Systems

Leadership—influencing others to move in a desired direction—doesn't necessarily mean being "the person in charge" and supervising hundreds (or even dozens) of subordinates. Sometimes, exerting leadership just means championing a new idea, and having the vision and then the drive, courage, conviction, and self-confidence to convince others to work with you to implement that vision.

Chris Sinton at Cisco Systems is a case in point. Just a few years ago, Chris may have been "one of the lowest tech people at Cisco," but he did know his customers. For example, he knew they hated wasting time phoning and faxing in orders and having to call only when the Cisco salespeople were available to take those orders. And while he may have been low-tech, he could already see—way back in 1995—that more and more people were using the Internet to place orders for various products with other companies.

At that time, although it was the leading firm in providing the various types of electronics that made the Internet work, Cisco Systems sold virtually none of its own products via the Internet. But Chris had a vision, and that vision was to have Cisco Systems set up Web sites so that customers could continually, at any time of the day, place orders via the Internet and check the status of those orders, without ever speaking directly to a salesperson. Chris first presented his vision to several marketing people two levels above him, and on that basis was given 15 minutes to present his idea at a meeting of senior Cisco executives. He urged the company to turn to e-commerce as a way of doing business, and to let customers e-purchase not only small items like Cisco Systems promotional T-shirts, but also technical support services and even $1.5 million worth of electronic routers.

Today Cisco, along with pioneers like Dell, "is proving that business to business selling is e-commerce's killer app [application]."[6] By 1999, Cisco was actually selling 80 percent of its products and services on the Web, thanks to the leadership of people like Chris Sinton.

Where is Chris Sinton today? He is overseeing the business-to-business e-commerce operation that was his brainchild. As he says, "I just knew the Net could be our business, that it could be a portal to our company."[7] The visionary proposal he wrote to the top executives at Cisco regarding the future of e-commerce is now preserved in the Smithsonian Institution archives.

As you can see, sometimes you don't have to be leading your own subordinates to be leading people. In championing Cisco Systems' move to e-commerce, Chris was able to get his bosses and the top executives at Cisco to become excited about his vision. Then, through the power of his personality, he was able to convince them to let him organize the resources that would enable Cisco to become a world leader in business-to-business e-commerce.

Thinking Like a Leader

Being a leader requires more than possessing book knowledge about leadership theories; the leader also needs **critical leadership thinking skills**. These allow the leader to examine a situation and dig out the underlying assumptions and values that are motivating subordinates, evaluate the evidence, and think through how to apply what he or she knows about leadership theory to solve the problem.

critical leadership thinking skills
Skills that allow a leader to examine a situation and dig out the underlying assumptions and values that are motivating subordinates, evaluate the evidence, and think through how to apply what he or she knows about leadership theory to solve the problem.

One way to view such critical leadership thinking skills is in terms of a three-step framework (see Figure 10.2). Specifically, review the leadership situation and (1) identify what is happening, (2) account for what is happening, and (3) decide on the leadership actions you will take.[8]

Identify What Is Happening. The first step is to identify issues or areas of concern that compel you as a leader to resolve an organizational problem. For example: "The employees here refuse to divulge bad news to their supervisors."

Account for What Is Happening. This and the next few chapters contain behavioural science theories and concepts that leaders need. For example, in this chapter you'll find a number of leadership theories that aim to explain what makes leaders effective, and in the following chapter there are theories that explain how to motivate employees. The main purpose of this step is to use behavioural science theories and similar concepts to account for *why* the issues you identified (like employees refusing to divulge bad news) are occurring.

Accounting for what is happening in a situation means asking yourself which theory or theories best explain what you see happening. In other words, this step identifies a cause-effect relationship between what has occurred and why. For example, "The employees here refuse to divulge bad news because they are punished when they do so by having the supervisors yell at them." The *effect* here is the employees' refusal to divulge bad news; the behavioural *cause*—in this case a motivational one—is the fact that they are "punished" when they do so.

To account for what is happening, you should view the situation as a coherent whole, while at the same time looking for a logical sequence of cause-effect events. You have to try to identify the root cause of the situation. For example, are the supervisors temperamentally unsuited for their jobs? Or are they just copying their own bosses' behaviour, reacting quickly and harshly to any negative news?

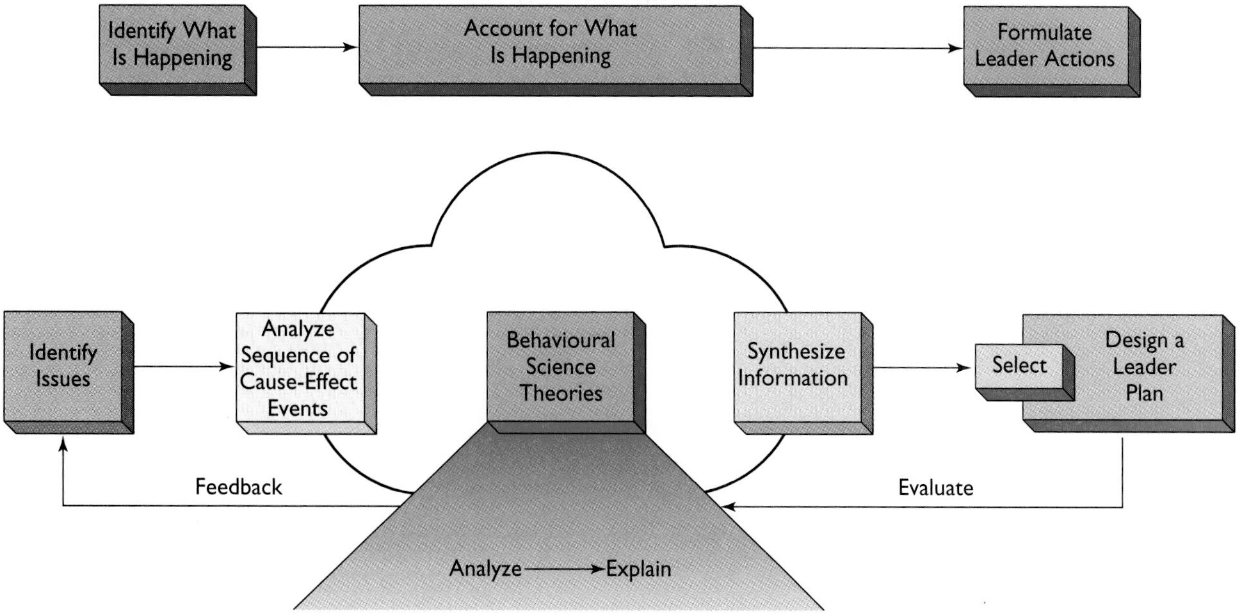

FIGURE 10.2
How to Think Like a Leader

In accounting for what is happening, you may well find that more than one leadership or behavioural science theory or concept applies. In this case, for instance, the supervisors may lack the required personality traits to do the job. Their own leaders may have inadvertently created a blame-oriented culture that signals that it is okay to dump on employees when they bring negative news.

There often is more than one way to explain or solve a leadership problem. This isn't a bad thing: if there is more than one behavioural science theory or concept you could apply to explain and solve the problem, you may combine several, or choose the one you'll take action on first.

Decide on the Leadership Actions You Will Take. After you have identified and accounted for what is happening, the next step is to decide on the leadership actions that will remedy the situation. Doing so will require applying all of the knowledge you gain in this and the other chapters, such as those on how to motivate employees and how to resolve and manage intergroup conflicts.

For example, what actions would you take to help resolve the problem of the employees who are afraid to report negative news to their supervisors? Your assessment of the situation is that (1) some of the current supervisors may be temperamentally unsuited for their jobs, and (2) there is a pervasive blame-oriented culture in the department. What actions would you take? Good possibilities include the following:

- Reassess the personality-based qualifications of the existing supervisors, to transfer or dismiss potential hotheads.
- Administer an attitude survey to all departmental employees to develop data that describe the current feelings about the blame-oriented atmosphere.
- Present this data to the top managers to encourage them to engage in a training program aimed at making them more open to receiving bad news and criticism.

Learning to think like a leader is just one step in developing leadership skills. You also need a sound understanding of what leaders do and what makes them successful. There are actually three types of leadership theories today—trait, behavioural, and situational—and we'll discuss them in the next few pages.

The Foundations of Leadership

Psychologists Shelley Kirkpatrick and Edwin Locke say that *personal traits* and *power* are two important foundations of leadership—in other words, two important prerequisites you'll need before you can lead.[9]

The Leader's Traits

Being a leader requires having the personality traits to do the job. Having "the right stuff" is thus an important component of being a leader. Identifying what those traits are is the aim of the **trait theory** of leadership.

trait theory
The idea that leaders are characterized by certain traits.

The Trait Theory. The idea that leaders are characterized by certain traits was initially inspired by a "great man" concept of leadership. This concept held that people like Microsoft's Bill Gates and Carly Fiorina—Hewlett-Packard's new president and CEO—are great leaders because they were born with certain definable personality traits. Early researchers believed that if they studied the personality and intelligence of great leaders, they would sooner or later stumble on the combination of traits that made these people outstanding.

Most of the early research was inconclusive. Specific traits were related to effectiveness in some situations, but none was related consistently to effectiveness in a variety of different studies and situations. However, recent research using a variety of methods "has made it clear that successful leaders are not like other people. The evidence indicates that there are certain core traits which significantly contribute to business leaders' success."[10] Six traits on which leaders differ from non-leaders include drive, the desire to lead, honesty/integrity, self-confidence, cognitive ability, and knowledge of the business. Let's see why each of these matters.

Leaders have drive.
Leaders are action-oriented people with a relatively high desire for achievement. They get satisfaction from successfully completing challenging tasks. Leaders are more ambitious than non-leaders. They have high energy, because "working long, intense work weeks (and many weekends for many years) requires an individual to have physical, mental, and emotional vitality."[11] Leaders are also tenacious and are better at overcoming obstacles than non-leaders.[12]

Leaders want to lead.
Leaders are motivated to influence others. They prefer to be in a leadership rather than in a subordinate role and willingly shoulder the mantle of authority.

Leaders have honesty and integrity.
Here's another way to state this: If your followers can't trust you, why should they follow you? Studies have found that leaders are generally rated more trustworthy and reliable in carrying out responsibilities than followers.[13]

Leaders have self-confidence.
As two experts summarize, "Self-confidence plays an important role in decision-making and in gaining others' trust. Obviously, if the leader is not sure of what decision to make, or expresses a high degree of doubt, then the followers are less likely to trust the leader and be committed to the vision."[14]

Leaders make good decisions.
By definition, a leader is the one who must pick the right direction and then put into place the mechanisms required to get there. Leaders, therefore, tend to have more "cognitive ability" than non-leaders, and a leader's intelligence and the subordinates' perception of his or her intelligence are generally highly rated leadership traits.[15]

Leaders know the business.
Effective leaders are extremely knowledgeable about the company and the industry; their information lets them make informed decisions and understand the implications of those decisions.[16] There are exceptions, however: Louis Gertsner, Jr., became IBM's chairman with no computer experience, and he has excelled at the job. However, these exceptions make the rule: Gerstner has high cognitive ability and quickly immersed himself in absorbing the details of IBM's business. (And he also had a degree in engineering!) Another example is Paul Tellier, who became CEO of CN even though he didn't have any experience in the railroad business, but had been a deputy minister, clerk of the Privy Council, and secretary to the federal Cabinet.

Personality Traits. A **personality trait** is any persisting characteristic or dimension of personality according to which individuals can be rated or measured.[17] Introversion, sociability, aloofness, and impulsiveness are examples.

personality trait
Any persisting characteristic or dimension of personality according to which individuals can be rated or measured.

Personality traits are just one means by which psychologists explain what personality is and why people act as they do. For example, you are probably familiar with the psychoanalytic personality theory of Sigmund Freud. Freud used building block concepts that he called *id, ego,* and *superego* to explain human personality and behaviour, basically in terms of our desire to maximize gratification while minimizing punishment or guilt. His theory did not depend on the concept of personality traits.

Personality trait theories are another approach that psychologists use to explain personality. To trait theorists, someone's personality is basically the sum total of the behaviours that a person with those traits persistently exhibits. Psychologist Raymond Cattell viewed personality traits as sets of polar opposites. Examples of so-called Cattell traits

Emotional Intelligence

The idea that great leaders have the "right stuff" is so seductive that the list of leadership traits is always growing. One of the most interesting lines of trait research focuses on what some experts call "emotional intelligence."[18] According to Daniel Goleman, the author of *Working with Emotional Intelligence*, traits like intelligence and technical knowledge do matter, but only as "threshold capabilities." In other words,

> they are the entry-level requirements for executive positions. But my research, along with other recent studies, clearly shows that emotional intelligence is the sine qua non of leadership. Without it, a person can have the best training in the world, an incisive, analytical mind, and an endless supply of smart ideas, but he [or she] still won't make a great leader.[19]

What is emotional intelligence? Basically, a bundle of people-oriented personality traits that, taken together, reflect a person's emotional maturity, empathy, and social skills. The five component traits of emotional intelligence at work (some of which, like motivation, consistently appear in earlier trait lists as well) are summarized in Table 10.1. They include self-awareness, self-regulation, motivation, empathy, and social skill. For example, says Goleman, "if there is one trait that virtually all the effective leaders have, it is motivation. They're driven to achieve beyond expectations—their own and everyone else's."[20]

TABLE 10.1 *The Five Components of Emotional Intelligence at Work*

	DEFINITION	HALLMARKS
Self-Awareness	– the ability to recognize and understand your moods, emotions, and drives, as well as their effect on others	– self-confidence – realistic self-assessment – self-deprecating sense of humour
Self-Regulation	– the ability to control or redirect disruptive impulses and moods – the propensity to suspend judgement—to think before acting	– trustworthiness and integrity – comfort with ambiguity – openness to change
Motivation	– a passion to work for reasons that go beyond money or status – a propensity to pursue goals with energy and persistence	– strong drive to achieve – optimism, even in the face of failure – organizational commitment
Empathy	– the ability to understand the emotional makeup of other people – skill in treating people according to their emotional reactions	– expertise in building and retaining talent – cross-cultural sensitivity – service to clients and customers
Social Skill	– proficiency in managing relationships and building networks – an ability to find common ground and build rapport	– effectiveness in leading change – persuasiveness – expertise in building and leading teams

include honest vs. dishonest, infantile vs. emotionally mature, thoughtful vs. unreflective, sociable vs. shy, responsive vs. aloof, deliberate vs. impulsive, and tidy vs. disorderly.[21] More recently, industrial psychologists have focused on what some call the "big five" personality dimensions: extroversion, emotional stability, agreeableness, conscientiousness, and openness to experience.[22]

Power

Perhaps you've had the unfortunate experience of being told you are in charge of something, only to find that your subordinates ignore you when you try to boss them around. Such an experience underscores an important fact of leadership: A leader without power is really not a leader at all, since he or she has zero chance of influencing anyone to do anything. Understanding the sources of leadership power is therefore important: It's a foundation of leadership.

From what sources can a leader's power derive? A leader's authority most commonly stems, first, from the *position* to which he or she is appointed. In other words, positions like sales manager or president have formal authority attached to them. As a leader you will also have power based on your authority to *reward* employees who do well or coerce or *punish* those who don't do well. As head of, say, the research lab you may also have *expert power* and be such an authority in your area that your followers do what you ask because of their respect for your expertise. If you are really lucky, you'll possess *referent power* based on your personal magnetism so your followers will follow you just because of your charisma.

Notice that whatever your source of power, it must be legitimate if you are to call yourself a leader. A mugger on the street may have a gun and the power to threaten your life, but he or she hardly qualifies as a leader, because leading means influencing people to work *willingly* towards achieving your objectives.

That is not to say that a little fear can't be a good thing, at least occasionally. The most famous comment on fear was made in the 16th century by the Italian writer Niccolò Machiavelli, in his book *The Prince:*

> One ought to be both feared and loved, but as it is difficult for the two to go together, it is much safer to be feared than loved…for love is held by a chain of obligation which, men being selfish, is broken whenever it serves their purpose; but fear is maintained by a dread of punishment which never fails.

But remember that while there's more than a germ of truth in what Machiavelli said, there's a danger in relying on fear. A shrewd executive named Chester Barnard wrote in his classic work, *The Functions of the Executive*, that managers are essentially powerless unless their followers grant them the authority to lead.[23] The reality of leading is that you're going to have to muster all of the legitimate power you can get, and that will often include convincing your followers that you have earned the right to lead them.

The issue of power and fear is especially tricky in today's downsized, flattened, and empowered organizations. Increasingly, as we've seen, the tendency is to delegate authority and organize around horizontal, self-managing teams in which the employees themselves have the information and skills they need to control their own activities. Influencing your people to get their jobs done by relying too heavily on your own formal authority or even on fear is therefore probably a much more imprudent tactic today than it would have been even a few years ago.

The idea that the "command-and-control" approach is increasingly unwieldy today is not just theoretical. No less an expert on power than General Peter Schoomaker, commander in chief of the U.S. Special Operations Command (which includes the Army's Delta Force, Green Berets, and Rangers and the Navy Seals), argues that the traditional military method of issuing orders that are then obeyed unquestioningly is often an outmoded, inaccurate, and dangerous model for leadership today.[24] That's because the armies (and companies) that win today will be those that marshal "creative solutions in ambiguous circumstances"—diffusing ethnic tensions, delivering humanitarian aid, and rescuing civilians trapped in an overseas uprising. And, in such circumstances, Schoomaker says, "everybody's got to know how to be a leader."[25] Power and the requisite leadership traits are not sufficient for successful leadership—they are only a foundation, a precondition. If you have the traits and you have the power, then you have the *potential* to be a leader.[26] As Kirkpatrick and Locke put it: "Traits only endow people with the potential for leadership. To actualize this potential, additional factors are necessary...."[27] Specifically, say Kirkpatrick and Locke, the leader must provide a vision and then engage in the behaviours required to get his or her people to implement that vision.

The Leader's Behaviour: How Leaders Act Like Leaders

Leadership researchers have formulated several theories to explain how a leader's style or behaviour is related to his or her effectiveness, and we can make two generalizations about their theories. First, they all focus on what the leader *does* and how he or she behaves in trying to influence followers. (Trait theory instead attempts to explain leadership on the basis of what the leader *is*.)

Second, the basic assumption underlying most behavioural leadership theories is that leaders perform two major functions—accomplishing the task and satisfying the needs of group members. Generally speaking, the functions of a task-oriented leader are to clarify the jobs to be done and force people to focus on their jobs. The role of a social or people-oriented leader is to reduce tension, make the job more pleasant, boost morale, and crystallize and defend the values, attitudes, and beliefs of the group.

Most experts believe that the task and people dimensions of leader behaviour are not mutually exclusive. In other words, most leaders exhibit degrees of both simultaneously.[28]

A number of different leadership styles are associated with these basic "task" and "people" dimensions. In the remainder of this section we'll describe some of the more popular leadership behaviour theories, as well as several offshoots.

Structuring and Considerate Styles

Initiating structure and *consideration* have been two of the most frequently used descriptions of leader behaviour. They developed out of a research project launched many years ago at Ohio State University.[29] A survey called the Leader Behavior Description Questionnaire (LBDQ) was developed and was further refined by subsequent researchers.[30] The two leadership factors it measures—consideration and initiating structure—have become synonymous with what experts call The Ohio State Dimensions of Leadership:

Consideration: Leader behaviour indicative of mutual trust, friendship, support, respect, and warmth.

Initiating structure: Leader behaviour by which the person organizes the work to be done and defines relationships or roles, the channels of communication, and ways of getting jobs done.

The research results unfortunately tend to be somewhat inconclusive. With respect to employee satisfaction, the findings led researcher Gary Yukl to conclude that "in most situations, considerate leaders will have more satisfied subordinates."[31] But the effects of such considerate leadership on employee performance are inconsistent.

Southwest Airline
www.iflyswa.com

However, it's obviously foolish to underestimate the importance of being considerate—at least as a rule. Some great leaders, such as Southwest Airline's Herb Kelleher, take great pains to emphasize the importance of being considerate of one's employees. As he says, "I've tried to create a culture of caring for people in the totality of their lives, not just at work....You have to recognize that people are still most important. How you treat them determines how they treat people on the outside."[32]

Yet leaders also have to remember to avoid what some leadership experts call a "country-club" style: in other words, all consideration, and no focus on doing the work.[33] Showing respect for employees, providing support, and generally being considerate of their material and psychological needs is certainly important. But setting goals and getting things done is the name of the game, and the leader's support must therefore generally be balanced with an expectation that employees are there to get their jobs done.

Yet the effects of initiating structure are also inconsistent with respect to performance and satisfaction. In one representative study, structuring activities by the leader and employee grievance rates were directly related: The more structuring the leader was, the more grievances were filed. However, where the leader was also very considerate, leader structure and grievances were *not* related.[34]

How can we explain such inconclusive findings? Part of the explanation—as we'll see in a moment—is that the leader style that is right for one situation might be wrong for another. Another reason, as mentioned above, is that it's generally a balance of these two styles that works best.

Participative and Autocratic Styles

Faced with the need to make a decision, the autocratic leader solves the problem and makes the decision himself or herself, using information available at the time.[35] Laurent Beaudoin of Bombardier Inc. is cited in the business press as being an autocratic leader.[36] Former Prime Minister Brian Mulroney was seen as an all-powerful leader who cracked the whip to make everybody jump.[37] At the other extreme, the participative leader shares the problem with subordinates, and together they generate and evaluate alternatives and attempt to reach a consensus on a solution.[38] Charles Hantho, CEO of Dominion Textile, is a democratic leader who readily delegates authority. Bob Hamaberg of Standard Aero Ltd. takes a collegial approach to running his company through a five-person executive committee.[39]

We know that encouraging employees to get involved in developing and implementing decisions affecting their jobs can have positive benefits. For example, employees who participate in setting goals tend to set higher goals than the supervisor would normally have assigned.[40] We've also seen that participation brings more points of view to bear and can improve the chances that participants will "buy into" the final decision. On the other hand, there are obviously some situations (like a sinking ship) in which being participative is inappropriate and too time consuming. The tricky part is deciding when to be participative and when not to be.

Leadership experts Victor Vroom, Arthur Jago, and Philip Yetton have developed a technique that enables a leader to analyze a situation and decide whether it is right for participation. The technique consists of three components: (1) a set of management decision styles, (2) a set of diagnostic questions, and (3) a decision tree for identifying how much participation the situation calls for.

The Management Decision Styles. Being participative is usually not an either/or decision, because there are different degrees of participation. These are summarized in Figure 10.3, which presents a continuum of five possible management decision styles. At one extreme is style I, no participation. Here the leader solves the problem and makes the decision himself or herself. Style V, total participation, is at the other extreme: Here the leader shares the problem with his or her subordinates and together they reach an agreement. You can see in Figure 10.3 that between these two extremes are style II, minimum participation; style III, more participation; and style IV, still more participation.

The Diagnostic Questions. In this leadership theory, the appropriate degree of participation depends on several attributes of the situation that can be quantified by asking a series of diagnostic questions (see Table 10.2). These situational attributes include the importance of the quality of the decision and the extent to which the leader possesses sufficient information to make a high-quality decision himself or herself. A typical diagnostic question is, "Do I have sufficient information to make a high-quality decision?"

The Decision Tree. The decision tree is actually a chart that enables the leader to determine the appropriate level of participation. It is presented in Figure 10.4. By starting on the left of the chart and answering each diagnostic question with a "yes" or "no," the leader can work his or her way across the decision tree and thus arrive at a decision regarding which style of participation (I to V) is best.

I. You solve the problem or make the decision yourself, using information available to you at that time.

II. You obtain the necessary information from your subordinates, then decide on the solution to the problem yourself. You may or may not tell your subordinates what the problem is when getting the information from them. The role played by your subordinates in making the decision is clearly one of providing the necessary information to you, rather than generating or evaluating alternative solutions.

III. You share the problem with relevant subordinates individually, getting their ideas and suggestions without bringing them together as a group. Then you make the decision, which may or may not reflect your subordinates' influence.

IV. You share the problem with your subordinates as a group, collectively obtaining their ideas and suggestions. Then you make the decision, which may or may not reflect your subordinates' influence.

V. You share a problem with your subordinates as a group. Together you generate and evaluate alternatives and attempt to reach agreement (consensus) on a solution. Your role is much like that of a chairperson. You do not try to influence the group to adopt "your" solution, and you are willing to accept and implement any solution that has the support of the entire group.

FIGURE 10.3
Five Types of Management Decision Styles

TABLE 10.2   *Diagnostic Questions Used in the Vroom-Jago-Yetton Model*

PROBLEM ATTRIBUTES (THESE DETERMINE THE DEGREE OF PARTICIPATION THAT IS APPROPRIATE)	DIAGNOSTIC QUESTIONS (THESE ENABLE YOU TO DIAGNOSE THE PRESENCE OR ABSENCE OF EACH ATTRIBUTE)
A. The importance of the quality of the decision	Is there a quality requirement such that one solution is likely to be more rational than another?
B. The extent to which the leader possesses sufficient information/expertise to make a high-quality decision by himself or herself	Do I have sufficient information to make a high-quality decision?
C. The extent to which the problem is structured	Is the problem structured?
D. The extent to which acceptance or commitment on the part of subordinates is critical to the effective implementation of the decision	Is acceptance of decision by subordinates critical to effective implementation?
E. The prior probability that the leader's autocratic decision will receive acceptance by subordinates	If you were to make the decision by yourself, is it reasonably certain that it would be accepted by your subordinates?
F. The extent to which the subordinates are motivated to attain the organizational goals as represented in the objectives explicit in the statement of the problem	Do subordinates share the organizational goals to be obtained in solving this problem?
G. The extent to which subordinates are likely to be in conflict over preferred solutions	Is conflict among subordinates likely in preferred solutions?

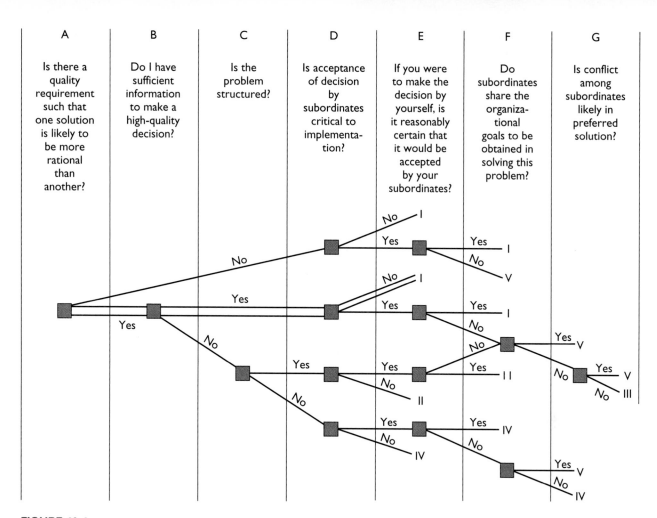

FIGURE 10.4
The Vroom-Jago-Yetton Model: Deciding Employee's Degree of Participation

Close vs. Laissez-Faire Styles

At about the same time that researchers at Ohio State were developing their Leader Behavior Description Questionnaire, a similar series of programs was beginning at the University of Michigan. Two sets of leadership styles emerged from the Michigan studies.

Job-Centred and Employee-Oriented. Rensis Likert and his associates at Michigan identified two leadership styles. **Employee-oriented leaders** focus on the individuality and personality needs of their employees and emphasize building good interpersonal relationships. Production or **job-centred leaders** focus on production and the job's technical aspects. Based on his review of the research results, Likert concluded:

> Supervisors with the best record of performance focus their primary attention on the human aspects of their subordinates' problems and on endeavoring to build effective work groups with high performance goals.[41]

Close and General. Other University of Michigan researchers conducted studies on what they called close and general leadership styles. **Close supervision,** according to these researchers, is at "one end of a continuum that describes the degree to which a supervisor specifies the roles of subordinates and checks up to see that they comply with these specifications."[42] The **laissez-faire leader** who follows a completely hands-off policy with subordinates is at the other extreme, while a **general leader** is somewhere in the middle of the continuum.

The research findings here are much clearer with respect to how close and general leaders affect employee morale than they are with respect to employee performance. Generally

employee-oriented leaders
Leaders who focus on the individuality and personality needs of their employees and emphasize building good interpersonal relationships.

job-centred leaders
Leaders who focus on production and the job's technical aspects.

close supervision
Leader specifies the roles of subordinates and regularly checks to see that they comply with these specifications.

laissez-faire leader
Leader follows a completely hands-off policy with subordinates.

general leader
Leader uses neither a close supervision strategy nor a hands-off strategy, but instead checks subordinates work only at intervals.

speaking, people do not like being closely supervised or having someone frequently checking up on them and telling them what to do. Close supervision is therefore usually associated with lower employee morale.[43] However, no consistent relationship emerged between closeness of supervision and employee performance.

Transformational Leadership Behaviour

James McGregor Burns' *Leadership* has had a major impact on the course of leadership theory.[44] Burns argued that leadership could be viewed as a transactional process or a transformational process.[45] Leader behaviours like initiating structure and consideration, he suggested, are essentially based on *quid pro quo* transactions.

Specifically, **transactional** behaviours are "largely oriented toward accomplishing the tasks at hand and at maintaining good relations with those working with the leader [by exchanging promises of rewards for performance]."[46] The key here is that transactional behaviours tend to focus more on accomplishing tasks, and perhaps on doing so by somehow adapting the leader's style and behaviour to the follower's expectations.

In today's rapidly changing world, Burns argued, it's often not a transactional but a **transformational** style of leadership that is required to manage change. "Transformational leadership refers to the process of influencing major changes in the attitudes and assumptions of organization members and building commitment for the organization's mission, objectives and strategies."[47] Transformational leaders are those who bring about "change, innovation, and entrepreneurship."[48] They are responsible for leading a corporate transformation that "recognizes the need for revitalization, creates a new vision, and institutionalizes change."[49]

What Do Transformational Leaders Do? Transformational leaders do several things. They encourage—and obtain—performance beyond expectations by formulating visions and then inspiring their subordinates to pursue them. In so doing, transformational leaders cultivate employee acceptance and commitment to those visions.[50] They "attempt to raise the needs of followers and promote dramatic changes of individuals, groups, and organizations."[51] For example, when Ted Newall took over as head of Alberta-based Nova Corporation in 1991, it was losing hundreds of millions of dollars a year. He conveyed his belief in the company to employees in a very dramatic way: He refused a salary and accepted only stock options and shares of Nova's stock as his compensation. Everyone knew that if the firm didn't make money that Newall would be working for nothing. By 1996 Newall was the highest-paid executive in the petroleum industry.[52]

Transformational leaders promote dramatic change by articulating a realistic vision of the future that can be shared, stimulating subordinates intellectually, and paying attention to the differences among these subordinates. Transformational leaders also provide a plan for attaining their vision and engage in "framing," which means giving subordinates the big picture so they can relate their individual activities to the work as a whole.[53]

From the vantage point of the followers, transformational leaders come across as charismatic, inspirational, considerate, and stimulating:[54]

- Transformational leaders are *charismatic*. Employees often idolize and develop strong emotional attachments to them.
- Transformational leaders are also *inspirational:* "the leader passionately communicates a future idealistic organization that can be shared. The leader uses visionary explanations to depict what the employee work group can accomplish."[55] The inspired employees are then motivated to achieve these organizational aims.
- *Individual consideration.* Transformational leaders treat employees as individuals and stress developing them in a way that encourages the employees to become all that they can be.
- Transformational leaders use *intellectual stimulation* to "encourage employees to approach old and familiar problems in new ways."[56] This enables employees to

transactional
Behaviours largely oriented towards accomplishing the tasks at hand and at maintaining good relations with those working with the leader by exchanging promises of rewards for performance.

transformational
The process of influencing major changes in the attitudes and assumptions of organization members and building commitment for the organization's mission, objectives and strategies.

Ellie Rubin's Entrepreneurial Rage

Ellie Rubin, former president and CEO of The Bulldog Group, Inc., demonstrated leadership with intensity. She made her formerly obscure design company in Toronto one of the most important media management companies on the planet.

In 1994, against the advice of family and friends, Rubin loaded the family car with her belongings and set out for Silicon Valley. "And no matter how many people told me I couldn't do it and I shouldn't do it and why am I doing it, it doesn't make sense, and I'm crazy, I already had my dream in my head. I was going there. I knew I was going to do it. And that's a very powerful formula that someone can't take away from you."

In *Bulldog Spirit of the New Entrepreneur* Rubin elaborates on her continuing philosophy of how to lead in business. She believes that passion, conviction, dedication, and invention are keys to entrepreneurial success. Rubin says, "You have to constantly reinvent yourself...I think you have to constantly take your knowledge and then twist it into a new something."

She has even coined "entrepreneuring" as a verb. The word in French means "between taking," which Rubin claims can also mean "giving." In this context entrepreneuring suggests creating opportunities, getting people jobs, and making those jobs exciting. Early in her book, Rubin introduces the term "entrepreneurial rage." In an interview she goes on to explain: "No matter how you look at it, this kind of entrepreneurial rage is good for all of us. It's kind of like my idea about being obsessed instead of being passionate...I really love what I'm doing."

Bulldog Group
www.bulldog.com

question their own beliefs and use creative ways to solve problems by themselves.

Examples of questions used to assess these four characteristics are:

1. *Charisma.* "I am ready to trust him or her to overcome any obstacle."

2. *Inspirational leadership.* "Provides vision of what lies ahead."

3. *Individualized consideration.* "Treats me as an individual rather than just as a member of the group."

4. *Intellectual stimulation.* "Shows me how to think about problems in new ways."[57]

Many leaders—some of whom you've probably heard of—have been described as transformational leaders. Former British Prime Minister Margaret Thatcher took over an industrially drifting nation and, by the power of her will, helped to transform it into one that fit her vision of a more privatized, competitive, hard-working nation. Apple's Steve Jobs is transforming his company into a highly competitive and "lean machine." Transformational leaders of an earlier day include India's Mahatma Gandhi and Martin Luther King, Jr.[58]

An example of a transformational leader, Steve Jobs, CEO of Apple, is committed to making his company a highly competitive force within the computer industry.

Studies of Transformational Leaders. Transformational leadership has been studied in many settings.[59] In one study, researchers found that high-performing managers in an express delivery firm used significantly more transformational leader behaviours than did less successful managers in the firm.[60] Another study found that successful champions of technological change used more transformational leader behaviours than did less successful champions.[61]

Other studies suggest that transformational leadership tends to be more closely associated with leader effectiveness and employee satisfaction than were transactional styles of leadership such as general or laissez-faire leadership.[62] It seems clear that a transformational style of leadership can be very effective, especially in situations that require managing dramatic change.

Are There Gender Differences in Leadership Styles?

Although the number of women in management jobs has risen to almost 40 percent, barely 2 percent of top management jobs are held by women.[63] Most women managers are still having trouble breaking through to the top executive ranks. Research evidence suggests that this disparity is caused not by some inherent inability of women to lead, but by institutional biases and persistent, if inaccurate, stereotypes. In other words, while there *are* a few differences in the way that men and women lead, they would not account for the slow career progress of most women managers. We can summarize some of the more relevant research findings as follows.

Persistence of Inaccurate Stereotypes. Women's promotions tend to be hampered first by inaccurate stereotypes. Managers tend to identify "masculine" (competitive) characteristics as managerial and "feminine" (cooperative and communicative) characteristics as non-managerial.[64] Women tend to be seen as less capable of being effective managers; men are viewed as "better" leaders. Another stereotype is that women managers tend to fall apart under pressure, respond impulsively, and have difficulty managing their emotions.[65] Such stereotypes usually don't hold up under the scrutiny of the researchers' microscope.

Leader Behaviours. Studies suggest few measurable differences in the leader behaviours that women and men managers use on the job. Women managers were found to be somewhat more achievement-oriented, and men managers more candid with co-workers.[66] In another study the only gender differences found were that women were more understanding.[67] Women and men who score high on the need for power (the need to influence other people) tend to behave more like each other than like people with lower power needs.[68]

Performance. How are women managers rated in terms of performance when compared with men? On the job and in joblike work simulations, women managers perform similarly to men. In actual organizational settings, "women and men in similar positions receive similar ratings."[69] In a special joblike simulation called an assessment centre in which managers must perform realistic leadership tasks (such as leading problem-solving groups and making decisions), men and women managers perform similarly. It is only in several off-the-job laboratory studies that men have scored higher in performance.[70]

A Gender Advantage. Interestingly, one often-noticed and scientifically supported difference between men and women leaders may actually prove to be a boon to women managers. Women often score higher on measures of patience, relationship development, social sensitivity, and communication. These may be precisely the skills that managers will need to manage diversity and the empowered members of self-managing teams.[71]

Situational Theories of Leadership

If only one conclusion could be drawn from studies of these various leadership style theories, it would be that the style of leadership right for one situation might not be right for another. Whether the styles are initiating structure and consideration, participative

Carol Stephenson of Lucent Technologies Canada has argued that women's interpersonal skills and aptitude for consensus-building give them an advantage as leaders.

and autocratic, employee-oriented and job-centred, or close and general, it seems apparent that the style that's best depends on the situation. This dependency helps to explain why structuring or job-centred leaders sometimes have high-performing groups and sometimes don't.

Research therefore has focused on trying to identify the situational factors that determined when one style or another is best. The Vroom-Yetton-Jago Theory discussed earlier is one example. Several other well-known situational leadership theories are presented next.

Fiedler's Contingency Theory of Leadership

Psychologist Fred Fiedler originally sought to determine whether a leader who was lenient in evaluating associates was more likely or less likely to have a high-producing group than a leader who was demanding and discriminating.[72] At the core of this research is the "least preferred co-worker" (or LPC) scale. The person who fills out the scale is asked to think of all the people with whom he or she has ever worked and to focus on the one person with whom he or she had experienced the most difficulty in getting a job completed, that is, focus on his or her least preferred co-worker. The rater is then asked to describe this person via a series of descriptive scales, for instance as:

Pleasant   Unpleasant

Smart   Stupid

Those who describe their least preferred co-worker favourably (pleasant, smart, and so on) are scored as "high LPC" and considered more people-oriented. "Low LPCs" describe least preferred co-workers unfavourably and are less people-oriented and more task-oriented.

According to Fiedler's theory, three situational factors combine to determine whether the high-LPC or the low-LPC leader style is appropriate:

1. *Position power:* the degree to which the position itself enables the leader to get his or her group members to comply with and accept his or her decisions and leadership.

2. *Task structure:* how routine and predictable the work group's task is.

3. *Leader–member relations:* the extent to which the leader gets along with workers and the extent to which they have confidence in and are loyal to him or her.

Fiedler initially concluded that the appropriateness of the leadership style "is contingent upon the favorableness of the group-task situation."[73] Basically, he argued that where the situation is either favourable or unfavourable to the leader (where leader-member relationships, task structure, and leader position power all are either very high or very low), a more task-oriented, low-LPC leader is appropriate. In the middle range, where these factors are more mixed and the task is not as clear-cut, a more people-oriented, high-LPC leader is appropriate. (These relationships are summarized in Figure 10.5.) Many research findings cast doubt on the validity of Fiedler's conclusions, and the usefulness of the theory, including its more recent variants, remains in dispute.[74]

The Path-Goal Model

Robert House has formulated a model of leadership that incorporates concepts from both the leader behaviour approach and from expectancy theory (discussed in Chapter 11).[75] The **path-goal model** suggests that the leader's job is to increase the payoffs to workers for achieving organizational goals. The leader accomplishes this by clarifying for workers what the path to these goals is, by reducing blockages that prevent workers from reaching their goals, and by behaving in a way that will increase worker satisfaction on the way to achieving goals.

path-goal model
A model that proposes that the leader's job is to increase the payoffs to workers for achieving organizational goals.

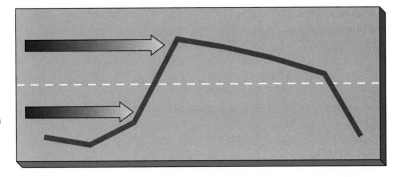

Leader-Member Relations	Good	Good	Good	Good	Poor	Poor	Poor	Poor
Task Structure	Structured		Unstructured		Structured		Unstructured	
Leader Position Power	Strong	Weak	Strong	Weak	Strong	Weak	Strong	Weak
	I	II	III	IV	V	VI	VII	VIII

FIGURE 10.5
How the Style of Effective Leadership Varies with the Situation

The path-goal model recognizes that the characteristics of the subordinates and of the task itself moderate the effects of the leader's behaviour. When workers feel that they are capable of accomplishing a task without direction from the boss, or when the task requirements are perfectly clear, directive leadership behaviour becomes unnecessary and causes dissatisfaction if implemented.

A basic assumption in the path-goal model is that high-level jobs are more ambiguous than low-level jobs. High-level employees, therefore, appreciate receiving leader-initiated structure, since it clarifies what behaviour is needed to attain their work goals. This reduces their sense of uncertainty. Since this clarification is helpful to high-level employees, the initiation of structure also increases their satisfaction. However, for routine, low-level jobs, initiating structure is not necessary and subordinates may even interpret it as a lack of trust. In these jobs, initiating structure may cause dissatisfaction. Yet, consideration may improve job satisfaction for these employees because it makes their jobs more "human" and therefore more bearable.

The path-goal model is helpful because it deals with specific leader behaviours and how they might influence employee satisfaction and performance. The model differs from others because it recognizes both situational variables and individual differences. But this model, like many others, seems able to predict employee satisfaction better than employee productivity.

Leader-Member Exchange (LMX) Theory

Although a leader may have one prevailing style like "participative" or "autocratic," most leaders don't treat all of their subordinates in the same way. Yet most of the leadership style theories we've discussed to this point imply that a leader exhibits a similar leadership style towards all members of his or her work group. The **leader-member exchange (LMX) theory** says that leaders may use different styles with different members of the same work group.[76]

This theory suggests that leaders tend to divide their subordinates into an "in" group and an "out" group. The in group gets more attention and a larger share of the resources than the out group, of course. What determines whether you're part of your leader's in group or out group? The leader's decision is often made with very little real

leader-member exchange (LMX) theory
A leadership theory that says that leaders may use different styles with different members of the same work group.

information, although perceived leader-member similarities—gender, age, or attitudes, for instance—can be enough.[77]

One study helps to illustrate what makes a follower (or member) fall into a leader's in group or out group.[78] In this study, completed questionnaires were obtained from 84 full-time registered nurses and 12 supervisors in 12 work groups at a large hospital. Eighty-three percent of the supervisors (leaders) were women with an average age of 39.4 years; the nurses (followers) were mostly women (88.1 percent), with an average age of 36.7 years. Various things were measured, including the strength and quality of leader-member relationships or exchanges (friendliness between leader and members, rewards given to members, and so on).

The quality of leader-member exchanges was found to be positively related to a leader's perceptions of two things: similarity of *leader-follower attitudes* and follower *extroversion*. Leaders were asked to assess the similarity between themselves and their followers in terms of their attitudes towards six items: family, money, career strategies, goals in life, education, and overall perspective. Not surprisingly, leaders were more favourably inclined towards those followers with whom they felt they shared similar attitudes. Followers were also asked to complete questionnaires that enabled the researchers to label them as introverted or extroverted. The extroverted nurses were more likely to have high-quality leader-member exchanges than were the introverts, presumably because they were more outgoing and sociable in general.

Findings like these suggest at least two practical implications. First, because members of the in group can be expected to perform better than those in the out group, leaders should strive to make the in group more inclusive. For employees the findings emphasize the (obvious) importance of being in your leader's in group and underscore the value of emphasizing similarities rather than differences in attitude—in politics, for instance—between you and your supervisor.

The Situational Leadership Model Approach

Start here

Other behavioural scientists have developed what they call a situational leadership model to describe how the leader should adapt his or her style to the task; their model is presented in Figure 10.6.[79] They identify four leadership styles:

■ The *delegating* leader lets the members of the group decide what to do themselves.
■ The *participating* leader asks the members of the group what to do but makes the final decisions himself or herself.

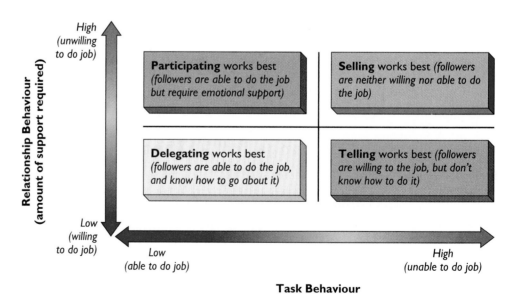

FIGURE 10.6
Situational Leadership Model

- The *selling* leader makes the decision himself or herself but explains the reasons.
- The *telling* leader makes the decision himself or herself, telling the group what to do.

According to the situational leadership model, each style is appropriate in a specific situation, as follows:

- Delegating works best where followers are willing to do the job and know how to go about doing it.
- Participating works best when followers are able to do the job but are unwilling, and so require emotional support.

SELF-ASSESSMENT EXERCISE:

Determining Your Leadership Style

To be able to identify and enact the most appropriate style of leadership in any given situation, it is first useful to understand the style to which you are already predisposed. This exercise will help you gain insight into your own leadership style.

DIRECTIONS

Following are eight hypothetical situations in which you have to make a decision affecting you and members of your work group. For each, indicate which of the following actions you are most likely to take by writing the letter corresponding to that action in the space provided.

A. Let the members of the group decide themselves what to do. (Delegating)

B. Ask the members of the group what to do, but make the final decision yourself. (Participating)

C. Make the decision yourself, but explain your reasons. (Selling)

D. Make the decision yourself, telling the group exactly what to do. (Telling)

_____ 1. In the face of financial pressures, you are forced to make budget cuts for your unit. Where do you cut?

_____ 2. To meet an impending deadline, someone in your secretarial pool will have to work late one evening to finish typing an important report. Who will it be?

_____ 3. As coach of a company softball team, you are required to trim your squad to 25 players from 30 currently on the roster. Who goes?

_____ 4. Employees in your department have to schedule their summer vacations so as to keep the office appropriately staffed. Who decides first?

_____ 5. As chair of the social committee, you are responsible for determining the theme for the company ball. How do you do so?

_____ 6. You have an opportunity to buy or rent an important piece of equipment for your company. After gathering all the facts, how do you make the choice?

_____ 7. The office is being redecorated. How do you decide on the colour scheme?

_____ 8. Along with your associates you are taking a visiting dignitary to dinner. How do you decide what restaurant to go to?

SCORING

1. Count the number of situations to which you responded by marking A. This is your *delegating* score.

2. Count the number of situations to which you responded by marking B. This is your *participating* score.

3. Count the number of situations to which you responded by marking C. This is your *selling* score.

4. Count the number of situations to which you responded by marking D. This is your *telling* score.

QUESTIONS FOR DISCUSSION

1. Based on this questionnaire, what was your most predominant leadership style? Is this consistent with what you would have predicted in advance?

2. According to Situational Leadership theory, in what kinds of situations would this style be most appropriate? Have you ever found yourself in such a situation, and if so, how well did you do?

3. Do you think that it would be possible for you to change this style if needed?

4. To what extent were your responses to this questionnaire affected by the nature of the situations described? In other words, would you have opted for different decisions in different situations?

FIGURE 10.7
Self-Assessment Exercise

- Selling works best where followers are neither willing nor able to do the job.
- Telling works best where followers are willing to do the job but don't know how to do it.

Figure 10.7 presents a self-assessment exercise you can use to gain perspective on whether you are primarily a delegating, participating, selling, or telling manager.

Being a Leader

Being a leader means taking the steps required to boost your effectiveness at filling the leader's role. No formula can guarantee that you can be a leader. However, based on the research presented in this chapter, there are some powerful actions you can take to improve the chances that in a leadership situation you will be a leader. These can be summarized as follows.

Think Like a Leader

We mentioned earlier that it is important to think like a leader, so that you can bring to bear what you know about leadership and behavioural theories rather than just react with a knee-jerk response. Thinking like a leader means doing at least these three things:

1. Apply the three-step model: Identify what is happening, account for what is happening by bringing to bear all of your knowledge of leadership and behavioural theory and concepts, and formulate a leadership response to address the issue.

2. Remember that behavioural science knowledge about leading is not limited to the material contained in this chapter. You will need to be able to apply the knowledge from the subsequent chapters on motivating, groups, conflict, and change, fitting it into your assessment of the issues as you account for what is happening and decide how to influence your followers to deal with the situation. Don't be overwhelmed by the number of theories and concepts that might apply; think of them as tools in your leadership toolbox. There may be—and probably is—more than one way to solve the problem.

3. In influencing your followers to move towards some goal, remember that you cannot ignore managerial planning, organizing, and controlling. In practice, moving followers from where they are to where you want them to be will require all of your management skills. To achieve your goals you will have to implement procedures, assign jobs, and monitor performance, for instance.

Develop Your Judgment

Possessing the traits of leadership gives someone the potential to be a leader. Your ability to be a leader can thus be improved by enhancing your existing leadership traits.

Some traits are easier to enhance than others, but all of them can be modified. For example, the leader's judgment is important because people will not follow a leader who makes too many bad decisions for long. In Chapter 4, we saw that several steps can improve your decision-making ability:

- *Correctly define the problem.* Remember: Don't install new elevators when mirrors will do!
- *Increase your knowledge.* The more you know about the problem and the more facts you can marshal, the more likely it is that your confidence in your decision will not be misplaced.

- *De-bias your judgment.* A number of cognitive or decision-making biases can distort a manager's judgment. De-biasing your judgment—reducing or eliminating biases like stereotyping from your judgment process—is, therefore, a crucial step towards making better decisions.
- *Be creative.* Creativity plays a big role in making better decisions. The ability to develop novel responses—creativity—is essential for decision-making activities like developing new alternatives and correctly defining the problem.
- *Use your intuition.* Many behavioural scientists argue that a preoccupation with analyzing problems rationally and logically can actually backfire by blocking someone from using his or her intuition.
- *Don't overstress the finality of your decision.* Remember that very few decisions are forever; there is more give in more decisions than we realize. Even major strategic decisions can often be reversed or modified as situations warrant.
- *Make sure the timing is right.* Most people's decisions are affected by their passing moods. Managerial decision makers should therefore take their emotions into account before making important decisions. Sometimes it's best just to sleep on decisions.

Develop Your Other Leadership Traits

Good judgment is just one of the leadership traits that you can enhance. For example, leaders also exhibit self-confidence (but not arrogance). Although developing self-confidence may be a lifelong process, you can enhance it in several ways. One is to focus more on those situations in which you are more self-confident to begin with, such as those in which you are an expert: A stamp collector might exhibit more self-confidence as president of his or her stamp club than in coaching a baseball team, for instance. You can act like a leader by exhibiting self-confidence when making decisions and by acting dignified rather than cracking jokes constantly with your subordinates. Your knowledge of the business is probably the easiest trait to modify; immerse yourself in the details of your new job and learn as much about the business as you can, as fast as you can.

Start to Build Your Power Base

Remember that a powerless leader is not a leader at all. Conversely, you can strengthen the foundation of your leadership by taking steps to enhance your authority and power. One way to do this is to start acting like a leader. Cracking jokes and being "one of the guys (or gals)" may get some laughs, but most leaders act at least somewhat reserved to maintain their power base. Table 10.3 shows the various bases of power to which managers have access.

Help Your Followers Share Your Vision

Leading means influencing people to work enthusiastically towards achieving an objective. Ensure that your subordinates know and understand the vision, mission, or objective and that you have clarified their assignments. As leadership expert John Kotter puts it, "great leaders are all good at getting relevant partners aligned with, buying into, believing in" the direction the leader has set.

Adapt Your Style and Actions to the Situation

We've seen in this chapter that no one leadership style is going to be appropriate for every situation in which you find yourself. Remember that the art of being a leader lies in your ability to identify the leadership-related issues and then to determine whether one or more leadership theories and concepts can be applied, and if so, how.

TABLE 10.3 *Managers' Bases of Power*

REWARD POWER

1. Increase pay levels.
2. Influence getting a raise.
3. Provide specific benefits.
4. Influence getting a promotion.

COERCIVE POWER (ETHICALLY QUESTIONABLE)

5. Give undesirable work assignments.
6. Make work difficult.
7. Make things unpleasant.
8. Influence getting a promotion.

LEGITIMATE POWER

9. Make others feel they have commitments to meet.
10. Make others feel they should satisfy job requirements.
11. Give the feeling that others have responsibilities to fulfil.
12. Make others recognize that they have tasks to accomplish.

EXPERT POWER

13. Give good technical suggestions.
14. Share considerable experience and/or training.
15. Provide sound job-related advice.
16. Provide needed technical knowledge.

REFERENCE POWER

17. Make employees feel valued.
18. Make employees feel that you approve of them.
19. Make employees feel personally accepted.
20. Make employees feel important.

Use Your Other Management Skills to Help You Lead

As we saw earlier in this chapter, leadership and management are inseparable: To get things done, leaders have to use their management skills. Research suggests that various management actions can actually function as effective "substitutes" for the leadership you may otherwise have to provide.[80] Here are a few examples.

Choose the Right Followers. If you select and train your followers well, there may be less reason for you to have to exercise leadership on a day-to-day basis. The greater your subordinates' ability, the greater their experience, the better their training, and the more professional their behaviour, the less direct supervision they will need. Some followers are inherently more effective than others: Choose followers who are cooperative, flexible, and trustworthy and who have initiative and are good at problem solving.[81]

Organize the Task Properly. You may also be able to modify organizational factors to reduce the need for day-to-day leadership. Jobs for which the performance standards are clear, or for which there is plenty of built-in feedback, may require less leadership.[82] Similarly, employees engaged in work that is intrinsically satisfying (work they love to do) require less leadership.[83] Cohesive work groups with positive norms also require less leadership (as do, by definition, self-managing teams).

The reward system is important, too: Some reward systems, like gainsharing programs that pay employees a percentage of any productivity improvement, leave the supervisor virtually out of the loop with regards to controlling rewards. Conversely, merit pay plans in which the leader's rating has a big impact on each follower's end-of-year raise require the leader to closely monitor performance and conduct appraisals.[84]

SUMMARY OF LEARNING OBJECTIVES

1. **Size up a situation like a leader.** Sizing up a situation and thinking like a leader means reviewing a leadership situation and identifying what is happening, accounting for what is happening (in terms of leadership and other behavioural science theories and concepts), and formulating leader actions.

2. **List the foundations of leadership.** Personal traits and power are the two important foundations (or prerequisites) of leadership. To be a leader one must have the potential to be a leader; that is, a person must have the "right stuff" in terms of personality traits. Traits on which leaders differ from non-leaders include drive, the desire to lead, honesty/integrity, self-confidence, cognitive ability, and knowledge of the business. Legitimate power and authority is the second element in the foundation of leadership, because a leader without power is not a leader at all. Sources of power include position, ability to give rewards or punishments, technical expertise, and referent power (personal magnetism).

3. **Provide a vision for an organization.** Leadership means influencing others to work willingly towards achieving objectives. Being a leader requires more than having a command of leadership theories. It also means managing organizational culture, motivating employees, managing groups, teams, and conflict, and facilitating organizational change. The leader must provide a direction that followers can work towards. This direction may be a statement of vision, mission, or objectives, depending largely on what the leader wants to achieve and the level at which he or she is acting.

4. **Compare the various styles a leader can use.** Leadership styles include (a) structuring (organizing the work to be done) and consideration (respecting subordinates and trusting them); (b) participative (letting subordinates get involved in making decisions) and autocratic (making all of the decisions yourself); (c) employee-oriented (focus on subordinates' individuality and needs) and job-centred (focus on the technical aspects of the job); (d) close (check on subordinates frequently) and laissez-faire (loosely supervise subordinates); and (e) transactional (focus on accomplishing the tasks at hand) and transformational (influence major changes in attitudes in subordinates).

5. **List the specific attributes of being a leader.** Leaders have drive, they want to lead, they are honest and possess integrity, they have self-confidence, they make good decisions, and they know the business.

Developing a plan and creating an organization is only part of the task a manager faces. Companies and other organizations are composed of people, and it's the manager's job to inspire, lead, and motivate these people to carry out the company's or the department's mission. In this chapter—the first in Part 4, Leading—we looked at what it takes to be a leader, in particular the traits and styles of effective leaders, and how to think like a leader and size up leadership situations. As you know from your own experience, one of the leader's biggest tasks involves actually motivating subordinates. So in the following chapter we'll turn to the important topic of motivating employees.

CRITICAL THINKING EXERCISES

1. Guidance, vision, culture, empowerment, personality, power, influence, charisma, the "right stuff," revolutionizing the behaviour of others: These seem to be evolving elements of leadership as we enter the next millennium. Rather than lifelong work in one company, we are also increasingly becoming independent workers or contractors, tied more to our own profession and skills than to any one company, or country for that matter.

Using the research presented in this chapter, develop a profile for the types of leaders needed for the following companies or leadership positions:

   • Prime Minister of Canada
   • CEO of Microsoft
   • Coach of an NHL team
   • Owner of a small business
   • CEO of Ford Motor Company in Brazil
   • Director of Consumer and Corporate Affairs
   • Director of the United Way

Be prepared to compare your profiles with those of your class members.

2. As a group, compare the perspectives noted below regarding leadership. What concepts from the chapter would help you to understand the various perspectives? Which sentiment do you like best and why?

   • "You can't succeed as a leader unless you're more concerned about people's performance than about their feelings. You must focus on people's output, not on their attitude towards their work. Reward the employees who get results, and don't pay much attention to employees who are sincere but incompetent."
   • "A leader must subscribe to the view that workers should share in the economic value they help to create. Stock options are a good way to do this, yet many business leaders do not make this available to their workers. When you decide to share the wealth with workers, you give them an incentive to succeed, so it is surprising that more companies don't do this."
   • "Leaders must have an overarching vision for their firm, but they must also have a clear understanding of where the company is now and how far it has to go to achieve its vision."
   • "The importance of leadership has been overstated. The leaders of business firms and other kinds of organizations make mistakes just like everybody else, and the ones who are successful just happen to be a little luckier than the ones who aren't."

1. Leaders come in all sizes, shapes, genders, and races. Research five of the following people and then write a brief analysis of what makes or made them leaders. After you have completed that portion of the task, explain what you think an "ideal" leader is and identify someone you think fits that profile best. Write no more than two pages of analysis.

   The leaders are Jean Chrétien, prime minister of Canada; Preston Manning, former leader of Canada's Reform party; Golda Meir, former leader of Israel; Bill Clinton, former president of the United States; Mao Zedong, the late communist leader of China; Bill Gates, chairman of Microsoft; Louis Gerstner, CEO of IBM; Helmut Kohl, former chancellor of Germany; Jesus Christ, religious leader; Paul Tellier, CEO of CN; and Larry Walker, baseball player.

2. The world has clearly changed in the last few decades. Many people argue that for families to maintain a decent standard of living, it is necessary for women to enter the labour market and stay there for many years. If Canada is to remain competitive on the international scene, the mixture of work and family is an issue we should address as a nation.

   In groups of four to six, including men and women, discuss the following questions:

   - What type of leadership do you think is needed in today's highly competitive workplace?
   - Are men and women using the same leadership styles? Should they?
   - Can women take their place in leadership positions under the current situation?

3. In their book entitled *The New Global Leaders*, Mansfried F.R. Kets de Vries and Elizabeth Florent-Treacy select Richard Branson of Virgin Airlines, Percy Barnevik of ASEA Brown Boveri, and David Simon of British Petroleum as the models for global leadership. Research each of these companies on the Internet or obtain a copy of *The New Global Leaders* from the library. Then write a comparative analysis of these individuals' leadership styles and why they are seen as models for the global marketplace.

4. The following self-assessment exercise can give you a feel for your readiness and inclination to assume a leadership role.

   Instructions. Indicate the extent to which you agree with each of the following statements, using the following scale: (1) disagree strongly; (2) disagree; (3) neutral; (4) agree; (5) agree strongly.

   1. It is enjoyable having people count on me for ideas and suggestions.
      1   2   3   4   5

   2. It would be accurate to say that I have inspired other people.
      1   2   3   4   5

   3. It's a good practice to ask people provocative questions about their work.
      1   2   3   4   5

   4. It's easy for me to compliment others.
      1   2   3   4   5

   5. I like to cheer people up even when my own spirits are down.
      1   2   3   4   5

   6. What my team accomplishes is more important than my personal glory.
      1   2   3   4   5

7. Many people imitate my ideas.
      1   2   3   4   5

8. Building team spirit is important to me.
      1   2   3   4   5

9. I would enjoy coaching other members of the team.
      1   2   3   4   5

10. It is important to me to recognize others for their accomplishments.
       1   2   3   4   5

11. I would enjoy entertaining visitors to my firm even if it interfered with my completing a report.
       1   2   3   4   5

12. It would be fun for me to represent my team at gatherings outside our department.
       1   2   3   4   5

13. The problems of my teammates are my problems, too.
       1   2   3   4   5

14. Resolving conflict is an activity I enjoy.
       1   2   3   4   5

15. I would cooperate with another unit in the organization even if I disagreed with the position taken by its members.
       1   2   3   4   5

16. I am an idea generator on the job.
       1   2   3   4   5

17. It's fun for me to bargain whenever I have the opportunity.
       1   2   3   4   5

18. Team members listen to me when I speak.
       1   2   3   4   5

19. People have asked me to assume leadership of an activity several times in my life.
       1   2   3   4   5

20. I've always been a convincing person.
       1   2   3   4   5

Total score: _____

Scoring and Interpretation. Calculate your total score by adding the numbers circled. A tentative interpretation of the scoring is as follows:

90–100	high readiness for the leadership role
60–89	moderate readiness for the leadership role
40–59	some uneasiness with the leadership role
39 or less	low readiness for the leadership role

If you are already a successful leader and you scored low on this questionnaire, ignore your score. If you scored surprisingly low and you are not yet a leader or are currently performing poorly as a leader, study the statements carefully. Consider changing your attitude or your behaviour so that you can legitimately answer more of the statements with a 4 or a 5.[85]

5. The following self-assessment exercise can give you a better feel for the steps you can take to enhance your power.

Directions. Circle the appropriate number of your answer, using the following scale: 5 = strongly agree, 4 = agree, 3 = neither agree nor disagree, 2 = disagree, 1 = strongly disagree.

AS A MANAGER, I CAN (OR, IF I'M NOT A MANAGER NOW, MY MANAGER CAN OR FORMER MANAGER COULD) …

REWARD POWER

1. Increase pay levels.	5	4	3	2	1
2. Influence getting a raise.	5	4	3	2	1
3. Provide specific benefits.	5	4	3	2	1
4. Influence getting a promotion.	5	4	3	2	1

COERCIVE POWER (ETHICALLY QUESTIONABLE)

5. Give undesirable work assignments.	5	4	3	2	1
6. Make work difficult.	5	4	3	2	1
7. Make things unpleasant.	5	4	3	2	1
8. Influence getting a promotion.	5	4	3	2	1

LEGITIMATE POWER

9. Make others feel they have commitments to meet.	5	4	3	2	1
10. Make others feel they should satisfy job requirements.	5	4	3	2	1
11. Give the feeling that others have responsibilities to fulfil.	5	4	3	2	1
12. Make others recognize that they have tasks to accomplish.	5	4	3	2	1

EXPERT POWER

13. Give good technical suggestions.	5	4	3	2	1
14. Share considerable experience and/or training.	5	4	3	2	1
15. Provide sound job-related advice.	5	4	3	2	1
16. Provide needed technical knowledge.	5	4	3	2	1

REFERENT POWER

17. Make employees feel valued.	5	4	3	2	1
18. Make employees feel that I approve of them.	5	4	3	2	1
19. Make employees feel personally accepted.	5	4	3	2	1
20. Make employees feel important.	5	4	3	2	1

Total score: _____

Scoring and Interpretation. Add all the circled numbers to calculate your total score. You can make a tentative interpretation of the score as follows:

90+	high power
70–89	moderate power
below 70	low power

Also, see whether you rated much higher on one type of power than on the others.[86]

INTERNET EXERCISE

You have read about leadership styles and issues. Now test your own leadership ability at www.leaderx.com/testyourlead.htm.

Complete the 15 questions as if you are a leader or manager in a company. Use your imagination a bit here. Then submit your responses to receive a customized response.

1. What do you believe are the most important skills or competencies in a leader? Why?

2. As a leader, what is important to motivate others?

3. How important is the leader in shaping the corporate culture of the organization? Explain.

CASE STUDY 10-1

The Ultimate Entrepreneur

Who is he? This entrepreneur started with little money but built a company up to $42 billion in revenues, created hundreds of thousands of jobs, and established a world-class name brand, all without charisma or big connections. High-tech whiz? Biotech inventor? No, he is Konosuke Matsushita, creator of Matsushita Electric, whose annual sales eventually exceeded the combined sales of Bethlehem Steel, Colgate-Palmolive, Gillette, Goodrich, Kellogg, Olivetti, Scott Paper, and Whirlpool.

Matsushita made a fortune and spent it on civic projects such as a Nobel prize–like organization and a school of government to reform Japan's political system. Today his spirit is still a part of the company he created. Matsushita's 265 000 workers worldwide start their day with the company song and from time to time recite its six business principles:

1. Treat the people you do business with as if they were a part of your family.

2. After-sales service is more important than assistance before sales.

3. Don't sell customers goods they are attached to; sell them goods that will benefit them.

4. Being out of stock is due to carelessness.

5. Think of yourself as being completely in charge of and responsible for your own work.

6. If we cannot make a profit, we are committing a crime against society, using precious resources that could be better used elsewhere.

Perhaps among all of Matsushita's lessons about business, the greatest was that life is growth—as a human being, as a businessperson, and as a leader.

Questions

1. How does Matsushita illustrate the traits and skills of a leader?

2. Do you think that Matsushita's culture made a difference in his leadership style? If so, how?

3. What are the lessons of leadership taught by Matsushita?

4. What do you think it would be like to work at Matsushita Electric?

5. What do you think it was about Matsushita that made him such a successful entrepreneur?

Leadership in the Canadian Forces

In 1993, soldiers of the Canadian Airborne Regiment who had been sent to Somalia on a United Nations humanitarian mission tortured and killed a teenaged Somali boy. Over the next few months, there was increasing publicity about the case, with most of it focussing on allegations that documents relating to the murder were tampered with and destroyed.

Colonel Geof Haswell, the only person actually charged with document tampering, claimed that General Jean Boyle, Chief of Defence Staff for the Canadian forces, knew that the documents had been tampered with before they were released in response to the CBC's access-to-information requests. Several other officers and civilian employees of the Defence Department supported this claim. Boyle denied that he had any knowledge of the document alteration. He did, however, admit that he had broken the spirit of the access-to-information law by failing to disclose certain other documents.

At an inquiry held during the summer of 1996, General Boyle said that he took responsibility for what happened in Somalia, but that he would not resign as Chief of Defence. When asked by members of the Somalia Inquiry Board if he was responsible for what he did and what his subordinates did, Boyle said "yes," but added that his responsibility for his subordinates' action depended on whether he knew about them. One commissioner said that the answer sounded like Boyle was trying to shift the blame onto his subordinates.

Boyle claimed that dishonest and cowardly subordinates conspired to betray him by altering documents relating to the Somalia incident. He therefore felt that he should not have to take responsibility for their actions. He also said that if Chiefs of Defence resigned every time a subordinate made an error, there would never be any leadership in the Canadian Forces.

Boyle was unable to explain how he could be unaware of document tampering while so many other people in the military knew about it. Observers felt that Boyle came across as not willing to accept responsibility for what happened.

As the inquiry progressed, General Boyle hinted that he might consider resigning if he though that his leadership capability was damaged in the eyes of his subordinates. On October 8, 1996, General Boyle did resign as Chief of Defence Staff. He said that the military deserved a leader who was not the focus of attention as he had been during the inquiry.

Observers of the case have varied opinions about what happened and who was responsible for what. A military historian who closely followed Boyle's testimony felt that General Boyle was the victim of a witch hunt. But several retired military said that Boyle was unfit to continue in his position, and that, because of the controversy, military personnel were ashamed to wear their uniforms in public. One general noted that there had been misconduct in Canadian troops in both Bosnia and Somalia, which he considered a result of leadership failure in the Canadian Forces. A 1995 survey of Canadian Forces personnel showed that only 17 percent had confidence in the most senior levels in the Department of Defence.

Questions

1. To what extent is a leader responsible for what his or her subordinates do? In this case, how responsible was Boyle?

2. How does a leader ensure that subordinates trust the leader? How effective was Boyle in generating trust and pride among his subordinates? Defend your answer.

3. Assuming that Boyle did not know that documents had been tampered with, should he have been held responsible for the actions of his subordinates? Defend your answer.

Michael Dorf Leads KnitMedia

If you were to fast-forward through KnitMedia's history, you'd find that it reflects the leadership of Michael Dorf: Dorf manages the band Swamp Thing and starts Flaming Pie Records in Madison, Wisconsin, in 1985; the first Knitting Factory opens in 1997; Dorf begins recording live Knitting Factory performances and offers them as a "Live at the Knitting Factory" radio series, in part by persuading 30 radio stations to pay $5 a week for the cost of duplication and mailings; Dorf begins KnitMedia's Internet operations; and Dorf and KnitMedia raise about $5 million and begin opening new Knitting Factory clubs abroad.

In other words, KnitMedia has always been driven by Michael Dorf's vision, and to a large extent, Dorf still exercises his leadership influence through that vision. As Allan Fried says, "I think Michael leads through his vision; he's got a really powerful instinct and vision for where we need to go, and of what drives our success aesthetically and commercially in terms of achieving our commercial goals as well as our artistic integrity."

However, as in Michael Dorf's case, it's usually not just vision that characterizes successful leaders, but also single-mindedness. Building a business from scratch means overcoming thousands of obstacles; an entrepreneur usually can't accomplish that if he or she is weak-willed or does not consistently demand perfection from those who are working for him or her.

This can translate into a sort of austere leadership style. For example, Mark Harabedian, the firm's vice-president of finance, says, "What kind of leader is Michael? He's rough. He expects a lot of you, probably more than is possible, and that might create, you know, problems since there's certain things that are physically impossible and that people simply can't do." Dorf himself would probably agree with this assessment. For example, when he left New York to open the Los Angeles Knitting Factory, he found that while he was gone people had to make decisions on their own and that, as a result, "some of our people completely failed, but [for] those who rose to the occasion, [their ability] was very clear. [My being away], I think, made the cream rise to the top and my being away sort of forced the issue, without having to wait two years to see how well people could do with some initiative."

This raises some questions for Michael Dorf and his management team, however. First, as the company grows, how can Dorf's vision continue to penetrate every nook and cranny of the company's worldwide operations so that he can continue to provide the sort of leadership he did during the firm's first 10 or 15 years? Second, what sort of effects do you think Dorf's single-mindedness and demanding style of leadership are liable to have—for good or for ill—on the company as it expands?

Team Exercises and Questions

Use what you learned in this chapter to answer the following questions from Michael Dorf and his management team:

1. What exactly can we do to make sure that Michael Dorf's vision does in fact penetrate every nook and cranny of the company as it grows?

2. How would you characterize Michael Dorf as a leader, based on the various styles and approaches that management experts use to describe leaders today?

3. What do you see as the pros and cons of this kind of leadership style in terms of the effects it will have on KnitMedia and its employees?

4. Should Michael Dorf modify his leadership style in any way? Why or why not? If so, how would you suggest that he go about doing so, and to what end?

Influencing Individual Behaviour and Motivation

A CEO Talks About Motivation

Jack Welch, the immensely successful CEO of General Electric Co., has some strong ideas about people and how to motivate them. He says that he spends at least 50 percent of his time on "people issues," and that his most important job is to assess and motivate the company's employees. At GE, each professional employee is given an annual "vitality rating" that is based on his or her performance. The rating scale runs from 1 to 5, with 1s being the top performers and 5s being the bottom performers. Grading is done on a curve, with about 10 percent of the employees receiving 1s, 15 percent 2s, 50 percent 3s, 15 percent 4s, and 10 percent 5s. So in a unit with 10 people, one person will be a 1 and one person will be a 5. A person who receives a 5 should start looking for a new job. Everyone is assigned a number each year so that they know where they stand.

A person's rating affects the chance that they will get stock options. All of the 1s get stock options. So will about 90 percent of the 2s and half of the 3s, but the 4s and 5s will not. In any given year, about one-third of employees actually get stock options. Welch thinks that giving people financial rewards for performance helps to motivate them, and Welch likes giving big raises as well. But money isn't enough. He says you have to reward a person's soul as well as their wallet.

Welch isn't particularly impressed by the idea of setting specific goals for employees. Rather, he thinks that the most important thing to do is to let people know whether they're on the right track or headed for a dead end. If they are on the right track, they will work hard and achieve goals. He also feels that managers don't have to hang around with subordinates, socialize with them, or be their buddies in order to be effective. But it is critical that people's values are the same, that they agree about how people should be treated, and that they agree about what behaviour they want to cultivate in the organization.

Welch encourages people to be seen and to make a statement. He also advises people not to allow themselves to become victims in an organization. As a practical test of this, Welch says that if a person feels like a victim at GE, that person should not be working at GE and therefore should seek a job at another organization where he or she will be happier.

General Electric
www.ge.com

After studying this chapter, you should be able to

1. Compare the three needs-based approaches to motivating employees.

2. Compare the three process approaches to motivating employees.

3. Explain the role of equity, goal setting, and expectations in employee motivation.

4. Illustrate the use of the behaviour modification approach in motivation.

5. Give examples of how to use 10 methods for influencing behaviour and motivating employees.

Imagine for a moment that you work for Jack Welch, General Electric's relentless CEO, a man who's been called "neutron Jack" (for the way he laid off 100 000 workers when he first took over GE) and who still grades each of GE's 85 000 professionals and managers. You know that while those in the top tier will receive bonuses, most of those in the bottom tier will be terminated.[1] The company Welch now manages strives for continuous progress towards perfection in the products that it makes, by continually eliminating defects and wasted effort through a process known as total quality management.

Your challenge is not just that you work for a demanding boss. You're building a product that should not have any defects. Those giant-jet engines that your plant builds will drive countless aircraft like the Boeing 777, so you certainly don't want any errors. For example, in measuring the huge two-metre circular rings that will seal the engine's gases, you know that the diameter can be off by no more than the width of half a human hair. This need for precision will take a degree of caution and responsibility on the part of employees that can't just be bought with money or assured by supervisors barking orders.

Indeed, your challenge is quite different from that facing the plant manager of the early auto plant shown in Figure 11.1. With relatively little competition and no one's life riding on the results, managers in plants like these could often rely on financial incentives and close supervision to ensure that the work got done, and done on time.

As a leader, you can't get away with that today. Somehow, you've got to organize the work and motivate the workers so that they're turned on by and committed to their jobs. Somehow, based on your experience and your understanding of human needs and motivation, you've got to organize the work so that the workers will do their jobs without supervision, as if they own the company.

motivation
The intensity of a person's desire to engage in some activity.

Motivation is the intensity of a person's desire to engage in some activity. **Extrinsic motivation** exists when a person works hard at a task because of the promise that some tangible reward will be given if the job is done well. **Intrinsic motivation**, on the other hand, exists if the person performs a task in the absence of any tangible reward. A salesperson who works hard to earn a large monetary bonus is likely to be extrinsically motivated, while a person working on a volunteer basis for the United Way is likely to be intrinsically motivated.

extrinsic motivation
Exists when a person works hard at a task because of the promise that some tangible reward will be given if the job is done well.

We know that employees can be motivated and that there are few more important leadership tasks than motivating subordinates. In Chapter 10 we discussed leadership, including how to size up and deal with a leadership situation that you may confront. Understanding how to motivate employees will play a central role in any such analysis. In this chapter, we'll turn to the organizational behaviour studies that help explain what motivates people, and to several specific methods that you as a leader can use to motivate subordinates.

intrinsic motivation
Exists if the person performs a task in the absence of any tangible reward.

FIGURE 11.1
An Early Auto Plant
Managers in plants like these could rely on close supervision to be sure the work got done right and on time.

Let us first look at three approaches that help explain what motivates people: needs-based, process-based, and learning/reinforcement-based. Each takes a different perspective in explaining how motivation occurs and how to motivate a person. All three approaches are used by managers.

Needs-Based Approaches to Motivating Employees

The defence attorney paced back and forth in front of the jury and asked, "Ladies and gentlemen, what possible motive would my client have for committing this crime?" That question is crucial: After all, if there is no motive, then why do it?

Motives and needs also play a central role on the job. A **motive** is something that incites a person to action or that sustains and gives direction to action.[2] When we ask why a defendant might have done what he did, or why a football player works to stay in shape all year, or why a sales manager flies all night to meet with a client, we are asking about motives.

A motive can be aroused or unaroused. Everyone carries within him or her **motivational dispositions**, or needs—motives that, like seeds in winter, remain unaroused until the proper conditions bring them forth. You may have a motivational disposition to enjoy yourself at the movies, but that motive is dormant until Saturday night, when you can put your studies aside. **Aroused motives** are motives that express themselves in behaviour.[3] When the conditions are right—when the studies are over, the quiz is done, and the weekend has arrived—the movie-attendance motive is aroused and you may be off to see your favourite flick.

Needs-based approaches to motivating employees focus on the role of needs or motivational dispositions in driving people to do what they do. Which needs or motivational dispositions are most important? How and under what conditions do they become aroused and translate into behaviour? These are the sorts of questions studied by psychologists like

motive
Something that incites a person to action or that sustains and gives direction to action.

motivational dispositions
Motives that remain unaroused until the proper conditions bring them forth.

aroused motives
Motives that express themselves in behaviour.

Abraham Maslow, David McClelland, and Frederick Herzberg. (See this chapter's appendix for an additional perspective on motives and behaviour.)

Maslow's Needs-Hierarchy Theory

Maslow's needs-hierarchy approach to motivation is typical of needs-based approaches and is the basis for the others discussed in this section. Maslow proposed that people have five increasingly higher-level needs: physiological, safety, social, self-esteem, and self-actualization. According to Maslow's *prepotency process principle*, people become motivated to satisfy the lower-order needs and then, in sequence, each of the higher-order needs.[4] (Psychologist Clay Alderfer, in a variation of this theory, emphasizes that all of the needs may be active to some degree at the same time.)

Maslow's hierarchy can be envisioned as a stepladder, as in Figure 11.2. The lower-level needs (once satisfied) become the foundations that trigger the potency of higher-order needs.[5]

Physiological Needs. People are born with certain physiological needs. These are the most basic needs, including the needs for food, drink, and shelter.

Safety Needs. Maslow says that when these physiological needs are reasonably satisfied—when a person is no longer thirsty and has enough to eat, for instance—then the safety needs become potent or aroused. In other words, if you are starving or in the middle of a desert with nothing to drink, the lower-level need for food or water will drive your behaviour, and you might even risk your life and safety by pursuing that need. But once you have enough to eat or to drink, your personal safety, security, and protection motivate your behaviour.

Social Needs. Once you feel reasonably secure and have had enough to eat and drink, social needs begin to drive your behaviour, says Maslow. These are the needs people have for affiliation, for giving and receiving affection, and for friendship.

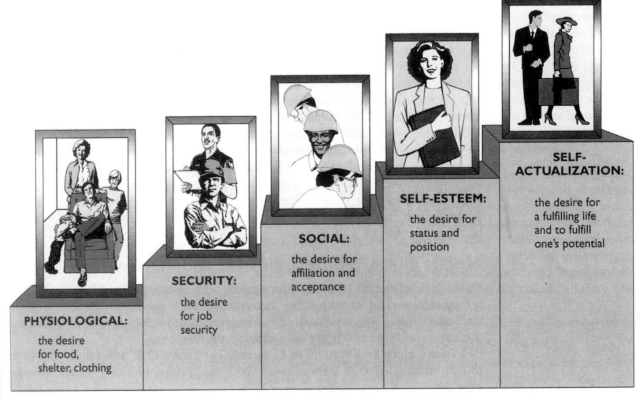

FIGURE 11.2
Maslow's Hierarchy of Needs

Self-Esteem Needs. At level four are the self-esteem needs. Psychologist Douglas McGregor says these include the following:

1. Those needs that relate to one's self-esteem—needs for self-confidence, independence, achievement, competence, and knowledge.

2. Those needs that relate to one's reputation—needs for status, recognition, appreciation, and the deserved respect of others.[6]

Like the social and safety needs, self-esteem needs only begin to motivate behaviour when the lower-level needs have been fairly well satisfied, according to Maslow. But McGregor and other psychologists argue that there is a big difference between self-esteem needs and lower-level physiological, safety, and social needs: Higher-level needs for things like self-respect and recognition are insatiable—we never get enough of such things. Lower-level needs are relatively easily satisfied.

Self-Actualization Needs. Finally, there is an ultimate need that only begins to dominate someone's behaviour once all lower-level needs have been reasonably well satisfied. This is the need for self-actualization or fulfilment, the need we all have to become the person we feel we have the potential to become. Self-actualization needs, as McGregor says, motivate us to realize our own potential, continue self-development, and be creative in the broadest sense of the word.

Herzberg's Two-Factor Approach to Motivation

Frederick Herzberg divides Maslow's hierarchy into a lower-level (physiological, safety, social) and a higher-level (ego, self-actualization) set of needs, and says that the best way to motivate someone is to offer to satisfy the person's higher-level needs.

Hygienes and Motivators. Herzberg believes that the factors (which he calls *hygienes*) that can satisfy lower-level needs are different from those (which he calls *motivators*) that can satisfy (or partially satisfy) a person's higher-level needs. He says that if hygiene factors (factors outside the job itself, such as working conditions, salary, and supervision) are inadequate, employees will become dissatisfied. But—and this is extremely important—adding more of these hygiene factors (like salary) to the job is a very bad way to try to motivate someone, because lower-level needs (such as physiological and security needs) are quickly satisfied. Next week or next month the employee is again dissatisfied, saying, in effect, "What have you done for me lately? I want another raise." Offering more hygienes is therefore an inefficient way to motivate employees. Robert Glegg, president of Glegg Water Conditioning Inc., agrees with Herzberg. He says that paying someone a lot of money is never enough by itself; it simply removes a possible negative.[7]

Glegg Water
Conditioning
www.glegg.com

On the other hand, says Herzberg, "job content" or "motivator" factors that are intrinsic to the work itself (like opportunities for achievement, recognition, responsibility, and more challenge) can motivate employees. They appeal to employees' higher-level needs for achievement and self-actualization. These are needs that are never completely satisfied and for which most people have an infinite craving. Thus, according to Herzberg, the best way to motivate employees is to build challenge and opportunities for achievement into their jobs. That way, even the prospect of doing the job may motivate the employee, much as the thought of doing a favourite hobby may motivate you.

Needs for Affiliation, Power, and Achievement

David McClelland and John Atkinson agree with Herzberg that higher-level needs are most important at work. They have studied three needs that they believe to be especially important—the needs for affiliation, power, and achievement. To understand the nature of these needs, try the following exercise.

Take a quick look (just 10 to 15 seconds) at Figure 11.3. Now, allow yourself up to five minutes to write a short essay about the picture, touching on the following questions:

FIGURE 11.3
What's Happening Here?

1. What is happening? Who are the people?

2. What has led up to this situation? That is, what happened in the past?

3. What is being thought? What is wanted? By whom?

4. What will happen? What will be done?

Remember that the questions are only guides for your thinking, so don't just answer each one. Instead, make your story continuous and let your imagination roam, since no one is going to see your essay except you. Once you have finished writing, resume reading with the next paragraph.

The picture in Figure 11.3 is one of a group of pictures that makes up a test called the Thematic Apperception Test, which McClelland and his associates use to identify a person's needs. You will notice that the picture is intentionally ambiguous, so when you wrote your essay you were supposedly reading into the picture ideas that reflected your own needs and drives. McClelland has found that this test can be useful for identifying the level of a person's achievement, power, and affiliation needs.[8]

The Need for Achievement. People who are high in the need to achieve have a predisposition to strive for success. They are highly motivated to obtain the satisfaction that comes from accomplishing a challenging task or goal. They prefer tasks in which there is a reasonable chance of success and avoid those that are either too easy or too difficult. Such people prefer getting specific, timely criticism and feedback about their performance. People with a high need for achievement like situations in which they can take personal responsibility for finding solutions to problems, prefer to set moderate achievement goals and take calculated risks, and want concrete feedback on how well they are doing.

Achievement motivation is present in your essay when any one of the following three things occurs:

1. Someone in the story is concerned about a standard of excellence: For example, he wants to win or do well in a competition, or has self-imposed standards for a good performance. Standards of excellence can be inferred by the use of words such as *good* or *better* to evaluate performance.

2. Someone in the story is involved in a unique accomplishment, such as an invention or an artistic creation.

3. Someone in the story is involved in a long-term goal, such as having a specific career or being a success in life.

The Need for Power. People with a strong need for power desire to influence others directly by making suggestions, giving their opinions and evaluations, and trying to talk others into things. They enjoy roles requiring persuasion, such as teaching and public speaking, as well as positions as leaders and clergymen. How the need for power manifests itself exactly depends on the person's other needs. Thus, a person with a high need for power but a low need for warm, supportive relationships might become dictatorial, while one with high needs for comradeship might become a clergyman or a social worker.

Power motivation is present in your essay when any of the following three things occurs:

1. Someone in the story shows affection or is emotionally concerned about getting or maintaining control of the means of influencing a person. Wanting to win a point, to show dominance, to convince someone, or to gain a position of control—as well as wanting to avoid weakness or humiliation—are obvious examples.[9]

2. Someone is actually doing something to get or keep control of the means of influence, such as arguing, demanding or forcing, giving a command, trying to convince, or punishing.

3. Your story involves an interpersonal relationship that is culturally defined as one in which a superior has control of the means of influencing a subordinate. For example, a boss is giving orders to a subordinate, or a parent is ordering a child to shape up.

The Need for Affiliation. People with a strong need for affiliation are highly motivated to maintain strong, warm relationships with friends and relations. In group meetings they try to establish friendly relationships, often by being agreeable or by giving emotional support.[10] Affiliation motivation is present in your essay when one of the following three things occurs:

1. Someone in the story is concerned about establishing, maintaining, or restoring a positive emotional relationship with another person. Friendship is the most basic example, such as when your story emphasizes that the individuals are friends. Other relationships, such as father–son, reflect affiliation motivation only if they have the warm, compassionate quality implied by the need for affiliation.

2. One person likes or wants to be liked by someone else, or someone has some similar feeling about another. Similarly, affiliation motivation is present if someone is expressing sorrow or grief about a broken relationship.

3. Affiliation motivation is also present if your essay mentions such affiliative activities as parties, reunions, visits, or relaxed small talk, as in a bull session. Friendly actions such as consoling or being concerned about the well-being or happiness of another person usually reflect a need for affiliation.

Remember that this exercise represents only one of several that constitute the Thematic Apperception Test, and it can therefore give you only the most tentative impressions about what your needs are. It should, however, give you a better understanding of what the needs for achievement, power, and affiliation are and how they manifest themselves.

Employee Needs and Common Sense

As you know from your own experience, what appeals to one person may be inconsequential to another, so you've got to use common sense when applying your knowledge of human motives and needs.

You see examples of this almost every day. One driver may find the risks involved with speeding and cutting from lane to lane to be exciting. Another prefers the security of a more temperate pace, and the quiet enjoyment of some music by Brahms. At work, one manager may drive herself relentlessly to obtain a promotion, while another manager, while equally secure, is happier on a slower track if that means spending more time with his spouse.

Different needs also drive our career choices, often without us even knowing it. For example, psychologist Edgar Schein says that as you learn more about yourself, it becomes apparent that you have a dominant *career anchor, a concern or value that you will not give up if a choice has to be made.* Based on his study of MIT graduates, Schein identified five career anchors.

Some people had a strong *technical/functional* career anchor. They made decisions that enabled them to remain in their chosen technical or functional fields. Some had *managerial competence* as a career anchor. They showed a strong motivation to become managers and (as we first mentioned in Chapter 1), they had the analytical, interpersonal, and emotional competence to be successful managers. Some of the graduates were driven by a need for expressing their *creativity.* Many of them went on to be successful entrepreneurs, or to somehow build their personal fortune by using their creative abilities (for example, by purchasing, restoring, and then renting homes).

Others made their career decisions based on their need for *autonomy* and *independence.* These people seemed driven by the need to be on their own, free from the dependence that can arise when a person elects to work in a large organization. Finally, some of the graduates were mostly concerned with long-term career stability and job *security;* they seemed willing to do what was required to maintain job security, a decent income, and a stable future in the form of a good retirement program and benefits.[11]

Findings like these mean that it's dangerous to generalize when it comes to talking about needs. One of your employees may be motivated by a significant raise, while another will prefer the security of an employment contract. People even differ in what they need to be recognized for. Some people value dependability and responsibility, and prefer that their supervisors recognize them for things like follow-through, dedication, and loyalty. Others value risk-taking action and the ability to act under pressure, and want to be recognized for responsiveness, cleverness, and ingenuity.[12] Thus, theories like those of Maslow, while useful as approximations, always need to be adjusted to the actual situation you face.

The bottom line is that you have to use common sense and apply your experience when thinking about and motivating employees. Teams, for instance, are so important at GE that the atmosphere has been described as like "tribal communities." For example, "there are rules, rituals, and folklore; there are tribal loyalties and tribal accountability."[13] This is obviously not the kind of atmosphere that appeals to everyone. The company therefore takes great pains to select employees whose needs—for affiliation and for security, for instance—are consistent with this kind of plant; mavericks and loners needn't apply.

Process Approaches to Motivating Employees

Process approaches to motivating employees explain motivation in terms of the decision-making process through which motivation takes place. Here we'll focus on the work of psychologists J.S. Adams, Edwin Locke, and Victor Vroom.

equity theory
A theory that assumes that people have a need for, and therefore value and seek, fairness at work.

Adams' Equity Theory

Adams' **equity theory** assumes that people have a need for, and therefore value and seek, fairness at work.[14] People are strongly motivated to maintain a balance between what they perceive as their inputs or contributions, and their rewards. Equity theory states that if a person perceives an inequity, a tension or drive will develop in the person's mind, and the person will be motivated to reduce or eliminate the tension and perceived inequity. The directors of MacMillan-Bloedel were embarrassed to read in the newspaper that their CEO was receiving substantially less compensation than other CEOs in the industry; they raised his salary by 60 percent.[15]

On the whole, empirical findings regarding underpayment, at least, are consistent with Adams' theory. For example, people paid on a piece-rate basis, per item produced, typically boost quantity and reduce quality when they believe that they are underpaid. Those paid a straight hourly rate tend to reduce both quantity and quality when they think they're underpaid. Unfortunately, overpayment inequity does not seem to have the positive effects on either quantity or quality that Adams' theory would predict.[16] (See Figure 11.4.)

Locke's Goal Theory of Motivation

The goal theory of motivation assumes that once someone decides to pursue a goal, the person regulates his or her behaviour to try to ensure that the goal is reached.[17] Locke and his colleagues contend that a person's goals provide the mechanism through which unsatisfied needs are translated into action.[18] In other words, unsatisfied needs prompt the person to seek ways to satisfy those needs; the person then formulates goals that prompt action.[19] For example, a person needs to self-actualize and wants to be an artist. To do so, she must go to college for a fine arts degree, so she sets the goal of graduating from McGill University's fine arts program. That goal (which is prompted by her need) then motivates her behaviour.

Most of the research in this area has been conducted in laboratory settings, with undergraduates as subjects. Although such findings may not necessarily apply to industrial settings, they do tend to support Locke's basic theory. The most consistent finding here is that people who are assigned or who adopt difficult and specific goals outperform people who are simply told to "do their best."[20]

Such findings have recently been extended to field settings. Here the evidence suggests rather strongly that people who are given or who adopt specific and difficult goals tend to outperform people without such performance goals.[21] At Campbell Soup's Toronto plant, for example, 120 000 cases of defective soup were sitting in the warehouse. Employees set a goal to cut that number in half within three months. The inventory was reduced to only 20 000 cases by the target date. Another goal was to reduce costs to the level of the most efficient Campbell's plant in the U.S. At that time, it cost $3.87 more to produce a case of soup in Ontario than it did in Campbell's North Carolina plant. Within one year, the difference had dropped to only 32 cents.[22]

Campbell Soup
www.campbellsoup. com

	Employee thinks he or she is underpaid	Employee thinks he or she is overpaid
Piece-rate Basis	Quality down Quantity the same or up	Quantity the same or down Quality up
Salary Basis	Quantity or quality should go down	Quantity or quality should go up

FIGURE 11.4
How a Perceived Inequity Affects Performance
According to equity theory, how a person reacts to under- or overpayment depends on whether he or she is paid on a piece-rate or salary basis.

Vroom's Expectancy Theory of Motivation

According to Victor Vroom, a person's motivation to exert a certain level of effort is a function of three things, expressed as follows: Motivation = E x I x V,[23] where

E represents the person's **expectancy** (in terms of probability) that his or her effort will lead to performance

I represents **instrumentality**, or the perceived relationship between successful performance and obtaining the reward

V represents **valence**, which represents the perceived value the person attaches to the reward.[24]

expectancy
The probability that a person's effort will lead to performance.

instrumentality
The perceived relationship between successful performance and obtaining a reward.

valence
The perceived value a person attaches to a reward.

If all three elements are high, a person will be very highly motivated. If any one of the three elements is close to zero, however, the person's motivation level will be very low. This is because the three variables are multiplied by each other, and any number multiplied by zero equals zero.

Consider, for example, what might happen in a course that you are not interested in but are forced to take as part of your curriculum. There may not be many desired outcomes for you in such a course (valence is low or negative). In addition, assume that you have heard that former students could not see any relationship between the amount of time they spent studying for exams in the course and the grade they got on exams (expectancy is low). This leads them to conclude that there is no connection between performance and rewards. In this situation, it is very likely that you will not be motivated to work hard in the course.

Research generally supports Vroom's theory, particularly in studies focusing on job choice. The results suggest that expectation, instrumentality, and valence combine to influence a person's motivation to choose specific jobs.[25] Recent studies of the expectancy approach also provide moderate to strong support for its usefulness in explaining and predicting work motivation.[26] Note that Vroom makes no mention of needs or motives.

Learning/Reinforcement Approaches to Motivating Employees

learning
A relatively permanent change in a person that occurs as a result of experience.

Learning can be defined as a relatively permanent change in a person that occurs as a result of experience.[27] For example, we learn as children that being courteous is rewarded by our parents, and so we may be motivated to be courteous throughout our lives. There are several theories about how people learn. In this section we'll focus on what may be called learning/reinforcement approaches to motivating employees, namely, on how people's behaviour is molded by the consequences or results of their actions.

Psychologist B.F. Skinner conducted many of the early studies in this area. Let's apply his theory to a simple example. Suppose you wanted to train your dog to roll over. How would you do it? In all likelihood, you would encourage the dog to roll over (perhaps by gently nudging it down and around) and then would reward it with some treat. Fairly quickly, no doubt, your dog would learn that if it wanted a treat it would have to roll over. Before you knew it, Fido would be rolling through your house.

operant behaviour
Behaviour in which one operates on one's environment.

contingent reward
A reward given only when a person exhibits a certain behaviour that is desired.

In Skinner's theory, the dog's rolling over would be called **operant behaviour**, because it *operates* on its environment, specifically by causing its owner to give it a treat. (So, who's training whom, you might ask!) In operant conditioning the main question is how to strengthen the association between the **contingent reward** (here the treat) and the operant behaviour.[28]

Behaviour Modification

The principles of operant conditioning are applied at work through behaviour modification. **Behaviour modification** means changing or modifying behaviour through the use of contingent rewards or punishment. It is built on two principles: (1) behaviour that appears to lead to a positive consequence (reward) tends to be repeated, whereas behaviour that appears to lead to a negative consequence (punishment) tends not to be repeated; and (2) therefore, by providing the properly scheduled rewards, it is possible to get a person to learn to change his or her behaviour.[29] There are two elements in behaviour modification: the types of reinforcement (reward or punishment) and the schedules of reinforcement.

Types of Reinforcement. There are several types of reinforcement. **Positive reinforcement** occurs when a pleasant stimulus is presented to a person. It increases the likelihood that a behaviour will be repeated. For example, if an employee does a job well and is complimented on it by the boss, the probability that the employee will repeat the behaviour is increased.

Negative reinforcement occurs when an unpleasant stimulus is withheld from a person. Negative reinforcement also increases the likelihood that a behaviour will be repeated, but here the individual exhibits the desired behaviour in order to avoid something unpleasant. Suppose an employee knows that arriving late will cause a reprimand from the boss. The employee arrives on time to avoid the reprimand.

Omission occurs when a pleasant stimulus is withheld from the person. Omission decreases the likelihood that behaviour will occur in the future. When a manager ignores an employee who spends a lot of time playing practical jokes, omission is occurring. Although this approach involves doing nothing, it does have an effect on behaviour. Since reinforced behaviour has a greater chance of recurring, it follows that not reinforcing behaviour reduces the chance that it will happen again.

Punishment occurs when an unpleasant stimulus is presented to a person. Punishment also decreases the likelihood of the behaviour occurring again. For example, when an employee arrives late to work, the boss may berate the employee. This decreases the chance the behaviour will recur in the future. Note that in punishment, an unpleasant stimulus is presented, while in negative reinforcement an unpleasant stimulus is withheld. Punishment discourages certain behaviours, while negative reinforcement encourages certain behaviours.

Schedules of Reinforcement. In this section, we look at the *timing* of the above-mentioned reinforcements. Two basic schedules can be used: continuous and intermittent. In a **continuous reinforcement schedule**, a reward or a punishment follows each time the behaviour of interest occurs. Thus, a parent may praise a child each time a puzzle is done correctly, or a boss may punish a worker each time an error is made. This type of schedule increases the desired response, but if the schedule is not maintained, the response decreases rapidly.

In a partial, or **intermittent reinforcement schedule**, the behaviour of interest is rewarded or punished only some of the time. The general result is that learning is more enduring in this type of schedule than in continuous schedules. Intermittent schedules of reinforcement are relatively slow in stimulating the desired behaviour, but once established, the behaviour tends to last. They are therefore useful for managers.

In a **fixed interval schedule**, a reinforcement is applied after a certain time period has passed, regardless of the number of responses that has occurred. A manager may visit a certain department once every fifth day, or workers may be paid once every two weeks. In a **variable interval schedule**, a reinforcement is applied after a varying amount of time has passed, regardless of the number of desired responses that has occurred. A manager may visit a certain department once a week, but subordinates don't know which day the visit will take place. Or, a manager may praise (or punish) a subordinate only some of the time the person does a good (or poor) job.

In a **fixed ratio schedule**, a reinforcement is applied after a fixed number of desired behavioural responses has occurred, regardless of the time that has passed. For example, the department manager may come to the department and congratulate the members

---

behaviour modification
Changing or modifying behaviour through the use of contingent rewards or punishment.

positive reinforcement
When a pleasant stimulus is presented to a person, the desired behaviour is likely to be repeated.

negative reinforcement
When a pleasant stimulus is withheld from a person, the desired behaviour will likely be repeated.

omission
Omission decreases the likelihood that a behaviour will occur in the future when a pleasant stimulus is withheld.

punishment
Punishment decreases the likelihood of a behaviour recurring when an unpleasant stimulus is presented.

continuous reinforcement schedule
According to this schedule, a reward or punishment follows each time the behaviour of interest occurs.

intermittent reinforcement schedule
When the behaviour of interest is rewarded or punished only some of the time.

fixed interval schedule
Regardless of the number of responses that has occurred, a reinforcement is employed after a set period of time has passed.

variable interval schedule
A reinforcement is used after a varying amount of time has passed, despite the number of desired responses that has occurred.

fixed ratio schedule
After a fixed number of desired behavioural responses has occurred, a reinforcement is applied, regardless of the time that has passed.

variable ratio schedule
Behaviour is reinforced
after a varying number of
responses has occurred.

every fourth time they achieve their production quota, or employees may be paid on a piece-rate or commission basis. In a **variable ratio schedule**, behaviours are reinforced after a varying number of responses has occurred; sometimes a reinforcement occurs after 3 responses, sometimes after 10, sometimes after 50, and so on. A manager following this schedule may come through a department irregularly, without the workers knowing why or when. All they know is that at apparently random times their boss visits and reinforces their behaviour (positively or negatively).

Does Behaviour Modification Improve Performance?

There seems little doubt that, used appropriately, organizational behaviour modification can significantly improve employee performance. One recent review of 19 prior studies of the effect of behaviour modification[30] yielded the following conclusions:[31]

1. Organizational behaviour modification is effective, regardless of the type of company and reward. Behaviour modification generally improves worker performance by 17 percent.

2. When financial rewards were used with non-financial ones (like recognition) there was a 30 percent performance improvement in service firms, almost twice the effect of the individual reinforcers.

3. Performance feedback—telling the employee how he or she is doing, and reinforcing performance—helped improve productivity in manufacturing firms by 41 percent on average.

4. Paying attention to employees and providing recognition raised productivity in service firms by 15 percent.

5. The effect of behaviour modification and how it's used seems to depend on the kind of company. Overall, organizational behaviour modification had stronger effects in manufacturing than in service organizations. In manufacturing firms, combining financial rewards with non-financial reinforcement (such as performance feedback) didn't seem to result in substantially higher performance than just using non-financial rewards themselves. On the other hand (as noted in 2, above), combining financial rewards with non-financial ones did create much stronger effects in service firms.

Motivation in Action: 10 Methods for Influencing Behaviour and Motivating Employees

Translating Theory into Practice

As a leader, you'll want to size up the leadership situation and (1) identify what is happening, (2) account for what is happening, and (3) formulate an action or response. Knowledge about things like perception, self-efficacy, self-concept, and the three approaches to motivating employees (needs-based, process-based, and learning/reinforcement) gives you tools for identifying what is happening and accounting for it. These behavioural tools can then also help you formulate an action or response, using one (or more) of the 10 motivation methods discussed in the next few pages.

One reason these motivation methods are widely used is the fact that they have strong foundations in organizational behaviour (OB) and motivation theory and research. Table 11.1 presents these foundations. For example, *empowering employees* (column 7) is based in part on self-efficacy—namely, on the idea that people differ in their estimates of how they'll perform on a task. Therefore, building their skills and self-confidence by empowering them should bolster their self-efficacy and thus their motivation.

Using Pay for Performance

Pay for performance is probably the first thing that comes to mind when most people think about motivating employees. Pay for performance refers to any compensation method that ties pay to the quantity or quality of work the person produces. (The People Side of Managing box on pages 354–55 describes the incentive programs that have been instituted at several Canadian companies as a means to motivate employees.) Piecework pay plans are probably the most familiar: Here earnings are tied directly to what the worker produces in the form of a "piece rate" for each unit he or she turns out. Thus, if Tom Smith gets 40 cents per piece for stamping out circuit boards, he would make $40 for stamping out 100 a day and $80 for stamping out 200. Sales commissions are another familiar example of pay for performance.

pay for performance
Any compensation method that ties pay to the quantity or quality of work the person produces.

Piecework plans have a firm foundation in motivation theory. Vroom's expectancy approach describes motivation as depending on employees seeing the link between performance and rewards, and pay for performance plans should emphasize precisely that. Similarly, behaviour modification emphasizes that people will continue behaviour that is rewarded, and pay for performance plans, of course, tie rewards directly to behaviour.

New pay for performance plans are becoming popular. **Variable pay plans**, for example, are essentially plans that put some portion of the employee's pay at risk, subject to the firm's meeting its financial goals. For example, employees might voluntarily place up to 5 percent of their base pay at risk. If they then meet the department's earnings projections, they would get that 5 percent back *plus* additional percentages, depending on how much the department exceeded its earnings projections.

variable pay plans
Plans that put some portion of the employee's pay at risk, subject to the firm's meeting its financial goals.

Other companies have gainsharing plans that engage many or all employees in a common effort to achieve a company's productivity goals.[32] Implementing a gainsharing plan requires several steps. Specific performance measures, such as cost per unit produced, are chosen, as is a funding formula, such as "47 percent of savings go to employees." Management thus decides how to divide and distribute cost savings between the employees and the company, and among employees themselves. If employees are then able to achieve cost savings in line with their performance goals, they share in the resulting gains.

Pay for performance plans of all types—including those that let employees share in profits by paying them with shares of company stock—are becoming more popular because they make sense.

A lot more employers are getting the stock options message. For example, when Jim Eckel went to his first interview with Starbucks in 1994 he didn't pay much attention to the stock option plan (affectionately known as Bean Stock within the company). But today, as manager of a Starbucks in Manhattan's Upper West Side, Jim Eckel is reportedly a champion of the plan.[33] In fact, as in an increasing number of companies such as IBM provide stock options to employees, Jim and about 30 000 other Starbucks "partners" are part of a new movement in compensation management: Stock options for everyone.

As Bradley Honeycutt, vice-president of human resources services at Starbucks puts it, "we established Bean Stock in 1991 as a way of investing in our partners and creating ownership across the company...it's been a key to retaining good people and building loyalty."[34] By letting all or most employees participate in this way, each employee has a built-in opportunity to see how performance and hard work translate into a rising stock price—and thus more rewards for them.

Not all pay for performance plans succeed. However, the following five suggestions make success more likely, given what we've discussed about motivation.

1. *Ensure that effort and rewards are directly related.* Your incentive plan should reward employees in direct proportion to their increased productivity. Employees

TABLE 11.1 *The Motivational Underpinnings of 10 Motivation Methods*

FOUNDATIONS OF BEHAVIOUR AND MOTIVATION	Pay for Performance	Merit Raises
Self-Concept: People seek to fulfil their potential.		
Self-Efficacy: People differ in their estimates of how they'll perform on a task; self-efficacy influences effort.		
Maslow Needs Hierarchy: High-level needs are never totally satisfied and aren't aroused until lower-level needs are satisfied.		X
Alderfer: All needs may be active, to some degree, at same time.		X
McClelland Ach, Pow, Aff: Needs for achievement, power, affiliation are especially important in work setting.		
Herzberg Dual Factor: Extrinsic factors just prevent dissatisfaction; intrinsic factors motivate workers.		
Vroom Expectancy Approach: Motivation is a function of expectancy that effort leads to performance, performance leads to reward, and reward is valued.	X	X
Locke Goal Setting: People are motivated to achieve goals they consciously set.		
Adams' Equity Theory: People are motivated to maintain balance between their perceived inputs and outputs.		X
Reinforcement: People will continue behaviour that is rewarded and cease behaviour that is punished.	X	X

must also perceive that they can actually do the tasks required. Thus the standard has to be attainable and you have to provide the necessary tools, equipment, and training.[35]

2. *Make the plan understandable and easily calculable by the employees.* Employees should be able to calculate easily the rewards they will receive for various levels of effort.

3. *Set effective standards.* The standards should be viewed as fair by your subordinates. They should be high but reasonable; there should be about a 50-50 chance of success. The goal should also be specific; this is much more effective than telling someone to "do your best."

4. *Guarantee your standards.* View the standard as a contract with your employees. Once the plan is operational use great caution before decreasing the size of the incentive in any way.[36]

5. *Guarantee a base rate.* It's often advisable to give employees a safety net by providing them with a base rate pay. They'll know that no matter what happens, they can at least earn a minimum guaranteed base rate.[37]

Using Merit Pay

Most employees, when they do a good job, expect to be rewarded with at least a merit raise at the end of the year. A merit raise is a salary increase—usually permanent—that

MOTIVATION METHODS							
Spot Rewards	Skill-Based Pay	Recognition Awards	Job Redesign	Empower Employees	Goal Setting	Positive Reinforcement	Lifelong Learning
	X	X	X	X			X
	X			X			X
X		X	X	X			X
X		X	X	X			X
	X	X	X	X			X
			X	X			X
X		X			X		
				X	X		
X		X					
X		X				X	

is based on the employee's individual performance. It is different from a bonus in that it represents a continuing increment, whereas the bonus represents a one-time payment. Gradually, however, traditional merit raises are being replaced by lump-sum merit raises, which are merit raises awarded in one lump sum that do not become part of the employee's continuing pay.[38]

To the extent that it is actually tied to performance, the prospect of a merit raise may focus the employee's attention on the link between performance and rewards, in line with the expectancy approach to motivation. If it is equitably distributed (which means, among other things, that performance must be evaluated fairly and accurately), a merit raise can enable employees to see the link between their perceived inputs and outputs, in line with Adams' equity approach to motivation.

However, relying too heavily on merit raises for rewards is a bit dangerous. A year is a long time to wait for a reward, so the reinforcement benefits of merit pay are somewhat suspect. You may also have personally experienced the questionable nature of some performance appraisal systems, including the fact that some supervisors take the easy way out and rate everyone's performance about the same, regardless of actual effort. Such problems can undermine the motivational basis for the merit plan and render it useless.[39]

Using "Spot Awards"

As its name implies, a spot award is a financial award given to an employee literally "on the spot," as soon as the laudable performance is observed. Programs like this have actually

Incentives and Motivations

Canadian companies are realizing that offering incentives beyond the normal benefits can result in creative ideas as well as in large increases in employee productivity. These incentives may be monetary or non-monetary. Consider the following:

Proctor & Redfern
www.pandrint.com

Pitney Bowes
www.pitneybowes.
com

Manitoba Telephone
System
www.mts.mb.ca

SkyDome
www.skydome.com

- At BC Tel (now called Telus), a suggestion system was implemented that gives cash rewards to employees for ideas that generate revenue or save the company money. The employee receives 10 percent of the money the company saves or the revenue generated (employees have received up to $20 000 for ideas).

- Drexis Inc. recently flew 12 employees and their families to Disney World as a reward for increasing sales by over 100 percent in one year.

- Proctor & Redfern Ltd., a consulting engineering firm, lets high achievers serve on committees with senior executives, represent the firm at outside functions, or enroll in development courses where the company pays the bill.

- Avatar Communications Inc. sent employees on a weeklong Outward Bound expedition into the wilderness. The trip had both reward and motivational components.

- Pitney Bowes Canada Ltd. sent 60 of its top salespeople and their spouses to Hong Kong after they achieved 135 percent of their sales quota (salespeople who achieved 112 percent received a trip to San Diego).

- Manitoba Telephone System instituted a suggestion system called IDEA$PLUS, which gives employees cash awards up to $10 000 for good ideas.

- At Toronto's SkyDome, employees are given coupons for exceptional service, such as finding a lost child or repairing a broken seat. The coupons can be used to accumulate points, which can be redeemed for prizes.

- At Ford Motor Company, workers are rewarded for suggestions that save the company money. For example, when a metal press operator found a way to save on the amount of sheet metal used in floor panels, the company gave $14 000 of the $70 000 first-year savings back to the worker. A recent study shows that activity like this has an effect—it takes workers at Ford one-third less time to build a car than workers at GM.

Incentives are important for top managers as well. The higher a manager is placed in a firm, the more likely it is that a good chunk of the manager's pay will be performance-based. A Conference Board of Canada study of executive compensation in Canada showed that up to 40 percent of top executives' total compensation comes in the form of incentives. For lower-level managers, the figure was 20 percent, and for other employees it was 10 percent. Top managers in the United States often receive up to 60 percent of their total compensation in the form of incentives. Most Canadian companies have set up some type of incentive plan for their senior executives.

Incentive systems must be carefully developed, or they will not motivate employee behaviour in the right direction. In addition to the usual sales and profit goals, firms are beginning to look at incentive systems that reward managers for achieving goals like effective downsizing, increasing environmental consciousness, and improving the corporate culture. A decision must also be made about whether the incentive system will be directed at individual employees or groups. Historically, incentives have been directed at individuals, but with the new emphasis on teamwork in organizations, this is changing.

→

Now, a group may get an incentive if it gets a new product launched on time.

Incentive systems must be used with care because they may unintentionally motivate employees to engage in undesirable behaviour. In the sale of mutual funds, for example, brokers are often given bonuses for making sales. Super salespeople may be given trips to exotic locations in return for making their sales goals. This may motivate the salesperson to push a product or service that doesn't really meet the customers' needs.

been around for some time. For example, Thomas J. Watson, Sr., founder of IBM, reportedly wrote cheques on the spot to employees who were doing an outstanding job.[40]

Such cash awards are increasingly used. At Federal Express, for example, workers receive immediate awards for outstanding performance. The average value of vouchers that are given out is about $50, and these may be in the form of a cheque or some other form of reward, such as dinner vouchers or theatre tickets.[41] At Remington Products, a $25 000 discretionary fund is maintained so that supervisors can give awards to workers who are spotted doing an exceptional job. The president of the firm then invites the winners to his office and gives them cheques ranging from $200 to $500.[42]

Remington Products
www.remington-products.com

In companies using spot rewards, the question of what qualifies for an award is up to the giver. There are no strict rules regarding what does or does not deserve a bonus, and a manager does not have to approve it. If the recipient (in the giver's eyes) does something exceptional—stays really late on a project, for instance, or meets an impossible deadline—the giver simply fills out a card indicating the amount of the bonus, and then the recipients can spend it as he or she likes. The award comes enclosed in a thank-you card that encourages the employee to pamper himself or herself in any way that he or she prefers. Most employees reportedly use the award for a fancy dinner, a show, or a day at a spa.

Spot rewards like these have a sound basis in what we know about motivation. For example, to the extent that the rewards are both contingent on good performance and awarded immediately, they are certainly consistent with equity theory, the expectancy approach, reinforcing desired behaviour, and providing the recognition that most people desire.

Using Skill-Based Pay

In most companies, pay is determined by the level of responsibility inherent in a particular job. Thus, presidents generally make more than vice-presidents, sales managers make more than assistant sales managers, and secretary IVs make more than secretary IIIs.

Skill-based pay is different in that you are paid for the range, depth, and types of skills and knowledge you are capable of using, rather than for the job you currently hold.[43] The difference is important: In a company with a skill-based pay plan it is conceivable that a secretary III could be paid more per hour than a secretary IV, for instance, if the person who happens to be the secretary III has more skills than the person in the secretary IV job.

General Mills
www.generalmills.com

A skill-based pay plan was implemented at a General Mills manufacturing facility.[44] In this case, General Mills was trying to boost the flexibility of its factory workforce by implementing a pay plan that would encourage all employees to develop a wider range of skills. In turn, that wider range of skills would make it easier for employees to take over whatever job needed to be done in the plant as the plant's needs changed.

In this plant, therefore, the workers were paid based on their attained skill levels. For each of the several types of jobs in the plant, workers could attain three levels of skill: limited ability (ability to perform simple tasks without direction); partial proficiency (ability to apply more advanced principles on the job); and full competence (ability to analyze

Going Online with Incentives

Check out popular Web sites today and you will see that many are using online incentives to attract crowds to their sites.[45] For example, online travel sites like Travelocity offer online-only specials and online bookstores like Amazon.com routinely use incentives to attract customers to their site. Amazon.com also runs contests, like one in which customers could win thousand-dollar prizes by helping to complete a story whose first paragraph was written by the famous author John Updike.

Chapter's online discount provides a real incentive to Web-savvy book lovers.

Companies are also using technology to improve the effectiveness of their employee incentive programs. For example, "New software charts participants' standings and painlessly tallies the final numbers, [and] e-mail can be used to send reminders and encouragement too—like '10 more days to sell, sell, sell!' or 'Think Hawaii!'"[46] Other companies are using their intranets to publicize incentive program rules, award details, prize catalogues, and current status to incentive-plan participants. They offer employees exotic prizes like a trip to Tahiti. Some companies use their intranets to provide links to the destination's Internet site.

Software packages help many companies to design and manage employee incentive programs. For example, ASPIRE 1.5 (Automated System Promoting Incentives that Reward Excellence) takes incentive planners through the steps required to design a corporate incentive program. The HR department can use the program to indicate how the winners will be judged (such as percentage of sales growth over past performance) and to choose the rewards from a menu of incentives options (such as travel, gifts, cheques, or even paid time off from the office). Another program, called Motivation Magic, helps incentive planners to custom design corporate award programs; it comes with a database containing suggestions for all types of incentives, as well as a design checklist, a program timeline, and functions for charting results. Another package—Bob Nelson's Reward Wizard— "keeps performance records for all employees in a department or organization, along with their career objectives, personal preferences, hobbies and family circumstances. Space is also provided to enter their accomplishments, award criteria, time allotted to win an award and individual award preferences."[47] Once it's up and running, Reward Wizard can generate prize suggestions adapted to each employee's needs, such as extra Mondays off for Gary and a bigger computer screen for Jeannine.

and solve problems associated with that job). After starting a job, workers were tested periodically to see whether they had earned certification at the next higher skill level. If so, they received higher pay even though they had the same job: In other words, higher-skilled workers on the same job received higher pay. Workers could then switch to other jobs in the plant, again starting at the lowest skill level and working their way up if they so desired. In this way the workers could earn more pay for more skills (particularly as they became skilled at a variety of jobs), and the company ended up with a more highly skilled and therefore more flexible workforce.

Skill-based pay makes sense in terms of what we know about motivation. People have a vision—a self-concept—of who they can be, and they seek to fulfil their potential. The individual development that is part and parcel of skill-based pay helps employees do exactly that. Skill-based pay also appeals to an employee's sense of self-efficacy in that the reward is a formal and concrete recognition that the person can do the more challenging job and do it well.

Using Recognition

If you've ever spent half a day cooking a meal for someone who gobbled it up without saying a word about it, or two weeks doing a report for a boss who didn't say, "Thanks" (let alone "Good job"), you know how important it can be to have your work recognized and appreciated.

Most people like to feel appreciated. In one study, respondents said that they highly valued day-to-day recognition from their supervisors, peers, and team members; over two-thirds said it was important to believe that their work was appreciated by others.[48]

Being recognized for a job well done—and not necessarily just financially—makes a lot of sense in terms of motivation theory. Immediate recognition can be a powerful reinforcer, for instance, and can provide some immediate outcomes to counterbalance the employees' inputs or efforts. Recognition also underscores the performance-reward-expectancy link, and it helps appeal to and satisfy the need that people have to achieve and to be recognized for their achievement.

At Cloverdale Paint, employees who come up with innovative ideas to improve customer service receive a personal letter from the president and a coffee mug or T-shirt bearing the company logo. The employee who makes the best suggestion of the year receives an engraved plaque, which is presented at a workplace ceremony. And Emery Apparel Canada Inc. conducts an annual "Oscar" awards ceremony. With great hoopla, the CEO asks for the envelope with the name of the winner of the top award. The Entrepreneurial Edge box examines one CEO's award-winning motivational strategies.

Using Job Redesign

Highly specialized, short-cycle, assembly-line jobs have long had a bad reputation among psychologists. Professor Chris Argyris, for instance, wrote that as people mature into adults they normally move from a position of dependence and narrow interests to one of

Rewards and recognition are important determinants of employee motivation. In 1998, the Financial Post *recognized Theresa Butcher, its head librarian, as an "unsung hero" for all of her help to reporters and editors over many years.*

Motivator of the Year

Eliassen Group
www.eliassen.com

Mona Eliassen, CEO and founder of the computer consulting firm Eliassen Group, won *Incentive* magazine's 1999 Motivator of the Year award. She started her business in 1989 with $50 000 that she borrowed from friends. Her company has expanded dramatically since then, with sales revenues of $29 million in 1997 and $40 million in 1998.

It is perhaps fitting that the *Mona Lisa* serves as this computer consulting and staffing firm's corporate symbol. While founder Mona Eliassen understands the need for basic incentive programs, she also recognizes that creative or artistic incentives are more effective and memorable. To achieve her goals, Eliassen rewards staff with "Mona Money," provides inspirational "Mona Messages," offers champagne toasts for a job well done, and encourages employees to "Devote-a-Day" to community service. "Mona is the driving force behind a lot of the community service events, but she's also a former salesperson who is very in tune with how to motivate salespeople. It's the best of both worlds with her," says Greg Hamilton, director of marketing for the company. "Some programs she developed on her own, others managers came up with. Regardless, she knows how to put us out of the daily grind."

In keeping with the company's corporate symbol (the *Mona Lisa* is a symbol of human talent, spirit, and achievement, according to Eliassen), a recent sales incentive sent a top earner to the Louvre in Paris to see the masterpiece. "At Eliassen we try to have a little fun rewarding employees," says Mona Eliassen. "We believe it's important not to offer trips here and there without purpose. Most of the awards are tied to a corporate theme, which we build upon during the year. The Louvre is a classic example of this. Such incentives clearly work in a high turnover industry. We have a very seasoned sales and recruiting staff."

The sales staff are not the only ones rewarded for their good work. The "Masterpiece Award" was created for office and administrative employees who "keep the machine oiled and running." Each month, a non-sales employee who has gone beyond the call of duty is recognized with a $25 gift certificate. At the end of the year, one of the 12 winners is randomly selected for an all-expenses-paid vacation in Bermuda.

Community service also plays an inspirational role at this thriving corporation. Employees are invited to "Devote-a-Day" to the community service program of their choice. In this way, it is not just about getting awards, but about giving back as well.

independence and broad interests and that specialized jobs fly in the face of individual development.[49] In fact, the negative impact of monotonous work has been substantiated. A recent study examined 1278 blue-collar workers in Israel.[50] The researchers concluded that (1) perceived monotony was moderately related to the objective work conditions, (2) some employees perceived even the same job as more monotonous than did other employees, (3) job satisfaction and psychological distress were related to perceived monotony, and (4) sickness absence was equally related to work conditions and to perceived monotony.

job design
The process of altering the nature and structure of jobs with the purpose of increasing employee satisfaction and productivity.

In the face of problems like these, many employers set up programs aimed at redesigning their workers' jobs. **Job design** is the process of altering the nature and structure of jobs with the purpose of increasing employee satisfaction and productivity. Many job design strategies have been tried, including job enlargement and job rotation, job enrichment, flextime, the compressed workweek, and job sharing.

Job Enlargement and Job Rotation. Initial attempts at job redesign centred on job enlargement and job rotation. **Job enlargement** assigns workers additional same-level tasks to increase the number of tasks they have to perform. For example, if the work is assembling chairs, the worker who previously only bolted the seat to the legs might take on the additional tasks of assembling the legs and attaching the back. **Job rotation** systematically moves workers from job to job. Thus, on an auto assembly line, a worker might spend an hour fitting doors, the next hour installing head lamps, the next hour fitting bumpers, and so on. At Abitibi-Price, lateral rotation of employees is done on a case-by-case basis. For example, a communication specialist might move temporarily into marketing or a human resources staff member might move into administration.[51]

Evidence regarding the effects of programs like these is somewhat contradictory. In one study the newly enlarged jobs initially led to improved job satisfaction, reduced boredom, and improved customer satisfaction (because one employee followed the customer's paperwork more or less from beginning to end).[52] However, in a follow-up study two years later, employee satisfaction had levelled off and boredom was on the rise again, suggesting that the motivational value of this technique may be short lived.[53]

Job Enrichment. Other psychologists, including Frederick Herzberg (recall his two-factor approach to motivating employees), contend that having several boring jobs to do instead of one is not what employees want. Psychologists like Herzberg, Maslow, and Alderfer believe that what employees want from their jobs is a sense of achievement from completing a challenging task successfully and the recognition that comes from using their skills and potential.

Job enrichment is the method that Herzberg recommends for applying his two-factor approach to motivation. **Job enrichment** means building motivators like opportunities for achievement into the job by making it more interesting and challenging. This is often accomplished by vertically loading the job, which means giving the worker more autonomy and allowing the worker to do much of the planning and inspection normally done by the supervisor. At Cadet Uniform of Toronto, for example, truck drivers have the authority to carry out some nontraditional functions, such as handling customer complaints.

Job enrichment can be accomplished in several ways:[54]

1. *Form natural work groups*. Change the job in such a way that each person is responsible for or "owns" an identifiable body of work. For example, instead of having the typist in a typing pool do work for all departments, make the work of one or two departments the continuing responsibility of each typist.

2. *Combine tasks*. Let one person assemble a product from start to finish, instead of having it go through several separate operations that are performed by different people. Combining tasks in this way is also often called job enlargement.

3. *Establish client relationships*. Let the worker have contact as often as possible with the client of that person's work. For example, let an assistant research and respond to customers' requests, instead of automatically referring all problems to his or her boss.

4. *Vertically load the job*. Have the worker plan and control his or her job, rather than letting it be controlled by others. For example, let the worker set a schedule, do his or her own troubleshooting, and decide when to start and stop working.

5. *Open feedback channels*. Finally, find more and better ways for the worker to get quick feedback on his or her performance.

Under what conditions would a leader want to consider implementing a job enrichment program? To find the answer, says one group of researchers, carefully diagnose the leadership situation, specifically addressing the following questions:[55]

1. Is motivation central to the problem? Or is there some other problem (a poorly designed flow of work in the office, for instance)?

2. Is *the job* low in motivating potential? Is the job the source of the motivation

job enlargement
Assigning workers additional same-level tasks to increase the number of tasks they have to perform.

job rotation
Systematically moving workers from job to job.

job enrichment
Building motivators like opportunities for achievement into the job by making it more interesting and challenging.

problem identified in step 1? Or, for instance, is it the fact that pay is unusually low, or that several members of the work group continually argue against working harder?

3. What specific aspects of the job are causing the difficulty, if it is the job? Here, consider inadequacies in the following core job dimensions:

—skill variety: to what degree does the job require the worker to perform activities that challenge his or her skills and abilities?

—task identity: to what degree does the job require completion of a whole, an identifiable piece of work?

—task significance: to what degree does the job have a substantial and perceptible effect on the lives of other people in the organization or the world at large?

—autonomy: to what degree does the job give the worker freedom and independence?

—knowledge of results: to what degree does the worker get information about the effectiveness of his or her job efforts?

4. How ready are the employees for change? Not all workers will prefer enriched jobs, and in any case some may not be ready to assume more responsibility. It may be futile to proceed with the change if the employees themselves will vigorously resist it.

Research results suggest that under the right conditions enrichment programs can be effective, particularly if implemented in association with other changes such as increasing pay in line with the increased levels of responsibilities.[56]

flextime
A system that allows workers increased discretion in deciding when they will be at their place of work.

Flextime. **Flextime** is a system that allows workers increased discretion in deciding when they will be at their place of work. Flextime does not involve changing the job itself, but it does affect how employees view their job. Management decides which hours of the day are "core hours" (times when it is absolutely essential that workers be on the job). In many firms these core hours are 10 a.m. to 2 p.m. Workers can then decide when to work the remaining number of required hours. 3M Canada and National Cash Register are among the companies that have adopted some form of flextime. A survey of 1600 Canadian companies showed that nearly half of them had some type of flextime program.[57]

compressed workweek
A work schedule in which employees work fewer days per week, but more hours on the days they do work.

The Compressed Workweek. In a **compressed workweek**, employees work fewer days per week, but more hours on the days they do work. The most popular compressed workweek is 4 days, 10 hours per day. The "weekend worker" program at 3M Canada in London, Ontario, offers workers 12-hour shifts on Saturdays and Sundays only, and pays workers the same wage as if they had worked normal hours on Mondays through Fridays.[58] Tellers at the Bank of Montreal in Oakville Place work long days (up to 14 hours), but enjoy a short workweek. Some tellers work 7 a.m. to 9 p.m. on Thursdays and Fridays, and 7:30 a.m. to 5:30 p.m. on Saturdays.[59]

job sharing
A program that allows two people to share one full-time job.

Job Sharing. As the name suggests, **job sharing** allows two people to share one full-time job. Kim Sarjeant and Loraine Champion, who are staff lawyers for NOVA Corp. in Calgary, share a position advising the human resources department. Sarjeant works Monday through Wednesday, and Champion works Wednesday through Friday.[60]

Using Empowerment

empowering
Giving employees the authority, tools, and information they need to do their jobs with greater autonomy, as well as the self-confidence required to perform the new jobs effectively.

Empowering employees is a popular phrase today; it means giving employees the authority, tools, and information they need to do their jobs with greater autonomy, as well as the self-confidence required to perform the new jobs effectively. Empowering is inherently a motivational approach: It boosts employees' feelings of self-efficacy and enables them to more fully use their potential, satisfying higher-level needs for achievement, recognition,

All jobs at Cin-Made are enriched when boss Bob Frey (standing) discusses the company's profit projections with employees. Frey operates under a philosophy of "open-book management," which assumes that if all employees act and think like businesspeople, the company will benefit. In order to do that, employees need the actual financial data that Frey provides.

and self-actualization. Figure 11.5 lists 10 principles for empowering people. Today, it's often work teams that are empowered.

At Saturn Corporation, for instance, empowered, self-managing work teams are responsible for a variety of duties. For each team, these duties include resolving its own conflicts, planning its own work schedule, determining its own job assignments, making selection decisions about new members, performing within its own budget, and obtaining its own supplies. Specific examples include:

- Using consensus decision making: No formal leader [will be] apparent in the process….All members of the work unit who reach consensus must be at least 70 percent comfortable with the decision, and 100 percent committed to its implementation.

- Making their own job assignments: A work unit…ensures safe, effective, efficient, and equal distribution of the work unit tasks to all its members.

- Planning their own work: The work unit assigns timely resources for the accomplishment of its purpose to its customers while meeting the needs of the people within the work unit.

---

1. Tell people what their responsibilities are.
2. Give them authority equal to the responsibilities assigned to them.
3. Set standards of excellence.
4. Provide them with training that will enable them to meet the standards.
5. Give them knowledge and information.
6. Provide them with feedback on their performance.
7. Recognize them for their achievements.
8. Trust them.
9. Give them permission to fail.
10. Treat them with dignity and respect.

FIGURE 11.5
Ten Principles for Empowering People

Self-managing work teams at Saturn have a great deal of discretion. They plan their own work schedules, decide which new team members will be added to the team, determine job assignments of team members, and resolve any conflicts within the team.

■ Designing their own jobs: This should provide the optimum balance between people and technology and include the effective use of labour power, ergonomics, machine use, quality, cost, job task analysis, and continuous improvement.

But empowering doesn't just mean assigning broad responsibilities. The teams also get the training, skills, and tools to empower them to do their jobs, such as in consensus decision making. Firms like Saturn also make sure their managers actually let their people do their jobs as assigned.

Not all empowerment programs are so comprehensive. At Scandinavian Air Systems (SAS), for instance, empowering the workforce meant letting employees make more decisions themselves. Ticket agents now have the authority to re-ticket a passenger or even move the passenger up a class, if they feel the situation warrants it. At one Marriott chain subsidiary, each and every hotel employee, from management to maintenance, is empowered to offer guests a free night's stay if, in the employee's opinion, the hotel has been lax in serving the guest. And at engine maker Pratt & Whitney, salespeople can now authorize multimillion-dollar repairs on the spot, instead of having to wait for approvals from up the line.

In virtually all such cases, employees find empowerment exciting, while employers find that it helps workers to self-actualize and exhibit self-efficacy, and thereby boosts motivation and employee commitment.[61]

Using Goal-Setting Methods

Have you ever set your sights on some goal—for example, aceing a course, graduating from college, or earning enough money for a trip abroad? What effect did setting the goal have on you? If you're like most people, it proved highly motivating. As Edwin Locke and his associates have shown time and again, people are strongly motivated to achieve goals that they consciously set. Setting specific goals with employees can be one of the simplest yet most powerful ways of motivating them.

The research on how to set goals that motivate employees is voluminous. Indeed, we discussed much of it in Chapter 5 in the context of goal setting for the purpose of planning. Here's a summary:

Scandinavian Air System
www.scandinavian.net

Pratt & Whitney
www.pratt-whitney. com

- *Be clear and specific.* Employees who are given specific goals usually perform better than those who are not.

- *Make goals measurable and verifiable.* Whenever possible, goals should be stated in quantitative terms and should include target dates or deadlines for accomplishment.

- *Make goals challenging but realistic.* Goals should be challenging but not so difficult that they appear impossible or unrealistic.

- *Set goals through participation.* Goals set through participation usually lead to higher performance, mostly because such goals tend to be more difficult.

- *Make sure your employee has the confidence to do the job.* Research studies show that self-efficacy, the person's perception of ability to do the job, has an important effect on whether he or she tries to attain the goal. In other words, ability and goal level are important determinants of performance, but having the confidence to do the job is important too. Therefore, building a person's confidence with honest and supportive comments can help determine if the goals the two of you set are translated into motivation and performance.[62]

Using Positive Reinforcement

Positive reinforcement programs (sometimes called organizational behaviour management or performance management programs) are widely used. They rely on operant conditioning principles to change behaviour.

As summarized in Figure 11.6, modifying behaviour with reinforcement is much like balancing a scale. Let's say that wearing a safety helmet is the desired behaviour and not wearing it is the undesired behaviour. One way to increase the desired behaviour (wearing the hat) is to add a positive consequence—for instance, by praising the worker each time he or she wears the hat. Another way to do so is to remove the negative consequences of wearing the hat, by lowering the temperature to cool the plant or by making the hat less cumbersome.

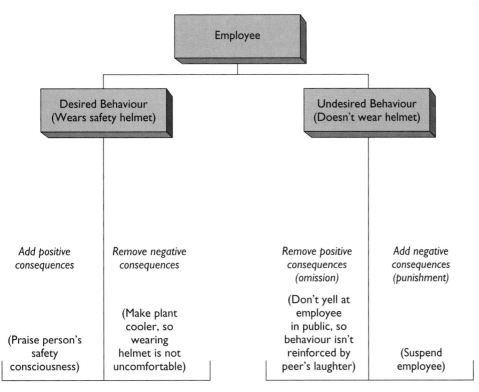

FIGURE 11.6
Options for Modifying Behaviour with Reinforcement

Most positive reinforcement/behaviour management experts say it's best to focus on improving desirable behaviours rather than on decreasing undesirable ones. If the employee regularly comes in late for work, stress improving the desired behaviour (coming to work punctually) rather than reducing the undesirable behaviour (coming to work late).

Types of Consequences. Obviously you needn't use just tangible rewards in these types of programs. *Social consequences* include peer approval, praise from the boss, letters of thanks from the company president, and a celebratory lunch. Intrinsic consequences include such intangibles as the enjoyment the person gets from engaging in a hobby and the sense of achievement from accomplishing a challenging task. *Tangible consequences* include outcomes like bonuses, incentive pay, and merit raises.

Behaviour Modification Programs at Work. Many employers have implemented positive reinforcement programs, and they have been used successfully in a multitude of applications. Probably the best known application in industry was implemented a number of years ago at Emery Air Freight Company.[63] The program grew out of management's discovery that the containers used to consolidate air freight shipments were not being fully used. In the air freight business, small shipments intended for the same destination fly at lower rates when shipped together in containers rather than separately. In this case, the workers used containers only about 45 percent of the time, while they reportedly thought they were using them about 90 percent of the time. Management wanted them to boost the actual usage rate to 90 to 95 percent.

A behaviour management program that showed managers how to use recognition and rewards was then implemented. In 80 percent of the offices where the program was implemented, container usage rose from 45 percent to 95 percent in a *single* day.

In another company, a behaviour management program was used to reduce absenteeism. Each day that an employee came to work on time, he or she received a playing card. At the end of the week, the highest poker hand received $20. Over a three-month period, the absenteeism rate decreased 18 percent.[64]

A telephone company identified several desirable behaviours among its operators and embarked on a behaviour management program to increase these behaviours. Praise and recognition were the main reinforcers that were used. Attendance improved 50 percent and productivity and efficiency levels rose above past standards.[65]

In a study involving a city transit company, behaviour management methods were applied to improve the safety record of bus drivers. The system reduced accident rates by nearly 25 percent.[66] At SAS Airlines, agents were trained to sell seats to customers who had simply called in for information. By the end of the program, agents had capitalized on 84 percent of the potential-offer opportunities, compared to only 34 percent at the beginning of the program.[67]

Using Lifelong Learning

Many employers today face a tremendous dilemma. On the one hand, remaining competitive requires highly committed employees who exercise self-discipline and basically do their jobs as if they owned the company. On the other hand, competitive pressures have forced many companies to continually downsize; this in turn causes employees to question whether it pays for them to work their hearts out for the company.

lifelong learning
Provides extensive continuing training, from basic remedial skills to advanced decision-making techniques, throughout the employees' careers.

Lifelong learning is one method increasingly used to address both of these issues simultaneously. **Lifelong learning** provides extensive continuing training, from basic remedial skills to advanced decision-making techniques, throughout the employees' careers.

The Benefits of Lifelong Learning. When implemented properly, lifelong learning programs can achieve three things. *First*, the training and education provide employees with the decision-making and other skills they need to competently carry out the demanding, team-based jobs that increasingly predominate, even on the factory floor. *Second*, the opportunity for lifelong learning is inherently motivational: It enables employees to develop and to see an enhanced possibility of fulfilling their potential; it boosts employees' sense of self-efficacy; and it provides an enhanced opportunity for the employee to self-actualize and gain the sense of achievement that psychologists like Maslow, Alderfer, McClelland, and Herzberg correctly argue is so important. *Third*, although lifelong learning may not cancel out the potential negative effects of downsizing, it might at least counterbalance them to some degree by giving the employee useful and marketable new skills.

An Example. One Canadian Honeywell manufacturing plant called its lifelong learning program the Honeywell-Scarborough Learning for Life Initiative.[68] It was "a concerted effort to upgrade skill and education levels so that employees can meet workplace challenges with confidence." This lifelong learning program had several components. It began with adult basic education. Here the company, in partnership with the employees' union, offered courses in English as a second language, basic literacy, numeracy, and computer literacy.

Next the factory formed a partnership with a local community college. Through that partnership all factory employees—hourly, professional, and managerial—have the opportunity to earn college diplomas and certificates. Included is a 15-hour "skills for success" program designed to refresh adults in the study habits required to succeed academically. All courses take place at the factory after work.

Finally, job training is provided for two hours every other week. These sessions focus on developing skills specifically important to the job, "such as the principles of just-in-time inventory systems, team effectiveness, interpersonal communication skills, conflict resolution, problem solving and dealing with a diverse work force."[69]

It's never easy to evaluate the success of a program like this because not all employees choose to participate, and many other factors will affect factory productivity and employee motivation. However, the evidence suggests that programs like these improve commitment, skills, and motivation, and possibly productivity too.[70]

In Conclusion: How Do You Motivate Today's Employees?

We covered many motivation techniques in this chapter, ranging from pay for performance to spot awards, merit pay, recognition, job redesign, empowerment, goal setting, positive reinforcement, and lifelong learning. All of these techniques can be effective; part of the art of managing is learning when to use—or not use—one or the other.

Another important aspect of motivating employees involves understanding their needs and using techniques like incentives and spot awards. However, motivation is not just a product of some technique. From your own experience, you know that it's the totality of how you're treated and not simply, say, a merit raise that determines whether you're motivated to get the job done.

Managers know that highly committed and self-motivated employees are their best competitive edge. They therefore work hard to earn commitment—an employee's identification with and agreement to pursue the company's or the unit's mission.[71]

Many of the motivation concepts and techniques discussed in this chapter have important roles to play in earning commitment. For example, appealing to employees higher-level needs and sense of responsibility and providing job enrichment fosters commitment.[72] However, earning commitment requires something more; specifically, a comprehensive management program that includes choosing the right employees to begin with and then doing things like encouraging extensive two-way communication, building a sense of shared fate and community, providing job security, and encouraging employees to self-actualize. Since earning commitment requires drawing on all of the management functions—from planning, to organizing, staffing, motivating, communicating, and controlling—we'll wait until Chapter 15, Controlling and Building Commitment, to discuss the mechanism of employee commitment more fully.

1. **Compare the three needs-based approaches to motivating employees.**
   Motivation is the intensity of a person's desire to engage in some activity. The three needs-based approaches to motivation (Maslow, Herzberg, and McClelland) all assume that human needs are an important element in motivation. Each approach proposes a different number of needs and different needs themselves; as well, Maslow assumes that needs are hierarchically arranged, while Herzberg and McClelland do not.

2. **Compare the three process approaches to motivating employees.** All of these approaches (equity theory, goal setting, and expectancy theory) assume that an employee's thought processes will influence motivation. Equity theory assumes that a person's desire to be treated equitably is of primary importance in motivating the person's behaviour. Goal setting theory argues that the setting of specific, quantifiable goals motivates individuals. Expectancy theory predicts that employees will be highly motivated if they see that desirable outcomes are attainable through hard work.

3. **Explain the role of equity, goal setting, and expectations in employee motivation.** People want to be treated equitably in their job. If they decide to pursue a specific goal, they will regulate their behaviour to ensure that the goal is reached. Their expectations—that effort will lead to performance, that performance will lead to rewards, and that the reward is valued—also influence motivation.

4. **Illustrate the use of the behaviour modification approach in motivation.** Behaviour modification means changing or modifying behaviour through the use of contingent rewards or punishment. Behaviour that appears to lead to a positive consequence or reward tends to be repeated, whereas behaviour that leads to a negative consequence or punishment tends not to be repeated.

5. **Give examples of how to use 10 methods for influencing behaviour and motivating employees.** Methods based on motivational approaches like Maslow's theory and behaviour modification include pay for performance, spot awards, merit pay, skill-based pay, recognition awards, job redesign, empowerment, goal setting, positive reinforcement, and lifelong learning.

TYING IT ALL TOGETHER

In Chapter 10, Being a Leader, we saw that a leader has to size up a situation by identifying what is happening, accounting for what is happening, and then formulating actions. When it comes to accounting for what is happening and formulating actions, the leader will need a firm understanding of human motivation—what motivates people and how motivation comes about. We therefore emphasized motivation in this chapter, including needs-based approaches to motivating employees, process approaches, learning/reinforcement approaches, and methods for actually influencing behaviour.

However, when it comes to motivating employees today, it's also important to take a broader view: Job enrichment and human needs are certainly important, but (as our discussions of the GE, and Saturn plants illustrate) it's really the entire management system, including communications and teamwork, that determine whether employees will be committed and self-motivated to do an exceptional job. Effective interpersonal and organizational communication plays an important role in this process, so we turn to this topic in the next chapter.

1. Are men and women motivated by the same things in the workplace? Are African women motivated by the same things that Korean men are? Are those who embrace the Muslim religion motivated by the same things as those who are Protestant? Do CEOs of large corporations seek the same rewards as Silken Laumann and Wayne Gretzky? What do you think? How do the theories presented in this chapter influence your answer?

2. It is said that the baby boomers (born 1946–64) "live to work" and that Generation Xers (born 1965–81) "work to live." What are the challenges in motivating the two groups? What if they are working on teams together? What job design challenges might you encounter as the team manager?

EXPERIENTIAL EXERCISES

1. Interview four or five friends, fellow workers, or fellow students about what motivates them. Record their responses. Then match the responses with the theories in this chapter. Be prepared to discuss in class what you find.

2. Read the business pages of your local newspaper for a week. Also read the sports pages for the same period. Then compare examples of motivation in each area. Is there a difference? How would you describe the differences? Construct a one-page explanation of your findings to share in class.

INTERNET EXERCISE

On the topic of individual motivation, find out if you are a worker or a shirker. Be honest, and complete the questionnaire located at www.reed.co.uk/tools/research/worker_or_shirker.htm. Once the form is completed, submit it electronically to obtain a personal profile.

1. What did you find most surprising? Why?

2. To what extent are you motivated by external factors (such as salary) or internal factors (such as pride in doing a job well)?

3. In this chapter you read about various ways to motivate employees. What do you think works best for you?

Galt Contracting

The Situation

Donald Galt, owner and manager of Galt Contracting, sat in his office in Kelowna, B.C., on a cold and rainy February day and pondered a serious problem that he was facing. The workers he had hired to plant trees during last summer's planting season had made far too many mistakes as they planted seedling trees. The lumber companies who had given Galt tree-planting contracts had threatened to withhold any more contracts if Galt was unable to solve the quality problem. Galt feared that the survival of his company was at stake, and he wondered what he could do.

Background

Galt Contracting is a small B.C.-based company that plants trees for lumber companies like Canfor, Gorman Brothers, and Riverside. In the spring of each year, Galt competitively bids on tree-planting contracts that will be available during the summer. Galt usually visits the block of land that is up for bid and looks it over with a lumber company representative. He then develops a bid and submits it to the lumber company. If he is awarded the job, he then hires tree planters to do the actual planting on the block of land. Galt decides how much he will pay his workers. The amount that Galt receives from the lumber company contracts minus the amount he has to pay his workers determines the profit that Galt Contracting makes each year.

Galt usually hires about 15 university students each summer who are looking for good-paying, short-term jobs. The work is very hard, but tree planters can make very good money because they are paid on a piece-rate system (i.e., they are paid a certain amount of

money for each tree they plant). Galt has been using this payment system for many years, but recently he has become very concerned about it, because trees are not being planted properly and they die soon after planting. Galt thinks this is happening because workers are stressing quantity at the expense of quality in order to earn a lot of money. At the end of last year's planting season, Galt was told in no uncertain terms by one lumber company that if he did not improve the quality of his tree planting, he would not get any more jobs. This year he has already lost one contract for 200 000 trees because of poor-quality planting that was done by his workers last year.

The problem is significant enough that Galt has been thinking about dropping the piece-rate pay system and moving towards a "flat rate" system, which would give the workers a fixed amount of pay for each day. Galt thinks that this would cause planters to take more time and care when planting each tree, since they would not have to worry about how much money they were going to make for the day. Before making this important decision, Galt reflects on how the tree-planting business works.

A Day in the Life of a Tree Planter

At Donald Galt's company, a typical day for a tree planter goes something like this:

TIME	ACTIVITY
4:45 a.m.	Get up
5:00 a.m.	Leave for storage site where trees are kept
5:30 a.m.	Arrive at storage site and load trees into truck
5:30 a.m. – 7:00 a.m.	Drive truck to planting site; everyone "bags up" (puts trees in planting bags) at the main tree cache
7:00 a.m. – 3:00 p.m.	Plant trees
3:00 p.m. – 4:30 p.m.	Return to storage site in preparation for driving home
4:30 p.m. – 5:30 p.m.	Drive home

→

Galt pays his tree planters between 16 and 32 cents per tree. The amount varies depending on terrain and the kind of tree being planted. Piece rates go above 16 cents per tree if the land to be planted has any of the following characteristics:

- it is uneven
- it has rocky soil
- it is covered with "slash" (branches lying on the ground)
- it is covered with high weeds (making it difficult to see where trees have been planted)
- it was logged more than 10 years ago (and there is new growth of alders and poplar)

When the land is particularly uneven, on some occasions Galt has paid a flat "day rate." He sometimes gets the impression that when he does this, workers don't seem to work as hard, and they take more breaks. Galt knows that workers like the piece-rate system because they can make good money. They also feel that it generates competition among planters to see who can be the most productive. This competition increases the number of trees that are planted. (A tree planter may plant as few as 1000 trees or as many as 2500 trees per day, depending on the terrain and the planter's experience. On an average day, a reasonably experienced tree planter can plant 1300 trees.)

When the piece-rate system is used, there is not much socializing among workers on the site, except when they are "bagging up" at the main cache at various times throughout the day. Tree bags hold about 400 seedlings. Planters do not have a set lunch break; instead, they eat lunch on the run. They usually leave their lunch boxes at the main cache, and eat about halfway through the day on one of their return trips to the cache to pick up more trees. Socializing is generally seen as counterproductive because workers who stand around and talk aren't planting trees, and this reduces the worker's pay.

The Production System

Trees are delivered to the planting site in boxes, with 360 trees per box. The seedlings range from 7.5 to 30 centimetres high and are called "plugs." The most common trees are lodgepole pine, spruce, Douglas fir, and larch.

Each planter is assigned a "piece" to plant for the day, usually an area equal in size to a football field, but not necessarily symmetrical. The limits of each planter's area are marked with flags by the planters as they

begin planting in the morning. The numbers in Figure 11.7 indicate the order in which trees are planted. Planters leave the main cache and begin planting trees in a straight line. As they plant they "flag a line," which indicates the boundaries of their piece. This involves staking out strips of brightly coloured tape close to the line of trees. The planter on piece 1, for example, would flag a line while planting trees 1 through 100. This line helps each of the planters to determine where their piece begins and ends. Planting is then done in a back-and-forth pattern within each piece as planters work towards the main cache. They monitor the number of trees left in their planting bags so they can end up near the main cache when they run out of trees. So, the planter on piece 1 might plant tree 400 near the main cache, then "bag up" and start the process all over again with tree 401. On non-symmetrical pieces, this process is more complicated.

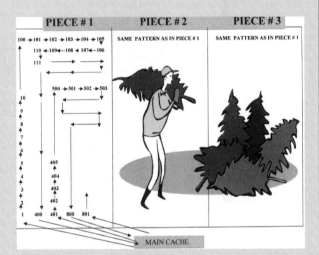

FIGURE 11.7
A Typical Tree Planting Route

Trees must be planted in different concentrations on different blocks, and a certain jargon has arisen to describe this activity. For example, if spacing is "2.9," this means that trees must be planted 2.9 metres apart; if spacing is "3.1," this means that trees must be planted 3.1 metres apart. Planters prefer "2.9 days" over "3.1 days" because they don't have to cover as much ground and can therefore plant more trees (and make more money).

A checker—who works for the lumber company—inspects the work of the planters to ensure that they are planting properly. Checkers use a cord to inscribe a circle on random pieces of ground. On "2.9 days," the checker will ensure that 7 trees are contained in the circle within the cord. The checker also determines whether the trees are planted properly; trees must not have any air pockets around the roots, there must be no "j-rooted" (crooked) roots, and trees must be planted on the south (sunny) side of any obstacles in the piece. Trees must also be planted close to obstacles so that they are not trampled by the cattle that graze in the area. If a planter consistently plants too many or too few trees on a piece, the checker can demand that the piece be replanted. This happens infrequently, but when it does, the planter's pay is sharply reduced.

Galt sometimes checks workers himself, especially if he has reason to believe that they are doing a sloppy job. The biggest problem he has encountered is workers who plant large numbers of trees, but do so very poorly. Planters know that if Galt is following them around for any significant period of time, he is suspicious about the quality of their planting. Planters are very hard on each other in terms of quality. They become very upset if one of their group tries to make more money by planting large numbers of trees by cutting corners. Planters put pressure on each other to do a good job because the reputation of the whole group suffers if one or two planters do poor-quality work. As well, planters resent those among them who make more money simply by planting large numbers of trees in a poor-quality way. A planter who is known to do a sloppy job or who is forced to replant an area might be nicknamed "j-root," for example.

Planters do not know when the checker will come by. If a planter "gets in good" with a checker, the checker may go easy when checking the planter's work. The checkers are themselves checked by other lumber company employees to ensure that they are doing reasonable quality control work. In turn, the lumber company is checked by the provincial government to see that trees are planted properly.

There is a real art to planting a tree. An experienced planter will push the shovel into the ground with one foot and hand and wiggle it back and forth to make a slit for the tree, while at the same time using the other hand to extract a tree from the tree bag and drop it into the newly created hole. The shovel is then pulled out, and the area around the newly planted tree is chopped up a bit with the shovel to aerate it. Using this system, an experienced worker planting trees on flat ground can plant over 300 trees per hour.

Donald Galt's Decision

As Galt considered all of these facts, he wondered what he should do regarding the payment system he uses for workers.

Questions

1. What are the advantages and disadvantages of paying tree planters on a piece-rate system? On a flat day-rate system?

2. What does each of the motivation theories in the chapter say (or imply) about Galt's idea of dropping the piece-rate system and paying tree planters a flat rate for each day of work?

3. Propose a payment system for the tree planters that minimizes negative consequences. Describe the impact of your proposal on the following: the motivation levels of the planters, the activities of the quality control checkers, the level of quality needed in tree planting, the needs of the lumber companies, and Galt Contracting's need for profit. Be specific.

CASE STUDY 11-2

Motivation at Intel—Guarding Against Complacency

Andy Grove is the CEO of Intel, the maker of the famous Pentium chip that drives most of today's desktop computers. Intel employs over 64 000 employees in what many consider to be the most complex industry in which to manage. It is not uncommon in this industry for new competitors to launch previously unheard-of technologies that can unseat market leaders. Grove developed a phrase that describes what he considers to be an essential way for managers of high-tech companies to operate. He later turned that phrase into a best-selling book: *Only the Paranoid Survive*.

The semiconductor industry is known for its breathtaking pace of change. Dot-com firms like Monster and Amazon can move from "start-ups" to publicly traded market leaders in the space of a few short years. As a $27-billion-a-year company with a great track record of success, it might be easy for Intel to become complacent; hence Grove's warning that "only the paranoid survive." In Grove's vocabulary, industries reach inflection points where the paradigm is about to shift. It would be easy for a manager to miss the new signals that consumers are sending, and as a result Intel could be driven from its "number 1" position.

In Grove's world, paranoia is healthy. He is not describing the irrational fear that a true paranoid would have; rather, what he is describing is the need for constant vigilance. To keep Intel's managers motivated to stay in constant touch with their changing world, the company has installed a comprehensive management and motivation system. The process begins before employment by first identifying and selecting employees with the highest potential for success. Central to the Intel system is the importance of rewarding excellence. Intel's merit-based performance system ties compensation increases and career advancement opportunities to employee performance.

Intel uses both bonuses and stock incentives. The bonus programs are generally profit-sharing programs that reward both company performance and the performance of the small group in which the employee participates. Stock programs include a stock option program and a stock participation plan. In both programs, Intel subsidizes the purchase of company stock. The value of share ownership among managers is well documented; the more shares that managers hold in Intel, the greater the effect of company performance on their compensation.

Intel also offers a variety of performance awards. Awards may or may not involve financial incentives, but they always involve personal recognition. Managers can achieve awards that lead to formal recognition at the corporate level or at the department level.

Many Intel sites also provide qualified child care. Where local child care is limited, child care facilities may be located on the Intel site. Intel also uses a number of alternative work schedule arrangements (each business group can establish their own methods and frameworks). The range of methods is quite broad and includes compressed workweeks, part-time positions, telecommuting, personal absence days, and family, medical, and personal leaves.

Intel is deeply concerned about the personal and intellectual renewal of its employees. In one of the more innovative programs, Intel offers all of its full-time U.S. employees the opportunity to take a sabbatical leave. Every seven years, all regular full-time employees are entitled to an eight-week sabbatical with pay, in addition to normal vacation and personal time off. Intel also encourages intellectual development in more traditional ways. In 1998, Intel spent more than $300 million on ongoing employee education. Under Grove's leadership, Intel has also developed a university that offers more that 3400 courses worldwide. Employees receive full reimbursement for tuition, books, and fees for university-level courses and programs that have present or future application at Intel. Finally, Intel has developed and launched a formal mentoring system.

So while Grove speaks of only the paranoid surviving, his company has invoked a full range of motivational methods to help its employees succeed. Still, the competitive dynamics in Intel's industry make it one of the most demanding competitive environments in the world.

Questions

1. Which of the 10 motivation methods described in this chapter do you see employed at Intel?

2. Which of the motivation methods do you believe will be most effective? Why?

3. Has Intel installed the correct mix of motivation methods to assure its survival and success? Are there other methods that might be more successful?

Intel
www.intel.com

Maintaining Motivation at KnitMedia

Developing a package of incentives with which to maintain the motivation of KnitMedia's managers, employees, and artists has become increasingly challenging over the past few years.

One problem, particularly recently, has been the explosion of new Internet start-ups, particularly in "Silicon Alley," the lower Manhattan neighbourhood in which many new Internet-related companies are setting up shop. Many of these start-ups are offering talented technical people and people with music experience big stakes in their companies in terms of stock options. KnitMedia has recently lost several high-potential employees to these start-ups, since it really can't compete with companies that give employees the chance to become multi-millionaires in a year or two.

Keeping top-notch artists is a similar but separate problem. KnitMedia recently raised about $5 million, but compared to giants like Warner Music and Universal it's still difficult, to say the least, to compete with major record labels' large cash advances. In the past few years, for instance, the company lost four of its rock artists and one jazz band to major labels after their contracts with KnitMedia expired. These artists had achieved significant success with KnitMedia, and used that success to sign with major labels. The artists who left included Eric Sanko, who signed with Capital Records for $1 million; Bill Ware, who moved to Warner Music; and the Jazz Passengers.

This, of course, could turn out to be a problem. The whole idea of KnitMedia is to attract and showcase new artists at the Knitting Factory clubs and then to develop them into successful recording artists who can be showcased on KnitMedia's record labels and Internet sites and sent on tours with KnitMedia festivals. That plan will obviously fail unless KnitMedia can retain the artists it identifies as high-potential performers.

As far as attracting and keeping lower-level employees is concerned, the company currently has few incentives. As Chuck Brownley, general manager of the New York club, puts it, to a large extent it's the image of the Knitting Factory itself that functions as a recruiting magnet, "by virtue of the scene that we create, by virtue of the reputation that we have." As far as the people who actually work as servers at the Knitting Factory, "generally the only incentives that we're utilizing are the potential of tips," a situation that is not at all unusual at clubs like these.

Michael Dorf and his management team have come to you for advice about what sort of incentive package they should put together.

Team Exercises and Questions

Use what you learned in this chapter to answer the following questions from Michael Dorf and his management team:

1. Based on what you know about motivation, how would you describe the motivational needs of recording artists and the other highly creative people who are associated with KnitMedia? What implications does this have for how we should motivate these people?

2. Based on whatever else you know about the music industry and KnitMedia, what exactly do you think we should do to ensure that we continue to attract and keep high-potential recording artists?

3. What incentive plan do you think would be effective in helping us to retain high-potential managers in the face of the sorts of incentives that Internet start-ups are offering?

Appendix

What Managers Should Know About Individual Behaviour

One of the paradoxes that leaders face is that what motivates one person might not motivate another. Any stimulus—an order from the boss, an offer of a raise, or the threat of being fired—will have different effects on different people. One person might leap at the chance for a $100 raise, while another might shun it. One might emerge from training with excellent skills, while another will learn nothing. One might jump whenever the boss gives orders, while another will laughingly ignore them.

To a large extent, these anomalies occur because of what psychologists call the **law of individual differences**, namely the fact that people differ in personalities, abilities, values, and needs. As illustrated in Figure 11A.1, these factors act much like filters, adding to, detracting from, and often distorting the effect of any stimulus. It is therefore important for managers to understand the nature of each of these factors.

law of individual differences
The fact that people differ in personalities, abilities, values, and needs.

PERSONALITY INFLUENCES BEHAVIOUR

Personality is probably the first thing that comes to mind when most people think about what determines behaviour. We tend to classify people as introverted, dominant, mature, or paranoid, for instance, and by and large these labels conjure up visions of particular kinds of behaviour.

Personality Defined

One way (but by no means the only way) to define **personality** is as "the characteristic and distinctive traits of an individual, and the way the traits interact to help or hinder the adjustment of the person to other people and situations." Psychologist Raymond Cattell used observations and questionnaires to identify 16 primary personality traits,[1] which he

personality
The characteristic and distinctive traits of an individual, and the way the traits interact to help or hinder the adjustment of the person to other people and situations.

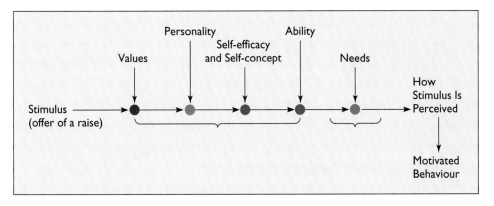

FIGURE 11A.1
Some Individual Determinants of Behaviour
A particular stimulus may evoke different behaviours among individuals, because each person's perceptions, personality, abilities, and needs will influence how he or she reacts to the stimulus.

then expressed in pairs of words, such as reserved/outgoing, submissive/dominant, and trusting/suspicious. Based on his work, Cattell and his colleagues developed a questionnaire that produced a personality profile for individuals. Figure 11A.2 shows the average personality profiles for people in two sample occupational groups: airline pilots and business executives.

Traits do not just represent characteristics that people possess. People do not possess "submissiveness" or "sensitivity"; instead, they act and feel submissive or sensitive. So one way to define personality is in terms of traits, since traits will generally influence how someone will act in a given situation.

Trait theories hold that someone's traits are a function of both genetic factors and learning, and that, as we saw above, behaviour reflects the person's traits—he or she is "extroverted," "agreeable," or "conscientious," for instance. Psychologists like Raymond Cattell and Gordon Allport describe an individual's personality in terms of a unique set of personality traits.

More recently, industrial psychologists have emphasized the "big five" personality dimensions as they apply to personnel testing: extroversion, emotional stability, agreeableness, conscientiousness, and openness to experience.[2] In one study of professionals, police officers, managers, sales workers, and unskilled and semi-skilled workers, *conscientiousness* showed a consistent relationship with all job performance criteria for all occupations. *Extroversion* was tied to performance for managers and sales employees, which of course are the two occupations in the study involving the most social interaction.[3]

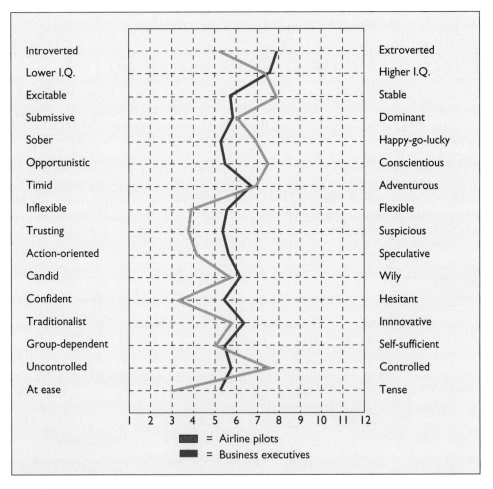

FIGURE 11A.2
Cattell's 16 Personality Factors
The personalities of various people and even various groups of people are characterized by particular packages of traits, such as introverted, dominant, excitable, and innovative.

Personality Types

At work, you will come across many unique personalities, but the following two types are useful examples. The **authoritarian personality** has been studied for at least 50 years. Such a person is rigid and intolerant of ambiguity, tends to stereotype people as good or bad, and conforms to the requirements of authority, perhaps while being dictatorial to subordinates. The **Machiavellian personality** (the name refers to the writings of the 16th-century political adviser Niccoló Machiavelli) tends to be oriented towards manipulation and control, with a low sensitivity to the needs of others.[4]

Measuring Personality

A test and scale known as the Myers-Briggs Type Indicator (MBTI) is one of the most popular tools for measuring personality, particularly in the work setting. The MBTI classifies people as extroverted or introverted (E or I), sensing or intuitive (S or N), thinking or feeling (T or F), and perceiving or judging (P or J). The person's answers to a questionnaire are classified into 16 different personality types (a four-by-four matrix); these 16 types in turn are classified into one of four cognitive (thinking or problem-solving) styles:

Sensation-thinking (ST)

Intuition-thinking (NT)

Sensation-feeling (SF)

Intuition-feeling (NF)

Classifying personality types and cognitive styles in this way has several applications. Some employers have found they can match the MBTI cognitive styles to particular occupations. This is illustrated in Figure 11A.3. People with the sensation-thinking approach to problem solving are often well suited to occupations like auditor and safety engineer, for instance.

ABILITIES INFLUENCE BEHAVIOUR

Individual differences in abilities also influence how we behave and perform.[5] Even the most highly motivated person will not perform well unless he or she also has the ability to do the job. Conversely, the most able employee will not perform satisfactorily if not motivated. Some experts summarize this interaction in the following way: Performance = Ability x Motivation.

There are many types of abilities. Mental abilities include intelligence and its building blocks, such as memory, inductive reasoning, and verbal comprehension. Mechanical ability would be important for mechanical engineers or machinists. Psychomotor abili-

authoritarian personality
A person who is rigid and intolerant of ambiguity, tends to stereotype people as good or bad, and conforms to the requirements of authority, perhaps while being dictatorial to subordinates.

Machiavellian personality
A person who tends to be oriented towards manipulation and control, with a low sensitivity to the needs of others.

	Thinking Style	Feeling Style
Sensation Style	People with this combined thinking/sensation style tend to be *thorough*, *logical*, and *practical* and to make good *CAs* or *safety engineers*.	People with this combined sensation/feeling style tend to be *conscientious* and *responsible* and to make *good social workers* and *drug supervisors*.
Intuitive Style	People with this combined intuitive/thinking style tend to be *creative*, *independent*, and *critical* and to make good *systems analysts, professors,* and *lawyers*.	People with this combined intuitive/feeling style tend to be *people-oriented, sociable,* and often *charismatic* and to make good *human resource managers, public relations directors,* and *politicians*.

FIGURE 11A.3
Four Examples of MBTI Styles and Some Corresponding Occupations

ties include dexterity, manipulative ability, eye-hand coordination, and motor ability; such abilities might be important for employees who have to put together delicate computer components or who work as croupiers in Las Vegas. People also differ in their visual skills; for example, in their ability to discriminate between colours and between black and white detail (called visual acuity).

In addition to these general abilities, people also have specific abilities learned through training, experience, or education. Employers test for these abilities when they are interested in determining a candidate's proficiency on a job such as computer programmer, word processor, or chemical engineer.

SELF-CONCEPT INFLUENCES BEHAVIOUR

Although it's true that everyone is different, there is one way in which we are all the same: We all have our own self-concepts. Humanist psychologists like Carl Rogers emphasize the role of self-concept in personality. Who we are and how we behave is largely driven, say humanist psychologists, by the perceptions we have of who we are and how we relate to other people and other things.

The very core of personality is to enhance the experiences of life through self-actualization—in other words, to strive to achieve our inborn potential and to become the people we believe we can become. Self-concept, in other words, is how we see ourselves, and how we see ourselves has a big influence on how we act and on how we react to the things that happen to us.

It's hard to overestimate the importance of self-concept in shaping the way we behave. Psychologist Saul Gellerman says that we all are driven in a constant quest to be ourselves or to be the kinds of individuals we think we should be.[6]

The next time you're in class or at work, stop and think about how you feel. Of all the people in the class or in the company cafeteria or in the office, around whom, more than anyone, does your world revolve? Who most occupies your thoughts? Would it bother you if your classmates or colleagues ignored you? How would you feel if you came to work every day and your boss or your boss's boss seemed to act as if you didn't exist, although you were knocking yourself out 10 hours a day for the company?

As a manager or future manager, you should keep in mind that every person you meet views himself or herself as being as special as you view yourself to be. The leader who doesn't recognize and act on that fact will be hampered in dealing effectively with people.

Some people have rigid self-concepts and are relatively unable to modify the way they view themselves.[7] Experiences that threaten such a person's self-concept will likely be screened out or distorted. Being turned down for promotion, for example, might be explained away in terms of politics or the supervisor's incompetence.

To some degree, everyone tries to protect his or her self-concept, and doing so is neither unnatural nor unhealthy, at least up to a point. However, most psychologists would probably agree that "people with healthy self-concepts can allow new experiences into their lives and can accept or reject them."[8] As these experts put it,

> Such people move in a positive direction. With each new experience, their self-concepts become stronger and more defined, and the goal of self-actualization is brought closer.[9]

In this view, *individual development* plays a major role in helping people to fulfil their self-concepts. The person with a healthy (and therefore somewhat flexible) self-concept is on a voyage of discovery, as his or her personality slowly evolves.

SELF-EFFICACY INFLUENCES BEHAVIOUR

self-efficacy
A person's belief about his or her own capacity to perform a task.

As we saw in Chapter 11, closely related to self-concept is the idea that people differ in their **self-efficacy**, or their belief about their own capacity to perform a task.[10] For a leader, this individual difference is important because self-efficacy has a big effect on how people perform and even on whether they'll try to accomplish the task.

As a familiar example of self-efficacy, in the movie *My Fair Lady* Professor Higgins convinces Eliza Doolittle that "she can do it"—and in short order she's speaking and acting like a proper upper-crust English lady. However, you don't have to rely on movies for proof that self-efficacy works. Research shows that self-efficacy is associated with high work performance in a wide range of settings: life insurance sales, faculty research productivity, career choice, learning and achievement, and adaptability to new technology, to name a few.[11]

PERCEPTION INFLUENCES BEHAVIOUR

The fact that we all differ in terms of things like personality and self-concept helps to explain why we perceive things differently. We all react to stimuli that reach us via our sense organs, but the way that we define or perceive these stimuli depends on what we bring with us from past experiences and what our present needs and personalities are.[12] In other words, our behaviour is motivated not just by stimuli, but also by our *perceptions* of those stimuli, by the way our personalities and experiences cause us to interpret them. **Perception** is the unique way that each person sees and interprets things.

You are probably familiar with the way that perceptual distortion clouds our view of inanimate objects. Consider what happens when we try to match the sizes of near objects with those of far ones. When we look down a row of arches, as in the photo, the farthest one usually looks smaller than the closest one, and its perspective size is in fact smaller (because it is farthest away).

Based on experience, however, we know that the arches are actually equal in size, so what we *perceive* is a compromise between the perspective size of the arch and its actual size. In the photo, the nearest arch seems about twice the size of the farthest arch. But if you measure the arches you will see that it is actually more than four times the size of the farthest arch. Our desire to see objects as we expect them to be causes us to perceive less difference in height than there really is.

Perception and People

Just as we read stable, specific characteristics into objects, we also read them into people. This process is called **stereotyping.** For example, some people tend to associate characteristics like industriousness and honesty with certain socio-economic classes but not with others. Some managers erroneously assume that women are fit for certain jobs but not for

How does perceptual distortion play a role in the visual perception of this image?

others. Similarly, we tend to stereotype people according to age, sex, race, or national origin and to attribute the characteristics of this stereotype to everyone we meet who is of that age, sex, race, or national origin. In other words, we all learn to associate certain meanings with certain groups of people.

This process helps us to deduce more quickly (but not always accurately) the important characteristics of the people we meet and to avoid having to make fresh guesses every time.[13] Thus, a manager might jump to the conclusion that an older job candidate would not be as flexible as a younger worker.[14]

Factors That Affect Perception

The way that we see or perceive the world is influenced by many things. Some important influences are:

- *Personality and needs.* Our needs affect our perceptions. For example, when shown fuzzy and ambiguous pictures of objects, hungry people tend to see them as food. Tell an insecure employee that you want to see him in your office later in the day and he might spend the hours worrying about being fired, although you only want to discuss vacation schedules.

- *Self-efficacy and abilities.* Someone confident about doing a job might welcome an assignment. Someone who believes that he or she will fail might be devastated by the same assignment. Our abilities influence our perceptions of our own success.

- *Values.* Perceptions are also influenced by values, the basic beliefs a person has about what he or she should or shouldn't do. Someone with a strong ethics code might be horrified at the suggestion of taking a bribe. Someone of lesser character might think, "That's not a bad idea."

- *Stress.* People who are under stress tend to perceive things less objectively than those who are not. In one experiment, a group of employment interviewers were put under pressure to hire more employees. They subsequently perceived candidates' qualifications as being much higher than did a group of interviewers who were not under pressure.

- *Experience.* Our perceptions are also influenced by experience. Based on our experiences, for example, we learn to associate certain groups with certain behaviours (in other words, we stereotype them). We then tend to expect everyone from that group to behave in the same fashion.

- *Position.* A person's position in the organization is another important factor. Production managers tend to see problems as production problems, while sales managers see them as sales problems.

- *Attribution.* People's perceptions are also strongly influenced by their **attributions**, or the meanings they give to actions. Suppose another car cuts you off as you are driving to work. If you attribute the driver's actions to his temporarily losing control of his car, you may drive on without giving it further thought. If you attribute his actions to his intentionally cutting you off in anger, you may take evasive action to avoid further encounters with someone you now perceive to be a hothead.

In summary, our behaviour is prompted by our perceptions, not by "reality," and our perceptions, even of the same event, can be different, since our personalities, values, experiences, and needs differ as well.[15]

ATTITUDES INFLUENCE BEHAVIOUR

A person's attitudes can and often will influence performance and behaviour at work. An **attitude** is a predisposition to respond to objects, people, or events in either a positive or a negative way.[16] When people say things like "I like my job" or "I don't care about my job," they are expressing attitudes, which are important because they can influence the way they behave on the job.

Because attitudes are important, many companies conduct periodic (and usually anonymous) attitude or opinion surveys of their workforces. IBM, for example, regularly asks employees their opinions about the company, its management, and their work life. The survey's stated purpose is "to aid management at all levels in identifying and solving problems."[17]

Job satisfaction is probably the most familiar example of attitudes at work. Job satisfaction reflects an employee's attitude about his or her job; in practice, measuring it usually means measuring several specific aspects of the job.

job satisfaction
Reflects an employee's attitude about his or her job.

International Survey Research surveyed thousands of Canadian and U.S. workers regarding their morale and job satisfaction. Interestingly, the survey showed that employee morale and job satisfaction are consistently and significantly higher in Canada than in the U.S.[18]

One popular job satisfaction survey, the Job Descriptive Index, measures the following five aspects of job satisfaction:

1. *Pay.* How much pay is received and is it perceived as equitable?

2. *Job.* Are tasks interesting? Are opportunities provided for learning and for accepting responsibility?

3. *Promotional opportunities.* Are promotions and opportunities to advance available and fair?

4. *Supervisor.* Does the supervisor demonstrate interest in and concern about employees?

5. *Co-workers.* Are co-workers friendly, competent, and supportive?[19]

Good (or bad) attitudes do not necessarily translate into good (or bad) performance.[20] Performance can be affected by many other factors. For example, engineers may continue to do their best regardless of how they feel about their employer, because their performance is governed mostly by professional standards of conduct. As another example, workers on a machine-paced assembly line may have so little discretion over the quantity or quality of what they do that their attitudes might not influence their performance.

Influencing Interpersonal and Organizational Communication

Store Walking at Home Depot

Home Depot, one of the most well-known "big box" retailers, operates more than 700 stores in Canada, the U.S., and Chile. The company employs 160 000 people and its annual sales revenue exceeds $30 billion. Co-

founders Bernie Marcus and Arthur Blank believe that poor communication between managers and employees can sink a company, so they have developed a technique—called the store walk—to make sure that managers hear what they need to hear from employees.

As the term implies, the store walk involves head office managers and district managers in a literal walk through Home Depot stores so they can see first-hand what merchandise is being offered, why it is being offered, how it is priced, and what the company expects from the manufacturers who supply the products. After a store walk is completed, Bernie Marcus fields questions from district managers. At these meetings, managers are given "immunity," meaning that they can ask blunt or potentially offensive questions without fear of reprisal. By the time these meetings are over, managers have received clear and direct answers to their questions, and they feel more secure about what they are doing. These meetings also help Home Depot to merchandise products that customers really want, because the local managers know customer needs better than head office managers do.

As part of the store walk, district managers meet with store associates without the store manager being present. The communication that goes on in these meetings can be very interesting. At one Canadian store where an employee stock ownership program (ESOP) had just been introduced, district managers discovered to their dismay that associates didn't know how to participate in the program because no one had explained it to them.

Unannounced store visits are also part of the program to improve communication within Home Depot. These unannounced visits can be made by head office managers or by district managers who walk the aisles, look at how the merchandise is displayed, and listen in on conversations between store employees and customers. These activities keep district managers and head office personnel "close to the customer." District managers also conduct announced

Home Depot
**www.homedepot.
com**

visits during which they put on orange aprons and wait on customers. They do this to model the proper behaviour for store employees (called associates). This activity effectively flattens the management pyramid and facilitates communication from the very top of the organization to its very bottom.

OBJECTIVES

After studying this chapter, you should be able to

1. Define communication and list the five elements in the communication process.

2. Understand how to improve your interpersonal communication.

3. List the barriers that undermine organizational communication.

4. Understand how to overcome the barriers that undermine organizational communication.

5. Give examples of how telecommunications improves communication within and among organizations.

A man drove up to a gasoline pump to fill his gas tank. The gas station attendant noticed three penguins in the back seat of the car and, curious, asked about them.

"I don't know how they got there," the driver said. "The penguins were there when I took the car out of the garage this morning."

The attendant thought for a moment. "Why don't you take them to the zoo?"

"Good idea," the driver said and drove away.

The next day, the same man returned to the gas station. In the back seat were the same three penguins, but now they wore sunglasses.

The attendant looked at the car in surprise. "I thought you took them to the zoo!" she exclaimed. "I did," the driver said. "And they had such a good time that today I decided to take them to the beach."

Communication is something that almost everyone agrees is a good thing; the problem is that (like our friend with the penguins) good communication can be hard to find. As you already know from your own experiences, many things—misunderstandings, semantics, or even fear—can distort the clarity of what you're trying to say. The result (as with the penguins) can range from laughable (if you're lucky) to disastrous. In the previous chapter we focused on motivating employees, and on the various techniques like job enrichment and recognition that companies use today. Influencing and motivating employees assumes, of course that you can effectively communicate what you want and understand the points of view of your bosses, colleagues, and subordinates. In this chapter, we'll therefore turn to the crucial topic of *communicating,* including communication barriers and how to overcome them.

A Communication Model

As the exchange of information and the transmission of meaning, **communication** is the very essence of managing.[1] Managers like Home Depot's Bernie Marcus manage based on information—about competitors' tactics, labour and materials, or assembly line delays. And it's not the events themselves that trigger management action, but the *infor-*

communication
The exchange of information and the transmission of meaning.

mation that managers receive about them. If that information arrives too late or is wrong or distorted, the company and its managers will suffer.

Studies of managers' communication patterns show that a large amount of time is spent on oral and written communication. An early study by Henry Mintzberg of McGill University showed that CEOs spent 78 percent of their time in oral communication.[2] This took place in situations like scheduled and unscheduled meetings, plant tours, and telephone conversations. A more recent study by other researchers showed that CEOs spent 74 percent of their time in oral communcation.[3] In both of these studies, executives spent about half of their time with subordinates, and the other half with peers, the board of directors, and people outside the company.

In fact, most studies of what managers do conclude that they spend most of their time communicating.[4] One study of supervisors in a DuPont lab found that they spent 53 percent of their time in meetings, 15 percent writing and reading, and 9 percent on the phone. If we include meetings, interacting with customers and colleagues, and other ways in which managerial communication takes place, managers spend 60 to 80 percent of their time communicating, mostly face to face.[5] Influencing people through communicating and managing communications is thus a fundamental part of what managers do.

As you can see in Figure 12.1,[6] there are five basic aspects to the communication process. The **sender** puts a message in understandable terms and then transmits it via a **communication channel**, a vehicle that carries the message. Face-to-face communication is the most familiar and widely used channel. Memos, reports, policies and procedures manuals, videotape reports, and e-mail are some other communication channels.

But managers (and the penguins' chauffeur) know that the information sent is not necessarily the same as that received. This is because information channels are all subject to "**noise**" and distortion. A face-to-face conversation in a restaurant can lead to misunderstandings when the message is overwhelmed by conversations from surrounding tables. Other "noise" includes ambiguities in the message and preconceptions on the part of the receiver.

The **receiver** is the person or persons to whom the message is sent. The receiver may interact face to face with the sender (for example, when a salesperson from the Great Canadian Travel Company tells a customer about a tour package to the Caribbean), or the

sender
Someone who puts a message in understandable terms and then transmits it.

communication channel
A vehicle that carries a message.

noise
Physical, personality, perceptual, or attitudinal factors that interfere with the communication process.

receiver
The person or persons to whom the message is sent.

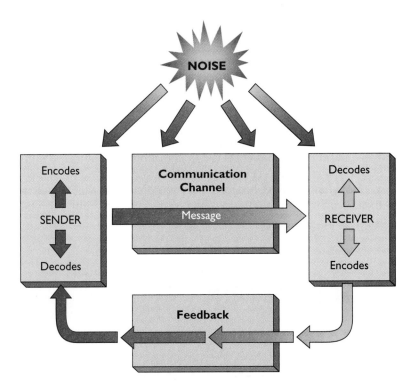

FIGURE 12.1
The Communication Process

sender may not be able to see the receiver (for example, when a Canadian Tire television advertisement is aired across Canada).

If noise or other barriers like stress or perceptual differences cause the person to decode or "hear" the message erroneously, feedback can save the situation. **Feedback** is the receiver's response. Air traffic controllers use feedback when they confirm and receive confirmation of messages they send.

Interpersonal and organizational communication barriers, discussed below, can lead to communications problems in any of these five elements. An event (like a big client lunching with one of your competitors) might be misperceived by you, the sender, as a cause for alarm. A restrictive communication channel (like the chain of command) could cause the message that you sent about the event to be delayed for several weeks. Noise (perhaps in the form of distractions) may further delay the message. And then the president, shocked at the long delay in receiving the message, might decode it erroneously and act as if it were accurate, although the lunch was innocent and the client was not thinking of switching accounts.

The communication model in Figure 12.1 graphically represents both interpersonal and organizational communication. **Interpersonal communication** occurs between two individuals. **Organizational communication** occurs among several individuals or groups. In this chapter, we'll discuss how managers in their leadership roles can better influence other people through both interpersonal and organizational communication techniques.

feedback
The receiver's response.

interpersonal communication
Communication that occurs between two individuals.

organizational communication
Communication that occurs among several individuals or groups.

Improving Interpersonal Communication

Because managers spend so much time communicating face to face, knowing how to improve interpersonal communication is an important management skill. However, let's look first at interpersonal communication barriers.

Barriers to Interpersonal Communication

Several interpersonal communication barriers can distort messages and inhibit communication.[7]

Perception. Perceptions are influenced by many factors, and it is probably safe to say that no two people will perceive the same stimulus or message in exactly the same way.

For one thing, people tend to perceive things in a manner consistent with what they *believe*. If you believe that people are good, trustworthy, and honest, then you may tend to perceive people's actions and their comments in a supportive way. People also perceive *selectively*. At the moment, for instance, you are probably concentrating on this book (we hope!) and may, therefore, be unaware of the radio blaring in the background. Similarly, people tend to select out messages they don't want to hear or simply tune out low-priority or unwelcome information.

Semantics. **Semantics**, the meaning of words, is another barrier, because words mean different things to different people. For example, you might tell an employee to "clean up that oil spill as soon as you can," only to find 10 minutes later that it has not been cleaned up and someone has slipped on it. The employee may say, "But you told me to do it as soon as I could, and I was busy." What you meant by "as soon as you can" was not the same thing as what the employee thought you meant.

semantics
The meaning of words.

Nonverbal Communication. People pick up cues to what you mean not just from your words but from your **nonverbal communication**—your manner of speaking, facial expressions, bodily posture, and so on. Thus, coming to work looking perturbed because you were caught in a traffic jam may communicate to employees that you are dissatis-

nonverbal communication
One's manner of speaking, facial expressions, bodily posture, and so on.

fied with their work, although you don't intend that message to be sent. According to one expert, "It has been estimated that in a conversation involving two people, verbal aspects of a message account for less than 35 percent of the social meaning, whereas nonverbal aspects of a message account for 65 percent of the social meaning."[8]

You're probably already aware of a lot of the nonverbal distractions that can trip a person up, but here's a sampling from one expert's list:

1. Scratching your head indicates confusion or disbelief;

2. Biting your lips signals anxiety;

3. Rubbing the back of your head or neck suggests frustration or impatience;

4. A lowered chin conveys defensiveness or insecurity;

5. Avoiding eye contact conveys insincerity, fear, evasiveness, or (at the very least) lack of interest in what's being discussed;

6. A steady stare suggests a need to control, intimidate, and dominate;

7. Crossing your arms in front of your chest communicates defiance, defensiveness, resistance, aggressiveness, or a closed mind;

8. Hand wringing is a strong sign of anxiety verging on terror;

9. At least in North America, getting a limp, dead-fish handshake is almost a disappointment;

10. Sighing will be interpreted as a sign of distress or of boredom.[9]

Ambiguity. Three types of ambiguity can distort messages. Ambiguity of *meaning* occurs when the person receiving the message isn't sure what was meant by the person who said or wrote the message. (For example, you might wonder whether "see me in my office as soon as you can" means immediately or next week, after you've finished your project.) Ambiguity of *intent* means that the words may be clear, but the sender's intentions aren't. (For example, you may ask, "Why does she want to see me in her office *now*?") Finally, ambiguity of *effect* represents the receiver's uncertainty about predicting what the consequences of responding to the message might be. (Thus, you might understand both your boss's note and her intentions but still not be able to gauge how noncompliance will affect you.)

Defensiveness. When confronted with information that may clash with their self-concept, many employees react defensively. Defences, or defence mechanisms, are adjustments people make, often unconsciously, to avoid having to recognize personal qualities that might lower their self-esteem. Defence mechanisms are very important. Everyone has a picture, real or not, of who they are and what they deserve, and most people try hard to screen out experiences that don't fit this ideal self-image; defence mechanisms are one way to do so.

Up to a point, screening can be useful: If people had to absorb the full impact of the problems and tensions of daily living, some might crack under the pressure. Defence mechanisms help people deflect a lot of the things that might otherwise diminish their self-esteem and raise their anxiety.

As a leader you will therefore find defences to be an important and familiar aspect of interpersonal relations. When someone is accused of poor performance, for instance, his or her first reaction will often be denial. By denying fault, the person avoids having to question or analyze his or her own competence. Still others react to criticism with anger and aggression. This helps them let off steam and postpone confronting the problem until they are better able to cope with it. Still others will react to criticism by retreating into a shell.

Ways to Improve Interpersonal Communication

Leaders depend on interpersonal communication skills to influence others in a variety of situations. The employee who breaks a rule may have to be disciplined; a new employee has to be shown how to improve her performance; a worker has to be persuaded

Not all communication is verbal. Gestures, posture, facial expressions, and even the distances between people all tell a part of the story.

to adopt a remedial plan of action; the sales manager wants to convince the production manager to get the order out a few days sooner—all are situations in which interpersonal communication is the key. The following guidelines should therefore be useful in improving your interpersonal communication skills.

Be an Active Listener. Communications pioneer Carl Rogers says that active listeners try to understand both the facts and the feelings in what they hear. The active listener doesn't just passively hear what the speaker is saying but also tries to understand and respond to the feelings behind the words—fear, anger, confusion, or tension, for instance.[10] The goal is to grasp what the person is saying from his or her point of view, and then convey that you understand. To do this,

- *Listen for total meaning.* For example, if the sales manager says "We can't sell that much this year," the active listener's response wouldn't be, "Sure you can." Instead, understand the underlying feelings, such as the pressure the sales manager might be under, and let the person know that his or her problem is understood.
- *Reflect feelings.* Reflecting the speaker's feelings is important because it helps the speaker to confront them. Reflecting feelings here might mean something like, "They're pushing you pretty hard, aren't they?"
- *Note all cues.* Remember that not all communication is verbal. Other cues such as facial expression and hand gestures portray the person's feeling, too.
- *Avoid passing judgment.* Being judged is almost invariably threatening to the other person's self-image.

Avoid Triggering Defensiveness. Criticizing, arguing, and even giving advice can trigger defensiveness as the person you're speaking with tries to protect his or her self-image. Attempting to influence someone in this way may, therefore, actually backfire. For the same reason, attacking a person's defences is unwise. For example, don't try to "explain a person to himself or herself" by saying things like, "You know the reason you're using that excuse is that you can't bear to be blamed for anything." Instead, concentrate on the act itself (low sales or poor attendance, for instance). Sometimes the best thing to do is nothing at all—postpone action. A cool-down period could give you a different perspective on the matter.

Clarify Your Ideas Before Communicating. Much miscommunication simply results from fuzzy thinking or poorly chosen words (consider our friend out on a drive with his three penguins, for instance). The way to avoid this problem is to "say what you mean and mean what you say," as someone once put it. If you mean "immediately," *say* "immediately," rather than "as soon as you can." Also keep in mind the underlying meaning of your message, and make sure that your tone, expression, and words all convey that same meaning.

Interpersonal Communication in Action

How can you apply what you know about interpersonal communication to some common business situations? Here are some suggestions from Jack Griffin.[11]

In Communicating with Your Supervisor. Your boss is a manager, and he or she is therefore responsible for getting results. In general, therefore, there are some key phrases to avoid when communicating with your boss, since they could be misinterpreted as a lack of responsibility on your part. These include "I'm only human," "I'm overworked," "it slipped past me," "not my fault," "not my problem," and "you don't appreciate me."

Similarly, whether you're requesting a raise or a day off next week, or discussing some other matter, body language to avoid includes cringing, looking down, rushing to be seated, slouching in your chair, bringing your hands to your face, mouth, or neck (since this suggests anxiety and evasion), and crossing your arms in front of your chest.

In Communicating with Colleagues. Getting along with colleagues is important for several reasons: You'll have to depend on them to get the job done, for one thing, and your career progress and day-to-day peace of mind will usually depend to a greater or lesser extent on how you get along with your peers. In general, therefore, unnecessarily belligerent-sounding words or phrases such as "absurd," "bad," "can't," "crazy," "doomed," "unworkable," and "are you out of your mind?" are usually best left unsaid. Body language no-nos include avoiding eye contact, frowning, shaking your head "no," and pushing gestures (that is, using the hands as if to push people or things away).

In Communicating with Subordinates. Your subordinates know that their appraisals and career success are in your hands. Knowing this makes them more sensitive to any indication of disrespect or unfairness on your part. Words to avoid with subordinates therefore include "blame," "catastrophe," "demand," "destroyed," "idiotic," and "misguided." Phrases to avoid include "better shape up," "don't come to me about it," "don't want to hear it," "figure it out for yourself," "you don't understand," and "you'd better." In terms of body language, Griffin says, "it pays to come across as open and receptive."[12] Therefore, maintain eye contact, smile, keep your hands away from your face and mouth, use many open-handed gestures, and (if you feel you must achieve a touch of a subtle domination) direct your glance at the subordinates forehead rather than meeting his or her eyes directly. And, of course (as the cartoon illustrates), don't lose your temper.

Negotiating. "Everything," someone once said, "is a negotiation." Whether you're buying a car, requesting a raise, trying to get a better seat on the airplane, or trying to get a cab driver to move faster or an employee to do a better job, negotiations are involved. And negotiations always mean interpersonal communication.

What is the key to being a good negotiator? Negotiating effectively of course starts with communicating effectively: In other words, actively listen so that you understand both the words and the feelings underlying what the other person has just said; avoid triggering defensiveness (since that will lead to arguments) and be clear and unambiguous in what you say.

Beyond this, there are several "tricks of the trade" that experienced negotiators recommend. For example, *leverage*, *information*, *credibility*, and *judgment* are four important negotiating skills. *Leverage* refers to the factors that either favour or disadvantage a party in a particular bargaining situation.[13] Necessity, desire, competition, and time are four important factors that can create leverage in a deal. For example, it's often the ability to walk away from a deal if acceptable terms can't be hammered out (or to *look* like you're able to walk away) that wins a negotiator the best terms. The seller who is forced to sell (out of necessity) is at an obvious disadvantage.

Similarly, who wants the deal more—*desire*—is another important leverage factor. That shiny new car in the automobile showroom may not be a necessity for you, but if your desire is too obvious, the chances are you won't be able to negotiate as good a deal.

Competition is important too, but then you probably already know that. In a negotiating situation, a critical factor is whether other potential buyers are vying for the right to make the acquisition; there is thus often no more effective ploy then convincing the other party that someone else is dying to make the deal.

Time (and particularly deadlines) can also tilt the tables for or against you. For example, if you've got a deadline that the other party is aware of but that does not particularly affect him or her, chances are you'll be at relative disadvantage. If the other party knows that your plane leaves tomorrow at 4 p.m. and that if you don't get the deal done you'll have to go back empty-handed, you can probably expect some "take it or leave it" demands as your departure approaches.

Information, *credibility*, and *judgment* are the other three basic negotiating skills. Going into the negotiation armed with information about the other side and about every aspect of the situation can put you at a relative advantage, while a lack thereof (or, even worse, having the other side have the information advantage on you) puts you at a distinct disadvantage. To some extent, all negotiations are a bit like poker games, so credibility can also be essential. In particular, the other side will always be assessing whether you're bluffing; convincing them that you're not is therefore an important negotiating skill. Finally, good negotiators always have outstanding judgment: They've got "the ability to strike the right balance between gaining advantages and reaching compromises, in the substance as well as in the style of [their] negotiating technique."[14]

So, how can you apply some of this, let's say when negotiating with your boss for a raise? First, gather all the information you can. Go back over your employment record and focus on how you meet—and exceed—the demands of your job. Make a list of your accomplishments during the preceding year, and research what others in similar positions with similar duties in similar companies are paid.[15]

"Knowledge is power," a philosopher once said, and that's certainly true when it comes to negotiating a raise. There's nothing quite as effective as making it clear what you're worth, and what others in similar situations are being paid for similar jobs. You'll therefore want to formulate a target salary level before you begin.

What will you do for leverage? While not without risks, having a counter-offer can certainly be effective. It's unfortunate but true that even if your relationship with your boss is great, there's a tendency for "the squeaky wheel to get the grease." It often happens in business that you get what you ask for, not just what you deserve. Having another job offer can therefore be an effective negotiating tool.

If you've done your homework (and have been doing a good job!), you've already gone a long way towards establishing your credibility. But there is still a lot that you can do. Your negotiating tactics and your body language will be important, too. For one thing, says one expert, "resolve not to 'ask' for a raise, since that can seem to put you in a subordinate position." Instead, remember that you're *negotiating* for a raise, and that the leverage you bring to the table means that you and your boss are two equal parties trying to work out an equitable deal.

Organizational Communication

While interpersonal communication occurs between two people, organizational communication is the exchange of information and transmission of meaning among several individuals or groups throughout the organization.

Organizational communication can flow downward, laterally, and upward. Downward communications are transmitted from superior to subordinate and consist of messages regarding things like corporate vision, what the job entails, procedures and practices to be followed, and performance evaluations. Lateral or horizontal communications are messages between departments or between people in the same department. Organizational communication can also flow upward. Upward communication (from subordinates to superiors) provides management with valuable insight into how the organization and its employees and competitors are functioning.

We can also distinguish between formal and informal organizational communication. **Formal communications** are messages recognized as official by the organization; they include orders (from superiors to subordinates) and various written and unwritten reports on sales levels, status of projects in progress, and so on. **Informal communication** is not officially sanctioned by the organization; the grapevine (or rumours) is the most familiar example.

Barriers to Organizational Communication

Because organizational communication happens between people, it is susceptible to all of the interpersonal communication problems discussed earlier. Noise, defensiveness, criticism, semantics, perception, and filtering also undermine organizational communication.

However, organizational communication is also plagued by some special problems because of the number of people involved and because they often work in different departments and at different organizational levels. Barriers that undermine organizational communication are as follows.

Distortion. The fact that a message has to be relayed from person to person creates many opportunities for the message to be filtered, embellished, or otherwise distorted. Most people are familiar with the party game in which seven or eight people line up and the first person is given a simple message to relay. Each person whispers the message to the next one in line and the final message usually bears little resemblance to the original one. Much the same phenomenon occurs in organizations. Messages that have to be transferred from person to person tend to be distorted, and the more people involved, the more distortion occurs.

Rumours and the Grapevine. Rumours are a good example of how messages are distorted in organizations. Rumours are spread by the organizational grapevine, often with alarming speed.[16] In one study of 100 employees, the researcher found that when management made an important change in the organization, most employees would hear the news first by grapevine. Hearing news from a supervisor and official memoranda ran a poor second and third, respectively.[17]

Researcher Keith Davis says that there are at least three reasons why rumours are started: lack of information, insecurity, and conflicts.[18] Lack of information contributes because when employees do not know what is happening in their world they are likely to speculate about a situation, and thus a rumour is born. For example, employees who observe an unscheduled disassembly of a machine may speculate that machines are being transferred to another plant and that workers will be laid off. Insecure, anxious employees are more likely to perceive events negatively and tell others of their worries.

Conflicts also foster rumours. For example, conflicts between union and management, or between two strong-willed executives, may trigger rumours as each side tries to interpret or distort the situation in a way most favourable to itself. Davis says that the best way to refute a rumour is to release the truth as quickly as possible, because the more that the rumour is repeated the more it will be believed and distorted.

Information Overload. Sometimes, usually around holidays, you may find that if you try to make a long-distance call you only get a rapid busy signal, because all of the circuits are busy. In this case, the phone lines leading across the country are overloaded and can handle no more messages. Similar problems occur in organizations. Supervisors can juggle only so many problems and make only so many decisions before they become over-loaded and incapable of handling any more messages.

Narrow Viewpoints. Organizational communication often connects people from different departments, each of whom has his or her own narrow viewpoint and specialty. Sales managers tend to see problems as sales problems, and production managers see them as production problems, for instance. These narrow viewpoints in turn can undermine organizational communication because they make it more difficult for each person to see or understand the other's point of view.

Status. The fact that each person in an organization holds a different status can also undermine organizational communication. On the organization chart, it is apparent that the president has more status than the vice-president, who in turn has more status than a sales manager, who in turn has more status than a salesperson.

Status differences can translate into communication breakdowns. Subordinates may prefer not to relate bad news to a boss, and thus hesitate to be candid about problems. The boss in his or her ivory tower may forget that subordinates down the line have a need to know what is happening in their world.

Organizational Culture. The organization's culture—its shared values and traditional ways of doing things—can influence the way that messages flow throughout the organization. When Jack Welch took over as GE's CEO, he inherited an organization that he felt did not adequately encourage lower-level employees to speak their minds. One of Welch's first tasks, therefore, was to re-create GE's culture to encourage all employees to communicate quickly, openly, and with candour.[19] He did this by emphasizing the value of open communication and by instituting organizational changes to encourage employees to speak up.

Hallmark Cards
www.hallmark.com

Structural Restrictions. The physical location of workers may have a restrictive effect on communication. At Hallmark Cards, it was taking 18 months to get a card from "concept to store," instead of the desired 6 months. To solve this problem, the card-creation process was redesigned. Artists and writers, who had previously been in separate buildings, were relocated to a central place where they could communicate easily with each other.

Diversity Issues. When many people and groups work together, there's a greater chance that diversity-driven differences in the way that messages are interpreted will undermine effective communication. What something means—whether it's a word, tone, hand gesture, or nonverbal behaviour—can be dramatically different among different ethnic and cultural groups. Consider these examples:

- In Canada, winking communicates friendship, but it is considered rude in Australia, Hong Kong, and Malaysia.
- Raising an eyebrow in Tonga means "I agree," but in Peru it means "pay me."
- Circling your ear with your finger means "crazy" in most European countries, but in the Netherlands it means "you have a phone call."
- Waving at someone is a sign of recognition in Canada, but it is considered a severe insult in Nigeria.
- Nodding your head means "yes" in Canada and the United States, but it means "no" in Bulgaria and Sri Lanka. In Turkey, people say "no" by shutting their eyes, raising their chin, and throwing their head back.
- Slapping a person on the back is inappropriate in Japan because touching is viewed as unacceptable.

Boundary Differences. Finally, remember (from Chapter 8, Designing Organizations to Manage Change) that boundary differences can inhibit communication. The authority, task, political, and identity boundaries must be pierced if communication is to flow freely.

For example, subordinates tend to be somewhat deferential towards their bosses, and may tell them what they want to hear or withhold unwelcome information. Employees also

In Canada, giving a person the "thumbs up" signal is a sign that things are going well, but in Bangladesh it is considered rude.

tend to be short-sighted when it comes to interpreting information and understanding organizational problems. The president's message that "costs are too high" might prompt the sales manager to claim that "production should get their costs under control," while the production manager might argue that "we are selling too many different products."[20]

Improving Organizational Communication

Different techniques exist for improving organizational communication in each direction in which it flows. For example, suggestion systems are useful for encouraging upward communication. And, some firms like Toyota install closed-circuit informational TV systems to enhance the information that top management can broadcast downward to the company's troops.

Influencing Upward Communication

Many organizations establish special methods through which employees can communicate their feelings and opinions upward to their superiors. Such methods can be beneficial. For example, they provide superiors with feedback about whether subordinates understand orders and instructions. They contribute to an acceptance of top management's decisions by giving subordinates a chance to "blow off steam." And they encourage subordinates to offer ideas of value to themselves and the organization. Special channels like these also provide supervisors with valuable information on which they can base decisions,[21] encourage gripes and grievances to surface,[22] and cultivate commitment by giving employees an opportunity to express their ideas and suggestions.[23] Upward communication can help employees "cope with their work problems and strengthen their involvement in their jobs and with the organization."[24]

Many firms also use upward communication to "take their pulse" by seeing how subordinates feel about their jobs, superiors, subordinates, and organization. For example, we saw that some companies periodically administer attitude surveys. In this way, management gets answers to questions like "Are working hours and shift rotations perceived as reasonable?" "Do employees feel that the boss has favourites?" and "Do employees consider cafeteria prices to be fair and the quality of the food to be good?" Managers can then assess the need for change and correct any problems that need solving.

At Imperial Oil, employees were asked to view the merger with Texaco Canada as an advantage because the new organization would have more opportunities for promotion. Employees filled out a questionnaire that asked them to indicate what positions they wanted in the new organization. Seventy-nine percent got their first choice, and 93 percent got one of their top three choices.[25]

Robert Glegg, president of Glegg Water Conditioning Inc., lunches regularly with small groups of employees to exchange ideas about projects, people, and problems. In one of these sessions, he heard objections from engineers about a proposed open-office concept and as a result changed the plans to satisfy their needs.[26]

George Cohon, president of McDonald's Restaurants of Canada, encourages upward communication by casually defining his office space. No doors or walls screen him from visitors. Employees are encouraged to talk to the boss whenever they feel the need.[27] Trevor Hayden, president of Ambassador Coffee Services, holds regular meetings with staff to keep them up to date on what is happening in the company, particularly during tough economic times.[28]

Imperial Oil
www.imperialoil.ca

Texaco
www.texaco.com

Methods for Encouraging Upward Communication. Many techniques are used to encourage upward communication. One expert says, "by far the most effective way of tapping the ideas of subordinates is sympathetic listening in the many day-to-day, informal contacts within the department and outside the workplace."[29] Here are other popular methods.

1. Social gatherings, including departmental parties, outings, picnics, and recreational events, provide good opportunities for informal, casual communication.

2. Union publications (in unionized organizations) can provide management with useful insights into employee attitudes.

3. Scheduled meetings. Particularly where subordinates are numerous, it can be easy to neglect contacting or communicating with them, especially the more introspective ones. For this reason, some experts suggest that supervisors keep a checklist of those subordinates that they have spoken with during the month so that meetings can be scheduled with any who might have been missed. Some supervisors formally schedule a monthly meeting with each of or all of their subordinates, in addition to the informal contacts that take place during the month.

4. Performance appraisal meetings usually provide good opportunities for seeking out an employee's opinions about his or her job and job attitudes.

5. Grievances should be monitored. Grievances are often symptoms of misunderstandings and provide top management with useful insights into problems at the operational level.

6. Attitude surveys can provide supervisors with useful information about employee morale.

7. A formal suggestion system—even one as simple as a suggestion box into which employees can anonymously drop comments—is another good way to encourage upward communication.

8. An "open door" policy, which allows subordinates to transmit concerns through a channel outside the normal chain of command, can act as a useful safety valve. Related to this is a formal appeals process (where no formal grievance process is in effect) that can show subordinates that their requests and complaints will receive fair treatment, even if they are not satisfied with the response of their immediate superior.

9. Finally, indirect measures, including monitoring absences, turnover rates, and

safety records, can be valuable indicators of unstated, uncommunicated problems that exist at the operational level.

Whichever of these mechanisms is used, at least three principles can boost their effectiveness. First, the system should be formalized—through scheduled meetings, suggestion plans, yearly surveys, and so on. Second, there must be a culture of trust in the organization, since subordinates are unlikely to speak freely (even anonymously) if they mistrust management's motives.[30]

Finally, management should react to the opinions and problems expressed in upward communication, even if just to acknowledge that they have been received. If the problem cannot be solved, it should be made clear why. If the problem can be eliminated, it should be. At Chrysler's Bramalea plant, suggestions are welcomed from workers, who fill out special forms describing problems they've noticed. Solutions to problems are also encouraged. The engineering staff, which is responsible for acting on these suggestions, acknowledges each request within a day, and responds with some type of action within 72 hours. When an employee's idea is adopted, a reward is given, ranging from a free lunch to the use of a Chrysler LH for the weekend.[31]

Here are three more examples of effective upward communication programs.

General Electric's Workout. To make General Electric more responsive to change, several years ago the company began a series of classroom sessions with executives that became known as the "pit."[32] In these sessions, GE executives were encouraged to put aside decorum and engage the firm's CEO, Jack Welch, in the "rough and tumble debate he relishes."[33] Soon, however, Welch became concerned that the candour he was experiencing with his executives in the pit meetings was not carrying over to lower-level GE employees, and the workout was born.

Like the pit, "workout" is basically a place. One observer described it as a forum in which participating employees get a mental workout while engaging in enthusiastic discussions aimed at taking unnecessary work out of their jobs and working out problems together.[34] A group of 40 to 100 employees, "picked by management from all ranks and several functions, goes to a conference center or hotel."[35] The three-day sessions are usually kicked off by a talk by the group's boss, who soon leaves.

An outside consultant/facilitator then breaks the group into five or six teams, each of which addresses problems, lists complaints, and debates solutions. Later the boss returns and the team spokesperson makes the team's proposals. Under workout's rules, the boss can make only three responses: He or she can agree on the spot, say no, or ask for more information.[36]

The workout sessions are useful for solving problems and for getting employees to express their ideas upward with openness and candour. As one GE electrician responded when told that his comments had made his boss "really sweat," "When you've been told to shut up for 20 years and someone tells you to speak up—you're going to let them have it."[37]

Federal Express's Guaranteed Fair Treatment Procedure. Federal Express's guaranteed fair treatment procedure is an upward communication process that contains three steps. In step 1, *management review,* the complainant submits a written complaint to a member of management. The manager reviews all relevant information, holds a conference with the complainant, and makes a decision to uphold, modify, or overturn the original supervisor's actions.[38]

In step 2, *officer review,* the complainant can submit a written complaint to a vice-president or senior vice-president of his or her division. That person reviews all relevant information, conducts an additional investigation, and makes a decision to uphold, overturn, or modify management's action.

In step 3, *executive appeals review,* the complainant can submit a written complaint that goes to an appeals board consisting of Federal Express's CEO, president, and chief personnel officer, as well as two other senior vice-presidents. They then review all relevant information and make a decision to uphold, overturn, or initiate an investigative board of review. (The latter is used when there is a question of fact.)

Toyota's Hotline. Toyota Motor Manufacturing tells its employees, "Don't spend time worrying about something...speak up!" At Toyota, the primary upward communication channel is called "Hotline." Its purpose is to give team members an additional channel for bringing questions or problems to the company's attention.

The hotline is available 24 hours a day. Employees are instructed to pick up any phone, dial the hotline extension (the number is posted on the plant bulletin board), and deliver their messages to the recorder. All inquiries are guaranteed to be reviewed by the human resources manager and to be thoroughly investigated.

If it is decided that a particular question would be of interest to other Toyota team members, then the question, along with the firm's response, is posted on plant bulletin boards. If a personal response is desired, employees must leave their names when they call. However, employees know that no other attempt will be made to identify a particular hotline caller.[39]

Appraising Your Boss. How would you like to appraise your supervisor, and how (if at all) do you think that knowing he or she will be appraised would influence the way he or she acts? A recent study sheds some interesting light on this upward communication technique.

Supervisors usually seem to react well to having subordinates appraise them, especially when the appraisals are not anonymous.[40] One study examined the effects of such upward feedback by collecting subordinates' ratings for 238 managers in a large corporation at two points in time, six months apart. Subordinates were asked to rate a variety of supervisory behaviours, such as "Regularly challenged me to continuously improve my effectiveness," "Took steps to resolve conflict and disagreement within the team," and "Treated me fairly and with respect."[41]

The study found that the performance of managers whose initial appraisal was high did not improve significantly in six months. However, there was a marked improvement in performance among managers whose initial appraisal was moderate or low. The researchers conclude that "this is encouraging because these are the managers that most need to improve from the organization's (as well as the subordinates') perspective."[42]

An interesting aspect of the findings was that the managers' performance improved whether or not they received the feedback. It's possible that the knowledge that their subordinates would appraise them was enough to get them to improve their behaviour at work.

Influencing Downward Communication

Downward communication includes a variety of essential types of information: job instructions, rationales for jobs (including how jobs are related to other jobs and positions in the organization), organizational policies and practices, employee performance, and the organization's mission.[43]

In addition to the usual channels (like face-to-face and written messages), firms today use many means to get data "down to the troops." At Saturn Corporation, assemblers describe communication as excellent and say, "We get information continuously via the internal television network and from financial documents."[44] The firm also has monthly town-hall-like meetings, usually with 500 to 700 people attending. The result is that all employees are familiar with Saturn's activities and performance.

Toyota has five-minute team information meetings at job sites twice a day, during which employees get the latest plant news. Toyota also puts a television set in each work site break area; the sets run continuously and present plant-wide information from the in-house Toyota Broadcasting Center. The company sponsors quarterly roundtable discussions between top management and selected non-supervisory staff, and an in-house newsletter. The hotline described earlier is another channel of top-down information, giving management a chance to answer publicly questions that team members might have.

Toyota's managers also practise what's become known as "managing by walking around." The plant's top management is often on the shop floor, fielding questions, providing performance information, and ensuring that all general managers, managers, and team members are "aware of Toyota's goal and where we are heading."[45]

Other companies are implementing a program called **open-book management**. As

open-book management
Literally opening the books of a company to the employees; financial data are shared, numbers are explained, and then workers are rewarded for improvements in the business performance.

An innovative form of downward communication, the in-house Toyota Broadcasting Center presents company news and information that employees can watch in their work site break areas.

its name implies, open-book management involves literally opening the books of a company to the employees. Financial data are shared, numbers are explained, and then workers are rewarded for improvements in business performance.[46] The basic goal of open-book management is to foster trust and commitment among employees by treating them, for informational purposes, more like partners than employees.

Influencing Horizontal Communication

It is also important for managers to pay attention to lateral, or horizontal, communication between departments. After Abitibi-Price and Stone Consolidated merged to form Abitibi-Consolidated, CEO Ronald Oberlander focused on improving communication between the manufacturing plants of the formerly separate companies. Managers also spent time developing a common vision for the company that everyone would understand.[47]

Managers use several techniques to improve horizontal communication. For example, managers traditionally use individuals or committees to bridge departments and improve the flow of communication between them, as follows:

■ *Liaison personnel.* A sales liaison person may be employed by the sales department, but be physically located in the factory to advise factory management about the sales department's priorities.

■ *Committees and task forces.* Interdepartmental committees, task forces, and teams are usually composed of representatives from several interdependent departments; the committees meet periodically to discuss and solve common problems and to ensure interdepartmental communication and coordination.

■ *Independent integrators.* Some companies boost interdepartmental communication by creating special independent integrators. A new-product development department is one example. This department's role is to facilitate communication and coordination among the activities of several other departments, such as research and development, sales, engineering, and manufacturing.

More informal techniques can also be effective (see the Entrepreneurial Edge box).

Encouraging Informal Communication

grapevine
The informal channel of communication in organizations.

As we saw in Chapter 7, the informal organization is an important part of everyday organizational activity. The **grapevine**, which is the informal channel of communication in or-

Fostering "Interdepartmental Empathy"

Adaptec
www.adaptec.com

While formal approaches are important, more and more companies today rely on informal means for improving interdepartmental communication. As the chief financial officer for the electronics firm Adaptec puts it: "We still look at teamwork as interdisciplinary empathy, not just slogans and well-coordinated efforts."[48] What this means in practice, he says, is that it's not enough for each department manager to look at decisions from his or her department's own point of view. Instead, each manager "must understand enough about the company's marketing, sales and operations [and finance]" to understand the impact of each department's activities on the decisions that need to be made.[49]

Adaptec fosters "interdisciplinary empathy" in several ways. Interdepartmental brainstorming sessions "let you bounce marketing's great idea off finance and operations, which may change the idea to align more closely with financial and operational realities."[50] Thus, when coordinating major product introductions, "members of the finance, engineering, manufacturing and marketing departments often meet bimonthly to brainstorm problems and solutions. Each participant assesses the situation and can then express an opinion on how, for example, a certain product packaging design could affect manufacturing or engineering processes or how the budget allotted for the project can help define product design or advertising."[51] What emerges from such sessions, says this executive, "is usually an idea or set of ideas that reflects the company's overall competencies better than ideas originating from any one department."

The company uses more formal interdepartmental communication programs as well. For example, their in-house legal department has developed a presentation to teach other departments about trademarks, and the finance department has provided financial training for other departments. "The cross-training sessions make it much easier to achieve understanding and buy-in to corporate strategies."

ganizations, is much faster than formal channels of communication. A survey of 393 Canadian companies that had reduced staff revealed that workers had heard the bad news unofficially in nearly half of the cases.[52]

The impact of the grapevine must be considered by managers as they plan their communication strategy, and managers are advised to plug into the grapevine to find out what kind of information is informally moving around the organization. They can also use it to squelch false rumours and to send out information that they want employees to hear.

In a study of innovative companies, Tom Peters and Robert Waterman found that these companies used informal, almost unorthodox, means of communicating to help them remain responsive and manage change.[53] Although some firms subsequently fell off most experts' lists of "excellent" companies, the techniques they used to encourage informal communication provide some useful insights:

> The excellent companies are a vast network of informal, open communications. The patterns and intensity cultivate the right people getting into contact with each other, regularly, and the chaotic/anarchic properties of a system are kept well under control simply because of the regularity of contact and its nature.[54]

In those outstanding and innovative companies, "the name of the success game" is rich, informal communication:

Walt Disney Company
disney.go.com

The astonishing byproduct is the ability to have your cake and eat it, too; that is, rich informal communication leads to more action, more experiments, more learning, and simultaneously to the ability to stay better in touch and on top of things.[55]

In excellent companies, say Peters and Waterman, the intensity and sheer volume of communication are unmistakable, and usually start with a stress on informality.[56] Specifically, they found that:

1. *Informality is emphasized.* At the Walt Disney Company, for instance, everyone from the president down wears a name tag with just his or her first name on it. (These are worn in the parks on a regular basis.) At 3M there are endless meetings, but few are scheduled; most are characterized by the casual getting together of people from different disciplines who talk about problems in a campus-like, shirt-sleeves atmosphere.

2. *Communication intensity is maintained at an extraordinary level.* At the more successful companies, meetings and presentations are held in which "the questions are unabashed; the flow is free; everyone is involved. Nobody hesitates to cut off the chairman, the president or board members."[57] What is encouraged, in other words, is an open confrontation of ideas in which people are blunt and straightforward in going after the issues. Meetings in these companies are not formal and politicized affairs. Instead, they are open, informative discussions in which all points of view can safely be aired.

3. *Communication is given physical support.* Blackboards and open offices facilitate and encourage frequent informal interaction. In one high-tech firm, for instance, all employees from the president down work not in offices but in two-metre-high doorless cubicles that encourage openness and interaction among employees. Corning Glass installed escalators rather than elevators in its new engineering building to increase the chance of face-to-face contact.[58] Another company got rid of its four-person dining room tables and substituted long rectangular ones that encourage strangers to come in contact, often across departmental lines. Managers are encouraged to get out of their offices, walk around, and strike up conversations with those both inside and outside their own departments.

Informal communication at Walt Disney Co. is exemplified by the employees' first-name-only name tags.

What all of this adds up to, say Peters and Waterman, is "lots of communication." In most of these firms, they say, you cannot wander around for long without "seeing lots of people sitting together in a room with blackboards working casually on problems."[59] (The People Side of Managing provides a possible rationale for keeping things so open.)

Communicating at the Speed of Thought

Telecommunications and the Internet play an important role in managing organizations today. Apparel manufacturer Levi Strauss uses a sophisticated telecommunications system to link its own inventory and manufacturing facilities with point-of-sale processing devices at retail stores. Detailed sales information is transmitted directly to headquarters, where it is analyzed for trends and buying patterns. Management can then make decisions regarding inventories and production plans. Similarly, retailers such as JC Penney use telecommunications to manage in-store inventories. Its buyers get instant access to sales information from the stores and can modify their purchasing accordingly.

As another example, Ford designers use computers to develop designs for new cars such as the Lincoln Continental. Digitized designs are sent via telecommunications and are reproduced at Ford's design facility in Turin, Italy, where Styrofoam mock-ups are made.

Telecommunications is also important to managers because more and more managerial computer system applications rely on it. Levi Strauss depends on telecommunications in its computerized inventory control system; radiologists rely on telecommunications for X-rays taken by their technologists, which can then be read from remote locations; your college or university may use telecommunications to allow you to access library information from your office or home; computer-assisted manufacturing systems rely on telecommu-

telecommunications
The electronic transmission of data, text, graphics, voice, or image over distance.

Applying Communication Research in Practice

What can research studies by communication experts tell us about staying more responsive by managing communication? Results from two lines of research—on communication networks and on "media richness"—are informative.

Communication Networks in Action. What happens when organizational communication is restricted to just a few allowable routes, as in more bureaucratic organizations? A classic study by psychologist Harold Leavitt addressed this question.[60]

Groups of five persons were arranged in one of the "communication networks" shown in Figure 12.2. Each person was placed in a compartment at a table in such a way that his or her communication was restricted. Each subject in the all-channel network could communicate with any other subject. Subjects in the wheel network could communicate only with the subject in the central position (hub) of the network, but this central person could communicate with all of the subjects in his network. (The lines show two-way linkages.) All each person knew was to whom messages could be sent and from whom messages could be received.

The researchers found that the best communication network depended on the nature of the problem that had to be solved. Where the problem was simple and amenable to a clear-cut, yes-or-no answer (such as "Is this marble blue?"), the wheel network worked best. But for complex, ambiguous problems that required lots of give and take among the subjects, the all-channel network worked best. Here, for instance, each person was given marbles that were difficult to describe. Two people looking at identical marbles could describe them quite differently; what one might view as "greenish-yellow," another might call "aqua." The person in the centre of the wheel network could not quickly decide what colour was com-

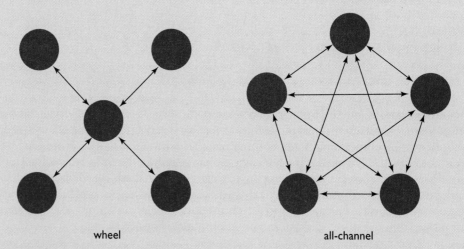

wheel   all-channel

FIGURE 12.2
Two Experimental Communication Networks
Note: In the "centralized" wheel network, each subject could communicate only with the hub subject; in the all-channel "decentralized" network, each subject could communicate with every other subject, so that ambiguous problems could be solved more quickly.

→

mon to all of the marbles. Rather, the all-channel network, in which communication could flow freely to everyone, arrived at the fastest decision for ambiguous problems.

Evidence from studies like Peters and Waterman's (discussed above) support the idea that lots of give and take is best when the company is faced with many ambiguous, unpredictable situations. In their study of quickly changing "organic" companies in the electronics industry, for instance, Burns and Stalker found "a lateral rather than a vertical direction of communication throughout the organization; communication between people of different rank, also resembling consultation rather than command; [and] a content of communication which consists of information and advice rather than instructions."[61]

The Media Richness Model. If you were an emergency room doctor and had to diagnose a patient who was obviously turning green, would you do it face to face or send impersonal notes back and forth?

The question highlights what communication researchers call the media richness model. Richard Daft and Robert Lengel say that the communication media or channels used—which may include face-to-face contact, telephone, personally addressed documents, or unaddressed documents—differ in their "media richness." This idea is summarized in Figure 12.3.[62] Media richness means the capacity of the media to resolve ambiguity. It is determined by four aspects: speed of feedback, the number of cues and channels employed, personalness of the source, and richness of the language used.

Face-to-face oral communication is the richest medium. As you know from your own experience, it provides instantaneous audio and visual feedback not just through the person's words but through his or her body language and tone as well. At the other extreme, unaddressed documents like company-wide memos impersonally distributed to all employees are lowest in media richness.

Do organizations and people rely more on rich media for addressing ambiguous situations? Yes and no. When it comes to traditional forms of communication such as face to face, telephone, and letters and memos, the answer is yes: The more ambiguous the situation to be addressed, the richer the media used in many companies. On the other hand, a recent entry in the communication media medley—e-mail—seems frequently to be used for addressing more emotional, ambiguous tasks even though it is relatively low in media richness.

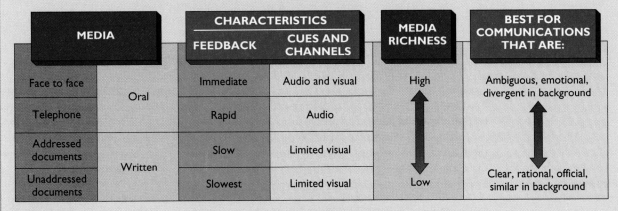

MEDIA		CHARACTERISTICS		MEDIA RICHNESS	BEST FOR COMMUNICATIONS THAT ARE:
		FEEDBACK	CUES AND CHANNELS		
Face to face	Oral	Immediate	Audio and visual	High	Ambiguous, emotional, divergent in background
Telephone		Rapid	Audio		
Addressed documents	Written	Slow	Limited visual		
Unaddressed documents		Slowest	Limited visual	Low	Clear, rational, official, similar in background

FIGURE 12.3
Hierarchy of Media Richness and Application for Managerial Applications

nications to transmit information from one location in the plant to another; and banks depend on telecommunications to make their remote automatic teller machines operational. Telecommunications also fosters the use of newer management computer system applications. We'll look at these on the next few pages.

Work Group Support Systems

Work groups and teams play an increasingly important role in managing organizations. The group might be a door-assembly team at Saturn cars, the sales department at a Levi Strauss subsidiary, or a project team set up in a manufacturing plant to solve a quality-control problem. It might be relatively permanent (as it would be if it were a sales department) or temporary (such as a group formed to solve a one-time quality problem). The team's members might all be at a single site, of they might be dispersed around the city or even around the world. All of the following work group support systems facilitate communication among a team's members.

Electronic Mail. Electronic mail (e-mail) is a computerized information system that lets group members electronically create, edit, and disseminate messages to each other, using electronic "mailboxes." E-mail's aim is to speed and facilitate intragroup communication and thereby bolster intragroup coordination. An **electronic bulletin board** is another example. It lets one or more group members file messages on various topics to be picked up later by other group members.

E-mail systems are not just for messages any more. For example, e-mail software called Eudora Pro helps Jim Le Goullon manage his sales operation. It lets him set up one computer to check all customer accounts every 10 minutes so he never misses a rush order. And it lets him sort messages based on key words like "brochure" (the requests for brochures are then automatically routed to the person in charge of mailing them).[63]

Videoconferencing. Videoconferencing is a telecommunications-based method that lets group members interact directly with or leave messages for a number of other group members via television links. Videoconferencing can significantly improve communication and coordination among the group members and help a work group achieve its aims more quickly than the group could otherwise. For example, the team developing the Boeing 777 made extensive use of videoconferencing for meetings with engine suppliers and key airlines regarding the new aircraft's design.[64]

Group Decision-Support Systems. A group decision-support system (GDSS) is an interactive computer-based system that facilitates the solution of unstructured problems by a team of decision makers.[65] The general aim of a GDSS is to allow a team of decision makers to get together (often in the same room) to facilitate making a particular decision or completing a particular task. To that end, the GDSS (as pictured in Figure 12.4) allows team members to interact via their computers and to use a number of software tools aimed at assisting them in their decision making or project completion.

Typical GDSS software tools include electronic questionnaires, electronic brainstorming tools, idea organizers (to help team members synthesize ideas generated during brainstorming), and tools for voting or setting priorities (so that recommended solutions can be weighted and prioritized).

Using GDSS helps a group avoid a lot of the group decision-making barriers that often occur in face-to-face groups. There's less likelihood that one assertive person will dominate the meeting, since all of the brainstorming and listing of ideas—and the voting—is governed by the computerized programs.

Other Work Group Support Systems. Other work group support systems are also available. **Collaborative writing systems** let a work group's members create long written documents (such as proposals) while working simultaneously at one of a number of interconnected or network computers. As team members work on different sections of the proposal, each member has automatic access to the rest of the sections and can modify his or her section to be compatible with the rest.

electronic bulletin board
A computerized information system that allows one or more group members to file messages on various topics to be picked up later by other group members.

collaborative writing systems
Allow a work group's members to create long written documents (such as proposals) while working simultaneously at one of a number of interconnected or network computers.

Communication at Nortel Networks

In 1895, a company called Northern Electric and Manufacturing began producing telephones. More than a century later, it has evolved into Nortel Networks, a company with 63 000 workers and a reputation as one of Canada's high-tech treasures. It is a world leader in phone switch technology, spending more on R&D than any other private company in Canada.

The rapid technological changes that are occurring in business are affecting Nortel just as they are other companies. Consider this: It is 11 a.m. on a recent Wednesday, and 42-year-old Dan Hunt, president of Nortel Networks' Caribbean and Latin American operations, is live on the air from the company's South Florida TV studio, answering questions from his far-flung employees. From Mexico, one employee wants to know how a new joint venture between Motorola and Cisco will affect Nortel. And so this topic goes on Hunt's once-a-month "corporate conversation," an hour-long program that enables him to interact live and informally with 2000 of his employees in 46 countries.

As Emma Carrasco, Hunt's marketing and communications vice-president, puts it: "We're always looking for ways to break down barriers in the company, and people are comfortable with a talk-show format."[66] This talk-show format lets Hunt and Nortel break down the typical one-way, top-down, rigid, corporate way of communicating. And it's why more and more smart companies are experimenting with live, interactive ways of communicating.

FIGURE 12.4
A Decision Support System
The Ventana Corporation demonstrates the features of its GroupSystems for Windows electronic meeting software, which helps people create, share, record, organize, and evaluate ideas in meetings, between offices, or around the world.

group scheduling system
Allows each group member to put his or her daily schedule into a shared database, which enables group members to identify the most suitable times for meetings or to attend currently scheduled meetings.

work flow automation system
Uses an e-mail-type system to automate paperwork flow.

telecommuting
The substitution of telecommunications and computers for the commute to a central office.

A **group scheduling system** lets each group member put his or her daily schedule into a shared database, which enables group members to identify the most suitable times for meetings or to attend currently scheduled meetings. The **work flow automation system** uses an e-mail-type system to automate paperwork flow.[67] For example, if a proposal requires four signatures, it can be sent electronically from mailbox to mailbox for the required signatures.

Telecommuting. Today, millions of people around the world do most of their work at home and commute to their work electronically. **Telecommuting** is the substitution of telecommunications and computers for the commute to a central office.[68] Nortel Networks has about 7000 telecommuters, one of whom is Dee McCrae. If she wants to do some work after dinner, she simply goes upstairs to her office in her home. She likes it because it saves wear and tear on her car. She also doesn't have to have such a big wardrobe.[69]

Telecommuting helps employees avoid driving a long way to work, but they often report feeling isolated and lonely. To avoid this problem, B.C. Tel and Bentall Development Inc. jointly developed a satellite telecommuting office in Langley, B.C. It allows workers who used to have to commute to Burnaby or Vancouver to reduce their travel time considerably and still be able to interact with other workers.[70]

The typical telecommuter falls into one of three categories. Some are not employees at all but are independent entrepreneurs who work out of their homes—perhaps developing new computer applications for consulting clients. The second (and largest) group of telecommuters includes professionals and highly skilled people who work at jobs that involve a great deal of independent thought and action. These employees—computer programmers, regional salespersons, textbook editors, or research specialists, for instance—typically work at home most of the time, coming into the office only occasionally, perhaps for monthly meetings.[71] The third telecommuter category includes workers who carry out relatively routine and easily monitored jobs such as data entry or word processing.[72]

Internet-Based Communication

While you are reading this page, millions of people are "on the Internet" searching through libraries, talking to friends, and buying and selling products and services. And at the same time, countless businesses are using the Internet to help them communicate—at the speed of thought.

The Internet provides enormous communication benefits to organizations. For one thing, since companies can, in a sense, get a "free ride" on the Internet, they can substantially reduce their communication costs. For instance, FedEx clients can track their own packages using FedEx's Web site instead of inquiring by telephone, thus saving FedEx millions of dollars per year.[73] Similarly, the Internet makes it easier and less expensive for companies to coordinate the work of small teams that may be opening new markets in isolated places.

Building Internet-Based Virtual Communities

Work group support systems and Internet-based communication systems provide a glimpse of how companies today are using the Internet to build virtual communities and networked, boundaryless organizations among their employees.

Companies want to build virtual communities for many reasons. For example, a company implements a new procedure and needs to make sure that the affected employees are communicating with each other to ensure that the procedure is implemented successfully.[74] In one case, a group of managers attended a series of management development courses; top management wanted to make sure they would continue to interact and to apply what they learned once they were back on the job. In this case, the goals included reinforcing and building on what the managers learned in the courses, and providing ongoing interactive ways for the managers to meet and learn from each other.[75]

The solution was an Internet-based application called Management University. This was basically a special Internet Web site that contained a "virtual library" that offered a pre-screened selection of books, articles, videos, and CD-ROMs on topics that complemented those in the management development course. Another part of the Web site was called Management Forum. It allowed those who attended the courses to interact and to share problems and examples of how they applied what they had learned.

With the need for such virtual communities booming, more companies are introducing Internet-based software applications to help organizations establish their own Internet-based virtual communities. Dubbed a "virtual community construction kit," one company has created an application called Tribal Voice. Its features include instant messaging (sending a message that will pop up on the receiver screens), text to speech (hearing text as it appears in a window), file transfer (exchanging files), buddy list (keeping track of regular online contacts), whiteboard (exchanging drawings), and cruising (starting a meeting or conversation with a few people and then directing their Web browsers to the pages of your choosing).[76]

Tribal Voice can help a company let a group of its employees who share a common interest get together via the Internet. For example, says the vice-president of marketing for the company that created Tribal Voice, "the sales department could hold forums and share information in an interactive community. A salesperson in a remote location could join this online department and ask for advice on a particular company he or she wants to call on."[77]

Is There a Company Portal in Your Future?

While most people today are using Web-based portals like Yahoo! to surf the Internet, more and more employees will soon be using their employers' special company-based business portals.

What is a business portal?[78] For one thing, it is, like other portals, a window to the Internet. However, for the companies that are increasingly setting them up for their employees, business portals are a great deal more. Through their business portals, categories of employees—secretaries, engineers, salespeople, and so on—will be able to access all of the corporate applications they need to use, as well as "get the tools [they] need to analyze data inside and outside [their] company, and see the customized content [they] need, like industry news and competitive data."[79]

Many companies are already rushing into the business of designing business portals for corporate customers. Netscape (which is now a division of America Online) has created business portals for employees at FedEx and Lucent. Another firm, Concur Technologies, just installed business portals for Hearst Corp.'s 15 000 employees. So, if communication is indeed "the exchange of information and the transmission of meaning," it looks like a company portal will soon be in most employees' future, helping them to zero in on just the information they need to do their jobs, and helping them to organize and make sense of all the information that's out there.

Netscape
www.netscape.com

Lucent
www.lucent.com

Concur Technologies
www.concur.com

SUMMARY OF LEARNING OBJECTIVES

1. **Define communication and list the five elements in the communication process.** Communication is the exchange of information and the transmission of meaning. It is the essence of managing. The five elements in the communication process are sender, communication channel, noise, receiver, and feedback.

2. **Understand how to improve your interpersonal communication.** You can improve your interpersonal communication by being an active listener, avoiding triggering defensiveness, and clarifying your ideas before communicating.

→

3. **List the barriers that undermine organizational communication.** Because organizational communication involves people, it is susceptible to all of the problems of interpersonal communication, as well as to some special problems, including distortion, rumours, the grapevine, information overload, narrow viewpoints, differences in status, organizational culture, structural restrictions, diversity issues, and boundary differences.

4. **Understand how to overcome the barriers that undermine organizational communication.** These barriers can be overcome by influencing upward communication (social gatherings, union publications, scheduled meetings, performance appraisal meetings, attitude surveys, formal suggestions systems, etc.), by influencing downward communication (job instructions, rationales for jobs, organizational policies and practices, team information meetings, management by walking around, open-book management, etc.), by influencing horizontal communication (using liaison personnel, committees and task forces, and independent integrators), and by encouraging informal communication (emphasizing informality, encouraging high communication intensity, giving communication physical support, etc.).

5. **Give examples of how telecommunications improves communication within and among organizations.** Levi Strauss uses a sophisticated telecommunications system to link its own inventory and manufacturing facilities with point-of-sale processing devices at retail stores. Retailers use telecommunications to manage in-store inventories. Ford Motor uses computers to develop designs for new cars, and these designs are sent via telecommunications to overseas design facilities. Electronic bulletin boards let group members file messages on various topics to be picked up later by other group members. Videoconferencing lets group members interact directly with other group members via television links. Group decision-support systems (GDSS) allow teams of decision-makers to get together to facilitate making a decision or completing a particular task. Telecommuting substitutes telecommunications and computers for the commute to a central office. Other electronic systems include collaborative writing systems, group scheduling systems, and work flow automation systems.

TYING IT ALL TOGETHER

Motivating and influencing employees is basically impossible if a leader can't effectively communicate with his or her employees, and so (having covered leadership and motivation in the previous two chapters) we turned in this chapter to how communication takes place in modern companies today. We began by discussing the barriers to interpersonal communication, improving interpersonal communication, and organizational communication and how it can be improved.

We also saw in this chapter that communicating today increasingly revolves around telecommunications (including, for instance, computer-based group decision support software and videoconferencing). In fact, along with the sorts of Internet-based applications that make virtual communities possible, it's hard to imagine how most of the 21st-century management techniques used today (such as networked and boundaryless organizations and virtual terms) would even be possible. Indeed, today's new telecommunications and Internet-based techniques are to a large extent the foundation around which modern companies are built. Having discussed the telecommunications and Internet bases for group work and virtual teams in this chapter, we'll turn in Chapter 13 to a closer look at how companies use teams today.

CRITICAL THINKING EXERCISES

1. For many of us, communication brings to mind technology. The uses of the computer, from e-mail to the Internet, shape our thinking patterns and, consequently, our communication. Everything is speeded up with electronic communication. Where will this electronic revolution take communication in the next 10 years? Will we all be e-mailing instead of writing letters, banking and shopping from home computers, doing business through our home pages on the Internet, and teleconferencing via video computer links? What do you think our patterns of communication will be as technology evolves?

2. English was the international language for the last half of the 20th century. In the 1980s English was used by at least 750 million people, and barely half of those people spoke it as their mother tongue. By 2000, millions of people from every continent and country spoke English. Countries such as Taiwan require English as a language, as do many other nations. *The Story of English*, by Robert Crum, William Cran, and Robert MacNeil, is a fascinating analysis of the growth and development of the English language. The book opens with the following passage:

> On 5 September 1977, the American spacecraft Voyager One blasted-off on its historic mission to Jupiter and beyond. On board was a recorded message greeting from the people of the planet Earth. Preceding a brief message in fifty-five different languages for the people of outer space, the gold-plated disk plays a statement from the Secretary-General of the United Nations, an Austrian named Kurt Waldheim, speaking on behalf of 147 member states—in English.

Since this observation was made, the world has increasingly embraced English as the language of communication and technology. This is fine for those who use English as their mother language, but what happens in an increasingly multi-language world? Americans tend to speak one language, but Canadians in some areas speak two, as do many Europeans. Obviously, this is true in many other nations that have adapted to English but still have a native tongue. More and more business is done globally, and increasing numbers of organizations are merging despite international borders. If these trends continue, what will it mean for the English language as a major language of communication? Should we all be learning other languages as the world globalizes to communicate more effectively? What are the cost and benefits of increasing your language base? Can you effectively negotiate if you do not understand the other person's language, nuances and all?

EXPERIENTIAL EXERCISES

1. Television is a powerful medium of communication, but, in general, it is a monologue, not a dialogue. Your challenge as a class is to break up into teams of four to five people. Each team member is then to be assigned one station to watch in terms of news for one week. You can choose any of the Canadian or American stations. At the end of the week, your team is to compare notes as to what news was communicated, how it was presented, who presented it, and how balanced it seemed to be. Then be prepared to make a team presentation to the class about your findings and how you see the news shaping our society through the way it is communicated.

2. Because actions speak louder than words, nonverbal communication can be confounding. Take international gestures. In Britain, secrecy or confidentiality is conveyed by a tap on one's nose, while in Italy this means a friendly warning. A nod in Bulgaria and Greece signifies "no"; in most other countries, it means "yes." Placing your thumb and forefinger in a circle and extending the other three fingers is widely accepted as the "okay" sign, except in Brazil, where it's considered vulgar or obscene.[80]

Gather 8 to 10 different gestures that mean different things in different nations. Interview classmates, friends, relatives, and co-workers and then come to class ready to discuss what you've discovered. Or brainstorm with a group of 4 to 6 classmates, generating a list of 8 to 10 Canadian gestures. Then divide the list and seek out what these gestures communicate in other cultures. Report to the class on your findings.

INTERNET EXERCISE

Communication in all forms, including on the Internet, is important for companies. View what Nortel Networks is doing is this area at www.nortelnetworks.com. Look at the general Web site. Also be sure to visit the corporate section, and once there take a look at the communication around ethics. In the ethics section, "Quick Reference" provides a comprehensive guide to employee behaviour in the company, and is worth browsing.

1. How is the information on the Web site structured? How effective is this?

2. Based on the information presented, what do you think is valued at Nortel?

3. What is the tone of the content?

CASE STUDY 12-1

Improving Communication and Performance with 360-Degree Feedback

As part of the plan to reinvent government, agencies have been moving to use more sophisticated appraisal and feedback systems. In the past, performance appraisals have been limited to a feedback process between employees and supervisors. With the increased focus on teamwork, employee development, and customer service, the emphasis has shifted to employee feedback from the full circle of contacts surrounding an employee. This multiple-input approach to performance feedback is sometimes called a 360-degree assessment. Will a 360-degree assessment really make employees more effective?

The circle of feedback sources consists of supervisors, peers, subordinates, customers, and one's self. Organizations do not find it necessary to include all of the feedback sources in a particular appraisal system.

Each organization is unique in culture and mission and, as a result, the feedback from various sources will differ across organizations. For example, subordinate assessments of a supervisor's performance can provide valuable developmental guidance, peer feedback can be the heart of excellence in teamwork, and customer service feedback focuses on the quality of the team's or agency's results.

Using Feedback Sources

Superiors—Superior evaluations are the most traditional source of employee feedback. The most common form of supervisor evaluation is the rating of individuals by supervisors on elements in an employee's performance plan.

Self-Assessment—This common form of performance information is often used only as an informal part of the supervisor-to-employee appraisal feedback session. In a 360-degree system, supervisors might ask employees to identify the key accomplishments they feel best represent their performance on important benchmarks.

Peers—As organizations increasingly use teams, team members often have the best perspective on their colleagues' performance. Peers often have a perspective different than that of management.

Subordinates—An upward appraisal process or feedback survey is an important and controversial feature of 360-degree performance evaluation programs. Evaluations of superiors by subordinates may provide valuable data concerning managerial behaviours. Not surprisingly, there is often great reluctance on the part of managers to use this method.

Customers—It is common to survey internal and external customers, publish customer service standards, and measure performance against these standards. Internal customers are defined as users of products or services supplied by another employee or group within the agency or organization. External customers are the traditional customers outside the organization.

Questions

1. In what ways might 360-degree feedback improve an employee's performance?

2. What problems or risks would managers perceive in implementing a 360-degree feedback system?

3. How would a 360-degree performance appraisal system work in a university or college? What would change in your performance if your school used 360-degree performance appraisal?

A Case of Good Intentions

Treeline Paper Ltd. employed 300 people. Management had always prided itself on the good relations that existed between the company and its employees. A strike had never taken place, and relations with the union were good.

The president of Treeline, Alex Kellner, had formed an executive committee that met every Tuesday morning to discuss specific issues facing management. These meetings also served to improve communications between managers since this was the only time they had the opportunity to meet together. At the most recent meeting, the committee was discussing how valuable the meetings had been and suggested that the company should examine ways of improving communication with the employees as well. One manager related an experience that seemed to sum up the lack of communication with employees: He had recently been talking with one employee who did not know who the president of the company was.

After considerable discussion, it was agreed that Treeline would embark on a program to improve communication with employees. Several ideas were put forth, and the executive committee eventually decided to start with a simple campaign that would give employees some basic statistics about the company and its operations. The centrepiece of this campaign would be three time series graphs that would summarize company operations. These graphs would show total sales, inventory levels, and total employment. The graphs would be updated weekly.

A memo was sent to all employees indicating that this decision had been made. Employees were encouraged to consult the graphs and to become better informed about the company they worked for.

After several months, the graphs looked like those on page 408.

About this time, Kellner had a visit from the president of the union. He was very agitated, and said that the union wanted to open up the job security clause of the collective agreement. Several supervisors also reported a noticeable drop in employee morale. One day in the cafeteria several employees confronted Kellner and demanded to speak to him about the rumour they had heard that the plant would be closing soon.

Questions

1. What has gone wrong here?

2. Using concepts introduced in the chapter, make suggestions about what Alex Kellner should do now.

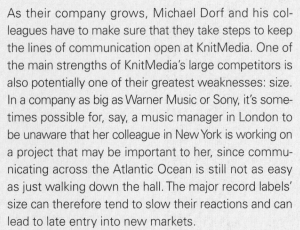

| Sales | Inventory | Number of Employees |

FIGURE 12.5
Treeline's Time Series Graphs

Keeping the Lines of Communication Open at KnitMedia

KNITMEDIA

As their company grows, Michael Dorf and his colleagues have to make sure that they take steps to keep the lines of communication open at KnitMedia. One of the main strengths of KnitMedia's large competitors is also potentially one of their greatest weaknesses: size. In a company as big as Warner Music or Sony, it's sometimes possible for, say, a music manager in London to be unaware that her colleague in New York is working on a project that may be important to her, since communicating across the Atlantic Ocean is still not as easy as just walking down the hall. The major record labels' size can therefore tend to slow their reactions and can lead to late entry into new markets.

Identifying new trends and hopping on these trends with new artists and new products is therefore at the heart of what music companies like KnitMedia must do. To accomplish that, they have to institute communication methods that enhance not only organizational communications within KnitMedia but also communication between KnitMedia and both its consumers and its artists.

The problem is that, as the company grows, this can actually become more difficult, not easier. For ex-

ample, consider the way in which Heather Stamm, production coordinator at the New York Knitting Factory club, describes how e-mail has affected communication at KnitMedia:

> I think it's cut down on face-to-face communication. We don't have time to schedule meetings to sit down and talk every five minutes, but we need to be in constant communication. Although we do have regular weekly meetings for production and weekly meetings for promotion where we talk to each other face to face, it's the ability to send instantaneous [e-mails] and to send [them] to more than one person at a time that's become important. Sometimes [though] I'm e-mailing Glen and he's only three feet away from me, but it's still a useful tool because you can go back and check to see what you said and how they responded. And with artists traveling all over the world all the time, it's a good way to keep in contact with the artists when they're touring.

→

Particularly as they've become an increasingly global operation, Michael Dorf and his team have recognized that other companies are using many approaches to keep their own lines of communication open. Dorf and his team have come to you for advice about implementing a new comprehensive communication package at KnitMedia.

Team Exercises and Questions

Use what you learned in this chapter to answer the following questions from Michael Dorf and his management team:

1. From what you know about our company, do you think interpersonal and organizational communication are currently adequate? Why or why not?

2. Based on what you know about communication from this chapter and based on a review of Internet- and non-Internet-based information, what methods are other music companies using to maintain open communication both within their organizations and between their organizations and their artists and consumers?

3. Which communication approaches and techniques do you think KnitMedia should implement, and how would you suggest we do so?

Leading Groups and Teams

Work Teams at Shell Canada Ltd.

Shell Canada's lubricants factory at Brockville, Ontario, was built at a cost of $75 million. It started operations in 1992, replacing older plants in Montreal and Toronto. The plant takes tankloads of base oils and mixes in various additives to make oil for automobiles, boats, and industrial applications. The heart of the blending process is an operations control centre where a bank of computers stores the "recipes" for 240 different oil blends. The computer also gives operators step-by-step directions on how to do the mixing.

The plant's 75 factory floor workers are grouped into three teams called "job families." Each team manages one of the plant's three basic activities—blending lubricants, packaging, and warehousing. Each worker must be able to perform all of the jobs allocated to her or his team. Operators are also expected to be knowledgeable about where raw materials come from and where final products are sold.

Teams are given the information and authority they need (including the right to talk to suppliers or customers) to make the plant perform up to standard. Missing from the plant are the traditional supervisors and superintendent who tell people what to do and how to do it. In their place is a system that turns all employees into supervisors by allowing them to tap into the information they need to manage themselves. Teams are responsible for cost control, developing vacation and training schedules, and disciplining non-performing workers. In essence, the old "command and control" hierarchy has been abandoned and has been replaced by a dynamic organizational structure that runs on worker commitment, enthusiasm, and group cohesiveness.

The Brockville plant produces about the same level of output as the Toronto and Montreal plants formerly did, but with half as many workers. It has also found customers in 44 different countries, whereas export sales were formerly a rarity. Absenteeism is at about one-third the normal rate in manufacturing.

Shell Canada Ltd.
www.shell.ca

OBJECTIVES

After studying this chapter, you should be able to

1. List and briefly describe the types of teams used at work.

2. Explain the causes and symptoms of unproductive teams.

3. Understand what is necessary to build team performance.

4. Describe the problems of making the transition from supervisor to team leader.

5. List the values that team leaders should have.

6. Use important team-leader coaching skills.

Teams like those at Shell Canada are becoming common in organizations. For example, work teams composed of 40 to 50 workers have been introduced at Imperial Oil's Dartmouth, Nova Scotia, refinery. Each team is responsible for an entire segment of the refinery's operations. The team responsible for first-stage conversion of crude oil into more useful forms is now headed by a single leader. Formerly, the work had been done by a variety of workers representing various trades and skills, each one reporting to a different manager. Under the new team approach, employees have taken on new responsibilities and a layer of supervision has disappeared.[1]

Teams: Employee Involvement in Action

You've probably already had some experience with teams yourself, perhaps as part of a classroom team assigned to make a presentation on some topic (such as "using the Internet as a management tool"). If so, you've also already experienced some of the things that we're going to address in this chapter: the importance of having a clear and agreed-upon goal; hammering out procedures for how the work will be done, and establishing milestones for getting there; making sure that everyone is pulling his or her own weight; and figuring out to how to motivate (or penalize) colleagues who aren't doing their jobs.

From your experience, you also probably know that doing work through teams has both pros and cons. In this chapter we'll therefore explain the methods and steps that leaders can take to make their teams more effective. And we'll see that to manage teams effectively, you must use many of the people skills that we've discussed in the previous three chapters: skills like choosing the right style, using recognition to motivate employees, and effectively communicating what you want done.

What Is Employee Involvement?

Work teams are examples of employee involvement programs. An **employee involvement program** is any formal program that lets employees participate in formulating important work decisions or in supervising all or part of their own work activities.[2]

Managers rate such programs as their biggest productivity boosters. For example, the editors of *National Productivity Review* mailed a survey to subscribers several years ago. They found that "increased employee involvement in the generation and implementa-

employee involvement program
Any formal program that lets employees participate in formulating important work decisions or in supervising all or part of their own work activities.

tion of ideas was ranked the highest priority productivity improvement action by the respondents." Employee involvement "was similarly ranked number one as the top cause of improvement over the past two years at these firms." (The other eight causes of improvement, in descending order, were quality programs, improved process methods, top management, equipment, technology, training, computers, and automation.)

Levels of Employee Involvement

Several levels or degrees of employee involvement are possible (see Figure 13.1).[3] The levels of employee involvement range from level 1, information sharing (managers make all important operational decisions, inform employees, and then respond to employee questions) to level 5, intergroup problem solving (experienced, trained, cross-functional teams meet regularly with a manager to work on problems across several organizational units),[4] to level 8, total self-direction ("every employee belongs to a self-directed team, starting with a highly interactive executive group").[5] Level 8 often means establishing a team-based organization. Here the company rearranges its organizational structure and systems around team-based work assignments. The managers then devote their major efforts towards coaching their subordinates to manage themselves.[6]

Group Dynamics: The Building Blocks of Groups

How do groups and teams differ, and how—if at all—are they alike?

Groups and Teams

A **group** is two or more persons who are interacting with one another in such a manner that each person influences, and is influenced by each other person.[7] **Formal groups**— for example, departments, task forces, quality circles, and project teams—are established to achieve certain organizational goals and are part of the formal structure of the orga-

group
Two or more persons who are interacting with one another in such a manner that each person influences, and is influenced by each other person.

formal group
A group established to achieve certain organizational goals; it is part of the formal structure of the organization.

**Employee Involvement in Your Company:
An Informal Checklist**

1. Information sharing: Managers make decisions on their own, announce them, then respond to any questions employees may have.
2. Managers usually make the decisions, but only after seeking the views of employees.
3. Managers often form temporary employee groups to recommend solutions for specified problems.
4. Managers meet with employee groups regularly—once a week or so—to help them identify problems and recommend solutions.
5. Intergroup problem solving: Managers establish and participate in cross-functional employee problem-solving teams.
6. Ongoing work groups assume expanded responsibility for a particular issue, like cost reduction.
7. Employees within an area function full-time with minimal direct supervision.
8. Total self-direction: Traditional supervisory roles do not exist; almost all employees participate in self-managing teams.

FIGURE 13.1
Eight Levels of Employee Involvement

nization. **Informal groups**—for example, a coffee-break group or a company bowling team—are set up to meet people's social needs and are not part of the formal structure of the organization. The leaders of informal groups can have a big impact on the formal organization because of the influence they have over the members of their informal group.

A **team** is always distinguished by the fact that its members are "committed to a common purpose, set of performance goals, and approach for which they hold themselves mutually accountable."[8] Groups in general need not have such unanimity of purpose, but since all teams are groups, we should briefly review some group concepts before moving on. Two aspects of groups are especially important: norms and cohesiveness.

Group Norms

Everyone knows that peer pressure is very important. To a greater or lesser extent, what we wear, what we drive, and how we behave is geared to make what we do look "right" to our peers. It generally takes a strong-willed person to deliberately go against the grain of the reference group we admire.

The fact that people are influenced by peer pressure is also certainly true at work. For example, in a study titled "Monkey See, Monkey Do: The Influence of Workgroups on the Antisocial Behavior of Employees," two researchers studied how individuals' anti-social behaviour at work was shaped by the anti-social behaviour of their co-workers. They found that "...a workgroup was a significant predictor of an individual's antisocial behavior at work," and that the more anti-social the group became the more it was able to influence its individual members' anti-social actions.[9] Neglecting the group's potential effects can therefore be calamitous.

It's largely through group norms that work groups can have such an impact. **Group norms** are "the informal rules that groups adopt to regulate and regularize group members' behavior."[10] They are "rules of behavior, proper ways of acting, which have been accepted as legitimate by members of a group [and that] specify the kind of behaviors that are expected of group members."[11]

By enforcing their norms, work groups can have an enormous impact on their members' behaviour.[12] In fact, studies show that "group norms may have a greater influence on the individual's performance than the knowledge, skills and abilities the individual brings to the work setting."[13] This fact was first revealed by a research project known as the Hawthorne studies. Here researchers described how production that exceeded the group's norms triggered what the workers called "binging," in which the producer's hand was slapped by other workers.

Group Cohesiveness

The extent to which a group can influence its members' behaviour depends largely on the attraction of the group for its members, or its **group cohesiveness**.[14]

Group cohesiveness depends on several factors. Proximity and contact are prerequisites for group cohesiveness; without them, individuals would have no opportunity to become attracted to one another. On the other hand, proximity is no guarantee that people will discover that they have something in common; if the individuals should find that they have little in common, the effect could be just the opposite.[15]

Cohesiveness also depends on the interpersonal attraction between the people involved. Similarly, individuals are usually attracted to the group itself because they find its activities or goals attractive, rewarding, or valuable, or because they believe that through the group they can accomplish something they could not accomplish on their own.

Several other things influence group cohesiveness. Intergroup competition can foster cohesiveness (particularly for the winning group), whereas intragroup competition (competition between the group's members) tends to undermine cohesiveness.[16] People join groups in part because they believe the group can help them accomplish their goals; agreement over goals therefore boosts cohesiveness, whereas differences reduce it.[17] Group cohesiveness also tends to decline as group size increases beyond about 20 members.[18] In summary, proximity, interpersonal attractiveness, homogeneity of interests or

informal group
A group set up to meet people's social needs; it is not part of the formal structure of the organization.

team
Always distinguished by the fact that its members are committed to a common purpose, set of performance goals, and approach for which they hold themselves mutually accountable.

group norms
The informal rules that groups adopt to regulate and regularize group members' behaviour.

group cohesiveness
The attraction of the group for its members.

Cohesiveness is essential to the success of many work teams, as much in traditional business settings as in such high-risk work as capping gushing oil wells.

**Outward Bound
Canada
www.outwardbound.ca**

goals, intergroup competition, and a manageable size tend to foster group cohesiveness and may therefore influence team performance as well.

Some firms make formal attempts to develop cohesive work groups because of the increased "energy" that is evident in such groups. For example, at Campbell Soup Canada, the president and six vice-presidents went on an Outward Bound program near Lake Superior. The trip included four days of canoeing, spending one day alone in the wilderness, and scaling a sheer granite cliff. After the group returned to work, they spent time discussing what they had learned and how it could be applied to business management.[19]

How to Use Teams at Work

In considering whether and how to rely more heavily on teams in the organization, the head of a company naturally must decide what sorts of teams to use. Here there are many choices, because teams can be used in various ways.

Team-expert James Shonk says that companies can use four basic types of teams: suggestion teams, problem-solving teams, semi-autonomous teams, and self-managing teams.[20]

suggestion teams
Short-term teams that exist to work on given issues such as how to cut costs or increase productivity.

Suggestion teams are usually short-term teams that exist to work on given issues such as how to cut costs or increase productivity.

problem-solving teams
Teams involved in identifying and researching activities and in developing effective solutions to work-related problems.

Problem-solving teams "are involved in identifying and researching activities and in developing effective solutions to work-related problems."[21] Most such teams consist of the supervisor and five to eight employees from a common work area; the quality circles described later are an example.

semi-autonomous teams
Teams that have a lot of input in managing the activities in their own work area but are still managed by a supervisor.

Semi-autonomous teams have a lot of input in managing the activities in their own work area but are still managed by a supervisor. Teams like this might establish their own goals, provide input into solving problems in their work area, and have a lot of input in daily operating decisions such as when to take breaks and which tasks to do first. However, they are still managed by a formal supervisor.

Self-managing teams are also called self-directed work teams. These teams are responsible for managing their work on a daily basis. For example, they schedule their own work, set their own goals, hire team members, and make operating decisions such as dealing with vendors if some parts are defective. These teams are a major element in helping companies to manage change. As Shonk puts it, "self-managing teams are also used where employees need freedom to act."[22] We'll look more closely at several specific types of work teams next.

self-managing teams
Teams responsible for managing their work on a daily basis; also called self-directed work teams.

Quality Circles

Companies have long used decision-making committees at the management level for analysis, advice, and recommendations. Often called task forces, project groups, or audit or safety groups, these committees identify problems or opportunities and recommend courses of action.[23]

Such teams have now become common in non-managerial ranks as well. The quality circle is the most familiar example. A **quality circle (QC)** is a team of 6 to 12 employees that meets once a week at work to solve problems affecting its work area.[24] Such teams are first trained in problem analysis techniques (including basic statistics). Then the quality circle is ready to apply the problem analysis process.[25] In practice, this process has five steps: problem identification, problem selection, problem analysis, solution recommendations, and solution review by top management.

quality circle (QC)
A team of 6 to 12 employees that meets once a week at work to solve problems affecting its work area.

At Great West Life Assurance Company, quality circles are composed of volunteers who meet once a week on company time to consider ways to do higher-quality, more-effective work. Each group has a leader who has received formal training in how to lead a QC. An agenda is prepared for each meeting. When a group has completed a given project—large projects may take six months or more—a presentation is made to management. All team members are encouraged to take part in these presentations.

Great West Life
Assurance Company
www.gwla.com

The original wave of employer enthusiasm and support for QC programs began to fade several years ago. Perhaps the biggest reason is that many circles failed to produce measurable cost savings. Some circles' bottom-line aims were too vague. In other firms, having the employees choose and analyze their own problems proved incompatible with the autocratic management styles and cultures in existence.[26]

Many firms today are taking steps to make their quality circles more effective. At

Members of a quality circle discuss ways to improve product quality and production efficiency.

Honeywell Corporation the firm has replaced about 700 of its original quality circles with about 1000 new work teams. These new teams are generally not voluntary; instead, they include most shop floor employees and, in contrast to the bottom-up approach of quality circles, they work on problems assigned by management.[27]

Project, Development, or Venture Teams

Teamwork is especially important for special projects like developing a new product. The tight coordination and open communication needed here make close-knit teams especially useful. Project and development teams are often composed of professionals (marketing experts or engineers, for example). They team up on specific projects such as designing new processes (process design teams) or products (new-product development teams).

A **venture team** "is a small group of people who operate as a semi-autonomous unit to create and develop a new idea."[28] The classic example was the IBM team that developed and introduced IBM's first personal computer. As is usually the case with venture teams, the unit was semi-autonomous in that it had its own budget and leader and the freedom to make decisions within broad guidelines.

As it turns out, IBM's PC venture team illustrates both the pros and cons of the venture team approach. Working semi-autonomously, the team was able to create a new computer system and bring it to market in less than two years. This might have taken IBM

venture team
A small group of people who operate as a semi-autonomous unit to create and develop a new idea.

IBM
www.ibm.com

"Hot" Groups

hot group
A lively, high-achieving, dedicated group, usually small, whose members are turned on to an exciting and challenging task.

If teams in general can be useful for getting things done, imagine how useful a "hot" group can be. A **hot group**, according to two experts, is just what the name implies: "a lively, high-achieving, dedicated group, usually small, whose members are turned on to an exciting and challenging task. Hot groups, while they last, completely captivate their members, occupying their hearts and minds to the exclusion of almost everything else."[29]

A hot group isn't so much a special use for a team as it is an especially vibrant and high-energy team. Thus, quality circles, new-product development teams, and self-directed work teams may also be hot teams (although hot teams do tend to focus on short-term projects or tasks). The thing that makes a team "hot," to repeat, is the fact that it is high-achieving, dedicated, and turned on to an exciting and challenging task.

Hot teams are especially important for 21st-century organizations, these experts say.[30] Tomorrow's organizations will require "both the capacity to keep up with an intense pace of change and the capacity to reshape themselves continually."[31] High-energy dedication helps hot team members challenge and pierce the "accepted organizational propriety" that might otherwise inhibit creative solutions. The hot group that developed Apple's flagship product, the Macintosh, a number of years ago is a classic example. As these experts describe it,

> Apple's early culture was exciting, urgent, flamboyant, defiant, ready to take on Big Blue (IBM) and anyone else in its path... It is not surprising, therefore, that Apple's flagship product, the Macintosh, was developed by a small group consisting of people from all over the company. Led primarily by the aggressive and charismatic Steve Jobs, the group was spurred on by the ennobling challenge of building small computers for the masses.[32]

Hot groups have a number of distinguishing characteristics that leaders should keep in mind:[33]

A total preoccupation with an important mission. The most distinguishing characteristic of a hot group is its total preoccupation with a task that for members has a higher meaning. The mission may be developing a vaccine for AIDS, or something less magnificent like instituting a 24-hour customer service system for a department store. Outsiders may not see the mission in the same way, but hot groups always feel that what they are doing is extremely relevant and important, and they think about their task constantly.

Intellectual intensity, integrity, and exchange of ideas. Hot groups work on problems in which all members have to use their heads, intensely and continuously. Debate among members is often loud and passionate.

Emotional intensity. Perhaps the best way to put this is that "hot group members behave like people in love. They are infatuated with the challenge of their task and often with the talent around them."[34] Even once they go home at night they may sacrifice their own personal preferences—say to attend a movie or a play—to continue trying to solve the problem at hand. Hot group members may then come in the next morning with a comment like "I was thinking about that problem in bed last night, and I had an idea. So I got up and tried a few things on my PC, and here's what I got. What do you all think?"[35]

Temporary structure/small size. Hot groups are usually small enough to permit close interpersonal relationships among their members (fewer than 30) and are also temporary and relatively short-lived: "They share the happy attribute of dissolving when they finish their work."[36]

Managers can provide several things to encourage the growth of hot groups:

Openness and flexibility. Companies in which hot groups thrive disdain bureaucracy and don't inhibit hot group members from seeking out information and advice anywhere in the company. Quite the opposite: Hot groups require "easy, informal access across hierarchical levels and across departmental, divisional, and organizational boundaries."[37]

Independence and autonomy. To help keep hot groups hot while they make their contributions, "it is wise to leave them alone for reasonable periods of time."[38] They need the independence and autonomy that IBM's Boca Raton PC development team received, for instance. And, they must not be unduly bound by restrictive company policies and procedures—like requiring hot team members to get approval ahead of time for just about every penny that they spend, for instance.

People first. Hot groups tend to thrive in companies that place a premium on putting their people first—on emphasizing respect for the individual and the importance of hiring high-potential people. Management then gives them the elbow room, opportunities, and training they need to become all that they can be.

The search for truth. Hot groups traditionally thrive in research-oriented companies like Bell Labs where the culture values the scientific method and the search for truth. What does this mean? It means valuing open debate of the issues; publicizing results; conducting objective, preferably measurable, studies to support one's conclusions; and accepting the fact that failures are an inescapable feature of the research process.

many years to accomplish under its usual hierarchical approach to product development.

However, many believe that the venture team's autonomy eventually backfired. Not bound by IBM's traditional policy of using only IBM parts, the team went outside IBM, both to Microsoft (for its DOS, or disk operating system) and to Intel (for the computer processor). This facilitated the early introduction of the IBM PC. Unfortunately for IBM, it also allowed Intel and Microsoft to sell the same PC parts to any manufacturer and led to the proliferation of IBM clones.[39]

Transnational Teams

transnational teams
Work groups composed of multinational members whose activities span many countries.

Xerox Corporation
www.xerox.com

What do you do, as the head of a multinational company, if you have a special project that involves activities in several countries at once? Increasingly, top executives are answering that question by creating **transnational teams**, work groups composed of multinational members whose activities span many countries.[40]

Transnational teams are being used in a variety of ways. For example, Fuji-Xerox sent 15 of its most experienced Tokyo engineers to a Xerox Corporation facility in Webster, New York. There they worked for five years with a group of U.S. engineers to develop a "world copier," a product that proved to be a huge success in the global marketplace.[41] A group of managers and technical specialists from IBM–Latin America formed their own multi-country team to market, sell, and distribute personal computers in 11 Latin American countries. A European beverage manufacturer formed a 13-member transnational team called the European Production Task Force with members from five countries. Its job was to analyze how many factories they should operate in Europe, what size and type they should be, and where they should be located. The common denominator in each case is that a multi-country team contributed to its company's efforts to globalize; that is, to extend the firm's products and operations into international markets.[42]

Transnational teams face some special challenges.[43] They typically work on projects that are highly complex and important compared to most other teams (projects like the world copier or multinational factory placement projects, for example). They are also obviously subject to what several experts have called the special demands of "multicultural dynamics"—in other words, the fact that they are made up of people with different languages, different interpersonal styles, different cultures, and a host of other differences, and are dealing with activities in multiple cultures as well.

What can you do to make such teams more effective? Recommendations include:

Establish the team's driving goal. Especially because the distances involved are so great, it's important that each team member's activities be focused like a laser on the group's overall goal. This means identifying, early in the process, the primary result towards which the team's resources should be applied.[44]

Provide communication. The communication system must enable geographically dispersed team members to communicate with each other, with others in the company, and with outsiders quickly and in a manner that provides for a full and rich understanding of the issues. The relevant information technology therefore typically includes videoconferencing as well as the more usual telephone, voice mail, e-mail, and fax. Group decision-support systems—PC-based "groupware" that permits, for instance, simultaneous computerized discussions of issues—are used as well.

Build teamwork. Facilitating group cohesiveness is particularly important, given the multicultural nature of these groups. "Successful [transnational] teams are characterized by leaders and members who trust each other, are committed to the team's mission, can be counted on to perform their respective tasks, and enjoy working with each other."[45] Team leaders and the company itself therefore have to work hard to provide the training and leadership that foster such characteristics.

Show mutual respect. For example, says one expert, rotate the times of conferences, so that the same members in a remote time zone don't always have to do business in the wee hours of the morning; hold staff meetings at various geographic locations; link employees at remote sites to the headquarters' e-mail system so they feel included; create office space for visiting team members; and learn words expressing respect and gratitude in the languages of other team members.[46]

Virtual Teams

In many cases today, transnational team members don't meet at all, but operate in a virtual environment. Their meetings take place entirely via telecommunications.

Teams like these are increasingly popular. For one thing, the increasing globalization of trade and corporate activity practically demands that teams be able to communicate continually regarding their projects and at great distances, but rarely face-to-face. Furthermore, the increasing emphasis today on strategic partnerships and joint ventures means that employees of various companies frequently must act together as a team, although they work for different companies and may be in different countries or continents.

Virtual teams "...are groups of geographically and/or organizationally dispersed co-workers that are assembled using a combination of telecommunications and information technologies to accomplish an organizational task. Virtual teams rarely, if ever, meet in a face-to-face setting. They may be set up as temporary structures, existing only to accomplish a specific task, or may be permanent structures, used to address ongoing issues, such as a strategic planning. Furthermore, membership is often fluid, evolving according to changing task requirements."[47]

Virtual teams depend for their existence on several types of information technology. Desktop videoconferencing systems (DVCS) are often the core system around which the rest of the virtual team's technologies are built. Systems like these "recreate the face-to-face interactions of conventional groups...," so that communication among team members can include the rich body language and nuances of "face-to-face" communications.[48]

Collaborative software systems (sometimes called group support systems, or group decision-support systems) further facilitate the group decision making in virtual teams. For example, one consulting team was able to use a collaborative software system to research and write a proposal for a major project by letting each member access the contribution of each other member in real time, while inputting his or her own contribution. Finally, com-

Not only an efficient means of communication, virtual and video telecommunication provides important face-to-face interaction, as well as the opportunity to glean information from another person's body language.

panies are creating their own intranets, linked to the Internet. With all of the virtual team's required forms and documents available on the company's internal Web sites, these intranets "allow virtual teams to archive text, visual, audio, and numerical data in a user-friendly format, [and] allow virtual teams to keep other organizational members and outside constituents such as suppliers and customers up-to-date on the team's progress..."[49]

Communications in such virtual teams need to acknowledge the cultural differences that often exist between team members. For example, one expert suggests eliminating cultural idioms (like "apples to oranges") and using multiple channels (such as phone and e-mail) to build in redundancy to ensure that the message is understood.[50]

Self-Directed Work Teams

In many firms today, **self-directed** (also called self-managing) **work teams** are the ultimate manifestation of employee involvement programs. When employees bought a 60 percent ownership share in Algoma Steel, self-directed work teams replaced the traditional top-down management style that had been used at the company. Now teams have the authority to decide many issues ranging from vacation schedules for workers to workplace redesign. At Johnsonville Foods, self-managing teams now recruit, hire, evaluate, and fire (if necessary) on their own. Many of the workers have little or no college background; however, they also "train one another, formulate and track their own budgets, make capital investment proposals as needed, handle quality control and inspection, develop their own quantitative standards, improve every process and product, and create prototypes of possible new products."[51]

Moving to Self-Directed Teams. Firms typically go through six phases in organizing the company's work around self-directed teams:

1. *Start-up*. First, an executive steering committee should establish the feasibility of a team-based organizational structure: develop a mission statement for the program, select the initial team sites, design a multi-level network of teams (to establish what tasks each team will do and how the teams will overlap), and assign employees to the teams. Then, at start-up, the teams and supervisors begin carving out their specific roles in the new teams. In summary, look at all of the work that must be done by the company (or the location that will be "teamed") and decide what kinds of teams will be assigned what tasks.

2. *Training*. Experts contend that "the dominant feature of start-up is intensive training for all involved." Team members must learn how to communicate and how to listen, how to use administrative procedures and budgets, and how to develop other similar skills. Supervisors must learn how to become facilitators and coaches rather than top-down supervisors.[52]

3. *Confusion*. Once the initial enthusiasm wears off, the organization and its teams may enter a period of some confusion. Team members may become concerned about whether their new (probably self-imposed) higher work standards are liable to backfire on them at compensation time; supervisors may become increasingly concerned about their apparently shrinking role in day-to-day operations.

4. *The move to leader-centred teams*. Ideally, the team's confidence should grow as members master their new skills and find better ways to apply their new authority and accomplish their work. The chief danger at this stage, according to experts, is that the teams become too reliant "on their internal leaders." Rather than remaining self-directed, some teams may slip into the habit of letting an elected team member carry out the former supervisor's role. One way to avoid this is "to make sure everyone continues to learn and eventually exercise leadership skills, ...[and] allow anyone to exercise leadership functions as needed."[53]

5. *Misplaced loyalty*. The teams, sometimes blinded by their newfound authority and ability to supervise themselves, may allow loyalty to their co-workers to

hide problems in the team. For example, team members might hide a poorly performing member to protect the person from outside discipline in a misguided show of loyalty. Management's job here is to re-emphasize both the need for intrateam cooperation and the team's responsibility to adequately supervise its own members.

6. *The move to self-directed teams.* Once the new teams rid themselves of the intense team-oriented loyalties that often accompany building self-directed teams, the organization can move to what researcher Jack Orsburn calls "the period of true self-direction."[54]

The empowerment of self-directed teams can reportedly be a heady experience for all concerned. Here's what one vice-president of a consumer goods company said about organizing his firm around teams: "People on the floor were talking about world markets, customer needs, competitors' products, making process improvements—all the things managers are supposed to think about."[55]

How to Build Productive Teams

Requiring several people to work together doesn't make the group a team, and certainly doesn't make it a productive one. An underperforming team might simply lack the sort of initiative and sense of urgency that coaches traditionally try to ignite during half-time breaks. But a lack of initiative is often just one of the problems with which teams must cope.

Does Teamwork Work?

The research regarding the effectiveness and productivity of teams is unfortunately mixed. Much of the anecdotal evidence is highly favourable. For example, after Kodak's consumer film finishing business division instituted a team-based structure, its division manager reported that unit costs declined by 6 percent per year over six years, and that productivity increased by over 200 percent in six years, from 383 units per employee to 836.[56]

One research study recently focused on the impact of work teams on manufacturing performance in a unionized plant.[57] During a 21-month period, the plant was converted to a team structure. The results of this study indicated that "quality and labor productivity improved over time after the introduction of work teams."[58]

Yet it's clear that team-based structures can also fail. One study surveyed plants of an automobile manufacturer in the early 1980s and found that work teams had a negative impact on plant productivity.[59] In that case, the researchers thought that the problems might simply be due to start-up, and that the team structures would eventually turn out to be effective.

One highly publicized work team program failure occurred in the mid-1990s at Levi Strauss & Company. In an industry famous for low wages and questionable working conditions, Levi's has always rightfully viewed itself as a major exception. However, as competitors with less expensive merchandise manufactured overseas made strong inroads into the Levi's brand, Levi's sought a way to keep its extensive network of U.S. factories going, but with higher productivity.

Levi Strauss
www.levistrauss.com

The idea Levi's hit on was the work team program. In the early 1990s, most of Levi's U.S. plants operated on the piecework system. The worker was paid a rate per piece for each specialized task (like attaching a belt loop) that he or she finished.[60] In the new team system, a pair of pants would be constructed by a group of 10 to 35 workers, who would share all of the tasks and be paid according to the total number of trousers the group finished each day. The idea was to boost productivity by, among other things, giving employees the flexibility to do several jobs instead of just one.

Unfortunately, it didn't quite work out that way. High-performing, faster workers in a group found their wages pulled down by slower-working colleagues (who, conversely, saw their hourly wages rise). Morale began to plummet, arguments ensued, and at some plants a pair of Dockers that previously had cost $5 to stitch together now cost 50 percent more.

The results weren't entirely bleak. Teams that were more homogeneous in terms of work skills did tend to perform better, and their productivity did rise. Furthermore, average turnaround—the time from when an order is received to when the products are shipped to retail stores—improved from nine weeks to seven.

Levi's intends to continue its team program at its remaining U.S. plants, but for 6000 of its U.S. employees, that is now irrelevant: In the past year or two, Levi's announced that it was closing 11 U.S. plants, laying off one-third of its U.S. employees. The moral seems to be that the team approach can be effective, but how it is implemented will determine whether it is successful.

Causes of Unproductive Teams

As you can see from these examples, many things can undermine the productiveness of a team. For example (as at Levi's), a group incentive plan that rewards slower workers at the expense of faster ones is obviously going to cause trouble.

The purpose of a team is to harness divergent skills and talents for specific objectives. However, *divergent points of view* may lead instead to tension and conflict.[61] *Power struggles*—some subtle, some not—can also undermine group effectiveness. Individual members may try to undermine potentially productive ideas with the implicit goal of winning their point rather than doing what's best for the team. In addition, some team members may be ignored, thus eliminating a potentially valuable resource.[62]

Irving Janis describes another team problem, one he calls **groupthink**: "the tendency for a highly cohesive group, especially one working on special projects, to develop a sense of detachment and elitism."[63] This sense of detachment, Janis found, can lead the group to press for conformity and to hesitate to examine different points of view. Just one powerful point of view prevails, even though cogent arguments against it may exist within the group.

Groupthink may seem academic, but it can actually have disastrous effects. For example, just before the explosion of the ill-fated *Challenger* flight in 1986, one engineer reportedly tried to tell colleagues and managers about his concerns that the low temperatures surrounding the shuttle could cause the engines' sealing rings to leak hot gas. As he put it, "I received cold stares.... With looks as if to say, 'Go away and don't bother us with the facts.' They just would not respond verbally to...me. I felt totally helpless at that moment and that further argument was fruitless, so I, too, stopped pressing my case."[64]

One expert says that the causes of a decline in team effectiveness can be summed up by three factors—leadership, focus, and capability—a point summarized in Figure 13.2.[65]

Leadership. Some problems have their genesis in a lack of leadership—lack of support, consistency of direction, vision, budget, or resources. The way to improve this situation is to ensure demonstrated leadership support, make the budget and resources available, boost communications and contact with the leader, and (if required) change leadership.

Focus. Lack of clarity or focus about team purpose, roles, strategy, and goals is the basis for several other problems that may undermine team performance. Improving the situation requires steps like clarifying the team's mission and charter, ensuring open channels of communication, clarifying team members' roles, and establishing regular team meetings.

Capability. Other problems (lack of training or lack of team member flexibility, for instance) stem from an overall "capability" problem—a lack of critical skills, knowledge, learning, and development. Improvement calls for such things as providing appropriate education and training, establishing a team development plan, establishing individual team member development plans, and regularly assessing team effectiveness.

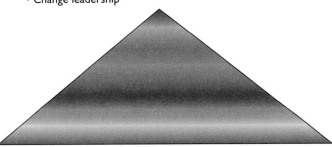

Leadership
Lack of support, consistency of direction, vision, budget, and resources.
Improvement strategy:
- Plan events to ensure demonstrated leadership support
- Increase availability of budget and resources
- Increase communication and contact with leader
- Change leadership

Focus
Lack of clarity about team purpose, roles, strategy, and goals.
Improvement strategy:
- Establish and clarify team charter
- Clarify boundary conditions
- Ensure open channels for communications and information transfer
- Clarify team member roles
- Establish regular team meetings

Capability
Lack of critical skill sets, knowledge, ongoing learning, and development.
Improvement strategy:
- Provide appropriate education and training
- Establish a team development plan
- Establish individual development plans
- Reflect on how group process can be improved
- Regularly assess team effectiveness

FIGURE 13.2
Leadership, Focus, and Capability Pyramid
Note: Traps that lead to a decline in team effectiveness typically are related to one of three factors: leadership, focus, or capability. Each of these three factors requires a different improvement strategy to overcome the trap.

Managers in their leadership roles can obviously influence team effectiveness. Doing so requires them to apply performance-building guidelines like those discussed here, and thereby avoid the three big failings—inadequate leadership, inadequate focus, and inadequate team member capabilities.

Symptoms of Unproductive Teams

As at Levi's, various symptoms make it easy to recognize unproductive teams.[66]

Non-accomplishment of goals. A team program should be implemented to accomplish specific measurable goals. If these aren't met, it's obvious that the program is not working.

Cautious or guarded communication. When people fear some form of punishment, ridicule, or negative reaction, they may say nothing or be guarded in what they do say.

Lack of disagreement. Lack of disagreement among team members may reflect an unwillingness to share true feelings and ideas.

Use of personal criticism. Personal criticism, such as "If you can't come up with a better idea than that, you'd better keep quiet," is a sign of unhealthy team member relations.

Malfunctioning meetings. Unproductive teams often have malfunctioning meetings characterized by boredom, lack of enthusiastic participation, failure to reach decisions, and dominance by one or two people.

Unclear goals. Productive teams have a clear sense of mission; members of unproductive teams are often unable to recite their own team's objectives.

Low commitment. Without a clear sense of purpose, unproductive teams tend to have low commitment. It's not clear what they should be committed to.

Conflict within the team. Unproductive teams are often characterized by a suspicious, combative environment and by conflict among team members.

Characteristics of Productive Teams

Of course, it is not unproductive teams you want but productive ones. A team, remember, is "a small number of people with complementary skills who are committed to a common purpose, set of performance goals, and approach for which they hold themselves mutually accountable."[67] The characteristics of productive teams are implicit in this definition. Specifically, based on an extensive study of teams at work, Katzenbach and Smith found that productive teams have five characteristics.

Commitment to a Mission. Katzenbach and Smith found that "the essence of a team is a common commitment. Without it, groups perform as individuals; with it, they become a powerful unit of collective performance." Teams must, therefore, have a clear mission to which to be committed, such as Saturn's "Let's beat the Japanese by producing a world-class quality car."[68] Katzenbach and Smith found that the most productive teams then developed commitment around their own definition of what management wanted their teams to do: "The best teams invest a tremendous amount of time and effort exploring, shaping, and agreeing on a purpose that belongs to them both collectively and individually."[69]

Specific Performance Goals. Productive teams translate their common purpose (such as "build world-class quality cars") into specific performance goals (such as "reduce new-car defects to no more than four per vehicle"). In fact, "transforming broad directives into specific and measurable performance goals is the surest first step for a team trying to shape a purpose meaningful to its members."[70]

Right Size, Right Mix. Best-performing teams generally have fewer than 25 people, and usually between 7 and 14 people. Team members also complement each other in terms of their skills. For example, accomplishing the team's mission usually calls for people strong in technical expertise as well as those skilled in problem solving, decision making, and interpersonal relationships.

A recent study illustrates the importance of the right mix of group members. The researchers studied the innovativeness of proposals made by top-management teams in 27 hospitals. The question was whether the teams' innovativeness reflected the individual innovativeness of the team members. Individual innovativeness was measured with a scale that asked such questions as "I suggest new working methods to the people I work with" and "I try to introduce improved methods of doing things at work."[71]

In this study the level of team innovation, and specifically the radicalness of the innovations introduced by the teams, apparently depended to a large extent on how individually innovative the team members were. The implication is that—at least when it comes to innovation—the team you put together had better have a mix that includes at least a few highly innovative people.

A Common Approach. Productive teams also agree on a common approach with respect to the way they will work together to accomplish their mission. For example, team members agree about who will do particular jobs; how schedules will be set and followed; what skills need to be developed; what members will have to do to earn continuing membership in the team; and how decisions will be made and modified.

Mutual Accountability. The most productive teams also develop a sense of mutual accountability. They believe "we are all in this together" and that "we all have to hold ourselves accountable for doing whatever is needed to help the team achieve its mission." Katzenbach and Smith found that such mutual accountability cannot be coerced. Instead, it emerges from the commitment and trust that come from working together towards a common purpose.

How to Build Team Performance

Productive teams don't emerge spontaneously; they're the result of careful selection, training, and leadership. Guidelines that leaders can use to build effective teams include:

Seek employee input. The basic reason for organizing work teams is to tap employees' self-motivation, commitment, and input. While the team structure can be organized unilaterally by management, it's probably best to start with a committee of employees. At Levi Strauss, for instance, consultants brought in after the teamwork problems surfaced recommended reorganizing the teams from scratch using worker input; by that time, productivity was so low that downsizings were already mandatory.

Establish demanding performance standards. All team members need to believe that the team has a worthwhile purpose, and they need to know what their performance standards are.

Select members for skill and skill potential. Choose people both for their existing skills and for their potential to improve existing skills and learn new ones.

Pay particular attention to first meetings and actions. Initial impressions always mean a lot. When potential teams first gather, everyone monitors the signals given by others to confirm, suspend, or dispel their assumptions and concerns. If a senior executive leaves the team's kickoff to take a phone call 10 minutes after the session begins and never returns, people get the message.

Set some clear rules for behaviour. All effective teams develop rules of conduct at the outset to help them achieve their purpose and performance goals. The most critical initial rules pertain to attendance (for example, "no interruptions to take phone calls"), discussion ("no sacred cows"), confidentiality ("the only things to leave this room are what we agree on"), analytic approach ("facts are friendly"), end-product orientation ("everyone gets assignments and does them"), constructive confrontation ("no finger pointing"), and, often the most important, contributions ("everyone does real work").

Move from "boss" to "coach." Self-directed work teams are by definition empowered: They have the confidence, authority, tools, and information to manage themselves. That means that the leader's job is not to boss but to support and to coach—to see that team members have the support they need to do their jobs.

Set a few immediate performance-oriented tasks and goals. Most effective teams trace their advancement to key accomplishments. Such accomplishments can be facilitated by immediately establishing a few challenging goals that can be reached early on.

Challenge the group regularly with fresh facts and information. New information (such as on how the company is doing) causes a team to redefine and enrich its understanding of the challenges it faces. It thereby helps the team shape its common purpose, set clearer goals, and improve its approach.

Spend lots of time together. Remember that proximity and interaction usually build cohesiveness. Team members should spend a lot of time together, both scheduled and unscheduled, especially in the beginning. This time need not always be spent together physically; electronic, fax, and phone time can also count as time spent together.

Exploit the power of positive feedback, recognition, and reward. Positive reinforcement works as well for teams as elsewhere. There are many ways to recognize and reward team performance beyond money. These include having a senior executive speak directly to the team about the urgency of its mission, and using awards to recognize contributions.

Shoot for the right team size.[72] Create teams with the smallest number of employees required to do the work. Large teams can reduce interaction and involvement and boost the need for excessive coordination.

Choose people who like teamwork. Do what companies like Toyota do: Recruit and select employees who have a history of preferring to work in teams and of being good team members. Loners and anti-social types don't usually make good team members.

Train, train, train. Ensure that team members have the training they need to do their jobs. Training should cover topics such as the philosophy of doing work through teams, how teams make decisions, interpersonal and communication skills for team members, and the technical skills team members will need to perform their jobs.

Cross-train for flexibility. Ideally, members of most teams should receive cross-training to learn the jobs of fellow team members, either informally or through scheduled rotating assignments. This can help reduce disruptions due to absenteeism and can boost flexibility, since all team members are always ready to fill in when needed.

Emphasize the task's importance. Team members need to know that what they're doing is important for the organization, so communicate that message whenever you can. For example, emphasize the task's importance in terms of its consequences for customers, other employees, the organization's mission, and the business' overall results.

Assign whole tasks. Try to make the team responsible for a distinct piece of work, such as an entire product or project or segment of the business. This can boost team members' sense of responsibility and ownership, in line with Herzberg's theory of job enrichment.

Build team spirit. Teams obviously should have a "can do" attitude and the confidence and sense of self-efficacy that they can and will be effective. Those managing and leading groups therefore have to focus on fostering a positive attitude. And, as we'll see below, they must provide the coaching and support needed to foster the self-confidence that's a big part of empowered work groups.

Encourage social support. Work teams, like any group, are more effective when members support and help each other. Therefore, set a good example by being supportive yourself, and take concrete steps to encourage and reinforce positive interactions and cohesiveness within the team.

Provide the necessary material support. Social support is important, but the results of a recent study showed that material support "...may be more important than ensuring group members are cohesive."[73] The researchers found that such material support includes timely information, resources, and rewards that encourage group rather than individual performance. "It also suggests organizations should determine if the necessary support resources are available before creating teams."[74]

Leading Productive Teams

You might say that leading productive teams is like leading anything—only more so. In other words, as we've just seen, leading a team also requires special team-building skills,

Published Image, Inc.

Almost from the day that he founded Published Image, Inc., and organized the newsletter into self-managed teams, Eric Gershman had in mind the time when his own position would become superfluous. His viewpoint was that employees capable of preparing their own work schedules, budgets, and bonuses certainly shouldn't have much use for a boss.

Gershman has always been something of a contrarian, dating back to his first job at a Boston ad agency. Luckily, he was resilient. Getting sacked didn't change his viewpoint in the least. "I always felt I had better ways of doing things than my boss," he says.

With the growth of mutual funds, Gershman correctly predicted the need for shareholder newsletters. He spent his entire savings getting Published Image off the ground. Even with 11 clients and $600 000 in revenue, things looked bleak: Turnover was high, morale was low, factual errors were commonplace, and one-third of his clients were leaving annually. Gershman came up with a 250-page plan of action. "We blew up the whole company and totally changed people's thinking about what their job is," Gershman says. Published Image was divided into four independent teams responsible for client relations, sales, editorial content, and production. Everyone performed a specialized task, but shared responsibility for daily deadlines as well. "We work like a unit and pitch in to get out on time whatever has to get done," says Shelley Danse. Her day as an account executive can cover tasks from research to proofreading to laying out artwork.

The team approach at Published Image fostered a sense of ownership of the collective output, as well as enhanced appreciation of the work of fellow members. Planning was easier and efficiency improved. Clients were also impressed. "We have one group of people who know all facets of our job, and we can contact any of them during the process," says Peter Herlihy, vice-president of mutual funds marketing at Fleet Financial Group.

Gershman soon got his wish of working himself out of a job. After revenues doubled to more than $4 million, his company was bought by Standard & Poors.

Rodel, Inc., a manufacturing firm in Delaware, ensures that its people are effective with a rigorous leadership training program aimed at building trust, teamwork, and leadership. The team members pictured here went through the program together.

Co-Worker Similarity and the Performance of the Team

How diverse should a team be? Co-worker diversity can be a tricky issue when it comes to team performance.[75] On the one hand, "a team with a variety of members whose skills and experiences differ and complement each other can take on a wide range of tasks."[76] On the other hand, "be on the alert…for teams whose membership is excessively varied, because conflict and communications breakdown can result."[77] What is a manager to do?

Part of the answer lies in a recent study that examined the impact of various types of similarities (demographics, values, and behavioural style preferences) on co-workers' attitudes and behaviours. The study was conducted in conjunction with a four-week training program for executives and surveyed 43 senior-level managers who were enrolled in the program and assigned to five- or six-person case study teams as part of their training.

Information about various dimensions of co-worker similarity was measured. Demographic characteristics included age, level of education, country of citizenship, and gender. Information about values included the relative importance that individuals placed on, for example, "a world at peace," "happiness," "freedom," and "self-determination." A psychological inventory known as the Myers-Briggs Type Indicator (discussed in Chapter 11 Appendix, page 375) was used to measure individuals' behavioural style preferences— for instance, in terms of sensing/intuition and thinking/feeling. Team members also rated how much they liked each team member and their willingness to work with each of them in the future. The basic research question was: How did co-workers' similarities influence how well they liked each other and how they felt about working with the other team members in the future? Co-worker similarities were important. For example, demographic similarity was the strongest predictor of social liking and co-worker preference, but only at the start of the training: three weeks after the teams had begun their work, demographic similarity ceased to contribute significantly to social liking and co-worker preference. Apparently, demographic differences among team members were overcome by the positive effects that came from the team members working together successfully to analyze their assigned case studies.

After three weeks of working together, however, similarities in personal values still predicted both liking and preference. Therefore, creating teams whose members share personal values—beliefs about what is good or bad and what one should or should not do—seems to be important for building long-term team cohesiveness. Differences in things like age, education, country of citizenship, and gender seem to fade in significance as the team works together successfully.

Myers-Briggs Type Indicator
www.keirsey.com/ keirsey.html

---

skills like building mutually supportive team–member relationships, building team members' self-confidence, and learning how to move from "boss" to "coach." In the remainder of this chapter we will turn briefly to a few of the uniquely team-related aspects of being a leader.

How Do Team Leaders Behave?

We've touched on this elsewhere, but a short review and elaboration is now in order. Team leaders

- coach, they don't boss. They assess their team members' skills and help members use them to the fullest.

- encourage participation. They solicit input into decisions, share decision-making responsibility, and delegate specifically identified decisions to the team—often a great many decisions, as in the case of self-directed, self-managing work teams.

- are boundary managers. The team leader has to manage the interaction of the team with its environment, which means with other teams and with management and those outside the company. As a boundary manager, the team leader must also provide his or her team with high-quality information so the team can make informed choices.[78]

- are facilitators.[79] The best team leaders see themselves as facilitators. They give the other team members the self-confidence, authority, information, and tools they need to get their jobs done. Team leaders don't view themselves as sitting atop an organizational pyramid with team members reporting to them. Instead, they view the pyramid as upside down, with their job being to support and facilitate so that their team can get the job done.

Typical Transition Problems

Moving from being a traditional in-charge supervisor to being a facilitator/coach team leader isn't easy. As one former executive put it:

> Working…under the autocratic system was a lot easier, particularly when you want something done quickly and you are convinced you know the right way to do it. It is a lot easier to say, "OK,…we're going to Toronto tomorrow," rather than sit down and say, "All right, first of all, do we want to go out of town? And where do we want to go—east or west?"[80]

Why is it so difficult to make the transition from supervisor to team leader? For at least four reasons, as follows:

The Perceived Loss of Power or Status. Making the transition from supervisor to team leader often involves a perceived loss of power or status.[81] One day you are the boss, with the authority to give orders and have others obey; the next day the pyramid is upside down and suddenly you're a facilitator/coach, trying to make sure your team members have what they need to do their jobs—to a large extent, without you. We've seen, for instance, that self-managing teams often schedule their own work priorities, hire their own co-workers, and decide themselves when to take their breaks.

What's worse, the perceived loss of power or status sometimes comes along with a real loss of supervisory perks. For example, the former boss (but now team leader) may find that he or she has had to relinquish that special parking spot or office that went along with being the boss. This is because the company is now operating in the new egalitarian climate most conducive to self-managing, empowered work teams.

Unclear Team Leader Roles. Some companies make the mistake of overemphasizing what the former supervisor (now team leader) is *not*: You're not the boss any more; you are not to control or direct any more; you are not to make all the hiring decisions any more. Just telling the new team leaders what they're not, without clarifying what they are, can cause unnecessary transition difficulties. It can exacerbate the new team leader's perceived loss of power or status. And of course it can leave the person with the very real and unnerving question, "What exactly am I supposed to be doing, anyway?"

This problem is easily avoided. We've seen that team leaders do have important duties to perform—for instance, as coaches, facilitators, and boundary managers. The company's job is to ensure that the new team leaders understand what their new duties are, and that they have the training they need to do their new jobs effectively.

Job Security Concerns. Telling some new team leaders that they're not in charge any more understandably undermines their sense of security. After all, it's not unreasonable for someone to ask, "Just how secure is the job of managing a self-managing team?" Some new team leaders will say, "Sure, I know that my new duties are to facilitate and coach, but that just doesn't make me feel as irreplaceable as I was when I was in charge."

There is a lot of truth in that. For example, General Mills claims that much of its productivity improvement from self-directed work teams came from eliminating middle managers. Insecurity is therefore not just a figment of supervisors' imaginations as companies move to self-managing teams.

Companies handle this problem in several ways. Many—perhaps most—of the resulting teams will still need someone as facilitator/coach, so many of the supervisors will in fact find new homes as effective team leaders. What happens when there are too many supervisors? As you know, many companies have been downsized, and many former supervisors or managers have unfortunately lost their jobs.

Other companies, reluctant to lose the enormous expertise their supervisors have, take steps to retain these valuable human assets. For example, when one manufacturing plant changed over to self-directing work teams, the redundant supervisors were turned into training coordinators and made responsible for managing the continuing educational requirements of the plant's new teams.[82] In another company, 15 of the 25 supervisors who were displaced by the move to self-directed work teams were guaranteed their existing salary packages if they became team members; if not, they had the option to transfer elsewhere in the company.

The Double Standard Problem. Many existing supervisors will feel that the company is treating them as second-class citizens compared with the employees who are being trained to be team members. Treating anyone—let alone the company's supervisors—so cavalierly can obviously make them annoyed and resistant. The smarter way to proceed is to create and implement a development and transition plan for the supervisors as well, one that clarifies their new team leadership duties, outlines how their security will be ensured, and identifies training they can expect to receive as they make the transition from supervisor to team leader.

What Are Team-Leader Values?

Not everyone is cut out to be an effective leader of self-managing teams. Self-managing teams are empowered to work with a minimum of supervision. Not every leader is philosophically prepared to surrender the trappings of "being a boss" that leading in such a situation requires.

In particular, being a leader of a self-managing team requires a special set of personal values, values that derive from the empowered nature of these teams. What personal values are consistent with building self-confidence, sharing authority, and ensuring that the team has the tools and information it requires? Important team-leader values include the following.

Saturn
www.saturn.com

Put Your Team Members First. Effective team leaders have an abiding respect for the individual. At Saturn, for instance, team members carry a card that lists the firm's values, one of which is set forth in these words:

> We have nothing of greater value than our people. We believe that demonstrating respect for the uniqueness of every individual builds a team of confident, creative members possessing a high degree of initiative, self-respect, and self-discipline.[83]

You'll find a similar stress on putting people first at companies like Toyota. Here's how one manager puts it:

> In all our meetings and in every way, all Toyota top managers continually express their trust in human nature. Mr. Cho [the chief executive of the company] continually reminds us that the team members must come first and that every other action we take and decision we make must be adapted to that basic idea; I must manage around that core idea.[84]

Team Members Can Be Trusted to Do Their Best. Some leaders have what Douglas McGregor called "Theory X" assumptions: They believe that people are lazy, need to be controlled, need to be motivated, and are not very smart.

Assumptions like those obviously won't work for leaders of self-managing teams. These leaders need what McGregor called "Theory Y" assumptions about human nature: that people like to work, have self-control, can motivate themselves, and are smart.

What this comes down to is that effective team leaders trust that their team members will do their best. They believe that team members can and want to do a good job, they trust them to do their best, and they focus much of their attention on ensuring that their team members have what they need to do their jobs.

Teamwork Is Important. Although it may seem obvious, effective team leaders should believe that teamwork is important. They can't just pay lip service to the value of teamwork; they really have to "walk the talk." Remember that much of the status and prestige of being a boss is stripped away in the transition from supervisor to team leader. Team leaders have to minimize status differences (like special parking spots and separate lunch rooms) when creating teams, and may even have to forgo mammoth salary differentials.[85]

Procter & Gamble
www.pg.com

Support Is Crucial. Team leaders value eliminating barriers to success and are often driven by the desire to do so.[86] At Procter & Gamble, for instance, some team leaders refer to themselves as "barrier busters" because "they recognize the primary importance of removing the things that get in the way of the success of their teams."[87]

Probably the single biggest difference between team leaders and supervisors is that the former view themselves as there to support their teams and therefore to eliminate barriers to their team's success. They believe that their primary responsibility is to make sure their teams can get their jobs done.

Developing Effective Coaching Skills

We've seen in this chapter that coaching is a big part of what team leaders do. That's why in his book *Team-Based Organizations*, James Shonk says that leading self-managing teams is a lot like coaching:

It involves assessing the team's skills and helping them to use them to the fullest. Employees tend to more effectively contribute when they are coached to make optimal use of all their strengths and resources.[88]

What is required to coach subordinates? Experts provide the following guidelines:[89]

- Know your people. Assess each employee's skills so you can help team members use them to the fullest. As Shonk put it, employees contribute more effectively when coached to use all of their strengths and resources.

- Coach, don't tell. Remember: Your role as coach is to help your people develop their skills and competencies. In other words, your job is not to tell people what to do or to sell your own ideas, but to help others define, analyze, and solve problems. The best way to influence subordinates in a coaching situation is *not* to tell them what to do. Instead, stimulate increased employee initiative and autonomy by raising questions, helping your people identify alternatives, providing general direction, encouraging employees to contribute their own ideas, and supplying feedback.[90]

- Give emotional support. Effective NHL and CFL coaches know when to back off and be more supportive. Particularly when an employee is new to the task and just developing his or her skills (like how to analyze problems), it's crucial to create a supportive environment. The way to influence employees is to let them know that you're not there to pass judgment or to place blame. Instead, provide the emotional support they need as they develop their skills and competencies.

- Provide specific feedback. Being supportive doesn't mean you shouldn't explain what improvements are required from your point of view. Letting subordinates flounder around trying to figure out where they fall short is no way to influence them; for example, if the team provides you with a recommendation that is lacking, be specific (but supportive) about why it needs improvement. Let them know that you are confident they will get it right the next time.

■ Use Socratic coaching. Try to refrain from making judgmental statements like, "That won't work." Instead, be Socratic, which means asking the questions that will lead your subordinates to find the answers for themselves. For instance, "What is the problem you want to solve?" or "How will you know when you have solved it?"[91]

■ Show that you have high expectations. The best coaches communicate the fact that they have high expectations for the team and its members. The heart of empowering employees is giving them not just the authority and tools but also the self-confidence to get the job done. That's why one expert says, "When I think back on people who have been great coaches in my life, they have always had very high expectations of me."[92]

SUMMARY OF LEARNING OBJECTIVES

1. **List and briefly describe the types of teams used at work.** Leaders can use four general types of teams in organizations: suggestion teams, problem-solving teams, semi-autonomous teams, and self-managing teams. Specific examples include quality circles; project, development, or venture teams; transnational teams; virtual teams; and self-directed work teams.

2. **Explain the causes and symptoms of unproductive teams.** Not all teams function effectively, and leaders can observe a number of symptoms of unproductive teams: non-accomplishment of goals, cautious or guarded communication, lack of disagreement, use of personal criticism, malfunctioning meetings, unclear goals, low commitment, and conflict within the team. The causes of unproductive teams are power struggles, groupthink, poor leadership, a lack of focus, and lack of team member capability.

3. **Understand what is necessary to build team performance.** Productive teams don't just happen; they are the result of careful selection, training, and leadership. Guidelines to build team performance include: seek employee input, establish demanding performance standards, select members for their skill and potential, pay particular attention to first meetings and actions, set some clear rules of behaviour, move from "boss" to "coach," set a few immediate performance-oriented tasks and goals, challenge the group regularly with fresh facts and information, spend lots of time together, exploit the power of positive feedback, recognition, and reward, shoot for the right team size, choose people who like teamwork, cross-train for flexibility, emphasize the task's importance, assign whole tasks, build team spirit, encourage social support, and provide material support.

4. **Describe the problems of making the transition from supervisor to team leader.** It can be difficult to make the transition from supervisor to team leader for several reasons: perceived loss of power or status; unclear team roles; job security concerns; and the double standard problem.

5. **List the values that team leaders should have.** Important team-leader values include the following: put your team members first; trust team members to do their best; and support team members.

6. **Use important team-leader coaching skills.** Important team-leader coaching skills include: know your people; coach, don't tell; give emotional support; provide specific feedback; use Socratic teaching; and show that you have high expectations.

Teamwork plays an important role in most companies today. In some companies the entire structure is organized around teams—as it was, for instance, at Published Image Inc. In other companies, such as General Electric and Johnsonville Foods, entire facilities are organized around teams; here self-managing teams of highly trained workers are responsible for (and hold themselves responsible for) discrete, self-contained tasks. For example, General Electric's aircraft engine plant has a team that builds an entire engine from beginning to end.

Managing teams like these requires all of the leadership skills discussed in the last three chapters. As any coach knows, the leadership style that works in one situation may not work in another. Even though coaching and support might be the usual prescriptions for leading a team at work, there'll be times when you size up the situation and recognize that some discipline is required. Similarly, motivating the team will require a shrewd balance of material rewards and recognition, and building an effective team will require all of the communication skills you can muster.

It often happens that teams are created as part of a broader organizational change and development program. Indeed (as companies like Levi Strauss have found), instituting teamwork without considering the broader context of the organization and the other changes that must also take place (in how employees are hired and appraised, for instance, or in the company's compensation plan) can lead to problems. In the following chapter we therefore turn to the topic of leading organizational change.

CRITICAL THINKING EXERCISES

1. Many girls are now expected to participate in sports to the same extent as boys. What impact do you think this will have on teamwork in organizations? What are the cultural and gender issues that arise around this trend and teamwork in general? Are teams the key to our economic present and future or just a passing fad?

2. One of the keys to effective teams is to assemble what Jennifer James, in *Thinking in the Future Tense*, calls thinking skills. She discusses a number of approaches, including evaluating and identifying your thinking.[93] Many of her points can be directly applied to teams in the future tense. Using Edward De Bono's hat analysis, James gives us an easy way to understand which approach to thinking people take by relating them to the imaginary hats they are wearing. This is a condensed version of De Bono's guide:

   - White Hat—the white-hat thinker is mainly concerned with facts and figures.
   - Red Hat—the red-hat thinker operates from an emotional source.
   - Black Hat—the black-hat thinker dwells on why something cannot be done.
   - Yellow Hat—the yellow-hat thinker is optimistic.
   - Green Hat—the green-hat thinker is creative and open to new ideas.
   - Blue Hat—the blue-hat thinker is concerned with control.

   Which hat do you wear at school, at work, at home, or with friends? Does the same hat always apply? If a team had one of each of these hat types, how do you think it would solve a problem such as downsizing or deciding to merge with another company? How would it work together on day-to-day projects? What would happen if only Green, Yellow, and Black Hats were on a team? What about if only White, Red, and Blue Hats were on a team? Be prepared to discuss and debate your thoughts in class.

1. Your class has just been appointed by the university administration to form teams to help address racial tensions and discrimination against minorities. Your goal is to create a plan to promote cultural awareness among the student body and to make positive links with the surrounding ethnically diverse community.

   The administration prefers that each team consist of students from several constituencies. Assume that those represented are to include the Asian Honour Society, the Aboriginal Outreach Group, the Disabled Students Coalition, the Gay and Lesbian Alliance, Christian Outreach, the Muslim Society, Young Conservatives, and the Older Students Awareness Association.

   Break into groups of five and select a team leader for each group. Then have each remaining member role-play as a representative of one of the groups listed above. Now create the plan requested by the administration.

2. Some companies have built their management foundation on teams and teamwork rather than introduce managers into a pre-existent bureaucratic structure. Individual effort and reward usually define work in a bureaucratic structure. Management was the only level that operated as a group, but not necessarily as a team. Some companies have decided against the bureaucratic structure and have adopted a team approach, but some companies have not had particularly good success with teams (e.g., Levi-Strauss). Research several companies that have introduced teams, and analyze the strengths and limitations of teams.

Teams are an important part of operating in a college or university environment, as well as in the world of work. Read about major issues facing teams and how to enhance team-building at www.poynter.org/research/lm/lm_team.htm. If you have operated as part of a team, consider the issues in the context of your past or present experience.

You may also want to test how your team is doing, if applicable. An inventory about teams and customized responses to your answers can be found at www.leaderx.com/testteamresp.htm.

Red Star Rising: How Do You Build a Team in a Nation Built on Secrecy?

With the breakup of the Soviet Union, challenges to rebuild the "new" countries into democracies and market economies multiplied. How do you manage in a country such as Russia, where the government has planned everything for years and entrepreneurship was unknown?

The answer for entrepreneur James Hickman was twofold. To start Rustel, a $40 million telephone company based in Moscow, he needed people who knew how to work the old bureaucratic system. But those he hired had a habit of secrecy. They left no records of their contacts when they left Rustel, and they devised incomplete plans.

In its second round of hiring, the company found some of its most important employees among the thousands of gypsy cab drivers who work Moscow's streets. Here were entrepreneurs with the work ethic Rustel needed. They might have lacked skills and training, but motivation and willingness to learn earned them important positions in the expanding Rustel and the growing market economy in Russia.

Questions

1. What barriers do you think there are to building a team in Russia today?

2. Rustel still hires experienced bureaucrats and new entrepreneurs. What would you do to forge a team using these two very different styles?

3. What are the differences between Canada and Russia in terms of building a team?

Merging Teams at Canadian National Railways

Over the last decade, the railway industry had been consolidating. There are fewer and fewer small companies, as large companies have acquired more and more firms. There was a clear message in the industry: Unless you were large or had a large partner, you were a likely target for a takeover of your firm. Canadian National Railways (CN) understood the market forces clearly. In order to grow in a consolidating industry, CN would need to acquire other railroads. CN had developed a strong team culture under the leadership of CEO Paul Tellier. Would CN be able to absorb another large railroad and still keep its team-oriented management style? If managers at newly acquired railroads feared for their jobs, would CN be able to get past this fear and build a single team?

The test came in 1998. First, CN merged with the Illinois Central (IC) Railroad. Then, the newly merged firm formed a marketing alliance with the Kansas City Southern Railroad. In the early stages of planning for mergers, Tellier had strong concerns. Regardless of industry forces, Tellier wanted all stakeholders to have a shared vision. He understood that IC provided a perfect complement to CN (because of their complementary assets) at the perfect time (NAFTA was increasing north–south rail traffic).

The second step that Tellier took in building a team was to seek high levels of commitment from top level managers. It was not enough for Tellier to envision the future of CN; the other senior executives also needed to be highly involved. The management team at CN also used proactive communication methods with their stakeholders. Within the first 48 hours of the CN–IC merger, Tellier's team made conference calls to employees in both organizations. They also installed a 1-800 number to handle employee questions about the merger. CN was very careful to establish communication early and to maintain it. CN was also proactive in eliciting commitment to a shared vision.

While post-acquisition integration can take years, it was apparent from company results that the two formerly separate companies were functioning well as a unit. In 1998, CN announced that it had won the Carrier of the Year award for 1998 from Occidental Chemical Corporation for the third consecutive year. CN had been rated first in performance, ranking ahead of eight other Class 1 railroads.

Questions

1. What concerns might IC managers have about forming teams with their new partner?
2. What steps did Tellier take to build his team?
3. What additional steps would you recommend he take in the future?

YOU BE THE CONSULTANT

Teamwork at KnitMedia

KNITMEDIA

One of the biggest challenges that KnitMedia faces over the next few years is maintaining the strong sense of team spirit and teamwork that the company had when it was small. Having team spirit when you're only 15 or 20 employees all working together in a small office above the Knitting Factory club in downtown Manhattan is one thing; keeping alive the spirit that "we're all in this together" is quite another when the company is large and people are scattered all over the world.

Heather Stamm, production coordinator of the New York club, puts it this way: "We do have teamwork, I think, especially in my department with programming and production and the sound stuff—we have pretty good teamwork going on. [However] there's a lot of people and a lot of departments, so you have to try really hard to make sure that everyone stays in communication, because the staff is just so large now and growing...."

Keeping the communication open is absolutely critical to the success of a small company like KnitMedia, since the company's size gives it one of its big advantages. Compared to its giant competitors, a small company like KnitMedia should have few of the functional boundaries that prevent departments from talking with each other. Emphasizing teamwork more and instituting concrete methods for building teamwork should therefore be very helpful for a company like KnitMedia. The question is: How does KnitMedia do this as it grows? Michael Dorf and his team want your advice.

Team Exercises and Questions

Use what you know and what you learned in this chapter to answer the following questions from Michael Dorf and his management team:

1. To what extent and in what manner would you say that KnitMedia is now using teams to accomplish its mission?
2. How exactly would you suggest we use teams to more effectively manage our transnational operations, and particularly our expansion into new Knitting Factory clubs abroad?
3. In general, what concrete recommendations would you make regarding how KnitMedia can make more extensive use of teams?

Leading Organizational Change

Big Changes in the Airline Industry

Throughout the 1990s, Canada's two premier airlines—Air Canada and Canadian Airlines International—were locked in a bitter competitive struggle for supremacy in the domestic airline market. Industry observers agreed that significant changes were needed and that the market could not support two national airlines in Canada. Other changes that were suggested included reducing costs, cutting employees, increasing revenues, reducing baggage-handling mistakes, and generally improving service.

Canadian Airlines, which was continuously on the brink of bankruptcy, considered several alternatives in an attempt to solve its problems, including asking for a federal bailout, merging with Air Canada, and partnering with a large U.S. airline. In 1999, Onex Corporation made a surprise bid to buy Canadian, and intended to follow that up with a bid for Air Canada so the two airlines could be merged. But a Quebec court ruled against that idea. Soon after, Air Canada made its own offer to buy Canadian and run it as a separate company. In January 2000, Air Canada announced that it had successfully completed the purchase of Canadian. The federal government and the Competition Bureau approved the deal.

This outcome probably means greater stability and security for employees of the newly merged company, since Air Canada will now control about 80 percent of all domestic air traffic. But consumers are worried that this dominance will result in higher airfares and reduced service. The federal government immediately responded to this concern by passing new price-gouging legislation. The legislation included a maximum prison sentence of five years and fines of up to $10 million if Air Canada did not live up to its promises to ensure competition in the industry. As well, the Canadian Transportation Agency has the power to reject or roll back fare increases, and it can order the airline to give refunds to customers. The government also indicated that if new domestic competitors don't emerge in the industry, U.S. airlines will be invited in to ensure that competition continues to exist.

What does the future hold for air travel in Canada? If Air Canada does not

Canadian
Transportation
Agency
www.cta-otc.gc.ca

WestJet
www.westjet.com

Air Canada
www.aircanada.ca

provide reasonably priced service, other new airlines will no doubt start up to compete in certain market niches. Discount airline WestJet is already planning significant expansion because it sees new opportunities in the market. Like everything else these days, the airline business is in a constant state of change.

The Challenge of Organizational Change

Why Should Organizations Change?

Fishery Products International
www.fpil.com

Organizations that do not adapt to their environments do not survive. Consider the difficulties that were encountered by Fishery Products International Ltd., Canada's largest fishing company. At one time it employed over 8000 Newfoundlanders and had revenues well over $300 million per year. But when the government imposed a moratorium on cod fishing, 6000 employees were laid off. However, the company did not give up. It survived by making the painful decision to shift its focus away from fish harvesting and towards fish trading and processing. It now processes fish that have been caught in other parts of the world.[1]

Many managers have chosen to try to change their organizations. As the *Harvard Business Review* recently put it: "Companies achieve real agility only when every function, office, strategy, goal, and process—when every person—is able and eager to rise to every challenge. This type and degree of fundamental change, commonly called *revitalization* or *transformation*, is what more and more companies seek but all too rarely achieve."[2] In the last few chapters we've seen how leaders motivate and influence individuals and teams; now we'll turn to an explanation of how to lead and influence organizational change.

What to Change?

What aspects of an organization can a manager actually change? The answer is the strategy, culture, structure, tasks, technologies, and attitudes and skills of the company's people.

strategic change
A shift in the firm's strategy, mission, and vision.

Strategic Change. Organizational change often starts with **strategic change**, a shift in the firm's strategy, mission, and vision. Strategic change may then lead to other organizational changes, for instance, in the firm's technology, structure, and culture.

Examples of strategic change abound. On becoming Kodak's CEO, for instance, one of the first strategic changes that George Fisher made was to refocus the company more fully on emphasizing digital cameras and photography. When Steve Jobs assumed the title of "interim CEO" of Apple Computer several years ago, one of his first strategic moves was to refocus Apple on a much narrower set of products and to emphasize the re-emergence of the Macintosh (iMac) computer. Whereas Microsoft's strategy had for-merly emphasized software for desktop computers, its new strategy is to provide the software that people will need to run their computers "anytime, anywhere"—including, for instance, cellphone-based Web browsers—to do Internet-based computing.

The strategic change initiated at Fuji-Xerox by President Yotaro Kobayashi provides another example.[3] Faced with declining market share, a dearth of new products, and more customer complaints, Kobayashi and his team created a new vision for Fuji-Xerox. They called this the New Xerox Movement; the strategy involved turning Fuji-Xerox into a total quality–based company. The core values of quality, problem solving, teamwork, and customer focus symbolized this new strategy and were aimed at making Fuji-Xerox a more competitive company.

Kodak
www.kodak.com

Implementing Strategic Organizational Change. Strategic organizational changes—redefining as they do the organization's basic direction—are among the riskiest but most important changes that managers can implement. What triggers such changes? Why are they risky? We can summarize some recent research findings as follows.

1. *Strategic organizational changes are usually triggered by factors outside the company.* External threats or challenges, such as deregulation, intensified global competition, and dramatic technological innovations (like those in the computer and telecommunications industries), are usually the ones that prompt organizations to embark on company-wide, strategic changes.[4]

2. *Strategic organizational changes are often required for survival.* Researchers found that making a strategic organizational change did not guarantee success, but firms that failed to change generally failed to survive. Specifically, they found that what they called "discontinuous" environmental change—change of an unexpected nature, such as happened when the Internet made obsolete many retail stores' traditional ways of doing business—required quick and effective strategic change for the firms to survive.

3. *Strategic, system-wide changes implemented under crisis conditions are highly risky.*

Changes in the external environment have motivated Chapters to introduce significant changes in the way that books are sold. The opening of book superstores and the introduction of on-line book selling are two examples of the major changes that have taken place at Chapters.

Chapters Innovates

Chapters
www.chapters.ca
www.chaptersglobe.
com

Early in 1995, SmithBooks and Coles Book Stores merged to create Chapters Inc., a Canadian company. Since then Chapters has been breaking new ground on a number of fronts. For starters, Chapters is the largest book retailer in Canada and the third largest in North America, operating 230 traditional bookstores under the banner of Coles or SmithBooks, and 70 book superstores under the Chapters banner. The company also manages five college bookstores through its Campus Bookstore Division, and offers books for sale online through two Internet sites.

Chapters had its early roots in two entrepreneurial companies: Coles and SmithBooks. Brothers Carl and Jack Cole opened the first Coles store in 1940 in Toronto. Coles expanded across Canada, bringing an inventive style to book retailing with stores that were enticing and accessible. Coles also created the popular Coles Notes student study guides. In 1980, Coles opened one of the original book superstores, the 57 000-square-foot World's Biggest Bookstore in downtown Toronto. Coles' co-partner is SmithBooks (originally called W.H. Smith), which opened in Toronto in 1950.

The tradition of leading organizational change continues with Chapters. The superstores are unique in layout and ambiance, and include Starbucks cafés and extended hours of operation. Some of the superstores have Internet cafés, community rooms, and "Hear Music" departments where customers can choose from over 15 000 CDs. Computer look-up stations are situated throughout each Chapters to give retail customers access to the same inventory of over 2.5 million titles available to online shoppers.

Expansion is a key component to the Chapters business strategy. During 2000, 7 to 10 new superstores were opened. With this intense activity, Chapters is well positioned to take advantage of more traditional retail needs, as well as the e-commerce boom.

Of all organizational changes, strategic, organization-wide ones initiated under crisis conditions and with short time constraints (like those of Kodak and Apple) were the riskiest. They involve changing more aspects of the organization, including its core values.[5] Because core values tend to be resistant to change, changing them tends to trigger the most serious resistance from employees.

Fuji
www.fujifilm.com

Cultural Change. Implementing a strategic change often requires changing the culture; in other words, changing the firm's shared values. For example, Fuji's executive team instituted what two experts referred to as a "dense infrastructure of objectives, measures, rewards, tools, education and slogans, all in service of total quality control and the 'new Xerox.'"[6] To help support the new strategy, they also created a new set of "heroes," individuals and teams that were publicly congratulated whenever their behaviour reflected the best of Fuji's new values.

Structural (Organizational) Change. Reorganizing means redesigning the organization's structure—that is, changing the departmentalization, coordination, span of control, reporting relationships, or centralization of decision making. It is a relatively direct and quick method for changing an organization.

Reorganizing is widely used and often effective, particularly given recent demands for leaner organizations. Seeing the need to put more emphasis on developing digital photography products, for instance, one of Fisher's first moves at Kodak was to group together in one new division all of the separate digital product teams.

Business Re-engineering

Organizational changes today are often driven by technological change. Perhaps a new technology (like Internet bookstores) have made your business (a retail bookstore) somewhat obsolete, or perhaps the availability of a new technology has raised the possibility that you can now manage your company more effectively. In any case, changing organizations today always means understanding how to manage at the speed of thought.

For example, "reorganizing" usually doesn't just mean pushing boxes around on an organization chart; instead, it means reorganizing the company in order to take advantage of some new technology. Business re-engineering is one example of this.

business re-engineering
The radical redesign of business processes, combining steps to cut waste and eliminate repetitive, paper-intensive tasks in order to improve cost, quality, and service, and to maximize the benefits of information technology.

Business re-engineering has been defined as "the radical redesign of business processes, combining steps to cut waste and eliminate repetitive, paper-intensive tasks in order to improve cost, quality, and service, and to maximize the benefits of information technology."[7] The approach is to (1) identify a business process to be designed (such as approving a mortgage application), (2) measure the performance of the existing processes, (3) identify opportunities to improve these processes, and (4) redesign and implement a new way of doing the work.

A re-engineering process at IBM Credit Corp., a financing subsidiary of IBM, is typical. The firm exists to provide a service: financing computers and software. But, previously, each financing request had to go through a cumbersome series of steps, even though must customers needed an immediate answer. After two managers decided to "walk through" a typical request, they discovered that the actual approval work took only 90 minutes. The rest of the time was spent shuffling forms between the various people who worked on the process. The managers' solution was to put one person in charge of all the steps. The result? A hundredfold increase in the number of requests handled.[8]

Re-engineering is also underway at Novacor Chemicals in Sarnia, Ontario. Over the past 10 years, the company acquired four different businesses, each with its own style, technology, and processes. It is now rethinking how it produces about 2 million tonnes of petrochemicals each year. In the process, it is finding that it can save millions of dollars by having the four businesses operate in a coordinated fashion rather than as separate entities. For example, when plants were shut down for maintenance, each one hired its own maintenance teams. Now, one team is hired and rotated among the four plants.[9]

Companies' experience with re-engineering underscores the importance of the organizational change process. While re-engineering with the aid of information technology has had its share of successes, some estimate failure rates to be as high as 70 percent.[10] When a re-engineering effort does fail, it is often due to behavioural factors. Sometimes (as in other change efforts) employees resist the change and deliberately undermine the revised procedures. If business processes are re-engineered without considering the new skill requirements, training, and reporting relationships involved, the usual employee resistance problems can be exacerbated. As John Champy, a long-time re-engineering proponent, has said:

> In short, reducing hierarchy, bureaucracy, and the rest of it is not just a matter of re-arranging the furniture to face our customers and markets. It is a matter of rear-ranging the quality of people's attachments—to their work and to each other. These are *cultural* matters....[11]

The aim today is often to create organic, more-responsive organizations. Here, as we've seen, committed and empowered cross-functional teams supervise their own efforts within the framework of top management's vision. Employees communicate with colleagues horizontally and vertically throughout the often boundaryless firm in these newly redesigned and more responsive structures.[12]

Task Redesign. The tasks and authority of individuals and teams within the organization are often changed as well. For example, to gain employees' commitment to quality, traditional assembly-line jobs were abolished at Saturn. Instead, work teams supervise their own work.

Technological Change. Technological changes are modifications to the work methods that the organization uses to accomplish its tasks. Such changes include new production technologies, new selection and screening procedures, and new performance appraisal methods. The new employee compensation plans and appraisal systems instituted by Yotaro Kobayashi at Fuji-Xerox illustrate technological change implemented to support cultural and strategic changes. So does Allen-Bradley Canada's introduction of new technology as part of an automated warehouse and shipping system.[13]

Changes in People: Attitudes and Skills. Sometimes the employees themselves must change.[14] Techniques such as lectures, conferences, and on-the-job training are often used to provide employees with the skills they need to perform their jobs adequately. At IBM Canada, 300 employees who used to work in manufacturing went through a 17-week retraining program to learn how to write software.[15] Digital Equipment of Canada puts every employee through a two-day "valuing diversity" training course that requires workers to examine their cultural attitudes. The seminar also presents hard facts about topics where misunderstandings often occur. For example, the session debunks myths about immigrants such as "they are unskilled refugees." In fact, fewer than 10 percent of immigrants are refugees, and most have skills that are in high demand.[16] **Organizational development interventions**—such as sensitivity training, discussed later in the chapter—are aimed at changing employees' attitudes, values, and behaviour.

organizational development interventions
Techniques aimed at changing employees' attitudes, values, and behaviour.

How Much Change?

Organizational changes differ in their breadth and urgency—changes can range from big to little, in other words. Some changes are limited and *incremental* in nature: They may require reorganizing just one department or establishing work teams in a single plant. At the other extreme, *strategic organizational changes* affect the entire company and usually change not just the company's strategy, but also its structure, culture, people, and processes.[17]

Some changes are *reactive* and reflect a sense of urgency in response to a crisis or threat; others are *anticipatory* and are initiated to prepare the company for the future. When Gil Amelio took over Apple Computer in 1996, organizational change was urgent, since Amelio had to react quickly to Apple's deteriorating market position. He apparently failed to move fast enough, and was replaced by Steve Jobs the next year.

Apple
www.apple.com/ca

Why Do People Resist Change?

Overcoming resistance is often the hardest part of leading change. As Niccolò Machiavelli, a shrewd observer of 16th-century Italian politics, once said: "There is nothing so difficult to implement as change, since those in favor of the change will often be small in number while those opposing the change will be numerous and enthusiastic in their resistance to change."[18] Indeed, even the best leaders would agree that implementing wide-scale change is enormously challenging: GE's Jack Welch once said that even after 10 years of continual change, he expected it would take at least 10 more years to rejuvenate GE's culture.[19]

The fact that a change is advisable or even mandatory doesn't mean that employees will accept it. In fact, it's often the company's key people—perhaps even some top and middle managers—who are the most resistant. They are the most supportive of (their and the company's) status quo, a fact that further complicates the change process.

It's actually not difficult to see how such resistance might arise. Take a personal example: Suppose that you've been attending a class in management with the school's best professor. Several weeks into the semester the dean comes in and announces that several students will have to be moved to another professor and class because the fire marshal says that the current lecture hall is overcrowded. You have been asked to move. How would you react? What would go through your mind?

Probably several things: that your grade might be adversely affected; that you don't want to leave the friends you've made in this class and start all over again; that it might be a tad embarrassing to have to get up and leave (although obviously it's not your fault); and that it's not fair that you should be one of the students singled out to leave. You don't want to go!

In his book *Beyond the Wall of Resistance*, author-consultant Rick Maurer says that resistance can stem from basically two sets of things. What he calls level 1 resistance is based on lack of information or on honest disagreement over the facts. In this type of resistance, everything is on the table and there are no hidden agendas. Level 2 resistance is more personal and emotional. Here, people are afraid—that the change may cost them their jobs, or cause them to lose face, or reduce their control (or in our example, lower their grades). Maurer points out that treating all resistance as if it were level 1 (simply caused by an honest disagreement and lack of information) can make a company miss the mark in its change efforts. For example, an employee may object to a transfer to another city on the grounds that he or she cannot afford the moving costs. When informed that the company will pay all of the moving costs, the employee may still oppose the change, saying that it will disrupt his or her personal life. These situations are very frustrating for managers because determining the real reason for an employee's resistance to change is difficult. Because of problems like this, it is important that we review some specific sources of resistance to change, and how managers can overcome them.

Habit. People become accustomed to the usual way of doing things; they may resist change solely because they assume that it is more convenient or less costly to keep doing things "the usual way."

Threats to Power and Influence. Professor Paul Lawrence says that it's usually not the technical aspects of a change that employees resist, but its social consequences, "the changes in their human relationships that generally accompany the technical change."[20] For example, they may see in the change diminished responsibilities for themselves and therefore lower status in the organization and less job security. Such real or perceived threats often underlie resistance to change.

Fear of the Unknown. Sometimes it's not fear of the change's obvious consequences but rather apprehension about its unknown consequences that produces resistance. For example, how much do you know about the professor who'll be teaching that class you're being moved to, and about the new classmates you'll be joining? Not much, unfortunately.

Changes in the "Personal Compact." Most people see themselves as having a written (or unwritten) "personal compact" with their companies. In other words, there are sets of reciprocal obligations and mutual commitments, both stated and implied, that define the employee-employer relationship.[21] Employees understandably resist any change that seems to alter what they view to be a personal compact.

There are formal, psychological, and social aspects to an employee's personal compact.[22] The *formal dimension* consists of the basic tasks and performance requirements for the job as defined by documents like job descriptions and employment contracts. It answers questions like "What am I supposed to do for the company?" and "What will I get to do the job?"

The *psychological dimension* "incorporates the elements of mutual expectation and reciprocal commitment that arise from feelings like trust and dependence between employee and employer."[23] For example, managers expect employees to be loyal and willing to do what it takes to get the job done; for their part, employees want to know, as part of the psychological dimension of their personal compact with the company, "How hard will

I really have to work? What recognition or other personal satisfaction will I get for my efforts? Are the rewards worth it?"

There's also a *social dimension* to these personal compacts. It reflects the degree to which employees view the firm's values and expectations as consistent with their own, and the degree to which management carries through on the values it espouses. For example, employees want to know "Are my values similar to those of others in the organization?" and "What are the real rules that determine who gets what in this company?" Moves on the company's part that violate what the employees have come to expect—as when Kodak, after years of protecting workers' jobs, began massive layoffs—risk triggering excessive resistance.

Personality. Last but not least, you've probably noticed that some people are inherently more resistant to change than others. At the extreme, in fact, some people are simply recalcitrant, which basically means that they'll almost always resist change as a knee-jerk reaction. People like these are continually "fighting the system" and, as you might imagine, are usually not the sorts of employees that contribute in a positive way to organizational change. Of course, you don't have to be recalcitrant to resist a change.

Some personalities are simply more open to change. One recent study took place in six organizations that included two large European companies, two Australian banks, a large American university, and a Korean manufacturing company. Its aim was to determine the extent to which managers' responses to organizational change were influenced by various personality traits. In this case, three factors—tolerance for ambiguity, having a positive self-concept, and being more tolerant of risk—significantly predicted both self-reports and independent assessments of managers' effectiveness in coping with change.[24] Personality is therefore another factor that needs to be considered when planning a change.

Overcoming Resistance to Change

Methods for Dealing with Resistance. What tools are available to overcome resistance to change? In Table 14.1, John Kotter and Leonard Schlesinger summarize the pros and cons of some of the methods that leaders use to deal with resistance to change. For example, *education and communication* are appropriate where inaccurate or missing information is contributing to employee resistance. When Inco Ltd. told 60 office workers (including 30 women) that they had to choose between accepting underground mining work or losing their jobs, the company tried to allay their fears about working underground by conducting mine tours, counselling sessions, and fitness training sessions.[25]

When employees are confronted with difficult changes in their working conditions, getting them to agree to the changes may be facilitated by education and communication.

TABLE 14.1 *Six Methods for Dealing with Resistance to Change*

APPROACH METHOD	COMMONLY USED IN SITUATIONS	ADVANTAGES	DRAWBACKS
Education + communication	Where there is a lack of information or inaccurate information and analysis.	Once persuaded, people will often help with the implementation of the change.	Can be very time consuming if lots of people are involved.
Participation + involvement	Where the initiators do not have all the information they need to design the change, and where others have considerable power to resist.	People who participate will be committed to implementing change, and any relevant information they have will be integrated into the change plan.	Can be very time consuming if participators design an inappropriate change.
Facilitation + support	Where people are resisting because of fear and anxiety.	No other approach works as well with employee adjustment problems.	Can be time consuming, expensive, and still fail.
Negotiation + agreement	Where someone or some group will clearly lose out in a change, and where that group has considerable power to resist.	Sometimes it is a relatively easy way to avoid major resistance.	Can be too expensive in many cases if it prompts others to negotiate.
Manipulation + co-optation	Where other tactics will not work, or are too expensive.	It can be a relatively quick and inexpensive solution to resistance problems.	Can lead to future problems if people feel manipulated.
Coercion	Where speed is essential, and the change initiators possess considerable power.	It is speedy, and can overcome any kind of resistance.	Can be risky if it leaves people angry at the initiators.

Participation and involvement can also be used effectively. At Allen-Bradley Canada, the company wanted to introduce a new automated warehouse and shipping system. It created a team that included shippers, information specialists, and other employees who would be involved in the actual operation of the new facility. The views of all employees who would be affected by the new equipment were carefully considered before any changes were made. Subsequently, the change was introduced successfully. Inventory levels decreased by 34 percent and on-time deliveries to customers improved from 50 to 75 percent.[26]

Negotiation and agreement may be appropriate if one group will clearly lose due to the change and that group has considerable power to resist. *Coercion*—simply forcing the change—can be a fast way of pushing through a change and is widely used, particularly when speed is essential. It can be effective when the manager has the power to force the change, but risky if it leaves influential employees with a residue of ill will.

Lewin's Process. Psychologist Kurt Lewin formulated a model to summarize what he believed to be the basic process for implementing a change with minimal resistance. To Lewin, all behaviour in organizations is a product of two kinds of forces: those striving to maintain the status quo and those pushing for change.

Implementing change thus means either reducing the forces for the status quo or building up the forces for change. Lewin's process consists of three steps: unfreezing, moving, and refreezing.

Unfreezing means reducing the forces that are striving to maintain the status quo, usually by presenting a provocative problem or event to get people to recognize the need for change and to search for new solutions. Without unfreezing, said Lewin, change will not occur. Attitude surveys, interview results, or participatory informational meetings are often used to provide such provocative events.

When he took over as CEO of Philips, the Dutch electronics firm, Jan Timmer invited the company's top managers to an off-site retreat. He tried to unfreeze the status quo

unfreezing
In Lewin's process, reducing the forces that are striving to maintain the status quo, usually by presenting a provocative problem or event to get people to recognize the need for change and to search for new solutions.

by having them consider a hypothetical press release that said that Philips was bankrupt. The managers were then asked to come up with ideas to bring the company back from the brink.[27]

moving
In Lewin's process, developing new behaviours, values, and attitudes, sometimes through structure changes.

refreezing
In Lewin's process, reinforcing the changes that have been introduced by instituting new systems and procedures that will support and maintain them.

Lewin's second step aims to shift or alter the behaviour of the people in the department or organization in which the changes are to take place. **Moving** means developing new behaviours, values, and attitudes, sometimes through structure changes and sometimes through the sorts of change and development techniques we'll cover later in this chapter.

Lewin assumed that organizations tended to revert to their former ways of doing things unless the changes were reinforced. This reinforcement is accomplished by **refreezing** the organization into its new state of equilibrium. Lewin advocated instituting new systems and procedures that would support and maintain the changes that were made.

The unfreezing-moving-refreezing model is helpful to managers because it suggests that change must be carefully thought out and implemented. But this model is becoming less useful because the rate of organizational change is now so fast. Robbins and Coulter use the metaphor of a ship sailing over calm waters to describe the organizations of the 1950s and 1960s.[28] But many organizations in the 21st century are more like a raft hurtling down a whitewater canyon. Managers in these organizations face chaotic situations, and a simple three-step change model may not be very helpful to them.

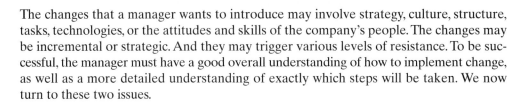

Leading Organizational Change

The changes that a manager wants to introduce may involve strategy, culture, structure, tasks, technologies, or the attitudes and skills of the company's people. The changes may be incremental or strategic. And they may trigger various levels of resistance. To be successful, the manager must have a good overall understanding of how to implement change, as well as a more detailed understanding of exactly which steps will be taken. We now turn to these two issues.

The Basic Change Process: An Overview

Implementing a change is like solving any problem: You have to become aware of the need for change, recognize the problem, diagnose it, and then formulate and implement a solution. In the case of organizational change, an overview of that basic process looks like this:

Become Aware of the Need for Change. Most organizational changes occur in reaction to or in anticipation of pressures from inside or outside the organization. Outside the organization, technological innovations like wireless Internet connections and automated factories force managers to confront a constantly changing competitive terrain. Within the firm, conflicts arise, employees retire or resign, and the company outgrows old ways of doing things.

Recognize and Accept the Need for Change. Even within the same industry, some leaders have been more adept at recognizing and accepting the need for change than others. Bill Gates at Microsoft successfully recognized and accepted the pressures driving the computer industry towards greater reliance on the Internet, and revamped his firm's offerings to make them more "Internet friendly." Ten years earlier, top executives at IBM, dramatically underestimating the effect that the personal computer would have on their industry, seemed to let the firm drift.

Diagnose the Problem. Recognizing that change is required isn't enough: The manager must also diagnose the problem to determine how change may affect the firm and what its consequences will be. After all, you don't want to implement a change aimed at solving the wrong problem. (We discussed problem solving in Chapter 4, Making Decisions.)

The breadth of the diagnosis will depend on how widespread the problem seems to be. In some cases, organizational analysis—in which the organization's goals, plans, environment, practices, and performance are studied—is appropriate. At other times, the problem may occur in just one department, group, or individual, and the diagnosis can appropriately focus just there.

Formulate the Change. The next step is to decide what to change and how to change it. We've seen that there are several things that leaders can change: the company's strategy, culture, structure, technology, and people. The change itself can therefore involve almost anything: reorganization, training programs, or new computer systems, for instance.

Implement and Lead the Change. Implementing and leading an organizational change can be tricky, even for a CEO with lots of clout. The change may be complex and require dozens or hundreds of managers to do their parts; resistance may be almost insurmountable; and the change may need to be carried out while the company continues to serve its customers.[29]

Eight Specific Steps for Leading Organizational Change

Create a Sense of Urgency. You've become aware of the need for change; what do you do now? Most experienced leaders instinctively know that they've got to "unfreeze" the old habits, often by creating a sense of urgency. Philips' CEO Jan Timmer knew he had to rouse his top managers out of their status-quo thinking. He did this with his hypothetical bankruptcy press release.

Urgency does more than overcome employees' traditional reasons for resisting change: It can also jar them out of their complacency. In organizations, several things can leave employees feeling "fat and happy.[30] These include the absence of a major and visible crisis, too many visible resources, low overall performance standards, and a lack of sufficient performance feedback from external sources. When complacency sets in, something must be done to create a sense of urgency so that employees will be more open to change.

How to create a sense of urgency?[31] A partial list includes:

- Make employees aware of the company's major weaknesses relative to competitors.
- Eliminate obvious examples of excess such as company-owned country club facilities, company aircraft, or gourmet executive dining rooms, in an effort to convey the need to develop more cost-effective company activities.
- Set challenging targets for revenue, income, productivity, customer satisfaction, and product development cycle time that can't be achieved by conducting "business as usual."
- Send data about customer satisfaction and financial performance to more employees, especially information that demonstrates weaknesses relative to competitors.

Create a Guiding Coalition and Mobilize Commitment. Major transformations—such as the one George Fisher accomplished in 1998 to transform Kodak into an Internet and digital-oriented company—are often associated with one highly visible leader. But no leader can accomplish a significant change alone. That's why most leaders create a guiding coalition of influential people who can be missionaries and implementers of change. The coalition should include people with enough power to lead the change effort, and it's essential to encourage the group to work together as a team.

In this process, the managers have to choose the right lieutenants. One reason for creating the coalition is to gather political support; the leader will therefore want to ensure that there are enough key players on board so that those left out can't easily block progress.[32] This step is especially important, given that it's often the firm's most influential people who prefer the status quo and may resist the change. The coalition's members should also have the expertise, credibility, and leadership skills to explain and implement the change.

Many leaders then create one or more broad-based task forces to diagnose the business' problems. This often produces a shared understanding of what can and must be improved, and thereby mobilizes the commitment of those who must actually implement the change.

Develop and Communicate a Shared Vision. In Chapter 10, Being a Leader, we saw that it's the leader's job to provide direction. Whether that "direction" is a statement of vision, mission, or objectives depends on what the leader wants to achieve and the level at which he or she is acting.

To transform an organization, a new vision is usually required, "a general statement of the organization's intended direction that evokes emotional feelings in organization members." For example, when Paul Tellier became CEO of CN he conveyed the vision of CN being a world-class competitor with leading North American railways.

Change expert John Kotter says that "the real power of a vision is unleashed only when most of those involved in an enterprise or activity have a common understanding of its goals and direction."[33] In other words, fostering support for the new vision is impossible unless the vision has been effectively communicated.

What are the key steps in effectively communicating a vision?

- *Keep it simple.* Here is an example of a good statement of vision: "We are going to become faster than anyone else in our industry at satisfying customer needs."
- *Use multiple forums.* Try to use every channel possible—big meetings and small, memos and newspapers, formal and informal interaction—to spread the word.
- *Use repetition.* Ideas sink in deeply only after they have been heard many times.
- *Lead by example.* "Walk your talk" so that your behaviours and decisions are consistent with the vision you espouse.

Empower Employees to Make the Change. Accomplishing a change that transforms an organization usually requires the assistance of the employees themselves. To get that assistance, change experts advise empowering the employees. As one expert explains:

> Major internal transformation rarely happens unless many people assist. Yet employees generally won't help, or can't help, if they feel relatively powerless. Hence the relevance of empowerment.[34]

The next step, therefore, is to empower employees to give them the wherewithal to help make the change, and this starts with removing the barriers to empowerment.

This idea is summarized in Figure 14.1. By now employees understand the vision and want to make it a reality, but they are boxed in: A lack of needed skills undermines action; formal structures, personnel, and information systems make it difficult to act; or bosses may discourage implementing the new vision. It's the leader's job to see to it that such barriers are removed.

There are many potential barriers, and therefore many ways to remove them. When he took over as CEO of Sony and its loss-making movie studios, Nobuyuki Idei proceeded, "in a most un-Japanese way," to fire all of the studio executives and install a new team of industry veterans, with a mandate to fix Sony's movie business.[35] Jacques Nasser, Ford Motor Co.'s newly appointed CEO, took a similar approach. His vision at Ford was aimed at getting employees "to think like shareholders" and at having the company as a whole respond swiftly to and anticipate customers needs.[36]

Sometimes "empowerment" just means letting the employees find their own way, rather than forcing the changes on them. In one successful change, an engineering department spent nearly a year analyzing how to implement the team concept: The engineers conducted surveys, held off-site meetings, and analyzed various alternatives before deciding on a matrix management approach that the department members felt would work for them.[37]

Canadian National
www.cn.ca

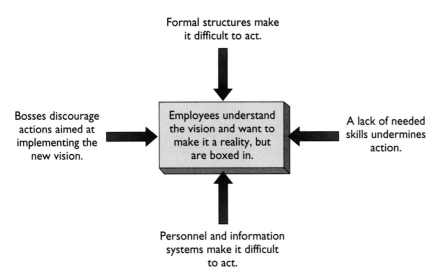

FIGURE 14.1
Barriers to Empowerment

Generate Short-Term Wins. Transforming a company can take time, but most people need reinforcement periodically to see that their efforts are working. Maintaining employees' motivation to stay involved in the change therefore requires planning for and creating short-term wins.

A leader can't just hope that short-term wins will simply materialize.[38] For example, the guiding coalition in one manufacturing company intentionally set its sights on producing one highly visible and successful new product about 20 months after the start of an organizational renewal effort.[39] The new product was selected in part because the coalition knew that its introduction was doable. And they knew that its introduction would provide the positive feedback required to renew a sense of urgency and motivation.

Consolidate Gains and Produce More Change. As momentum builds and changes are made, the leader has to guard against renewed complacency. That's why it's crucial, while employees are generating short-term wins, to consolidate the gains that have been made and produce even more change. How?

One approach is to use the increased credibility that comes from short-term wins to change all of the systems, structures, and policies that don't fit well with the company's new vision. In one company, for example, when a vice-president for operations saw the handwriting on the wall and left the firm, the position was left vacant; the two departments that had reported to him—engineering and manufacturing—now reported to the general manager. This helped to formalize the cross-functional nature of the new team approach at this firm.[40]

Other actions can be taken. For example, firms can continue to consolidate gains and produce more change by hiring, promoting, and developing new people who can implement the company's new vision; identifying a few employees who can champion the continuing changes; and providing additional opportunities for short-term wins by employees.

Anchor the New Ways of Doing Things in the Company's Culture. The organizational change won't survive without a corresponding change in employees' shared values. A "team-based, quality-oriented, adaptable organization" is not going to happen if the company's shared values still emphasize selfishness, mediocrity, and bureaucratic behaviour. We'll look more closely at how to mold company culture later in the chapter.

Monitor Progress and Adjust the Vision as Required. Finally, it's essential that the company have a mechanism for monitoring the effectiveness of the change and for recommending remedial actions. One firm appointed an oversight team composed of managers, a union representative, an engineer, and several others to monitor the functioning of its new self-managing teams. In another firm, regular morale surveys were used to monitor employee attitudes.

The Leader's Role in Organizational Change

Organizational changes usually don't take place spontaneously. Instead, they are triggered by problems and opportunities, and then driven by leaders.

When it comes to organizational change, the "leader" doesn't necessarily mean just the CEO or top executive. While the person leading the change is often the CEO (like Kodak's George Fisher) the leader may also be an office manager, or perhaps just a champion who assumes the role of cajoling, inspiring, and negotiating a new product successfully through the firm until it's produced.

Whatever the case, such leaders—called change advocates or champions—play a major role in any organizational change. We should therefore look more closely at the unique aspects of what the person leading the change is expected to do.

Influencing Strategic Change

Nowhere is the role of leadership more obvious or more important than in the sorts of organization-wide strategic changes implemented at firms like Kodak, Apple, and IBM. A careful analysis of leaders in firms like these suggests three crucial roles for change leaders: charismatic leadership, instrumental leadership, and missionary leadership.[41]

Charismatic Leadership. Successful leadership for change requires charismatic leaders who possess "a special quality that enables the leader to mobilize and sustain activity within an organization."[42]

charismatic leadership
Leadership composed of three behaviours: envisioning, energizing, and enabling.

Charismatic leadership is composed of three behaviours: envisioning, energizing, and enabling. As summarized in Figure 14.2, the charismatic leader is an *envisioning* leader who

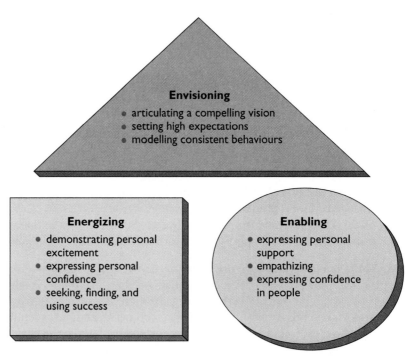

Envisioning
- articulating a compelling vision
- setting high expectations
- modelling consistent behaviours

Energizing
- demonstrating personal excitement
- expressing personal confidence
- seeking, finding, and using success

Enabling
- expressing personal support
- empathizing
- expressing confidence in people

FIGURE 14.2
What Charismatic Leadership Is
Charismatic leadership plays a major role in driving through a change. Its components are envisioning, energizing, and enabling.

is capable of articulating a compelling vision, setting high expectations, and modelling behaviours that are consistent with that compelling vision.

The charismatic leader is also an *energizing* leader who is able to demonstrate personal excitement, express personal confidence, and seek, find, and use success among his or her colleagues. Finally, the charismatic leader is an *enabling* leader who is able to express personal support, empathy, and confidence in people and thereby inspire them to undertake the required changes.

Instrumental Leadership. Charismatic leadership alone doesn't explain the sort of success that executives like Louis Gerstner had in turning IBM around. Effective leaders of change must also "build competent teams, clarify required behavior, build in measurements, and administer rewards and punishments so that individuals perceive that behavior consistent with the change is essential for them in achieving their own goals." Nadler and Tushman call this the change leader's **instrumental leadership role**: the managerial aspect of change leadership that puts the instruments in place through which the employees can accomplish their new tasks.

There are three aspects to instrumental leader behaviour. The first is *structuring*. Leaders must ensure that the necessary structure is in place to carry out the change and must invest in building teams, creating new organizational structures, setting goals, establishing standards, and defining roles and responsibilities.[43] Instrumental change leadership also means establishing successful *controlling* mechanisms. Finally, instrumental change leadership means *rewarding*, instituting the material (and nonmaterial) rewards and punishments needed to reinforce behaviours consistent with (or discourage behaviours inconsistent with) the desired organizational change.[44]

Missionary Leadership. Few leaders can turn an organization around by themselves; instead, as we've seen, they must enlist the aid of others. They must then depend on this new coalition to spread the top manager's vision.

In practice, successful leaders extend their new visions to three groups: their own senior team, senior management, and leadership throughout the organization. They generally look first for opportunities to extend and institutionalize their vision for the firm to the group of individuals who comprise their own senior team. (This, in part, is why CEOs seeking to implement major changes often seek out and hire new subordinates whose values and visions are consistent with theirs. For example, Louis Gerstner quickly hired several new senior vice-presidents for finance, human resource management, and several other functions within months of assuming the reins at IBM.)

When the senior management team at Labatt Breweries met to make decisions about major corporate restructuring, a change agent from People Tech Consulting sat in on the discussions. The change agent helped company executives play their roles more effectively, and got them to think through the human side of the organization. As a result of the meetings, the company's president went on a cross-country tour to talk with employees about what restructuring would mean. People Tech Consulting also arranged workshops on change in each of the company's four divisions.[45]

The change leader CEO must then encourage senior managers just below the top executive team to buy into his or her vision and plans and become missionaries for change. Unfortunately, those below the top management level often feel they are not in positions to lead such change. They may even feel more like unwitting participants or observers. As a result, "the [leader's] task is to make this group feel like [top] management, to get them signed up for the change, and to motivate and enable them to work as an extension of the senior team."[46]

Finally, the vision and details of the change need to be "sold" and spread throughout the organization. This means creating cadres of employees who are capable of helping to lead the change and are eager to do so. Ford does this, for instance, with its "teaching" programs, by annually training hundreds of employees, not just managers but engineers, chemists, and others throughout the firm. In this way, Ford provides employees with the values and skills they will need to make their units consistent with Nasser's vision of a lean, competitive, agile organization.

instrumental leadership role
The managerial aspect of change leadership that puts the instruments in place through which the employees can accomplish their new tasks.

Training Leaders to Lead Change

Can leaders be trained to be better leaders of change? The answer, based on one recent study, is yes.

Much of what change leaders do—being charismatic, exercising instrumental leadership, and missionary leadership, for instance—is part of what being a transformational leader is all about. We've seen (in Chapter 10) that transformational leaders can be influential in shaping organizational change. Transformational leadership tends to be positively correlated with subordinates' satisfaction, organizational commitment, and performance.[47]

But can a person be trained to be more transformational? The results of one study suggest that the answer is a definite yes.[48] The study took place in one of the five largest banks in Canada. The managers of the 20 branches in one region were randomly assigned to receive transformational leadership training or not to receive it. The "training" group ended up with five male and four female managers; the "no training" group had six male and five female managers.

There was a two-part training program. The first part consisted of a one-day training session that familiarized participants with the meaning of transformational leadership and explained and illustrated how it might be implemented in the managers' branches. The second part consisted of several one-on-one "booster" sessions. Here a trainer met individually with each of the managers to go over the latter's leadership style and to develop personal action plans for the manager to become more of a goal-oriented, transformational leader.

The results of this study clearly indicate that managers can be trained to be transformational leaders. For example, the subordinates of the managers who received the training subsequently perceived their managers as higher on intellectual stimulation, charisma, and individual consideration than did subordinates of managers in the no-training group.

Concepts like charismatic or transformational or instrumental leadership, therefore, aren't just theoretical. Behaviours like these can be developed, and developing them begins with an understanding—which you now should have—of what these concepts are and how they can be used.

Influencing Organizational Culture

organizational culture
The characteristic traditions, norms, and values that employees share.

Leaders who effectively transform their organizations all recognize the important role that organizational culture always plays in such a process. As we saw in Chapter 3, **organizational culture** can be defined as the characteristic traditions, norms, and values that employees share. Values and norms (such as "be honest," "be thrifty," and "don't be bureaucratic") are basic beliefs about what you should or shouldn't do, and what is or is not important.

Norms and values guide and channel all of our behaviour, and so successfully changing organizations (for instance, changing it from "bureaucratic" and "stick to the chain of command" to "let's be responsive and get the job done") requires a new set of values—a new culture—as well. As re-engineering advocate John Champy was quoted as saying on page 441, reducing hierarchy and bureaucracy is not just a matter of rearranging the furniture: It is a cultural matter.

You know from your own experience that changing someone's values involves a lot more than just talk. Parents might tell their children repeatedly to eat only healthy foods, but if the children see their parents saying one thing and doing another, chances are it's the parents actions that will mold their child's eating habits, not simply what the parents say.

Much the same is true when it comes to creating or changing a company's culture. When he decided to transform Kodak, for instance Fisher knew he had to do a lot more than talk. Top executives who weren't performing were replaced; new incentive plans were instituted; and new, more results-oriented appraisal systems were introduced. The net effect was to send a strong signal to employees throughout the firm that the values of being efficient, effective, and responsive were a lot more important than they'd been the week before.

Creating and Sustaining the Corporate Culture. Realistically, there are several steps a leader can take to create and sustain the desired corporate culture. In many companies, for instance, publishing a formal *core value statement* is a logical first step in creating a culture. The leaders' own *words and actions* are important, too. For example, the foundation of Wal-Mart's values can be traced to the late Sam Walton's personal values of "hard work, honesty, neighborliness, and thrift." Under Walton's leadership, the firm developed an almost religious zeal for doing things efficiently, and hard work became a requirement for getting promoted. Symbolism—what the manager says and does, and the signals that he or she sends—ultimately does the most to create and sustain the company's culture.

Your *management practices* also send a strong signal about what you do and do not think is important. For example, at Toyota (where quality and teamwork are essential), much of the training process focuses on how to work in teams and how to solve quality problems. Similarly, one of the first things that Louis Gerstner did when he took over as CEO of IBM was to institute a new bonus-based approach to paying employees, one that emphasized performance much more heavily than did the compensation plan in the "old," more ponderous IBM.

How to Change a Company's Culture. Two experts say that regardless of the industry, "the single most visible factor that distinguishes major cultural changes that succeed from those that failed was competent leadership at the top."[49] The competent leaders "knew how to produce change and were willing to do just that."[50] In each instance the leader created a team that established a new vision and a set of strategies for achieving that vision. Each new leader succeeded in persuading important groups and individuals in the firm to commit themselves to that new direction and to energize the personnel sufficiently to make it happen, despite all obstacles. Ultimately, hundreds (or even thousands) of people helped to make all of the changes in strategies, product structures, policies, personnel, and (eventually) culture. But often, just one or two people seemed to have been essential in getting the process started.[51]

Imagine that you are swept into the CEO's position in a company long known for its culture of backbiting, bureaucratic behaviour, and disdain for clients. What steps would you take to change your company's culture? Management expert Edgar Schein has proposed a sort of shorthand list of mechanisms that leaders can use to establish, embed, and reinforce organizational culture.[52]

Schein advocates five "primary embedding mechanisms." To change culture, he says, you should:

1. *Make it clear to your employees what you pay attention to, measure, and control.* For example, you can direct the attention of your employees towards controlling costs or serving customers if those are the values you want to emphasize.

2. *React appropriately to critical incidents and organizational crises.* For example, if you want to emphasize the value that "we're all in this together," don't react to declining profits by laying off operating employees and middle managers while leaving your top managers intact.

3. *Deliberately model, teach, and coach the values you want to emphasize.* For example, at Four Seasons Hotels and Resorts, managers act as role models and employees take their cues from them. The culture of the firm motivates employees to "go the extra mile" when providing service to customers. CEO Isadore Sharp says that the firm's first concern is winning customers.

4. *Communicate your priorities by the way you allocate rewards and status.* Leaders communicate their priorities by the way they link pay raises and promotions (or the lack thereof) to particular behaviours. For example, when the top management at General Foods decided several years ago to reorient its strategy from cost control to diversification and sales growth, it revised the compensation system to link bonuses to sales volume (rather than just to increased earnings) and to new-product development.

   As another example, Frank Stronach, CEO of the large Canadian auto parts firm Magna International, is well known for his strong views about employees, working conditions, and profit distribution (20 percent to shareholders, 2 percent to charities, 7 percent to R&D, 10 percent to employees, 2 percent to Stronach, and the remainder reinvested).

5. *Make your HR procedures and criteria consistent with the values you espouse.* When he became chairperson and CEO of IBM, Louis Gerstner brought in a new top management team whose values were consistent with shaking up IBM's traditionally bureaucratic and politicized culture.

Schein suggests not stopping there. As you can see in Table 14.2, he also recommends using secondary mechanisms—such as a redesign of the organizational structure, new organizational systems, and a redesign of physical space—to further reinforce the desired cultural changes. However, Schein believes that these secondary mechanisms are just that—secondary, because they work only if consistent with the five primary mechanisms listed above.

TABLE 14.2 *Mechanisms for Embedding and Reinforcing Organizational Culture*
PRIMARY EMBEDDING MECHANISMS
1. What leaders pay attention to, measure, and control
2. Leader reactions to critical incidents and organizational crises
3. Deliberate role modelling, teaching, and coaching
4. Criteria for allocation of rewards and status
5. Criteria for recruitment, selection, promotion, retirement, and dismissal
SECONDARY ARTICULATION AND REINFORCEMENT MECHANISMS
1. Organization design and structure
2. Organizational systems and procedures
3. Design of physical space, facades, buildings
4. Stories about important events and people
5. Formal statements of organizational philosophy, creeds, charters

Using Organizational Development to Change Organizations

What Is Organizational Development?

Organizational development (OD) is a special approach to organizational change in which the employees themselves formulate the change that's required and implement it, often with the assistance of a trained "facilitator." As an approach to changing organizations, OD has several distinguishing characteristics:

1. It is usually based on **action research**, which means collecting data about a group, department, or organization, and then feeding that data back to employees so they can analyze them and develop hypotheses about what the problems in the unit might be.

2. It applies behavioural science knowledge for the purpose of improving the organization's effectiveness.

3. It changes the attitudes, values, and beliefs of employees so that the employees themselves can identify and implement the technical, procedural, structural, or other changes needed to improve the company's functioning.

4. It changes the organization in a particular direction—towards improved problem solving, responsiveness, quality of work, and effectiveness.[53]

Types of OD Applications

The number and variety of OD applications (also called OD *interventions* or *techniques*) have increased substantially over the past few years. OD got its start with what were called **human process interventions**. These interventions were aimed at helping employees better understand and modify their own and others' attitudes, values, and beliefs, and thereby improve the company.

Today, as illustrated in Table 14.3, a much wider range of applications is available. Indeed, the once-clear lines between OD and other types of organizational change efforts (such as reorganizing) are starting to blur. This is happening because OD practitioners have become increasingly involved not just in changing participants' attitudes, values, and beliefs, but also in directly altering the firm's structure, practices, strategy, and culture.

There are four types of OD applications: human process, technostructural, human resource management, and strategic applications. All are based on getting the employees themselves to collect the required data and to create and implement the solutions.

Human Process Applications. The human process OD techniques generally aim first at improving employees' human relations skills. The goal is to provide employees with the insight and skills required to analyze their own and others' behaviour more effectively so they can solve interpersonal and intergroup problems more intelligently. Sensitivity training, team building, confrontation meetings, and survey research are in this category.

Sensitivity training.
Sensitivity, laboratory, or t-group training (the *t* is for training) was one of the earliest OD techniques. Although its use has diminished, it is still found today. **Sensitivity training**'s basic aim is to increase the participant's insight into his or her own behaviour and the behaviour of others by encouraging an open expression of feelings in the group.

---

organizational development (OD)
A special approach to organizational change in which the employees themselves formulate the change that's required and implement it, often with the assistance of a trained "facilitator."

action research
Collecting data about a group, department, or organization, and then feeding that data back to employees so they can analyze them and develop hypotheses about what the problems in the unit might be.

human process interventions
Interventions aimed at helping employees better understand and modify their own and others' attitudes, values, and beliefs, and thereby improve the company.

sensitivity training
Training aimed at increasing the participant's insight into his or her own behaviour and the behaviour of others by encouraging an open expression of feelings in the group.

TABLE 14.3 *Examples of OD Interventions and the Organizational Levels They Affect*

Interventions	PRIMARY ORGANIZATIONAL LEVEL AFFECTED		
	Individual	Group	Organization
HUMAN PROCESS			
T-groups	X	X	
Process consultation		X	
Third-party intervention	X	X	
Team building		X	
Organizational confrontation meeting		X	X
Intergroup relations		X	X
TECHNOSTRUCTURAL			
Formal structural change			X
Differentiation and integration			X
Cooperative union-management projects	X	X	X
Quality circles	X	X	
Total quality management		X	X
Work design	X	X	
HUMAN RESOURCE MANAGEMENT			
Goal setting	X	X	
Performance appraisal	X	X	
Reward systems	X	X	X
Career planning and development	X		
Managing workforce diversity	X		
Employee wellness	X		
STRATEGIC			
Integrated strategic management			X
Culture change			X
Strategic change			X
Self-designing organizations		X	X

Typically, 10 to 15 people meet, usually away from the job, and no activities or discussion topics are planned. The focus is on the here and now (specifically, on the feelings and emotions of the members in the group). Participants are encouraged to portray themselves as they are now rather than in terms of past experiences or future problems. The t-group's success depends largely on the participants' willingness to expose their feelings.[54] Since t-group training is obviously very personal in nature, it's not surprising that it is a controversial technique, and that its use has diminished markedly since its heyday back in the 1970s. Participation should therefore always be voluntary.[55]

Team building.

The characteristic OD stress on action research is perhaps most evident in **team building**, which refers to the process of improving the effectiveness of a team. Data concerning the team's performance are collected and then fed back to the members of the group. The participants examine, explain, and analyze the data and develop specific action plans or solutions for solving the team's problems.

According to experts French and Bell, the typical team-building meeting begins with the consultant interviewing each of the group members and the group leader prior to the meeting.[56] All are asked what their problems are, how they think the group functions, and what obstacles are keeping the group from performing better. The consultant might then categorize the interview data into themes and present the themes to the group at the beginning of the meeting. (Themes like lack of time or lack of cohesion might be culled from such statements as "I don't have enough time to get my job done" or "I can't get any cooperation around here.")

The themes are ranked by the group in terms of importance; the most important themes become the agenda for the meeting. The group then explores and discusses the issues, examines the underlying causes of the problems, and begins working on some solutions.

Confrontation meetings.

Other human process interventions aim to bring about intergroup or organization-wide change. Organizational **confrontation meetings** can help clarify and bring into the open misperceptions and problems so that conflicts can be resolved. The basic approach here is that the participants themselves provide the data for the meeting and then (with the help of a facilitator/moderator) confront and discuss any misperceptions in an effort to reduce tensions.

Survey research requires that employees throughout the organization fill out attitude surveys. The data are then used as feedback to work groups who use it as a basis for problem analysis and action planning. In general, such surveys are a convenient and widely used method for unfreezing an organization's management and employees by providing a lucid, comparative, graphic illustration of the fact that the organization does have problems that should be solved.

team building
The process of improving the effectiveness of a team.

confrontation meetings
Help clarify and bring into the open misperceptions and problems so that conflicts can be resolved.

survey research
A convenient and widely used method for unfreezing an organization's management and employees by providing a lucid, comparative, graphic illustration of the fact that the organization does have problems that should be solved.

Members of a confrontation meeting openly discuss misperceptions and problems, working towards the common goal of conflict resolution.

Technostructural Applications. OD practitioners are increasingly involved in efforts to change the structures, methods, and job designs of firms. Compared with human process interventions, technostructural interventions (as well as the human resource management interventions and strategic interventions described in the following sections) generally focus more directly on productivity improvement and efficiency.

OD practitioners use a variety of technostructural interventions. For example, in a **formal structural change** program, employees collect data on existing structures and analyze them. The purpose is to jointly redesign and implement new organizational structures. OD practitioners also assist in implementing employee-involvement programs, including quality circles and job redesign.

formal structural change
Changes in the formal hierarchical structure of the organization that are designed to improve its efficiency and effectiveness.

Human Resource Management Applications. OD practitioners increasingly use action research to enable employees to analyze and change personnel practices. Targets of change include the performance appraisal system and reward system. Changes might include instituting workforce diversity programs aimed at boosting cooperation among a firm's diverse employees.

strategic interventions
Organization-wide interventions aimed at bringing about a better fit between a firm's strategy, structure, culture, and external environment.

Strategic Applications. Among the newest OD applications are **strategic interventions**, organization-wide interventions aimed at bringing about a better fit between a firm's strategy, structure, culture, and external environment. **Integrated strategic management** is one example of using OD to create or change a strategy. This intervention consists of four steps:

integrated strategic management
A four-step OD process that helps to create or change a strategy, and that facilitates strategic interventions.

1. *Analyze current strategy and organizational design.* Senior managers and other employees use models such as the SWOT matrix (explained in Chapter 6) to analyze the firm's current strategy, as well as its organizational design.

2. *Choose a desired strategy and organizational design.* Based on the analysis, senior management formulates a strategic vision, objectives, and a plan, and an organizational structure for implementing them.

3. *Design a strategic change plan.* The group designs a strategic change plan, which "is an action plan for moving the organization from its current strategy and organizational design to the desired future strategy and design."[57] The plan explains how the strategic change will be implemented, including specific activities as well as the costs and budgets associated with them.

4. *Implement a strategic change plan.* The final step is actually implementing a strategic change plan and measuring and reviewing the results of the change activities to ensure that they are proceeding as planned.[58]

Conflict in Organizations

Conflict can be a cause or a result of organizational change. Sometimes, for instance, conflict makes the need for change apparent, as when two departments resist working cooperatively to achieve some goal. Sometimes, on the other hand, an organizational change (like a new strategy) may trigger conflict, as two or more managers or units see in the change an opportunity or need to get more power or resources for themselves. In any case, conflict management is an important aspect of leading organizational change.

Conflict: Pros and Cons

Conflict, as you probably know, can have dysfunctional effects on the organization and its employees. Opposing parties in conflicts tend to put their own aims above those of the organization, and the organization's effectiveness suffers. Time that could have been used productively is wasted as people hide valuable information and jockey for position. Opponents can become so personally involved in the tensions produced by conflict that they undermine their emotional and physical well-being.

Perhaps the most insidious effect of conflict is that it doesn't remain organization-bound for long. Its effects are observed by customers and stockholders and are taken home by the opponents, whose families are caught in the fallout.

Despite its adverse effects, conflict is viewed by most experts today as a potentially useful aspect of an organization because it can, if properly channelled, be an engine of innovation and change. This view explicitly encourages a certain amount of controlled conflict in organizations. The basic case for it is that a lack of active debate can permit the status quo or mediocre ideas to prevail.

This more positive view of conflict is supported by surveys of management practice. In one survey of top and middle managers, for example, managers rated "conflict management" as of equal or slightly higher importance than topics like planning, communication, motivation, and decision making. The managers spent about 20 percent of their time on conflicts, yet they did not consider the conflict level in their organization to be excessive. Instead, they rated it as about right—that is, at the midpoint of a scale running from "too low" to "too high."

Individual, Interpersonal, and Intergroup Organizational Conflict

Three types of conflict—individual, interpersonal, and intergroup organizational—exist in organizations.

Individual Conflict. **Role conflict** is a familiar example of conflict "within" the individual. It occurs when a person is faced with conflicting orders, such that compliance with one would make it difficult or impossible to comply with the other. Sometimes role conflict arises out of obviously conflicting orders, as when a corporal receives orders from a captain that would force her to disobey an order from her sergeant.

Sometimes, however, the role conflict's source is not so obvious: Obeying an order might force a person to violate his or her own cherished values and sense of right and wrong. In any case, role conflict is a serious problem in organizations, one that can be stressful to the people involved and can adversely affect morale and performance.[59]

While the term "role conflict" can sound theoretical, its effects in practice are very real. This is illustrated by a study that included, among others, 68 supervisors employed by a large university.[60] The basic question in this study was whether the stress resulting from supervisors experiencing role conflict would result in a deliberate inflation of performance ratings for the subordinates they were rating.

Surveys were used to measure two things: the extent to which the supervisors experienced role conflict, and the degree to which their subordinates' performance ratings were inflated. An example of a survey item used to measure the self-reported tendency to deliberately inflate performance ratings is "At times I find it necessary to deliberately inflate performance evaluation ratings of my subordinates." An example of an item used to measure the supervisor's role conflict is "I receive incompatible requests from two or more people."[61]

The findings show the sorts of subtle but serious consequences that role conflict can have. In this case, role conflict and inflated appraisals went hand in hand. The more supervisors saw themselves as receiving conflicting orders and instructions, the more leniently they tended to appraise their own subordinates. Why might that be the case? It's not clear, but perhaps the supervisors with more role conflict felt that their own authority was less clear and secure, so they were less apt to take a chance on being strict with subordinates.

Interpersonal Conflict. Conflicts in organizations can also be interpersonal and occur between individuals or between individuals and groups. Sometimes, of course, such conflicts arise from legitimate sources, as when real differences in goals or objectives exist be-

role conflict
Conflict that occurs when a person is faced with conflicting orders, such that compliance with one would make it difficult or impossible to comply with the other.

interpersonal conflict
Conflict that occurs between individuals or between individuals and groups.

tween the parties involved. Often, however, they arise not from legitimate differences but from personalities. Some people are more aggressive and prone to conflict than others, and some are so hypersensitive that every comment is viewed as an insult that provokes a response.

Intergroup Organizational Conflicts. These are conflicts such as those between line and staff units or between production and sales departments. Effectively managing intergroup conflict is especially crucial today as firms increasingly try to manage change by moving towards boundaryless organizations. We will focus on the causes and management of intergroup conflict in the remainder of this section.

Causes of Intergroup Conflict

There are many causes of intergroup conflict, but research suggests that four factors create most of the problems: interdependencies and shared resources; differences in goals, values, or perceptions; authority imbalances; and ambiguities.

Interdependencies and Shared Resources. Groups that do not have to depend on each other or compete for scarce resources will generally not get involved in intergroup conflict. Conversely, groups who work interdependently or who must compete for scarce resources may eventually come into conflict.[62]

Examples of how interdependency or competition for scarce resources leads to conflict are common. Conflicts are often a way of life for members of quality control and production departments, sales and production departments, and other departments that depend on each other. On the other hand, intergroup conflict is less likely to occur between the finance and quality control departments, since the people in these departments are not as interdependent. Competition for scarce resources, such as when two or more departments must compete for limited funds or for the services of a typing pool, often leads to "office politics," hiding of information, and conflict.

Of course, interdependence doesn't have to lead to conflict. If the situation is managed correctly, or if the groups' overall aims are similar, interdependence can provide an incentive for collaboration rather than conflict. This is one reason why the conflict management techniques we discuss later in this chapter are so important.[63]

Intergroup Differences in Goals, Values, or Perceptions. Persons who agree in terms of their goals, values, or perceptions are less likely to find themselves arguing than are those with fundamental differences.

There are numerous examples. For instance, Walton and Dutton found that the preference of production departments for long, economical runs conflicted with the preference of sales units for quick delivery to good customers, and that these differing goals often led to intergroup conflict.[64] Other differences in goals that lead to intergroup conflicts include those between flexibility and stability, between short-run and long-run performance, between measurable and intangible results, and between organizational goals and societal needs.[65]

In any case, the bottom line is that when the goals of two groups are similar or identical, there is little chance of serious conflict arising; when there is a fundamental difference in goals, conflicts are likely to arise.

Lawrence and Lorsch found that what they call "organizational differentiation" is another source of intergroup conflict.[66] As each department in an organization tries to cope with the unique demands of its own environment, it necessarily develops its own procedures, cherished values, and points of view.

For example, a research department in a chemical firm might be run very democratically, and its employees might develop a rather long-term time perspective, because most of the things they are working on will not reach fruition for years. The production department might be run more autocratically, and its managers might be expected to put more emphasis on immediate results. Lawrence and Lorsch believe that the greater the differentiation between co-workers' departments, the more potential for conflict there is.

Authority Imbalances. We also know that when a group's actual authority is inconsistent with its prestige, intergroup conflicts are more likely to arise. For example, a researcher found that in one company, the production department had to accept instructions from a production engineering department composed of employees with skills no greater than (and, in fact, quite similar to) those possessed by production employees. As a result, "production managers spent an inordinate amount of time checking for consistency among the various items produced by production engineering,"[67] in order to catch the engineers in a mistake.

Ambiguity. Ambiguity—for instance, regarding who does what, or in assigning credit or blame between two departments—increases the likelihood of conflict between units. If both the quality control and production departments can claim credit for the cost savings resulting from a change in production procedures, a conflict may well result. Similarly, if it's hard to place the blame for a problem, conflicts may emerge as departments attempt to shed the blame, say, for a cost overrun or a machine breakdown. Conflict can also occur where power vacuums arise, as each department fights to fill those power vacuums by assuming increased responsibilities.

Techniques for Managing Intergroup Conflict

The many techniques for managing or resolving conflicts generally fall into two categories: structural approaches and interpersonal approaches.

Structural Approaches. Various conflict-management methods are based on using the organization's structure (See Table 14.4). For example, the most frequent way of resolving disagreements between departments is still to refer them to a common superior. If the vice-presidents for sales and finance cannot reach agreement on some point, they would typically refer their disagreement to the president for a binding decision.

Another structural way to reduce the potential for conflict is to reduce the interdependencies or the need to compete for scarce resources. Sometimes the changes are as simple as separating the units physically, so that the members of one group no longer have to confront members of the other group each day.[68] Another change is to increase the available resources so that both groups can get what they want.

Lawrence and Lorsch, in the study mentioned earlier, found that many companies reduced interdepartmental conflict by setting up special liaisons between warring departments. In the high-tech plastics industry, for example, successful companies set up special "integrator" new-product development departments, whose job was to coordinate the work of the research, sales, and manufacturing departments.

Interpersonal Approaches. There are different ways to settle an argument. For example, having both parties meet to confront the facts and hammer out a solution is usually more effective than simply smoothing over the conflict by sweeping problems under a rug. Popular interpersonal conflict-resolution styles are described in Table 14.5.

The style you use will depend on several things, including your personality, your success or failure with particular styles, and the response you get (or expect to get) from the other party. The latter is illustrated in Figure 14.3, where the wife's use of "avoidance" depends on which of three different response styles her husband uses.

Which Conflict-Resolution Style is Best? A recent study of how supervisors and subordinates actually handled conflicts provides an interesting perspective on which conflict-resolution styles are best. The fact is, people usually don't rely on a single conflict-resolution mode. In other words, they don't just confront or smooth over a situation, but rather use these and other approaches together to some degree.[69]

In the study, the researchers focused on seven possible conflict-resolution styles: forcing, confronting, process controlling, problem solving, compromising, accommodating, and avoiding. The basic question that the researchers wanted to study was whether some combinations of these styles was more effective than others. To answer this question they

TABLE 14.4 Structural Conflict Resolution Techniques

TECHNIQUE	DESCRIPTION	EXAMPLE
1. Procedural changes	Work procedures are changed to resolve conflict.	A sales manager argues that a credit manager is cancelling too many deals for credit reasons. The dispute is resolved by involving the credit manager earlier in the process of selling.
2. Personnel changes	Individuals are transferred into or out of a department in order to resolve personality clashes.	A personality clash between two high-performing workers is disrupting departmental productivity. One of the workers is transferred to another department, and both workers are now able to make a positive contribution to the organization.
3. Authority changes	Authority lines are changed or clarified to reduce conflict.	The head of industrial engineering complains that production managers do not listen to his advice about new high-tech machinery. The head of industrial engineering is given functional authority over the production managers on the issue of new machinery procedures.
4. Layout changes	The work space is rearranged to resolve conflict.	Two work groups harass each other continually. A wall is built between the two groups so they can no longer interact.
5. Resource changes	Resources are expanded so that the disputing parties can each have what they want.	The dean of a business school gets a commitment from the provincial government for funds to hire additional faculty members. This reduces the dispute between department heads because they each get to hire two more faculty members.

analyzed videotapes of 116 male police sergeants handling a standardized, scripted conflict with either a subordinate or a superior.

It was clear that to resolve the conflict most effectively, the sergeant had to use several styles at once. For example, problem solving tended to enhance the sergeant's effectiveness, especially if he combined it with much forcing. However, process controlling—dominating the conflict-resolution process to one's own advantage—was even more effective than trying to force the issue by insisting that the adversary do what he or she was told. In this study the sergeants also enhanced their conflict-management effectiveness by being somewhat accommodating.

The bottom line seems to be that for these police sergeants, the use of three conflict-resolution styles together—problem solving while being moderately accommodating and still maintaining a strong hand in controlling the conflict-resolution process—was an especially effective combination. Whether this combination would prove equally effective for other types of supervisors would have to be addressed by other studies.

TABLE 14.5 Interpersonal Conflict Resolution Techniques

TECHNIQUE	DESCRIPTION	EXAMPLE
1. Forcing	Managerial authority is used to compel a resolution of the conflict.	A manager orders two disputing subordinates to stop their interpersonal conflict on company time because it is disrupting the work of the department.
2. Smoothing	The manager tries to convince the disputing parties that they really don't have anything to fight about.	A manager tries to calm two disputing subordinates by pointing out all the areas where they are in agreement, and down-playing the one area in which they disagree.
3. Avoidance	The conflicting parties avoid each other.	Two managers who are trying to increase the budget for their respective departments begin avoiding each other because every time they meet they get into an argument.
4. Compromise	Each side gives up some of what it wants in order to resolve the conflict.	During collective bargaining, the union demands a 10 percent increase while management offers only 2 percent. Eventually they agree on a 6 percent increase.
5. Mediation	A neutral third party tries to help the disputing parties work out a resolution of the conflict.	During a strike, a mediator is called in to help labour and management reach a settlement. The mediator has no authority to force a settlement.
6. Arbitration	A neutral third party imposes a binding resolution on the disputing parties.	An arbitrator imposes a new collective agreement on a company where there has been a major labour–management dispute. The arbitrator's decision is binding on both parties in the dispute.
7. Superordinate goal	An agreed upon goal by the disputing parties is used to override the conflict.	Arab states in the Middle East may not see eye-to-eye on many issues, but they join OPEC to achieve a superordinate goal of high oil prices.
8. Majority rule	The side with the most votes gets its way.	At a committee meeting, a motion to resolve a dispute is passed by a vote of 8–7.
9. Confrontation	The opposing sides openly state their views to each other.	In a marriage counselling session, the husband and wife state how they really feel about each other. Each spouse is likely to hear things they have never heard before.
10. Integration	The disputing parties try to find solutions that generate both their desires so that a "win–win" solution can be developed.	The board of directors of a church resolves a dispute about musical style by having two worship services, one with traditional music, and one with contemporary music.
11. Consensus	The disputing parties must attempt to reach a consensus on what should be done to resolve conflict.	At a meeting of the new product committee, seven new product ideas are prioritized in order of importance after a three-hour discussion where each person indicates his or her preferences.
12. Accommodation	Giving in to the other person	The manager of one department agrees to do some paperwork for the manager of another department after a conflict develops over who is responsible for the paperwork.

Husband confronts wife about her parents giving their children expensive gifts.

Avoidance—Accommodation

W: "I don't want to talk about this."
H: "All right, maybe we'll talk about it later."

Avoidance—Competitive

W: "I don't want to talk about this."
H: "You never want to talk about anything."
W: "That's not true. You're the one avoiding problems."
H: "Look, if you're not going to discuss this rationally, I don't want to hear from you about it later."
W: "Don't blame me for this."

Avoidance—Collaborative

W: "I don't want to talk about this."
H: "I know you're upset with me, and I can understand why."
W: "There's no problem here. Just drop it."
H: "Does it bother you when I criticize your parents' attitude towards the kids?"
W: "Yes, of course it does."
H: "Why do you think they bring them so much?"
W: "It makes them happy to give the things. After all they don't get to see them very often."
H: "Well, that's true. And certainly they're not to blame for that. Our career choices have caused us to move so far away. I just don't want the kids to think that their love of their grandparents is dependent on gifts."
W: "I think we could find a way to let the children know, without changing my parents, don't you?"

FIGURE 14.3
Sample Conflict-Resolution Styles

1. **List the things that managers can change in organizations.** Managers in their leadership roles can focus on various change targets. They can change the strategy, culture, structure, tasks, technologies, or attitudes and skills of the people in their organization.

2. **Explain why employees resist change.** The hardest part of leading a change is overcoming resistance to change. Resistance stems from several sources, including habit (people resist changing the way they do things simply because it is not convenient for them to do so), threats to power and influence (people may fear diminished status and authority for themselves as the result of a change), fear of the unknown (people are apprehensive about the unknown consequences of a proposed change), and changes in the "personal compact" (people resist altering the unwritten "personal compact" they have with the company that defines the employee-employer relationship).

3. **Give examples of each of the eight steps for leading organizational change.** The eight steps and an example of each are as follows: (1) create a sense of urgency (e.g., the CEO of Philips presented his managers with a hypothetical press release that the company had gone bankrupt); (2) create a guiding coalition and mobilize commitment (e.g., choose the right supporters to gather political support for the change); (3) develop and communicate a shared vision (e.g., CN's CEO, Paul Tellier, conveyed a vision of CN being a world-class railroad); (4) empower employees to make the change (e.g., the newly appointed CEO of Ford got employees to think like shareholders); (5) generate short-term wins (e.g., in one company the goal was to produce just one successful new product within a certain time frame); (6) consolidate gains and produce more changes (e.g., hire, promote, and develop new people who can implement the company's new vision); (7) anchor the new ways of doing things in the company's culture (e.g., reward those individuals who demonstrate behaviour consistent with the new way of doing things); and (8) monitor progress and adjust the vision as required (e.g., appoint an oversight team to monitor newly formed self-managing teams).

4. **Identify four basic organizational development techniques to change organizations.** There are four basic types of organizational development applications: (1) human process interventions (which try to improve employees' human relations skills); (2) technostructural applications (which involve changing the structures, methods, and job design of firms); (3) human resource management applications (which help employees to analyze and change personnel practices); and (4) strategic applications (which are organization-wide interventions aimed at bringing about a better fit between a firm's strategy, structure, culture, and external environment).

5. **Illustrate three techniques for overcoming individual, interpersonal, and intergroup organizational conflicts.** Techniques include establishing superordinate goals (finding a common ground on which the parties can agree), structural approaches (revising the structure and reporting relationships in order to resolve conflicts), and conflict-resolution modes (which address the way that people deal with others during a conflict).

Managers plan, organize, lead, and control. *Planning* (the subject of Chapters 4 to 6) involves making decisions, laying plans and setting goals, and developing a strategy and mission for the firm. *Organizing* (Chapters 7 to 9) means putting an organization in place to implement those plans by creating reporting relationships, delegating authority, writing job descriptions, and hiring and training the employees who will staff those positions and implement the plans. With the employees in place, the manager's *leadership* role becomes more important. Organizations are not just organization charts and machines but people, and it's the manager in his or her leadership role who is responsible for influencing and motivating the company's employees to achieve their goals.

Leadership therefore involves the distinctly interpersonal aspects of what managers do. In Chapters 10 to 14 we therefore focused on the people side of the manager's job, including leadership style, motivation, communication, groups and teams, and now, in the current chapter, on leading organizational change.

In the following chapter (Controlling and Building Commitment) we'll turn to the fourth and "last" of a manager's functions. But in fact control is, in most respects, inseparable from and largely an extension of the other three functions. Controlling, for instance, traditionally means setting standards, measuring performance, and then taking corrective action as required. Thinking of controlling separately from planning (and setting standards) is therefore somewhat meaningless. Similarly, controlling is, to a large extent, an extension of the manager's leadership or people-oriented duties.

You know from your own experience that the best way to "control" someone is to get that person to control themselves, so that they do the job right because they want to. To that extent, controlling, as we'll see, really calls on all the leadership skills that you can muster. Indeed, particularly in today's fast-changing empowered companies, it's best not to think of control as a mechanical process imposed on your employees. Keeping track of what's happening in your organization will always be important, of course, but more often than not the key to "control" is getting employees to want to excel. That is why the following chapter is not called Controlling, but Controlling and Building Commitment.

CRITICAL THINKING EXERCISES

1. MIT economist Lester Thurow is well known for his views on the economics of change. In *Rethinking the Future*, edited by Rowan Gibson,[70] Thurow contributes an article entitled "Changing the Nature of Capitalism." He argues that there are five economic "tectonic plates" that are driving all of the current economic changes and fundamentally remaking the economic surface of the earth. These are (1) the end of communism; (2) the movement from natural resource–based industries to brainpower industries; (3) world population growth, mobility, and aging; (4) a genuinely global economy; and (5) a world in which we will not have one dominant economic, political, or military power. Thurow argues that these changes are shaking the foundations of 21st-century capitalism. But what we don't know is the exact shape of the future, because that's not determined by the stars; instead, it's determined by "what we do." What do you think of Thurow's analysis? How do the tools and concepts presented in this chapter help us shape what we do? What new assumptions and tools might be needed?

2. Many authors have identified the change from a brawn-based economy to a brain- and knowledge-based economy. In *The New Realities*, Peter Drucker noted that only one of the 19th-century business builders had any advanced schooling. That was J.P. Morgan and he was a college dropout. By the latter part of the 20th century knowledge had become the capital of a developed economy, and blue-collar workers are now a social problem. This change has occurred in one generation. What are the implications of leadership in this brave new world of knowledge capital? How will those trained and educated in another era survive

the changes of today? What techniques discussed in this chapter may help leaders find their way and influence others?

1. Management guru Peter Drucker, who is in his mid-eighties, has witnessed, experienced, and analyzed a great deal of organizational change in this century. In a recent interview he was asked a series of questions about the changes he sees in our post-capitalist world; that is, a world based on knowledge as the economic driving force, rather than on assets or brawn.[71] Read the following questions and then interview five people you know between the ages of 35 and 60. Ask them to respond to the questions. Compare their answers. Be prepared to discuss your findings in class.

   • If a "man in a grey flannel suit" represents yesterday's typical corporate type, what is today's symbol?

   • How does one prepare for this new kind of managerial career?

   • What do you think is the biggest challenge in leading organizational change in Drucker's post-capitalist companies?

2. At Shell International, the giant oil and petroleum multinational with headquarters in both The Hague and London, the global scale of operations is evident. In fact, with operations in more than 120 countries, Shell may have more expatriates, or employees stationed outside their native countries, than any other company in the world.

   Shell conducted a survey to chart demographic and social trends among expatriates. They noted increasing numbers of women in the workforce, more aged dependents, greater travel opportunities and chances to experience other cultures, and concern about the unknown effects of expatriation on children separated from their parents.[72]

   Your team has been asked to advise Shell. Write a two- to three-page report about how the firm might integrate these external trends into its internal management policies and strategies. What is the leadership challenge here? What concepts from this chapter can help Shell management develop an effective way to manage changes?

3. In *Owning the Future*,[73] Seth Shulman warns that freely shared knowledge is fast becoming a valuable commodity. We face imminent threats from innovation and new monopolies that concentrate vital information in the hands of a few. Shulman writes of today's battles for control over the intangible new assets—genes, software, databases, and scientific information—that make up the lifeblood of our new economy. What do you think of his warnings? Interview one person in each of these four areas and be prepared to discuss the issues in class.

In today's rapidly paced environment, change is the norm. View the path to change at Magna International Inc.'s Web site at www.magnaint.com. Browse the general site, and then read about the company's history at www.magnaint.com/Magna.nsf/Pages/M2-History.

1. What do you think the cornerstones of change at Magna have been?

2. To what extent are organizational changes incremental (and therefore relatively slow) versus transforming?

3. Does change operate differently in technology-based companies than it does in other types of firms?

Conflict and Change at Parallax Systems

Janet Palica was the assistant to the president of Parallax Systems Ltd. In this staff position, Palica worked on a variety of projects for the president. Recently, she had been asked to draw up plans for renovations to the company's administrative offices. The president stressed how important it was that the renovations proceed efficiently and on time. Palica was looking forward to this project because one of the outcomes would be a new office for her.

Because Palica wanted to make a good impression on the president, she immediately put the project at the top of her priority list. She gave considerable thought to what should be included in the renovations and then contacted a local architect and had him draw up renovation plans. When the blueprints were ready, she circulated a memo to all those who would be affected by the renovations, and invited them to a meeting to announce the changes that would be made.

At the meeting, everything went wrong. Several secretaries who were going to have to move their workstations as a result of the renovations were very upset. After they had received Palica's memo, they had met (on their own time) and drawn up an alternate plan. Palica saw that their plan was better than hers, but she said nothing at the meeting. The secretaries argued that the renovations should be delayed until everyone had a chance to comment on them.

Several other groups were also upset. The drafting department members complained that their proposed new quarters were unacceptable and that no one had consulted them about the specialized type of space they needed. The marketing people complained that there was no area where sales meetings could be held. They reminded Palica that the president had promised that a large meeting room would be included when renovations were made. By the end of the meeting, Palica was exhausted. She was concerned that the president would hear about the negative tone of the meeting, and that it would reflect badly on her management skills. She also felt obliged to consult with several of the groups that had been very vocal at the meeting. She realized that the renovation project could not possibly be completed by the time the president wanted. Palica thought to herself, "If only I had talked to some of these people before I had the renovation plans drawn up!"

Questions

1. Why has the problem arisen for Janet Palica?
2. Why did some groups react so vigorously to the proposed changes?
3. What should Palica do now?

PricewaterhouseCoopers— Consulting on Strategic Change

How important is it for a company to constantly change and improve? On their Web site for strategic consulting, PricewaterhouseCoopers (PWC) notes that "Of the 100 largest companies at the turn of the 20th century, only 16 are still in business." The message is clear: Adapt or fail. PWC is a consultant to major companies on strategic change. In what ways can a consultant lead a company in a change process?

Consulting organizations are uniquely positioned to help clients adjust to change. Since they often have a wider geographic presence than the firms they consult with, they can spot trends that might be occurring in distant parts of the globe. Consulting firms can also generalize the experiences of their clients and spot trends that are particularly important. Their work with a broad range of firms also deepens their experience; they can therefore pass on their accumulated know-how to their clients. In essence, a consultant can broker the content of their learning and experience.

PricewaterhouseCoopers recognized three key trends at the end of the 20th century: growth, globalization, and e-business. During the early 1990s, many firms focused on process re-engineering to improve profit performance and to get more done with fewer resources. The new century, however, will bring renewed attention to growth.

Globalization is clearly a major force in business. Of the top 100 "economies" in the world, 49 belong to countries and 51 belong to global corporations. It is estimated that the combined sales of the top 200 global businesses account for about one-quarter of the world's gross national product (GNP). PWC believes that globalization will continue to be a powerful force even in the largest firms. Their experience has shown that the cost differentials between operations in different countries are still so substantial that companies must rethink their entire processes on a worldwide scale to capture the highest returns.

Through their business experience, PWC has identified two programs for strategic change that have been broadly successful: (1) mergers, acquisitions, and alliances; and (2) strategic enterprise architecture. Mergers, acquisitions, and alliances are tools that can help firms enter new markets or diversify some of the risk associated with market-specific downturns. Strategic enterprise architecture helps companies to accumulate knowledge as their information is carefully integrated and communicated across departmental boundaries. While these strategies have general application to executives leading their organizations in changing environments, PWC recognizes differences in individual companies. PWC's literature boasts, "We do strategy with, and not to our clients."

Questions

1. According to the description above, at what level(s) of the organization does PricewaterhouseCoopers intervene?

2. What advantages might a consulting firm like PWC bring to the process of influencing change?

3. Consider a firm that has not done business beyond its national borders. At what levels in the organization would change need to take place for that firm to be successful?

4. Assume that a consulting firm like PWC has recommended a significant strategic change for a company. Describe some specific steps that managers in the firm could take to make sure that the change actually gets implemented.

How Can We Keep the Spirit of Change Alive?

To see how important the spirit of change can be at a company like KnitMedia, consider the following comments from John Swenson, KnitMedia's senior editor at jazze.com:

> It's a new Web site we started up at Thanksgiving, and it's going to be the most comprehensive jazz and blues Web site. We're going to have over 20 000 titles. We've only been going since Thanksgiving, so we're building as we go. We're about 20 percent completed with a biography section. We donated daily news updates and there will be live music clips and videos available for downloading.... Working here is like being in a beehive. Everybody's constantly busy whirling around: If you go out for lunch, when you come back, somebody will be working on your computer because there aren't enough to go around. I mean, we probably need about twice as much office space for the amount of activity that's going on here. But surprisingly, everybody's very industrious and polite, contrary to what you might expect under the circumstances.... I love editing a jazz Web site on a day-to-day basis.

Of course, a lot of that spirit goes back to the culture—the underlying values—that Michael Dorf has cultivated at KnitMedia. In terms of values, for instance, Michael has said, "We always allow, we hope, for caprice, spontaneity, and the unexpected.... The secret is improvisation, and constant improvising."

The potential problem for KnitMedia, of course, is that a creative, improvisational culture becomes increasingly difficult to sustain as a company grows, and as employees become further removed from a visionary leader—in this case, Michael Dorf. The last thing Dorf and his team want is a "that's not my job, you'll have to do your job alone" type of culture. But that's the risk they take as more managers and employees are brought in. Needless to say, Dorf and his team want to make sure that doesn't happen, and have come to you for advice.

Team Exercises and Questions

Use what you learned in this chapter to answer the following questions from Michael Dorf and his management team:

1. What is KnitMedia's culture? In answering, please make sure to tell us the underlying values and assumptions, as well as any of the physical or procedural manifestations of that culture.

2. Do you see any need for us to change KnitMedia's culture? Why or why not? If so, what suggestions for change would you make?

3. Michael Dorf is both the company's visionary leader and the main person molding the company's culture. How can Dorf ensure that KnitMedia's culture continues to reflect his vision, and continues to provide the guidance for all employees that it has in the past?

4. Do you see any reason to institute a formal organizational change program? If so, how would you suggest we proceed? Please explain your answer.

The Trouble with Teams

Workplace democracy sounds like a very attractive idea, and the idea of teams—where members can influence how work is done—is consistent with the idea of introducing more democracy in the workplace. In the 1980s, business gurus and academics told managers that teams were the wave of the future. Teams were suggested as a way to solve the problems of autocratic management. People power was "in."

The first large-scale use of teams occurred in the automobile industry, when it was trying to cope with increasing competition from Japanese auto makers. It was known that Japanese workers worked in small groups and were allowed flexibility that was unheard of in North America. For example, Japanese workers actually made suggestions about how to improve productivity, rather than simply assembling automobiles. They also rotated through various jobs, learning them all. The key to success was thought to be the teamwork that occurred in these small work groups. The conventional wisdom at the time was that Japan's economic success could be attributed to the emphasis on teamwork in so many of its companies.

A good illustration of the current use of teams in Canada can be found at Quaker Canada. This company uses teams and reports steady productivity gains from year to year. At Quaker, workers switch jobs (for example, from packaging to quality testing), and teams have taken over supervisory functions (for example, determining their own schedules and ordering supplies). Through the use of teams, the company has cut its management costs by two-thirds. The company is happy with its results, but admits that getting teams up and running takes a lot of work.

In the early years of the 21st century, people are beginning to have second thoughts about teams. Consider the case of ESG of Kingston, Ontario, a manufacturer of sound monitoring systems that are used in underground mining. A few years ago, the company's top management laid out the company plan— five equal partners making decisions in a democratic environment with a great team dynamic. But practical problems have arisen with their team approach, and the managers are wondering whether teamwork

can really work. They, too, feel that teamwork takes a great deal of effort to make it work, so much so that they are considering changing to another approach. They have found that it takes a long time to make suggestions and achieve consensus.

Auto makers Ford and GM haven't been able to use teams as much as they originally wanted to: when workers are in team meetings, they obviously are not producing cars. As well, much training is needed for workers to function effectively in teams.

There is actually very little hard evidence that shows that teams improve company performance in the long run. A study of European parts suppliers, carried out by the Massachusetts Institute of Technology, found that the most productive and best-quality manufacturing plants were in Spain—where they didn't use teams at all. Companies cannot conclude that using teams will automatically lead to increased productivity and quality. Rather, they need to discover the conditions under which teams are and are not effective.

One of the important points that should not be ignored is that our society ranks individual stars above true team players. We have an individualistic culture, which may make it harder for teams to work. Peter Drucker, a leading management expert, was formerly a big supporter of teams, but now says that leaders are actually the key to organizational success.

Questions

1. What is the definition of a team? How well do the teams at Quaker Canada and ESG fit the definition?

2. Four basic types of teams are described in Chapter 13. What type of team approach is used at Quaker Canada? At ESG?

3. What are the causes of unproductive teams? What symptoms can be observed in unproductive teams?

4. What can leaders do to build productive teams?

5. What can managers do to motivate individuals to work as a team rather than try to be individual stars?

Video Resource: "The Trouble with Teams," *Venture* #716 (March 9, 1999).

Rocky Mountain Creativity

Question: For what reason, besides the love of skiing, would executives from across Canada take 10 days out of their busy schedules and pay $4000 to come to Banff, Alberta, in the middle of winter?

Answer: To attend the Banff School of Management, one of Canada's most innovative executive training programs.

The Banff School of Management, situated in Canada's beautiful Rocky Mountains, is fast achieving a national reputation for its creative approach to management development. Managers come from across the country in search of something "extra" in leadership training.

The school's director, Doug Macnamara, advises students to "expect an intense experience." Macnamara claims that the school's training helps make managers into better leaders. One of the ways the school accomplishes this is by emphasizing creativity. The focus is not altogether surprising, given the school's home in the Banff Centre of Creative Arts. Doug sees the school's mission as helping bring creativity back to business. According to one student, the emphasis on creativity is essential, since "Creativity is a tool that a lot of businesses have not enhanced...they've actually depressed it."

The focus on encouraging creativity calls for a different pedagogical approach, since, according to Macnamara, people "can't figure out how to be creative by lecture." The course typically involves a wide variety of hands-on exercises emphasizing teamwork and collaborative problem solving. One class began its session with a semi-structured orienteering exercise carried out in the middle of the night. The exercise was intended to replicate some key conditions of the workplace, including hidden goals and confusing directions, while encouraging cooperation and team-building.

Outdoor exercises comprise only part of the course though, with nearly half of it taking place in the classroom, where top-flight instructors from across the country provide a theoretical grounding for the practical side of management. Emphasis is on understanding personal behaviour, in this case both the student's and that of fellow team members, in order to understand basic principles of why people behave the way they do. Role playing is often used, as well as direct and sometimes confrontational feedback. For some, the program is too "touch-feely." This route should not be interpreted as a substandard teaching mode, however. According to Macnamara, the Banff School seeks to "push people beyond their envelope." The director continues, arguing that "the best learning happens when you're active in it."

The course's training exercises range from yoga and ceramics to interpretive dance and improvisation. One reason for the inclusion of such "artsy" activities arises from the on-site presence of some of Canada's leading artists. The school doesn't hesitate to co-opt the artists into the program, since they are an excellent resource for alternative ideas, insights, and paradigms. According to Macnamara, "An excellent leader and excellent artist are actually very, very close to the same type." Therefore, since "we are called to be creative starting at 8:30 in the morning until whenever," it only makes sense to stimulate the creative juices using whatever is inherently creative and, in this case, readily accessible.

Questions

1. What is the difference between a leader and a manager? The director of the Banff School of Management says that the school's training helps make managers into better leaders. Do you agree with this statement? Why or why not?

2. What is the difference between a transactional leader and a transformational leader? What kind of leader is the Banff School of Management apparently focusing on?

3. Describe the various aspects of an organization that managers can actually change. To what extent will the training provided by the Banff School of Management facilitate making changes in each of these areas?

4. List and briefly describe the four types of organization development (OD) applications. To what extent does the training offered by the Banff School of Management facilitate each of these four types of OD?

Video Resource: "Rocky Mountain Leaders," *Venture* #637 (April 6, 1997).

Leading and Motivating

It would be difficult to imagine how KnitMedia's successful start-up and subsequent growth could have been accomplished without the vision and leadership of Michael Dorf. Dorf's love for a particular kind of music, his vision of the Knitting Factory club as an incubator for talent—and eventually as a brand name for the many new ventures that became KnitMedia, Inc.—and his energy and commitment to sharing that vision with others are widely acknowledged as the organization's single guiding force.

It becomes clear from listening to KnitMedia's managers, employees, and artists that all of them share Dorf's love of jazz music. Music is what draws many people to work at KnitMedia, and it is very often what keeps them there. The chance to bring non-commercial music to the widest possible audience, to participate in Dorf's creative vision, is a major motivator, particularly when coupled with the organization's ambitious plans to tap cutting-edge media such as Webcasting and new ventures like e-commerce.

None of this heady appeal should suggest that KnitMedia is all play and no work. A strong degree of self-motivation is needed to survive in the organization's growing and evolving culture. Most of the managers try to hire people with experience and specific technical skills, and hard work and a certain level of intensity and dedication—along with the camaraderie inspired by Dorf's shared vision—are the norm.

Dorf himself is known as a very demanding leader who admits to being somewhat difficult to work for. He has been criticized, even by those who admire him, for being a workaholic with unrealistic expectations of others. He is also recognized as brilliant, inspiring, and a savvy business thinker. As Ed Greer, senior vice-president of club operations, sees it, creating the new position of chief operating officer, now held by Allan Fried, was a necessary step in creating a kind of buffer between Dorf and the rest of the company. This change has allowed Dorf to do what he does best—that is, go out and "challenge the world" on behalf of KnitMedia—

while Fried undertakes the day-to-day operation of the firm, making sure, as he puts it, that Dorf's "vision gets implemented."

Ed Greer sees himself as another facilitating leader, pointing people in the right direction, checking that they are doing what they need to do, but refraining from micromanaging or telling people in detail what to do. His hope is that he can develop his employees sufficiently so they can see for themselves what needs to be done and be able to do it independently.

Dave Brenner, vice-president of new media, describes himself as the first to come in to work and the last one to leave, a leader "by example." He relies on his interpersonal skills to help him work with people on a day-to-day basis, letting his staff know what is expected of them and finding out what their concerns are in return.

For Stephanie Oxley, vice-president of KnitMedia Labels, who runs what she calls "a tight ship," leadership means motivating people to feel as if the company were their own. The factors that make that happen, she feels, are being honest and straightforward with her staff, offering encouragement, and making it known that her expectations are very high. Although two of her staff members work in the Amsterdam office, Oxley feels there is a high degree of closeness and cohesion in her group. Those team members who work in New York often socialize together, for example.

Questions

Based on this case, the video, the text chapters you've read so far, and your knowledge from other sources, answer the following:

1. Evaluate Michael Dorf's leadership style and characteristics.

2. Contrast the styles of the KnitMedia managers.

3. What motivating factors do you think keep people at KnitMedia?

PART

5 Controlling

Part 5: Controlling provides an overview of the controlling process and the techniques that mangers use to ensure that what is supposed to happen actually *does* happen.

In Chapter 15, **Controlling and Building Commitment**, we describe the five-step control process, providing practical examples. Inputs, processes, and output must be controlled so that organizational goals are achieved. Several traditional approaches to control are described, as well as the typical human reactions to these traditional approaches. Commitment-based control systems provide a way to encourage employee self-control and motivation.

The final Appendix of this text focuses on information and information technology, and how rapid developments in these areas affect the controlling aspect of the manager's job. We begin by noting the increasing importance of knowledge management and then move on to explain what a management information system is. We also describe how systematic mobilization of information helps executives make better decisions; included here is a discussion of decision support systems, executive support systems, artificial intelligence, and expert systems. The Appendix concludes with a look at the impact of the Internet on the manager's job.

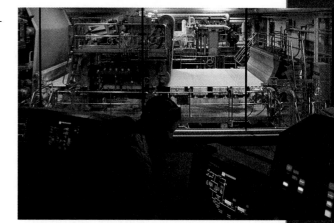

Controlling and Building Commitment

United Parcel Service

United Parcel Service (UPS) is the world's largest air and ground package distribution company, delivering more than 3 billion parcels and documents each year in over 200 countries. Perhaps the most distinguishing feature

of the company is the rigid control that it maintains over every aspect of its operations. Time and motion studies have been conducted on virtually every task that workers do. For example, delivery people are supposed to walk one metre per second, hold their key rings with their middle finger, and fold their money face up, ordered sequentially. Drivers are instructed to climb aboard their trucks with their left foot first to avoid wasted steps. Packages are arranged in a precise fashion in the trucks, which have overhead lights so the drivers can read the addresses better.

Workers at sorting centres are carefully timed according to strict standards for each task. Drivers are closely timed also; each delivery is timed with a stopwatch. All trucks are washed every day, and they are kept on a strict maintenance schedule.

United Parcel
Service
www.ups.com

Critical to UPS's success is the $10 billion the company invested in information technology since 1986. UPS drivers use a hand-held computer called a Delivery Information Acquisition Device to capture customers' signatures along with pick-up, delivery, and time card information and to transmit this information back to headquarters automatically via a cellular telephone network.

Through TotalTrack, its automated package-tracking system, UPS can control packages throughout the delivery process. And with its own global communication network called UPSnet, UPS not only tracks its packages, but electronically transmits documentation on each shipment directly to customs officials prior to arrival. Shipments are therefore either cleared for shipment or flagged for inspection before they arrive.

Today, UPS uses the Internet to help it and its customers monitor and control the progress of all those millions and millions of packages. For example, the UPS Internet-based tracking system lets a customer store up to 25 tracking numbers and then monitor the progress of each package. That not only lets the customer (and UPS) keep on top of each package's progress, it also is a value-added feature for the customer, who in turn can easily keep its own customers informed about the progress of the package.

After studying this chapter, you should be able to

1. Explain each of the five steps in the traditional control process.

2. Compare traditional control methods and commitment-based control methods.

3. Give examples of "traditional" diagnostic, boundary, and interactive control methods.

4. List the unintended behavioural consequences of controls.

5. Illustrate how managers can use belief systems and employee commitment to maintain better control.

6. Give examples of the factors that contribute to employee commitment.

Control: A Central Issue in Management

After plans have been made and the organization has been designed and staffed with motivated employees, it's time to ensure that the employees are actually doing what they're supposed to be doing, and that the plans you set up are being carried out. **Control** is the task of ensuring that activities are providing the desired results. In its most general sense, *controlling* means setting a target, measuring performance, and taking corrective action as required.

Managers need controls for two main reasons. One is that employees must be influenced to do what they are supposed to do:

> If all personnel always did what was best for the organization, control—and even management—would not be needed. But, obviously, individuals are sometimes unable or unwilling to act in the organization's best interest, and a set of controls must be implemented to guard against undesirable behavior and to encourage desirable actions.[1]

But in today's fast-changing world, there's also a second need for control. Plans can quickly become outdated as unanticipated events occur; when that happens, control is required to inform management that the plan needs changing. As control expert Kenneth Merchant says, "The goal [of the control system] is to have no unpleasant surprises in the future."[2]

What is the best way to "stay in control"? As we'll see in this chapter, there are two basic options: the **traditional control process** and **commitment-based control methods**. The first, traditional control, involves setting targets and then ensuring that employees adhere to them. The second, commitment-based control, means fostering employee self-control.

control
The task of ensuring that activities are providing the desired results.

traditional control process
Setting targets and then ensuring that employees adhere to them.

commitment-based control methods
Fostering employee self-control.

The Traditional Control Process

Five Key Steps

What's the first thing you think of when someone mentions the word "control"? Chances are, you think of somehow exerting influence to ensure that some person or group is doing what he or she is supposed to do. When most people think of control, in other words, they generally think of some kind of external process that's somehow used to keep a person's behaviour in line. Therefore, whether you're "controlling" your neighbour down the block, or the sales team at your company, or the City of Vancouver, control traditionally includes five steps:

1. Identify the areas that need to be controlled.

2. Set performance standards.

3. Measure performance.

4. Compare actual performance to the standard.

5. Take corrective action as necessary.

The controlling process is shown in Figure 15.1 and explained in the following paragraphs.

Identify the Areas that Need to Be Controlled. The controlling process starts with a clear understanding of the tasks that are being performed, and an acceptance of the basic idea that some sort of control must be exercised over the people who do these tasks. To do this step properly, managers must focus not only on the obvious things that must be controlled, but on *all* aspects of a task from start to finish.

This understanding of the total task system is necessary if the manager hopes to develop efficient and effective controls. However, such understanding may not be easy, particularly when new initiatives are started and the organization has no expertise or understanding of how to do the work. For example, when Samsung first started making microwave ovens, no one in the company knew much about them. It took several years before Samsung finally became successful in that market. Along the way, identifying the things that needed to be controlled was one of the many difficulties that managers had to cope with.

Samsung
www.samsung.com

standards
Criteria for evaluating the quality and quantity of the products or services produced by employees.

Set Performance Standards. To be effective, both managers and workers must know what is expected of them. Standards convey these expectations. **Standards** are criteria for evaluating the quality and quantity of the products or services produced by employees. Ideally, standards are set and communicated to employees during the planning process. Standards are most helpful in directing employee behaviour when they are stated in quantitative terms. A standard of "20 sales calls each week" guides behaviour much more specifically than a standard of "maximum sales calls each week." Quantitative standards give clear, objective guidance to employees, and allow management to assess performance

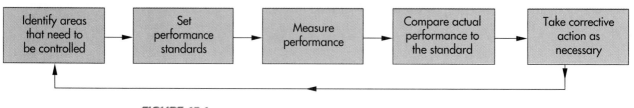

FIGURE 15.1
The Controlling Process

accurately.[3] A manufacturing firm like Dofasco sets a standard relating to the amount of steel produced in a certain time period. Revenue Canada sets a standard stating the number of clients that should be served every day. Victoria Hospital sets a standard for occupancy rates. Royal Airlines has set a goal to fill every seat on every flight. Its average seat use is 86 percent, the highest in the industry.[4]

AMP of Canada Ltd. produces electrical interconnection devices. In this highly competitive market, it is imperative that the company find out what customers want and then give it to them. To achieve this, standards of performance have been set for all marketing jobs.[5] McDonald's is legendary for its adherence to standards. The company's training manual, for example, sets standards on hundreds of activities, ranging from the cooking time for french fries to the cleanliness of the restrooms.

Many types of standards are used in organizations.[6] **Time standards** state the length of time it should take to complete a task. At American Express of Canada Inc., customer contact personnel are required to respond to customer inquiries within 24 hours.[7] Time standards are relevant for many other types of workers, including auto mechanics (time standards for tune-ups, engine scope checks, engine rebuilding, and other repairs), airline pilots (time standards for trips between various cities), and production workers (time standards for the work they do, and for the length of time they can spend on a coffee break). Setting time standards can result in significant increases in profitability. Hewlett-Packard discovered that when a new product was late getting to the market, it lost 30 percent of the product's profitability over its life. In contrast, a 50 percent cost overrun in research and development led to only a 3 percent loss.[8]

Output standards state the quantity of the product or service that employees should be producing. At a General Motors Canada plant, for example, the overall output standard might be 60 compact cars per hour. At a McDonald's outlet, the standard might be that no more than four people are standing in any line waiting to be served.

Cost standards state the maximum cost that should be incurred in the course of producing goods and services. A customer who buys stock from a broker will normally state the maximum price per share he or she is willing to pay. A volunteer organization will state the maximum salary it is willing to pay its executive director. A manufacturing firm will state the maximum price it is willing to pay for raw materials.

Royal Airlines is a charter company that focuses on cost control. Royal knows that aircraft fuel is a very important cost to control. A 1 percent drop in the price of fuel, for example, boosts Royal's annual profit by a quarter of a million dollars. The company's profit-sharing plan motivates everyone, including flight attendants, to focus on cost control in other areas as well.[9]

Quality standards define the level of quality that is to be maintained in the production of goods and services. McDonald's sets quality standards for the meat it buys. Asics sets quality standards for the material it uses in its "Gel" running shoe. Legal and accounting firms set quality standards for the services they provide to their clients. At American Express of Canada Inc., quality standards are high: Customer-contact employees are to provide information that is 100 percent accurate.[10]

Behavioural standards state the types of behaviour that are acceptable for employees. Most organizations have standards dealing with smoking, employee dress, use of foul language in front of customers, and so forth.

Often, control tolerances are necessary in addition to standards. **Control tolerances** state the degree of deviation from the standard that is permissible. For example, a company may require all employees to be at their workstation by 8:30 a.m. If an employee doesn't arrive until 8:32 a.m., this may be tolerated, but any employee who arrives after 8:35 a.m. will have their pay docked. Both standards and control tolerances should be clearly communicated to workers.

Measure Performance. The goal of this phase of the controlling process is to measure accurately the output that has resulted from employees' efforts. In many situations, such a measurement is simple. The number of letters typed, the number of hamburgers cooked, the number of automobiles produced, and the number of income tax forms processed can be determined with a high degree of accuracy. But measuring employee output in certain other situations may be problematic. Determining the output level of a psycho-

time standards
State the length of time it should take to complete a task.

American Express of Canada Inc.
www.americanexpress. com

output standards
State the quantity of the product or service that employees should be producing.

cost standards
State the maximum cost that should be incurred in the course of producing goods and services.

quality standards
Define the level of quality that is to be maintained in the production of goods and services.

behavioural standards
State the types of behaviour that are acceptable for employees.

control tolerances
State the degree of deviation from the standard that is permissible.

Quality standards are important in today's highly competitive global marketplace. This employee is checking to see whether these laptop computers are up to the standards demanded by the company.

analyst, a university professor, a management consultant, or a researcher in a laboratory may be difficult because of the nature of the work these people are doing. For example, measuring the effect of psychotherapy is difficult because improvements may not be attributable solely to the therapy; other factors, such as the person's home situation, also influence the person's life.

Managers can measure output in various ways. One is through personal observation of the performance of subordinates. At American Express of Canada, for example, supervisors tap into the calls of customer-contact employees 20 times per month to determine if they are dealing properly with customers. Monthly evaluations of customer complaints are also carried out.[11] Personal observation gives the manager first-hand information about subordinates. However, it is not always practical or advisable for a manager to use this approach since it is very time-consuming. A second approach is to use written reports of employee performance. For example, a manager may require an annual report of activity from an employee. This approach gives the manager a permanent record of employee performance, but has the disadvantage of requiring the employee to do additional work. A third approach is for the manager to require oral reports from subordinates about their performance. This has the advantage of getting the manager and subordinate together for a face-to-face meeting, but problems may develop if the subordinate feels intimidated by the boss. Because each approach has both strong and weak points, it is best to use them in combination.

If standards have been clearly stated, the measurement of performance is much easier. However, even if standards are explicitly defined, management cannot simply assume that the reported performance has actually occurred. Employees might have made honest errors when reporting their performance, output might have been at the expense of quality standards, or employees might have deliberately falsified reports of their performance.

Compare Performance with Standards. In this step, the manager essentially compares "what is" with "what should be." Since the performance of human beings varies, it is necessary for the manager to determine control tolerances. Only if performance is outside the acceptable range of deviation does the manager take further action. If the preceding steps in the control process have been carried out properly, the comparison of performance with standards is straightforward. Comparison is also easier if quantitative standards have been set.

Take Corrective Action as Necessary. The final phase in the controlling process requires the manager to decide what corrective action (if any) is required. When making this decision, the manager must ensure that the real cause of the deviation from the standard is identified. For example, if the output of a certain product is below standard, it must be determined whether the cause is human failure or machine failure. The corrective action that is necessary will depend on the cause of the deviation.

When comparing performance with the standard, the manager will find that it exceeds, meets, or falls short of the standard. If performance exceeds the standard, the manager must first ensure that the standard is actually reasonable. Once this has been done, the employee should be praised. If performance meets the standard, no further action needs to be taken.

When performance falls short of the standard, the manager must decide whether the shortfall is significant enough to demand corrective action. For example, if instructors in a college or university must achieve at least a 3.0/5.0 on student evaluations, and an instructor receives a 2.9/5.0, the department head will have to decide whether this deviation is significant enough to warrant a talk with the instructor. This process is simplified if control tolerances have already been stated.

When performance is not up to standard, managers can choose one of the following actions: (1) take corrective action, (2) change the standard, or (3) do nothing and hope things will improve. If the manager decides to take corrective action, two alternatives are available—immediate and long-term. **Immediate corrective action** solves the problem immediately and gets output back to the desired level. If management discovers that a major project is behind schedule and is therefore going to hold up other high-priority projects, immediate corrective action is taken. The top priority is getting the project back on schedule, rather than attaching blame for its lateness. Actions such as adding more personnel to the project, authorizing overtime, giving priority in the secretarial pool for project typing needs, and assigning an expediter to speed up the project are all examples of such action.

immediate corrective action
Solves the problem immediately and gets output back to the desired level.

Long-term corrective action determines why deviations occur and what can be done to prevent the problem from happening in the future. Many managers focus too much of their effort on immediate responses and not enough on long-term corrective action. Consider this example: A manager of a department with high turnover finds that she is spending a great deal of her time recruiting new members for the department (immediate corrective action). But the manager never stops to figure out why so many people are leaving the department (long-term corrective action). Unless long-term corrective action is taken, this manager will continually be trying to cope with problems she does not understand.

long-term corrective action
Determines why deviations occur and what can be done to prevent the problem from happening in the future.

The Controlling Process in Action: An Example

Here is how the five steps in the controlling process usually unfold in an academic setting.

1. *Identify the areas that need to be controlled.* Your instructors do not try to control every aspect of your life (although sometimes it may seem that they are). Certain important elements of the learning process remain under your control: You decide whether to cram for an exam or keep up with your readings, whether to use a highlighter or take notes, whether to belong to a study group or work on your own, and so on. But instructors do implement controls to ensure that you do certain things, like reading the assigned chapters, because they have identified these things as definitely needing to be controlled.

2. *Set performance standards.* Your instructors typically want you to demonstrate that you can do several things: think critically, understand the course material, apply the material to real-world management situations, and so on. These skills are crucial for your success as a manager, and that is why standards are in place.

3. *Measure performance.* Your performance is measured through assignments, exams, class participation, and group projects.

4. *Compare actual performance to the standard.* Once the instructor has observed your performance, he or she must determine whether you have met the performance standard. This may appear to be a very subjective process if the instructor does not clearly state the standard. For example, consider the comment of one instructor who said, "When I was a student, I never could quite see how a professor could distinguish a B paper from a C+ paper, but now that I'm grading papers, the distinction is crystal clear." The instructor must convey that distinction to students.

5. *Take corrective action as necessary.* Feedback to students in the form of grades provides a clear signal regarding the acceptability of their performance in relation to the standard. The extreme corrective action is requiring the student to take the course over again because the deviation from the standard is unacceptable.

Many people think that the controlling process shown in Figure 15.1 (see page 478) is a rather mechanical series of steps that managers work through, like following a cookbook recipe when baking a cake. But this academic example shows that the controlling process (like the decision-making process discussed in Chapter 4) is not so simple. At each step, numerous things can go wrong, and the people who are being controlled can become very upset.

Controlling Inputs, Processes, and Outputs

Controls can be applied before the production process starts (input controls), during the production process (process controls), or after the production process has been completed (output controls).

Controlling Inputs

input controls
Monitor the material, human, and capital resources that come into the organization.

Managers use input controls primarily as a preventive measure. **Input controls** (also called feedforward or preventive controls) monitor the material, human, and capital resources that come into the organization. For example, Four Seasons Hotels Inc. places strong emphasis on controlling inputs so that customers get the service they expect. This emphasis is evident even before the construction of a hotel starts. Developers who approach the company must buy land that meets Four Seasons' specifications. The company then puts together a detailed operating plan. On the human side, prospective employees go through as many as four screenings and interviews. When hiring, the company emphasizes character and personality rather than technical skills.[12]

inventory
The items an organization keeps on hand either for use in the production process or as a result of the production process.

raw materials inventory
The basic inputs into the production process.

goods-in-process inventory
Those items that are partway through the production process.

finished goods inventory
Those items that have passed through the entire production process and are ready to be sold to customers.

Inventory Control. **Inventory** refers to the items an organization keeps on hand either for use in the production process or as a result of the production process. **Raw materials inventory** consists of the basic inputs into the production process. At McDonald's raw materials include potatoes, meat, milk, and hamburger buns. At Northern Paint, raw materials include petroleum distillate, linseed oil, and pigment. **Goods-in-process inventory** includes those items that are partway through the production process. At Chrysler Canada, goods-in-process inventory includes engine blocks, tires, transmissions, and dashboards. At Wendy's, goods-in-process includes hamburgers cooking on the grill and baked potatoes in the microwave. **Finished goods inventory** includes those items that have passed through the entire production process and are ready to be sold to customers. New Buicks in an automobile dealer's showroom, french fries sitting under a heat lamp at Burger King, running shoes at Athlete's Wear, and computers on the counter at Computerland are finished goods inventory.

Inventory is also necessary in service operations. Magicuts Inc. introduced computers to record customer arrival and departure times, keep track of inventory, and record how demand for hairstyling services ebbs and flows over the course of a day. This helps the company to serve customers better by maintaining proper inventory, knowing a given customer's history at the shop, and matching available stylists with customer traffic patterns so that customers don't have to wait for service.[13]

Until recently, many organizations carried large amounts of inventory. Assembly line operations in particular stressed carrying inventory so their operations would not be disrupted if a supplier experienced a strike or failed to deliver inventory on time. Increasingly, however, managers have come to the conclusion that inventory should be minimized, and cite several reasons for this decision. First, inventories require an investment of money. If a company can avoid this investment, it will be more efficient and will make a greater profit. Second, inventories take up space. Space costs money, so a company that is able to carry less inventory will be more efficient. Third, inventory may deteriorate, be stolen, or be damaged, again costing money. Finally, inventory may become obsolete and hence unusable.

In the **just-in-time (JIT) inventory system**, inventory is scheduled to arrive just in time to be used in the production process. This system, which was pioneered by Toyota, is based on the idea that very little inventory is actually necessary if it is scheduled to arrive at precisely the time it is needed. Properly managed, the JIT system saves the company considerable money because inventory levels can be drastically reduced. In addition, all of the risks normally associated with inventory—obsolescence, theft, deterioration, or damage—can be avoided.

In the JIT system, production at one workstation is triggered by demand for its output by the next workstation. In an automobile manufacturing plant, for example, as the chassis moves down the production line, a signal goes out for the door subassembly unit to send doors to the assembly line. The doors would have been scheduled to be completed just as they were needed in the main assembly line. What number and type of door to send at this time has been determined in Japanese automobile plants by the *kanban* system. The ***kanban* system** specifies how many and what kind of items are to be produced. The JIT and *kanban* systems work in conjunction with each other.

JIT is also useful in the service sector. For example, when a pair of jeans is sold in a retail outlet, the bar code on the jeans is read by the cash register. This information can then be transmitted directly to the manufacturer to let them know that another pair of jeans is needed.

Mount Sinai Hospital uses a JIT system by storing its inventory at a nearby facility. Orders are delivered once a day, as well as in emergency situations.

Cassidy's Recipe for Failure

Although little known outside the restaurant industry, Cassidy's is a 199-year-old business, cited as the third oldest in Canada, that began in the early 1800s by importing china and glass goods from Britain. Based in Brossard, Quebec, and managed from Toronto, the company employed 400 people across Canada, distributing glassware, dishes, and cutlery to the tables of thousands of restaurants. However, Cassidy's, which once held an estimated 20 percent of Canada's food service supply market, is in receivership. Its inventories and other assets are being sold off.

What caused the demise of this almost two-century-old business that survived Confederation, the Depression, and changing tastes? It could not endure the e-commerce and re-engineering revolutions of the late 1990s.

Cassidy's passing underscores the challenges of an Old Economy supplier in an era of electronic commerce. "This was an old-line distribution company that had not kept up with the times," says Jim Stewart, who recently stepped into the company as the chief restructuring officer. As a traditional distributor, Cassidy's maintained a large and expensive sales force to keep contact with customers. "But my vision was to have most orders handled on the Internet, instead of by shoe leather on the pavement," Stewart commented.

However, Cassidy's was too slow to embrace the changes required for survival. The Bordeurs had owned this publicly traded but family-controlled company since the early 1950s and were hesitant to shake off obsolete business models. For years, Cassidy's was a decentralized operation with more than 20 branches nationwide. Through the 1990s, the company embarked on an acquisition drive and bought smaller distributors in cities such as Calgary and Winnipeg. The aim was to be the industry consolidator. "We want Cassidy's not only to survive, but to become the category killer, as was Wal-Mart in the department store field," former president Ralph Edwards said in May 1998.

Sales exceeded $120 million in the 1998 fiscal year, but the company was losing money. Sales and general administration expenses remained too high. "It's a watching-pennies kind of business," says Toronto restaurant consultant Elizabeth Hollyer of FHG Inc. "If a glass costs $1.98 instead of $1.90, it makes a difference."

In the end, several factors killed Cassidy's. Gross margins in the hotel and restaurant supply industry came under increased attack. Manufacturers began to sell directly to restaurants, and they could rely increasingly on business-to-business orders on the Web—therefore cutting out intermediaries such as Cassidy's. In addition, competing distributors were moving to a faster and more efficient sales model, based on new computer technology. Although Cassidy's had been an innovator in introducing computers to its operations, the company did not keep up to date.

The distribution network also became a major problem. New management tried to centralize operations and closed down parts of the unwieldy branch network. But Cassidy's lacked the information systems necessary to cope with the bigger warehouses, and lost control of its inventory. The company began short-shipping some customers, which meant restaurants could no longer rely on obtaining supplies when they were needed. Clients started leaving, as did some top sales representatives.

Cassidy's needed to spend money on new technology, but the fix would take time—and time was quickly running out. Gross margins in the industry plunged in 1999, and Ideal Food Service, a major Toronto competitor, closed. Cassidy's costs remained too high, and the capital base quickly eroded. Although the owners delayed the inevitable, the business closed in December 1999. Lorne Weidman, a senior manager in the company says they had no choice—they had to walk away.

Mount Sinai Hospital, in downtown Toronto, also uses a JIT system. Here's how it works. Individual suppliers no longer come to Mount Sinai to deliver their items. Instead, all suppliers deliver their products to Livingston Healthcare Services Inc. in Oakville, Ontario. Livingston stores these items and fills Mount Sinai's orders once a day. The orders are put into plastic boxes that are delivered to specific nursing stations at the hospital.

The new system is highly computerized. Clerks carry scanners as they tour the stockrooms of each nursing station. Each product has a bar code, and the computer indicates how many of each item are in stock. If more product is needed, that information is transmitted to the hospital's central computer. The computer assembles data from all of the nursing stations and transmits a blanket order to Livingston's warehouse and distribution centre. If there is a crisis, Livingston can deliver within one hour.

Mount Sinai Hospital
www.mtsinai.on.ca

Livingston Healthcare Services
www.livgroup.com

Controlling Processes

Process controls focus on the activities that transform inputs into outputs. **Process controls** (also called steering or concurrent controls) are applied while the product or service is produced. Interaction between bosses and subordinates provides control by keeping both up to date on the production of goods or services. Interaction makes both managers and workers aware of problems as they develop; it also suggests actions that might be necessary to get work back on track. For many lower- and middle-level managers, this form of process control takes up a substantial part of their time each day. Other process controls include rules, policies, and procedures (see Chapter 5).

process controls
Controls that are applied while the product or service is produced.

Process control is relevant for all sorts of jobs. Consider college students who are taking a course that requires them to read the management literature in a certain area and then write a paper on what they have learned. If the instructor in this situation wanted to exercise process control, he or she could require the students to first develop a written plan of the work that is to be done. The instructor could then make periodic checks to see if the actual work matches what was planned. Students who are not guided by process control often find to their dismay that their finished paper is not acceptable to the professor.

Controlling Output

Managers use output controls to assess the results of the production process. **Output controls** (also called comparison or yes-no controls) are used to determine whether deviations from standards have occurred in a product or service. Examples of output controls include a coach assessing a basketball player's offensive and defensive statistics, a manager surveying users of the firm's products, and a teacher reading final examination papers. Output controls normally contain guidelines for correcting any deviations and returning the operation to standard.

output controls
Controls that are used to determine whether deviations from standards have occurred in a product or service.

Serious difficulties arise when companies do not properly control output. In 1999, for example, Coca-Cola received very bad publicity when people in Europe became ill after drinking Coke. The Belgian health minister banned Coke products until the problem could be resolved. Coke was eventually forced to recall 14 million cases of Coke, and its profits were reduced by $35 million. It was later discovered that quality control procedures were inadequate, and that this lapse had allowed Coke products to become contaminated.[14]

Quality and Quality Control. In the years following the Second World War, a U.S. consultant named W. Edwards Deming tried to convince U.S. firms of the value of high-quality products. He was not successful in the United States, but he did convince the Japanese. His work there transformed the phrase "Made in Japan" from a synonym for shoddy merchandise into a hallmark of reliability and quality. Now, Japan's highest award for industrial achievement is the Deming Award for Quality.

Deming developed 14 points on how to improve quality, including:[15]

1. Make a long-term commitment to improving quality.

2. Reduce dependence on inspection after the product is produced; instead, build quality into the product.

3. Minimize total cost by constantly improving the production system.

4. Be concerned about quality.

5. If you are a leader, you should help workers do a better job.

Deming's ideas gained prominence in Canada and the United States during the economic troubles of the 1970s and 1980s, and emphasis on quality manufacturing in the United States and Canada still continues to increase. In the United States, the Malcolm Baldridge Quality Award signifies the highest level of quality processes in manufacturing. In Canada, the Awards for Business Excellence acknowledge those businesses that increase Canada's competitiveness in international business. The Gold Plant Quality Award was given to the workers of Toyota's Cambridge, Ontario, plant in 1991 and 1995. This award honours the plant as the top-quality producer of automobiles in North America. The award is proof of Toyota's emphasis on *kaizen* (continual search for improvement) and *jidoka* (defect detection).

total quality management (TQM)
Based on the idea that no defects are tolerable, and that employees are responsible for maintaining quality standards.

Standard Aero
www.standardaero.ca

Motorola
www.motorola.ca

Total Quality Management. The **total quality management (TQM)** concept is based on the idea that no defects are tolerable, and that employees are responsible for maintaining quality standards.[16] Traditionally, organizations formed separate departments (quality control) and set up specific jobs (quality-control inspector) to monitor quality levels. The workers' responsibility was to make the product, and the quality-control department's responsibility was to check the work. TQM does away with this distinction and makes each worker responsible for achieving high-quality standards. For example:

- At Standard Aero in Winnipeg, the impetus to submit a bid to the U.S. Air Force for aircraft overhaul work came from employees, not managers. Standard Aero got the contract. The only definition of quality that really counts at Standard Aero is "what the customer wants."[17]

- At Toyota's Cambridge, Ontario, plant, workers can push a button or pull a rope to stop the production line when something is not up to standard.[18]

- Motorola has achieved a level of "six-sigma quality," which translates into just over three defects per million parts produced.

- When Levi Strauss introduced an "alternative work styles" program, it required workers to inspect their own output. Since the program began, there has been a 50 percent decline in defective pieces.[19]

The introduction of a TQM program is no guarantee that a company will be successful, because an emphasis on quality is just one component of TQM. It must be combined with allowing employees to try new ideas and a recognition system that rewards them when they are successful. Some managers have difficulty adapting to TQM because they deal with workers using a "leave your brains at home and do what I say" management philosophy. Workers may also resist the move to TQM because they fear it will lead to a reduction in the number of jobs. When TQM is introduced, companies typically find that about 5 to 10 percent of the employees are enthusiastic, 5 to 10 percent are totally opposed, and the rest are somewhere in between.[20]

Three Traditional Control Systems

There are three main types of traditional control systems: diagnostic control systems, boundary control systems, and interactive control systems.

Diagnostic Control Systems

When most people think of controls, they think of **diagnostic control systems**. These aim to ensure that important goals are being achieved and that any variances are explained. Budgets and performance reports are examples.

One of the main purposes of diagnostic controls is to reduce the need for managers to constantly monitor everything.[21] Once targets have been set, managers can (at least in theory) leave the employees to pursue the goals, supposedly secure in the knowledge that if the goals are not being met, the deviations will show up as variances that have to be explained.

This idea is at the heart of what management experts call the principle of exception. The **principle of exception** (or "management by exception") holds that to conserve managers' time, only significant deviations or exceptions from the standard, "both the especially good and bad exceptions," should be brought to the managers' attention.[22]

Diagnostic control systems are based on several assumptions. One is that the results reported by the employees (like reported sales) are accurate and, in particular, that employees don't work to get around or fudge the control system. It's also assumed that the goals or targets are still valid. If they're not, what's the sense in comparing the company's actual results to an outdated goal?

Unfortunately, assumptions like these are often not valid in today's fast-changing world. Nevertheless, diagnostic control systems remain important and widely used. Let's look at some examples.

Budgets and Performance Reports. **Budgets** are formal financial expressions of a manager's plans. They show target numbers for such yardsticks as revenues, cost of materials, expenditures, and profits, usually in dollars.

Budgets are widely used. Each manager, from first-line supervisor to top manager, usually has his or her own budget.[23] However, creating the budget (as shown in Figure 15.2)

diagnostic control systems
Control systems that aim to ensure that important goals are being achieved and that any variances are explained.

principle of exception
To conserve managers' time, only significant deviations or exceptions from the standard should be brought to the managers' attention.

budgets
Formal financial expressions of a manager's plans.

BUDGET FOR MACHINERY DEPARTMENT, JUNE 2000	
Budgeted Expenses	**Budget**
Direct Labour	$2107
Supplies	$3826
Repairs	$ 402
Overhead (electricity, etc.)	$ 500
TOTAL EXPENSES	$6835

FIGURE 15.2
Example of a Budget

is just the standard-setting step in the control process. Actual performance still must be measured and compared to the budgeted standards. Then corrective action can be taken.

The organization's accountants are responsible for collecting data on actual performance. They compile the financial data and feed them back to the appropriate managers. The most common form of feedback is a performance report, such as the one shown in Figure 15.3. The manager typically receives a report like this for his or her unit at the end of some time period (say, each month).

As in Figure 15.3, the performance report shows budgeted or planned targets. Next to these figures, it shows the department's actual performance. The report also lists the differences between budgeted and actual amounts; these are usually called **variances**. A space on the report is sometimes provided for the manager to explain any variances. After reviewing the performance report, the manager can then take corrective action.

Zero-Based Budgeting.
In traditional budgeting, funding requests are often based on ongoing projects, although sometimes these projects may no longer be needed. For example, many federal government programs are routinely continued from year to year simply because "they've always been in the budget."

Zero-based budgeting is a technique that forces managers to defend their budgeted programs every year and to rank them in order of priority based on the ratio of benefits and costs. This exercise gives top management an opportunity to re-evaluate ongoing programs, compare ongoing programs to proposed programs, and consider reducing or eliminating the funding for ongoing programs so that new programs with higher priorities can be implemented.[24]

Ratio Analysis and Return on Investment.
Most managers achieve control in part by monitoring various **financial ratios**, which compare one financial indicator to another. The rate of return on investment (ROI) is one such ratio: It is a measure of overall company performance and equals net income divided by total investment. Return on investment views profit (net income) not as an absolute figure, but rather in relation to the total investment in the business. A $1 million profit, for example, would be more impressive in a business with a $10 million investment than in one with a $100 million investment. Figure 15.4 presents some commonly used financial ratios.

Figure 15.5 shows how some companies combine these ratios for control. For example, sales by itself is less informative than the ratio of sales to total investment (or capital turnover). Similarly, sales divided by earnings (the profit margin) reflects management's success or failure in maintaining satisfactory cost controls. As another example, note how ROI can be influenced by factors like excessive investment. In turn, excessive investment might reflect inadequate inventory control, accounts receivable, or cash.[25]

The Corporate Scorecard.
As the head of a company, how would you like to have the equivalent of a set of cockpit displays that you could use to help you pilot your company? Today, more and more companies are experimenting with a diagnostic control tool called a corporate scorecard. Its basic purpose is to provide managers with an overall impression of how their companies are doing.[26]

variances
The differences between budgeted and actual amounts.

zero-based budgeting
A technique that forces managers to defend their budgeted programs every year and to rank them in order of priority based on the ratio of benefits and costs.

financial ratios
Compare one financial indicator to another.

PERFORMANCE REPORT FOR MACHINERY DEPARTMENT, JUNE 2000

	Budget	Actual	Variance	Explanation
Direct Labour	$2107	$2480	$373 over	Had to put workers on overtime.
Supplies	$3826	$4200	$374 over	Wasted two crates of material.
Repairs	$ 402	$ 150	$252 under	
Overhead (electricity, etc.)	$ 500	$ 500	0	
TOTAL	$6835	$7330	$495 over	

FIGURE 15.3
Example of a Performance Report

Corporate scorecards (which are usually computerized models) put a new twist on traditional control tools. Like other traditional diagnostic control tools, they measure how the company has been doing and help managers diagnose exactly what (if anything) has gone wrong. However, they differ from their simpler control cousins, such as budgets, in several ways.

First, they mathematically trace a multitude of performance measures simultaneously, and show the interactions between these various measures. Second, the manager generally gets several measures of overall performance, rather than just one or two. At Shell Oil, for instance, the Shell Business Model (as the Shell scorecard is called) shows revenue growth, overall company market value, rate of return compared to the cost of borrowing money, and rate of return of the firm as a whole.

NAME OF RATIO	FORMULA	INDUSTRY NORM (ASSUMED MERELY AS ILLUSTRATION)
1. Liquidity Ratios (measuring the ability of the firm to meet its short-term obligations)		
Current ratio	$\dfrac{\text{Current assets}}{\text{Current liabilities}}$	2.6
Acid-test ratio	$\dfrac{\text{Cash and equivalent}}{\text{Current liability}}$	1.0
Cash velocity	$\dfrac{\text{Sales}}{\text{Cash and equivalent}}$	12 times
Inventory to net working capital	$\dfrac{\text{Inventory}}{\text{Current assets} - \text{Current liabilities}}$	85%
2. Leverage Ratios (measure the contributions of financing by owners compared with financing provided by creditors)		
Debt to equity	$\dfrac{\text{Total debt}}{\text{Net worth}}$	56%
Coverage of fixed charges	$\dfrac{\text{Net profit before fixed charges}}{\text{Fixed charges}}$	6 times
Current liability to net worth	$\dfrac{\text{Current liability}}{\text{Net worth}}$	32%
Fixed assets to net worth	$\dfrac{\text{Fixed assets}}{\text{Net worth}}$	60%
3. Activities Ratios (measuring the effectiveness of the employment of resources)		
Inventory turnover	$\dfrac{\text{Sales}}{\text{Inventory}}$	7 times
Net working capital turnover	$\dfrac{\text{Sales}}{\text{Net working capital}}$	5 times
Fixed-assets turnover	$\dfrac{\text{Sales}}{\text{Fixed assets}}$	6 times
Average collection period	$\dfrac{\text{Receivables}}{\text{Average sales per day}}$	20 days
Equity capital turnover	$\dfrac{\text{Sales}}{\text{Net worth}}$	3 times
Total capital turnover	$\dfrac{\text{Sales}}{\text{Total assets}}$	2 times

(continued)

FIGURE 15.4
Widely Used Financial Ratios

NAME OF RATIO	FORMULA	INDUSTRY NORM
4. Profitability Ratios (indicating degree of success of achieving desired profit levels)		
Gross operating margin	$\dfrac{\text{Gross operating profit}}{\text{Sales}}$	30%
Net operating margin	$\dfrac{\text{Net operating profit}}{\text{Sales}}$	6.5%
Sales margin	$\dfrac{\text{Net profit after taxes}}{\text{Sales}}$	3.2%
Productivity of assets	$\dfrac{\text{Gross income less taxes}}{\text{Total assets}}$	10%
Return on investment	$\dfrac{\text{Net profit after taxes}}{\text{Total investment}}$	7.5%
Net profit on working capital	$\dfrac{\text{Net operating profit}}{\text{Net working capital}}$	14.5%

FIGURE 15.4
Widely Used Financial Ratios

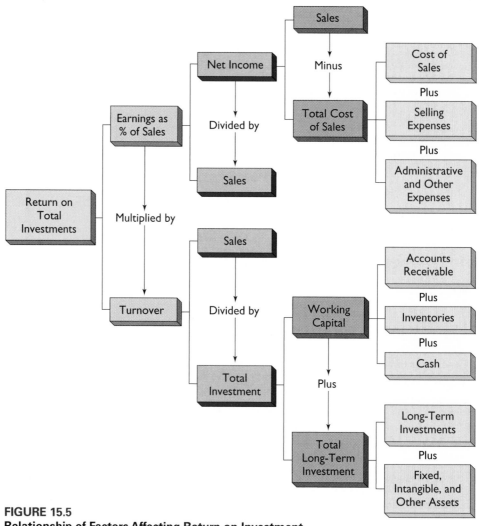

FIGURE 15.5
Relationship of Factors Affecting Return on Investment
The firm's overall profitability—its return on total investments—can be better understood by analyzing its components, including earnings as a percentage of sales and turnover.

Like your car's dashboard, the corporate scorecard can help a manager better analyze and control what's happening in the company. For example, before using their model, Shell's managers didn't understand the mathematical link between revenue growth and shareholder value. As a result, they wouldn't try to rush a new oil rig into operation, since fast growth was not so important to them. With the new scorecard model, they can see that faster growth translates into higher shareholder value, so they're more anxious to get those oil rigs online quickly.

Enterprise Resource Planning Systems. Corporate scorecards are actually components of larger control systems known today as enterprise resource planning systems. Systems like these are produced by companies like SAP of Germany, Oracle, and PeopleSoft. They are basically company-wide integrated computer systems that integrate a firm's individual systems (such as order processing, production control, and accounting) in order to give managers "real-time," instantaneous information regarding the costs and status of every activity and project in the business.[27]

Using one of these products, for example, the cheque-printing company Deluxe Paper Payment Systems was able to "get a clearer picture of which of its customers were profitable and which were not."[28] When it discovered how much more profitable an order from a bank for cheques could be when it came via electronic ordering, the company launched a campaign to increase electronic ordering—particularly by 18 000 bank and small-business customers. As a result, the percentage of cheques ordered electronically jumped from 48 to 62 percent in just a few months, dramatically improving profits at Deluxe.

With results like that, some glowingly refer to enterprise software as "the stuff that puts the information age to work for corporations."[29] By integrating all of the company's various systems, "managers will now be able to receive daily online reports about the costs of specific business processes, for example, and on the real-time profitability of individual products and customers."[30]

On September 30, 1999, SAP, the market leader of inter-enterprise software solutions, launched a new Web site, called "mysap.com." Companies of all sizes and industries can use that site to download SAP software components, as well as to link with other companies that are using SAP in order to interact more seamlessly with them.[31]

SAP
www.mysap.com

Oracle
www.oracle.com

PeopleSoft
www.peoplesoft.com

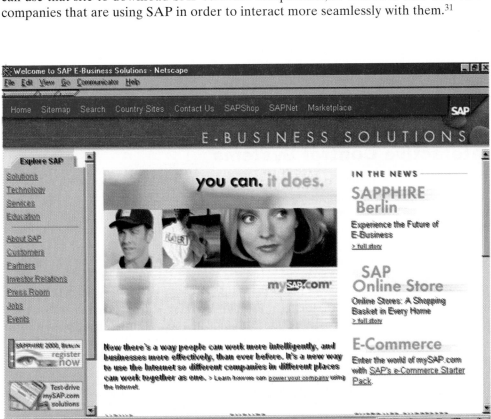

The Web site of SAP of Germany promotes its enterprise resource planning system.

Boundary Control Systems

Boundary control systems are a second traditional approach to maintaining control. They "establish the rules of the game and identify actions and pitfalls that employees must avoid."[32] Examples include standards of ethical behaviour and codes of conduct to which employees are encouraged to adhere.

Johnson & Johnson's credo illustrates the heart of a boundary control system. The credo contains fundamental ethical guidelines (such as "We believe our first responsibility is to the doctors, nurses, and patients...who use our products" and "our suppliers and distributors must have an opportunity to make a fair profit") that are supposed to provide the boundaries over which Johnson & Johnson employees are not to step. For example, selling a product that might be harmful would obviously be out of bounds. This helps account for the fact that when confronted by several bottles of poisoned Tylenol some years back, Johnson & Johnson's managers elected to recall the entire stock of the product.

Ethical or boundary control systems require more than just drawing up a list of guidelines. In Chapter 3, for instance, we emphasized that fostering ethics at work involves at least these five steps:

1. Emphasize top management's commitment.
2. Publish a "code."
3. Establish compliance mechanisms.
4. Involve personnel at all levels.
5. Measure results.

Boundary control systems are important for any company, but they're especially important for firms that depend on trust.[33] Large consulting firms like McKinsey & Company must be able to assure clients that the highly proprietary strategic data they will review will never be compromised. They must therefore enforce strict boundaries "that forbid consultants to reveal information—even the names of clients—to anyone not employed by the firm, including spouses."[34]

The "boundaries" that a firm lays down are not limited to ethical guidelines. For example, "strategic boundaries focus on ensuring that people steer clear of opportunities that could diminish the business's competitive position."[35] Thus managers at Automatic Data Processing (ADP) use a strategic boundary list that lays out the types of business opportunities that ADP managers should avoid. Another company, a large Netherlands-based multinational, has a strategic policy of discouraging its executives from forming joint ventures with firms in the United States because of the greater possibility of litigation in U.S. courts.

Interactive Control Systems

The typical small, entrepreneurial company has at least one big control advantage over its huge multinational competitors: Mom and Pop can talk face to face with almost everyone in the firm to find out immediately how everything is going. Indeed, such face-to-face interaction is at the heart of how most smaller companies traditionally maintain control.

Of course, as companies grow and expand, this kind of direct interaction becomes more difficult, since there are so many people, often far away, to keep track of. However, just because it's difficult doesn't mean that interactive, primarily face-to-face controls cannot and should not be used, and most firms do use them. *Interactive strategic control* is one example. It is a real-time, usually face-to-face method of monitoring both a strategy's effectiveness and the underlying assumptions on which the strategy is built.[36]

The basic intention of using interactive controls for strategic purposes is twofold: (1) to give senior managers a formal procedure through which they can monitor information of strategic importance to the firm; and (2) to get a feel for the importance of that information by interacting, primarily face to face, with key subordinates. Such controls can be very useful for managing change.

Human Reactions to Traditional Control

Every organization has to ensure that its employees are performing as expected. Every day managers are faced with questions like "How can I make sure that Marie files her sales reports on time?" and "How can I make sure that John doesn't close the store before 10 p.m.?" To a large extent, the answer to both questions is: "By imposing controls."

If tightly controlling employees were the only (or the best) way to ensure effective performance, we could disregard more than half of this book. For example, we would not need to know very much about what motivates people, which leadership style is best, or how to win employees' commitment.

But the fact is that managers can't rely on controls for keeping employees in line. For one thing (even with enterprise software), it's impossible to have a system of rules and controls so complete that you can keep track of everything that employees say and do. This is one reason why as a manager you will have to rely more on self-control, like that fostered with the motivational practices outlined in Chapter 11.

Furthermore, a manager cannot rely just on controls because employees can and will retaliate, using what will often seem to be extraordinarily ingenious techniques. Consider this true story: The owner of a chain of dry cleaning stores tried to control stealing by requiring store managers to give a cash register receipt to each and every customer. To reinforce this policy, the owner placed a large sign by the register that said: "If you don't get a cash receipt, your order is free. Please call us at 555-6283."

Sure that he could now account for all of the cash coming into the store, every night the owner handed over the store to his store manager at 5 p.m. and happily went home. But every evening at 5:15 sharp, the store manager pulled out his own cash register, which he had secreted away during the day, and spent about an hour happily taking in cash and giving each satisfied customer a cash register receipt. Then he replaced the owner's cash register and pocketed his loot.[37]

As you can see, a big problem with overreliance on traditional controls is that they can lead to unintended, undesirable, and often harmful consequences. Professor Kenneth Merchant classifies these employee reactions as behavioural displacement, gamesmanship, operating delays, and negative attitudes.[38] Reduced empowerment is a fifth unwanted reaction.

Behavioural Displacement. Employees who feel pressured to look good in terms of the control standards may concentrate their efforts where results are measured, disregarding the company's more important goals. **Behavioural displacement** occurs when the behaviours encouraged by the controls are inconsistent with what the company actually wants to accomplish.

behavioural displacement
Occurs when the behaviours encouraged by the controls are inconsistent with what the company actually wants to accomplish.

This problem stems mostly from focusing too narrowly on one or two control standards. For example, Nordstrom, a retailer famed for its extraordinary customer service, recently found itself involved in a series of lawsuits related to its policy of controlling sales per hour of performance.[39]

Unfortunately, tracking the performance of its empowered salespeople by simply monitoring sales per hour backfired. Without other, counterbalancing measures the sales per hour system blew up: Some employees claimed that first-line supervisors were pressuring them to underreport their hours on the job to boost reported sales per hour. Nordstrom ended up settling those claims for over $15 million.

Gamesmanship. **Gamesmanship** refers to management actions aimed at improving the manager's performance in terms of the control system without producing any economic benefits for the firm. For example, a manager depleted his stocks of spare parts and heating oil at year's end although he knew these stocks would have to be replenished shortly thereafter at higher prices. By reducing his stocks, the manager reduced his expenses for the year and made his end-of-year results look better, although in the long run the company lost out.[40] In another example, a division overshipped products to its distributors at year end. The aim was to ensure that management could meet its budgeted sales targets, even though the managers knew that the products would be returned.[41]

gamesmanship
Management actions aimed at improving the manager's performance in terms of the control system without producing any economic benefits for the firm.

Personality and How People React to Control

locus of control
The extent to which individuals believe that they control their lives.

To psychologists like Julian Rotter, who first studied this phenomenon, **locus of control** means the extent to which individuals believe that they control their lives.[42] Some people, called internals, "have an internal locus of control and believe that they can control what happens to them. Others, called externals, have an external locus of control and tend to think that what happens to them is determined by fate or luck."[43] To psychologists, locus of control is basically a personality trait—people are either "internals" or "externals," for instance. To examine locus of control, Rotter developed a test consisting of a series of statements about oneself and other people. Here is a sampling. With which statement in each pair do you agree?

With enough effort, we can wipe out political corruption.	vs.	It is difficult to have much control over the things politicians do while in office.
There is a direct connection between how hard I study and the grade I get	vs.	Sometimes I can't understand how teachers arrive at the grades they give.
What happens to me is my doing.	vs.	Sometimes I feel that I don't have enough control over the direction my life is taking.
People's misfortunes result from the mistakes they make.	vs.	Many of the unhappy things in people's lives are partly due to bad luck.[44]

Statements like these, says Rotter, help distinguish between internals and externals. Internals tend to agree with the statements on the left, whereas externals agree with those on the right. Internals generally feel they are able to control their environments; externals believe that they have little control over their lives.

You are probably thinking that a clever manager can influence the degree to which employees react badly to being controlled by choosing employees more carefully. If so, you are right. For example, internals tend to be more independent and more reliant on their own judgment, and may be best for low-supervision jobs. Externals expect to be controlled and may be better suited for jobs that will be closely supervised.[45]

Operating Delays. Operating delays can be another unfortunate and unintended consequence of many control systems. They are especially dangerous when quick, responsive decisions are required. When he became CEO of General Electric, for instance, Jack Welch knew that it sometimes took a year or more for division managers to get approval to introduce new products because of a long list of required approvals.

Negative Attitudes. In addition to displacement, gamesmanship, and operating delays, controls can have a more insidious effect by undermining employees' attitudes. In one study that focused on first-line supervisors' reactions to budgets, Professor Chris Argyris found that the budgets were viewed as pressure devices. The supervisors came to see budgets as prods by top management and in turn used them to prod their own subordinates. As a result of this pressure, employees formed anti-management work groups and the supervisors reacted by increasing their compliance efforts.[46]

"Intelligent" employee ID badges provide another example of a control tool that may elicit negative attitudes. Italy's Olivetti holds the basic patent on the Active-Badge System and began marketing it commercially around the beginning of 1993. The Active-Badge looks like a clip-on ID card. It's actually a small computer that emits infrared signals to strategically located sensors, which can then effectively track the wearer anywhere within an equipped facility. The system can also keep tabs on most visitors. Knowing where people are avoids interruptions, wasted phone calls, and useless trips to empty offices.

Olivetti
www.olivetti.it

But questions remain: How much privacy can managers expect employees to surrender in the name of control? How much control is too much? And what effect will these badges have on morale and performance? Proponents say that effective safeguards can be implemented. Critics fear that once such a system is in place, there will be no defence against abuse.[47]

THE CHALLENGE OF CHANGE

Electronic Performance Monitoring and Control

When it comes to monitoring employees electronically, computerized badges are the tip of the iceberg. Many workers are subject to electronic performance monitoring (EPM) on the job—such as having supervisors monitor through electronic means the amount of computerized data an employee is processing per day.[48]

Jeffrey Stanton and Janet Barnes-Farrell studied the effects of EPM on individuals working on computers in an office-like environment.[49] The 108 participants were recruited from introductory psychology classes. The researchers wanted to study several things, including whether a worker's feelings of personal control were affected by having the ability to lock out the performance monitoring and whether informing the person that he or she was being monitored affected performance.

The results show why it's important for employees to believe that they have some personal control over their environments. "Participants with the ability to delay or prevent electronic performance monitoring indicated higher feelings of personal control and demonstrated superior task performance."[50] The findings also suggest that if you *are* going to monitor employees' performance electronically, it's probably best not to let them know when they're actually being monitored. Participants who knew when they were being monitored expressed lower feelings of personal control than did those who were not told when they were being monitored.

By the way, managers can't assume that EPM will apply only to subordinates. For example, the Japanese company that controls 7-Eleven is gradually trying to impose an EPM system on its store managers both in Japan and in the United States. Like all 7-Eleven stores, the ones belonging to Michiharu Endo use a "point-of-sale" computer to let headquarters know each time he makes a sale. In the case of 7-Eleven's new EPM system, headquarters also monitors how much time Endo spends using the analytical tools built into the computerized cash register to track product sales, and how effective he is at weeding out underproductive products. Headquarters then ranks stores by how often their operators use the computer, as a sort of measure of how efficient they are.

Perhaps not surprisingly, the system has run into particular resistance in the United States. Many 7-Eleven managers, thinking that they had escaped the bureaucratic rat race by agreeing to take over their own stores, have been surprised at the degree of control to which this new EPM system has exposed them.[51]

Anti-Empowerment. If controls can reduce employees' feelings of personal control, they can obviously also undermine a company's empowerment efforts. Maintaining control in an age of empowerment can therefore be very tricky. Too much control can undermine your empowerment efforts. After all, empowerment basically means that employees self-manage their jobs, and they can hardly do this (or be motivated to do so) if someone is closely monitoring every decision they make. But empowerment without control can be equally deadly. Recall the overenthusiastic Nordstrom supervisors, for instance, whose empowerment and lack of oversight may have allowed them to pressure subordinates to underreport actual hours worked.

What is a manager to do? The answer is that managers can no longer rely just on traditional diagnostic, boundary, or even interactive control techniques, with all of their unintended consequences. In an age of empowered employees, managers must also emphasize employees' self-control, and their commitment to do their best for the company even if they're half a world away and out of sight of the headquarters staff.

Management writer Tom Peters put it this way:

> You are out of control when you are "in control." You are in control when you are "out of control." [The executive] who knows everything and who is surrounded by layers of staffers and inundated with thousands of pages of analyses from below may be "in control" in the classic sense but in fact really only has the illusion of control. The manager has tons of after-the-fact reports on everything, but (almost) invariably a control system and organization that's so ponderous that it's virtually impossible to respond fast enough even if a deviation is finally detected....In fact, you really are in control when thousands upon thousands of people, unbeknownst to you, are taking initiatives, going beyond job descriptions and the constraints of their box on the organization chart, to serve the customer better, improve the process, [or] work quickly with a supplier to nullify a defect.[52]

Commitment-Based Control

As companies expand worldwide and compete in fast-changing markets, the problems of relying on traditional controls have become increasingly apparent. In England several years ago the great banking firm Barings—almost 400 years old—was virtually destroyed by the trading practices of a lone rogue trader in Singapore named Nicholas Leeson. In the U.S., Sears took a $60 million charge against earnings after it admitted that some of its service writers and mechanics had recommended unnecessary automobile repairs to customers. In Canada, a great deal of damage was done to the Better Business Bureau when public questions were raised about whether large amounts of money that were paid to its president were properly authorized.

Problems like these were not—and probably could not have been—anticipated by traditional controls like budgets and accounting reports. Particularly today, when markets change quickly and more employees are empowered, managers need a way to ensure that employees won't let activities slip out of control, or that, if they do, the managers will discover it before catastrophe strikes. Harvard professor and control expert Robert Simons puts it this way:

> A fundamental problem facing managers [today] is how to exercise adequate control in organizations that demand flexibility, innovation, and creativity....In most organizations operating in dynamic and highly competitive markets, managers cannot spend all their time and effort making sure that everyone is doing what is expected. Nor is it realistic to think that managers can achieve control by simply hiring good people, aligning incentives, and hoping for the best. Instead, today's managers must encourage employees to initiate process improvements and new ways of responding to customers' needs—but in a controlled way.[53]

Companies are therefore increasingly relying on employees' self-control to keep things "under control." One sign of this is the widespread use of empowerment self-managing teams—giving the self-confidence, tools, training, and information they need to do their jobs as if they owned the firm. However, "managing yourself" is inconsistent with being controlled and monitored: You can't require or force people to be creative, for example. Control in an age of empowerment, as Robert Simons puts it, therefore requires new types of commitment-based control systems to "reconcile the conflict between creativity and control."[54]

Commitment-Based Control Systems

Managers use at least three systems for encouraging self-control and employee commitment: motivation techniques, belief systems, and commitment-building systems. Obviously, highly motivated employees are more likely to do their jobs correctly. We discussed motivation techniques at length in Chapter 11. In the remainder of this chapter we'll focus on using belief systems and commitment-building systems to encourage self-control.

Using Belief Systems and Values to Maintain Control

As we saw in Chapter 14, Leading Organizational Change, shared values can make it easier for companies to maintain control. Shared values like Wal-Mart's "hard work, honesty, neighborliness, and thrift" provide a common ideology. Shared values give all employees a sort of built-in compass, one that gives them the direction and sense of purpose that's required to do the job right, no matter how far away from headquarters they are, and without a rule book or a supervisor to watch their every move.

The idea that shared values work in this way is not just theoretical. For example, Burns and Stalker, in their study of British industry, found that organic (highly innovative) organizations achieved coordinated action in the absence of formal rules and a chain of command by relying

> on the development of a common culture, of a dependable constant system of shared values about the common interests of the working community and about the standards and criteria used in it to judge achievement, individual contributions, expertise, and other matters by which a person or a combination of people are evaluated. A system of shared values of this kind is expressed and visible in a code of conduct, a way of dealing with other people.[55]

In a study of successful and long-lived companies, James Collins and Jerry Porras made precisely the same observations. In their book *Built to Last* they describe how firms like Boeing, Disney, General Electric, Merck, and Motorola put enormous effort into creating shared values, values that answer questions such as "What are we trying to achieve together?" and "What does this organization stand for?"[56] As they say,

> More than at any time in the past companies will not be able to hold themselves together with the traditional methods of control: hierarchy, systems, budgets, and the like. Even "going into the office" will become less relevant as technology enables people to work from remote sites. The bonding glue will increasingly become *ideological.*[57]

In explaining why shared values and organizational culture are so important for managing change, writers like Burns and Stalker emphasize that a strong set of shared values "allows for coordination without control, adaptation without chaos."[58] In other words, employees who "buy into" your company's values don't need to be coaxed, prodded, or controlled into doing the right thing: They'll do the right thing because they believe that it's the right thing to do.

What sorts of shared values and beliefs do change-oriented, responsive companies encourage? Core values in firms like these emphasize caring deeply about not just customers, but stockholders and employees too, and valuing the processes—such as empowerment—that can create useful change. They also value willingly initiating change when needed, even if this might entail some risks. Teamwork, openness, candour, trust, and being number one are other values that are stressed.

Commitment-Building Systems

Most experts would probably agree that the most powerful way for a firm to get things done is to synchronize its goals with those of its employees. Creating such a synthesis is essentially what building commitment is all about.[59]

commitment
The relative strength of an individual's identification with and involvement in an organization.

Researcher Richard Steers defines **commitment** as the relative strength of an individual's identification with and involvement in an organization. He says that commitment is characterized by a strong belief in and acceptance of the organization's goals and values, a willingness to exert considerable effort on behalf of the organization, and a strong desire to maintain membership in the organization.[60] Employee commitment therefore exists when an employee comes to think of the organization's goals in personal terms and to incorporate them into his or her own goals.[61]

Creating commitment means taking the steps needed to synthesize employee and company goals and create self-motivated employees. It requires a multi-faceted, systematic approach, one that depends on using virtually all of the management skills you've learned in this book. In particular, you'll have to tie together what you know about planning, organizing, and staffing, and what you know about people. Steps for building employee commitment include the following.

Foster People-First Values. Building employee commitment usually starts by establishing a strong foundation of "people-first values." Firms that hold to these values literally put their people first: They trust them, assume that their employees are their most important assets, believe strongly in respecting their employees as individuals and treating them fairly, and maintain a relentless commitment to each employee's welfare.

Research indicates that firms do at least four things to institutionalize such values and create a people-first culture: "they clarify what they want, they codify it, they hire and indoctrinate, and they walk the talk."

Encourage Two-Way Communication. Commitment is built on trust, and trust requires two-way communication. Managers in firms like Saturn, Federal Express, and GE do more than express a willingness to hear and be heard. They also establish programs that guarantee two-way communications. As explained in Chapter 12, at least four types of programs are typically employed: guaranteed fair treatment programs for filing grievances and complaints, "speak up" programs for voicing concerns and making inquiries, periodic survey programs for expressing opinions, and various top-down programs for keeping employees informed.

Build a Sense of Shared Fate and Community. Firms that score highly on commitment also work hard to encourage a sense of community and shared fate. They do so by pursuing what Rosabeth Moss Kanter calls commonality, communal work, and regular work contact and ritual.[62]

They usually start by instituting policies that emphasize to employees that "we're all in this together." In many new Internet companies, for instance, there's a deliberate effort to avoid status differences, and all of the managers and employees often just share one large space, perhaps (as at Sears) just with some movable cubicles. At Toyota motor manufacturing in Lexington, Kentucky, all of the office employees (including the president) similarly share one large space with no cubicles or offices at all. You've probably noticed that many employers today have eliminated status differences like executive washrooms and executive parking spaces; these, too, are usually efforts at building a sense of community, a sense, in other words, that "we're all in this together."

Managers can further emphasize this sense of community by encouraging joint effort and communal work. At Saturn, new employees are quickly steeped in the terminology and techniques of teamwork: There are no employees in the plant, only team members working together on "communal tasks" (like installing all dashboard components).

Team training begins during the employees' initial orientation, as new members meet their teams and are trained in the interpersonal techniques that make for good teamwork. The resulting closeness is then enhanced by empowering work teams to recruit and select their own new members. Periodic job rotation reinforces the sense that everyone is sharing all of the work.

Rosabeth Moss Kanter found that the feeling of "we're all in this together" is further enhanced by bringing individual employees into regular contact with the group as a whole.[63] Ben & Jerry's hosts monthly staff meetings in the receiving bay of its Waterbury, Vermont, plant. It also has a "joy gang," whose function is to organize regular "joy events," including Cajun parties, ping-pong contests, and "manufacturing appreciation day."

Ben & Jerry's
www.benjerry.com

Thanks to the Internet, employees don't necessarily have to be at the same location in order to feel that they're part of a close-knit community. For example, we saw that by using Internet-based group communication systems such as Tribal Voice (see Chapter 12, page 403), companies can build virtual communities by letting teams of employees communicate easily and in real time, even if their members are dispersed around the globe.[64] For example, as one expert put it, "the sales department could hold forums and share information in an interactive community."

Particularly given the ability of today's Internet software to provide video-based links, real-time voice messaging, instant messaging, and text-to-speech facilities, belonging to a virtual community can help build the feeling that the employees are "in the same boat together" and are members of a community. As one observer put it, "when people interact in a virtual community, there is an exchange of ideas and information, which becomes powerful and generates excitement."[65]

Provide a Vision. Committed employees need missions and visions to which to be committed, missions and visions that they can say "are bigger than we are." Having such missions means that workers become almost soldiers in a crusade that allows them to redefine themselves in terms of an ideology. Commitment in high-commitment firms thus derives in part from the power of the firm's mission and from the willingness of the employees to acquiesce, if need be, to the needs of the firm for the good of achieving its mission.

As we saw in Chapter 9, many firms today practise **value-based hiring**. Instead of looking just at an applicant's job-related skills, these firms try to get a sense of the individual's personal qualities and values; identify common experiences and values that may signal the applicant's fit with the firm; give applicants realistic previews of what to expect; and usually end up rejecting a large number of applicants. In short, they foster commitment in part by putting enormous effort into interviewing and screening to find people whose values are already consistent with the firm's.

value-based hiring
Putting enormous effort into interviewing and screening to find people whose values are already consistent with the firm's.

Use Financial Rewards and Profit Sharing. Although you may not be able to buy commitment, most firms don't try to build it without good financial rewards. Intrinsic motivators like work involvement, a sense of achievement, and a feeling of oneness are not enough. To paraphrase psychologist Abraham Maslow, you can't appeal to someone's need to achieve until you've filled his or her belly and made that person secure. That is why Rosabeth Moss Kanter says that "entrepreneurial incentives that give teams a piece of the action are highly appropriate in collaborative companies."[66]

Encourage Employee Development and Self-Actualization. Few needs are as strong as the need to fulfil our dreams, to become all that we are capable of being. In Chapter 11, we saw that Abraham Maslow said that the ultimate need is "the desire to become more and more what one is, to become everything that one is capable of becoming." Self-actualization, to Maslow, meant that "what man can be, he *must* be...it refers to the desire for self-fulfillment, namely, to this tendency for him to become actualized in what he is potentially."[67]

At work, actualizing does not just mean promotions. Certainly, promotions are important. But the real question is whether employees get the opportunity to develop and use all of their skills and become, as Maslow would say, all that they can be. Training employees to expand their skills and to solve problems, enriching their jobs, empowering employees to plan and inspect their own work, and helping them to continue their education and to grow are some other ways to accomplish employee self-actualization. One Federal Express manager described his firm's commitment to actualizing employees as follows:

> At Federal Express, the best I can be is what I can be here. I have been allowed to grow with Federal Express. For the people at Federal Express, it's not the money that draws us to the firm. The biggest benefit is that Federal Express…gave me the confidence and self-esteem to become the person I had the potential to become.[68]

Summary: Earning Employee Commitment

"Achieving control in an age of empowerment" depends on fostering employees' self-control. Motivation techniques (like those discussed in Chapter 11) and building belief systems are two important ways to tap such self-control. Another powerful way to do so is to get the employees to actually think of the company's goals as their own—to get their commitment to the company and its mission, in other words. Doing so isn't easy; it will require most of your management skills and the creation of an integrated commitment-oriented management system, since you must

- foster people-first values
- encourage extensive two-way communication
- build a sense of shared fate and community
- provide a vision
- use value-based hiring
- use financial rewards and profit sharing
- encourage self-actualizing

Doing this is obviously not as easy as just monitoring everything that employees do, or raking them over the coals when they don't reach their budgets or when some other problem means that "things are out of control." But in an age of self-managing teams, fostering self-control is an increasingly important approach for ensuring that activities produce the desired results.

dards of ethical behaviour and codes of conduct to which employees are expected to adhere. Interactive controls involve managers talking face to face with employees to find out how everything is going. Interactive strategic control is an example; it is a real-time method of monitoring both a strategy's effectiveness and the underlying assumptions on which the strategy is built.

4. **List the unintended behavioural consequences of controls.** A big problem with relying on traditional controls is that they can lead to unintended, undesirable, and often harmful employee reactions, such as behavioural displacement, gamesmanship, operating delays, negative attitudes, and reduced empowerment.

5. **Illustrate how managers can use belief systems and employee commitment to maintain better control.** Shared values can make it easier for companies to maintain control. Shared values provide a common ideology. They give all employees a sort of built-in compass, one that gives them the direction and sense of purpose that is required to do the job right, even if no supervisor is watching them. Achieving control in an age of empowerment means relying on employees' self-control. Motivation techniques and building belief systems are two important ways to tap such self-control. Another powerful way is to get employees to actually think of the company's goals as their own (commitment).

6. **Give examples of the factors that contribute to employee commitment.** Employee commitment is characterized by a strong belief in, and acceptance of, the organization's goals and values. Commitment can be increased by fostering people-first values, encouraging two-way communication, building a sense of shared fate and community, providing a vision, using financial rewards and profit sharing, and encouraging employee development and self-actualization.

TYING IT ALL TOGETHER

In this book—and in this and the preceding 14 chapters—we talked about the management process, namely planning, organizing, leading, and controlling. Since this is a textbook, we necessarily covered the topics sequentially, one topic at a time, but as you can probably imagine, that's not the way managers really manage on a day-to-day basis. In other words, you generally won't have the luxury of spending Monday planning, Tuesday organizing, Wednesday and Thursday leading, and Friday controlling. Instead, you'll be doing all of these tasks simultaneously. For example, as part of your planning function you'll be sitting with your subordinates trying to formulate goals and to motivate them to accept them. You may be monitoring and controlling the progress of a project, only to discover that the people staffing the project are not up to the job, or that the milestones you set when the project was planned are no longer valid. Management is really an integrated, "tying it all together" process, in other words.

That fact is particularly evident when it comes to controlling and building commitment, the subject of the present chapter. For one thing, planning and controlling are merely two sides of the same coin: What you control and how you're doing depends entirely on where you want to go, so that deciding where planning leaves off and controlling begins is bound to be somewhat arbitrary.

Similarly, effectively controlling your organization will demand all of the people skills you can muster. For one thing, employees can be enormously creative when it comes to getting around control systems; getting them to *not* want to get around those systems is therefore a very demanding task. For another (and perhaps more important), "controlling someone" is usually not the best way to stay in control, particularly today. You can lower your "control costs"—not to mention your aggravation level—enormously, by getting your employees to want to do a great job; doing this is essentially a behavioural, not a technical, process.

When you ask most people how they maintain control, their first responses might be "we use budgets," "we use time clocks," or "we watch what our people are doing." But getting employees to want to do a great job is in many respects the best way to keep your firm under control, and doing so, as we saw, relies on behavioural activities like fostering people-first values, encouraging two-way communications, and building a sense of shared fate and community. And its just such "integrating the people side of management into all that they do" that many top managers do best.

CRITICAL THINKING EXERCISES

1. The traditional approach in the 20th century was to control as many aspects of the workplace as possible by attempting to control and predict behaviour and by structuring behaviour in hierarchical organizations with little freedom for individuals to express their own ideas beyond the rules, procedures, and regulations. Changing times are calling for new forms of control in organizations based on teams, knowledge workers, and discontinuous change; that is, the status quo is not just moved forward but new questions and answers are needed. If we have flat organizations, leaders as coaches, workers in autonomous teams, employees changing jobs frequently, a globalized economy, and uncertainty in world affairs, what new forms of control do we need? Speculate on the means and ends for change in the 21st century.

2. We are increasingly dependent on technology and the flow of information provided by means such as the Internet. Yet there is ongoing debate about the control and privacy aspects of both the Internet and intranets. What do you think about using electronic monitoring technology as a control device? What about the privacy issues involved? Should anyone be able to monitor us and our use of computers?

EXPERIENTIAL EXERCISES

1. You are one of the founding engineers of your six-month-old firm, and you brought to the firm values of environmental awareness, quality, and excellence. These values have united the original members, but you are concerned that they might change with the addition of 50 new people needed by your quickly growing company to meet demand. What type of control system would you develop to ensure that your values are adhered to, based on the concepts discussed in this chapter?

2. When you next eat at a fast food restaurant, or go to the gas station to fill up your tank or get service, or go shopping at the grocery store, note the control systems in place. Then be prepared to discuss them in class in terms of what you have read in this chapter.

INTERNET EXERCISE

Building organizational commitment is central to all companies. At the heart of Magna International's operating structure is an entrepreneurial culture that builds ownership and inspires pride in its employees. Visit Magna's Web site at www.magnaint.com. Once there, check out "Culture: Magna's Corporate Constitution" and "Foundation: Magna Employee's Charter."

1. What is it about Magna, and what it offers, that builds commitment?

2. Which of the benefits offered would be most important to you?

3. In what ways does the development of the culture and values of the company operate as a form of control?

Second Cup Ltd.

With 177 retail outlets, Second Cup Ltd. is one of Canada's dominant retailers of specialty coffee. Specialty retailing is a competitive business, and Second Cup has its share of competitors: A.L. Van Houtte Ltd. (Montreal), Timothy's Coffees of the World Inc. (Toronto), and Starbucks Coffee Co. (Toronto). With about 40 percent of its sales coming from specialty coffee, the company actively seeks out contracts with suppliers of high-quality beans to attract customers.

Almost all of Second Cup's retail outlets are franchised. Since the average transaction is small, customer loyalty is extremely important. If a franchisee loses a customer, it is not just a $2 sale that is being lost. It could mean $2 per day for 10 years, or almost $5000.

New franchisees must attend Coffee College, which includes sessions on how to recognize high-quality coffee. A company consultant taste-tests every sample of beans purchased by the company. In fact, each batch of product is tested at least 70 times before it is sent to the retail outlets. One weekend, two head office employees went to a mall to conduct a taste-test between a Second Cup blend and a supermarket coffee. Consumers overwhelmingly selected the Second Cup offering.

It can cost franchisees as much as $225 000 to open a store (including a $20 000 franchising fee). A typical franchisee keeps about 20 percent of revenue as profit. Franchisees are expected to be absolutely dedicated to the business. Applicants are screened closely and interviewed at least three different times. The company receives over 100 franchise applications each year, but accepts only about one-quarter of them.

Second Cup demands that its franchisees work full-time in their store and have no other business on the side. They must also agree to run their franchise *exactly* as Second Cup stipulates, including passing the course at Coffee College. And, they must *love* to drink coffee. The company feels that franchisees will not be truly dedicated unless they love the product. Franchisees are also exhorted to apply high standards when hiring employees. Second Cup tells them to hire employees with four qualities: a happy face, good grooming, a high energy level, and a love of coffee.

To check up on how franchisees are operating, head office sends out "mystery shoppers" to test staff members and rate the store's appearance. Field consultants from head office also visit the various retail outlets to assess how things are going. Some franchisees object to both of these tactics, arguing that it is too authoritarian and restricts their freedom. Other franchisees say that while they may be a bit upset when a visit occurs, they recognize that their store will be more profitable if they stick to the company plan.

Questions

1. Discuss the various control techniques that are being employed by the head office of Second Cup.

2. At what stage in the controlling process are each of these control techniques being used?

Second Cup Ltd.
www.secondcup.com

Belief Systems and Controls at Intel

In Case 11-2, we considered motivation at Intel. Here we look at the same case with a focus on the control issues covered in this chapter.

Andy Grove, CEO of Intel, once called his company the laboratory of contemporary management. The maker of the famous Pentium chip that drives most of today's desktop computers employs over 64 000 employees to launch previously unheard of technologies that can unseat market leaders. Grove developed a phrase that described what he considered to be an essential way for managers of high-tech companies to operate: "only the paranoid survive." Could Intel control its managers in a "paranoid" environment? Were values and norms going to be sufficiently strong to keep the managers in a high-powered company in line?

The semiconductor industry is known for its tremendous pace of change. As a $27-billion-a-year company with a great track record of success, it might be easy for Intel to become complacent; hence Grove's warning, "only the paranoid survive." To Grove, paranoia is healthy. To be sure, he is not describing the irrational fear a true paranoid would have. What he is describing is a need for constant vigilance. To keep their managers motivated to stay in constant touch with their changing world, Intel has installed a complex management motivation and control system.

Intel has grouped its human resource practices into three areas: benefits, and compensation, flexible work options and benefits and personal development and training. Central to the Intel system is the value of rewarding individual excellence. Intel's merit-based performance system ties compensation increases and career advancement opportunities to personal performance.

Intel uses three basic types of incentive programs: an employee cash bonus program, a general bonus program, and stock incentives. The bonus programs are generally profit-sharing programs with the unique twist of rewarding both company performance and the performance of the small group in which the employee participates. Stock programs included a stock options program and stock participation plan. In both programs, Intel subsidizes the purchase of company stock. The value of share ownership among managers is well documented; the more shares a manager holds in Intel, the greater the effect of company performance on that employee's compensation.

Intel also offers a variety of performance awards. Awards may or may not involve financial incentives, but they always involve personal recognition. Managers can achieve awards that lead to formal recognition at the corporate level or spontaneous employee to employee awards at the department level. Intel also uses a number of alternative work schedule arrangements (each business group can establish their own methods and frameworks). The range of methods is quite broad and includes compressed workweeks; part-time positions; telecommuting; personal absence days; and family, medical, and personal leaves.

Intel is involved closely with the intellectual renewal of its employees, its core resource. In 1998, Intel spent more than $300 million for ongoing employee education. Under Grove's leadership, Intel has developed a university that offers more than 3400 courses worldwide; employees may also receive full reimbursement for tuition, books, and fees for university level courses and programs that have present or future application at Intel. Intel has also developed and launched a formal mentoring system.

While there are formal control systems at Intel, there is also a great reliance on the individual self-control of managers and professional staff. By sharing their vision and values, and developing incentives to reinforce those values, the top management team at Intel is expressing their belief that motivated employees will control themselves to the good of the firm. So while Grove speaks of only the paranoid surviving, his company has invoked a full range of control mechanisms to help its employees succeed. Still, the competitive dynamics in Intel's industry make it one of the most demanding competitive environments in the world. Has Intel installed the correct mix of motivational methods to assure its survival and success?

Questions

1. In what ways do Intel's compensation packages function as a control system?
2. To what extent do you feel a company can rely on the self-control of its employees?
3. Would traditional control systems work in the "high-velocity" environment in which Intel operates?

Keeping Things Under Control at KnitMedia

KnitMedia's plans to establish a network of Knitting Factory clubs around the world means that it will need sophisticated new methods for maintaining control. That was one of the reasons why Mark Harabedian was asked to join the management team. Harabedian has an accounting degree and about 15 years of strong systems background in various companies ranging from start-ups to rapidly growing firms. When he came in, the first thing he needed to do was "some cleanup work," as well as to choose an auditor to review the company's financial situation.

Harabedian has already made many control systems changes. For example, he instituted an accounts payable approval process: A manager now needs to approve every bill that has to be paid. He also installed a new budgeting process: "All the managers came back to me with information that we put into financial plans, and we put a budget together. There's a budget of employee spending, capital improvements, and so on. There are also budgets for the Web site activity, the festival activity, and the club activity." These new systems, says Harabedian, help show the management team what they're going to spend for things like capital improvements in the future. Now they can ensure that money is available, and also that budget figures are not exceeded.

That's just the tip of the iceberg when it comes to maintaining control at KnitMedia. As Harabedian points out, the company also has extensive retail sales of things like CDs. And it has to be able to monitor the finances of the Knitting Factory clubs in Los Angeles and Berlin, since the cash coming in—when people pay admission, for example, or buy a soft drink—can "disappear" if the company isn't careful. KnitMedia therefore should have a way for each individual club to report to company headquarters in New York the exact ticket, merchandise, and bar sales on each night. That way Michael Dorf and his staff can keep a firm grip on revenues generated by each club. The management team would like you to review its current control efforts and to make some recommendations regarding possible improvements.

Team Exercises and Questions

Use what you learned in this chapter to answer the following questions from Michael Dorf and his management team:

1. How do other companies, including specifically restaurants and nightclubs, maintain control over their national or global locations?

2. Given what you know about the enthusiasm with which managers and employees work for KnitMedia and about our culture, to what extent do you think we can rely on employee commitment to ensure that things stay under control?

3. What specifically would you suggest we do to foster increased commitment? Which of our company's values do you think would be most influential in keeping things under control? Why?

4. Finding out two weeks later that an employee may have run off with several days' worth of club receipts is pretty useless, since at that point the money is probably gone for good. What controls would you suggest we implement to try to ensure that (1) an employee can't hide any significant amount of money that comes into a club, and (2) if someone does manage to hide some cash, we can find out about it as quickly as possible?

5. We know that boundary control systems basically lay out the boundaries within which employees must operate, for example, in terms of the ethical and other rules of behaviour that employees are required to follow. What are some of the important ethical and other rules you think we should enforce to ensure that things stay under control?

Managing Change with Information Technology

MANAGEMENT IN THE INFORMATION AGE

Throughout this book, we've seen how managers are using information technology like computers and the Internet to increase their effectiveness. In this appendix, we'll take a closer look at what information technology is, and how it is used to manage organizations.

Information technology refers to any processes, practices, or systems that facilitate processing and transporting information. You are already very familiar with information technology's modern components (e.g., personal computers, management information systems, cellular phones, facsimile machines, e-mail, and voice mail). Information technologies like these have dramatically altered the way that people do their jobs and the way that companies are managed.

The Nature of Information

Information is data presented in a form that is meaningful to the recipient.[1] "Information," as Peter Drucker has said, "is data endowed with relevance and purpose."[2] Knowledge, on the other hand, has been defined as "information…distilled via study or research and augmented by judgment and experience."[3]

To put these definitions into managerial terms, consider this example. PepsiCo, Inc., wants to determine why consumers are not buying its new Pepsi Light clear drink. To search for an answer, the company's market researchers conduct a survey containing 25 multiple-choice questions. The answers to the questions are put on computer disks, where by themselves they would appear to the untrained eye as nothing but long streams of unrelated numbers.

When market researchers summarize these *data* for presentation to management, the result is *information*, such as graphs showing average responses by age level and other demographic traits for each question. The marketing department can then apply its *knowledge* to draw meaningful conclusions, such as, in PepsiCo's case, a hypothesis about why older consumers seem less inclined to purchase Pepsi Light than are younger ones.

Playdium Entertainment Corp. of Toronto operates game parks offering video and virtual reality games for people in the 18 to 34 age bracket. Some Canadian companies send their employees to these game parks to build team spirit or to increase their confidence as individuals. Customers can play any game they want by inserting a "Playcard" into a game. From these Playcards, Playdium can gather all sorts of demographic data about its customers. This information allows the company to specifically target the needs of its customers. For example, Playdium might create a "nightclub" atmosphere on Friday nights and a more "family-oriented" atmosphere on Saturday mornings.[4]

What Is "Information Quality"?

Managers are inundated with information all the time. What they need is high-quality information. High-quality information has several characteristics.[5] As in the PepsiCo example, high-quality information must be *pertinent* and related to the problem at hand. It also must be *timely*. For example, the Pepsi Light survey information would be useless if it came in two years after the product was pulled off the shelf. Good information also must be *accurate*. Finally, good information reduces *uncertainty*, which we can define as the

information technology
Any processes, practices, or systems that facilitate processing and transporting information.

information
Data presented in a form that is meaningful to the recipient.

Playdium
Entertainment Corp.
www.playdium.com

absence of information about a particular area of concern.[6] In the PepsiCo example, to meet these last criteria the survey information should help the marketing manager answer the question "Why aren't people buying Pepsi Light the way we thought they would?"

Yet, even good information is relatively useless without the knowledge that comes from analysis, interpretation, and explanation.[7] The role of organizational information technology is thus not just to generate and transfer more (or even better-quality) information. It is to contribute to the manager's knowledge of what is happening, through analysis, interpretation, and explanation. Its ultimate aim is to make the manager's company more competitive.

Data mining is one example.[8] This means using special computer software to analyze vast amounts of customer data stored in a company's data banks to obtain information the firm can use to be more competitive. When it comes to making decisions, managers usually don't want to be deluged with truckloads of numbers; they want to receive reports that let them see meaningful patterns and relationships. New data-mining software products like Intelligent Miner from IBM let them do just that.

Knowledge Management

Knowledge—no matter how high-quality it is—is totally useless if the people who need that knowledge don't know that it exists or can't get to it. This fact has given rise to a new area called **knowledge management**, which one expert refers to as "the task of developing and exploiting organizations' tangible and intangible knowledge resources."[9] The company's tangible knowledge assets include things like patents, licences, and information on customers and competitors. Intangible knowledge assets refer to the knowledge that employees possess, including their experiences and the methods they've discovered for solving problems. The basic purpose of knowledge management "is to leverage and reuse resources that already exist in the organization so that people will seek out best practices rather than reinvent the wheel."[10]

knowledge management
The task of developing and exploiting organizations' tangible and intangible knowledge resources.

As we noted in earlier chapters, using computerized systems to enable employees to easily access their companies' knowledge bases has proved to be quite a boon to companies. For example, IBM consultants reportedly cut their proposal-writing time from an average of 200 to 30 hours because they can now share information.[11] The sales and technical support reps at Dell Computer Corp.'s call centres solve more problems more easily thanks to a central knowledge base that advises them on what questions to ask and what solutions to suggest. Xerox Corp.'s copier repairers have reduced average repair time by 50 percent thanks to knowledge based on suggestions and solutions from the company's repair staff.

Managers' Requirements for Information

Managers at different levels in the organization require different types of information.[12] First-line managers (like the front-desk manager at a Four Seasons Hotel) tend to focus on short-term, operational decisions. At this level, information should emphasize operational activities such as accounts receivable, order entry, inventory control, and cash management.

Middle managers tend to focus more on intermediate-range decisions, like events that might affect the company in the coming year or so. They therefore require information for use in budget analysis, short-term forecasting, and variance analysis. A marketing manager, for example, needs consumer data to plan for the next advertising campaign.

Top managers (including the firm's CEO and vice-presidents) focus more on long-range, strategic decisions. They therefore need information that enables them to make decisions on factory location, mergers and acquisitions, and new-product planning. These different information requirements mean that there is a need for different types of information systems at each level of the organization.

INFORMATION SYSTEMS FOR MANAGING ORGANIZATIONS

What Is an Information System?

An **information system** is a set of people, data, technology, and organizational procedures that work together to retrieve, process, store, and disseminate information to support de-

information system
A set of people, data, technology, and organizational procedures that work together to retrieve, process, store, and disseminate information to support decision making and control.

cision making and control.[13] We'll focus here on *managerial* information systems, which are systems that support managerial decision making and control.

Information systems are more than computers. The information system also usually includes the organization or major parts of it, such as the employees who input data into the system and retrieve its output. Managers are (or should be) part of the information system, since it's their specific need for information that the information system is designed to serve.

Levels of Information Systems.

transaction processing systems
Provide detailed information about most short-term, daily activities, such as accounts payables and order status.

management information systems
Provide middle managers with reports regarding matters such as current versus historical sales levels.

decision-support systems
Provide middle managers with reports regarding matters such as current versus historical sales levels.

Because information requirements at each organizational level tend to be unique to that level, there is a corresponding hierarchy of information systems: from strategic-level decisions systems at the top of the organization to operational systems at the bottom of the organization.[14] As shown in Figure 15A.1, executive support systems provide information for strategic-level decisions on matters such as five-year operating plans. **Transaction processing systems** provide detailed information about short-term, daily activities, such as accounts payables and order status. **Management information systems** and **decision-support systems** provide middle managers with reports regarding matters such as current versus historical sales levels.

Transaction Processing Systems

A *transaction* is an event that affects the business. Hiring an employee, selling merchandise, paying an employee, and ordering supplies are transactions. In essence, transaction processing systems collect and maintain detailed records regarding the organization's transactions. These records are generally used to make operational-level decisions. For example, a university must know which students have registered, which have paid fees, which members of the faculty are teaching, and what secretaries are employed in order to conduct its business.

TYPES OF SYSTEMS

Executive Support Systems (ESS)

Strategic-Level Systems				
5 year	**5 year**	**5 year**	**Profit**	**Labour**
sales trend forecasting	operating plan	budget forecasting	planning	planning

Management Information Systems (MIS)

Decision-Support Systems (DSS)

Management-Level Systems				
Sales management	**Inventory control**	**Annual budgeting**	**Capital investment analysis**	**Relocation analysis**
Sales region analysis	Production scheduling	Cost analysis	Pricing/profitability analysis	Contract cost analysis

Knowledge Work Systems (KWS)

Office Automation Systems (OAS)

Knowledge-Level Systems		
Engineering workstations	**Graphics workstations**	**Managerial workstations**
Word processing	Document imaging	Electronic calendars

Transaction Processing Systems (TPS)

Operational-Level Systems				
Sales and Marketing	**Manufacturing**	**Finance**	**Accounting**	**Human Resources**
	Machine control	Securities trading	Payroll	Compensation
Order tracking	Plant scheduling		Accounts	Training and development
Order processing	Material movement control	Cash management	Accounts receivable	Employee record keeping

FIGURE 15A.1
Objectives of Information Systems of Each Organizational Level

The collection and maintenance of such day-to-day transactions were two of the first procedures to be computerized in organizations. As is still the case today, early transaction processing systems automated the collection, maintenance, and processing of mostly repetitive transactions. Examples include computing withholding taxes and net pay, and processing accounts payable cheques.

Transaction processing systems (TPS) can be put to five uses.[15] They may be used to *classify data* based on common characteristics of a group (such as finding all sales employees with five years' service). They are used to do *routine calculations* (such as computing net pay after taxes and deductions for each employee) and can be used for *sorting* (for instance, grouping invoices by postal code). The TPS can also be used for *summarization* (such as summarizing for each department's manager what his or her average payroll is compared to the other departments). Finally, the TPS can be used for *storage* (for example, storing payroll information for the past five years).

Management Information Systems

A management information system (MIS) provides decision support for managers by producing standardized, summarized reports on a regular basis.[16] It generally produces reports for longer-term purposes than typical transaction processing systems. In a university, for instance, a TPS is used to print class rolls and grade rolls. An MIS, in contrast, can measure and report class size and enrolment trends by department and by college. The deans can then use the MIS reports to increase or decrease class sizes or to drop some courses from next semester's schedule while adding others. Management information systems condense, summarize, and manipulate information derived from the organization's transaction processing systems. They then present the results in the form of routine summary reports to management, often with exceptions flagged for control purposes.[17]

Decision-Support Systems

Decision-support systems (DSS) "assist management decision making by combining data, sophisticated analytical models, and user-friendly software into a single powerful system that can support semi-structured or unstructured decision making."[18] In other words, systems like these can help managers make decisions that are relatively unstructured when compared to those addressed by the typical MIS. At a university, for instance, an MIS is used to make course addition and deletion decisions, decisions that are fairly routine. However, suppose the university's faculty threatens to strike. The university could use a decision-support system to estimate the impact on university revenues of having to drop various combinations of classes.

An MIS differs from a DSS in several ways.[19] A DSS is more capable of analyzing alternatives because decision-support systems let the user (in this case, the vice-president for academic affairs) include different subprograms showing how various components of the university (such as revenues and enrolments in various courses) are related. Furthermore, a DSS does not just rely on internal information from the transaction processing system the way that an MIS typically does. Instead, a DSS is built to absorb new external information in the analysis. Thus, our university's academic vice-president, faced with a strike, may want to include in her or his analysis an estimate of the likelihood that a number of the university's students will move across town to a competing school, given the competing school's ability (or inability) to expand its class offerings.

Table 15A.1 gives some examples of how companies use their DSS systems.

Executive Support Systems

Executive support systems (ESS) are information systems designed to help top-level executives acquire, manipulate, and use the information they need to maintain the overall strategic effectiveness of the company. Such systems often focus on providing top management with information to make strategic decisions. They help top management match changes in the firm's environment with the firm's existing and potential strengths and weaknesses.[20]

A university president could thus use an ESS to keep tabs on and analyze the following questions:

TABLE 15A.1 *Examples of DSS Systems Uses*

Airlines	Price and route selection
Petroleum Companies	Corporate planning and forecasting
Financial Corporations	Investment evaluation
Consumer Products Companies	Price, advertising, and promotion selection
Lumber Companies	Production optimization
Retail Companies	Price evaluation
Industrial Companies	Corporate planning and forecasting
Railways	Train dispatching and routing
Oil and Gas Exploration	Evaluation of potential drilling sites
Department of Defence	Defence contract analysis

Is the average student taking fewer courses?

Are costs for maintenance labour substantially higher than they have been in the past?

Is there a significant shift in the geographic areas from which most of our students come?

An ESS also makes it easy for executives to browse through the data. One executive describes the capability this way:

> I like to take a few minutes to review details about our customers, our manufacturers or our financial activities first hand. Having the details flow across the screen gives me a feel for how things are going. I don't look at each record, but glance at certain elements as they scroll by. If something looks unusual, it will almost jump out at me and I can find out more about it. But if nothing is unusual, I will know that, too.[21]

The top executive can also use an ESS to monitor a situation. Thus, a university president could use an ESS to monitor the new dining facilities management firm running the student cafeteria by reviewing information such as student usage, student complaints, and revenues. Executives also use ESS to facilitate environmental scanning. For example, a wealth of information is available in commercial computerized data banks, including financial information on tens of thousands of companies. Executives can use an ESS to tap into such data banks in order to glean competitive data regarding other firms in their industry. An ESS can also support analytical needs. For example, it may allow our university president to create "what if" scenarios that show the probable effects on university revenues of increasing faculty salaries or adding new programs. Finally, an ESS may enable the executive to get at data directly. Using their terminals and telephone lines, executives can use an executive support system to tap directly into the company's data files in order to get specific information that may be of interest, without waiting for others to assemble it.[22]

When executives at Montreal-based Teleglobe Inc. want answers to certain questions about financial matters, they can access the information almost immediately on their computers. By pressing the touch-sensitive screen, the executive can choose from various items on the menu (for example, current sales of an important product, or customer satisfaction levels). Information officers in each division of the company prepare the information in a form that can easily be retrieved by the CEO. Managers are not restricted to historical information; they can also make predictions by calling up the spreadsheet that forecasts next quarter's sales and then asking several "what if" questions to see how those changes will affect the financial results.[23]

Artificial Intelligence and Expert Systems

Artificial intelligence (AI) is the field of study that tries to simulate intelligent human thought with a computer. The application of AI that is most relevant to management is the expert system. An **expert system** duplicates the thinking processes of an expert in a particular area by using decision rules that are built into the system. Stated another way, expert systems allow managers to get advice from a computer that is much like the advice they would get from a human expert.

An expert system was created at Campbell's Soup when Aldo Cimino, a production engineer who knew more about soup making than anyone else, decided to retire. A computer programmer picked Cimino's brain to devise a system that would mimic his decision-making processes while he was making soup. After seven months of close cooperation between Cimino and the programmer, the project was completed. Now, Campbell Soup has all of the soup-making knowledge that Cimino possessed, even though he has long since retired.[24]

Enterprise-Wide Information Systems and the Company's "Digital Nervous System"

As we saw in Chapter 15, companies today are increasingly implementing enterprise-wide information systems. Basically, systems like these—produced by companies like SAP of Germany—are company-wide integrated computer systems that integrate firm's individual systems (such as order processing, production control, and accounting) to give managers "real-time," instantaneous information regarding the costs and status of every activity and project in the business.

Today, in other words, more and more managers don't rely on the sorts of executive management and transaction information systems that parallel the company's executive, managerial, and operational levels. Instead, enterprise-wide systems are being used to integrate these various systems. For example, a point-of-sale device at a Wal-Mart store might signal Levi Strauss to produce 50 more size-34 501 jeans. Levi's enterprise-wide system then automatically acknowledges the order, produces a production schedule, monitors the order's process, and provides top managers with real-time information regarding the profitability of that order as well as total Wal-Mart orders by geographic region for that day.

Bill Gates, Microsoft's chairman, says, "Like a human being, the company has to have an internal communication mechanism, a 'nervous system,' to coordinate its actions."[25] Like world-class athletes, world-class companies need superfast reflexes. And just as it's hard for someone to have great reflexes with a malfunctioning nervous system, companies with inadequate "digital nervous systems" can't respond quickly enough to customers' requests or competitors' moves. Enterprise-wide information systems like the one at Levi's can form the backbone of the digital nervous system. It's easier for companies with systems like these to literally "do business at the speed of thought."

And systems like these are already in place and working effectively at many firms. For example, Harmon Music Group uses a type of enterprise-wide system to integrate its order processing, production scheduling, and accounting systems and to thereby run its business very efficiently. Similarly, Deluxe Paper Payment Systems was able to dramatically improve its profitability by using information from its enterprise-wide information system to get many of its smaller customers to switch over to electronic clock ordering.

Yet installing one of these highly integrated systems can also be fraught with peril. For example, October 31, 1999, turned out to be a scary Halloween for Hershey Foods Corp. During the summer, "Hershey flipped the switch on a $112 million computer system that was supposed to automate and modernize everything from taking candy orders to putting pallets on trucks."[26] But instead of speeding the flow of orders and information, the system has apparently gummed up the works. Orders, even from huge customers like Wal-Mart, were being delayed, and Hershey sales reps had to call customers to find out what products they'd received, because the new information system couldn't tell which orders

artificial intelligence
The field of study that tries to simulate intelligent human thought with a computer.

expert system
A system that duplicates the thinking processes of an expert in a particular area by using decision rules that are built into the system.

Hershey's
www.hersheys.com

Hershey had delivered and which it had not. The snafu was a boon to competitors like Mars Inc. and Nestle, both of which saw their Halloween chocolate orders jump as customers scrambled to keep their shelves stocked with candy.

Part of the problem, experts now say, may be that Hershey tried to implement its system all at once, putting it online in what computer people call a "big bang" approach. Whatever the cause, it's apparent that while enterprise-wide information systems can certainly help managers to manage, implementing a project of that magnitude requires the most effective planning, organizing, leading, and controlling (in other words, management) skills that the company can muster.

NETWORKS FOR MANAGING ORGANIZATIONS

network
A group of interconnected computers, work stations, and computer devices (such as printers and data storage systems).

Organizations make extensive use of networks to manage their operations better. A **network** "is a group of interconnected computers, work stations or computer devices (such as printers and data storage systems)."[27] Local area networks (LANs), wide area networks (WANs), and distributed networks are three examples of managerial networks.

Local Area Networks

local area network (LAN)
A network that spans a limited distance, such as a building or several adjacent buildings, using the company's own telecommunications links.

A **local area network (LAN)** spans a limited distance, such as a building or several adjacent buildings, using the company's own telecommunications links (rather than common-carrier links such as those provided by Bell Canada's phone lines). In an office, a LAN may be used to support a work group information system such as e-mail, and a factory may use a LAN to link computers with computer-controlled production equipment.

More generally, LANs are used for one or more of the following reasons: to distribute information and messages (including e-mail); to drive computer-controlled manufacturing equipment; to distribute documents (such as engineering drawings from one department to another); to interconnect the LAN's computers with those of a public network such as Prodigy or the Internet; and, given the high cost of certain equipment such as laser printers, to make equipment sharing possible (including not just printers but disk storage file servers, for instance).

Wide Area Networks

wide area network (WAN)
A network that serves microcomputers over larger geographic areas, spanning distances that can cover a few kilometres or circle the globe.

Wide area networks (WANs) are networks that serve microcomputers over larger geographic areas, spanning distances that can cover a few kilometres or circle the globe. Early WANs used common-carrier networks; however, many firms today own their own wide area networks, which are essentially private, computerized telecommunications systems. The Benetton retail store chain uses its WAN to enable both store managers and headquarters staff to identify local trends and improve inventory and production management. The stores accumulate sales data during the day and keep them on computer disks. At night, another, larger computer at corporate headquarters polls the individual retail stores' computers, accessing data that are then transmitted over telephone lines back to headquarters. Here, the information is processed and a summary of sales trends is forwarded to headquarters and individual store managers.[28]

Benetton
www.benetton.com

As at Benetton, wide area networks are often used to achieve distributed processing. **Distributed processing** generally uses small local computers (such as point-of-sale systems) to collect, store, and process information, with summary reports and information sent to headquarters as needed.[29]

distributed processing
Uses small local computers (such as point-of-sale systems) to collect, store, and process information, with summary reports and information sent to headquarters as needed.

Managing and the Internet

While you are reading this page, millions of people around the world are "on the Internet," searching through libraries, talking to friends, and buying and selling products and services from firms ranging from Chapters to Sony. The value of the Internet lies in its ability to easily and inexpensively connect so many people from so many places. The miracle of the Internet is that no one owns it and it has no formal management structure. Instead, to become part of the Internet, an existing network simply pays a small registration fee and agrees to comply with certain electronic standards known as the Transmission Control Protocol/Internet Protocol (TCP/IP).

The boom in e-commerce has turned most businesspeople into Web believers. Soon it will be harder to find companies that don't use the Web than those that do. Consider just a few specific examples: Hershey Foods Corp. offers a personal address book and gift reminder service that reminds users of special dates and anniversaries, thus allowing them to conveniently send Hershey gifts to special people on special occasions. In July 1999, Barnes & Noble.com launched its music site. Another site, Online Office Supplies.com, is open 24 hours a day, 7 days a week, offering more than 30 000 products at reduced prices, again via the Internet.[30]

But these Internet-based sales sites are only the tip of the iceberg when it comes to managerial uses of the Internet. For one thing, since companies can, in a sense, get a "free ride" on the Internet, they can substantially reduce their communications costs by building their management systems around the Internet.

Other companies use the Internet for strategic planning. With so many firms having Web sites today, the Internet has become a useful device for collecting information on competitors, for example. One company, visiting a competitor's site, reportedly found a preview of an upcoming promotional campaign and was able to quickly revise its own plans to get a jump on its competitor.[31] Other companies actually build Web pages to help employees gather information about competitors or customers; the Web pages contain, for instance, links to published news accounts, press releases, and government statistics.[32]

The bottom line is that information technology and the Internet are literally helping managers to manage "at the speed of thought." Many or most of today's virtual corporations and strategic alliances—all of which depend for their existence on rapid, relatively inexpensive multimedia communications—would be impossible without such tools. Similarly, many team-based organizations would be unmanageable without systems such as Lotus Notes groupware, through which geographically dispersed team members can communicate virtually, "face to face." Indeed, when it comes to leading and influencing employees, information technology and the Internet now almost always play a major role.

When the president of Xerox recently wanted to motivate his troops, he sent them all what Xerox calls a "v-mail," a voice mail note that goes automatically to each employee's voice mailbox. Dell Computer, the direct-sales computer firm, relies heavily on information technology to stay close to its customers and to control the progress of its orders. For example, employees who take customers' calls work on PCs linked by a network to a large central computer that contains the company's customer database. As the calls come in, the telephone representatives input the information to the database and follow up on inquiries by triggering the mailing of customized sales letters to these customers. Customers can then easily track the progress of their orders on Dell's Web site, and can do this without tying up a Dell telephone representative's time. Thus, whether a manager is planning, organizing, leading, or controlling, information technology and the Internet are vital management tools today.

Getting Good Information from Focus Groups

Focus groups are often used by companies to gather information from a sample of consumers. For example, Happy Planet, a Vancouver-based juice company, used a focus group to determine what kind of people were most likely to buy its products. Focus groups usually involve 6 to 15 people in a discussion about a product or service offered by a company. A moderator leads the group discussion, and employees from the sponsoring company watch from behind a one-way mirror. After the session, researchers go through the data and try to find themes. Companies then make strategic decisions based on what they have heard from the focus group.

The idea behind focus groups is to allow people to interact in a fairly informal setting and then determine what they like and don't like about a company's product. But coordinators of focus groups say it's not that easy. People often cannot explain why they decide to buy certain products and services. It is also possible that people will lie about their preferences, or deceive themselves about their product preferences. Another challenge is the questionable recruiting of subjects. Some people actively seek out focus groups and become "regulars"; a focus group with several "regulars" is not representative of the general population, and may therefore render skewed results. One focus group, composed of young adults, viewed a proposed advertisement showing a couple engaging in passionate moments. They thought the advertisement was fine, but when it was actually aired many complaints came in—apparently older people thought the advertisement was in bad taste.

Because of these problems, people who run focus groups try to use several different methods to cross-reference their feedback and see if it makes sense. One technique involves "stacking" the focus group with some people who are there specifically to make positive statements about the company's product. The other people in the group (who are not aware that the group is stacked) will then argue with these people if they disagree with them. Another technique involves following consumers around for an entire day and looking for clues as to why they make certain purchases. Other focus groups involve the participants in different kinds of games to subtly glean information about peoples' attitudes towards products and services.

Properly used, focus groups can be very helpful. One focus group made up of snowboarders was given cameras and asked to document its leisure activity. The members came back with the expected pictures of beer and good times, but they also took pictures of expensive sports cars and stereo equipment. Based partly on these pictures, Option Snowboards (the sponsor of the focus group) developed an advertising campaign that appealed to mainstream attitudes about success. Geoff Power, president of Option, said there was no question that the advertising campaign had a positive impact on sales.

Questions

1. What is the difference between "data" and "information"? How is the activity (processes and outcomes) of focus groups related to these two terms? (Read the appendix to Chapter 15 before answering this and the following questions.)

2. Managers need high-quality information. What are the characteristics of high-quality information? Does the output of focus groups qualify as high-quality information? Explain.

3. Is the output of focus groups a tangible or intangible knowledge asset? Explain.

Video Resource: "Behind the Glass," *Venture* #734 (January 11, 2000).

Forensic Accounting

We've just gotten over the Livent scandal and then along comes Cinar, the Quebec animation house, with all of its various problems. Who's watching the numbers? Is anyone trying to do something? As it turns out, someone *is*. It is Al Rosen, Canada's leading forensic accountant (also known as "The Enforcer"). He has been busy ferreting out fast and loose accounting practices that make a company look better than it actually is. He is working hard to alert the world to these scam artists. Rosen is a frequent expert witness in court cases, and he has given so much information about questionable accounting practices at various firms to *Canadian Business* magazine that he is now on their masthead.

People have described Rosen as hard-nosed, a corporate muckraker, tough, arrogant, bitter, dark, and gloomy. He isn't deterred, he says, because these people haven't seen the evidence he has seen. If a client is caught playing fast and loose with accounting rules, lawyers rush to Rosen's office for advice.

Rosen is an expert at explaining how a company can play with numbers to make its dismal financial statement glow. Rosen's concern is that this can be easily achieved using Generally Accepted Accounting Principles (GAAP), the accountant's "Bible." He says that "crooked" companies look at GAAP and say, "Wow, I can use this stuff to make my company look good."

Rosen wants to blow the whistle on suspicious accounting, and one of the ways he is doing so is by writing a monthly exposé for mutual fund managers. So far he has examined 20 companies in detail. He gives an opinion on whether a given company is on the level, whether it should be watched carefully, or whether it is already a disaster. In the early 1990s, he offered the view that the accounting numbers generated by Cott Corp., the generic cola maker, were not telling the whole story, and the company was not as strong as it appeared. Cott, which was then a stock-market darling, blasted Rosen for his views, but time has proved Rosen right. Cott's stock dropped from nearly $40 per share in 1994 to just $10 per share in 1999.

Another company that's unhappy with Rosen is ski-resort operator Interwest. The company complained that Rosen's newsletter caused its stock to drop by 20 percent. It claims it was rock-solid, but that it was "bushwacked" by Rosen, simply because Rosen has a vendetta against standard accounting practices.

Rosen's mutual fund clients seek his advice regarding which companies are good and which ones are questionable. And, indeed, Rosen says that there are many strong Canadian companies that are perfectly good investments. Still, he will continue to do everything he can to make sure that people receive his message that accounting numbers may not be what they seem. At York University, he tells aspiring accountants not to "play the game." He suggests thinking beyond the numbers, and encourages them to think in non-traditional ways about accounting. He warns that a business deal can easily fall prey to slippery accounting practices.

Rosen is keen to be a source for the media. One of his favourite words in describing manipulators is "scumbag." He recognizes that many people think that his perspective is too negative, but he says there are plenty of cheerleaders for companies and someone needs to do serious analyses of their soundness. He says there are 1,000 cheerleaders, but no one (except him) is taking care of the other side.

So, corporate Canada beware: The Enforcer is watching.

Questions

1. What are the steps in the controlling process of management? What role does accounting play in this process?

2. At what stage of the production process (inputs, process, output) is accounting important?

3. What are the three main types of traditional control systems? In which of these three systems is accounting activity most obvious?

4. "As companies expand worldwide and compete in fast-changing markets, the problems of relying on traditional control systems have become apparent. Since accounting is very much a traditional system, the former emphasis on accounting should be replaced with a greater emphasis on methods of gaining employee commitment to the organization." Comment.

Video Resource: "On the Case with Al Rosen," *Venture* #745 (March 28, 2000).

Controlling and Building Commitment

For a growing organization like KnitMedia, the checks and balances of an effective control process become more important all the time. If they performed no other function than to let managers know when it is time to revise or change their plans, controls would still perform a valuable service. At most organizations, however, they do much more.

We've seen that a high degree of employee commitment to the brand, the product, or the organizational vision exists at KnitMedia. Vice-President of KnitMedia Labels Stephanie Oxley wants her staff members to feel that the company is their own, and that kind of identification with the organization is an equally strong goal among her colleagues. So employee commitment can already operate as a control in situations involving productivity and team effort, particularly in the more creative aspects of the organization.

As new Knitting Factory clubs are opened, both in the United States and abroad, a dual set of more traditional controls comes into play. Each club has its own local manager who is responsible for overseeing operations. These managers report to Ed Greer, senior vice-president of club operations. Greer has written a new operations manual for running the clubs that includes all kinds of housekeeping details, spelling out standards for cleaning and maintenance that are the responsibility of the club managers and night managers. At weekly management meetings for the New York staff, Greer personally reinforces the standards. He encourages his staff to walk frequently through the club (particularly before the doors open) to make sure that all is in order, from the supply of toilet paper in the rest rooms to the replacement of a broken light bulb. The artists' dressing rooms get the same meticulous attention as the rest of the club.

While "production rests completely in attention to details," as Greer says, it also begins at the top, with the simple question of whether the club is clearly visible from 100 metres away. Greer continually works with his staff to ensure that they can see the club's facilities as he sees them—and as expectant customers see them—and that they can follow through on their responsibilities for ensuring that every visitor's experience is a pleasant one.

Mark Harabedian, vice-president of finance, describes the ways in which cash inflows and outflows are controlled in the club's bar. Cash disappears easily, he admits, and it is necessary to have strong control systems to ensure that it all ends up in the safe at the end of the night. New cash registers have arrived that use touch screens; they also boast many inventory features and controls that will simplify the process of accurately measuring nightly cash income. In addition, weekly meetings keep the staff "ahead of the snowball," and monthly reports on bar performance are generated that measure average dollar spent, types of drinks sold and in what quantities, and so on.

A cheque approval process operates to control the outflow of funds, and stricter budgets are now drawn up, particularly for larger projects like building a new Web site, upgrading the organization's office computers, or adding to staff. CEO Michael Dorf jokes that the process of budgeting is so new that he still has trouble pronouncing the word, and sometimes has trouble adhering to the plan as well. But there is no question that this kind of financial control tool is critical to KnitMedia's future success.

Questions

Based on this case, the video, the text chapters, and your knowledge from other sources, answer the following:

1. Describe the types of controls at KnitMedia.
2. Do you think that the right types are being used in each area?
3. Could there be a downside to the increasing use of controls at KnitMedia?

Glossary

360-degree feedback An appraisal technique in which performance information is collected "all around" an employee, from his or her supervisors, subordinates, peers, and internal or external customers.

A

accommodation Can help calm an opponent who is not uncontrollably irate, but this is only a stop-gap measure, since the disagreement itself remains unresolved.

action research Collecting data about a group, department, or organization, and then feeding that data back to employees so they can analyze them and develop hypotheses about what the problems in the unit might be.

anchoring Unconsciously giving disproportionate weight to the first information you hear.

application form Requests information about factors like education, work history, and hobbies.

aroused motives Motives that express themselves in behaviour.

artificial intelligence The field of study that tries to simulate intelligent human thought with a computer.

attitude A predisposition to respond to objects, people, or events in either a positive or a negative way.

attributions The meanings given to actions.

authoritarian personality A person who is rigid and intolerant of ambiguity, tends to stereotype people as good or bad, and conforms to the requirements of authority, perhaps while being dictatorial to subordinates.

authority The right to take action, to make decisions, and to direct the work of others.

authority boundary The boundary at which superiors and subordinates always meet.

avoidance Usually won't resolve a conflict and may actually make it worse if bad feelings fester.

B

behaviour modification Changing or modifying behaviour through the use of contingent rewards or punishment.

behavioural displacement Occurs when the behaviours encouraged by the controls are inconsistent with what the company actually wants to accomplish.

behavioural standards State the types of behaviour that are acceptable for employees.

benchmarking A process in which a company learns how to become the best in one or more areas by carefully analyzing the practices of other companies who excel in that area.

benefits What a firm offers its workers other than wages and salaries in return for their labour.

bona fide occupational requirement When an employer may choose one applicant over another based on overriding characteristics of the job.

boundaryless organization An organization in which the widespread use of teams, networks, and similar structural mechanisms means that the boundaries that typically separate organizational functions and hierarchical levels are reduced and made more permeable.

bounded rationality A manager's decision making is only as rational as his or her unique values, capabilities, and limited capacity for processing information permit him or her to be.

brainstorming A group problem-solving technique whereby group members introduce all possible solutions before evaluating any of them.

break-even analysis A decision-making aid that enables a manager to determine whether a particular volume of sales will result in losses or profits.

break-even chart A graph that shows whether a particular volume of sales will result in profits or losses.

break-even point The point at which the total-revenue line crosses the total-costs line.

budget A plan stated in financial terms.

business re-engineering The radical redesign of business processes, combining steps to cut waste and eliminate repetitive, paper-intensive tasks in order to improve cost, quality, and service, and to maximize the benefits of information technology.

C

cafeteria benefits A flexible approach to providing benefits in which employees are allocated a certain sum to cover benefits and can "spend" this allocation on the specific benefits they prefer.

Canadian Human Rights Act Ensures that any individual who wishes to obtain a job has an equal opportunity to apply for it.

career anchor A concern or value that a worker will not give up if a choice has to be made.

cash cow A business in a low-growth industry that enjoys a high relative market share.

category killer Retailers who carry large selections with competitive prices in order to attract buyers.

causal forecasting Estimates the company factor (such as sales) based on other factors (such as advertising expenditures, or level of unemployment).

causal method Develops a projection based on the mathematical relationship between a company factor and those variables that management believes influence or explain the company factor.

cellular organization A structure in which independent companies or self-managing teams (cells) are self-sufficient and perform specialized functions. Each cell contributes to the overall functioning of the company.

centralization Occurs when top management makes all decisions regarding the hiring and firing of personnel, the purchasing of equipment and supplies, and other key decisions.

certainty Knowing in advance the outcome of the decision.

chain of command The path a directive should take in travelling from the president to employees at the bottom of the organization chart, or from employees at the bottom to the top of the organization chart.

close supervision Leader specifies the roles of subordinates and regularly checks to see that they comply with these specifications.

cohesiveness The attraction of the group for its members.

collaborating Often the best approach, especially when differences are confronted and aired in a civil, problem-solving manner.

collaborative writing systems Allow a work group's members to create long written documents (such as proposals) while working simultaneously at one of a number of interconnected or network computers.

commitment The relative strength of an individual's identification with and involvement in an organization.

commitment-based control methods Fostering employee self-control.

common market A level of economic integration in which no trade barriers exist among members, and a common external trade policy is in force.

communication The exchange of information and the transmission of meaning.

communication channel A vehicle that carries a message.

comparable worth A legal idea that aims to pay equal wages for work of equal value.

compensation system What a firm offers its employees in return for their labour.

competition Presumes a win-lose situation and sometimes works best when it's all right to resolve the conflict with a clear winner or loser, such as in sports.

competitive advantage   A basis on which to identify a relative superiority over competitors.

competitive intelligence   A systematic way to obtain and analyze public information about competitors.

competitive strategy   Identifies how to build and strengthen the business' long-term competitive position in the marketplace.

compressed workweek   A work schedule in which employees work fewer days per week, but more hours on the days they do work.

compromise   Each person gives up something in return for reaching agreement.

confrontation   Requires the disputing parties to openly state their views to each other in an attempt to understand the basic causes of the conflict.

confrontation meetings   Help clarify and bring into the open misperceptions and problems so that conflicts can be resolved.

conglomerate diversification   Diversifying into products or markets that are *not* related to the firm's present businesses or to one another.

contingency planning   Identifying possible future outcomes and then developing a plan for coping with them.

contingent reward   A reward given only when a person exhibits a certain behaviour that is desired.

continuous reinforcement schedule   A reward or punishment is given each time a behaviour of interest occurs.

control   The task of ensuring that activities are providing the desired results.

control tolerances   State the degree of deviation from the standard that is permissible.

coordination   The process of achieving unity of action among interdependent activities.

core competencies   The collective learning in the organization, especially knowing how to coordinate diverse production skills and integrate multiple streams of technologies.

corporate-level strategy   Identifies the group of businesses that will comprise the corporation, and the ways in which these businesses will relate to each other.

corporate social audit   An accounting by companies that they uphold acceptable social practices.

corporate stakeholder   Any group vital to the survival and success of the corporation.

cost leadership   A competitive strategy in which a company aims to become *the* low-cost leader in an industry.

cost standards   State the maximum cost that should be incurred in the course of producing goods and services.

creativity   The process of developing original, novel responses to a problem.

critical leadership thinking skills   Skills that allow a leader to examine a situation and dig out the underlying assumptions and values that are motivating subordinates, evaluate the evidence, and think through how to apply what he or she knows about leadership theory to solve the problem.

cultural artifacts   The obvious signs and symbols of corporate culture, such as written rules, office layouts, organizational structure, and dress codes.

customer departmentalization   Used when an organization wants to focus on the needs of specific types of customers.

customs union   A level of economic integration in which members dismantle trade barriers among themselves and establish a common trade policy with respect to non-members.

D

decentralization   Occurs when the right to make decisions is pushed down to the middle and lower levels of the management hierarchy.

decision   A choice from among the available alternatives.

decision making   The process of developing and analyzing alternatives and making a choice.

decision support systems   Provide middle managers with reports regarding matters such as current versus historical sales levels.

decision tree   A technique for making a decision under conditions of risk in which an expected value can be calculated for each alternative.

delegation   The pushing down of authority from supervisor to subordinate.

departmentalization   The process through which an enterprise's activities are grouped together and assigned to managers.

deregulation   A reduction in the number of laws affecting business activity and in the powers of government enforcement agencies.

descriptive plan   A plan that states in words what is to be achieved and how.

diagnostic control systems   Control systems that aim to ensure that important goals are being achieved and that any variances are explained.

differentiation strategy   A competitive strategy in which a firm seeks to be unique in its industry along some dimensions that are valued by buyers.

discipline without punishment   A discipline technique that makes the employee aware that a company rule has been broken, but that does not monetarily punish the employee for having broken the rule.

discrimination   Taking specific actions towards or against a person based on the person's group.

dismissal   The involuntary termination of an employee's employment with the firm.

distributed processing   Uses small local computers (such as point-of-sale systems) to collect, store, and process information, with summary reports and information sent to headquarters as needed.

diverse   Comprised of two or more groups, each of whose members are identifiable and distinguishable based on demographic or other characteristics.

diversification   A strategy of expanding into related or unrelated products or market segments.

divestment   Selling or liquidating individual businesses.

divisionalization   Exists when the firm's major departments are organized so that each can manage all of the activities needed to develop, manufacture, and sell a particular product, product line, or service.

dog   A low-market-share business in a low-growth, unattractive industry.

downsizing   Dramatically reducing the size of a company's workforce.

E

economic integration   Occurs when two or more nations obtain the advantages of free trade by minimizing trade restrictions between them.

electronic brainstorming   A form of brainstorming in which group members type ideas into a computer.

electronic bulletin board   A computerized information system that allows one or more group members to file messages on various topics to be picked up later by other group members.

employee involvement program   Any formal program that lets employees participate in formulating important work decisions or in supervising all or part of their own work activities.

employee-oriented leaders   Leaders who focus on the individuality and personality needs of their employees and emphasize building good interpersonal relationships.

Employment Equity Act of 1986   Federal legislation that designates four groups as employment disadvantaged—women, visible minorities, aboriginal people, and people with disabilities.

empowering   Giving employees the authority, tools, and information they need to do their jobs with greater autonomy, as well as the self-confidence required to perform the new jobs effectively.

empowerment   Authorizing and enabling workers to do their jobs.

equity theory   A theory that assumes that people have a need for, and therefore value and seek, fairness at work.

escalation of commitment   The situation in which a manager becomes increasingly committed to a previously chosen course of action even though it has been shown to be ineffective.

ethics   The principles of conduct governing an individual or a group and, specifically, the standards used to decide conduct.

ethnocentric   A type of management philosophy that results in a home-market-oriented firm.

ethnocentrism   A tendency to view members of one's own group as the centre of the universe and to view other social groups less favourably than one's own.

exchange rate   The rate at which one country's currency can be exchanged for another country's currency.

executive A manager at the top of a firm.

executive recruiter An agency retained by employers to seek out top management talent.

expectancy The probability that a person's effort will lead to performance.

expected value The probability of the outcome multiplied by the benefit or cost of that outcome.

expert system A system that duplicates the thinking processes of an expert in a particular area by using decision rules that are built into the system.

exporting Selling abroad, either directly to target customers or indirectly by retaining foreign sales agents and distributors.

external environment The set of forces with which that organization interacts.

extinction The process by which an undesired behaviour disappears because reinforcement is withheld.

extrinsic motivation Exists when a person works hard at a task because of the promise that some tangible reward will be given if the job is done well.

F

federal organization An organization in which power is distributed between a central authority and a number of constituent units, but the central unit's authority is intentionally limited.

feedback The receiver's response.

financial ratios Compare one financial indicator to another.

finished goods inventory Those items that have passed through the entire production process and are ready to be sold to customers.

first-line manager A manager lower on the management ladder; often called a supervisor.

fixed interval schedule A reinforcement is applied after a certain time period has passed, regardless of the number of responses that has occurred.

fixed ratio schedule A reinforcement is applied after a fixed number of desired behavioural responses has occurred, regardless of the time that has passed.

flextime A system that allows workers increased discretion in deciding when they will be at their place of work.

focus strategy A competitive strategy in which a firm selects a market segment and builds its competitive strategy on serving the customers in its market niche better or more cheaply than its competitors.

forcing Can be effective as a brute show of power, but it can backfire if the person "forced" has the option of wiggling out of the deal.

forecasting To estimate or calculate in advance or to predict.

foreign direct investment Operations in one country that are controlled by entities in a foreign country.

formal communication Messages recognized as official by the organization.

formal group A group established to achieve certain organizational goals and part of the formal structure of the organization.

formal organizational network A recognized group of managers assembled by the CEO and the senior executive team and drawn from across the company's functions, business units, and geography, and from different levels of the hierarchy.

formal structural change Changes in the formal hierarchical structure of the organization that are designed to improve its efficiency and effectiveness.

franchising The granting of a right by a parent company to another firm to do business in a prescribed manner.

free trade Occurs when two or more countries sign an agreement to allow the free flow of goods and services, unimpeded by trade barriers such as tariffs.

free trade area A level of economic integration in which barriers to trade among member countries are removed, so that goods and services are traded more freely.

functional authority The ability to issue orders down the chain of command within the very narrow limits of his or her authority.

functional departmentalization Grouping activities around basic functions like manufacturing, sales, and finance.

functional strategy Identifies the basic courses of action that each functional department will pursue to contribute to attaining the business' competitive goals.

G

gain-sharing plan An incentive program in which employees receive a bonus if the firm's costs are reduced because of greater worker efficiency and/or productivity.

gamesmanship Management actions aimed at improving the manager's performance in terms of the control system without producing any economic benefits for the firm.

gender-role stereotype The tendency to associate women with certain (frequently non-managerial) jobs.

general leader Leader uses neither a close supervision strategy nor a hands-off strategy, but instead checks subordinates work only at intervals.

geographic expansion Expanding a company into new geographic areas or foreign countries.

global corporation A corporation that operates as if the entire world (or major regions of it) were a single entity.

global mercantilism A scenario in which regional conflicts and frustration with international failures lead to more government intervention in managing international trade.

globalization The integration of markets globally.

globalization of production Dispersing parts of a firm's production process to various locations around the globe.

goal (objective) A specific result you want to achieve.

goods-in-process inventory Those items that are partway through the production process.

grapevine The informal channel of communication in organizations.

graphic plan A plan that shows in charts what is to be achieved and how.

grievance A complaint that an employee lodges against an employer, usually regarding wages, hours, or some condition of employment like unfair supervisory behaviour.

group Two or more persons who interact together for some purpose and in such a manner that each person influences and is influenced by each other person.

group cohesiveness The attraction of the group for its members.

group norms The informal rules that groups adopt to regulate and regularize group members' behaviour.

group scheduling system Allows each group member to put his or her daily schedule into a shared database, which enables group members to identify the most suitable times for meetings or to attend currently scheduled meetings.

groupthink The tendency for a highly cohesive group, especially one working on special projects, to develop a sense of detachment and elitism.

H

heuristics Shortcuts, or rules of thumb, used when solving problems.

hierarchy of plans Broad and specific plans that work together to achieve overall organizational goals.

horizontal corporation A structure organized around customer-oriented processes such as new-product development, sales and fulfilment, and customer support.

horizontal integration Acquiring ownership or control of competitors in the same or similar markets with the same or similar products.

hot group A lively, high-achieving, dedicated group, usually small, whose members are turned on to an exciting and challenging task.

human capital The knowledge, training, skills, and expertise of a firm's workers.

human process interventions Interventions aimed at helping employees better understand and modify their own and others' attitudes, values, and beliefs, and thereby improve the company.

human resource management (HRM) The management function devoted to acquiring, training, appraising, and compensating employees.

hyperarchy A network so complete that everyone can communicate with anyone else, and is encouraged to do so.

I

identity boundary The boundary identifying those who share values and experiences from those who do not.

immediate corrective action   Solves the problem immediately and gets output back to the desired level.

incentive program   Any program in which a company offers its workers additional pay over and above the normal wage or salary level in order to motivate them to perform at a higher-than-normal level.

independent integrator   An individual or group that coordinates the activities of several interdependent departments.

individualism vs. collectivism   The degree to which ties between individuals are normally loose or close.

informal communication   Not officially sanctioned by the organization; for example, the grapevine.

informal group   A group set up to meet people's social needs and not part of the formal structure of the organization.

informal organization   The informal, habitual contacts, communications, interpersonal relationships, and ways of doing things that employees always develop.

informal organizational network   A group of cooperating individuals who are interconnected only informally and who share information and help solve each other's problems based on their personal knowledge of each other's expertise.

information   Data presented in a form that is meaningful to the recipient.

information system   A set of people, data, technology, and organizational procedures that work together to retrieve, process, store, and disseminate information to support decision making and control.

information technology   Any processes, practices, or systems that facilitate processing and transporting information.

input controls   Monitor the material, human, and capital resources that come into the organization.

instrumental leadership role   The managerial aspect of change leadership that puts the instruments in place through which the employees can accomplish their new tasks.

instrumentality   The perceived relationship between successful performance and obtaining a reward.

integrated strategic management   A four-step OD process that helps to create or change a strategy, and that facilitates strategic interventions.

intermittent reinforcement schedule   The behaviour of interest is rewarded only some of the time.

international management   Carrying out the management functions of planning, organizing, leading, and controlling on an international scale.

interpersonal communication   Communication that occurs between two individuals.

interpersonal conflict   Conflict that occurs between individuals or between individuals and groups.

intrinsic motivation   Exists if the person performs a task in the absence of any tangible reward.

intuition   A cognitive process whereby a person unconsciously makes a decision based on accumulated knowledge and experience.

intuitive decision-makers   Those who use a more trial-and-error approach.

inventory   The items an organization keeps on hand either for use in the production process or as a result of the production process.

J

job analysis   The procedure used to determine the duties of jobs and the kinds of people (in terms of skills and experience) who should be hired for them.

job analysis questionnaire   A questionnaire used by managers and administered to employees to determine the duties and functions of a job.

job-centred leaders   Leaders who focus on production and the job's technical aspects.

job description   A list of duties showing what the job entails.

job enlargement   Assigning workers additional same-level tasks to increase the number of tasks they have to perform.

job enrichment   Building opportunities for achievement into a job by making it more interesting and challenging.

job posting   Publicizing an open job to employees and listing its attributes, such as qualifications, supervisor, working schedule, and pay rate.

job rotation   Systematically moving workers from job to job.

job satisfaction   Reflects an employee's attitude about his or her job.

job sharing   A program that allows two people to share one full-time job.

job specifications   A list of the skills and aptitudes sought in people hired for the job.

joint venture   A type of longer-term strategic alliance in which there is an equity contribution by the partners.

jury of executive opinion   A qualitative forecasting technique that involves asking a "jury" of key executives to forecast sales for, say, the next year.

just-in-time (JIT) inventory system   A system in which inventory is scheduled to arrive just in time to be used in the production process.

K

kanban system   Specifies how many and what kind of items are to be produced.

knowledge management   The task of developing and exploiting organizations' tangible and intangible knowledge resources.

L

laissez-faire leaders   Leader follows a completely hands-off policy with subordinates.

law of individual differences   The fact that people differ in personalities, abilities, values, and needs.

leader-member exchange (LMX) theory   A leadership theory that says that leaders may use different styles with different members of the same work group.

leadership   One person influencing another to work towards some predetermined objective.

learning   A relatively permanent change in a person that occurs as a result of experience.

leverage   Concentrating limited organizational resources on a few key strategic goals.

licensing   An arrangement whereby a company grants a foreign firm the right to use intangible property for a specified period of time, usually for a fee or for a percentage of the earnings.

lifelong learning   Provides extensive continuing training, from basic remedial skills to advanced decision-making techniques, throughout the employees' careers.

line managers   Managers in charge of essential activities and authorized to issue orders to subordinates.

linear programming   A mathematical method used to solve resource allocation problems.

line-staff conflict   Disagreements between a line manager and the staff manager who is giving him or her advice.

local area network (LAN)   A network that spans a limited distance, such as a building or several adjacent buildings, using the company's own telecommunications links.

locus of control   The extent to which individuals believe that they control their lives.

long-term corrective action   Determines why deviations occur and what can be done to prevent the problem from happening in the future.

M

Machiavellian personality   A person who tends to be oriented towards manipulation and control, with a low sensitivity to the needs of others.

management   The process of planning, organizing, leading, and controlling a business' financial, physical, human, and information resources in order to achieve designated goals.

management assessment centre   An approach to selection in which about a dozen management candidates spend two or three days performing realistic management tasks under the observation of expert appraisers.

management by objectives (MBO)   A technique used by many firms to assist in the process of setting organization-wide objectives and goals for subsidiary units and their employees.

management information systems   Provide middle managers with reports regarding matters such as current versus historical sales levels.

management process   The manager's four basic functions of planning, organizing, leading, and controlling.

manager   Someone who plans, organizes, leads, and controls the people and the work of an organization with the aim of ensuring that the organization achieves its goals.

managerial competence   The ability to operate effectively across multiple managerial functions.

managing diversity   Planning and implementing organizational systems and practices to manage people so that the potential advantages of diversity are maximized while its potential disadvantages are minimized.

market economy   An economic system in which the quantities and nature of the goods and services produced are not planned by anyone.

market penetration   Taking steps to boost sales of present products by more aggressively selling and marketing into the firm's current markets.

marketing channel   The conduit through which a manufacturer distributes its products to its ultimate customers.

marketing-channel departmentalization   In which top-level departments are organized around each of the firm's marketing channels.

marketing research   The procedures used to develop and analyze new customer-related information that helps managers make decisions.

masculinity vs. femininity   The degree to which assertiveness ("masculinity") or quality-of-life issues ("femininity") are valued.

matrix organization (matrix management)   The imposition of one form of departmentalization on top of another.

mechanistic organization   An organization that stresses highly structured work, clearly stated authority relations, centralized authority, and vertical communication.

mentoring   A relationship between a younger adult and an older, more experienced adult in which the mentor provides support, guidance, and counselling to enhance the protégé's success at work and in other arenas of life.

middle manager   A manager who usually reports to an executive.

mission statement   A statement that broadly outlines the organization's future course and serves to communicate who the organization is, what it does, and where it's headed.

mixed economy   An economic system in which some sectors of the economy are left to private ownership and free market mechanisms, while others are largely owned by and managed by the government.

moral minimum   The idea that a firm is free to strive for profits as long as no harm is committed.

morality   Society's accepted ways of behaviour.

motivation   The intensity of a person's desire to engage in some activity.

motivational dispositions   Motives that remain unaroused until the proper conditions bring them forth.

motive   Something that incites a person to action or that sustains and gives direction to action.

moving   In Lewin's process, developing new behaviours, values, and attitudes, sometimes through structure changes.

multinational corporation (MNC)   An internationally integrated business controlled by a parent corporation, and owned and managed by the nationals of its home country.

mutual adjustment   Achieving coordination by relying on face-to-face interpersonal interactions in both simple and complex situations.

N

negative reinforcement   The likelihood that a behaviour will be repeated increases when an unpleasant stimulus is withheld from a person.

network   A group of interconnected computers, work stations, and computer devices (such as printers and data storage systems).

noise   Physical, personality, perceptual, or attitudinal factors that interfere with the communication process.

non-programmed decision   A unique and novel decision that relies on judgment.

nonverbal communication   One's manner of speaking, facial expressions, bodily posture, and so on.

normative judgment   A judgment that implies that something is good or bad, right or wrong, better or worse.

norms   The informal rules that groups adopt to regulate and regularize members' behaviour.

O

objectives   Specific results a leader wants the group to achieve.

off-the-job training   Training that is performed at a location away from the work site.

omission   The likelihood that a behaviour will occur again decreases when a pleasant stimulus is withheld from a person.

on-the-job training   Training that occurs while the employee is actually at work.

open-book management   Literally opening the books of a company to the employees; financial data are shared, numbers are explained, and then workers are rewarded for improvements in the business performance.

operant behaviour   Behaviour in which one operates on one's environment.

operational planning   Shorter-term planning by first-line managers regarding staffing and production levels, for example.

organic organization   An organization that puts little emphasis on hierarchical authority and encourages managers and subordinates to work together as a team to solve problems.

organization   People with formally assigned roles who must work together to achieve stated goals.

organization chart   Shows the structure of the organization, specifically, the key positions in the organization and interrelationships among them.

organizational communication   Communication that occurs among several individuals or groups.

organizational culture   The characteristics, traditions, and values that employees share.

organizational development (OD)   A special approach to organizational change in which the employees themselves formulate the change that's required and implement it, often with the assistance of a trained "facilitator."

organizational development interventions   Techniques aimed at changing employees' attitudes, values, and behaviour.

organizing   The process of deciding which specific functions must be performed, and how these functions should be coordinated so that organizational goals are achieved.

orientation   Providing new employees with basic information about the employer.

output controls   Controls that are used to determine whether deviations from standards have occurred in a product or service.

output standards   State the quantity of the product or service that employees should be producing.

P

participative management   A method of increasing employees' job satisfaction by giving them a voice in how they do their jobs, and how the company is managed.

patterns of behaviour   Include ceremonial events, written and spoken comments, and the actual behaviours in which the firm's managers and other employees engage.

pay for performance   Any compensation method that ties pay to the quantity or quality of work the person produces.

perception   The selection and interpretation of information we receive through our senses and the meaning we give to the information.

performance appraisal   Evaluating an employee's current or past performance relative to his or her performance standards.

personality   The characteristic and distinctive traits of an individual, and the way the traits interact to help or hinder the adjustment of the person to other people and situations.

personality trait   Any persisting characteristic or dimension of personality according to which individuals can be rated or measured.

personnel planning   Forecasting personnel requirements (in terms of future open positions); forecasting the supply of outside candidates and internal candidates; and producing plans that describe how candidates will be hired, trained, and prepared for the jobs that will be opening up.

plan   A method formulated beforehand for achieving a desired result.

planned economy   An economic system in which central planning agencies such as the government try to determine how much is produced and for whom, by which sectors of the economy, and by which plants.

planning   The process of establishing objectives and courses of action, prior to taking action.

policy   A guide to action.

political boundary   The boundary defining what different departments want, based on who will benefit from an activity and who will not.

polycentric   A type of management philosophy that limits a company to several individual foreign markets.

positive reinforcement   A form of reinforcement that occurs when a pleasant stimulus is presented to a person to increase the likelihood that a behaviour will be repeated.

power distance   The extent to which the less powerful members of institutions accept and expect that power will be distributed unequally.

prejudice   A bias that results from prejudging someone on the basis of some trait.

premises   Assumptions made about the future.

primary data   Information specifically collected to solve a current problem.

principle of exception   To conserve managers' time, only significant deviations or exceptions from the standard should be brought to the manager's attention.

problem-solving teams   Teams involved in identifying and researching activities and in developing effective solutions to work-related problems.

procedure   Specifies how to proceed if some specific situation arises.

process controls   Controls that are applied while the product or service is produced.

product development   Developing improved products for current markets.

profit-sharing plan   An incentive program in which employees receive a bonus depending on the firm's profits.

programmed decision   A decision that is repetitive and routine and that can be solved through mechanical procedures such as by applying rules.

promotion   Rewarding an employee's efforts by moving that person to a job with increased authority and responsibility.

punishment   An unpleasant stimulus, presented to a person when undesirable behaviour occurs, to ensure that the behaviour will not be repeated.

Q

qualitative forecasting   Forecasting methods that emphasize human judgment.

quality circle (QC)   A team of 6 to 12 employees that meets once a week at work to solve problems affecting its work area.

quality standards   Define the level of quality that is to be maintained in the production of goods and services.

quantitative forecasting   Using statistical methods to examine data and find underlying patterns and relationships.

question mark   A business in a high-growth industry, but with low market share.

quota   A legal restriction on the import of particular goods.

R

raw materials inventory   The basic inputs into the production process.

receiver   The person or persons to whom the message is sent.

recruiting   Attracting a pool of viable job applicants.

refreezing   In Lewin's process, reinforcing the changes that have been introduced by instituting new systems and procedures that will support and maintain them.

regiocentric (or geocentric)   A type of management philosophy that may lead a manager to create a more integrated worldwide production and marketing presence.

related diversification   Adding new, but related, products or services to an existing business.

retrenchment   The reduction of activity or operations.

risk   Being able to assign probabilities to each outcome.

rites and ceremonies   Company activities such as conferences or annual parties that reinforce the corporate culture.

role ambiguity   A lack of clarity regarding what the employee is to do or how he or she is to do it.

role conflict   A situation in which two or more sets of demands are placed on an employee in such a manner that compliance with one demand makes it difficult to comply with the other.

rule   A highly specific guide to action.

S

salary   Dollars paid at regular intervals in return for doing a job, regardless of the amount of time or output involved.

sales force estimation   A qualitative forecasting technique that gathers the opinions of the sales force regarding what they think sales will be in the forthcoming period.

satisfice   Discovering and selecting satisfactory alternatives, rather than finding optimal alternatives.

secondary data   Information that has been collected or published already.

self-directed work team   A highly trained group of six to eight employees, on average, fully responsible for turning out a well-defined segment of finished work.

self-efficacy   A person's belief about his or her own capacity to perform a task.

self-managing teams   Teams responsible for managing their work on a daily basis; also called self-directed work teams.

semantics   The meaning of words.

semi-autonomous teams   Teams that have a lot of input in managing the activities in their own work area but are still managed by a supervisor.

sender   Someone who puts a message in understandable terms and then transmits it.

sensitivity training   Training aimed at increasing the participant's insight into his or

her own behaviour and the behaviour of others by encouraging an open expression of feelings in the group.

signs and symbols   The activities in an organization such as profit sharing or managers' actions that symbolize what is valued.

simulation   Developing a model of an actual situation and working through the simulation to see what kind of outcome results.

single-use plan   A plan developed for a specific, one-time purpose that will not be used again.

smoothing over   Usually won't resolve a conflict and may actually make it worse if bad feelings fester.

social responsibility   The extent to which companies should and do channel resources towards improving one or more segments of society other than the firm's own stockholders.

span of control   The number of subordinates that report directly to a manager.

staff managers   Managers who assist and advise line managers.

staffing   Filling a firm's open positions.

standards   Criteria for evaluating the quality and quantity of the products or services produced by employees.

standing plan   A plan, such as a policy, procedure, or rule, intended for repeated usage.

star   A business in a high-growth industry in which the company has a high relative market share.

statistical decision theory techniques   Decision-making techniques used to solve problems for which information is incomplete or uncertain.

stereotyping   A process in which specific behavioural traits are ascribed to individuals on the basis of their apparent membership in a group.

stories   Company tales that reinforce the company's history and values.

strategic alliance   A reciprocal arrangement in which partners pool, exchange, or integrate specified business resources for mutual gain.

strategic business unit (SBU)   An organizational entity that contains several related businesses.

strategic change   A shift in the firm's strategy, mission, and vision.

strategic control   Assessing progress towards strategic goals and taking corrective action as needed.

strategic human resource management   The linking of HRM with strategic goals and objectives in order to improve business performance and develop organizational cultures that foster innovation and flexibility.

strategic interventions   Organization-wide interventions aimed at bringing about a better fit between a firm's strategy, structure, culture, and external environment.

strategic management   The process of identifying and pursuing the organization's mission by aligning the organization's internal capabilities with the external demands of its environment.

strategic plan   A plan that specifies the business or businesses a firm will be in, and the major steps it must take to get there.

strategic planning   The process of identifying the business of the firm today and the business it wants for the future, and then identifying the course of action it will pursue, given its opportunities, threats, and weaknesses.

strategy   A course of action that explains how the enterprise will move from the business it is in now to the business it wants to be in (as stated in its mission), given its opportunities and threats and its internal strengths and weaknesses.

subsidy   A direct payment made by a country to domestic producers in an effort to make them more cost competitive.

suggestion teams   Short-term teams that exist to work on given issues such as how to cut costs or increase productivity.

survey research   A convenient and widely used method for unfreezing an organization's management and employees by providing a lucid, comparative, graphic illustration of the fact that the organization does have problems that should be solved.

sustainable world   A scenario in which international economic frictions are resolved and economic trade flows freely.

SWOT analysis   A strategic planning tool used to list and consolidate information regarding a firm's external opportunities and threats and internal strengths and weaknesses.

systematic decision-makers   Those who tend to take a more logical, structured, step-by-step approach to solving a problem.

T

tactical (functional) plan   A plan that shows how top management's plans are to be carried out at the departmental level.

tariff   Governmental taxes levied on goods shipped internationally; the most common trade barrier.

task boundary   The boundary defining how employees from different departments feel about "who does what" as the necessary work is divided up.

team   A group of people who work together and share a common work objective.

team-based organization   A company in which work is organized around teams.

team building   The process of improving the effectiveness of a team.

technological innovation   Product and service innovation resulting from the use of technology.

technology transfer   The transfer of systematic knowledge for the manufacture of a product, for the application of a process, or for the rendering of a service; does not extend to the mere sale or lease of goods.

telecommunications   The electronic transmission of data, text, graphics, voice, or image over distance.

telecommuting   A type of work in which people do some or all or their work away from the office using fax, phone, and computer.

test   A sample of a person's behaviour.

time series   A set of observations taken at specific times, usually at equal intervals.

time standards   State the length of time it should take to complete a task.

tokenism   Occurs when a company appoints a small group of women or minority-group members to high-profile positions, rather than more aggressively seeking full workgroup representation for those groups.

total quality management (TQM)   Based on the idea that no defects are tolerable, and that employees are responsible for maintaining quality standards.

trade barrier   Governmental influences usually aimed at reducing the competitiveness of imported products or services.

traditional control process   Setting targets and then ensuring that employees adhere to them.

training program   A program aimed at ensuring that the new employee has the basic knowledge required to perform the job satisfactorily.

trait theory   The idea that leaders are characterized by certain traits.

transaction processing systems   Provide detailed information about most short-term, daily activities, such as accounts payables and order status.

transactional   Behaviours largely oriented towards accomplishing the tasks at hand and at maintaining good relations with those working with the leader by exchanging promises of rewards for performance.

transformational leadership   The process of influencing major changes in the attitudes and assumptions of organization members and building commitment for the organization's mission, objectives, and strategies.

transnational teams   Work groups composed of multinational members whose activities span many countries.

U

uncertainty   Being unable to even assign probabilities to the likelihood of the various outcomes.

uncertainty avoidance   The extent to which people in a society are uncomfortable with unstructured situations in which unknown, surprising, novel incidents occur.

unfreezing   In Lewin's process, reducing the forces that are striving to maintain the status quo, usually by presenting a provocative problem or event to get people to recognize the need for change and to search for new solutions.

V

valence   The perceived value a person attaches to a reward.

value-based hiring   Putting enormous effort into interviewing and screening to find people whose values are already consistent with the firm's.

values and beliefs   Guiding standards that lay out "what ought to be, as distinct from what is."

variable interval schedule   A reinforcement is applied after a varying amount of time has passed, regardless of the number of desired responses that has occurred.

variable pay plans   Plans that put some portion of the employee's pay at risk, subject to the firm's meeting its financial goals.

variable ratio schedule   Behaviours are reinforced after a varying number of responses has occurred.

variances   The differences between budgeted and actual amounts.

venture team   A small group of people who operate as a semi-autonomous unit to create and develop a new idea.

vertical integration   Owning or controlling the inputs to the firm's processes and/or the channels through which the products or services are distributed.

virtual corporation   A temporary network of independent companies—suppliers, customers, even erstwhile rivals—linked by information technology to share skills, costs, and access to one another's markets.

virtual organization   An organization where employees communicate electronically with the office, lab, or factory by means of their PCs at home.

vision   A general statement of the organization's intended direction that evokes positive emotional feelings in organization members.

W

wages   Dollars paid based on the number of hours worked or the number of units produced.

waiting-line/queuing techniques   Mathematical decision-making techniques for solving waiting-line problems.

whistle-blowing   The activities of employees who try to report organizational wrongdoing.

wholly owned subsidiary   A company that is 100 percent owned by a foreign firm.

wide area network (WAN)   A network that serves microcomputers over larger geographic areas, spanning distances that can cover a few kilometres or circle the globe.

work flow automation system   Uses an e-mail-type system to automate paperwork flow.

Z

zero-based budgeting   A technique that forces managers to defend their budgeted programs every year and to rank them in order of priority based on the ratio of benefits and costs.

Sources

Chapter 1

Chapters Turns Over a New Leaf Adapted from Mark Evans, "Chapters Turns Over New Leaf," *Globe and Mail*, May 13, 1999, p. T2. **Table 1.2** *Fortune*, May 24, 1999, p. 107. © 1999 Time Inc. Reprinted by permission. **Figure 1.1** American Management Association International, "What Has the CEO's Attention?" *Management Review*, September 1998, p. 12. **Case Study 1-1** Adapted from Mary Janigan, "Going E-postal," *Maclean's*, September 13, 1999, pp. 34–36. **Case Study 1-2** Adapted from Danny Kucharsky, "Future Shop Avoids Retail Web Woes," *Marketing*, November 22, 1999, p. 3.

Chapter 1 Appendix

Figure A1.1 Thomas A. Stewart, "The All-Time Greatest Hits of Managing," *Fortune*, March 29, 1999, p. 192.

Chapter 2

Bombardier Is Buzzing Summarized from www.bombardier.com (refer to Corporate Profile and "Bombardier at a Glance"); Konrad Yakabuski, "Bombardier Soars on Jet Orders, but Turbulence May Loom Ahead," *The Globe and Mail*, February 22, 1999, pp. B1, B5; Heather Scoffield, "Bombardier-Embraer Dogfight Heats Up," *The Globe and Mail*, February 15, 1999, pp. B1, B6. **Case Study 2-1** Summarized from www.nortelnetworks.com. **Case Study 2-2** Adapted from Frederick A. Starke and Robert W. Sexty, *Contemporary Management*, Third Edition (Scarborough: Prentice-Hall Canada, 1998), pp. 146–47; and Geoffrey York, "Russians Accuse McDonald's of Union Bashing," *The Globe and Mail*, June 14, 1999, p. A17.

Chapter 3

Business Ethics in the Canadian Context Adapted from Kathleen Sibley, "Technology Complicates Work Ethics: KPMG Survey," *Computer Dealer News*, June 15, 1998, pp. 14–15. **Figure 3.1** © 1999 *The Economist* newspaper group, Inc. Reprinted with permission. Further reproduction is prohibited. **Figure 3.2** Courtesy of Johnson & Johnson. **Figure 3.4** Reprinted with permission of the publisher. From *Cultural Diversity in Organizations: Theory, Research and Practice*, copyright © 1993 by Taylor Cox, Jr. Berrett-Koehler Publishers, Inc., San Francisco, CA. All rights reserved. **Case Study 3-1** Adapted from Peter Verburg, "Going to the Wall with China," *Canadian Business*, February 12, 1999, pp. 26–38. **Case Study 3-2** Adapted from Paul Maasland, "How to Build an Employee-centric Culture," *Computing Canada*, July 9, 1999, pp. 33–34. **CBC Video Case 1-1** "E-Commerce," *Venture* #723 (October 5, 1999); also "Retailing Online Can Mean a World of Difference," *The Globe and Mail*, December 1, 1999, p. D2; Erica Goode, "Tough and Impatient Online Shoppers," *The Globe and Mail*, December 1, 1999, p. D17; http://cism.bus.utexas.edu. **CBC Video Case 1-2** "The Pressure to be Positive," *Venture* #725 (October 19, 1999); also Natalie Southworth and Janet McFarland, "RCMP Says It Won't Lay Charges in Bre-X Case," *The Globe and Mail*, May 13, 1999, p. B1; Gayle MacDonald, "Drabinsky Denies Fraud Allegations," *The Globe and Mail*, May 13, 1999, pp. B1, B12; Gayle MacDonald, "Livent VP Puts Blame on Bosses for Accounting," *The Globe and Mail*, June 26, 1999, p. B3. **KnitMedia Video Case** Prepared by D.T. Ogilvie, Rutgers University.

Chapter 4

Decision Making in a Crisis Summarized from William M. Carley, "Swissair Pilots Differed on How to Avoid Crash," *The Wall Street Journal*, January 21, 1999, pp. B1, B10. **Table 4.1** Stephen P. Robbins and Mary Coulter, *Management*, Fifth Edition (Upper Saddle River, NJ: Prentice-Hall, 1996), p. 193. **Figure 4.1** *Management,* Fifth Edition, by Robbins/Coulter, © 1996. Reprinted by permission of Prentice-Hall, Inc., Upper Saddle River, NJ. **Figure 4.2** *Management,* Fifth Edition, by Robbins/Coulter, © 1996. Reprinted by permission of Prentice-Hall, Inc., Upper Saddle River, NJ. **Figure 4.3** Lester A. Lefton and Laura Valvatine, *Mastering Psychology*, 4th ed. Copyright © 1992 by Allyn & Bacon. Reprinted by permission. **Figure 4.4** Max H. Bazerman, Judgment in Managerial Decision Making. Copyright © 1994 by John Wiley & Sons, Inc., p. 93. Reprinted by permission of John Wiley & Sons, Inc. **The People Side of Management** Frederick A. Starke and Robert W. Sexty, *Contemporary Management,* Third Edition (Scarborough: Prentice Hall Canada, 1998), p. 266. **Figure 4.5** *Applied Human Relations*, Fourth Edition, by Benton/Halloran, © 1991. Reprinted by permission of Prentice-Hall, Inc., Upper Saddle River, NJ. **Figure 4.6** Adapted and reproduced by special permission of the Publisher, Psychological Assessment Resources, Inc., Odessa FL 33556, from the Personal Style Inventory by William Taggart, Ph.D., and Barbara Hausladen, Copyright 1991, 1993 by PAR, Inc. **Table 4.4** Summarized from I. Janis, *Victims of Groupthink* (Boston: Houghton-Mifflin, 1973). **Table 4.5** Summarized from I. Janis, *Victims of Groupthink* (Boston: Houghton-Mifflin, 1973). **Experiential Exercise 2** Adapted from Benjamin Hoff, *The Tao of Pooh* (New York: Viking, 1982), p. 42. **Case Study 4-1** Summarized from Allan Robinson, "Inco President Willing to Compromise on Voisey's Bay," *The Globe and Mail*, April 29, 1999, pp. B1, B4; Allan Robinson, "Inco to Halt Voisey's Bay Work," *The Globe and Mail*, July 28, 1998, pp. B1, B6; "Giant Newfoundland Nickel Project May Soon Proceed," *Winnipeg Free Press*, November 23, 1999, p. B8; Allan Robinson, "Inco Chairman Defends Actions," *The Globe and Mail*, April 23, 1998, p. B3.

Chapter 5

The Rise and Fall of Loewen Group Inc. Summarized from Ann Gibbon, "Funeral King Has His Judgment Day," *The Globe and Mail*, October 12, 1998, p. B5; also Ann Gibbon, "Possible Sale Breathes Life Into Loewen Stock," *The Globe and Mail*, July 24, 1998, pp. B1, B10; Brian Milner, "The Dying Game," *The Globe and Mail*, December 16, 1995, pp. B1, B4; Brian Milner, "Loewen Settles Mississippi Suit," *The Globe and Mail*, January 30, 1996, pp. B1, B4; Brian Milner, "Loewen Licks Its Wounds," *The Globe and Mail*, January 31, 1996, pp. B1, B4. **Figure 5.1** Frederick A. Starke and Robert W. Sexty, *Contemporary Management*, Third Edition (Scarborough: Prentice Hall Canada, 1998), p. 189. **Table 5.1** Reprinted with permission from George Morrisey, *A Guide to Long-Range Planning*. Copyright © 1996 Jossey-Bass, Inc., Publishers. All rights reserved. **Table 5.5** Reprinted with permission from George Morrisey, *A Guide to Tactical Planning*. Copyright © 1996 Jossey-Bass, Inc, Publisher. All rights reserved. **Figure 5.3** Reprinted from Adam Kahan, "Scenarios for Energy: Sustainable World vs. Global Mercantilism," *Long Range Planning*, vol. 25, no. 4, p. 41, with permission from Elsevier Science. **Case Study 5-2** Adapted from Shona McKay, "High Spirits," *Report on Business Magazine*, October 1992, pp. 92–99.

Chapter 6

Planning and Strategy at Seagram Summarized from Allan Swift, "Polygram Bid Heats Up," *Winnipeg Free Press*, November 5, 1998, p. B12; also Brian Milner, "Seagram's Top Gun Shoots for the Stars," *The Globe and Mail*, June 6, 1998, pp. B1, B6; also "Investors Expected to Snap Up Tropicana IPO," *The Globe and Mail*, June 12, 1998, p. B12; also Brian Milner, "Seagram Snares Polygram," *The Globe and Mail*, May 22, 1998, pp. B1, B4; also Brian Milner, "The Selling of Edgar Bronfman Jr.," *The Globe and Mail*, February 15, 1999, p. B15. **Figure 6.5** Michael Porter, *Competitive Strategy: Techniques for Analyzing Industries and Competitors* (New York: The Free Press, 1980), p. 365. **Figure 6.7** Reprinted with the permission of The Free Press, a division of Simon & Schuster from *Competitive*

Strategy: Techniques for Analyzing Industries and Competitors by Michael E. Porter. Copyright © 1980 by The Free Press. **The Entrepreneurial Edge** Adapted from Anonymous, "Women Entrepreneurs Focus on Key Business Growth," *Computer Dealer News*, May 28, 1999. **CBC Video Case 2-1** Written by Reg Litz of the University of Manitoba. Video Resource: "Earth Buddy," *Venture* #518 (December 11, 1994). **CBC Video Case 2-2** "High Flyers," *Venture* (February 15, 2000).

Chapter 7

Starbucks on the Move Summarized from information contained on the Starbucks Web site at www.starbucks.com; also Jennifer Reese, "Starbucks: Inside the Coffee Cult," *Fortune*, December 9, 1996, pp. 190–200. **Figure 7.8** Adapted from Montreal Trust, *Annual Report*, 1989. **Figure 7.9** Adapted from Air Canada, *Annual Report*, 1995, p. 52.

Chapter 8

Restructuring at Canadian Pacific Summarized from Ann Gibbon, "CP Rail Moving to Calgary," *The Globe and Mail*, November 21, 1995, pp. B1, B19; also Ann Gibbon, "Reorganization of CP Draws Applause," *The Globe and Mail*, November 22, 1995, p. B2. **The Entrepreneurial Edge** Summarized from Suan Scheck, "Eicon Finds that Teamwork Builds a Better Diva," *Electronic Engineering Times*, March 15, 1999, pp. 92–94. **Figure 8.1** Adapted from James H. Shonk, *Team-Based Organizations* (Homewood, IL: Irwin, 1997), p. 36. **Figure 8.2** Reprinted by permission of *Harvard Business Review*. From "How Networks Reshape Organizations—For Results," by Ram Charan, September–October 1991. Copyright © 1991 by the President and Fellows of Harvard College; all rights reserved. **Figure 8.4** Reprinted by permission of *Harvard Business Review*. "The Four Organizational Boundaries that Matter." From "The New Boundaries of the 'Boundaryless' Company," by Larry Hirschorn and Thomas Gilmore, May–June 1992. Copyright © 1992 by the President and Fellows of Harvard College. All rights reserved. **Figure 8.5** John A. Byrne, "The Horizontal Corporation," *Business Week*, December 20, 1993, p. 80. **Figure 8.6** Reprinted from December 20, 1993, issue of *Business Week* by special permission. Copyright © 1993 by the McGraw-Hill Companies, Inc. **Figure 8.8** Reprinted with permission of the *Academy of Management Executive*, from "Organizing in the Knowledge Age: Anticipating the Cellular Form," Raymond Miles, vol. 11, no. 4, © 1997; permission conveyed through Copyright Clearance Center, Inc.

Chapter 9

Cisco Systems Summarized from www.Cisco.com. **Figure 9.4** Bennett Mechanical Comprehension Test. Copyright © 1968 by The Psychological Corporation, a Harcourt Assessment Company. Reproduced by permission. All rights reserved. **Figure 9.6** H. Lee Rust, *Job Search, The Complete Manual for Job Seekers* (New York, AMACOM, 1991), pp. 232–33. **Figure 9.7** H. Lee Rust, *Job Search, The Complete Manual for Job Seekers* (New York, AMACOM, 1991), pp. 234–35. **Figure 9.8** Joseph Famularo, *Handbook of Modern Personnel Administration* (McGraw-Hill, © 1985). **Figure 9.10** *Human Resource Management: 7/E* by Gary Dessler, © 1997. Reprinted by permission of Prentice-Hall, Inc., Upper Saddle River, NJ. **CBC Video Case 3-1** "Revenge of Middle Managers," *Venture* (October 12, 1999). **CBC Video Case 3-2** "Keepers Inc.," *Venture* #742 (March 7, 2000).

Chapter 10

Breaking the Glass Ceiling Summarized from Andrea Orr, "H-P Names Carly Fiorina CEO," *The Globe and Mail*, July 20, 1999, p. B12; also Anita Lahey, "Homegrown," *Canadian Business*, August 13, 1999, pp. 33–35; also Ian Austen, "Problem Child," *Canadian Business*, March 26, 1999, pp. 22–28; also John Heinzl, "Women Take Charge at Canadian Units," *The Globe and Mail*, November 29, 1996, p. B10; also Greg Keenan, "Ford Canada Gets New CEO," *The Globe and Mail*, April 9, 1997, p. B1; also Joseph White and Carol

Hymowitz, "Watershed Generation of Women Executives is Rising to the Top," *The Globe and Mail*, February 10, 1997, pp. A1, A6; also Greg Keenan, "Woman at the Wheel," *The Globe and Mail*, July 8, 1995, pp. B1, B6; also Greg Keenan and Janet McFarland, "The Boys' Club," *The Globe and Mail*, September 27, 1997, pp. B1, B5; also Belle Rose Ragins, "Gender Gap in the Executive Suite: CEOs and Female Executives report on breaking the Glass Ceiling," *Academy of Management Executive*, February 1998, pp. 28–42. **Figure 10.1** Adapted from Jeffrey A. McNally, Stephen J. Gerra, and R. Craig Bollis, "Teaching Leadership at the U.S. Military Academy at West Point," *Journal of Applied Behavioral Science*, 32:2, p. 181, copyright © 1996 by Sage Publications. Reprinted by permission of Sage Publications, Inc. **Figure 10.2** Adapted from an idea presented in Shelley Kirkpatrick and Edwin A. Luke, "Leadership: Do Traits Matter?" *Academy of Management Executive*, 5, no. 2 (May 1991), pp. 47–60. **Figure 10.3** Adapted from Jeffrey A. McNally, Stephen J. Gerra, and R. Craig Bollis, "Teaching Leadership at the U.S. Military Academy at West Point," *Journal of Applied Behavioral Science*, 32:2, p. 178, copyright © 1996 by Sage Publications. Reprinted by permission of Sage Publications. **Table 10.1** Reprinted with permission of the *Harvard Business Review*. An exhibit from "What Makes a Leader," by Daniel Goleman, November–December 1998. Copyright © 1998 by the President and Fellows of Harvard College. All rights reserved. **The Entrepreneurial Edge** Summarized from www.janmag.com/profiles/rubin.html. **Figure 10.4** Adapted and reprinted by permission of the *Harvard Business Review*. "How the Style of Effective Leadership Varies with the Situation" from "Engineer the Job to Fit the Manager" by Fred E. Fiedler, September–October 1965. Copyright © 1965 by the President and Fellows of Harvard College; all rights reserved. **Figure 10.5** *Managing Behavior in Organizations: Science in Service* by Jerald Greenberg, © 1996. Reprinted by permission of Prentice-Hall, Inc., Upper Saddle River, NJ. **Figure 10.6** *Managing Behavior in Organizations* by Jerald Greenberg, © 1996. Reprinted by permission of Prentice-Hall, Upper Saddle River, NJ. **Figure 10.7** Jerald Greenberg. *Managing Behavior in Organizations: Science in Service* (Upper Saddle River, NJ: Prentice Hall, 1996). Reprinted by permission. **Case Study 10-1** Summarized from John P. Kotter, "Matsushita: The World's Greatest Entrepreneur?" *Fortune*, March 31, 1997, pp. 105–11. **Case Study 10-2** Summarized from Jeff Sallot, "Boyle Leaves Defence Post," *The Globe and Mail*, October 9, 1996, pp. A1, A5; also Paul Koring, "General's Ejection Inevitable," *The Globe and Mail*, October 9, 1996, p. A4; also "Former Military Leaders Criticize Boyle," *The Globe and Mail*, September 23, 1996, p. A5; also Murray Campbell, "Boyle Entwined in 'Ethical Malaise,'" *The Globe and Mail*, September 16, 1996, p. A8; also Paul Koring, "Collenette's Praise for General Draws Fire," *The Globe and Mail*, August 29, 1996, pp. A1, A3; also Paul Koring, "Boyle Blames his Subordinates," *The Globe and Mail*, August 21, 1996, pp. A1, A4; also Paul Koring, "Boyle Admits Breaking 'Spirit' of Law," *The Globe and Mail*, August 15, 1996, pp. A1, A4; also Paul Koring, "Boyle Gets Rough Ride at Inquiry," *The Globe and Mail*, August 14, 1996, pp. A1, A4; also Paul Koring, "Boyle Breaks Somalia Silence," *The Globe and Mail*, August 13, 1996, pp. A1, A3.

Chapter 11

A CEO Talks About Motivation Summarized from Carol Hymowitz and Matt Murray, "Raises and Praise or Out the Door," *The Wall Street Journal*, June 21, 1999, pp. B1, B4. **Figure 11.1** Warner Pflug, *The UAW in Pictures* (Detroit: Wayne State University Press, 1971), p. 14. **Figure 11.2** *Fundamentals of Organizational Behavior* by Carrell/Jennings/Heavrin, © 1997. Reprinted by permission of Prentice-Hall, Inc., Upper Saddle River, NJ. **Figure 11.3** David A. Kolb, Irwin M. Rubin, and James M. McIntyre, *Organizational Psychology: An Experiential Approach* (Englewood Cliffs, NJ: Prentice-Hall, 1971), p. 55. **Table 11.1** Copyright © 1997 by Gary Dessler, Ph.D. **The People Side of Management** Adapted from Bruce McDougall, "Perks with Pizzazz," *Canadian Business*, June 1990, pp. 78–79; also Don Champion, "Quality—A Way of Life at BC Tel," *Canadian Business Review*, Spring 1990, p. 33; also Margot Gibb-Clark, "Companies Find Merit in Using Pay as a Carrot," *The Globe and Mail*, August 10, 1990, p. B5; also Peter Matthews, "Just Rewards—The Lure of Pay for Performance," *Canadian Business*, February 1990, pp. 78–79; also Bud Jorgensen, "Do Bonuses Unscrupulous Brokers Make?" *The Globe and Mail*, May 28, 1990, p. B5; also David Evans, "The Myth of Customer Service," *Canadian Business*, March 1991, pp. 34–39; also Ian Allaby, "Just Rewards," *Canadian Business*, May 1990, p. 39; also Wayne Gooding, "Ownership is the Best Motivator," *Canadian Business*, March 1990, p. 6; also Neal Templin, "Ford Giving Every Worker a Purpose," *The Globe and Mail*, December 28, 1992, p. B6. **The Entrepreneurial Edge** Adapted from Vincent Alonzo, "1999 Motivator of the Year," *Incentive*, April 1999, pp. 39–46. **Figure 11.5** Diane Tracey, *10 Steps to Empowerment* (New York: William Morrow, 1990), p. 163. Copyright © 1990 by Diane Tracey. By permission of William Morrow & Co., Inc.

Chapter 11 Appendix

Figure 11A.2 Adapted from Gregory Northcraft and Margaret Neale, *Organizational Behavior* (Fort Worth, TX: The Dryden Press, 1994), p. 87.

Chapter 12

Store Walking at Home Depot Summarized from Arthur Blank, "They Sweat the Small Stuff," *Canadian Business*, May 28, 1999, pp. 51–55. **Figure 12.1** *Fundamentals of Organizational Behavior* by Carrell/Jennings/Heavrin, © 1997. Reprinted by permission of Prentice-Hall, Inc., Upper Saddle River, NJ. **Figure 12.3** Adapted from Richard L. Daft and Robert H. Lengel, "Information Richness: A New Approach to Managerial Information Processing and Organization Design." In Barry Staw and Larry L. Cummings (eds.), *Research in Organizational Behavior*, vol. 6 (Greenwich, CT: JAI Press, 1984), pp. 191–233. Reprinted from R. Daft and R. Steers, *Organizations: A Micro/Macro Approach* (Glenview, IL: Scott, Foresman, 1986), p. 532. **Case Study 12-2** Frederick A. Starke and Robert W. Sexty, *Contemporary Management*, Third Edition (Scarborough: Prentice Hall Canada, 1998), pp. 532–33.

Chapter 13

Work Teams at Shell Canada Ltd. Adapted from Bruce Little, "How to Make a Small, Smart Factory," *The Globe and Mail*, February 2, 1993, p. B24. **Figure 13.1** Jack Osborn et al., *Self-Directed Work Teams* (Homewood, IL: Business One Irwin, 1990), p. 30. **Figure 13.2** Steven Rayner, "Team Traps: What They Are, How to Avoid Them," *National Productivity Review* (Summer 1996), p. 107. Reprinted by permission of John Wiley & Sons, Inc. **The Entrepreneurial Edge** Summarized from Michael Selz, "Testing Self-Managing Teams, Entrepreneur Hopes to Lose Job," *Wall Street Journal,* January 11, 1994, p. B1; and Sally Goll Beatty, "Standard & Poors Acquires Published Image, Inc." *The Wall Street Journal*, July 2, 1997, p. B7. **Case Study 13-1** Summarized from James L. Hickman, "Red Star Rising," *Inc.*, August 1995, pp. 19–20.

Chapter 14

Big Changes in the Airline Industry Summarized from Sandra Cordon, "Feds Rein in Air Monopoly," *Winnipeg Free Press*, February 18, 2000, pp. B1–B2; also Gillian Livingstone, "Done Deal: Canadian Airlines Sold January 5," *Winnipeg Free Press*, December 24, 1999, p. B1; also Gillian Livingstone, "Air Canada's Cards on Table," *Winnipeg Free Press*, November 16, 1999, p. B3; also Conway Daly, "Air Canada Strikes Back," *Winnipeg Free Press*, October 20, 1999, pp. B1–B2; also Jacquie McNish, "CAI Lashes Out at Air Canada," *The Globe and Mail*, September 25, 1999, pp. B1, B9; also Andrew Willis, "Institutions Favour Merged Airline," *The Globe and Mail*, August 25, 1999, pp. B1, B6. **The Entrepreneurial Edge** Summarized from www.chaptersinc.com/corppro.htm. **Table 14.1** Adapted and reprinted by permission of *Harvard Business Review*. "Six Methods for Dealing with Change," from "Choosing Strategies for Change," by John P. Kotter and Leonard A. Schlesinger, March–April 1979. Copyright © 1979 by the President and Fellows of Harvard College; all rights reserved. **Figure 14.1** Reprinted by permission of Harvard

Business School Press. From John P. Kotter, *Leading Change* (Boston: 1996), p. 102. Copyright © 1996 by the President and Fellows of Harvard College; all rights reserved. **Figure 14.2** Copyright © 1990, by The Regents of the University of California. Reprinted from the *California Management Review*, Vol. 32, No. 2. By permission of The Regents. **Table 14.2** Reprinted with permission from E.H. Schein, *Organizational Culture and Leadership*. Copyright © 1985 Jossey-Bass Inc., Publishers. All rights reserved. **Figure 14.3** *Fundamentals of Organizational Behavior* by Carrell/Jennings/Heavrin, © 1997. Reprinted by permission of Prentice-Hall, Inc., Upper Saddle River, NJ. **Case Study 14-1** Frederick A. Starke and Robert W. Sexty, *Contemporary Management*, Third Edition (Scarborough: Prentice-Hall Canada, 1998), p. 569. **CBC Video Case 4-1** *Venture* (March 9, 1999). **CBC Video Case 4-2** Written by Professor Reg Litz of the University of Manitoba. Video Resource: "The Banff Experience," *Venture* #637 (April 6, 1997).

Chapter 15

The Entrepreneurial Edge Adapted from Stacy Baker, "Danier Leather: Vertical and Loving It," *Apparel Industry Magazine*, September 1999, pp. 102–104. **CBC Video Case 5-1** "Source Groups," *Venture* (January 11, 2000). **CBC Video Case 5-2** "On the Case with Al Rosen," *Venture* (March 28, 2000).

Chapter 15 Appendix

Figure 15A.1 Adapted from *Management Information Systems*, 6/e by Laudon/Laudon (Upper Saddle River, NJ; Prentice-Hall, 1996).

Endnotes

Chapter 1

1 Adrian Hosford and Richard Woods, "Tracking trends into the future," *Marketing*, August 5, 1999, pp. 22–26.

2 www.dofasco.ca/news (November 1999).

3 David Kirkpatrick, "The Second Coming of Apple," *Fortune*, November 9, 1998, pp. 87–104.

4 Joan Magretta, "The Power of Virtual Integration: An Interview with Dell Computer's Michael Dell," *Harvard Business Review*, March–April 1998, pp. 73–84.

5 Don Sheehy and Bryan Walker, "First Things First," CA *Magazine*, August 1999.

6 Henry Mintzberg, "The Manager's Job: Folklore and Fact," *Harvard Business Review*, July–August 1975, pp. 489–561.

7 See, for example, Henry Mintzberg, "The Manager's Job: Folklore and Fact," *Harvard Business Review*, July–August 1975, pp. 489–561, and George Copeman, *The Chief Executive* (London: Leviathan House, 1971), p. 271.

8 John Helyar and Joann Lubin, "Do You Need an Expert on Widgets to Head a Widget Company?" *The Wall Street Journal*, January 21, 1998, pp. A1, A10.

9 Geoffrey Colvin, "How to be a great ECEO," *Fortune*, May 24, 1999, pp. 104–110.

10 G. William Dauphinais and Colin Price, "The CEO as a Psychologist," *Management Review*, September 1998, pp. 1–15.

11 Phillip Crawley, "The Executive View," *The Globe and Mail*, October 27, 1999, p. E2.

12 Casey Mahood, "Dot-coms Turn Up the Heat on Compensation," *The Globe and Mail*, April 28, 2000.

13 These are based on Henry Mintzberg, "The Manager's Job: Folklore and Fact," *Harvard Business Review*, July–August 1975, pp. 489–561.

14 Sumatra Ghoshal and Christopher Bartlett, "Changing the Role of Top Management: Beyond Structure to Processes," *Harvard Business Review*, January–February 1995, pp. 86–96.

15 Sumatra Ghoshal and Christopher Bartlett, "Changing the Role of Top Management: Beyond Structure to Processes," *Harvard Business Review*, January–February 1995, p. 89.

16 Sumatra Ghoshal and Christopher Bartlett, "Changing the Role of Top Management: Beyond Structure to Processes," *Harvard Business Review*, January–February 1995, p. 91.

17 Sumatra Ghoshal and Christopher Bartlett, "Changing the Role of Top Management: Beyond Structure to Processes," *Harvard Business Review*, January–February 1995, p. 96.

18 Sumatra Ghoshal and Christopher Bartlett, "Changing the Role of Top Management: Beyond Structure to Processes," *Harvard Business Review*, January–February 1995, p. 94.

19 Peter Wilson, "Canadian Execs Don't See the Value of the Internet," *Vancouver Sun*, October 7, 1999, p. E4.

20 John Holland, *Making Vocational Choices: A Theory of Careers* (Upper Saddle River, NJ: Prentice-Hall, 1973); see also John Holland, *Assessment Booklet: A Guide to Educational and Career Planning* (Odessa, FL: Psychological Assessment Resources, Inc., 1990).

21 Adapted from Jonathan Harris, "The Most Annoying Company in Canada," *Canadian Business*, December 26, 1997/January 16, 1998, used with permission; and www.infolinkca.com.

22 Edgar Schein, *Career Dynamics: Matching Individual and Organizational Needs* (Reading, MA: Addison-Wesley, 1978), pp. 128–29.

23 A. Howard and D.W. Bray, *Managerial Lives in Transition: Advancing Age and Changing Times* (New York: Guilford, 1988); discussed in Dwayne Schultz and Sydney Ellen Schultz, *Psychology and Work Today* (New York: Macmillan Publishing Co., 1994), pp. 103–104.

24 A. Howard and D.W. Bray, *Managerial Lives in Transition: Advancing Age and Changing Times* (New York: Guilford, 1988); discussed in Dwayne Schultz and Sydney Ellen Schultz, *Psychology and Work Today* (New York: Macmillan Publishing Co., 1994), p. 104.

25 www.cibc.com. Address by A.L. Flood, October 8, 1998.

26 Frederick Starke and Robert Sexty, *Contemporary Management in Canada*, Third Edition (Scarborough: Prentice Hall Canada, 1998) p. 340; www.cibc.com.

27 Nina Munk, "How Levi's Trashed a Great American Brand," *Fortune*, April 12, 1999, pp. 83–90.

28 Henry Mintzberg, "The Manager's Job: Folklore and Fact," *Harvard Business Review*, July–August 1975, pp. 489–561.

29 www.bombardier.com, November 4, 1999.

30 Frederick Starke and Robert Sexty, *Contemporary Management in Canada*, Third Edition (Scarborough: Prentice Hall Canada, 1998), pp. 146–47, 170.

31 Dianne Cyr, "Organizational Transformation at Skoda in the Czech Republic: An HRM Perspective." In M. Mendenhall and G. Oddou (eds.), *Readings and Cases in International Human Resource Management*, Third Edition (South-Western, 2000), pp. 379–93.

32 Bryan O'Reilly, "Your New Global Workforce," *Fortune*, December 14, 1992, pp. 52–66.

33 www.nortelnetworks.com.

34 www.bombardier.com.

35 Dianne Cyr, "Organizational Transformation at Skoda in the Czech Republic: An HRM Perspective." In M. Mendenhall and G. Oddou (eds.), *Readings and Cases in International Human Resource Management*, Third Edition (South-Western, 2000), pp. 379–93.

36 Richard Crawford, *In the Era of Human Capital* (New York: Harper, 1991), p. 10.

37 James Brian Quinn, *Intelligent Enterprise* (New York: The Free Press, 1992), p. 3.

38 Bill Gates, *Business @ the Speed of Thought* (New York: Warner Books, 1999), p. 289.

39 Francis Fukuyama, "Are We at the End of History?" *Fortune*, January 15, 1990, p. 68.

40 Bryan Dumaine, "What the Leaders of Tomorrow See," *Fortune*, July 3, 1989, p. 58.

41 Tom Peters, *Liberation Management* (New York: Alfred Knopf, 1992), p. 9.

42 Eryn Brown, "Nine Ways to Win on the Web," *Fortune*, May 24, 1999, p. 125.

43 Mary Janigan, "Going E-Postal," *Maclean's*, September 13, 1999, pp. 34–36.

44 www.sierrasystems.com.

45 Tom Peters, *Liberation Management* (New York: Alfred A. Knopf, 1992), p. 9.

46 Ricky Griffin, Ronald Ebert, and Frederick Starke, *Business*, Third Canadian Edition (Scarborough: Prentice Hall Canada, 1999), p. 297.

47 www.nortelnetworks.com/corporate/global/emea/press/news.html.

48 Stratford Sherman, "A Master Class in Radical Change," *Fortune*, December 13, 1993, p. 82.

49 Rosabeth Moss Kanter, "The New Managerial Work," *Harvard Business Review*, November–December 1989, p. 88.

50 Rosabeth Moss Kanter, "The New Managerial Work," *Harvard Business Review*, November–December 1989, p. 88.

51 Peter Drucker, "The Coming of the New Organization," p. 45.

52 Thomas Stewart, "How GE Keeps Those Ideas Coming," *Fortune*, August 12, 1991, p. 42.

53 Peter Drucker, "The Coming of the New Organization," p. 43.

54 Anonymous, "High Tech Sector Discovers the Wonders of Rural Newfoundland," *Financial Post*, September 30, 1999, p. C5.

55 Bryan Dumaine, "The New Non-Managers," *Fortune*, February 22, 1993, p. 81.

56 Karl Albrecht, *At America's Service: How Corporations Can Revolutionize the Way They Treat Their Customers* (Homewood, IL: Dow-Jones Irwin, 1998).

57 Bryan Dumaine, "What the Leaders of Tomorrow See," *Fortune*, July 3, 1989, p. 51.

58 Michael Dorf, *Knitting Music* (New York: Knitting Factory Works, 1992), p. 4.

Chapter 1 Appendix

1 Alvin Toeffler, *Future Shock* (New York: Bantam Books, 1971), p. 43.

2 Adam Smith, *An Inquiry into the Nature and Causes of Wealth of Nations*, Fourth Edition (Edward Cannan, ed.) (London: Methuen, 1925). Published originally in 1776.

3 Alfred Chandler, *Strategy and Structure* (Cambridge, MA: MIT Press, 1990); see also Daniel Wren, *The Evolution of Management Thought* (New York: John Wiley, 1979).

4 D.S. Pugh, *Organization Theory* (Baltimore: Penguin, 1971), pp. 126–27.

5 Claude George, Jr., *The History of Management Thought* (Upper Saddle River, NJ: Prentice-Hall, 1972), pp. 99–101.

6 Richard Hopeman, *Production* (Columbus, OH: Charles Merrill, 1965), pp. 478–85.

7 Henri Fayol, *General and Industrial Management* (Constance Storrs, trans.) (London: Sir Isaac Pitman, 1949), pp. 42–43.

8 Based on Richard Hall, "Intra-Organizational Structural Variation: Application of the Bureaucratic Model," *Administrative Science Quarterly*, Vol. 7, No. 3 (December 1962): pp. 295–308.

9 William Scott, *Organization Theory* (Homewood, IL: Richard D. Irwin, 1967).

10 F.L. Roethlisberger and William Dickson, *Management and Worker* (Boston: Graduate School of Business, Harvard University, 1947), p. 21.

11 Alfred Chandler, *Strategy and Structure* (Cambridge, MA: MIT Press, 1990), pp. 19–51.

12 Warren G. Bennis, "Organizational Development and the Fate of Bureaucracy." Address at the Division of Industrial and Business Psychology, American Psychological Association, September 5, 1964. Reprinted in L.L. Cummings and W.E. Scott, Jr., *Organizational Behavior and Human Performance* (Homewood, IL: Richard D. Irwin and Dorsey, 1969), p. 436.

13 Douglas McGregor, "The Human Side of Enterprise." In Edward Deci, B. Von haller Gilmer, and Harry Kairn (eds.), *Readings in Industrial and Organizational Psychology* (New York: McGraw-Hill, 1972), p. 123.

14 R. Likert, *New Patterns of Management* (New York: McGraw-Hill, 1961), p. 6.

15 R. Likert, *New Patterns of Management* (New York: McGraw-Hill, 1961), p. 103.

16 Chris Argyris, *Integrating the Individual and the Organization* (New York: John Wiley, 1964).

17 R. Likert, *New Patterns of Management* (New York: McGraw-Hill, 1961), p. 91.

18 R. Likert, *New Patterns of Management* (New York: McGraw-Hill, 1961), p. 100.

19 R. Likert, *New Patterns of Management* (New York: McGraw-Hill, 1961), p. 100.

20 R. Likert, *New Patterns of Management* (New York: McGraw-Hill, 1961), p. 100.

21 Chester Barnard, *The Functions of the Executive* (Cambridge: Harvard University Press, 1968), p. 84.

22 Chester Barnard, *The Functions of the Executive* (Cambridge: Harvard University Press, 1968), p. 167.

23 Chester Barnard, *The Functions of the Executive* (Cambridge: Harvard University Press, 1968), p. 143.

24 Herbert A. Simon, *Administrative Behavior* (New York: Free Press, 1976), p. 11.

25 C. West Churchman, Russell Ackoff, and E. Linard Arnoff, *Introduction to Operations Research* (New York: John Wiley, 1957), p. 18.

26 Daniel Wren, *The Evolution of Management Thought* (New York: John Wiley, 1979), p. 512.

27 C. West Churchman, *The Systems Approach* (New York: Delta, 1968).

28 Joan Woodward, *Industrial Organizations: Theory and Practice* (London: Oxford University Press, 1965), pp. 64–65.

Chapter 2

1 Anonymous, "High-tech Sector Discovers the Wonders of Rural Newfoundland," *Financial Post*, September 30, 1999, p. C5.

2 Mark MacKinnon, "Foreign Ownership on the Rise," *The Globe and Mail*, February 1, 1999, pp. B1, B7.

3 Bruce Little, "Canada Ranks 10th in Competitiveness Study," *The Globe and Mail*, April 21, 1999, p. B7; Heather Scoffield, "Canada Lowest of G7 in Business Costs," *The Globe and Mail*, March 11, 1999; Barrie McKenna, "Canada Slips in Ability to Innovate," *The Globe and Mail*, March 12, 1999, p. B3; Shawn McCarthy, "Growth in Productivity Outpaces U.S.," *The Globe and Mail*, March 24, 1999, pp. B1, B8.

4 Dianne Cyr, *The Human Resource Challenge of International Joint Ventures* (Westport, CT: Quorum Books, 1995).

5 David H. Freedman, "Culture and Urgency," *Forbes*, pp. 25–28; William Tyler, "At Verifone It's a Dog's Life," *Fast Company*, 1, no. 1, 1995.

6 Steven Edwards, "The Corporate Engines that Drive Globalization," *Financial Post*, September 29, 1999, p. C15.

7 Theodore Levitt, "The Globalization of Markets," *Harvard Business Review*, May–June 1983, pp. 92–102.

8 Paul Doremus, William Keller, Louis Pauly, and Simon Reich, *The Myth of the Global Corporation* (Princeton: Princeton University Press, 1998).

9 For a discussion see, for example, Michael Czinkota, Pietra Rivoli, and Ilka Ronkinen, *International Business* (Fort Worth: The Dryden Press, 1992), Chapter 2.

10 Michael Czinkota, Pietra Rivoli, and Ilka Ronkinen, *International Business* (Fort Worth: The Dryden Press, 1992), p. 116.

11 John Daniels and Lee Radebaugh, *International Business* (Reading, MA: Addison-Wesley, 1994), p. 409.

12 Molly O'Meara, "Riding the Dragon," *World Watch*, March/April 1997, pp. 8–18.

13 Heather Scoffield, "Canada Adjusts to Free-Trade Realities," *The Globe and Mail*, December 31, 1998, pp. B1, B4.

14 Paul Dickens, *Global Shift* (New York: Guilford Press, 1992), p. 45; reprinted in Charles Hill, *International Business* (Burr Ridge, IL: Irwin, 1994).

15 See, for example, Susan Lee, "Are We Building New Berlin Walls?" *Forbes*, vol. 7, January 1991, pp. 86–89; Tom Reilly, "The Harmonization of Standards in the European Union and the Impact on U.S. Business," *Business Horizons*, March/April 1995.

16 John Daniels and Lee Radebaugh, *International Business* (Reading, MA: Addison-Wesley, 1994), pp. 9–10.

17 www.labatt.com; Fred Starke and Robert Sexty, *Contemporary Management*, Third Edition (Scarborough: Prentice-Hall, 1998), p. 150.

18 "The Car Is Born," *Economist*, September, 13, 1997, p. 68; Kathleen Kerwin, "GM's New Promised Land," *Business Week*, June 16, 1997, p. 34.

19 Ted Rakstis, "Going Global," *Kiwanis Magazine*, October 1981, pp. 39–43.

20 www.eicon.com.

21 Thomas Clasen, "An Exporter's Guide to Selecting Foreign Sales Agents and Distributors," *The Journal of European Business*, vol. 3, no. 2, November–December 1991, pp. 28–32.

22 Charles Hill, *International Business* (Burr Ridge, IL: Irwin, 1994), p. 402.

23 See, for example, John Daniels and Lee Radebaugh, *International Business* (Reading, MA: Addison-Wesley, 1994), p. 544.

24 Fred Starke and Robert Sexty, *Contemporary Management*, Third Edition (Scarborough: Prentice-Hall, 1998), p. 70.

25 David Jordan, "Creo Battles Asian Partner," *Business in Vancouver*, September 28–October 4, 1999, pp. 1, 8, 9.

26 Michael Czinkota, Pietra Rivoli, and Ilka Ronkinen, *International Business* (Fort Worth: The Dryden Press, 1992), p. 278.

27 Mark McKinnon, "Foreign Ownership on the Rise," *The Globe and Mail*, February 1, 1999, pp. B1, B7.

28 Margaret Cauley De La Sierra, *Managing Global Alliances: Key Steps for Successful Collaboration* (Wolkinham, England: Addison-Wesley Publishing Company, 1995), p. 4.

29 www.star-alliance.com.

30 Dianne Cyr, "High Tech, High Impact: Creating Canada's Competitive Advantage Through Technology Alliances," *Academy of Management Executive*, 1999, 13(2), pp. 17–26.

31 Kenichi Ohmae, "The Global Logic of Strategic Alliances," *Harvard Business Review*, March–April 1989, pp. 143–54.

32 Katherine Rudie Harrigan, "Joint Ventures and Global Strategies," *Columbia Journal of World Business*, 19 (Summer 1984): pp. 7–16; Michael Czinkota, Pietra Rivoli, and Ilka Ronkinen, *International Business* (Fort Worth: The Dryden Press, 1992), p. 320.

33 www.ballard.com.

34 Kenichi Ohmae, "The Global Logic of Strategic Alliances," *Harvard Business Review*, March–April 1989, p. 143.

35 Dianne Cyr, "Organizational Transformation at Skoda in the Czech Republic: An HRM Perspective." In M. Mendenhall and G. Oddou (eds.), *Readings and Cases in International Human Resource Management,* Third Edition (South-Western, 2000) pp. 379–393.

36 Wilfred Vanhonacker, "Entering China: An Unconventional Approach," *Harvard Business Review*, March–April 1997, pp. 130–140.

37 *Maclean's*, September 13, 1999.

38 Jeremy Main, "How to Go Global—and Why," *Fortune*, August 28, 1989, p. 70.

39 Karen Lee, "NTS's Marketplace Includes the World," *Business in Vancouver*, August 31–September 6, 1999, p. 24; David Jordan, "Finding the Best Way to Grow," *Business in Vancouver*, August 31–September 6, 1999, p. 29.

40 Charles Hill, *International Business* (Burr Ridge, IL: Irwin, 1994), pp. 5–6.

41 www.purdy's.com; Ricky Griffin, Ronald Ebert, and Frederick Starke, *Business,* Third Edition (Scarborough: Prentice-Hall, 1999), p. 91.

42 Charles Hill, *International Business* (Burr Ridge, IL: Irwin, 1994), p. 6; Michael McGrath and Richard Hoole, "Manufacturing's New Economies of Scale," *Harvard Business Review*, May–June 1992, p. 94.

43 www.mccain.com.

44 Kasra Ferdows, "Making the Most of Foreign Factories," *Harvard Business Review*, March–April 1997, pp. 80–81.

45 Based on Brian O'Reilly, "Your New Global Workforce," *Fortune*, vol. 14, December 1992, pp. 52–66.

46 Mariah E. DeForest, "Thinking of a Plant in Mexico?" *Academy of Management Executive*, vol. 8, no. 1, February 1994, pp. 33–40.

47 Mariah E. DeForest, "Thinking of a Plant in Mexico?" *Academy of Management Executive*, vol. 8, no. 1, February 1994, p. 34.

48 Mariah E. DeForest, "Thinking of a Plant in Mexico?" *Academy of Management Executive*, vol. 8, no. 1, February 1994, p. 37.

49 Mariah E. DeForest, "Thinking of a Plant in Mexico?" *Academy of Management Executive*, vol. 8, no. 1, February 1994, p. 38. See also Randall S. Schuler, Susan E. Jackson, Ellen Jackofsky, and John W. Slocum, "Managing Human Resources in Mexico: A Cultural Understanding," *Business Horizons*, 39, no. 3 (May 1996), pp. 55–61.

50 Robert Reich, "Who Is Them?" *Harvard Business Review*, March–April 1991, pp. 77–88.

51 Philip Harris and Robert Moran, *Managing Cultural Differences* (Houston: Gulf Publishing Company, 1979), p. 1.

52 Dianne Cyr, "Organizational Transformation at Skoda in the Czech Republic: An HRM Perspective." In M. Mendenhall and G. Oddou (eds.), *Readings and Cases in International Human Resource Management,* Third Edition (South-Western, 2000) pp. 379–393.

53 Gail Dutton, "Building a Global Brain," *Management Review*, May 1999, p. 35.

54 Gail Dutton, "Building a Global Brain," *Management Review*, May 1999, p. 36.

55 Gail Dutton, "Building a Global Brain," *Management Review*, May 1999, p. 37.

56 Gail Dutton, "Building a Global Brain," *Management Review*, May 1999, p. 35.

57 Gail Dutton, "Building a Global Brain," *Management Review*, May 1999, p. 35.

58 Gail Dutton, "Building a Global Brain," *Management Review*, May 1999, p. 35.

59 Gretchen Spreitzer, Morgan McCall, Jr., and Joan Mahoney, "Early Identification of International Executive Potential," *Journal of Applied Psychology*, 82, no. 1 (February 1997), pp. 6–29.

60 Note that there are few, if any, "pure" market economies or command economies any more. For example, much of the French banking system is still under government control. And it was only several years ago that the government of England privatized (sold to private investors) British Airways.

61 Jeffrey Garten, "Troubles Ahead in Emerging Markets," *Harvard Business Review*, May–June 1997, pp. 38–48.

62 "Countries with Highest Gross Domestic Product and Per-Capita GDP," *The World Almanac and Book of Facts, 1998* (Mahwah, NJ: K-III Reference Corporation, 1997), p. 112.

63 David Kemme, "The World Economic Outlook for 1999," *Business Perspectives*, January 1999, vol. 11, no. 2, pp. 6–9.

64 John Daniels and Lee Radebaugh, *International Business* (Reading, MA: Addison-Wesley, 1994), p. 138.

65 Michael Czinkota, Pietra Rivoli, and Ilka Ronkinen, *International Business* (Fort Worth: The Dryden Press, 1992), p. 640.

66 Benjamin Weiner, "What Executives Should Know About Political Risk," *Management Review*, January 1992, pp. 19–22.

67 Laura Pincus and James Belohlav, "Legal Issues in Multinational Business Strategy: To Play the Game, You Have to Know the Rules," *Academy of Management Executive*, 10, no. 3 (November 1996), pp. 52–61.

68 Philip Harris and Robert Moran, *Managing Cultural Differences* (Houston: Gulf Publishing Company, 1979), pp. 227–28. See also Jack N. Behrman, "Cross-cultural Impacts on International Competitiveness," *Business and the Contemporary World*, 7, no. 4 (1995), pp. 93–113; Lorna Wright, "Building Cultural Competence," *Canadian Business Review*, 23, no. 1 (Spring 1996), p. 29.

69 Catherine Tinsley, "Models of Conflict Resolution in Japanese, German, and American Cultures," *Journal of Applied Psychology*, vol. 83, no. 2, 1998, pp. 316–322.

70 Catherine Tinsley, "Models of Conflict Resolution in Japanese,

German, and American Cultures," *Journal of Applied Psychology*, vol. 83, no. 2, 1998, p. 321.

71 Geert Hofstede, "Cultural Dimensions in People Management." In Vladimir Pucik, Noel Tichy, and Carole Barnett (eds.), *Globalizing Management* (New York: John Wiley & Sons, Inc., 1992), pp.139–58.

72 Geert Hofstede, "Cultural Dimensions in People Management." In Vladimir Pucik, Noel Tichy, and Carole Barnett (eds.), *Globalizing Management* (New York: John Wiley & Sons, Inc., 1992), p. 143.

73 Geert Hofstede, "Cultural Dimensions in People Management." In Vladimir Pucik, Noel Tichy, and Carole Barnett (eds.), *Globalizing Management* (New York: John Wiley & Sons, Inc., 1992), p. 143.

74 Geert Hofstede, "Cultural Dimensions in People Management." In Vladimir Pucik, Noel Tichy, and Carole Barnett (eds.), *Globalizing Management* (New York: John Wiley & Sons, Inc., 1992), p. 147.

75 Michael Czinkota, Pietra Rivoli, and Ilka Ronkinen, *International Business* (Fort Worth: The Dryden Press, 1992), p. 205.

76 United Nations, *Draft International Code of Conduct on the Transfer of Technology* (New York: United Nations, 1981), p. 3; quoted in Michael Czinkota, Pietra Rivoli, and Ilka Ronkinen, *International Business* (Fort Worth: The Dryden Press, 1992), p. 313.

77 Michael Czinkota, Pietra Rivoli, and Ilka Ronkinen, *International Business* (Fort Worth: The Dryden Press, 1992), p. 314.

78 Arvind Phatak, *International Dimensions of Management* (Boston: PWS-Kent, 1989), pp. 46–49.

79 John Rossant, "After the Scandals," *Business Week*, November 22, 1993, pp. 56–57.

80 Anant Negandhi, *International Management* (Newton, MA: Allyn & Bacon, Inc., 1987), p. 61. See also Keith W. Glaister and Peter J. Buckley, "Strategic Motives for International Alliance Formation," *Journal of Management Studies*, 33, no. 3 (May 1996), pp. 301–22.

81 See also S.M. Davis, "Managing and Organizing Multinational Corporations." In C.A. Bartlett and S. Ghoshal (eds.), *Transnational Management* (Homewood, IL: Richard D. Irwin, 1992); and Arvind Phatak, *International Dimensions of Management* (Boston: PWS-Kent, 1989), pp. 78–104.

82 Paul Blocklyn, "Developing the International Executive," *Personnel*, March 1989, p. 44. Overseas assignments can also be risky for the manager who's sent abroad, with one recent study concluding that their employers don't reward their international experience. See Linda Grant, "That Overseas Job Could Derail Your Career," *Fortune*, April 14, 1997, p. 167. See also Martha I. Finney, "Global Success Rides on Keeping Top Talent," *HRMagazine*, 41, no. 4 (April 1996), pp. 69–72; and Reyer A. Swaak, "Expatriate Failures: Too Many, Too Much Cost, Too Little Planning," *Compensation and Benefits Review*, 27, no. 6 (November 1995), pp. 47–55.

83 Jackqueline Heidelberg, "When Sexual Harassment Is a Foreign Affair," *Personnel Journal*, April 1996.

84 Madelyn Callahan, "Preparing the New Global Manager," *Training and Development Journal*, March 1989, p. 30. See also Charlene Marmer Solomon, "Big Mac's McGlobal HR Secrets," *Personnel Journal*, 75, no. 4 (April 1996), p. 46; and Lorna Wright, "Building Cultural Competence," *Canadian Business Review*, 23, no. 1 (Spring 1996), pp. 29.

85 Dianne Cyr, *The Human Resource Challenge of International Joint Ventures* (Westport, CN: Quorum Books, 1995), p. 149.

Chapter 3

1 "A Global War Against Bribery," *Economist*, January 16, 1999, pp. 22–24.

2 Manuel Velasquez, *Business Ethics: Concepts and Cases* (Upper Saddle River, NJ: Prentice-Hall, 1992), p. 9; Kate Walter, "Ethics Hot Lines Tap into More Than Wrongdoing," *HR Magazine*, vol. 40, no. 9 (September 1995), pp. 79–85.

3 The following, except as noted, is based on Manuel Velasquez, *Business Ethics: Concepts and Cases* (Upper Saddle River, NJ: Prentice-Hall, 1992), pp. 9–12.

4 Manuel Velasquez, *Business Ethics: Concepts and Cases* (Upper Saddle River, NJ: Prentice-Hall, 1992), p. 9.

5 Based on Manuel Velasquez, *Business Ethics: Concepts and Cases* (Upper Saddle River, NJ: Prentice-Hall, 1992), pp. 12–14.

6 Manuel Velasquez, *Business Ethics: Concepts and Cases* (Upper Saddle River, NJ: Prentice-Hall, 1992), p. 12. For further discussion, see Kurt Baier, *Moral Points of View*, abbreviated edition (New York: Random House, 1965), p. 88.

7 For further discussion of ethics and morality, see Tom Beauchamp and Norman Bowe, *Ethical Theory and Business* (Upper Saddle River, NJ: Prentice-Hall, 1993), pp. 1–19.

8 See Michael McCarthy, "James Bond Hits the Supermarket: Stores Snoop on Shoppers' Habits to Boost Sales," *Wall Street Journal*, August 25, 1993, p. B12.

9 Gayle Macdonald and Paul Waldie, "Gottlieb Suing Six Ex-Livent Managers for Fraud," *The Globe and Mail*, February 18, 1999, pp. B1, B6; Paul Waldie and Gayle Macdonald, "A Quest for Profit from a Livent Loss," *The Globe and Mail*, February 17, 1999, pp. B1, B4.

10 Sar Morris et al., "A Test of Environmental, Situational, and Personal Influences on the Ethical Intentions of CEOs," *Business and Society*, 34, no. 2 (August 1995), pp. 119–47.

11 Justin Longnecker, Joseph McKinney, and Carlos Moore, "The Generation Gap in Business Ethics," *Business Horizons*, September–October 1989, pp. 9–14.

12 Justin Longnecker, Joseph McKinney, and Carlos Moore, "The Generation Gap in Business Ethics," *Business Horizons*, September–October 1989, p. 10. For a discussion of the development of a scale for measuring individual beliefs about organizational ethics, see Kristina Froelich and Janet Kottke, "Measuring Individual Beliefs About Organizational Ethics," *Educational and Psychological Measurement*, 51 (1991), pp. 377–83.

13 Thomas Tyson, "Does Believing that Everyone Else is Less Ethical Have an Impact on Work Behavior?" *Journal of Business Ethics*, 11 (1992), pp. 707–17.

14 Lynn Sharp Paine, "Managing for Organizational Integrity," *Harvard Business Review*, March–April 1994, p. 106.

15 Lynn Sharp Paine, "Managing for Organizational Integrity," *Harvard Business Review*, March–April 1994, pp. 107–17.

16 Lynn Sharp Paine, "Managing for Organizational Integrity," *Harvard Business Review*, March–April 1994, p. 108.

17 "Firms Go on Offensive in HR War," *The Globe and Mail*, September 23, 1999, p. T6.

18 Lynn Sharp Paine, "Managing for Organizational Integrity," *Harvard Business Review*, March–April 1994, p. 108. For a recent analysis of the financial consequences of illegal corporate activities, see Melissa Baucus and David Baucus, "Paying the Piper: An Empirical Examination of Longer-term Financial Consequences of Illegal Corporate Behavior," *Academy of Management Journal*, 40, no. 1 (February 1997), pp. 129–51; Dale Kurschner, "Five Ways Ethical Business Creates Fatter Profits," *Business Ethics*, 10, no. 2 (March 1996), p. 20; James Hunter, "Good Ethics Means Good Business," *Canadian Business Review*, 23, no. 1 (Spring 1996), pp. 14–17.

19 Emily Nelson and Joann Lublin, "How Whistle-Blowers Set Off a Fraud Problem that Crushed Cendant," *The Wall Street Journal*, August 13, 1998, pp. A1, A8.

20 Summarized from R. Craig Copetas, "Olympic Investigations Sprawl Far Abroad, Vexing a Stressed IOC," *The Wall Street Journal*, March 3, 1999, pp. A1, A6; also Craig Copetas and Roger Thurow, "Torch and Burn, or Behind the Scenes at the IOC Meeting," *The Wall Street Journal*, February 4, 1999, pp. A1, A16; also Craig Copetas, "A Preliminary Report on Salt Lake Scandal Certain to Rile the IOC," *The Wall Street Journal*, January 20, 1999, pp. A1, A8; also Stephen Moore, "For the Olympics, Worrisome Clouds over its Lofty Image," *The Wall Street Journal*, January 6, 1999, pp. A1, A10.

21 Leanne Yohemas-Hayes, "Defence Admits Records Purged," *Winnipeg Free Press*, July 23, 1999, p. B1.

22 Melissa Baucus and David Baucus, "Paying the Piper: An Empirical Examination of Longer-term Financial Consequences of Illegal Corporate Behavior," *Academy of Management Journal*, 40, no. 1 (February 1997), p. 149.

23 For a discussion, see Steen Brenner and Earl Molander, "Is the Ethics of Business Changing?" *Harvard Business Review*, January–February 1977, pp. 57–71; Robert Jackyll, "Moral Mazes: Bureaucracy and Managerial Work," *Harvard Business Review*, September–October 1983, pp. 118–30; see also Ishmael P. Akaah, "The Influence of Organizational Rank and Role of Marketing Professionals' Ethical Judgements," *Journal of Business Ethics*, 15, no. 6 (June 1996), pp. 605–14.

24 From Guy Brumback, "Managing Above the Bottom Line of Ethics," *Supervisory Management*, December 1993, p. 12.

25 Deon Nel, Leyland Pitt, and Richard Watson, "Business Ethics: Defining the Twilight Zone," *Journal of Business Ethics*, 8 (1989), p. 781; Steen Brenner and Earl Molander, "Is the Ethics of Business Changing?" *Harvard Business Review*, January–February 1977, pp. 57–71.

26 Mark Schwartz, "Heat's on to Get an Effective Code," *The Globe and Mail*, November 27, 1997, pp. 102–118.

27 Robert Sweeney and Howard Siers, "Survey: Ethics in Corporate America," *Management Accounting*, June 1990, pp. 34–40.

28 Robert Sweeney and Howard Siers, "Survey: Ethics in Corporate America," *Management Accounting*, June 1990, p. 34.

29 Robert Sweeney and Howard Siers, "Survey: Ethics in Corporate America," *Management Accounting*, June 1990, p. 35.

30 Rochelle Kelin, "Ethnic versus Organizational Cultures: The Bureaucratic Alternatives," *International Journal of Public Administration*, 19, no. 3 (March 1996), pp. 323–44.

31 Discussed in Samuel Greengard, "Cheating and Stealing," *Workforce*, October 1997, pp. 45–53.

32 Samual Certo, Carol Sales, and Frances Owen, *Modern Management in Canada: Diversity, Quality, Ethics, and the Global Environment*, Canadian Seventh Edition (Scarborough: Prentice Hall Canada, 1997), pp. 436, 475.

33 *Corporate Ethics: A Prime Business Asset* (New York: The Business Round Table, February 1988), p. 81

34 www.us.kpmg.com/ethics; also see www.ethics.ubc.ca/resources/business.

35 For a discussion, see, for example, Alan Rowe et al., *Strategic Management: A Methodological Approach* (Reading, MA: Addison-Wesley Publishing Co., 1994), p. 101.

36 Alan Rowe et al., *Strategic Management: A Methodological Approach* (Reading, MA: Addison-Wesley Publishing Co., 1994), p. 6.

37 Kate Walters, "Ethics Hot Lines Tap into More Than Wrongdoing," *HR Magazine*, 40, no. 9 (September 1995), pp. 79–85.

38 Alan Rowe et al., *Strategic Management: A Methodological Approach* (Reading, MA: Addison-Wesley Publishing Co., 1994), p. 7; see also John J. Quinn, "The Role of 'Good Conversation' in Strategic Control," *Journal of Management Studies*, 33, no. 3 (May 1996), pp. 381–95.

39 Alan Rowe et al., *Strategic Management: A Methodological Approach* (Reading, MA: Addison-Wesley Publishing Co., 1994), p. 9.

40 Sandra Gray, "Audit Your Ethics," *Association Management*, 48, no. 9 (September 1996), p. 188.

41 Rosi Lombardi, "Web Monitoring: Who's in Control at the Office?" *Computing Canada*, November 26, 1999, pp. 28–29.

42 Rosi Lombardi, "Web Monitoring: Who's in Control at the Office?" *Computing Canada*, November 26, 1999, pp. 28–29.

43 *Maclean's*, September 1999.

44 James G. Hunt, *Leadership* (Newbury Park, CA: Sage Publications, 1991), pp. 220–24. One somewhat tongue-in-cheek writer describes culture as a sort of organizational DNA, since "it's the stuff, mostly intangible, that determines the basic character of a business." See James Moore, "How Companies Have Sex," *Fast Company*, October–November 1997, pp. 66–68.

45 James G. Hunt, *Leadership* (Newbury Park, CA: Sage Publications, 1991), p. 221. For a recent discussion of types of cultures, see, for example, "A Quadrant of Corporate Cultures," *Management Decision*, 34, no. 5 (September 1996), pp. 37–40.

46 Ricky Griffin, Ronald Ebert, and Frederick Starke, *Business*, Third Canadian Edition (Scarborough: Prentice Hall Canada, 1999), p. 186.

47 Frederick Starke and Robert Sexty, *Contemporary Management*, Third Edition (Scarborough: Prentice Hall Canada, 1998), p. 573.

48 Richard Osborne, "Core Value Statements: The Corporate Compass," *Business Horizons*, September–October 1991, p. 29.

49 Frederick Starke and Robert Sexty, *Contemporary Management*, Third Edition (Scarborough: Prentice Hall Canada, 1998), p. 574.

50 Gary Dessler, *Winning Commitment: How to Build and Keep a Competitive Work Force* (New York: McGraw-Hill, 1993), p. 85.

51 Ricky Griffin, Ronald Ebert, and Frederick Starke, *Business*, Third Canadian Edition (Scarborough: Prentice Hall Canada, 1999), p. 139.

52 Example is based on Daniel Denison, *Corporate Culture and Organizational Effectiveness* (New York: John Wiley and Sons, 1990), pp. 147–74.

53 Daniel Denison, *Corporate Culture and Organizational Effectiveness* (New York: John Wiley and Sons, 1990), p. 148.

54 Daniel Denison, *Corporate Culture and Organizational Effectiveness* (New York: John Wiley and Sons, 1990), p. 148.

55 Daniel Denison, *Corporate Culture and Organizational Effectiveness* (New York: John Wiley and Sons, 1990), p. 151.

56 Daniel Denison, *Corporate Culture and Organizational Effectiveness* (New York: John Wiley and Sons, 1990), p. 151.

57 Daniel Denison, *Corporate Culture and Organizational Effectiveness* (New York: John Wiley and Sons, 1990), p. 151.

58 Daniel Denison, *Corporate Culture and Organizational Effectiveness* (New York: John Wiley and Sons, 1990), p. 154.

59 Daniel Denison, *Corporate Culture and Organizational Effectiveness* (New York: John Wiley and Sons, 1990), p. 155.

60 "Sweatshop Wars," *Economist*, February 27, 1999, pp. 62–63.

61 Milton Friedman, *Capitalism and Freedom* (Chicago: University of Chicago Press, 1962), p. 133.

62 Tom Beauchamp and Norman Bowie, *Ethical Theory and Business* (Upper Saddle River, NJ: Prentice Hall, 1993), pp. 49–52.

63 Tom Beauchamp and Norman Bowie, *Ethical Theory and Business* (Upper Saddle River, NJ: Prentice Hall, 1993), p. 79.

64 Tom Beauchamp and Norman Bowie, *Ethical Theory and Business* (Upper Saddle River, NJ: Prentice Hall, 1993), p. 60.

65 Tom Beauchamp and Norman Bowie, *Ethical Theory and Business* (Upper Saddle River, NJ: Prentice Hall, 1993), p. 54.

66 Adapted from Wayne Kondro, "Taking the V-Chip to TV Violence," *The Globe and Mail*, January 25, 2000.

67 William Evan and R. Edward Freeman, "A Stakeholder Theory of the Modern Corporation: Kantian Capitalism," *Ethical Theory of Business*, p. 82. See also Kenneth Goodpaster, "Business Ethics and Stakeholder Analysis," *Business Ethics Quarterly*, 1 (January 1991), pp.53–73.

68 John Simon, Charles Powers, and John Gunnermann, "The Responsibilities of Corporations and Their Owners." In *The Ethical Investor: Universities and Corporate Responsibility* (New Haven, CT: Yale University Press, 1972); reprinted in Beauchamp and Bowie, *Ethical Theory of Business* (Upper Saddle River, NJ: Prentice Hall, 1993), pp. 60–65.

69 www.bombardier.com.

70 Jo-Ann Johnston, "Social Auditors: The New Breed of Expert," *Business Ethics*, 10, no. 2 (March 1996), p. 27.

71 Karen Paul and Steven Ludenberg, "Applications of Corporate Social Monitoring Systems: Types, Dimensions and Goals," *Journal of Business Ethics*, 11 (1992), pp. 1–10.

72 Karen Paul, "Corporate Social Monitoring in South Africa: A Decade of Achievement, an Uncertain Future," *Journal of Business Ethics*, 8 (1989), p. 464.

73 Karen Paul, "Corporate Social Monitoring in South Africa: A Decade of Achievement, an Uncertain Future," *Journal of Business Ethics,* 8 (1989), p. 464. See also John S. North, "Living Under a Social Code of Ethics: Eli Lilly in South Africa Operating Under the Sullivan Principles," *Business and the Contemporary World,* 8, no. 1 (1996), pp.168–80; and S. Prakash Sethi, "Working with International Codes of Conduct: Experience of U.S. Companies Operating in South Africa Under the Sullivan Principles," *Business and the Contemporary World,* 8, no. 1 (1996), pp. 129–50.

74 Janet Near, "Whistle-blowing: Encourage It!" *Business Horizons,* January–February 1989, p. 5. See also Robert J. Paul and James B. Townsend, "Don't Kill the Messenger! Whistle-blowing in America: A Review with Recommendations," *Employee Responsibilities and Rights,* 9, no. 2 (June 1996), pp. 149–61.

75 Janet Near, "Whistle-blowing: Encourage It!" *Business Horizons,* January–February 1989, p. 5. See also Robert J. Paul and James B. Townsend, "Don't Kill the Messenger! Whistle-blowing in America: A Review with Recommendations," *Employee Responsibilities and Rights,* 9, no. 2 (June 1996), pp. 149–61.

76 Janet Near, "Whistle-blowing: Encourage It!" *Business Horizons,* January–February 1989, p. 6.

77 Kathleen Sibley, "Technology Complicates Work Ethics: KPMG Survey," *Computer Dealer News,* June 15, 1998, pp. 14–15.

78 *CBC Magazine,* November 22, 1999.

79 Government of Canada publications at www.odci.gov/cia/publications/factbook/ca.html.

80 See, for example, Taylor Cox, Jr., *Cultural Diversity in Organizations* (San Francisco: Berrett-Koehler Publishers, Inc., 1993), p. 3.

81 Taylor Cox, Jr., *Cultural Diversity in Organizations* (San Francisco: Berrett-Koehler Publishers, Inc., 1993), p. 3. See also T. Horowitz and C. Forman, "Clashing Cultures," *The Wall Street Journal,* August 14, 1990, p. A1.

82 Taylor Cox, Jr., *Cultural Diversity in Organizations* (San Francisco: Berrett-Koehler Publishers, Inc., 1993), pp. 3–4.

83 Francis Milliken and Luis Martins, "Searching for Common Threads: Understanding the Multiple Effects of Diversity in Organizational Groups," *Academy of Management Review,* vol. 21, no. 2 (1996), p. 415; see also Patricia Nemetz and Sandra Christensen, "The Challenge of Cultural Diversity: Harnessing a Diversity of Views to Understand Multiculturalism," *Academy of Management Review,* July 21, 1996, pp. 434–62.

84 Taylor Cox, Jr., *Cultural Diversity in Organizations* (San Francisco: Berrett-Koehler Publishers, Inc., 1993), p. 11.

85 Michael Carrell, Daniel Jennings, and Christina Heavrin, *Fundamentals of Organizational Behavior* (Upper Saddle River, NJ: Prentice-Hall, 1997), pp. 282–83.

86 Vivian Smith, "Breaking Down the Barriers," *The Globe and Mail,* November 17, 1992, p. B24.

87 George Kronenberger, "Out of the Closet," *Personnel Journal,* June 1991, pp. 40–44.

88 Taylor Cox, Jr., *Cultural Diversity in Organizations* (San Francisco: Berrett-Koehler Publishers, Inc., 1993), p. 88.

89 Taylor Cox, Jr., *Cultural Diversity in Organizations* (San Francisco: Berrett-Koehler Publishers, Inc., 1993), p. 89.

90 J.H. Greenhaus and S. Parasuraman, "Job Performance Attributions and Career Advancement Prospects: An Examination of Gender and Race Affects," *Organizational Behavior and Human Decision Processes,* 55, no. 2 (July 1993), pp. 273–98.

91 Adapted from Taylor Cox, Jr., *Cultural Diversity in Organizations* (San Francisco: Berrett-Koehler Publishers, Inc., 1993), p. 64.

92 Taylor Cox, Jr., *Cultural Diversity in Organizations* (San Francisco: Berrett-Koehler Publishers, Inc., 1993), pp. 179–80.

93 Madeleine Heilmann and Lewis Saruwatari, "When Beauty is Beastly: The Effects of Appearance and Sex on Evaluation of Job Applicants for Managerial and Nonmanagerial Jobs," *Organizational Behavior and Human Performance,* 23 (June 1979), pp. 360–72; see also Tracy McDonald and Milton Hakel, "Effects of Applicant Race, Sex, Suitability, and Answers on Interviewer's Questioning Strategy and Ratings," *Personnel Psychology,* 38, no. 2 (Summer 1985), pp. 321–34.

94 "Women in High Tech," www.pacifictech.net, November 24, 1999.

95 Patricia Digh, "Coming to Terms with Diversity," *HR Magazine,* November 1998, p. 119.

96 Taylor Cox, Jr., *Cultural Diversity in Organizations* (San Francisco: Berrett-Koehler Publishers, Inc., 1993), p. 236.

97 Patricia Digh, "Coming to Terms with Diversity," *HR Magazine,* November 1998, p. 119.

98 K. Kram, *Mentoring at Work* (Glenview, IL: Scott Foresman, 1985); Taylor Cox, Jr., *Cultural Diversity in Organizations* (San Francisco: Berrett-Koehler Publishers, Inc., 1993), p. 198.

99 Jules Oliver, "Seeking Greater Diversity Connectivity: A Canadian Experience," *Diversity Factor,* Winter 1999.

100 Jules Oliver, "Seeking Greater Diversity Connectivity: A Canadian Experience," *Diversity Factor,* Winter 1999.

Chapter 4

1 Max Bazerman, *Judgment in Managerial Decision Making* (New York: John Wiley & Sons, Inc., 1994), p. 3.

2 See, for example, Herbert Simon, *The New Science of Management Decision* (Englewood Cliffs, NJ: Prentice Hall, 1971), pp. 45–47.

3 Larry Long and Nancy Long, *Computers* (Upper Saddle River, NJ: Prentice-Hall, 1996), p. M-7.

4 Mairead Browne, *Organizational Decision Making and Information* (Norwood, NJ: Ablex Publishing Corporation, 1993), p. 6.

5 Richard Evans, "Advanced RISC Machines," *Fortune,* October 28, 1996, pp. 162–68.

6 Max Bazerman, *Judgment in Managerial Decision Making* (New York: John Wiley & Sons, Inc., 1994), p. 5.

7 For a discussion see, for example, Max Bazerman, *Judgment in Managerial Decision Making* (New York: John Wiley & Sons, Inc., 1994), pp. 4–5.

8 Max Bazerman, *Judgment in Managerial Decision Making* (New York: John Wiley & Sons, Inc., 1994), p. 4.

9 Heath Row, "Chumbo Rewrites the Software Code," *Fast Company,* September 1999, pp. 70–72.

10 Max Bazerman, *Judgment in Managerial Decision Making* (New York: John Wiley & Sons, Inc., 1994), p. 4.

11 James G. Miller, "Adjusting to Overloads of Information," in Joseph A. Litterer, *Organizations: Structure and Behavior* (New York: John Wiley, 1969), pp. 313–22. See also Jennifer Laabs, "Overload," *Workforce,* January 1999, pp. 30–37.

12 Dewitt Dearborn and Herbert A. Simon, "Selective Perception: A Note on the Departmental Identification of Executives," *Sociometry,* vol. 21, 1958, pp. 140–44. For a recent study of this phenomenon, see Mary Waller, George Huber, and William Glick, "Functional Background as a Determinant of Executives' Selective Perception," *Academy of Management Journal,* August 1995, pp. 943–94. While not completely supporting the Dearborn findings, these researchers did also conclude that managers' functional backgrounds affected how they perceived organizational changes. See also Paul Gamble and Duncan Gibson, "Executive Values and Decision Making: The Relationship of Culture and Information Flows," *Journal of Management Studies,* March 1999, pp. 217–40.

13 See also Janice Beyer et al., "The Selective Perception of Managers Revisited," *Academy of Management Journal,* June 1997, pp. 716–37.

14 Kenneth Laudon and Jane Price Laudon, *Management Information Systems* (Upper Saddle River, NJ: Prentice Hall, 1996), p. 125. See also Bob F. Holder, "Intuitive Decision Making," *CMA,* October 1995, p. 6.

15 Joan Johnson et al., "Vigilant and Hypervigilant Decision Making," *Journal of Applied Psychology,* vol. 82, no. 4, pp. 614–22.

16 Max Bazerman, *Judgment in Managerial Decision Making* (New York: John Wiley & Sons, Inc., 1994), pp. 6–8.

17 John Hammond, Ralph Keeney, and Howard Raiffa, *Smart Choices* (Boston: Harvard Business School Press, 1999), p. 16.

18 Lester Lefton and Laura Valvatne, *Mastering Psychology* (Boston: Allyn and Bacon, 1992), pp. 248–49. See also Daphne Main and Joyce Lambert, "Improving Your Decision Making," *Business and Economic Review,* April 1998, pp. 9–12.

19 James March and Herbert Simon, *Organizations* (New York: John Wiley, 1958), pp. 140–41.

20 Max Bazerman, *Judgment in Managerial Decision Making* (New York: John Wiley & Sons, Inc., 1994), p. 93.

21 Quoted from Max Bazerman, *Judgment in Managerial Decision Making* (New York: John Wiley & Sons, Inc., 1994), pp. 105–106.

22 Quoted from Max Bazerman, *Judgment in Managerial Decision Making* (New York: John Wiley & Sons, Inc., 1994), p. 108.

23 Prased Padmanabhan, "Decision Specific Experience in Foreign Ownership and Establishment Strategies: Evidence from Japanese Firms," *Journal of International Studies,* Spring 1999, pp. 25–27.

24 Jean Benoit Nadeau, "The Making of a Super Grocer," *The Financial Post Magazine,* May 1998, pp. 14–20.

25 Quoted in Robert L. Heilbroner, "How to Make an Intelligent Decision," *Think,* December 1990, pp. 2–4.

26 Robert L. Heilbroner, "How to Make an Intelligent Decision," *Think,* December 1990. See also Theodore Rubin, *Overcoming Indecisiveness: The Eight Stages of Effective Decision Making* (New York: Avon Books, 1985). See also John Hammond, Ralph Keeney, and Howard Raiffa, *Smart Choices* (Boston: Harvard Business School Press, 1999).

27 See, for example, William Taggart and Enzo Valenzi, "Assessing Rational and Intuitive Styles: A Human Information Processing Metaphor," *Journal of Management Studies,* March 1990, pp. 150–71; Christopher W. Allinson and John Hayes, "The Cognitive Style Index: A Measure of Intuition-Analysis for Organizational Research," *Journal of Management Studies,* January 1996, pp. 119–135.

28 This and the following guideline are from Robert L. Heilbroner, "How to Make an Intelligent Decision," *Think,* December 1990.

29 Ian Austen, "Internet or Bust," *Canadian Business,* March 6, 2000, pp. 24–30.

30 Helga Drummond, "Analysis and Intuition I Technological Toys: Lessons of Taurus," *International Journal of Technology Management,* April 1999, pp. 459–67.

31 Harvey Enchin, "Consensus Management? Not for Bombardier's CEO," *The Globe and Mail,* April 16, 1990, p. B1.

32 Fred Moody, "No Ordinary Ambassador," *Canadian Transportation,* August 1990, p. 13.

33 James Bowditsch and Anthony Buono, *A Primer on Organizational Behavior* (New York: John Wiley & Sons Inc., 1994), pp. 171–72.

34 Michael Carrell, Daniel Jennings, and Christine Heavrin, *Fundamentals of Organizational Behavior* (Upper Saddle River, NJ: Prentice Hall, 1997), p. 346.

35 For a discussion of these and the following points see, for example, Michael Carrell, Daniel Jennings, and Christine Heavrin, *Fundamentals of Organizational Behavior* (Upper Saddle River, NJ: Prentice Hall, 1997), p. 346.

36 I. Janis, *Victims of Groupthink* (Boston: Houghton-Mifflin, 1972); for an alternate view of decision-making problems in groups, see Glen Whyte, "Group-Think Reconsidered," *Academy of Management Review,* 14 (1989), pp. 40–56.

37 For an additional perspective on many of these see Randy Hirokawa and Marshall Scott Poole, *Communication and Group Decision Making* (Thousand Oaks, CA: Sage Publications, Inc., 1996), pp. 354–64. See also John O. Whitney and E. Kirby Warren, "Action Forums: How General Electric and Other Firms Have Learned to Make Better Decisions," *Columbia Journal of World Business,* 30, no. 4 (Winter 1995), pp. 18–27; Steven G. Rogelberg and Steven M. Rumery, "Gender Diversity, Team Decision Quality, Time on Task, and Interpersonal Cohesion," *Small Group Research,* 27, no. 1 (February 1996), pp. 79–90; Beatrice Shultz, Sandra M. Ketrow, and Daphne M. Urban, "Improving Decision Quality in the Small Group: The Role of the Reminder," *Small Group Research,* 26, no. 4 (November 1995), pp. 521–41.

38 See, for example, Lester Lefton and Laura Valvatne, *Mastering Psychology* (Boston: Allyn and Bacon, 1992), p. 249.

39 Jerald Greenberg and Robert Baron, *Behavior in Organizations* (Englewood Cliffs, NJ: Prentice-Hall, 1995), p. 393.

40 See Ron Zemke, "In Search of Good Ideas," *Training,* January 1993, pp. 46–52; R. Brent Gallupe, Lana Bastianutti, and William Cooper, "Unblocking Brainstorms," *Journal of Applied Psychology* (January 1991), pp. 137–42.

41 Gerry Blackwell, "You, Too, Can Be an Einstein," *Canadian Business,* May 1993, pp. 66–69.

42 See, for example, Jerald Greenberg and Robert Baron, *Behavior in Organizations* (Englewood Cliffs, NJ: Prentice-Hall, 1995), pp. 399–400.

43 See S.G. Rogelberg, J.L. Barnes-Farrell, and C.A. Lowe, "The Stepladder Technique: An Alternative Group Structure Facilitating Effective Group Decision Making," *Journal of Applied Psychology,* 57 (1992), pp. 730–37.

44 Norman R.F. Maier and E.P. McRay, "Increasing Innovation in Change Situations Through Leadership Skills," *Psychological Reports,* 31 (1972), pp. 30–43.

Chapter 4 Appendix

1 The break-even point is also sometimes defined more technically as the quantity of output or sales that will result in a zero level of earnings before interest or taxes. See, for example, J. William Petty et al., *Basic Financial Management* (Englewood Cliffs, NJ: Prentice Hall, 1993), p. 932.

2 Jay Heizer and Barry Render, *Production and Operations Management* (Upper Saddle River, NJ: Prentice Hall, 1996), pp. 240–50.

Chapter 5

1 George L. Morrisey, *A Guide to Tactical Planning* (San Francisco: Jossey-Bass, 1996), p. 61.

2 R.R. Donnelley and Sons Company Web site, 10 November 1999. www.rrdonnelley.com.

3 Harvey Kahalas, "A Look at Planning and Its Components," *Managerial Planning,* January–February 1982, pp. 13–16; reprinted in Phillip DuBose, *Readings in Management* (Englewood Cliffs, NJ: Prentice Hall, Inc., 1988), p. 49.

4 Peter Drucker, "Long Range Planning," *Management Science,* 5 (1959), pp. 238–49.

5 Oliver Bertin, "A Global Gamble," *The Globe and Mail,* August 24, 1996, pp. B1, B3.

6 Tamsen Tillson, "On a Wing and a Prayer," *Canadian Business,* October 1995, pp. 90–100.

7 Andre Picard, "Turn Green or Wilt, Business Told," *The Globe and Mail,* October 13, 1990, p. B6.

8 Merle MacIsaac, "Born-Again Basket Case," *Canadian Business,* May 1993, pp. 38–44.

9 See, for example, Bill Vlasic, "Can Chrysler Keep It Up?" *Business Week,* November 25, 1996, pp. 108–20.

10 This is from George Morrisey, *A Guide to Long-Range Planning* (San Francisco: Jossey-Bass, 1996), pp. 72–73.

11 Leonard Goodstein, Timothy Nolan, and Jay William Pfeiffer, *Applied Strategic Planning* (New York: McGraw-Hill, Inc., 1993), p. 170.

12 Gayle MacDonald, "The Eye of a Storm," *The Globe and Mail*, January 11, 1996, p. B13.

13 Martin Cash, "MTS Locks in Clients in Face of Deregulation," *Winnipeg Free Press*, November 20, 1990, p. 17.

14 Peter F. Drucker, *The Effective Executive* (New York: Harper & Row, 1966); quoted in Keith Curtis, *From Management Goal Setting to Organizational Results* (Westport, CT: Quorum Books, 1994), p. 101.

15 Peter Drucker, *The Practice of Management* (New York: Harper, 1954), pp. 62–87.

16 Gary Latham and J. James Baldes, "The Practical Significance of Locke's Theory of Goal Setting," *Journal of Applied Psychology*, 60, no. 1 (February 1975).

17 See, for example, Gary Latham and Gary Yukl, "A Review of Research on the Application of Goal Setting in Organizations," *Academy of Management Journal*, 18, no. 4 (1964), p. 824; Gary Latham and Terrance A. Mitchell, "Importance of Participative Goal Setting and Anticipated Rewards on Goal Difficulty and Job Performance," *Journal of Applied Psychology*, 63 (1978), pp. 163–71; and Sondra Hart, William Moncrief, and A. Parasuraman, "An Empirical Investigation of Sales People's Performance, Effort, and Selling Method During a Sales Contest," *Journal of the Academy of Marketing Science*, 17, no. 1 (Winter 1989), pp. 29–39.

18 The rest of this section, except as noted, is based on Gary Yukl, *Skills for Managers and Leaders* (Englewood Cliffs, NJ: Prentice Hall, 1991), pp. 132–33.

19 Gary Yukl, *Skills for Managers and Leaders* (Englewood Cliffs, NJ: Prentice Hall, 1991), p. 133; and Miriam Erez, Daniel Gopher, and Nira Arzi, "Effects of Goal Difficulty, Self-Set Goals, and Monetary Rewards on Dual Task Performance," *Organizational Behavior & Human Decision Processes*, 47, no. 2 (December 1990), pp. 247–69.

20 See, for example, Stephan Schiffman and Michele Reisner, "New Sales Resolutions," *Sales & Marketing*, 33, no. 1 (January 1992), pp. 15–16; and Steve Rosenstock, "Your Agent's Success," *Manager's Magazine*, 66, no. 9 (September 1991), pp. 21–23.

21 Gary Yukl, *Skills for Managers and Leaders* (Englewood Cliffs, NJ: Prentice Hall, 1991), p. 133.

22 Gary Latham and Lise Saari, "The Effects of Holding Goal Difficulty Constant on Assigned and Participatively Set Goals," *Academy of Management Journal*, 22 (1979), pp. 163–68; and Mark Tubbs and Steven Ekeberg, "The Role of Intentions in Work Motivation: Implications for Goal Setting Theory and Research," *Academy of Management Review*, 16, no. 1 (January 1991), pp. 180–99.

23 See Gary Latham and Lise Saari, "The Effects of Holding Goal Difficulty Constant on Assigned and Participatively Set Goals," *Academy of Management Journal*, 22 (1979), pp. 163–68.

24 Gary Latham, Terence Mitchell, and Denise Dorsett, "Importance of Participative Goal Setting and Anticipated Rewards on Goal Difficulty and Job Performance," *Journal of Applied Psychology*, 63 (1978), p. 170.

25 See, for example, Anthony Mento, Norman Cartledge, and Edwin Locke, "Maryland Versus Michigan Versus Minnesota: Another Look at the Relationship of Expectancy and Goal Difficulty to Task Performance," *Organizational Behavior and Human Performance*, 25, no. 3 (June 1980), pp. 419–40.

26 William Werther, "Workshops Aid in Goal Setting," *Personnel Journal*, 68 (November 1989), pp. 32–38.

27 Based on interviews with Sterling McLeod and Wayne Walker, vice-presidents of sales at Investors Group.

28 Steven Carroll and Henry Tosi, *Management by Objectives* (New York: Macmillan, 1973).

29 Mark McConkie, "A Clarification of the Goal Setting and Appraisal Processes in MBO," *Academy of Management Review*, 4 (December 1991), pp. 29–40.

30 *Webster's Collegiate Dictionary of American English* (New York: Simon & Schuster, Inc., 1988).

31 Rona Maynard, "The Pain Threshold," *Canadian Business*, February 1993, p. 24.

32 Murray R. Spiegel, *Statistics* (New York: Schaum Publishing, 1961), p. 283.

33 See, for example, Moore, *Handbook of Business Forecasting*, p. 5.

34 George Kress, *Practical Techniques of Business Forecasting* (Westport, CT: Quorum Books, 1985), p. 13. See also Diane Painter, "The Business in Economist at Work: Mobil Corp.," *Business Economics*, April 1999, pp. 52–55.

35 K. Romain, "Killer Computer is Making Pilots Sweat," *The Globe and Mail*, September 27, 1985, p. B12.

36 Kenneth Laudon and Jane Laudon, *Management Information Systems* (Upper Saddle River, NJ: Prentice Hall), p. 598; and "Wal-Mart to Triple Size of a Warehouse," *TechWeb*, http://192.215.17.45/,lewsflash/nf617/0210—st6.htm, February 10, 1999.

37 A. Chairncross, quoted in Thomas Milne, *Business Forecasting*, p. 42.

38 John Chambers, Santinder Mullick, and Donald Smith, "How to Choose the Right Forecasting Technique," *Harvard Business Review*, July–August 1971, pp. 45–74; and Moore, *Handbook of Business Forecasting*, pp. 265–290. See also John Mentzer et al., "Benchmarking Sales Forecasting Management," *Business Horizons*, May–June 1999, pp. 48–57. This study of 20 leading U.S. firms found widespread dissatisfaction regarding their current sales forecasting techniques.

39 Philip Kotler, *Marketing Management* (Upper Saddle River, NJ: Prentice Hall, 1997), p. 113.

40 Gina Mallet, "Greatest Romance on Earth," *Canadian Business*, August 1993, pp. 19–23.

41 Herman Kahn and Anthony Weiner, *The Year 2000: A Framework for Speculation on the Next Thirty-Three Years* (New York: Macmillan, 1967), p. 6; quoted in George A. Steiner, *Strategic Planning: What Every Manager Must Know* (New York: The Free Press, 1979), p. 237; and Nikcholas Georgantzas and William Acar, *Scenario-Driven Planning* (Westport, CT: Quorum Books, 1995).

42 Adam Kahane, "Scenarios for Energy: Sustainable World vs. Global Mercantilism," *Long-Range Planning*, 25, no. 4 (1992), pp. 38–46.

43 E. Jerome McCarthy and William Perreault, Jr., *Basic Marketing* (Homewood, IL: Irwin, 1990), pp. 131–32.

44 Stan Crock et al., "They Snoop to Conquer," *Business Week*, October 28, 1996, p. 172.

45 Melanie Warner, "Nightmare on Net Street," *Fortune*, September 6, 1999, pp. 285–86.

46 Arthur Little, *Global Strategic Planning* (New York: Business International Corporation, 1991), p. 3.

47 Arthur Little, *Global Strategic Planning* (New York: Business International Corporation, 1991), p. 3.

48 General Electric Corporation, *Annual Report*, 1998.

49 Andrew Campbell, "Tailored, Not Benchmarked: A Fresh Look at Corporate Planning," *Harvard Business Review*, March–April 1999, pp. 41–50.

50 Andrew Campbell, "Tailored, Not Benchmarked: A Fresh Look at Corporate Planning," *Harvard Business Review*, March–April 1999, p. 42.

51 Andrew Campbell, "Tailored, Not Benchmarked: A Fresh Look at Corporate Planning," *Harvard Business Review*, March–April 1999, p. 42.

52 Andrew Campbell, "Tailored, Not Benchmarked: A Fresh Look at Corporate Planning," *Harvard Business Review*, March–April 1999, p. 43.

53 Teri Lammers, "The One-Page Strategy Guide," *Inc.*, September 1992, pp. 135–38.

54 Eric Matson, "Now That We Have Your Complete Attention," *Fast Company*, February/March 1997.

Chapter 6

1 Peter Drucker, *Management: Tasks, Responsibilities, Practices.* (New York: Harper & Row, 1974), p. 611.

2 Andrew Campbell and Marcus Alexander, "What's Wrong with Strategy?" *Harvard Business Review,* November–December 1997, p. 48.

3 See, for example, Allan J. Rowe, et al., *Strategic Management* (Reading, MA: Addison-Wesley Publishing Co., 1989), p. 2; James Higgins and Julian Vincze, *Strategic Management* (Fort Worth: The Dryden Press, 1993), p. 5; Peter Wright, Mark Kroll, and John Parnell, *Strategic Management Concepts* (Englewood Cliffs, NJ: Prentice Hall, 1996), pp. 1–15.

4 Arthur Thompson and A.J. Strickland, *Strategic Management* (Homewood, IL: Irwin, 1992), p. 4; Fred R. David, *Concepts of Strategic Management* (Upper Saddle River, NJ: Prentice Hall, 1997), pp. 1–27. See also Bob Dust, "Making Mission Statements Meaningful," *Training & Development Journal,* 50, no. 6 (June 1996), p. 53.

5 James Higgins and Julian Vincze, *Strategic Management* (Fort Worth: The Dryden Press, 1993), p. 5.

6 Warren Bennis and Bert Manus, *Leaders: The Strategies for Taking Charge* (New York: Harper & Row, 1985); quoted in Andrew Campbell and Sally Yeung, "Mission, Vision and Strategic Intent," *Long-Range Planning,* 24, no. 4, p. 145.

7 Arthur Thompson and A.J. Strickland, *Strategic Management* (Homewood, IL: Irwin, 1992), p. 4. See also George Morrisey, *A Guide to Strategic Planning* (San Francisco: Jossey-Bass, 1996), p. 7.

8 Andrew Willis, "New CEO Pledges to Redefine B of M," *The Globe and Mail,* February 24, 1999, p. B7.

9 David Berman, "Hold the Fries," *Canadian Business,* January 30, 1998, pp. 32–34.

10 Susanne Craig, "Hunkin Takes Charge of CIBC Renovation," *The Globe and Mail,* June 28, 1999, pp. B1, B4.

11 Susanne Craig, "CIBC's New Chief Makes Bold Debut," *The Globe and Mail,* June 4, 1999, pp. B1, B4.

12 Claytton Christensen, "Making Strategy: Learning by Doing," *Harvard Business Review,* November–December 1997, pp. 141–56.

13 Gary Himel, "Killer Strategies That Make Shareholders Rich," *Fortune,* June 23, 1997, p. 83.

14 Gary Himel, "Killer Strategies That Make Shareholders Rich," *Fortune,* June 23, 1997, p. 83.

15 Gary Himel, "Killer Strategies That Make Shareholders Rich," *Fortune,* June 23, 1997, p. 83; see also Gary Hamel, "Strategies as Revolutions," *Harvard Business Review,* July–August 1996, pp. 69–82.

16 Philip Evans and Thomas Wurster, "Strategy and the New Economics of Information," *Harvard Business Review,* September–October 1997, p. 72.

17 Philip Evans and Thomas Wurster, "Strategy and the New Economics of Information," *Harvard Business Review,* September–October 1997, p. 72.

18 Hugh Courtney, Jane Kirkland, and Patrick Viguerie, "Strategy Under Uncertainty," *Harvard Business Review,* November–December 1997, p. 69.

19 This is quoted from, and this section is based on, Allan J. Rowe, Richard O. Mason, Carl E. Dickel, Richard B. Mann, and Robert J. Mockler, *Strategic Management: A Methodological Approach* (Reading, MA: Addison-Wesley Publishing Co., 1994), pp. 114–16.

20 Margot Gibb-Clark, "Hospital Managers Gain Tool to Compare Notes," *The Globe and Mail,* September 9, 1996, p. B9.

21 This is based on Allan J. Rowe, Richard O. Mason, Carl E. Dickel, Richard B. Mann, and Robert J. Mockler, *Strategic Management: A Methodological Approach* (Reading, MA: Addison-Wesley Publishing Co., 1994), p. 116; and Stephen George and Arnold Weimerskirch, *Total Quality Management* (New York: John Wiley & Sons, 1994), pp. 207–21.

22 Oliver Bertin, "Rail Deal Makes Shipping Giant," *The Globe and Mail,* December 20, 1999, p. B1.

23 This is based on James Higgins and Julian Vincze, *Strategic Management* (Fort Worth: The Dryden Press, 1993), pp. 200–204.

24 Allan J. Rowe, Richard O. Mason, Carl E. Dickel, Richard B. Mann, and Robert J. Mockler, *Strategic Management: A Methodological Approach* (Reading, MA: Addison-Wesley Publishing Co., 1994), pp. 246–47.

25 Steven Chase, "It's a For-Letter Word to Investors," *The Globe and Mail,* August 14, 1999, p. B4.

26 John Byrne, Richard Brandt, and Otis Port, "The Virtual Corporation," *Business Week,* February 8, 1993, p. 99.

27 See also J. Carlos Jarillo, "On Strategic Networks," *Strategic Management Journal,* 9 (1988), pp. 31–41; and William Davidow and Michael Malone, "The Virtual Corporation," *California Business Review,* November 12, 1992, pp. 34–42.

28 John Byrne, Richard Brandt, and Otis Port, "The Virtual Corporation," *Business Week,* February 8, 1993, p. 99.

29 John Byrne, Richard Brandt, and Otis Port, "The Virtual Corporation," *Business Week,* February 8, 1993, p. 100.

30 John Byrne, Richard Brandt, and Otis Port, "The Virtual Corporation," *Business Week,* February 8, 1993, p. 100.

31 Virtual corporations should not be confused with the Japanese Keiretsus strategy. Keiretsus are tightly knit groups of firms governed by a supra-board of directors concerned with establishing the long-term survivability of the Keiretsus organization. Interlocking boards of directors and shared ownership help distinguish Keiretsus from other forms of strategic alliances, including virtual corporations. See, for example, John Byrne, Richard Brandt, and Otis Port, "The Virtual Corporation," *Business Week,* February 8, 1993, p. 101; Arthur Thompson and A.J. Strickland, *Strategic Management* (Homewood, IL: Irwin, 1992), p. 216; and Kenichi Ohmae, "The Global Logic of Strategic Alliances," *Harvard Business Review,* March–April 1989, pp. 143–54.

32 Unless otherwise noted, the following is based on Michael E. Porter, *Competitive Strategy* (New York: The Free Press, 1980); and Michael E. Porter, *Competitive Advantage* (New York: The Free Press, 1985).

33 Michael E. Porter, *Competitive Advantage* (New York: The Free Press, 1985), p. 14.

34 John Geddes, "'Good Book' Good Business for Paper Makers," *The Financial Post,* January 8, 1989, pp. 1, 4.

35 Michael E. Porter, *Competitive Strategy: Techniques for Analyzing Industries and Competitions* (New York: The Free Press, 1980).

36 Michael E. Porter, *Competitive Strategy: Techniques for Analyzing Industries and Competitions* (New York: The Free Press, 1980), p. 17.

37 Michael E. Porter, "What is Strategy?" *Harvard Business Review,* November–December 1996, pp. 61–80.

38 Interprovincial Pipeline System Inc., *1992 Annual Report,* pp. 4–6.

39 Peter Verburg, "Reach for the Bottom," *Canadian Business,* March 6, 2000, pp. 43–47.

40 For a discussion of core competencies see, for example, C.K. Prahalad and Gary Hamel, "The Core Competence of a Corporation," *Harvard Business Review,* May–June 1990, pp. 80–82.

41 Gary Hamel and C.K. Prahalad, "Strategy as Stretch and Leverage," *Harvard Business Review,* March–April 1993, pp. 75–84.

42 Gary Hamel and C.K. Prahalad, "Strategy as Stretch and Leverage," *Harvard Business Review,* March–April 1993, p. 77.

43 C.K. Prahalad and Gary Hamel, "The Core Competence of a Corporation," *Harvard Business Review,* May–June 1990, p. 82.

44 C.K. Prahalad and Gary Hamel, "The Core Competence of a Corporation," *Harvard Business Review,* May–June 1990, p. 82.

45 Alan D. Gray, "Arrow Takes Aim," *Montreal Gazette,* September 5, 1995, pp. C3–C4.

46 Gary Yukl, *Managerial Leadership,* 269: "A Review and Theory of Research," *Journal of Management,* 15, no. 2 (1989).

47 Except as noted, the next several leader characteristics are based on Michael E. Porter, "What is Strategy?" *Harvard Business Review*, November–December 1996, p. 77.

48 Michael E. Porter, "What is Strategy?" *Harvard Business Review*, November–December 1996, p. 77.

49 See, for example, Clay Carr, "Seven Keys to Successful Change," *Training*, February 1994, pp. 55–60; Guvenc G. Alpander and Carroll R. Lee, "Culture, Strategy and Teamwork: The Keys to Organizational Change," *Journal of Management Development*, 14, no. 8 (1995), p. 418.

50 Thomas Cummings and Christopher Worley, *Organization Development and Change* (Minneapolis: West Publishing Company, 1993).

Chapter 7

1 James P. Sterba, "At the Met Opera, It's Not Over till the Fat Man folds," *The Wall Street Journal*, January 5, 1998, pp. 1, 6.

2 Bombardier Annual Report.

3 Daniel Stoffman, "Mr. Clean," *Canadian Business*, June 1996, pp. 59–65.

4 "How Can Big Companies Keep the Entrepreneurial Spirit Alive?" *Harvard Business Review*, November–December 1995, pp. 188–89.

5 David Yoffie, "Building a Company on Internet Time: Lessons from Netscape," *California Management Review*, Spring 1999, p. 8.

6 David Yoffie, "Building a Company on Internet Time: Lessons from Netscape," *California Management Review*, Spring 1999, p. 8.

7 Brian S. Akre, "GM Names Wagoner President; Reorganizes Auto Units," *The Globe and Mail*, October 7, 1998, p. B11.

8 Rekha Balu, "Heinz's Johnson to Divest Operations, Scrap Management of Firm by Regions," *The Wall Street Journal*.

9 Tara Parker-Pope and Joann Lublin, "P&G Will Make Jurgen Feel Ahead of Schedule," *The Wall Street Journal*, September 10, 1998, pp. B-1, B-8.

10 Kenneth and Jane Laudon, *Management Information Systems*, 5th edition (Upper Saddle River, NJ: Prentice Hall, 1998), p. 323.

11 Richard Blackwell, "New CIBC Boss Promises Shakeup," *The Globe and Mail*, April 2, 1999, pp. B1, B4.

12 See, for example, Lawton Burns and Douglas Wholey, "Adoption and Abandonment of Matrix Management Programs: Effects of Organizational Characteristics and Interorganizational Networks," *Academy of Management Journal*, 36, no. 1 (February 1993), pp. 106–38.

13 Interview with Tom Ward, operations manager for Genstar Shipyards Ltd.

14 *Organizing for International Competitiveness: How Successful Corporations Structure Their Worldwide Operations* (New York: Business International Corp., 1988), p. 117.

15 Lawton Burns and Douglas Wholey, "Adoption and Abandonment of Matrix Management Programs: Effects of Organizational Characteristics and Interorganizational Networks," *Academy of Management Journal*, 36, no. 1 (February 1993), p. 106.

16 Robert Hercz, "Shooting for Profits," *Canadian Business*, June 12, 1998, pp. 71–73.

17 John Partridge, "Abitibi Dares to Digest Another Deal," *The Globe and Mail*, February 27, 1998, p. B27.

18 Henry Mintzberg, *Structure in Fives: Designing Effective Organizations* (Englewood Cliffs, NJ: Prentice-Hall, 1983), p. 4.

19 Paul Lawrence and Jay Lorsch, *Organization and Environment* (Cambridge, MA: Harvard University Press, 1967).

20 Paul Lawrence and Jay Lorsch, *Organization and Environment* (Cambridge, MA: Harvard University Press, 1967), p. 6.

21 Christopher A. Bartlett and Sumantra Ghoshal, "Matrix Management: Not a Structure, a Frame of Mind," *Harvard Business Review* (July–August 1990), pp. 138–45.

22 Christopher A. Bartlett and Sumantra Ghoshal, "Matrix Management: Not a Structure, a Frame of Mind," *Harvard Business Review* (July–August 1990), pp. 143–44.

23 Jacquie McNish, "A Chairman with Worries Lots of Others Would Like," *The Globe and Mail*, April 14, 1990, p. B6.

24 Ann Gibbon, "CN's New Boss Takes Hard Line," *The Globe and Mail*, February 8, 1993, pp. B1–B2.

25 A. Ross, "BMO's Big Bang," *Canadian Business*, January 1994, pp. 58–63.

26 Peter Larson, "Winning Strategies," *Canadian Business Review*, Summer 1989, p. 41.

27 Ian Allaby, "The Search for Quality," *Canadian Business*, May 1990, pp. 31–42.

28 Mario Shao, "For Levi's, a Flattering Fit Overseas," *Business Week*, November 5, 1990, pp. 76–77.

29 "Can Japan's Giants Cut the Apron Strings?" *Business Week*, May 14, 1990, pp. 105–106.

30 "A Circus Juggles HR Worldwide," *Workforce*, February 1997, p. 50.

31 The foundation study for this conclusion is Alfred Chandler, *Strategy and Structure* (Cambridge: MIT Press, 1962); for a recent literature review and test of the strategy-structure link see Terry Amburgey and Tina Dacin, "As the Left Foot Follows the Right? The Dynamics of Strategic and Structural Change," *Academy of Management Journal*, 37, no. 6 (1994), pp. 1427–52.

32 Terry Amburgey and Tina Dacin, "As the Left Foot Follows the Right? The Dynamics of Strategic and Structural Change," *Academy of Management Journal*, 37, no. 6 (1994), pp. 1427–52.

33. Alfred Chandler, *Strategy and Structure* (Cambridge: MIT Press, 1962), p. 14.

34 Alfred Chandler, *Strategy and Structure* (Cambridge: MIT Press, 1962), p. 366.

35 Y. Ono and M. Brauchli, "Japan Cuts the Middle Management Fat," *The Wall Street Journal*, August 8, 1989, p. B1.

36 J.S. McClenahen, "Managing More People in the '90's," *Industry Week*, March 20, 1989, p. 30.

37 Randall Litchfield, "Trouble is my Business," *Canadian Business*, February 1993, pp. 31–32.

38 For a definition of stress see, for example, James Bowditch and Anthony Buono, *A Primer on Organization Behavior* (New York: John Wiley, 1994), p. 439.

39 Jerald Greenberg and Robert Baron, *Behavior in Organizations* (Englewood Cliffs, NJ: Prentice-Hall, 1995), p. 244.

40 J.D. Quick, R.S. Horn, and J.C. Quick, "Health Consequences of Stress," *Journal of Organizational Behavior Management*, 8 (1986), pp. 19–36.

41 Margot Gibb-Clark, "The Case For a Mentally Healthy Office," *The Globe and Mail*, October 20, 1998, p. B12.

42 Robert Vecchio, *Organizational Behavior* (Chicago: Dryden Press, 1991), quoted in Michael Carrell, Daniel Jennings, and Christina Heavrin, *Fundamentals of Organizational Behavior* (Upper Saddle River, NJ: Prentice-Hall, 1997), p. 144.

43 David Myers, *Social Psychology*, Third Edition (New York: McGraw-Hill, 1990), pp. 178–79.

Chapter 8

1 Tom Peters, *Liberation Management* (New York: Alfred A. Knopf, 1992), p. 9; see also Bart Ziegler, "Gerstner's IBM Revival: Impressive, Incomplete," *Wall Street Journal*, March 27, 1997, pp. 81, 84.

2 Shona McKay, "The Challenge in Change," *The Financial Post Magazine*, April 1992, pp. 43–44.

3 Tom Peters, *Liberation Management* (New York: Alfred A. Knopf, 1992), p. 310.

4 Except as noted, this section is based on Tom Peters, *Thriving on Chaos* (New York: Harper & Row, 1987), pp. 425–38; and Tom

Peters, *Liberation Management* (New York: Alfred A. Knopf, 1992), pp. 90–95.

5   Jerry Ross, "Review of *Rogue Trader: How I Brought Down Barings Bank and Shook the Financial World*, by Nicholas Leeson," *Academy of Management Review*, October 1997, p. 10.

6   "How Can Big Companies Keep the Entrepreneurial Spirit Alive?" *Harvard Business Review*, November–December 1996, pp. 188–89.

7   Tom Peters, *Liberation Management* (New York: Alfred A. Knopf, 1992), pp. 49–50.

8   James O'Toole, *Work and the Quality of Life: Resources Papers for Work in America* (Boston: MIT Press, 1994), pp. 18–29.

9   Tom Peters, *Thriving on Chaos* (New York: Harper & Row, 1987), p. 256.

10 Gordon Pitts, "The Cheese Plant Nobody Wanted," *The Globe and Mail*, February 16, 1993, p. B24.

11 William H. Miller, "Chesebrough-Pond's at a Glance," *Industry Week*, October 19, 1992, pp. 14–15.

12 Except as noted, the remainder of this section is based on James Shonk, *Team-Based Organizations* (Chicago: Irwin, 1997).

13 James Shonk, *Team-Based Organizations* (Chicago: Irwin, 1997), pp. 35–38.

14 *Webster's New World Dictionary*, 3rd College ed. (New York: Simon and Schuster, Inc., 1988), p. 911. For a discussion of networked organizations, see James Brian Quinn, *Intelligent Enterprise* (New York: Free Press, 1992), pp. 213–40.

15 Ram Charan, "How Networks Reshape Organizations—For Results," *Harvard Business Review*, September–October 1991, pp. 104–15.

16 Ram Charan, "How Networks Reshape Organizations—For Results," *Harvard Business Review*, September–October 1991, pp. 106–07.

17 Ram Charan, "How Networks Reshape Organizations—For Results," *Harvard Business Review*, September–October 1991, p. 106.

18 Christopher Bartlett and Sumantra Ghoshal, "What Is a Global Manager?" *Harvard Business Review*, September–October 1992, pp. 62–74.

19 Tom Lester, "The Rise of the Network," *International Management*, June 1992, p. 72.

20 Paul Evans, Yves Doz, and Andre Laurent, *Human Resource Management in International Firms* (London: Macmillan, 1989), p. 123.

21 Chandler Harrison Stevens, "Electronic Organization and Expert Networks: Beyond Electronic Mail and Computer Conferencing," Sloan School of Management Working Paper No. 1794-86, Massachusetts Institute of Technology, Management in the 1990s Research Program, May 1986. Reprinted in Tom Peters, *Liberation Management* (New York: Alfred A. Knopf, 1992), pp. 123–24.

22 David Kilpatrick, "Groupware Goes Boom," *Fortune*, December 27, 1993, pp. 99–101.

23 Kenneth Laudon and Jane Laudon, *Essentials of Management Information Systems* (Upper Saddle River, NJ: Prentice-Hall, 1997), pp. 413–416.

24 *Harvard Business Review,* September–October 1997, p. 75.

25 Bill Gates, *Business @ the Speed of Thought* (New York, Warner Books, 1999), pp. 238–239.

26 Mary Anne Devanna and Noel Tichy, "Creating the Competitive Organization of the 21st Century: The Boundaryless Corporation," *Human Resource Management*, 29, no. 4 (Winter 1990), pp. 455–71.

27 Larry Hirschhorn and Thomas Gilmore, "The New Boundaries of the 'Boundaryless' Company," *Harvard Business Review*, May–June 1992, p. 104. See also Daniel Denison, Stuart Hart, and Joel Kahn, "From Chimneys to Cross-Functional Teams: Developing and Validating a Diagnostic Model," *Academy of Management Journal*, 39, no. 4 (August 1996), pp. 1005–23.

28 This is based on Larry Hirschhorn and Thomas Gilmore, "The New Boundaries of the 'Boundaryless' Company," *Harvard Business Review*, May–June 1992, pp. 104–108.

29 Except as noted, the remainder of this section is based on Larry Hirschhorn and Thomas Gilmore, "The New Boundaries of the 'Boundaryless' Company," *Harvard Business Review*, May–June 1992, pp. 107–108.

30 Larry Hirschhorn and Thomas Gilmore, "The New Boundaries of the 'Boundaryless' Company," *Harvard Business Review*, May–June 1992, p. 107.

31 Larry Hirschhorn and Thomas Gilmore, "The New Boundaries of the 'Boundaryless' Company," *Harvard Business Review*, May–June 1992, p. 108.

32 Larry Hirschhorn and Thomas Gilmore, "The New Boundaries of the 'Boundaryless' Company," *Harvard Business Review*, May–June 1992, p. 109.

33 Except as noted, this section is based on John A. Byrne, "The Horizontal Corporation," *Business Week*, December 20, 1993, pp. 76–81.

34 Michael Hammer and James Champy, *Reengineering the Corporation* (New York: HarperBusiness, 1994), 35; Ann Majchrzak and Quinwei Wang, "Breaking the Functional Mind-Set of Process Organizations," *Harvard Business Review* (September–October 1996), pp. 93–99.

35 Ann Majchrzak and Quinwei Wang, "Breaking the Functional Mind-Set of Process Organizations," *Harvard Business Review* (September–October 1996), pp. 96–99.

36 Ann Majchrzak and Quinwei Wang, "Breaking the Functional Mind-Set of Process Organizations," *Harvard Business Review* (September–October 1996), pp. 96–99.

37 Frederick Herzberg, One More Time, How Do You Motivate Workers? See also Judith A. Kolb, "Let's Bring Structure Back: A Commentary," *Management Communications Quarterly*, 9, no. 4 (May 1996), pp. 452–65.

38 *Changing Nature of Work, 1993*. American Psychological Society Observer Special Issue: HCI Report I. See also Jeffrey Edwards, "An Examination of Competing Versions of the Person–Environment Fit Approach to Stress," *Academy of Management Journal*, 39, no. 2 (April 1996), pp. 292–339.

39 Except as noted, this section is based on Jia Lin Xie and Gary Johns, "Job Scope and Stress: Can Job Scope Be Too High?" *Academy of Management Journal*, 38, no. 5 (1995), pp. 1288–1309.

40 See, for example, *Webster's New Collegiate Dictionary* (Springfield, MA: G&C Miriam Company, 1973), p. 420.

41 Marie-Claude Boudreau et al., "Going Global: Using Information Technology to Advance the Competitiveness of the Virtual Transnational Organization," *Academy of Management Executive*, 1998, vol. 12, no. 4, pp. 121–22.

42 Marie-Claude Boudreau et al., "Going Global: Using Information Technology to Advance the Competitiveness of the Virtual Transnational Organization," *Academy of Management Executive*, 1998, vol. 12, no. 4, pp. 121–22.

43 Marie-Claude Boudreau et al., "Going Global: Using Information Technology to Advance the Competitiveness of the Virtual Transnational Organization," *Academy of Management Executive*, 1998, vol. 12, no. 4, p. 122.

44 See, for example, Gail Dutton, "The New Consortiums," *Management Review*, January 1999, pp. 46–50.

45 Raymond Miles et al., "Organizing in the Knowledge Age: Anticipating the Cellular Form," *Academy of Management Executive*, 1997, vol. 11, no. 4, pp. 7–24.

46 Raymond Miles et al., "Organizing in the Knowledge Age: Anticipating the Cellular Form," *Academy of Management Executive*, 1997, vol. 11, no. 4, p. 13.

47 Raymond Miles et al., "Organizing in the Knowledge Age: Anticipating the Cellular Form," *Academy of Management Executive*, 1997, vol. 11, no. 4, p. 13.

48 Raymond Miles et al., "Organizing in the Knowledge Age: Anticipating the Cellular Form," *Academy of Management Executive*, 1997, vol. 11, no. 4, p. 13.

49 Tom Burns and G.M. Stalker, *The Management of Innovation* (London: Tavistock, 1961), p. 1.

50 Tom Burns and G.M. Stalker, *The Management of Innovation* (London: Tavistock, 1961), p. 1.

51 Tom Burns and G.M. Stalker, *The Management of Innovation* (London: Tavistock, 1961), p. 80.

52 Emery and Trist, two other British researchers, referred to this innovative environment as a "turbulent field" environment because changes often come not from a firm's traditional competitors, but from out of the blue: Often, in fact, the changes seem to "arise from the field itself," in that they result from interaction between parts of the environment. The very "texture" of a firm's environment changes because previously unrelated or (from the point of view of the firm) irrelevant elements in its environment become interconnected. F.E. Emery and E.C. Trist, "The Causal Texture of Organizational Environments," *Human Relations* 18 (August 1965), pp. 20–26. As another example, after 1970 (when digital watches were introduced) calculator firms like Texas Instruments suddenly and unexpectedly became competitors in the watch industry.

53 Tom Burns and G.M. Stalker, *The Management of Innovation* (London: Tavistock, 1961), p. 92.

54 Tom Burns and G.M. Stalker, *The Management of Innovation* (London: Tavistock, 1961), p. 92.

55 Adapted from Tom Burns and G.M. Stalker, *The Management of Innovation* (London: Tavistock, 1961), pp. 119–22.

56 Peter Blau, Cecilia Falbe, William McKinley, and Phelps Tracy, "Technology and Organization in Manufacturing," *Administrative Science Quarterly,* March 1976.

57 However, Allen found that "characteristics, beliefs, and strategies of top management groups were found to be fully as important as contextual factors in predicting organizational choices." Stephen A. Allen, "Understanding Reorganizations and Divisionalized Companies," *Academy of Management Journal,* December 1979, pp. 641–71.

58 How can we explain the fact that an organization's environment and technology influence its structure? One plausible explanation is that some environments and technologies require managers to handle more unforeseen problems and decisions than do others. And, since each person's capacity for juggling problems and making decisions is limited, an overabundance of problems forces managers to respond—often by reorganizing. Thus, when a manager finds himself or herself becoming overloaded with problems, one reasonable response is to give subordinates more autonomy, to decentralize (thus letting employees handle more problems among themselves), and to reorganize around self-contained divisions. By reorganizing in these ways, the manager may surrender some direct control but at least the organization avoids becoming unresponsive, as might otherwise have been the case.

59 Rosabeth Moss Kanter, Barry Stein, and Todd Jick, *The Challenge of Organizational Change* (New York: The Free Press, 1992), p. 225.

60 John Case, "The Open-Book Management Revolution," *Inc.,* June 1995, pp. 26–43.

61 KnitMedia prospectus, pp. 31–32.

Chapter 9

1 Catherine Truss and Lynda Gratton, "Strategic Human Resource Management: A Conceptual Approach," *International Journal of Human Resource Management*, 5, no. 3 (September 1994), p. 663.

2 Based on Gary Dessler, *Human Resource Management*, Seventh Edition (Upper Saddle River, NJ: Prentice-Hall, 1997), pp. 20–22.

3 John Partridge, "B of M lauded for promoting women's careers," *The Globe and Mail*, January 7, 1994, p. B3.

4 Vivian Smith, "Breaking down the barriers," *The Globe and Mail*, November 17, 1992, p. B24.

5 Bob Cox, "Women gaining on men's wages," *The Globe and Mail*, January 18, 1994, p. B4.

6 *Statistics Canada Survey of Labour and Income Dynamics: Moving Out of Low-paid Work, 1993–1995.*

7 Gordon Pitts, "Equal Pay Issue: Business Uneasy," *The Financial Post*, August 31, 1985, pp. 1–2.

8 Margot Gibb-Clark, "Harassment Cases Can Also Hurt Employers," *The Globe and Mail*, September 16, 1991, p. B24.

9 This section is based on Gary Dessler, *Human Resource Management*, Seventh Edition (Upper Saddle River, NJ, Prentice-Hall, 1997), pp. 40–42; see also Commerce Clearing House, *Sexual Harassment Manual*, p. 8.

10 Ted Kennedy, "Beware of Health and Safety Law: It Could Bite You," *Canadian Business*, December 1990, p. 19.

11 Moira Farr, "Work that Wounds and How to Cure It," *Canadian Business*, December 1991, p. 90; also "Industrial Workers Learn to Stretch and Save," *Canadian Business*, October 1991, p. 15.

12 For a discussion see Gary Dessler, *Human Resource Management*, Seventh Edition (Upper Saddle River, NJ, Prentice-Hall, 1997), pp. 632–33.

13 Wayne Cascio, *Applied Psychology in Personnel Management* (Reston, VA: Reston, 1978), p. 132.

14 Donald Harris, "A Matter of Privacy: Managing Personnel Data in Company Computers," *Personnel*, February 1987, p. 37.

15 See, for example, William Bridges, "The End of the Job," *Fortune*, September 19, 1994, p. 64.

16 See Gary Dessler, *Human Resource Management*, Seventh Edition (Upper Saddle River, NJ, Prentice-Hall, 1997), pp. 108–10.

17 Arthur R. Pell, *Recruiting and Selecting Personnel* (New York: Regents, 1969), pp. 10–12; see also Katherine Tyler, "Employees Can Help Recruiting New Talent," *HRMagazine,* September 1996, pp. 57–61.

18 Arthur R. Pell, *Recruiting and Selecting Personnel* (New York: Regents, 1969), p. 11.

19 "Search and Destroy," *The Economist,* June 27, 1998, p. 63.

20 "Search and Destroy," *The Economist,* June 27, 1998, p. 63.

21 Sara Rynes, Marc Orlitzky, and Robert Brett, Jr., "Experienced Hiring versus College Recruiting: Practices and Emerging Trends," *Personnel Psychology*, vol. 50 (1997), pp. 309–39.

22 See, for example, Richard Becker, "Ten Common Mistakes to College Recruiting—or How to Try Without Really Succeeding," *Personnel*, March–April 1975, pp. 19–28. See also Sara Rynes and John Boudreau, "College Recruiting in Large Organizations: Practice, Evaluation, and Research Implications," *Personnel Psychology*, Winter 1986, pp. 729–57.

23 Nancy Austin, "First Aide," *Inc.,* September 1999, pp. 68–71.

24 Nancy Austin, "First Aide," *Inc.,* September 1999, p. 78.

25 Nancy Austin, "First Aide," *Inc.,* September 1999, p. 72.

26 "Internet Recruitment Survey," *BNA Bulletin to Management,* May 22, 1997, pp. 164–65.

27 Julia King, "Job Networking," *Enterprise Networking,* January 26, 1995; see also David Schulz, "Internet Emerging as a Major Vehicle for Mid-Level Retail Recruiting," *Stores,* June 1999, pp. 70–73.

28 Gillian Flynn, "Cisco Turns the Internet Inside (and) Out," *Personnel Journal,* October 1996, pp. 28–34.

29 "Retirees Increasingly Reentering the Workforce," *BNA Bulletin to Management*, January 16, 1997, p. 17.

30 Diane Cyr, "Lost and Found—Retired Employees," *Personnel Journal*, November 1996, p. 41.

31 Harold E. Johnson, "Older Workers Help Meet Employment Needs," *Personnel Journal* (May 1988), pp. 100–105.

32 This is based on Robert W. Goddard, "How to Harness America's Gray Power," *Personnel Journal* (May 1987), pp. 33–40.

33 Samuel Greengard, "At Peoplesoft, Client/Server Drives the HR Office of the Future," *Personnel Journal,* May 1996, p. 92; see also Bill Gates, *Business @ the Speed of Thought* (New York: Warner Books, 1999), pp. 41–42.

34 Herbert Greenberg, "A Hidden Source of Talent," *HRMagazine,* March 1997, pp. 88–91.

35 "Welfare-to-Work: No Easy Chore," *BNA Bulletin to Management,* February 13, 1997, p. 56.

36 Stephen J. Vodanovich and Rosemary H. Lowe, "They Ought to Know Better: The Incidence and Correlates of Inappropriate Application Blank Inquiries," *Public Personnel Management*, 21, no. 3 (Fall 1992), p. 363.

37 See Paul Blocklyn, "Pre-Employment Testing," *Personnel* (February 1988), pp. 66–68.

38 Bruce McDougall, "The Thinking Man's Assembly Line," *Canadian Business*, November 1991, p. 40.

39 Mel Kleiman, "Employee Testing Essential to Hiring Effectively in the '90s," *Houston Business Journal*, 22, no. 38 (February 8, 1993), p. 31; and Gerald L. Borofsky, "Pre-Employment Psychological Screening," *Risk Management*, 40, no. 1 (January 1993), p. 47.

40 Louis Olivas, "Using Assessment Centers for Individual and Organizational Development," *Personnel*, 57 (May–June 1980), pp. 63–67; Tim Payne, Neil Anderson, and Tom Smith, "Assessment Centres, Selection Systems and Cost-Effectiveness: An Evaluative Case Study," *Personnel Review*, 21, no. 4 (Fall 1992), p. 48; and Roger Mottram, "Assessment Centres Are Not Only for Selection: The Assessment Centre as a Development Workshop," *Journal of Managerial Psychology*, 7, no. 1 (January 1992), p. A1.

41 Rose Fisher, "Screen Test," *Canadian Business*, May 1992, pp. 62–64.

42 This is based on Daniel Goleman, "Forget Money; Nothing Can Buy Happiness, Some Researchers Say," *Wall Street Journal*, August 16, 1996, pp. B5, B9. See also Shari Caudron, "Hire for Attitude," *Staffing: A Workforce Supplement*, August 1997, pp. 20–26.

43 Daniel Goleman, "Forget Money; Nothing Can Buy Happiness, Some Researchers Say," *Wall Street Journal*, August 16, 1996, p. B9.

44 Source for questions: Daniel Goleman, "Forget Money; Nothing Can Buy Happiness, Some Researchers Say," *Wall Street Journal*, August 16, 1996; and Dr. Richard Davidson, University of Wisconsin.

45 For a full discussion of this, see Gary Dessler, *Human Resource Management*, Sixth Edition (Englewood Cliffs, NJ: Prentice-Hall, 1994), Chapter 6.

46 R.E. Carlson, "Selection Interview Decisions: The Effects of Interviewer Experience, Relative Quota Situation, and Applicant Sample on Interview Decisions," *Personnel Psychology*, 20 (1967), pp. 259–80.

47 William Tullar, Terry Mullins, and Sharon Caldwell, "Effects of Interview Length and Applicant Quality on Interview Decision Time," *Journal of Applied Psychology*, 64 (December 1979), pp. 669–74.

48 Edwin Walley, "Successful Interviewing Techniques," *The CPA Journal* (September 1992), p. 29.

49 Pamela Paul, "Interviewing is Your Business," *Association Management* (November 1992), p. 29.

50 Gary Dessler, *Human Resource Management*, Seventh Edition (Upper Saddle River, NJ: Prentice-Hall, 1997), pp. 242–43.

51 Wayne F. Cascio and Val Silbey, "Utility of the Assessment Center as a Selection Device," *Journal of Applied Psychology*, April 1979, pp. 107–18. See also Paul R. Sackett, "Assessment Centers and Content Validity: Some Neglected Issues," *Personnel Psychology*, vol. 40, Spring 1981, pp. 55–64.

52 "Database Helps Employers Screen Applicants for Theft," *BNA Bulletin to Management,* June 12, 1997, p. 186.

53 "Database Helps Employers Screen Applicants for Theft," *BNA Bulletin to Management,* June 12, 1997, p. 191.

54 John Jones and William Terris, "Post-Polygraph Selection Techniques," *Recruitment Today* (May–June 1989), pp. 25–31.

55 Gilbert Fuchsberg, "Prominent Psychologists Group Gives Qualified Support to Integrity Tests," *Wall Street Journal*, March 7, 1991, pp. B2, B7.

56 Malcolm McKillip, "An Employer's Guide to Drug Testing," *The Globe and Mail*, April 9, 1998, p. B13.

57 Margot Gibb-Clark, "Ruling Narrows Options for Drug Testing," *The Globe and Mail*, July 28, 1998, p. B11.

58 Bruce Little, "A Factory Learns to Survive," *The Globe and Mail*, May 18, 1993, p. B22.

59 Jerry Zeidenberg, "Extra-Curricular," *Canadian Business*, February 1991, pp. 66–69.

60 Scott Feschuk, "Phi Beta Cuppa," *The Globe and Mail*, March 6, 1993, pp. B1, B4.

61 Gordon Pitts, "Stepping on the Quality Ladder," *The Globe and Mail*, June 30, 1992, p. B20.

62 Jane Allen, "Literacy at Work," *Canadian Business*, February 1991, pp. 70–73.

63 Harvey Enchin, "Employee Training a Must," *The Globe and Mail*, May 15, 1991, p. B6.

64 Kenneth Nowack, "360-Degree Feedback: The Whole Story," *Training and Development,* January 1993, p. 69. For a description of some of the problems involved in implementing 360-degree feedback, see Matthew Budman, "The Rating Game," *Across the Board,* February 1994, pp. 35–38.

65 Katherine Romano, "Fear of Feedback," *Management Review,* December 1993, p. 39.

66 Katherine Romano, "Fear of Feedback," *Management Review,* December 1993, p. 39.

67 See, for instance, Gerry Rich, "Group Reviews—Are You Up to It?" *CMA Magazine,* March 1993, p. 5.

68 Summarized from Tom Davis and Michael Landa, "Pat or Slap: Do Appraisals Work?" *CMA Management*, March 1999, pp. 24–26.

69 Randall Echlin, "Why Firms Need Performance Reviews," *The Globe and Mail*, December 14, 1998, p. B15.

70 Paul Waldie, "Canadian CEOs in Middle of Pay Pack," *The Globe and Mail*, April 26, 1999, p. B6; also Mark MacKinnon, Canada's Biggest Paycheques," *The Globe and Mail*, April 26, 1999, pp. B1, B4.

71 David Roberts, "A Long Way from Cambodia," *The Globe and Mail*, July 5, 1994, p. B18.

72 C.D. Fisher, L. Schoenfeldt, and B. Shaw, *Personnel/Human Resources Management* (Boston: Houghton-Mifflin, 1990).

73 Matt Rothman, "Into the Black," *Inc.*, January 1993, pp. 59–65. For a good discussion of what other employers are doing to improve benefits, see, for example, Kimberly Seals McDonald, "Your Benefits," *Fortune*, March 3, 1997, pp. 199–201.

74 "Ouch! The Squeeze on Your Health Benefits," *Business Week*, November 29, 1989, pp. 110–116.

75 Bruce McDougall, "The Thinking Man's Assembly Line," *Canadian Business*, November 1991, p. 40.

76 Terrence Belford, "Flex Plans Now Offer What Employee Really Want: Cash," *The Globe and Mail*, May 13, 1998, p. B27.

77 "Canadians Are Retiring Earlier," *Winnipeg Free Press*, June 12, 1997, p. B12.

78 Michael Moss, "For Older Employees, On-the-Job Injuries Are More Often Deadly," *The Wall Street Journal*, June 17, 1997, pp. A1, A10.

79 Thomas Claridge, "Fired Jumbo Boss Awarded $226,000," *The Globe and Mail*, May 31, 1995, p. B5.

80 Dianne Forrest, "Guess Who You Can't Fire," *Canadian Business*, November 1991, pp. 97–100.

81 "Transplanting Corporate Cultures Globally," *Personnel Journal* (October 1993).

Chapter 10

1 For example, see Renato Tagiuri, "Managing People: Ten Essential Behaviors," *Harvard Business Review,* January–February 1995, pp. 10–11.

2   Renato Tagiuri, "Managing People: Ten Essential Behaviors," *Harvard Business Review,* January–February 1995, pp. 10–11.

3   M.S. Lel-Namaki, "Creating a Corporate Vision," *Long-Range Planning,* 25, no. 6 (1979), p. 25.

4   M.S. Lel-Namaki, "Creating a Corporate Vision," *Long-Range Planning,* 25, no. 6 (1979), p. 25.

5   Arthur Thompson and A.J. Strickland, *Strategic Management* (Homewood, IL: Irwin, 1992), p. 7.

6   Shawn Tully, "How Cisco Mastered the Net," *Fortune,* August 17, 1998, pp. 207–10.

7   Shawn Tully, "How Cisco Mastered the Net," *Fortune,* August 17, 1998, p. 210.

8   Jeffrey McNally, Stephen Gerras, and R. Craig Bullis, "Teaching Leadership at the U.S. Military Academy at West Point," *Journal of Applied Behavioral Science,* 32, no. 2 (June 1996), p. 178.

9   Shelley Kirkpatrick and Edwin A. Locke, "Leadership: Do Traits Matter?" *Academy of Management Executive,* May 1991, p. 49. See also Edwin A. Locke and Associates, *The Essence of Leadership: The Four Keys to Leading Successfully* (New York: Lexington/Macmillan, 1991). See also Ruth Tait, "The Attributes of Leadership," *Leadership and Organization Development Journal,* vol. 17, no.1 (1996), pp. 27–31; and David L. Cawthon, "Leadership: The Great Man Theory Revisited," *Business Horizons,* May 1996, pp. 1–4; See also Robert Baum, "A Longitudinal Study of the Relation of Vision and Vision Communication to Venture Growth in Entrepreneurial Firms," *Journal of Applied Psychology,* February 1998, pp. 43–55.

10 Shelley Kirkpatrick and Edwin A. Locke, "Leadership: Do Traits Matter?" *Academy of Management Executive,* May 1991, p. 49.

11 Shelley Kirkpatrick and Edwin A. Locke, "Leadership: Do Traits Matter?" *Academy of Management Executive,* May 1991, p. 50.

12 Except as noted, this section is based on Shelley Kirkpatrick and Edwin A. Locke, "Leadership: Do Traits Matter?" *Academy of Management Executive,* May 1991, pp. 48–60; see also Ross Laver, "Building a Better Boss: Studies Show That the Personality of a Chief Executive Can Have a Major Impact on Profits and Productivity," *Maclean's,* September 30, 1996, p. 41.

13 Shelley Kirkpatrick and Edwin A. Locke, "Leadership: Do Traits Matter?" *Academy of Management Executive,* May 1991, p. 53.

14 Shelley Kirkpatrick and Edwin A. Locke, "Leadership: Do Traits Matter?" *Academy of Management Executive,* May 1991, p. 54.

15 Shelley Kirkpatrick and Edwin A. Locke, "Leadership: Do Traits Matter?" *Academy of Management Executive,* May 1991, p. 55.

16 Shelley Kirkpatrick and Edwin A. Locke, "Leadership: Do Traits Matter?" *Academy of Management Executive,* May 1991, pp. 5–6.

17 Ernest Hilgard, *Introduction to Psychology* (New York: Harcourt, Brace and World, 1962), p. 635; see also Lester Lefton and Laura Valvatne, *Mastering Psychology* (Boston: Allyn and Bacon, 1992), p. 419.

18 Daniel Goleman, "What Makes a Leader?" *Harvard Business Review,* November–December 1998, pp. 93–99.

19 Daniel Goleman, "What Makes a Leader?" *Harvard Business Review,* November–December 1998, p. 94.

20 Daniel Goleman, "What Makes a Leader?" *Harvard Business Review,* November–December 1998, p. 99.

21 R.B. Cattell, *Personality* (New York: McGraw-Hill, 1950), pp. 37–41.

22 Grant Marshall et al., "The Five-Factor Model of Personality as a Framework for Personality-Health Research," *Journal of Personality and Social Psychology,* vol. 67, no. 2 (1994), pp. 278–86.

23 Chester Barnard, The *Functions of the Executive* (Cambridge, MA: Harvard University Press, 1938). See also Roger Dawson, *Secrets of Power Persuasion* (Upper Saddle River, NJ: Prentice-Hall, 1992); Sydney Finkelstein, "Power in Top Management Teams: Dimensions, Measurement, and Validation," *Academy of Management Journal,* August 1992; and Jeffrey Pfeffer, *Managing with Power: Politics and Influence in Organizations* (Boston: Harvard Business School Press, 1992).

24 Eli Cohen and Noel Tichy, "Operation: Leadership," *Fast Company,* September 1999, p. 280.

25 Eli Cohen and Noel Tichy, "Operation: Leadership," *Fast Company,* September 1999, p. 280.

26 See, for example, Shelley Kirkpatrick and Edwin A. Locke, "Leadership: Do Traits Matter?" *Academy of Management Executive,* vol. 5, no. 2 (May 1991), p. 49.

27 Shelley Kirkpatrick and Edwin A. Locke, "Leadership: Do Traits Matter?" *Academy of Management Executive,* vol. 5, no. 2 (May 1991), p. 56.

28 For a discussion of this issue, see Peter Wissenberg and Michael Kavanagh, "The Independence of Initiating Structure and Consideration: A Review of Evidence," *Personnel Psychology,* vol. 25 (1972), pp. 119–30. See also Gary A. Yukl, *Leadership in Organizations,* 3rd ed. (Upper Saddle River, NJ: Prentice-Hall, 1994). For an interesting example of what can go wrong when the leader uses the wrong leadership style, see Thomas Ricks, "Army at Odds: West Point Posting Becomes a Minefield for 'Warrior' Officer," *Wall Street Journal,* March 13, 1997, pp. A1, A9.

29 Ralph Stogdill and A.E. Koonz, "Leader Behavior: Its Description and Measurement" (Columbus: Bureau of Business Research, Ohio State University, 1957). See also Bernard M. Bass, *Bass & Stogdill's Handbook of Leadership: Theory, Research, & Managerial Applications,* 3rd ed. (New York: The Free Press, 1990).

30 Ralph Stogdill, *Managers, Employees, Organizations* (Columbus: Bureau of Business Research, Ohio State University, 1965).

31 Gary Yukl, "Towards a Behavioral Theory of Leadership," *Organizational Behavior and Human Performance,* 6, no. 4 (July 1971), pp. 414–40. See also Gary A. Yukl, *Leadership in Organizations,* 3rd ed. (Englewood Cliffs, NJ: Prentice-Hall, 1994).

32 Hal Lancaster, "Herb Kelleher Has One Main Strategy: Treat Employees Well," *Wall Street Journal,* August 31, 1999, p. B1.

33 Blake and Mouton, *The Managerial Grid.*

34 Chester Schriesheim, Robert J. House, and Steven Kerr, "Leader Initiating Structure: A Reconciliation of Discrepant Research Results and Some Empirical Tests," *Organizational Behavior and Human Performance,* 15, no. 2 (April 1976). See also Bernard M. Bass, *Bass & Stogdill's Handbook of Leadership: Theory, Research, & Managerial Applications,* 3rd ed. (New York: The Free Press, 1990).

35 Victor Vroom and Arthur Jago, "On the Validity of the Vroom-Yetton Model," *Journal of Applied Psychology,* vol. 63, no. 2 (1978), pp. 151–62; Madeleine Heilman et al., "Reactions to Prescribed Leader Behavior as a Function of Role Perspective: The Case of Vroom-Yetton Model," *Journal of Applied Psychology,* vol. 69, no. 1 (February 1984), pp. 50–60. See also Donna Brown, "Why Participative Management Won't Work Here" *Management Review* (June 1992).

36 Harvey Enchin, "Consensus Management? Not for Bombardier's CEO," *The Globe and Mail,* April 16, 1990, p. B1.

37 Michael Stern, "New Tory Chief Must Motivate by Leading," *The Globe and Mail,* March 29, 1993, p. B4.

38 Victor Vroom and Arthur Jago, "On the Validity of the Vroom-Yetton Model," *Journal of Applied Psychology,* vol. 63, no. 2 (1978), pp. 151–62.

39 M. Love, "Let's Forget Tradition," *Winnipeg Business People,* August–September 1990, p. 11.

40 See, for example, Mark Tubbs and Steven Akeberg, "The Role of Intentions in Work Motivation: Implications for Goal Setting Theory and Research," *Academy of Management Review,* vol. 16, no. 1 (January 1991), pp. 180–99.

41 Rensis Likert, *New Patterns of Management* (New York: McGraw-Hill, 1961).

42 Robert Day and Robert Hamblin, "Some Effects of Close and Punitive Styles of Leadership," *American Journal of Psychology,* vol. 69 (1964), pp. 499–510.

43 See, for example, Nancy Morse, *Satisfactions in the White Collar Job* (Ann Arbor, MI: Survey Research Center, University of Michigan, 1953).

44 J.M. Burns, *Leadership* (New York: Harper, 1978).

45 Joseph Seltzer and Bernard Bass, "Transformational Leadership: Beyond Initiation and Consideration," *Journal of Management,* vol. 4 (1990), p. 694. See also Bernard M. Bass, "Theory of Transformational Leadership Redux," *Leadership Quarterly,* Winter 1995, pp. 463–78.

46 Gary Yukl, "Managerial Leadership," p. 269.

47 N.M. Tichy and M.A. Devanna, *The Transformational Leader* (New York: Wiley, 1986).

48 Joseph Seltzer and Bernard Bass, "Transformational Leadership: Beyond Initiation and Consideration," *Journal of Management,* vol. 4 (1990), p. 694.

49 Deluga, p. 457.

50 Frances Yamarino and Bernard Bass, "Transformational Leadership and Multiple Levels of Analysis," *Human Relations,* vol. 43, no.10 (1990), p. 976; See also David Walman, "CEO Charismatic Leadership: Levels of Management and Levels of Analysis Effects," *Academy of Management Review,* April 1999, pp. 266–68.

51 J.A. Conger, "Inspiring Others: The Language of Leadership," *Academy of Management Executive,* vol. 5 (1991), pp. 31–45; See also Linda Hill, "Charismatic Leadership in Organizations," *Personnel Psychology,* October 1999, pp. 767–68.

52 Brent Jang, "Nova's Newall a $6.3 Million Dollar Man," *The Globe and Mail,* March 20, 1997, pp. B1, B6.

53 Bernard Bass, *Leadership and Performance Beyond Expectations* (New York: The Free Press, 1985); and Deluga, pp. 457–58; See also Boas Shamir, "Correlates of Charismatic Leader Behavior in Military Units: Subordinates Attitudes, Unit of Characteristics, and Superiors Appraisals of Leader Performance," *Academy of Management Journal,* August 1998, pp. 387–410.

54 Deluga, p. 457.

55 Deluga, p. 457.

56 Frances Yamarino and Bernard Bass, "Transformational Leadership and Multiple Levels of Analysis," *Human Relations,* vol. 43, no.10 (1990), p. 981.

57 For a review, see Robert Keller, "Transformational Leadership and the Performance of Research and Development Project Groups," *Journal of Management,* vol. 18, no. 3 (1992), pp. 489–501.

58 Thomas Stewart, "How to Lead a Revolution," *Fortune,* vol. 28 (November 1994), p. 61.

59 J.J. Hater and Bernard Bass, "Superiors' Evaluations and Subordinates' Perceptions of Transformational and Transactional Leadership," *Journal of Applied Psychology,* vol. 73 (1988), pp. 695–702.

60 J.M. Howell and C.A. Higgins, "Champions of Technological Innovation," *Administrative Science Quarterly,* vol. 35 (1990), pp. 317–41.

61 Frances Yamarino and Bernard Bass, "Transformational Leadership and Multiple Levels of Analysis," *Human Relations,* vol. 43, no.10 (1990), p. 981.

62 C.M. Solomon, "Careers Under Glass," *Personnel Journal,* vol. 69, no.4 (1990), pp. 96–105.

63 See, for example, James Bowditch and Anthony Buono, *A Primer on Organizational Behavior* (New York: John Wiley, 1994), p. 238.

64 Russell Kent and Sherry Moss, "Effects of Sex and Gender Role on Leader Emergence," *Academy of Management Journal,* vol. 37, no.5 (1994), pp. 1335–46; Jane Baack, Norma Carr-Ruffino, and Monica Pelletier, "Making It to the Top: Specific Leadership Skills," *Women in Management Review,* vol. 8, no.2 (1993), pp. 17–23.

65 S.M. Donnel and J. Hall, "Men and Women as Managers: A Significant Case of No Significant Difference," *Organizational Dynamics,* vol. 8 (1980), pp. 60–77. See also Jennifer L. Berdahl, "Gender and Leadership in Work Groups: Six Alternative Models," *Leadership Quarterly,* Spring 1996, pp. 21–40.

66 M.A. Hatcher, "The Corporate Woman of the 1990s: Maverick or Innovator?" *Psychology of Women Quarterly,* vol. 5 (1991), pp. 251–59.

67 D.G. Winter, *The Power Motive* (New York: The Free Press, 1975).

68 L. McFarland Shore and G.C. Thornton, "Effects of Gender on Self and Supervisory Ratings," *Academy of Management Journal,* vol. 29, no.1 (1986), pp. 115–29; quoted in Bowditch and Buono, p. 238.

69 G.H. Dobbins and S.J. Paltz, "Sex Differences in Leadership: How Real Are They?" *Academy of Management Review,* vol. 11 (1986), pp. 118–27; R. Drazin and E.R. Auster, "Wage Differences Between Men and Women: Performance Appraisal Ratings versus Salary Allocation as the Locus of Bias," *Human Resource Management,* vol. 26 (1987), pp. 157–68. See also Nancy DiTomaso and Robert Hooijberg, "Diversity and the Demands of Leadership," *Leadership Quarterly,* Summer 1996, pp. 163–87 and Chao C. Chen and Ellen Van Velsor, "New Directions for Research and Practice in Diversity Leadership," *Leadership Quarterly,* Summer 1996, pp. 285–302.

70 M. Jelinek and N.J. Alder, "Woman: World-Class Managers for Global Competition," *Academy of Management Executive,* vol. 2, no.1 (1988), pp. 11–19; J. Grant, "Women as Managers: What Can They Offer to Organizations?" *Organizational Dynamics,* vol. 16, no.3 (1988), pp. 56–63. On the other hand, one author suggests that women should be more Machiavellian: "War favors the dangerous woman. Women may love peace and seek stability, but these conditions seldom serve them." Harriet Rub in *The Princessa: Machiavelli for Women* (New York: Doubleday/ Currenly, 1997), quoted in Anne Fisher, "What Women Can Learn from Machiavelli," *Fortune,* April 1997, p. 162.

71 Frederick E. Fiedler, *A Theory of Leadership Effectiveness* (New York: McGraw- Hill, 1967), p. 147; See also David Stauffer, "Once a Leader, Always a Leader?" *Across the Board,* April 1999, pp. 14–19.

72 Frederick E. Fiedler, *A Theory of Leadership Effectiveness* (New York: McGraw-Hill, 1967), p. 147.

73 Frederick E. Fiedler, *A Theory of Leadership Effectiveness* (New York: McGraw-Hill, 1967), p. 147.

74 See, for example, Robert J. House and J.V. Singh, "Organizational Behavior: Some New Directions for I/O Psychology," *Annual Review of Psychology,* 38 (1987), pp. 669–718; L.H. Peters, D.D. Hartke, and J.T. Pohlmann, "Fiedler's Contingency Theory of Leadership: An Application of the Meta-Analytic Procedures of Schmidt and Hunter," *Psychological Bulletin,* 97 (1985), pp. 274–85. Also, Fred Fiedler and J.E. Garcia, *New Approaches to Effective Leadership: Cognitive Resources and Organizational Performance* (New York: John Wiley and Sons, 1987); and Robert T. Vecchio, "Theoretical and Empirical Examination of Cognitive Resource Theory," *Journal of Applied Psychology* (April 1990), pp. 141–47. See also Robert Vecchio, "Cognitive Resource Theory: Issues for Specifying a Test of the Theory" *Journal of Applied Psychology* (June 1992).

75 R. House, "A Path-Goal Model of Leader Effectiveness," *Administrative Science Quarterly,* 16 (1971), pp. 321–28.

76 G.B. Graen and T.A. Scandura, "Toward a Psychology of Daidic Organizing." In *Research in Organizational Behavior,* vol. 9, edited by L.L. Cummings and B.M. Staw (Greenwich, CT: J.A.I. Press, 1987), p. 208. Also, Antoinette Phillips and Arthur Bedeian, "Leader-Follower Exchange Quality: The Role of Personal and Interpersonal Attributes," *Academy of Management Journal,* 37, no. 4 (1994), pp. 990–1001.

77 Jerald Greenberg, *Managing Behavior in Organizations* (Upper Saddle River, NJ: Prentice-Hall, 1996), p. 215.

78 Antoinette Phillips and Arthur Bedeian, "Leader-Follower Exchange Quality: The Role of Personal and Interpersonal Attributes," *Academy of Management Journal,* 37, no. 4 (1994), pp. 990–1001.

79 See Robert P. Vecchio, "Situational Leadership Theory: An Examination of a Prescriptive Theory," *Journal of Applied Psychology* (August 1987), pp. 444–51; and Jerald Greenberg, *Managing Behavior in Organizations* (Upper Saddle River, NJ: Prentice-Hall, 1996), p. 226.

80   David Alcorn, "Dynamic Followership: Empowerment at Work," *Management Quarterly*, Spring 1992, pp. 11–13.

81   Jon Howell, David Bowen, Peter Dorfman, Steven Ken, and Philip Podsakoff, "Substitutes for Leadership: Effective Alternatives to Ineffective Leadership," *Organizational Dynamics*, Summer 1990, p. 23.

82   Jon Howell, David Bowen, Peter Dorfman, Steven Ken, and Philip Podsakoff, "Substitutes for Leadership: Effective Alternatives to Ineffective Leadership," *Organizational Dynamics*, Summer 1990, p. 23.

83   "What It Means to Lead," *Fast Company*, February–March 1997.

84   See, for example, P.M. Podsakoff, P.B. Niehoff, S.B. MacKenzie, and M.L. Williams, "Do Substitutes for Leadership Really Substitute for Leadership? An Empirical Examination of Kerr and Jermier Situational Leadership Model," *Organizational Behavior and Human Decision Processes*, vol. 54 (1993), pp. 1–44.

85   Andrew Dubrin, *Leadership: Research Findings, Practice, and Skills* (Boston: Houghton-Mifflin, 1995), pp. 10–11.

86   Adapted from "Development and Application of New Scales to Measure the French and Raven (1959) Bases of Social Power," by Thomas R. Hinkin and Chester A. Schriescheim, *Journal of Applied Psychology* (August 1989), p. 567. Copyright 1989 by the American Psychological Association. Adapted by permission. Found in Andrew DuBrin, *Leadership: Research in Findings, Practice, and Skills* (Boston: Houghton-Mifflin, 1995), pp. 146–47. (The actual scale presents the items in random order. They are classified here according to the power source for your convenience.)

Chapter 11

1   "The Powerhouse That Jack Built," *Economist*, September 18, 1999, p. 26.

2   Ernest R. Hilgard, *Introduction to Psychology* (New York: Harcourt Brace and World, 1962), pp. 124–25.

3   Ernest R. Hilgard, *Introduction to Psychology* (New York: Harcourt Brace and World, 1962), p. 124.

4   See, for instance, Kanfer, "Motivation Theory," in *Handbook of Industrial and Organizational Psychology, 1990*. See also Robert Hersey, "A Practitioner's View of Motivation," *Journal of Managerial Psychology* (May 1993), pp. 110–15, and Kenneth Kovatch, "Employee Motivation: Addressing a Crucial Factor in Your Organization's Performance," *Employment Relations Today*, 22 (Summer 1995), pp. 93–107.

5   See Douglas M. McGregor, "The Human Side of Enterprise." In Michael Matteson and John M. Ivancevich (eds.), *Management Classics* (Santa Monica, CA: Goodyear, 1977), pp. 43–49.

6   Douglas M. McGregor, "The Human Side of Enterprise." In Michael Matteson and John M. Ivancevich (eds.), *Management Classics* (Santa Monica, CA: Goodyear, 1977), p. 45.

7   Ian Allaby, "The Search for Quality," *Canadian Business*, May 1990, pp. 31–42.

8   This is based on David Kolb, Irwin Rubin, and James McIntyre, *Organizational Psychology: An Experiential Approach* (Englewood Cliffs, NJ: Prentice-Hall, 1971), pp. 65–69.

9   These are all from David Kolb, Irwin Rubin, and James McIntyre, *Organizational Psychology: An Experiential Approach* (Englewood Cliffs, NJ: Prentice-Hall, 1971).

10   George Litwin and Robert Stringer, Jr., *Motivation and Organizational Climate* (Boston: Harvard University, 1968), pp. 20–24.

11   Edgar Schein, *Career Dynamics: Matching Individual and Organizational Needs* (Reading, MA: Addison-Wesley, 1978); and Thomas Earth, "Career Anchor Theory," *Review of Public Personnel Administration*, vol. 13, no. 4, 1993, pp. 127–42; see also Jeffrey Colvin, "Looking to Hire the Very Best? Ask the Right Questions, Lots of Them," *Fortune*, June 21, 1999, pp. 19–21.

12   Bob Nelson et al., "Motivate Employees According to Temperament," *HRMagazine*, March 1997, pp. 51–56; See also

Donna McNeese-Smith, "The Relationship Between Managerial Motivation, Leadership, Nurse Outcomes and Patient Satisfaction," *Journal of Organizational Behavior*, March 1999, p. 243.

13   *Fast Company*, October 1999, p. 186.

14   Kanfer, "Motivation Theory," in *Handbook of Industrial and Organizational Psychology, 1990*, p. 102. See also Robert Bretz and Steven Thomas, "Perceived Equity, Motivation, and Final-Offer Arbitration in Major League Baseball," *Journal of Applied Psychology* (June 1992), pp. 280–89.

15   Patricia Lush, "Bargain MacBlo Chief Got Big Raise," *The Globe and Mail*, March 21, 1996, pp. B1, B6.

16   See, for example, J. Greenberg, "A Taxonomy of Organizational Justice Theories," *Academy of Management Review*, 12 (1987), pp. 9–22.

17   For a discussion, see Kanfer, "Motivation Theory," in *Handbook of Industrial and Organizational Psychology, 1990*, p. 124.

18   Edwin A. Locke and D. Henne, "Work Motivation Theories," in C.L. Cooper and I. Robertson (eds.), *International Review of Industrial and Organizational Psychology* (Chichester, England: Wiley, 1986), pp. 1–35.

19   Kanfer, "Motivation Theory," in *Handbook of Industrial and Organizational Psychology, 1990*, p. 125.

20   A.J. Mento, R.P. Steel, and R.J. Karren, "A Meta-analytic Study of the Effects of Goal Setting on Task Performance: 1966–1984," *Organizational Behavior and Human Decision Processes*, 39 (1987), pp. 52–83.

21   Gary Latham and T.W. Lee, "Goal Setting." In Edwin A. Locke (ed.), *Generalizing from Laboratory to Field Settings* (Lexington, MA: Lexington Books, 1986), pp. 101–19.

22   Wendy Trueman, "Alternate Visions," *Canadian Business*, March 1991, pp. 29–33.

23   Kanfer, "Motivation Theory," in *Handbook of Industrial and Organizational Psychology, 1990*, p. 113.

24   For a discussion, see John P. Campbell and Robert Pritchard, "Motivation Theory in Industrial and Organizational Psychology." In Marvin Dunnette (ed.), *Industrial and Organizational Psychology*, pp. 74–5; and Kanfer, "Motivation Theory," in *Handbook of Industrial and Organizational Psychology, 1990*, pp. 115–16.

25   See, for example, Terrence Mitchell, "Expectancy-Value Models in Organizational Psychology." In N.P. Feather (ed.), *Expectations and Actions: Expectancy-Value Models in Psychology* (Hillsdale, NJ: Erlbaum, 1982), pp. 293–312. See also Mark Tubbs et al., "Expectancy, Valence, and Motivational Force Functions in Goal Setting Research: An Empirical Test," *Journal of Applied Psychology* (June 1993), pp. 36–49.

26   Mark Tubbs, Donna Boehne, and James Dahl, "Expectancy, Valence, and Motivational Force Functions in Goal Setting Research: An Empirical Test," *Journal of Applied Psychology*, 78, no. 3 (June 1993), pp. 361–73; Wendelien Van Eerde and Hank Thierry, "Vroom's Expectancy Models and Work-Related Criteria: A Meta-Analysis," *Journal of Applied Psychology*, 81, no. 5 (October 1996), pp. 575–86.

27   For a definition of learning, see Lester Lefton and Laura Valvatne, *Mastering Psychology* (Boston: Allyn and Bacon, 1992), p. 161.

28   For a recent review of operant conditioning, see Fred Luthans and R. Kreitner, *Organizational Behavior Modification and Beyond: An Operant and Social Learning Approach* (Glenview, IL: Scott, Foresman, 1985).

29   W. Clay Hamner, "Reinforcement Theory in Management and Organizational Settings." In Henry Tosi and W. Clay Hamner (eds), *Organizational Behavior and Management: A Contingency Approach* (Chicago: Saint Claire, 1974), pp. 86–112. See also Donald J. Campbell, "The Effects of Goal-Contingent Payment on the Performance of a Complex Task," *Personnel Psychology*, 37, no. 1 (Spring 1984), pp. 23–40.

30   Alexander Stajkovic and Fred Luthans, "A Meta-Analysis of the Effects of Organizational Behavior Modifications on Task Performance, 1975–1976," *Academy of Management Journal*,

1997, vol. 40, no. 5, pp. 1122–49; See also Robert Taylor, "Preventing Employee Theft: A Behavioral Approach," *Business Perspectives,* June 1998, pp. 9–14.

31 Cheryl Comeau-Kirschner, "Improving Productivity Doesn't Cost a Dime," *Management Review,* January 1999, p. 7.

32 Barry Thomas and Madeline Hess Olson, "Gainsharing: The Design Guarantees Success," *Personnel Journal,* 67 (May 1988), pp. 73–79. One of the most well-known and well-established plans of this type is in place at the Lincoln Electric Company. See, for example, Kenneth Chilton, "Lincoln Electric's Incentive System: A Reservoir of Trust," *Compensation and Benefits Review,* 26, no. 6 (November 1994), pp. 29–34.

33 James Lardner, "Okay Here Are Your Options," *U.S. News and World Report,* March 1, 1999, p. 44.

34 Naomi Weiss, "How Starbucks Impassions Workers to Drive Growth," *Workforce,* August 1998, pp. 61–63.

35 See, for example, James Gutherie and Edward Cunningham, "Pay for Performance: The Quaker Oats Alternative," *Compensation & Benefits Review,* 24, no. 2 (March–April 1992), pp. 18–23.

36 See, for example, Graham O'Neill, "Linking Pay to Performance: Conflicting Views and Conflicting Evidence," *Asia Pacific Journal of HRM,* 33, no. 2 (Winter 1995), pp. 20–35.

37 See, for example, Kent Romanoff, "The Ten Commandments of Performance Management," *Personnel,* 66, no. 1 (January 1989), pp. 24–28.

38 For a discussion see, for example, Gary Dessler, *Human Resource Management* (Upper Saddle River, NJ: Prentice-Hall, 1997), pp. 466–67.

39 James Brinks, "Is There Merit in Merit Increases?" *Personnel Administrator,* 25 (May 1980), p. 60. See also Atul Migra et al., "The Case of the Invisible Merit Raise: How People See Their Pay Raises," *Compensation and Benefits Review,* 27, no. 3 (May 1995), pp. 71–76.

40 Bob Nelson, *1001 Ways to Reward Employees* (New York: Workmen Publishing, 1994), p. 47.

41 Federal Express Corporation, *Blueprints for Service Quality,* pp. 34–35.

42 Bob Nelson, *1001 Ways to Reward Employees* (New York: Workmen Publishing, 1994), p. 47.

43 Gerald Ledford, Jr., "Three Case Studies on Skill-Based Pay: An Overview," *Compensation & Benefits Review,* 23 (March–April 1991), pp. 11–23.

44 Gerald Ledford, Jr., and Gary Bergel, "Skill-Based Pay Case No. 1: General Mills," *Compensation & Benefits Review,* 23 (March–April 1991), pp. 24–38.

45 Sarah Braley, "Getting Technical: The Incentive Business Gets Wired Slowly," *Meetings and Conventions,* October 1997, pp. 13–16.

46 Sarah Braley, "Getting Technical: The Incentive Business Gets Wired Slowly," *Meetings and Conventions,* October 1997, p. 13.

47 Sarah Braley, "Getting Technical: The Incentive Business Gets Wired Slowly," *Meetings and Conventions,* October 1997, p. 43.

48 Bob Nelson, *1001 Ways to Reward Employees* (New York: Workmen Publishing, 1994), p. 19.

49 Chris Argyris, *Integrating the Individual and the Organization* (New York: John Wiley, 1964).

50 Samuel Melamed, Irit Ben-Avi, Jair Luz, and Manfred Green, "Objective and Subjective Work Monotony: Effects on Job Satisfaction, Psychological Distress, and Absenteeism in Blue Collar Workers," *Journal of Applied Psychology,* 80, no. 1 (February 1995), pp. 29–42.

51 Wendy Cuthbert, "Corporate Life After Downsizing," *The Financial Post,* March 20, 1993, p. 8.

52 M.A. Campion and C.L. McClelland, "Interdisciplinary Examination of the Costs and Benefits of Enlarged Jobs: A Job Design Quasi-experiment," *Journal of Applied Psychology,* 76 (1991), pp. 186–98.

53 M.A. Campion and C.L. McClelland, "Follow-up and Extension of the Interdisciplinary Costs and Benefits of Enlarged Jobs," *Journal of Applied Psychology,* 78 (1993), pp. 339–51.

54 See, for example, J. Richard Hackman et al., "A New Strategy for Job Enrichment," *California Management Review,* 17, no. 4 (1973), pp. 57–71.

55 J. Richard Hackman et al., "A New Strategy for Job Enrichment," *California Management Review,* 17, no. 4 (1973), pp. 57–71.

56 See, for example, J. Richard Hackman and Greg Oldham, "Motivation Through the Design of Work: Test of a Theory," *Organizational Behavior and Human Performance,* 16, no. 2 (August 1976), pp. 250–79; and J.R. Hackman and G. Oldham, *Work Redesign* (Reading, MA: Addison-Wesley, 1980).

57 J. McBride-King and H. Paris, "Balancing Work and Family Responsibilities," *Canadian Business Review,* Autumn 1989, p. 21.

58 Robert White, "Changing Needs of Work and Family: A Union Response," *Canadian Business Review,* Autumn 1989, pp. 31–33.

59 Margot Gibb-Clark, "Banks' Short Work Week Improves Service," *The Globe and Mail,* September 23, 1991, p. B4.

60 "Slaves of the New Economy," *Canadian Business,* April 1996, pp. 86–92.

61 See, for example, Kenneth Thomas and Betty Velthouse, "Cognitive Elements of Empowerment: An Interpretive Model of Intrinsic Task Motivation," *Academy of Management Review,* vol. 15, no. 4, 1990, pp. 666–81. See also Allan J.H. Thorlackson and Robert P. Murray, "An Empirical Study of Empowerment in the Workplace," *Group and Organization Management,* March 1996, pp. 670–83.

62 Gene Phillips and Stanley Gully, "Role of Goal Orientation, Ability, Need for Achievement, and Locus of Control in the Self-Efficacy and Goal Setting Process," *Journal of Applied Psychology,* vol. 82, no. 5, 1997, pp. 780–82.

63 This is based on W. Clay Hamner and Ellen Hamner, "Behavior Modification on the Bottom Line," *Organizational Dynamics* (Spring 1976). For recent applications, see Greg LaBar, "Safety Incentives: Q & A Reveals Best Practices," *Occupational Hazards,* 58, no. 11 (November 1996), pp. 51–56.

64 Ed Pedalinoa and Victor Gamboa, "Behavior Modification and Absenteeism," *Journal of Applied Psychology* (1974), pp. 694–698.

65 W. Clay Hamner and Ellen P. Hamner, "Behavior Modification and the Bottom Line," *Organizational Dynamics,* 4 (1976), p. 12.

66 R.S. Haynes, R.C. Pine, and H.G. Fitch, "Reducing Accident Rates with Organizational Behavior Modification," *Academy of Management Journal,* 25 (1982), pp. 407–16.

67 E.J. Feeney, J.R. Staelin, R.M. O'Brien, and A.M. Dickinson, "Increasing Sales Performance Among Airline Reservation Personnel." In O'Brien, Dickinson, and Rosow (eds.), *Industrial Behavior Modification,* pp. 141–58.

68 This is based on Norman Nopper, "Reinventing the Factory with Lifelong Learning," *Training,* May 1993, pp. 55–57.

69 Norman Nopper, "Reinventing the Factory with Lifelong Learning," *Training,* May 1993, p. 57. For other examples see Kevin Kelly and Peter Burrows, "Motorola: Training for the Millennium," *Business Week,* March 28, 1994, pp. 158–60; and "Some Nuts and Bolts of Lifelong Learning," *Training,* March 1994, p. 30.

70 Norman Nopper, "Reinventing the Factory with Lifelong Learning," *Training,* May 1993; and Gary Dessler, *Winning Commitment: How to Build and Keep a Competitive Workforce* (New York: McGraw-Hill, 1993), pp. 133–50.

71 Gary Dessler, "How to Earn Your Employees Commitment," *Academy of Management Executive,* vol. 13, no. 2, 1999, pp. 58–67.

72 Joann Davy, "Online at the Office: Virtual Communities Go to Work," *Managing Office Technology,* vol. 43, no. 6, July–August 1998, pp. 9–11.

Chapter 11 Appendix

1 R. Cattel, *The Scientific Analysis of Personality* (Baltimore: Penguin Books, 1965). See also G. Northcraft and M. Neale, *Organizational Behavior* (Hinsdale, IL: Dryden Press, 1994), pp. 64–240.

2 See, for example, Jesus Delgado, "The Five Factor Model of Personality and Job Performance in the European Community," *Journal of Applied Psychology,* vol. 82, no.1, 1997, pp. 30–43.

3 Murray Barrick and Michael Mount, "The Big Five Personality Dimension and Job Performance: A Meta-Analysis," *Personal Psychology,* Spring 1991, pp. 1–26.

4 James Bowditch and Anthony Buono, *A Primer on Organizational Behavior* (New York: John Wiley, 1994), p. 115.

5 Based on Ernest J. McCormick and Joseph Tiffin, *Industrial Psychology* (Upper Saddle River, NJ: Prentice-Hall, 1974), pp. 136–74. See also Marilyn Gist and Terence Mitchell, "Self-Efficacy: A Theoretical Analysis of its Determinants and Malleability," *Academy of Management Review,* April 1992, pp. 183–202.

6 Saul Gellerman, *Motivation and Productivity* (New York: AMACOM).

7 Lester Lefton and Laura Valvatne, *Mastering Psychology* (Boston: Allyn and Bacon, 1992), p. 412.

8 Lester Lefton and Laura Valvatne, *Mastering Psychology* (Boston: Allyn and Bacon, 1992), p. 412.

9 Lester Lefton and Laura Valvatne, *Mastering Psychology* (Boston: Allyn and Bacon, 1992), p. 412.

10 Marilyn Gist and Terence Mitchell, "Self-Efficacy: A Theoretical Analysis of its Determinants and Malleability," *Academy of Management Review,* April 1992, p. 183.

11 For a review and listing of these studies, see Marilyn Gist and Terence Mitchell, "Self-Efficacy: A Theoretical Analysis of its Determinants and Malleability," *Academy of Management Review,* April 1992, pp. 183–211.

12 Ernest R. Hilgard, *Introduction to Psychology* (New York: Harcourt Brace and World, 1962), p. 86.

13 Timothy Costello and Sheldon Zalkind, *Psychology in Administration* (Upper Saddle River, NJ: Prentice-Hall, 1963), pp. 315-16.

14 Benson Rosen and Thomas Jerdee, "The Influence of Age Stereotypes on Managerial Decisions," *Journal of Applied Psychology,* August 1976, pp. 428–32.

15 Ernest R. Hilgard, *Introduction to Psychology* (New York: Harcourt Brace and World, 1962), p. 476; see also R. Heneman et al., "Attributions and Exchanges: The Effects of Interpersonal Factors on the Diagnosis of Employee Performance," *Academy of Management Journal,* June 1989, pp. 466–78; and Mary Ann Glynn, "Effects of Work Task Cues and Play Task Cues on Information Processing, Judgment and Motivation," *Journal of Applied Psychology,* February 1994, pp. 34–46.

16 Martin Fishbein and Icek Ajzen, *Attitude, Intention and Behavior: An Introduction to Theory and Research* (Reading, MA: Addison-Wesley, 1975).

17 All About Your Company, *IBM Employee Handbook,* p. 184.

18 Margot Gibb-Clark, "Worker Morale Higher in Canada than U.S.: Survey," *The Globe and Mail,* February 10, 1999, p. B11.

19 The Job Descriptive Index is copyrighted by Bowling Green State University, and can be obtained from Dr. Patricia C. Smith, Department of Psychology, Bowling Green State University, Bowling Green, Ohio, 43403.

20 See, for example, M.T. Iaffaldano and M.P. Muchinsky, "Job Satisfaction and Job Performance: A Meta-Analysis," *Psychological Bulletin,* March 1985, pp. 251–73.

Chapter 12

1 Daniel Katz and Robert Kahn, *The Social Psychology of Organizations* (New York: Wiley, 1966).

2 H. Mintzberg, *The Nature of Managerial Work* (New York: Harper & Row, 1973).

3 L.B. Kurke and H. Aldrich, "Mintzberg Was Right! A Replication and Extension of *The Nature of Managerial Work,*" *Management Science,* 29 (1983), p. 979.

4 George Miller, *Language and Communication* (New York: McGraw-Hill, 1951), p. 10, discussed in Gary Hunt, *Communication Skills in the Organization,* 2nd ed. (Upper Saddle River, NJ: Prentice-Hall, 1989), p. 29.

5 This is discussed in and based on Fred Luthans and Janet Larsen, "How Managers Really Communicate," *Human Relations,* 1986, p. 162.

6 This model is based on the classic and best-known communication model by Claude E. Shannon and Warren Weaver and is adapted by using several improvements suggested by Sanford, Hunt, and Bracey. Both models are presented in Gary Hunt, *Communication Skills in the Organization,* 2nd ed. (Upper Saddle River, NJ: Prentice-Hall, 1989), pp. 34–36.

7 This section on dealing with communication barriers is based on R. Wayne Pace and Don Faules, *Organizational Communication* (Englewood Cliffs, NJ: Prentice Hall, 1989), pp. 150–62, unless otherwise noted. See also Tom Geddie, "Leap Over Communications Barriers," *Communication World,* April 1994, pp. 12–17.

8 R. Wayne Pace and Don Faules, *Organizational Communication* (Englewood Cliffs, NJ: Prentice Hall, 1989), p. 153.

9 Carey Goldberg, "Windfall Sets Off a Blizzard of Bonuses for a Company," *New York Times,* December 25, 1996, p. A16.

10 For instance, see Jay Knippn and Thad Green, "How the Manager Can Use Active Listening," *Public Personnel Management,* 23, no. 2 (Summer 1994), pp. 357–59.

11 Jack Griffin, *How to Say It at Work* (Paramus, NJ: Prentice Hall Press, 1998), pp. 86–220.

12 Jack Griffin, *How to Say It at Work* (Paramus, NJ: Prentice Hall Press, 1998), p. 178.

13 James C. Freund, *Smart Negotiating* (New York: Simon & Schuster, 1992), pp. 42–46.

14 James C. Freund, *Smart Negotiating* (New York: Simon & Schuster, 1992), p. 33.

15 Jack Griffin, *How to Say It at Work* (Paramus, NJ: Prentice Hall Press, 1998), pp. 107–09.

16 Bob Smith, "Care and Feeding of the Office Grapevine," *American Management Association,* February 1996, p. 6.

17 Eugene Walton, "How Efficient Is the Grapevine?" *Personnel,* March/April 1961, pp. 45–49, reprinted in Davis, *Organizational Behavior: A Book of Readings.*

18 Keith Davis, "Cut Those Rumors Down to Size," *Supervisory Management,* June 1975, p. 206.

19 Thomas Stewart, "How G.E. Keeps Those Ideas Coming," *Fortune,* August 12, 1991, pp. 41–49.

20 Edwin A. Locke and D. Henne, "Work Motivation Theories," in *International Review of Industrial and Organizational Psychology,* C.L. Cooper and I. Robertson (eds.) (Chichester, England: Wiley, 1986), pp. 1–35.

21 Jitendra Sharma, "Organizational Communications: A Linking Process," *The Personnel Administrator,* 24 (July 1979), pp. 35–43. See also Victor Callan, "Subordinate-Manager Communication in Different Sex Dyads: Consequences for Job Satisfaction," *Journal of Occupational and Organizational Psychology* (March 1993), pp. 13–28.

22 William Convoy, *Working Together . . . Communication in a Healthy Organization* (Columbus, OH: Charles Merrill, 1976). See also David Johnson et al., "Differences Between Formal and Informal Communication Channels," *Journal of Business Communication* (April 1994), pp. 111–24.

23 Gary Dessler, *Winning Commitment: How to Build and Keep a Competitive Workforce* (New York: McGraw-Hill, 1993).

24 R. Wayne Pace and Don Faules, *Organizational Communication* (Englewood Cliffs, NJ: Prentice Hall, 1989), pp. 105–6. See also

Joanne Yates and Wanda Orlinkowski, "Genres of Organizational Communication: A Structurational Approach to Studying Communication and Media," *Academy of Management Review*, 17 (April 1992), pp. 299–327.

25 Joanne Sisto, "Onward and… Oops," *Canadian Business*, July 1990, pp. 70–71.

26 Ian Allaby, "The Search for Quality," *Canadian Business*, May 1990, pp. 31–42.

27 Patrick Conlon, "Open for Business," *Report on Business*, June 1990, p. 75.

28 Murray McNeill, "Slump Called Opportunity to Trim Fat," *Winnipeg Free Press*, September 21, 1990, p. 68.

29 Earl Plenty and William Machaner, "Stimulating Upward Communication." In Jerry Gray and Frederick Starke (eds.), *Readings in Organizational Behavior* (Columbus, OH: Merrill, 1977), pp. 229–40. See also R. Wayne Pace and Don Faules, *Organizational Communication* (Englewood Cliffs, NJ: Prentice Hall, 1989), pp. 153–60.

30 For a discussion of this see Karlene Roberts and Charles O'Reilly III, "Failures in Upward Communication in Organizations: Three Possible Culprits," *Academy of Management Journal*, vol. 17, no. 2, June 1974, pp. 205–15.

31 Gordon Brockhouse, "Can This Marrriage Succeed?" *Canadian Business*, October 1992, pp. 128–35.

32 Based on Stewart, "How GE Keeps Those Ideas Coming."

33 Stewart, "How GE Keeps Those Ideas Coming," p. 42.

34 Stewart, "How GE Keeps Those Ideas Coming," p. 42.

35 Stewart, "How GE Keeps Those Ideas Coming," p. 42.

36 Stewart, "How GE Keeps Those Ideas Coming," p. 43.

37 Stewart, "How GE Keeps Those Ideas Coming," p. 43.

38 *Federal Express Employee Handbook*, p. 89.

39 Toyota Motor Manufacturing, USA, *Team-Member Handbook*, February 1988, pp. 52–53.

40 For a recent review and a discussion of the current study see James Smither et al., "An Examination of the Effects of an Upward Feedback Program Over Time," *Personnel Psychology*, vol. 48, 1995, pp. 1–34.

41 James Smither et al., "An Examination of the Effects of an Upward Feedback Program Over Time," *Personnel Psychology*, vol. 48, 1995, pp. 10–11.

42 James Smither et al., "An Examination of the Effects of an Upward Feedback Program Over Time," *Personnel Psychology*, vol. 48, 1995, p. 27.

43 R. Wayne Pace and Don Faules, Organizational Communication, (Upper Saddle River, NJ: Prentice Hall, 1989), pp. 99–100.

44 Personal interview, March 1992.

45 Personal interview, March 1992.

46 "Employers Profit from Opening the Books," *Bureau of National Affairs Bulletin to Management*, September 5, 1999, p. 288.

47 John Partridge, "Abitibi Dares to Digest Another Deal," *The Globe and Mail*, February 27, 1998, p. B27.

48 Paul Hansen, "Getting Your Team on the Same Side," *Financial Executive*, March–April 1994, pp. 43–48.

49 Paul Hansen, "Getting Your Team on the Same Side," *Financial Executive*, March–April 1994, p. 43.

50 Paul Hansen, "Getting Your Team on the Same Side," *Financial Executive*, March–April 1994, p. 44.

51 Paul Hansen, "Getting Your Team on the Same Side," *Financial Executive*, March–April 1994, p. 45.

52 Margot Gibb-Clark, "Most Job Losers find out Second-Hand," *The Globe and Mail*, April 14, 1993, pp. B1, B4.

53 This is based on Tom Peters and Robert Waterman, *In Search of Excellence* (New York: Harper & Row), pp. 119–218. On the other hand, creating too much emphasis on "free speech" can make firms vulnerable to lawsuits and other problems if employees are to quick to speak their minds, according to one expert. See Scott Hayes, "Censored! Free speech at work," *Workforce*, September 1999, pp. 34–38.

54 Tom Peters and Robert Waterman, *In Search of Excellence* (New York: Harper & Row), p. 122.

55 Tom Peters and Robert Waterman, *In Search of Excellence* (New York: Harper & Row), p. 124.

56 Tom Peters and Robert Waterman, *In Search of Excellence* (New York: Harper & Row), pp. 218–20, 122–23.

57 Tom Peters and Robert Waterman, *In Search of Excellence* (New York: Harper & Row), p. 219.

58 Tom Peters and Robert Waterman, *In Search of Excellence* (New York: Harper & Row), p. 22.

59 Tom Peters and Robert Waterman, *In Search of Excellence* (New York: Harper & Row), pp. 122–23.

60 Harold Leavitt, "Some Effects of Certain Communication Patterns on a Group Performance," *Journal of Abnormal and Social Psychology*, 46 (1972), pp. 38–50.

61 Tom Burns and G.M. Stalker, *The Management of Innovation* (London: Tavistock Publications, 1961), pp. 120–25.

62 R.L. Daft and R.H. Lengel, "Information Richness: A New Approach in Managerial Behavior and Organization Design." In Larry Cummings and Barry Staw (eds.), *Research in Organizational Behavior* (Greenwich, CT: JAI Press, 1984), pp. 190–233, discussed in Janet Fulk and Bryan Boyd, "Emerging Theories of Communication in Organizations," *Journal of Management*, 17, no. 2 (1991), pp. 409–11. See also Susan Strauss and Joseph McGrath, "Does the Medium Matter? The Intersection of Task Type and Technology on Group Performance and Member Reactions," *Journal of Applied Psychology* (February 1994), pp. 87–99.

63 Sarah Schafer, "E-mail Grows Up," *Inc. Technology*, vol. 1, 1997, pp. 87–88.

64 Paul Saffo, "The Future of Travel," *Fortune*, Autumn 1993, p. 119.

65 Kenneth Laudon and Jane Laudon, *Essentials of Management Information Systems* (Upper Saddle River, NJ: Prentice-Hall, 1997), p. 413.

66 Paul Roberts, "Live! From Your Office!" *Fast Company*, October 1999, p. 152.

67 David Kroenke and Richard Hatch, *Management Information Systems* (New York: McGraw-Hill, 1994), p. 359.

68 Robert Ford and Michael Butts, "Is Your Organization Ready for Telecommuting?" *SAM Advanced Management Journal*, Autumn 1991, p. 19; and Kenneth Laudon and Jane Laudon, *Essentials of Management Information Systems* (Upper Saddle River, NJ: Prentice-Hall, 1997), pp. 413–16.

69 "Telecommuting Causing Work Condition Worries," *The Globe and Mail*, January 7, 2000, p. B8.

70 Margot Gibb-Clark, "Satellite Office a Hit With Staff," *The Globe and Mail*, November 18, 1991, p. B4.

71 Robert Ford and Michael Butts, "Is Your Organization Ready for Telecommuting?" *SAM Advanced Management Journal*, Autumn 1991, p. 19; and Kenneth Laudon and Jane Laudon, *Essentials of Management Information Systems* (Upper Saddle River, NJ: Prentice-Hall, 1997), pp. 413–16.

72 See Sandra Atchison, "The Care and Feeding of Loan Eagles," *Business Week*, November 15, 1993, p. 58.

73 David Kirkpatrick, "Hot New PC Services," *Fortune*, November 1992, p. 108. See also Amy Cortese, "Here Comes the Intranet," *Business Week*, February 1996.

74 Nopper, "Reinventing the Factory"; and Dessler, *Winning Commitment: How to Build and Keep a Competitive Workforce* (New York: McGraw-Hill, 1993), pp. 133–50.

75 Amy Newman, "How to Create a Virtual Learning Community," *Training & Development*, July 1999, p. 44.

76 Joann Davy, "Online at the Office: Virtual Communities Go to Work," *Managing Office Technology*, July–August 1998, pp. 9–11.

77 Joann Davy, "Online at the Office: Virtual Communities Go to Work," *Managing Office Technology*, July–August 1998, pp. 9–11.

78 David Kirkpatrick, "The Portal of the Future? Your Boss Will Run It," *Fortune*, August 2, 1999, pp. 222–27.

79 David Kirkpatrick, "The Portal of the Future? Your Boss Will Run It," *Fortune*, August 2, 1999, pp. 222–27.

80 Roger E. Axtell (ed.), *Do's and Taboos Around the World* (New York: John Wiley & Sons, Inc., 1985), pp. 37–48.

Chapter 13

1 Merle MacIsaac, "Born-Agan Basket Case," *Canadian Business*, May 1993, pp. 38–44.

2 For employee involvement survey data, see Lee Towe, "Survey Finds Employee Involvement a Priority for Necessary Innovation," *National Productivity Review*, Winter 1989–90, pp. 3–15. See also Bradley Kirkman and Benson Rosen, "Beyond Self-Management: Antecedents and Consequences of Team Empowerment," *Academy of Management Journal*, February 1999, pp. 58–74.

3 Jack Orsburn, Linda Moran, Ed Musselwhite, John Zenger, and Craig Perrin, *Self-Directed Work Teams: The New American Challenge* (Homewood, IL: Business One Irwin, 1990), pp. 30–34.

4 Jack Orsburn, Linda Moran, Ed Musselwhite, John Zenger, and Craig Perrin, *Self-Directed Work Teams: The New American Challenge* (Homewood, IL: Business One Irwin, 1990), p. 33.

5 Jack Orsburn, Linda Moran, Ed Musselwhite, John Zenger, and Craig Perrin, *Self-Directed Work Teams: The New American Challenge* (Homewood, IL: Business One Irwin, 1990), p. 33.

6 Jack Orsburn, Linda Moran, Ed Musselwhite, John Zenger, and Craig Perrin, *Self-Directed Work Teams: The New American Challenge* (Homewood, IL: Business One Irwin, 1990), p. 34. See also Charles Manz, "Self-Leading Work Teams: Moving Beyond Self-Management Myths," *Human Relations*, 45, no. 11 (1992), pp. 1119–41.

7 These definitions are from Marvin E. Shaw, *Group Dynamics: The Psychology of Small Group Behavior* (New York: McGraw-Hill, 1976), p. 11.

8 See, for example, John Katzenbach and Douglas Smith, "The Discipline of Teams," *Harvard Business Review* (March–April 1993), pp. 112–13. Note that many researchers do not, however, distinguish between groups and teams. See, for example, Gary Coleman and Eileen M. VanAken, "Applying Small-Group Behavior Dynamics to Improve Action-Team Performance," *Employment Relations Today* (Autumn 1991), pp. 343–53.

9 Sandra Robinson and Ann O'Leary-Kelly, "Monkey See, Monkey Do: The Influence of Workgroups on the Antisocial Behavior of Employees," *Academy of Management Journal*, vol. 41, no.6, 1988, p. 667.

10 Daniel Feldman, "The Development and Enforcement of Group Norms," *Academy of Management Review*, vol. 9, no.1, 1984, pp. 47–53.

11 A.P. Hare, Handbook of Small Group Research (New York: The Free Press, 1962), p. 24. See also S. Barr and E. Conlon, "Effects of Distribution of Feedback in Work Groups," Academy of Management Journal, June 1994, pp. 641–56.

12 See Stephen Worchel, Wendy Wood, and Jeffrey Simpson, *Group Process and Productivity* (Newbury Park, CA: Sage Publications, 1992), pp. 245–50.

13 See Stephen Worchel, Wendy Wood, and Jeffrey Simpson, *Group Process and Productivity* (Newbury Park, CA: Sage Publications, 1992), p. 245.

14 For a discussion of the difficulty of measuring and defining cohesiveness, see Peter Mudrack, "Group Cohesiveness and Productivity: A Closer Look," *Human Relations*, 42, no. 9 (1989), pp. 771–85. See also R. Saavedra et al., "Complex Interdependence in Task-Performing Groups," *Journal of Applied Psychology* (February 1993), pp. 61–73.

15 See Marvin Shaw, *Group Dynamics* (New York: McGraw-Hill, 1976), Chapter 4.

16 Robert Blake and Jane Mouton, "Reactions to Inter-Group Competition under Win-Lose Conditions," *Management Science*, 7 (1961), p. 432.

17 John R.P. French, Jr., "The Disruption and Cohesion of Groups," *Journal of Abnormal and Social Psychology*, 36 (1941), pp. 361–77.

18 Stanley C. Seashore, *Group Cohesiveness in the Industry Work Group* (Ann Arbor, MI: Survey Research Center, University of Michigan, 1954), pp. 90–95; and Joseph Litterer, *The Analysis of Organizations* (New York: Wiley, 1965), pp. 91–101; and J. Haleblian and S. Finkelstein, "Top Management Team Size, CEO Dominance, and Firm Performance: The Moderating Roles of Environmental Turbulence and Discretion," *Academy of Management Journal* (August 1993), pp. 844–64.

19 Dorothy Lipovenko, "One Way to Cut Management Flab," *The Globe and Mail*, January 1, 1987, pp. B1–B2.

20 This material is based on James H. Shonk, *Team-Based Organizations* (Chicago: Irwin, 1997), pp. 27–33.

21 James H. Shonk, *Team-Based Organizations* (Chicago: Irwin, 1997), p. 28.

22 James H. Shonk, *Team-Based Organizations* (Chicago: Irwin, 1997), p. 29.

23 John Katzenbach and Douglas Smith, "The Discipline of Teams," *Harvard Business Review* (March–April 1993), pp. 116–18.

24 Everett Adams, Jr., "Quality Circle Performance," *Journal of Management*, 17, no. 1 (1991), pp. 25–39.

25 Everett Adams, Jr., "Quality Circle Performance," *Journal of Management*, 17, no. 1 (1991), pp. 25–39.

26 See, for example, Everett Adams, Jr., "Quality Circle Performance," *Journal of Management*, 17, no. 1 (1991); and Gilbert Fuchsberg, "Quality Programs Show Shoddy Results," *Wall Street Journal*, May 14, 1992, pp. B-1, B-4.

27 Gopal Pati, Robert Salitore, and Saundra Brady, "What Went Wrong with Quality Circles?" *Personnel Journal* (December 1987), pp. 83–89.

28 Philip Olson, "Choices for Innovation Minded Corporations," *Journal of Business Strategy* (January–February 1990), pp. 86–90.

29 Harold J. Leavitt and Jean Lipman-Blumen, "Hot Groups," *Harvard Business Review* (July–August 1995), p. 109.

30 Harold J. Leavitt and Jean Lipman-Blumen, "Hot Groups," *Harvard Business Review* (July–August 1995), p. 165.

31 Harold J. Leavitt and Jean Lipman-Blumen, "Hot Groups," *Harvard Business Review* (July–August 1995), p. 165.

32 Harold J. Leavitt and Jean Lipman-Blumen, "Hot Groups," *Harvard Business Review* (July–August 1995), p. 113.

33 The remainder of this section is based on Harold J. Leavitt and Jean Lipman-Blumen, "Hot Groups," *Harvard Business Review* (July–August 1995), pp. 110–16.

34 Harold J. Leavitt and Jean Lipman-Blumen, "Hot Groups," *Harvard Business Review* (July–August 1995), p. 111.

35 Harold J. Leavitt and Jean Lipman-Blumen, "Hot Groups," *Harvard Business Review* (July–August 1995), p. 111.

36 Harold J. Leavitt and Jean Lipman-Blumen, "Hot Groups," *Harvard Business Review* (July–August 1995), p. 112.

37 Harold J. Leavitt and Jean Lipman-Blumen, "Hot Groups," *Harvard Business Review* (July–August 1995), p. 112.

38 Harold J. Leavitt and Jean Lipman-Blumen, "Hot Groups," *Harvard Business Review* (July–August 1995), p. 113.

39 In many firms, the concept of a venture team is taken to what may be its natural conclusion in that new-venture units and new-venture divisions are established. These are separate divisions devoted to new-product development. See, for example, Christopher Bart, "New Venture Units: Use Them Wisely to Manage Innovation," *Sloan Management Review*, 35 (Summer 1988), pp. 35–43; and Robert Burgelman, "Managing the New

Venture Division: Research Findings and Implications for Strategic Management," *Strategic Management Journal*, 6 (1985), pp. 39–54.

40 Charles Snow, Scott Snell, Sue Canney Davison, and Donald Hambrick, "Use Transnational Teams to Globalize Your Company," *Organizational Dynamics* (Spring 1996), pp. 50–67.

41 Charles Snow, Scott Snell, Sue Canney Davison, and Donald Hambrick, "Use Transnational Teams to Globalize Your Company," *Organizational Dynamics* (Spring 1996), p. 50.

42 Charles Snow, Scott Snell, Sue Canney Davison, and Donald Hambrick, "Use Transnational Teams to Globalize Your Company," *Organizational Dynamics* (Spring 1996), p. 50.

43 Charles Snow, Scott Snell, Sue Canney Davison, and Donald Hambrick, "Use Transnational Teams to Globalize Your Company," *Organizational Dynamics* (Spring 1996), pp. 53–57.

44 Lynda McDermott, Bill Waite, and Nolan Brawley, "Putting Together a World-Class Team," *Training and Development*, January 1999, p. 48.

45 Charles Snow, Scott Snell, Sue Canney Davison, and Donald Hambrick, "Use Transnational Teams to Globalize Your Company," *Organizational Dynamics* (Spring 1996), p. 61.

46 Based on suggestions by David Armstrong, "Making Dispersed Teams Work," *Bureau of National Affairs Bulletin to Management,* May 23, 1996, p. 168.

47 Anthony Townsend, Samuel DiMarie, and Anthony Hendrickson, "Virtual Teams: Technology and the Workplace of the Future," *Academy of Management Executive*, vol. 12, no. 3, 1998, pp. 17–29.

48 Anthony Townsend, Samuel DiMarie, and Anthony Hendrickson, "Virtual Teams: Technology and the Workplace of the Future," *Academy of Management Executive*, vol. 12, no. 3, 1998, p. 20.

49 Christa Degnan, "ActiveProject Aids Teamwork," *PC Week*, May 31, 1999, pp. 21–22

50 Rochelle Garner, "Round-the-World Teamwork," *Computerworld*, May 24, 1999, p. 46.

51 Tom Peters, *Liberation Management* (New York: Alfred Knopf, 1992), pp. 238–239.

52 Jack Orsburn, Linda Moran, Ed Musselwhite, John Zenger, and Craig Perrin, *Self-Directed Work Teams: The New American Challenge* (Homewood, IL: Business One Irwin, 1990), pp. 20–27.

53 Jack Orsburn, Linda Moran, Ed Musselwhite, John Zenger, and Craig Perrin, *Self-Directed Work Teams: The New American Challenge* (Homewood, IL: Business One Irwin, 1990), p. 21.

54 Jack Orsburn, Linda Moran, Ed Musselwhite, John Zenger, and Craig Perrin, *Self-Directed Work Teams: The New American Challenge* (Homewood, IL: Business One Irwin, 1990), p. 22.

55 Jack Orsburn, Linda Moran, Ed Musselwhite, John Zenger, and Craig Perrin, *Self-Directed Work Teams: The New American Challenge* (Homewood, IL: Business One Irwin, 1990), pp. 22–23.

56 "Kodak's Team Structure is Picture Perfect," *Bureau of National Affairs Bulletin to Management,* August 15, 1996, p. 264.

57 Rojiv Banker, Roger Schroeder, and Kingshuk Sinha, "Impact of Work Teams on Manufacturing Performance: A Longitudinal Field Study," *Academy of Management Journal*, vol. 39, no. 4, 1996, pp. 867–88.

58 Rojiv Banker, Roger Schroeder, and Kingshuk Sinha, "Impact of Work Teams on Manufacturing Performance: A Longitudinal Field Study," *Academy of Management Journal*, vol. 39, no. 4, 1996, pp. 887–88.

59 Rojiv Banker, Roger Schroeder, and Kingshuk Sinha, "Impact of Work Teams on Manufacturing Performance: A Longitudinal Field Study," *Academy of Management Journal*, vol. 39, no. 4, 1996, p. 870.

60 Ralph King, Jr., "Levi's Factory Workers are Assigned to Teams, and Morale has Taken a Hit," *Wall Street Journal,* May 20, 1998, pp. A-I, A-6.

61 Based on Erin Neurick, "Facilitating Effective Work Teams," *SAM*

Advanced Management Journal, Winter 1993, pp. 22–26. See also Margarita Alegria, "Building Effective Research Teams When Conducting Drug Prevention Research with Minority Populations," *Drugs & Society,* 1999, vol. 14, no.1–2, pp. 227–45. George Neuman and Julie Wright, "Team Effectiveness: Beyond Skills and Cognitive Ability," *Journal of Applied Psychology,* June 1999, pp. 376–89.

62 Erin Neurick, "Facilitating Effective Work Teams," *SAM Advanced Management Journal,* Winter 1993, p. 23.

63 Suchitra Mouly and Jayaram Sankaran, "Barriers to the Cohesiveness and Effectiveness of Indian R&D Project Groups: Insights from Four Federal R&D Organizations," in John Wagner et al., *Advances in Qualitative Organization Research,* vol. 2 (Stanford, CT: A.I. Press, 1999), pp. 221–43.

64 Discussed in Paul Mulvey, John Veiga, and Priscilla Elsass, "When Teammates Raise the White Flag," *Academy of Management Executive,* vol. 10, no.1, 1996, p. 40. See also Richard Hackman, "Why Teams Don't Work," in R. Tindale et al., *Theory and Research on Small Groups: Social Psychological Applications in Social Issues,* vol. 4 (Plenum Press, New York, 1998), pp. 245–67.

65 The following, except as noted, is based on Glenn H. Varney, *Building Productive Teams: An Action Guide and Resource Book* (San Francisco: Jossey-Bass Publishers, 1989), pp. 11–18. See also P. Bernthal and C. Insko, "Cohesiveness without Group Think: The Interactive Effects of Social and Task Cohesion," *Group and Organization Management,* March 1993, pp. 66–68. See also Vanessa Druskat, "The Antecedents of Team Competence: Toward a Fine-Grained Model of Self-Managing Team Effectiveness," *Research on Managing Groups and Teams: Groups in Context,* vol. 2, 1999, pp. 201–31.

66 John Katzenbach and Douglas Smith, "The Discipline of Teams," *Harvard Business Review* (March–April 1993), p. 112. See also C. Meyer, "How the Right Measures Help Teams Excel," *Harvard Business Review* (May–June 1994), pp. 95–106.

67 John Katzenbach and Douglas Smith, "The Discipline of Teams," *Harvard Business Review* (March–April 1993), p. 112.

68 See G.T. Shea and R.A. Guzzo, "Groups as Human Resources." In K.M. Roland and G.R. Ferris (eds.), *Research in Personnel and Human Resources Management,* Vol. 5 (Greenwich, CT: JAI Press, 1987), pp. 323–56. See also Eric Sundstrom, Kenneth DeMeuse, and David Futrell, "Workteams: Applications and Effectiveness," *American Psychologist,* February 1990, p. 123.

69 John Katzenbach and Douglas Smith, "The Discipline of Teams," *Harvard Business Review* (March–April 1993), p. 113.

70 John Katzenbach and Douglas Smith, "The Discipline of Teams," *Harvard Business Review* (March–April 1993), p. 113. The evaluation process is important as well. See R. Saavedra and S. Kwun, "Peer Evaluation in Self-Managing Work Groups," *Journal of Applied Psychology* (June 1993), pp. 450–63.

71 Michael West and Neil Anderson, "Innovation in Top Management Teams," *Journal of Applied Psychology,* 81, no. 6 (December 1996), pp. 680–93.

72 The remaining items in this section, except as noted, are quoted from or based on Michael A. Campion and A. Catherine Higgs, "Design Work Teams to Increase Productivity and Satisfaction," *HR Magazine,* October 1995, pp. 101–7. See also Steven G. Rogelberg and Steven M. Rumery, "Gender Diversity, Team Decision Quality, Time on Task, and Interpersonal Cohesion," *Small Group Research,* 27, no. 1 (February 1996), pp. 79–90; Steven E. Gross and Jeffrey Blair, "Reinforcing Team Effectiveness Through Pay," *Compensation and Benefits Review,* 27, no. 5 (September 1995), pp. 34–38; and Joan M. Glaman, Allan P. Jones, and Richard M. Rozelle, "The Effects of Co-Worker Similarity on the Emergence of Affect in Work Teams," *Group and Organization Management,* 21, no. 2 (June 1996), pp. 192–215.

73 David Hyatt and Thomas Ruddy, "An Examination of the Relationship Between Workgroup Characteristics and Performance: Once More into the Breach," *Personnel Psychology,* 50, 1997, p. 577.

74 David Hyatt and Thomas Ruddy, "An Examination of the Relationship Between Workgroup Characteristics and Performance: Once More into the Breach," *Personnel Psychology,* 50, 1997, p. 578.

75 See Michael A. Campion and A. Catherine Higgs, "Design Work Teams to Increase Productivity and Satisfaction," *HR Magazine*, October 1995, pp. 102–103. See also Michael Campion, Ellen Papper, and Gina Medsker, "Relations Between Work Team Characteristics and Effectiveness: A Replication and Extension," *Personnel Psychology*, 49, no. 2 (Summer 1996), pp. 429–52.

76 Michael A. Campion and A. Catherine Higgs, "Design Work Teams to Increase Productivity and Satisfaction," *HR Magazine*, October 1995, p. 102.

77 Michael A. Campion and A. Catherine Higgs, "Design Work Teams to Increase Productivity and Satisfaction," *HR Magazine*, October 1995, pp. 103–104.

78 These are based on James H. Shonk, *Team-Based Organizations* (Chicago: Irwin, 1997), pp. 133–38.

79 Kimball Fisher, *Leading Self-Directed Work Teams* (New York: McGraw-Hill, 1993), pp. 151–53.

80 Kimball Fisher, *Leading Self-Directed Work Teams* (New York: McGraw-Hill, 1993), p. 44.

81 These are based on Kimball Fisher, *Leading Self-Directed Work Teams* (New York: McGraw-Hill, 1993), pp. 48–56.

82 Kimball Fisher, *Leading Self-Directed Work Teams* (New York: McGraw-Hill, 1993), p. 53.

83 Gary Dessler, *Winning Commitment* (New York: McGraw-Hill, 1992), p. 28.

84 Gary Dessler, *Winning Commitment* (New York: McGraw-Hill, 1992), p. 30.

85 For a discussion see Kimball Fisher, *Leading Self-Directed Work Teams* (New York: McGraw-Hill, 1993), p. 106.

86 Kimball Fisher, *Leading Self-Directed Work Teams* (New York: McGraw-Hill, 1993), pp. 110–11.

87 Kimball Fisher, *Leading Self-Directed Work Teams* (New York: McGraw-Hill, 1993), p. 110.

88 James H. Shonk, *Team-Based Organizations* (Chicago: Irwin, 1997), p. 133.

89 See James H. Shonk, *Team-Based Organizations* (Chicago: Irwin, 1997), pp. 133–38; Andrew DuBrin, *Leadership: Research Findings, Practice and Skills* (Boston: Houghton-Mifflin, 1995), pp. 224–27.

90 James H. Shonk, *Team-Based Organizations* (Chicago: Irwin, 1997), p. 133.

91 Kimball Fisher, *Leading Self-Directed Work Teams* (New York: McGraw-Hill, 1993), pp. 143–44.

92 Kimball Fisher, *Leading Self-Directed Work Teams* (New York: McGraw-Hill, 1993), p. 143.

93 Jennifer James, *Thinking in the Future Tense* (New York: Simon & Schuster, 1996), pp. 190–206.

Chapter 14

1 Kevin Cox, "Sea Change," *The Globe and Mail*, May 17, 1994, p. B24.

2 Melanie Warner, "Nightmare on Net Street," *Fortune*, September 6, 1999, pp. 285–88.

3 Based on David Nadler and Michael Tushman, "Beyond the Charismatic Leader: Leadership and Organizational Change," *California Management Review*, Winter 1990, pp. 77–97.

4 Based on David Nadler and Michael Tushman, "Beyond the Charismatic Leader: Leadership and Organizational Change," *California Management Review*, Winter 1990, p. 80; and Alfred Marcus, "Responses to Externally Induced Innovation: To their Effects on Organizational Performance," *Strategic Management Journal*, vol. 9 (1988), pp. 194–202. See also Steve Crom, "Change Leadership: the Virtues of Obedience," *Leadership & Organization Development Journal*, March–June 1999, pp. 162–68.

5 David Nadler and Michael Tushman, "Beyond the Charismatic Leader: Leadership and Organizational Change," *California Management Review*, Winter 1990, p. 80.

6 David Nadler and Michael Tushman, "Beyond the Charismatic Leader: Leadership and Organizational Change," *California Management Review*, Winter 1990, p. 78. See also Guvenc G. Alpander and Carroll R. Lee, "Culture, Strategy and Teamwork: The Keys to Organizational Change," *Journal of Management Development*, vol. 14, no. 8, 1995, pp. 4–18; and Benjamin Schneider, Arthur P. Brief, and Richard A. Guzzo, "Creating a Climate and Culture for Sustainable Organizational Change," *Organizational Dynamics*, vol. 24, no. 4, Spring 1996, pp. 7–19.

7 Gary Dessler, *Winning Commitment: How to Build and Keep a Competitive Work Force* (New York: McGraw-Hill, 1993), p. 85.

8 Michael Hammer and James Champy, "The Promise of Reengineering," *Fortune*, May 3, 1993, pp. 94–97; also Thomas A. Stewart, "Reengineering: The Hot New Managing Tool," *Fortune*, August 23, 1993, pp. 41–48; also Ronald Henkoff, "The Hot New Seal of Quality," *Fortune*, August 23, 1993, pp. 116–18.

9 Cathryn Mottherwell, "How to Fix a Model of a Muddle," *The Globe and Mail*, November 22, 1994, p. B30.

10 Gary Dessler, *Winning Commitment: How to Build and Keep a Competitive Work Force* (New York: McGraw-Hill, 1993), p. 85. See also Varun Grover, "From Business Reengineering to Business Process Change Management: A Longitudinal Study of Chen Trends and Practices," *IEEE Transactions on Engineering Management*, February 1999, p. 36.

11 Denison, *Corporate Culture*, p. 12. For a recent discussion see also Daniel Denison, "What Is the Difference between Organizational Culture and Organizational Climate? A Native's Point of View on a Decade of Paradigm Wars," *Academy of Management Review*, July 1996, pp. 619–54.

12 See, for example, Brian Dumaine, "The Bureaucracy Busters," *Fortune*, June 17, 1991, pp. 36–50.

13 Peter Larson, "Winning Strategies," *Canadian Business Review*, Summer 1989, pp. 41–42.

14 Roger Harrison, "Choosing the Depth of Organization Intervention," *Journal of Applied Behavioral Science*, 2, April–May–June 1970, pp. 181–202.

15 Karen Howlett, "IBM Canada Realigns: Staff to Go Back to School," *The Globe and Mail*, March 17, 1987, pp. B1–B2.

16 Michael Crawford, "The New Office Etiquette," *Canadian Business*, May 1993, pp. 22–31.

17 David Nadler and Michael Tushman, "Beyond the Charismatic Leader: Leadership and Organizational Change," *California Management Review*, Winter 1990, p. 79.

18 Niccolo Machiavelli (trans. W.K. Marriott), *The Prince* (London: J.M. Dent & Sons, Ltd., 1958).

19 Richard Osborne, "Core Values Statements: The Corporate Compass," *Business Horizons*, September–October 1991, pp. 28–34.

20 Paul Lawrence, "How to Deal with Resistance to Change," *Harvard Business Review*, May–June 1954. See also Andrew W. Schwartz, "Eight Guidelines for Managing Change," *Supervisory Management*, July 1994, pp. 3–5; Thomas J. Werner and Robert F. Lynch, "Challenges of a Change Agent," *Journal for Quality and Participation*, June 1994, pp. 50–54; Larry Reynolds, "Understand Employees' Resistance to Change," *HR Focus*, June 1994, pp. 17–18; and Kenneth E. Hultman, "Scaling the Wall of Resistance," *Training & Development Journal*, October 1995, pp. 15–18. See also Eric Dent, "Challenging Resistance to Change," *Journal of Applied Behavioral Science*, March 1999, p. 25.

21 Paul Strebel, "Why Do Employees Resist Change?" *Harvard Business Review*, May–June 1996, pp. 86–92.

22 Paul Strebel, "Why Do Employees Resist Change?" *Harvard Business Review*, May–June 1996, p. 87.

23 Paul Strebel, "Why Do Employees Resist Change?" *Harvard Business Review*, May–June 1996, p. 87.

24 Timothy Judge et al., "Managerial Coping with Organizational Change: A Dispositional Perspective," *Journal of Applied Psychology*, vol. 84, no.1, 1999, pp. 107–22.

25 "30 Women Opt to Become Miners," *The Globe and Mail*, February 24, 1993, p. B1.

26 Peter Larson, "Winning Strategies," *Canadian Business Review*, Summer 1989, pp. 41–42.

27 Kurt Lewin, "Group Decision and Social Change," in T. Newcomb and E. Hartley (eds.), *Readings in Social Psychology* (New York: Holt Rinehart & Winston, 1947). See also Thomas Cummings and Christopher Worley, *Organization Development and Change* (Minneapolis: West Publishing Company, 1993), p. 53. See also Terry Neese, "Convincing Your Employees to Accept Change," *LI Business News*, March 7, 1999, p. 41.

28 Stephen Robbins and Mary Coulter, *Management* (Englewood Cliffs, NJ: Prentice-Hall, 1996), pp. 423–25.

29 The ten steps are based on Michael Beer, Russell Eisenstat, and Burt Spector, "Why Change Programs Don't Produce Change," *Harvard Business Review*, November–December 1990, pp. 158–66; Thomas Cummings and Christopher Worley, *Organization Development and Change* (Minneapolis: West Publishing Company, 1993); John P. Kotter, "Leading Change: Why Transformation Efforts Fail," *Harvard Business Review*, March–April 1995, pp. 59–66; and John P. Kotter, *Leading Change* (Boston: Harvard Business School Press, 1996).

30 John P. Kotter, *Leading Change* (Boston: Harvard Business School Press, 1996), pp. 40–41.

31 John P. Kotter, *Leading Change* (Boston: Harvard Business School Press, 1996), p. 44.

32 John P. Kotter, *Leading Change* (Boston: Harvard Business School Press, 1996), p. 57.

33 John P. Kotter, *Leading Change* (Boston: Harvard Business School Press, 1996), pp. 90–91.

34 John P. Kotter, *Leading Change* (Boston: Harvard Business School Press, 1996), pp. 101–02.

35 Kathryn Harris, "Mr. Sony Confronts Hollywood," *Fortune*, December 23, 1996, p. 36.

36 Suzy Wetlaufer, "Driving Change: An Interview with Ford Motor Co.'s Jacques Nasser," *Harvard Business Review*, March–April 1999, pp. 77–88.

37 Beer, Eisenstat, and Spector, p. 163.

38 This is based on John P. Kotter, *Leading Change* (Boston: Harvard Business School Press, 1996), pp. 61–66.

39 John P. Kotter, *Leading Change* (Boston: Harvard Business School Press, 1996), p. 65.

40 Beer, Eisenstat, and Spector, p. 164.

41 The following is based on David Nadler and Michael Tushman, "Beyond the Charismatic Leader: Leadership and Organizational Change," *California Management Review*, Winter 1990, pp. 77–97.

42 David Nadler and Michael Tushman, "Beyond the Charismatic Leader: Leadership and Organizational Change," *California Management Review*, Winter 1990, p. 82.

43 David Nadler and Michael Tushman, "Beyond the Charismatic Leader: Leadership and Organizational Change," *California Management Review*, Winter 1990, p. 85.

44 The perceptive reader will note that Nadler and Tushman's concept of instrumental leadership is in some respects the same as saying that the successful executive leader of change is really a successful manager in that he or she is able to successfully plan, organize, staff, lead, and control the various elements of the change.

45 Shona McKay, "The Challenge in Change," *The Financial Post Magazine*, April 1992, pp. 43–44.

46 David Nadler and Michael Tushman, "Beyond the Charismatic Leader: Leadership and Organizational Change," *California Management Review*, Winter 1990, p. 92.

47 For a discussion see Julian Barling, Tom Weber, and E. Kevin Kelloway, "Effects of Transformational Leadership Training on Attitudinal and Financial Outcomes: A Field Experiment," *Journal of Applied Psychology*, December 1996, pp. 827–32.

48 Julian Barling, Tom Weber, and E. Kevin Kelloway, "Effects of Transformational Leadership Training on Attitudinal and Financial Outcomes: A Field Experiment," *Journal of Applied Psychology*, December 1996, pp. 827–32.

49 John Kotter and James Heskett, *Corporate Culture and Performance* (New York: The Free Press, 1992), p. 84.

50 John Kotter and James Heskett, *Corporate Culture and Performance* (New York: The Free Press, 1992), p. 84.

51 John Kotter and James Heskett, *Corporate Culture and Performance* (New York: The Free Press, 1992), p. 84.

52 See, for example, John Rizzo, Robert J. House, and Sydney I. Lirtzinan, "Role Conflict and Ambiguity in Complex Organizations," *Administrative Science Quarterly*, June 15, 1970, pp. 150–63. For additional views on sources of conflict, see Patricia A. Gwartney-Gibbs and Denise H. Lach, "Gender Differences in Clerical Workers' Disputes Over Tasks," *Human Relations*, June 1994, pp. 611–40; and Kevin J. Williams and George Alliger, "Role Stressors, Mood Spillover, and Perceptions of Work-Family Conflict in Employed Parents," *Academy of Management Journal*, August 1994, pp. 837–69.

53 Thomas Cummings and Christopher Worley, *Organization Development and Change* (Minneapolis: West Publishing Company, 1993), p. 3.

54 Based on J.T. Campbell and M.D. Dunnette, "Effectiveness of T-Group Experiences in Managerial Training and Development" *Psychological Bulletin*, 7, 1968, pp. 73–104, reprinted in W.E. Scott and L.L. Cummings, *Readings in Organizational Behavior and Human Performance* (Homewood, IL: Irwin, 1973), p. 571.

55 Robert J. House, *Management Development* (Ann Arbor, MI: Bureau of Industrial Relations, University of Michigan, 1967), p. 71; Louis White and Kevin Wooten, "Ethical Dilemmas in Various Stages of Organizational Development," *Academy of Management Review*, vol. 8, no. 4 (1983), pp. 690–97.

56 Wendell French and Cecil Bell, Jr., *Organization Development* (Upper Saddle River, NJ: Prentice-Hall, 1995), pp. 171–93.

57 Thomas Cummings and Christopher Worley, *Organization Development and Change* (Minneapolis: West Publishing Company, 1993), p. 501.

58 For a description of how to make OD a part of organizational strategy, see Aubrey Mendelow and S. Jay Liebowitz, "Difficulties in Making OD a Part of Organizational Strategy," *Human Resource Planning*, vol. 12, no. 4 (1995), pp. 317–29.

59 See, for example, John Rizzo, Robert J. House, and Sydney I. Lirtzinan, "Role Conflict and Ambiguity in Complex Organizations," *Administrative Science Quarterly*, June 1970, pp. 150–63. For additional views on sources of conflict, see Patricia A. Gwartney-Gibbs and Denise H. Lach, "Gender Differences in Clerical Workers' Disputes Over Tasks," *Human Relations*, June 1994, pp. 611–40; and Kevin J. Williams and George Alliger, "Role Stressors, Mood Spillover, and Perceptions of Work-Family Conflict in Employed Parents," *Academy of Management Journal*, August 1994, pp. 837–69. See also Howard Guttman, "Conflict at the Top," *Management Review*, November 1999, p. 49.

60 Yitzhak Fried and Robert B. Tiegs, "Supervisors' Role Conflict and Role Ambiguity: Differential Relations with Performance Ratings of Subordinates and the Moderating Effect of Screening Ability," *Journal of Applied Psychology*, April 1995, pp. 282–91.

61 Yitzhak Fried and Robert B. Tiegs, "Supervisors' Role Conflict and Role Ambiguity: Differential Relations with Performance Ratings of Subordinates and the Moderating Effect of Screening Ability," *Journal of Applied Psychology*, April 1995, p. 291.

62 See, for example, Richard Walton and John Dutton, "The Management of Interdepartment Conflict: A Model and Review," *Administrative Science Quarterly*, March 1969, pp. 73–84.

63 See, for example, Richard Walton and John Dutton, "The Management of Interdepartment Conflict: A Model and Review," *Administrative Science Quarterly*, vol. 14, no. 1, March 1969, pp. 73–84.

64 John Dutton and Richard Walton, "Interdepartmental Conflict and Cooperation: Two Contrasting Studies," *Human Organization*, vol. 25, 1966, pp. 207–20.

65 H.A. Lansberger, "The Horizontal Dimensions in a Bureaucracy," *Administrative Science Quarterly*, vol. 6, 1961, pp. 298–333.

66 Paul Lawrence and Jay Lorsch, *Organization and Environment* (Boston: Harvard University, Graduate School of Business Administration, Division of Research, 1967).

67 John A. Seiler, "Diagnosing Interdepartmental Conflict," *Harvard Business Review,* September–October 1963, pp. 121–32.

68 Eric Neilson, "Understanding and Managing Intergroup Conflict," in Paul Lawrence and Jay Lorsch, *Organizational Behavior and Administration* (Homewood, IL: Irwin, 1976), p. 294. See also Robin L. Pinkley and Gregory B. Northcraft, "Conflict Frames of Reference: Implications for Dispute Processes and Outcomes," *Academy of Management Journal,* February 1994, pp. 193–206.

69 This section is based on Evert Van De Vliert, Martin Euwema, and Sipke Huismans, "Managing Conflict with a Subordinate or a Superior: Effectiveness of Conglomerated Behavior," *Journal of Applied Psychology*, April 1995, pp. 271–81.

70 Rowan Gibson (ed.), *Rethinking the Future* (Nicholas Breakely, 1998).

71 T. George Harris, "The Post-Capitalist Executive: An Interview with Peter F. Drucker," *Harvard Business Review* (May–June 1993), pp. 115–22.

72 Charlene Marmer Solomon, "Expats Say: Help Make Us Mobile," *Personnel Journal* (July 1996), pp. 47–52.

73 Seth Shulman, *Owning the Future* (New York: Houghton Mifflin Company, 1999).

Chapter 15

1 Kenneth Merchant, "The Control Function of Management," *Sloan Management Review,* Summer 1982, p. 43.

2 Kenneth Merchant, "The Control Function of Management," *Sloan Management Review,* Summer 1982, p. 44.

3 S.M. Klein and R.R. Ritti, *Understanding Organizational Behavior* (Boston: Kent Publishing, 1984), p. 509.

4 Tamsen Tillson, "On a Wing and a Prayer," *Canadian Business*, October 1995, pp. 95–100.

5 Barrie Whittaker, "Increasing Market Share Through Marketing Excellence," *Canadian Business Review,* Spring 1990, pp. 35–37.

6 R. Wayne Mondy, Arthur Sharplin, Robert E. Holmes, and Edwin Flippo, *Management Concepts and Practice* (Boston: Allyn and Bacon, 1986), p. 416.

7 Eva Kiess-Moser, "Customer Satisfaction," *Canadian Business Review,* Summer 1989, pp. 44–45.

8 John Gilks, "Total Quality: A Strategy for Organizational Transformation," *Canadian Manager,* Summer 1990, pp. 19–21.

9 Tamsen Tillson, "On a Wing and a Prayer," *Canadian Business*, October 1995, pp. 90–100.

10 Eva Kiess-Moser, "Customer Satisfaction," *Canadian Business Review,* Summer 1989, p. 44.

11 Eva Kiess-Moser, "Customer Satisfaction," *Canadian Business Review,* Summer 1989, p. 44.

12 Paul King, "Building a Team the Sharp Way," *Canadian Business,* November 1990, pp. 96–102.

13 Adapted from Gordon Pitts, "Cassidy's Recipe for Failure," *The Globe and Mail*, March 15, 2000, p. M1.

14 Carolyn Leitch, "The Hair-Cutting Edge," *The Globe and Mail*, April 27, 1993, p. B22.

15 "Anatomy of a Recall: How Coke's Controls Fizzled Out in Europe," *The Wall Street Journal*, June 29, 1999, pp. A1, A6.

16 W. Edwards Deming, *Out of the Crisis* (Cambridge, MA: Center for Advanced Engineering Study, 1986).

17 Richard J. Schonberger, "Production Workers Bear Major Quality Responsibility in Japanese Industry," *Industrial Engineering*, December 1982, pp. 34–40.

18 Ted Wakefield, "No Pain, No Gain," *Canadian Business,* January 1993, pp. 50–54.

19 Bruce McDougall, "The Thinking Man's Assembly Line," *Canadian Business,* November 1991, p. 40.

20 Chris Argyris, *Personality and Organization* (New York: Harper, 1957).

21 Carey French, "A Question of Survival," *The Globe and Mail,* October 26, 1993, p. B27.

22 For example, see Robert Simons, *Levers of Control: How Managers Use Innovative Control Systems to Drive Strategic Renewal* (Boston: Harvard Business School Press, 1995), p. 82.

23 Daniel Wren, *The Evolution of Management Thought* (John Wiley & Sons, 1994), p. 115.

24 Charles Horngren, *Accounting for Management Control* (Upper Saddle River, NJ: Prentice Hall, 1975), p. 188.

25 Mark Dirsmith and Stephen Jablonski, "Zero Based

26 For a discussion, see Kenneth Merchant, *Modern Management Control Systems* (Upper Saddle River, NJ: Prentice Hall, 1998), pp. 542–45.

27 Joel Kurtzman, "Is Your Company Off Course? Now You Can Find Out Why," *Fortune,* February 17, 1997, pp. 128–30.

28 See for example Matt Hicks, "Tuning into the Big Picture for a Better Business," *PC Week,* July 15, 1999, p. 69.

29 Matt Hicks, "Tuning into the Big Picture for a Better Business," *PC Week,* July 15, 1999, p. 69.

30 "The S-Ware War," *Fortune,* December 7, 1998, p. 102.

31 Robin Cooper and Tobert Kaplan, "The Promise and Peril of Integrated Costs Systems," *Harvard Business Review,* July–August 1998, p. 109.

32 Stephen Baker and Steve Hamm, "A Belated Rush to the Net," *Business Week,* October 25, 1999, pp. 152–58.

33 Robert Simons, *Levers of Control: How Managers Use Innovative Control Systems to Drive Strategic Renewal* (Boston: Harvard Business School Press, 1995), p. 81.

34 Robert Simons, *Levers of Control: How Managers Use Innovative Control Systems to Drive Strategic Renewal* (Boston: Harvard Business School Press, 1995), p. 84.

35 Robert Simons, *Levers of Control: How Managers Use Innovative Control Systems to Drive Strategic Renewal* (Boston: Harvard Business School Press, 1995), pp. 84–95.

36 Robert Simons, *Levers of Control: How Managers Use Innovative Control Systems to Drive Strategic Renewal* (Boston: Harvard Business School Press, 1995), p. 86.

37 These characteristics are based on Robert Simons, *Levers of Control: How Managers Use Innovative Control Systems to Drive Strategic Renewal* (Boston: Harvard Business School Press, 1995), p. 87.

38 This discussion is based on Robert Simons, *Levers of Control: How Managers Use Innovative Control Systems to Drive Strategic Renewal* (Boston: Harvard Business School Press, 1995), pp. 87–88.

39 Robert Simons, *Levers of Control: How Managers Use Innovative Control Systems to Drive Strategic Renewal* (Boston: Harvard Business School Press, 1995), pp. 84–95.

40 Kenneth Merchant, *Control in Business Organizations* (Boston: Pitman, 1985), p. 98.

41 Kenneth Merchant, *Control in Business Organizations* (Boston: Pitman, 1985), p. 98.

42 As described by the owner of a chain of dry cleaning stores to the author. For a discussion of how to evaluate standards, see Dennis Arter, "Evaluate Standards and Improve Performance with a Quality Audit," *Quality Progress,* 22, no. 9 (September 1989): pp. 41–43.

43 The following, except as noted, is based on Kenneth Merchant, *Control in Business Organizations* (Boston: Pitman, 1985), pp. 71–120. See also Robert Kaplan, "New Systems for Measurement and Control," *The Engineering Economist,* vol. 36, no. 3, Spring 1991, pp. 201–18.

44 Lester Lefton and Laura Valvatne, *Mastering Psychology* (Boston: Allyn and Bacon, 1992), pp. 426–7.

45 Robert Simons, *Levers of Control: How Managers Use Innovative Control Systems to Drive Strategic Renewal* (Boston: Harvard Business School Press, 1995), p. 84.

46 "Did Warner-Lambert Make a $468 Million Mistake?" *Business Week,* November 21, 1983, p. 123; quoted in Kenneth Merchant, *Control in Business Organizations* (Boston: Pitman, 1985), pp. 98–99.

47 Chris Argyris, "Human Problems with Budgets," *Harvard Business Review,* January–February 1953, pp. 97–110.

48 Peter Coy, "Big Brother, Pinned to Your Chest," *Business Week,* August 17, 1992, p. 38.

49 Jeffrey Stanton and Janet Barnes-Farrell, "Effects of Electronic Performance Monitoring on Personal Control, Task Satisfaction, and Task Performance," *Journal of Applied Psychology,* December 1996, p. 738; and Paul Greenlaw, "The Impact of Federal Legislation to Limit Electronic Monitoring," *Public Personnel Management,* Summer 1997, pp. 227–45.

50 Jeffrey Stanton and Janet Barnes-Farrell, "Effects of Electronic Performance Monitoring on Personal Control, Task Satisfaction, and Task Performance," *Journal of Applied Psychology,* December 1996, pp. 738–45.

51 Jeffrey Stanton and Janet Barnes-Farrell, "Effects of Electronic Performance Monitoring on Personal Control, Task Satisfaction, and Task Performance," *Journal of Applied Psychology,* December 1996, p. 738.

52 Norihiko Shirouzu and Jon Bigness, "'7-Eleven' Operators Resist System to Monitor Managers," *Wall Street Journal,* June 16, 1997, pp. B-l–B-6.

53 Tom Peters, *Liberation Management* (New York: Alfred A. Knopf, 1992), pp. 465–66.

54 Robert Simons, *Levers of Control: How Managers Use Innovative Control Systems to Drive Strategic Renewal* (Boston: Harvard Business School Press, 1995), p. 80.

55 Robert Simons, *Levers of Control: How Managers Use Innovative Control Systems to Drive Strategic Renewal* (Boston: Harvard Business School Press, 1995), p. 80.

56 Tom Peters, *Liberation Management* (New York: Alfred A. Knopf, 1992), pp. 465–66.

57 Tom Burns and G.M. Stalker, *The Management of Innovation* (London: Tavistock, 1961), p. 119.

58 This quote is based on William Taylor, "Control in an Age of Chaos," *Harvard Business Review* (November–December 1994), pp. 70–71. James Collins and Jerry Porras, *Built to Last: Successful Habits of Visionary Companies* (New York: Harper and Row, 1994).

59 William Taylor, "Control in an Age of Chaos," *Harvard Business Review* (November–December 1994), p. 71.

60 William Taylor, "Control in an Age of Chaos," *Harvard Business Review* (November–December 1994), p. 72.

61 Except as noted, this section is based on Gary Dessler, *Winning Commitment: How to Build and Keep a Competitive Work Force* (New York: McGraw-Hill, 1993).

62 Richard Steers, "Antecedents and Outcomes of Organizational Commitment," *Administrative Science Quarterly,* 22 (March 1977). For an additional view, see R. Hackett et al., "Further Assessments of Meyer and Allen's (1991) Three Component Model of Organizational Commitment," *Journal of Applied Psychology,* 79 (February 1994), pp. 15–24.

63 Rosabeth Moss Kanter, *Commitment and Community* (Cambridge, MA: Harvard University Press, 1972), pp. 24–25.

64 See Gary Dessler, *Winning Commitment: How to Build and Keep a Competitive Work Force* (New York: McGraw-Hill, 1993), p. 64.

65 JoAnn Davy, "Online at the Office: Virtual Communities Go to Work," *Managing Office Technology,* July–August 1998, pp. 9–11.

66 Rosabeth Moss Kanter, *Commitment and Community* (Cambridge, MA: Harvard University Press, 1972), p. 91.

67 Abraham Maslow, *Motivation and Personality* (New York: Harper & Row, 1954), p. 336.

68 Personal interview, March 1992.

Chapter 15 Appendix

1 James Senn, *Information Systems in Management* (Belmont, CA: Wadsworth Publishing Co., 1990), p. 58.

2 Peter F. Drucker, "The Coming of the New Organization," *Harvard Business Review* (January–February 1988), p. 45.

3 Carroll Frenzel, *Management of Information Technology* (Boston: Boyd & Fraser, 1992), p. 10.

4 Geoffrey Rowan and Gayle MacDonald, "Playdium Has Fun and Games in Mind for Edmonton," *The Globe and Mail,* March 18, 1998, p. B3; also Shawna Steinberg, "Playing for Keeps," *Canadian Business,* June 12, 1998, pp. 74–78.

5 See, for example, David Kroenke and Richard Hatch, *Management Information Systems* (New York: McGraw-Hill, 1994), p. 20.

6 James Senn, *Information Systems in Management* (Belmont, CA: Wadsworth Publishing Co., 1990), p. 58.

7 Kenneth Laudon and Jane Price Laudon, *Management Information Systems* (New York: Macmillan Publishing, 1991), p. 25.

8 The following is based on Kenneth Laudon and Jane Price Laudon, *Management Information Systems* (Upper Saddle River, NJ: Prentice-Hall, 1996), pp. 11, 41–46. See also John Verity, "Coaxing Meaning out of Raw Data," *Business Week,* February 3, 1997, pp. 134, 138.

9 Jenny McCune, "For Knowledge," *Management Review,* April 1999, p. 10.

10 Louisa Wah, "Behind the Buzz," *Management Review,* April 1999, p. 17.

11 Jenny McCune, "For Knowledge," *Management Review,* April 1999, p. 11.

12 Carroll Frenzel, *Management of Information Technology* (Boston: Boyd & Fraser, 1992), p. 11.

13 Based on James Senn, *Information Systems in Management* (Belmont, CA: Wadsworth Publishing Co., 1990), p. 8; and Kenneth Laudon and Jane Price Laudon, *Management Information Systems* (Upper Saddle River, NJ: Prentice-Hall, 1996), p. 5.

14 Kenneth Laudon and Jane Price Laudon, *Management Information Systems* (Upper Saddle River, NJ: Prentice-Hall, 1996), p. 7.

15 James Senn, *Information Systems in Management* (Belmont, CA: Wadsworth Publishing Co., 1990), pp. 14–15.

16 See, for example, David Kroenke and Richard Hatch, *Management Information Systems* (New York: McGraw-Hill, 1994), p. 51.

17 Kenneth Laudon and Jane Price Laudon, *Management Information Systems* (Upper Saddle River, NJ: Prentice Hall, 1996), p. 24.

18 Kenneth Laudon and Jane Laudon, *Essentials of Management Information Systems* (Upper Saddle River, NJ: Prentice-Hall, 1997), p. 405.

19 See, for example, Kenneth Laudon and Jane Price Laudon, *Management Information Systems* (Upper Saddle River, NJ: Prentice Hall, 1996), p. 24.

20 Larry Long and Nancy Long, *Computers* (Upper Saddle River, NJ: Prentice-Hall, 1996), p. 18.

21 James Senn, *Information Systems in Management* (Belmont, CA: Wadsworth Publishing Co., 1990), p. 576.

22 This discussion is based on James Senn, *Information Systems in Management* (Belmont, CA: Wadsworth Publishing Co., 1990), pp. 576–77.

23 Howard Druckman, "Infotech: Helping Hands," *Canadian Business,* July 1989, pp. 57–59.

24 Emily Smith, "Turning an Expert's Skills Into Computer Software," *Business Week,* October 7, 1985, pp. 104–107.

25 Bill Gates, *Business @ the Speed of Thought* (New York: Warner Books, 1999), p. 22.

26 Emily Nelson and Evan Ramstad, "Hershey's Biggest Dud Has Turned Out to Be New Computer System," *The Wall Street Journal,* October 29, 1999, p. A1.

27 James Senn, *Information Systems in Management* (Belmont, CA: Wadsworth Publishing Co., 1990), p. 415.

28 See, for example, James Senn, *Information Systems in Management* (Belmont, CA: Wadsworth Publishing Co., 1990), p. 418.

29 James Senn, *Information Systems in Management* (Belmont, CA: Wadsworth Publishing Co., 1990), p. 427.

30 Microsoft Corp., Special Informational Advertising, *Fortune*, November 8, 1999.

31 Kenneth Laudon and Jane Laudon, *Management Information Systems* (Upper Saddle River, NJ: Prentice Hall, 1998), p. 608.

32 Kenneth Laudon and Jane Laudon, *Management Information Systems* (Upper Saddle River, NJ: Prentice Hall, 1998), p. 608.

Name Index

K

Kaiser, Karl, 157
Kanter, Rosabeth Moss, 19, 214, 498–99
Kasba Lake Lodge, 102
Katzenbach and Smith, 424–25
Kelleher, Herb, 316
Kelley Blue Book, **115**
Kellner, Alex, 407
Kennedy, Margret, 179
Kentucky Fried Chicken (KFC), 172
King, Martin Luther, Jr., 321
Kirkpatrick, Shelley, 312, 316
Kmart, 173, 180, 188–89
KnitMedia, 24, 39, 66, 92, 96–97, 125–26,
        158, 186–87, 190, 197, 226, 256–57,
        299–302, 338, 372, 408–09, 436, 470,
        473, 505, 516
Knitting Factory, 24, 125, 338
Kobayashi, Yotaro, 438, 442
Kodak, 421, 440, 447, 450, 453
Kotter, John, 329, 444, 448
KPMG, 68, 85, 292
Kraft, **306**
Kucharsky, Danny, 23

L

L.L. Bean, 170
Labatt Breweries, **44**, 451
Land, Dr. Edwin, 163
Latham, Gary, 141
Lawrence, Paul, 443, 460–61
Le Goullon, Jim, 400
Leeson, Nicholas, 229–30, 496
Lehman Brothers, 272
Lengel, Robert, 399
Lessard, Pierre, 115
Levac Supply Ltd., 263
Levi Strauss & Co., 12, 13, 216, 397, 400,
        421–25, 486, 511
Levy, Dr. Julia, 47
Lewin, Kurt, 445 46
Lexis–Nexus, 78
Likert, Rensis, 32, 319
Linamar Corp., 306
Lindahl, Goran, 224, 225
Lions Gate Entertainment Corp., **255**
Livent Inc., 71
Livingstone Healthcare Services, **485**
Locke, Edwin, 141, 312, 316, 347, 356, 362
Loewen Group Inc., **132**
Loewen Ray, 132
Logistec Corp., 180
London Stock Exchange, **115**
Lorsch, 460–61
Lotus, 260
Lowe, Stefan, 100
LSI Logicorp, 272
Lucent, **403**
Lufthansa, 47
Lycos, **115**

M

Maasland, Paul, 93
Machiavelli, Niccolo, 315, 375, 442
Maclean Hunter, 13
MacMillan–Bloedel, 347
Macnamara, Doug, 472
Magicuts Inc., 483
Magna International, **79**, 454, 467, 502–03
Major Electronics, 211
Mandalay Pictures, **255**
Manitoba Hydro, **208**–09

Manitoba Telephone System, 140, **354**
Manus, Bert, 162
Maple Leaf Foods Inc., 163
Maple Leaf Gardens Ltd., 173
Marathon Realty, 228
Marcus, Bernie, 380–81
Marlin Fast Freight, 140
Marriott International, 273, 362
Mars Inc., **230**
Marubeni Trading Co., 174
Maslow, Abraham, 342–43, 359, 365–66,
        499–500
Matsushita Electronic Industrial Co., 174, 245,
        336
Matsushita, Konosuke, 336
Mattel, 82, 84
Maurer, Rick, 443
Max, Glen, 25
McCain Foods Ltd., 50
McCain, Wallace, 163
McClelland, 342–44, 365–66
McCrae, Dee, 402
McDonald's Corp., 15, 37, 46, **65**, 172–73,
        179, 285, 479, 482
McGovern, Gail, 306
McGregor, Douglas, 31–32, 343, 431
McKinsey & Company, 492
Mercedes–Benz, 176
Mercer, Stephen, 19
Merchant, Kenneth, 477, 493
Merck, 497
Metropolitan Life, **120**
Metro–Richelieu, 115
Microsoft Corp., **16**, 78–79, 111, 168–69, 172,
        174–75, 439, 446
Midas Muffler, 173
Ministry of Labour, 264
Minolta, **50**
Mintzberg, Harry, 9, 382
Monster.com, 298–99
Montreal Trust, 205, **209**
Monty, Jean, 115, 202
Moore's, 172
Morkunas, Vida, 23
Motorola, 401, 486, 497
Mount Sinai Hospital, **485**
Mulroney, Brian, 317
Multimedia Inc., 37
Munk, Peter, 291
Munn, Cathy, 87
Murdoch, Rupert, 163

N

NAFTA, **43**–44, 435
NASA, 118
Nasser, Jacques, 448, 451
National Cash Register, 360
National Productivity Review, 411
NEC Electronics, **272**
Netscape, 169, 172, 202–03, **403**
New United Motor Manufacturing, Inc.
        (NUMMI), 48
New York Metropolitan Opera, 196
New York Times, 166
Newall, Ted, 320
Noranda Inc., **5**
Nordstrom, 493, 496
Nortel Networks, **15**, 18–19, 39, 44, 47, 51,
        63, 68, 75, 115, 202, 275, 287, 401–02
North Atlantic Inc., 201–02
Northern Paint, 482
NOVA Corp., 320, 360
Novacor Chemicals, 441
Noverco, 163
NTS Computer Systems, 49

O

Oberlander, Ronald, 210, 394
Office Depot, 15
Office Overload, 215
Ohio State University, 316, 319
Olivetti, 235
Olson, Ken, 146
Ontario Human Rights Commission, 75
Ontario Hydro, 145
Ontario Ministry of Labour, **262**
Ontario Workers Compensation Board, 145
Oracle, **491**
Ostroff, Frank, 253
Ouellet, Andre, 23
Outward Bound Canada, **414**
Ovitz, Michael, 71
Oxley, Stephanie, 473, 516

P

Palica, Janet, 468
Palliser Furniture Ltd., 292
PanCanadian Petroleum, 228
Paquin, Madeleine, 180
Parallax Systems Ltd., 468
Pavarotti, Luciano, 196
Pea in the Pod, **172**, 176
Pecault, David, 94
People Tech Consulting, 228, 451
PeopleSoft, **491**
Pepperidge Farm Cookies, 173
PepsiCo Inc., 159–60, 506–07
Personnel Systems, 73
Peters, Tom, 214, 229, 395–97, 496
Petro–Canada, 20
Peugeot, **45**
Phillips, 180, 235, 445–47, 465
Pitney Bowes Canada Ltd., 354
Playdium Entertainment Corp., 506
Polygram, 159, **160**
Porras, Jerry, 497
Porter, Michael, 175–76, 178, 182
Portera, **151**
Pound, Richard, 74
Prahalad, C.K., 180
Prais, David, 106
Pratt & Whitney, **362**
PricewaterhouseCoopers, 7, 236, 469
Procter & Gamble, 81, 206, 431
Procter & Redfern, **354**
Public Service Commission, **89**
Published Image, Inc., 427, 433
Purdy's Chocolates, 40, 50
Purolator, 260

Q

QLT Phototherapeutics, 47
Quaker Canada, 471
Quebec North Shore Paper Company, 262
Quinn, James Brian, 16

R

Rabie, Anton, 188–89
Reebok, 275
Remington Products, **355**
Revenue Canada, 479
Revlon, **205**
Reynolds Aluminum, 218
Ricoh, **50**
Ritchie, Cedric, 215
Robbins and Coulter, 446

product (divisionalization), 201–03
Deregulation
defined, 14
Descriptive plans, 135
Determining your leadership style
self assessment, 327
Development, organizational (OD)
confrontation meetings, 457
defined, 455
examples of, 456
interventions, 442, 455
types of applications, 455–58
Devil's advocate
approach to decision making, 120
Diagnostic control systems, 487–92
Differences
individual, 108
Differentiation
strategy, 176
Discipline
employee, 294
Discrimination, 87
Distortion
organizational communication and,
388
Distributed processing, 512
Diversification
conglomerate, 173
defined, 173
related, 173
Diversity
bases for, 86
barriers to, 87–88
boosting performance by, 88–89
managing, 85–86
organizational communication and,
389
recruiting, 273
Divestment, 174
Divisionalization. *See* Product departmentalization
Dogs
businesses as, 171
Dot-coms
incentives and compensation
packages, 8
Downsizing
defined, 229
information technology and, case
study, 300–01
Downward communication, 393

E

Earth Buddy
case study, 188
e-CEO, 7–8
compared to traditional, 7
Economic development, 54–55
Economic integration
defined, 41
development and benefits of, 41
free trade and, 41–44
levels of, 42
Economy
market, 54
mixed, 54
planned, 54
Electronic brainstorming, 120–21
Electronic bulletin board, 400
Electronic networking, 236–37
Electronic performance monitoring (EPM),
495
Emotional intelligence, 314
Empathy
fostering interdepartmental, 395

Employee
appraisal, 288
commitment, earning, 500
involvement checklist, 412
needs, 345–46
Employee centered organization, 32
case study, 93
Employee oriented leadership, 319
Employment equity act of 1986, 262
Empowerment, employee, 20
barriers to, 449
defined, 215
motivation and, 360–61
organizational change and, 448–49
Enterprise resource planning systems, 491
Entrepreneur
case study, 336
example of, 321
Environment
organization and, 247–51
socio-cultural, 56
technological, 57
Environmental monitoring, 495–96
Environmental scanning
of an organization, 167–69
E-postal, 22–23
Equality theory of motivation, 346–47
Escalation of commitment
decision making and, 111
Ethics, 68
characteristics of ethical people,
70–72
codes of, 75–77
corruption index, 69
defined, 71
emerging issues, 77–78
generation gap in, 72
how to foster, 76–77
individual standards of, 71–72
law and, 71
leadership and, 74–75
nature of, 71
resources website, 77
what determines whether behaviour
is ethical, 70–71
Ethnocentrism, 52, 87
EU (European Union)
member countries, 43
Exchange rate, 55
Executive recruiters, 271
Executive support systems (ESS)
defined, 509
using, 509–11
Expectancy theory of motivation, 348
Expected value, 130
Expert systems
defined, 511
using, 511
Exporting, 45–46
Extrinsic motivation, 340

F

Federal organizations, 245
Feedback
360 degree, 288–289
case study, 406–07
communication, 383
Figurehead role, 9
Finality of decision making, 115–16
Financial incentives, 292, 499
Financial ratios
analysis of, 488–91
Finished goods inventory, 482
Five forces model of competitive analysis,
176–77

Fixed interval schedule, 349
Fixed ratio schedule, 349
Flat versus tall organizations, 217–18
Flatter structures
centralized monitoring and, 493
Flextime, 360
Focus groups
case study, 514
Focus strategy, 176
Forecasting techniques. *See* Sales
forecasting techniques
Forecasting, 145
Foreign direct investment
and the multinational enterprise,
46–47
Foreign ownership, 39
Formal groups, 412
Formal organizational networks, 234–35
Formal structure change program, 458
Framing
decision making and, 109–10
Franchising
of international companies, 46
Free Trade
area, 41
defined, 41
development and benefits of, 41
economic integration and, 41–44
Freelancing
case study, 297–98
Functional (tactical) plans, 135
Functional authority, 214
Functional departmentalization
advantages of, 199, 201
defined, 198
disadvantages of, 200–01
Functional strategies, 177–78
defined, 172

G

Gain-sharing plans, 292
Gamesmanship, 493
GE Business Screen, 170
Gender
leadership styles and, 322–23
role stereotyping and, 87
sexual harassment, 263–64
General and Industrial Management (Fayol),
28–29
General leader style of leadership, 319
Geocentric philosophy, 52
Geographic departmentalization, 206–07
advantages of, 205–06
defined, 205
disadvantages of, 205–06
Geographic expansion, 173
Glass ceiling
breaking, 306–07
Global brain, 52–53
Global business. *See* International business
Global corporation(s), 40–41
Global marketing, 49–50
staffing, 51–52
Global mercantilism scenario, 147
Globalization, 13–14, 37. *See also*
International business
defined, 13
demands of, 37–38
production 50–51
Goal setting methods, 362–63
Goal theory of motivation, 347
Goals. *See* Objectives
Goods in process inventory, 482
Grapevine
communication and, 194–95

Photo Credits

Chapter 1

p. 1 Bruce Ayres/Tony Stone Images; **p. 2** Tony Bock/Canapress; **p. 3** Courtesy of Dofasco Inc.; **p. 9** SuperStock; **p. 11** Photo by Doug Forster, *Canadian Business*, used with permission; **p. 14** © John Dakers/Eye Ubiquitous/CORBIS

Chapter 2

p. 36 Courtesy of Bombardier Inc.; **p. 40** F.L. Avery/Verifone, Inc.; **p. 44** Courtesy of Labatt Brewing Company Ltd.; **p. 48** Courtesy of Ballard Power Systems; **p. 49** Yiu Chun Ma/The Image Bank; **p. 50** Courtesy of McCain Foods (Canada)

Chapter 3

p. 68 Dick Hemingway; **p. 70** Jeff Greenberg/Unicorn Stock Photo; **p. 74** Fabrice Coffrini/Associated Press/Canapress; **p. 77** Centre for Applied Ethics, University of British Columbia; **p. 80** Colin McConnell/Canapress; **p. 86** Stacy Pick/Stock Boston

Chapter 4

p. 99 Paul Avis/Gamma-Liaison, Inc.; **p. 100** USA Navy Visual News Service (CHINFO); **p. 103** Dick Hemingway; **p. 111** Infoline/Vancouver Sun; **p. 118** Michael Newman/PhotoEdit

Chapter 5

p. 132 Rick Loughran/The Province; **p. 134** Dick Hemingway; **p. 137** Chrysler Corporation; **p. 149** Michael Krasowiotz/FPG International; **p. 153** Jim Leynse/SABA Press Photos, Inc.

Chapter 6

p. 159 Paul Chiasson/Canapress; **p. 162** Courtesy of Toyota; **p. 162** Courtesy of Ferrari North America; **p. 164** Adrian Wyld/Canapress; **p. 169** ONG & Associates; **p. 175** Lawrence Migdale/Stock Boston; **p. 180** The Gazette/Montreal

Chapter 7

p. 193 Jose L. Pelaez/The Stock Market; **p. 194** Jon Anderson for Black Star; **p. 198** Jon Riley/Tony Stone Images; **p. 200** (a) M. Douglas/The Image Works, (b) IBM, (c) Jose L. Pelaez/The Stock Market, (d) L. Skoogfors/Woodfin Camp & Associates; **p. 208** Courtesy of Manitoba Hydro; **p. 212** SuperStock Inc.; **p. 216** Duo Trapeze Act from the "Otm" Show Bellagio. © 1998 Cirque du Soliel Inc. Photo: Veronnique Lemieux

Chapter 8

p. 227 Courtesy of Canadian Pacific Railway; **p. 231** Prentice Hall Archives; **p. 232** Eicon Technology; **p. 238** M.A. Malfavon Y Assoc., Rio Guadalquivir 83. 6' Piso Colonia Cuauhtemoc Mexico

Chapter 9

p. 258 These materials have been reproduced by Karen Taylor Permissions and Photo Research with the permission of Cisco Systems Inc. COPYRIGHT © 2000 CISCO SYSTEMS, INC. ALL RIGHTS RESERVED; **p. 260** Summer Productions; **p. 265** Dick Hemingway; **p. 273** Screen shot courtesy of Workopolis.com; **p. 285** Frank Gunn/Canapress; **p. 285** Internal & External Communication, Inc.; **p. 293** Dave Starrett Photo

Chapter 10

p. 305 Byron/Monkmeyer Press; **p. 306** Nina Long/The Tenessean/AP Photo; **p. 309** Ryan Remiorz/Canapress; **p. 321** No.1 national best selling author, international speaker, national columnist and co-founder, The Bulldog Group Inc.; **p. 322** Stuart Ramson/Canapress; **p. 323** Jeff Goode/Canapress

Chapter 11

p. 339 Beth A. Keiser/AP Photo; **p. 356** Chapters www.chapters.ca; **p. 357** The Financial Post; **p. 361** Jim Callaway Photography; **p. 362** Courtesy of Saturn Corporation; **p. 368** Courtesy of Fred Starke

Chapter 12

p. 380 Alene M. McNeill; **p. 385** Byron/Monkmeyer Press; **p. 390** Dick Hemingway; **p. 394** Toyota Motor Manufacturing, Inc., Kentucky; **p. 396** Lisette Lebon/SuperStock; **p. 397** © Disney Enterprises, Inc.

Chapter 13

p. 410 T. Cariou/First Light; **p. 414** Steve Lehman/SABA Press Photos, Inc.; **p. 415** SuperStock; **p. 419** SuperStock; **p. 427** Steve Lehman/SABA Press Photos, Inc.

Chapter 14

p. 437 Andrew Vaughan/Canapress; **p. 439** Alene M. McNeill; **p. 444** Richard Heinzen/SuperStock; **p. 457** Fransisco Cruz/SuperStock

Chapter 15

p. 475 © Arthur Meyerson. Courtesy S.D. Warren Company; **p. 476** UPS.com/Canada; **p. 480** SuperStock; **p. 483** Dick Hemingway; **p. 484** © Owen Franken/CORBIS; **p. 491** Copyright © 2000 SAP AG